THE

INTERNATIONALISTS

HOW A RADICAL PLAN TO OUTLAW
WAR REMADE THE WORLD

OONA A. HATHAWAY
AND SCOTT J. SHAPIRO

SIMON & SCHUSTER

NEW YORK LONDON TORONTO SYDNEY NEW DELHI

Simon & Schuster
1230 Avenue of the Americas
New York, NY 10020

Copyright © 2017 by Oona A. Hathaway and Scott J. Shapiro

All rights reserved, including the right to reproduce this book or portions
thereof in any form whatsoever. For information, address
Simon & Schuster Subsidiary Rights Department,
1230 Avenue of the Americas, New York, NY 10020.

First Simon & Schuster hardcover edition September 2017

SIMON & SCHUSTER and colophon are registered trademarks of Simon & Schuster, Inc.

For information about special discounts for bulk purchases, please contact
Simon & Schuster Special Sales at 1-866-506-1949 or business@simonandschuster.com.

The Simon & Schuster Speakers Bureau can bring authors to your live event.
For more information or to book an event, contact the
Simon & Schuster Speakers Bureau at 1-866-248-3049
or visit our website at www.simonspeakers.com.

Interior design by Ruth Lee-Mui
Maps by Paul J. Pugliese

Manufactured in the United States of America

1 3 5 7 9 10 8 6 4 2

Library of Congress Cataloging-in-Publication Data is available.

ISBN 978-1-5011-0986-7
ISBN 978-1-5011-0988-1 (ebook)

For Ava and Owen
and
Liza and Drin

CONTENTS

INTRODUCTION

Crowds gathered outside the Quai d'Orsay to watch the world leaders arrive. Onlookers stood wherever they could: on the sidewalk, on taxis, on trucks, on the parapets of the Seine. An extra squad of police mobilized just to remove the people who had climbed streetlamps to get a better view. Dignitaries and journalists pressed through the crowds and handed the ushers their invitations, yellow cards printed for that date, August 27, 1928, with the words: "*Signature du pacte générale renonciation à la guerre*"—"The Signing of the General Pact for the Renunciation of War."[1]

The ushers led the guests into the grand Salle de l'Horloge, the "Clock Room," deep within the immense Foreign Ministry. Enormous chandeliers hung from the hall's shining gold ceiling, and blood-red drapes sealed off the outside world. Four colorful cartouches, each depicting one of the "Four Continents," were poised on the exquisitely carved moldings. The entire chamber appeared to have been designed to send one message: The Law of the World is made here.

And, indeed, for generations, it had been. In this lavishly appointed hall, the international community established a uniform system of measurements for commerce and science in 1875.[2] The League of Nations, instituted to resolve disputes between states, first assembled here in 1920.[3] And it was here, only a decade earlier, that the victorious nations dictated the terms of the peace to a defeated Germany.[4]

It was a balmy day outside but hellishly hot inside the Salle de l'Horloge. Blazing klieg lights set up to film the ceremony had turned the Clock Room into an oven, roasting the dignitaries in their formal attire. At precisely 3:01, the procession began. Swiss guards carrying medieval halberds led the emissaries into the room. Just as the guests rose, the shouting began. "Sit! Sit!" the cameramen barked in many different languages. The guests were blocking the shot. Stunned by the incivility of the photographers but obeying orders, they returned to their seats.

Aristide Briand, the French foreign minister, was the master of ceremonies. Briand did not look like a statesman. He was neither tall nor striking. A long drooping mustache obscured a good portion of his grizzled face, and he often seemed bored. Yet Briand was no jaded diplomat. He was an indefatigable defender of France who had spent the decade since Germany's defeat working to spare his country another bloody conflict. Just two years earlier, in 1926, he had won the Nobel Peace Prize for brokering the Locarno Treaties, an interlocking set of agreements designed to prevent the major European powers from waging war with each other. Now Briand, together with his American counterpart, Frank Kellogg, the U.S. secretary of state, aimed to spread the "Spirit of Locarno" to the entire globe.[5]

As Briand rose to speak, the camera crews switched off the bright klieg lamps and replaced them with a softer spotlight focused on Briand. He began by warmly acknowledging Kellogg on his left, and Gustav Stresemann, the German foreign minister, on his right. This day, he declared, "marks a new date in the history of mankind" and the end of "selfish and willful warfare." From this moment, the nations of the world will no longer treat war as a lawful means to resolve disputes. The treaty will attack "the evil at its very root" by depriving war of "its legitimacy."[6] The room burst into applause. Tears ran down Kellogg's cheeks.

The klieg lights reignited. Blinded, Briand asked that they be switched off, but the cameramen refused. Briand then turned and bowed to Stresemann, who rose and approached the treaty. His head and neck glistening with perspiration, Stresemann sat down at a small table on which the parchment document lay and lifted a foot-long gold fountain pen, a recent gift to Kellogg from the town of Le Havre. The pen was decorated with laurel wreaths and inscribed with the phrase: "*Si vis pacem, para pacem*"—"If you want peace, prepare for peace"—a play on the celebrated maxim usually attributed to the Roman military theorist Vegetius: "If you want peace, prepare for war."[7]

Kellogg was next. Unable to get the unwieldy pen to work, he grimaced with irritation and gave it a vigorous shake.

After Kellogg, Paul Hymans, the Belgian minister of foreign affairs, signed the treaty for Belgium and Briand signed for France. The U.K.'s acting foreign secretary, Lord Cushendun, then signed for Great Britain and Northern Ireland. The plenipotentiaries of Canada, New Zealand, South Africa, Australia, the Irish Free State, India, Italy, Japan, Poland, and Czechoslovakia followed suit.[8]

The entire ceremony took less than an hour. At 3:57 p.m., a Swiss Guard banged his halberd on the floor, the cameras stopped rolling, and, for the first time in the history of the world, war was declared illegal.

You don't have to be an expert in international relations to know that the agreement signed that day—the Paris Peace Pact—failed to end war. Three years after the grand pronouncement, Japan invaded China. Four years after that, Italy invaded Ethiopia. Four years later, Germany invaded Poland and then most of Europe. With the exception of Ireland, every one of the states that had gathered in Paris to renounce war was *at war*. And the ensuing catastrophe was far more destructive than the one that preceded it. The death toll of the Second World War was five times that of the First World War—an unimaginable seventy million people.[9] It was the deadliest conflict in over a thousand years.[10] Nor did the Pact stop the Korean War, the Arab-Israeli conflict, the Indo-Pakistani wars, the Vietnam War, the breakup of Yugoslavia, the genocide in Rwanda, the "war on terror," or the current conflicts in Ukraine and Syria.

The Paris Peace Pact was, at the time, the most ratified treaty in history, having been joined by sixty-three nations.* Today, however, it is largely forgotten. Few people have heard of it. Most historians ignore it. Neither *The Penguin History of the World* nor Oxford's *The History of the World*, each over 1,200 pages, mentions it even once.[11] When the Peace Pact (known in the United States as the Kellogg-Briand Pact) is mentioned, it is usually to dismiss it as an embarrassing lapse in the serious business of international affairs, a naive experiment that should never be repeated. Former secretary of state Henry Kissinger mocked the effort to outlaw war as being "as irresistible as it was meaningless."[12] The Cold War strategist George Kennan described it as "childish, just childish."[13] In his otherwise excellent book, *To Hell and Back*, the British historian Ian Kershaw described the Peace Pact as "singularly vacuous."[14] The diplomat Kenneth Adelman judged it "a laughingstock," and James M. Lindsay, of the Council on Foreign Relations, called it "the international equivalent of an air kiss."[15]

Perhaps the most damning indictment of the Peace Pact was made by the Belgian filmmaker Henri Storck. In 1932, Storck took the footage of the signing of the Peace Pact and spliced it with scenes from newsreels from 1928: snippets of British dreadnoughts firing their enormous guns; German military officers parading in Pickelhauben, their iconic pointed helmets; and Benito Mussolini defiantly shaking his fist. The film had no narration, but its message was clear: the solemn ceremony in the Clock Room was pure political theater. The Great Powers had absolutely no intention of renouncing war; on the contrary, they were busily preparing for it. The French government was so stung by the satire that it censored the

*By 1934, the following countries had become parties to the Pact: Afghanistan, Albania, Australia, Austria, Belgium, Brazil, Bulgaria, Canada, Chile, China, Colombia, Costa Rica, Cuba, Czechoslovakia, Danzig, Denmark, Dominican Republic, Ecuador, Egypt, Estonia, Ethiopia, Finland, France, Germany, Greece, Guatemala, Hayti, Hejaz, Honduras, Hungary, Iceland, India, Iraq, Irish Free State, Italy, Japan, Latvia, Liberia, Lithuania, Luxembourg, Mexico, The Netherlands, New Zealand, Nicaragua, Norway, Panama, Paraguay, Persia, Peru, Poland, Portugal, Roumania, Siam, South Africa, Soviet Union, Spain, Sweden, Switzerland, Turkey, United Kingdom, United States of America, Venezuela, and Yugoslavia. Barbados joined in 1971, Antilles and Aruba in 1986, Commonwealth of Dominica in 1988, and Bosnia and Herzegovina in 1994.

film before its release. It only debuted in 1959, by which time Storck had added marching music to underscore the farcical nature of the proceedings.[16]

The Peace Pact is not reviled like the Treaty of Versailles of 1919 or the Munich Agreement of 1938, both of which are often blamed for contributing to the Second World War. No one actually cares enough to blame or revile it. When we wrote an op-ed in *The New York Times* praising the Pact,[17] the international relations scholar Daniel Drezner remarked, "This might be the first positive mention of the Kellogg-Briand pact in an op-ed that I've ever read. I don't mean that in a snarky way, either—I've honestly never seen that treaty talked about favorably."[18]

The argument of this book is that it should be. The Peace Pact quite plainly did not create world peace. Yet it was among the most transformative events of human history, one that has, ultimately, made our world far more peaceful. It did not end war between states, but it marked the beginning of the end—and, with it, the replacement of one international order with another.

The "beginning of the end of war between states"? The "creation of a new international order"? These are strong claims, and they understandably provoke skepticism. After all, even as we write these words, many parts of the world are embroiled in brutal, devastating conflicts. Syria is in the midst of the bloody civil war that has already claimed half a million lives. The Kurds are fighting Turkey for independence. Russia has seized Crimea and is currently supporting armed separatists in Eastern Ukraine. The Islamic State has spread from Iraq to Syria and now has control of significant territory in Libya as well. Nigeria is battling the terrorist group Boko Haram. The number of casualties from these conflicts is horrifying. In 2015, there were three armed conflicts—Syria, Iraq, Afghanistan—that had battle-related deaths greater than ten thousand. In Syria alone, the annual toll exceeded thirty thousand. An additional six conflicts, raging on three different continents, had at least one thousand fatalities: Nigeria, South Sudan, and Somalia (Africa); Pakistan and Yemen (Asia); and Ukraine (Europe).[19]

But the chief basis of skepticism about the Peace Pact is not simply that it didn't work but that it *couldn't* work, that outlawing war is a fool's errand in a world of power politics. The idea that war could be ended by declaring it illegal has been routinely dismissed as preposterously naive. As Senator Henry Cabot Lodge put the point, "renouncing war by governmental fiat seems inherently absurd."[20] Peace-loving states do not need an agreement to keep them from going to war, and warmongers will not be stopped from pursuing their interests by a thin piece of paper.

Our book explains why this skeptical reaction, while reasonable, is wrong. Outlawing war only seems ridiculous to us because ours is a world in which war has already been outlawed. It is difficult to imagine war serving any legitimate function other than a defensive one. Today, war is regarded as a departure from civilized politics. But this has not always been so. Before 1928, every state accepted the opposite position. War wasn't a departure from civilized politics; it *was* civilized politics. Indeed, states could not imagine doing without it.

Those who signed the Pact sought to end war between states by renouncing war as an instrument of national policy. This renunciation was the beginning of a transformation, not the end. Much like the U.S. Declaration of Independence, the Pact was a decisive break with the past. It was also a promise of a new legal and political order—but one that was still unformed. Just as it took the Revolutionary War, the collapse of the first constitution of the United States (known as the Articles of Confederation), and the ratification of a second constitution in 1789 for the Declaration's promise to be realized, it would take two decades of struggle, including a world war, the collapse of the League of Nations, and the establishment of the United Nations for the promise of the Pact to become a reality.

And it *did* become reality. Drawing on an extensive body of statistical and historical research, we will show that the Pact succeeded in ways few appreciate—not immediately and not precisely as the assembled delegates might have hoped, but over time and in ways that have profoundly shaped the world we live in. Our evidence will reveal not just that the deadliest conflicts *have* become less common, but, more important, that the nature of conflict has changed fundamentally. The Pact was aimed at ending war *between states* and, in that, it proved remarkably successful. But it has certainly not ended all armed conflict. Paradoxically, by removing war from states' legal toolkit and reinforcing their sovereignty, it even may have made some conflicts more difficult to resolve.

The Pact outlawed war. But it did more than that. By prohibiting states from using war to resolve disputes, it began a cascade of events that would give birth to the modern global order. As its effects reverberated across the globe, it reshaped the world map, catalyzed the human rights revolution, enabled the use of economic sanctions as a tool of law enforcement, and ignited the explosion in the number of international organizations that regulate so many aspects of our daily lives.

The Internationalists begins by recovering the now forgotten universe of pre-1928 that we call the "Old World Order"—the legal regime European states adopted in the seventeenth century and spent the next three centuries imposing on the rest of the globe. It formed the basis of what we now call "international law." The rules that defined the Old World Order evolved informally, through a gradual process of improvisation and acculturation. That the rules developed by custom rather than by treaty does not mean, however, that they were any less binding. The rules of the Old World Order were understood to be obligatory, and sovereigns largely obeyed them.

The rules differed starkly from the ones that govern today. The Old World Order was defined first and foremost by the belief that war is a legitimate means of righting wrongs. The inhabitants of the Old World Order would have found the famous maxim from Carl von Clausewitz's *On War* to be incontrovertibly true: *War is simply the continuation of politics by other means.*[21] Resorting to arms did not signal a failure in the system: It was how the system worked. War was an instrument of justice. *Might was Right.*

But it is not just that the Old World Order sanctioned war: It relied on and rewarded it. All states had the right of conquest: Any state that claimed it had been wronged by another state, and whose demands for reparations were ignored, could retaliate with force and capture territory as compensation. The conquering state thereby became the new sovereign of the captured territory: It owned all public property and possessed the legal authority to rule over its subjects. Nearly every border in the world today bears witness to some such past battle—including that of the United

States. Arizona, California, Nevada, Utah, and parts of Colorado, New Mexico, and Wyoming, are no longer part of Mexico because the United States launched a war in 1846 over unpaid debts.

Not only did states have the legal right to wage war to redress wrongs, they could also *threaten* to wage war for the same purpose. When Japan refused to trade with the United States in the nineteenth century, violating its obligation to participate in global commerce, the United States sent Commodore Matthew Perry with a fleet of gunboats to offer a "treaty of friendship." He left no doubt that the alternative to friendship was war.

The Old World Order also granted immunities to those who waged war—in effect, authorizing mass homicide. If an ordinary person killed another outside of war, it was a murderous crime. If an army killed thousands during a war, it was not only lawful but glorious. To wage war was to be *necessarily* immune from criminal prosecution.

While waging war was legal, economic sanctions by neutrals against belligerents were prohibited. A state that favored one side over another in an ongoing war could be punished, even if it never fired a shot. Thus, if a neutral state traded with a belligerent but refused to trade with its opponent (or traded, but on less favorable terms), it violated its duty of neutrality and could be attacked in retaliation. Had the United States traded with Great Britain but refused to trade with Germany when the First World War began, it would have violated its duty of neutrality and Germany would have been entitled to strike. It was for this reason that President Woodrow Wilson, who ran for reelection in 1916 on the slogan "He Kept Us Out of War," called on Americans to remain "impartial in thought as well as in action."

The Peace Pact was naive—but not for the reason most think. Outlawing war did work. If anything, it worked too well. The problem with the Peace Pact was that it was purely destructive. By outlawing war, states renounced the principal means they had for resolving their disputes. They demolished the existing system, which had allowed states to right wrongs with force, but they failed to replace it with a new system. This was in part because there already was an institution—the League of Nations—that seemed poised to resolve disputes. But the League was built on Old

World Order principles. It, too, relied on war and the threat of war to right wrongs and enforce the rules. In a world in which war was outlawed, however, the League's enforcement mechanism was grounded in a power that states were reluctant to wield.

Thus, when the Japanese invaded Manchuria in 1931, the League was paralyzed. After all, nearly all its members had just renounced war. The *prohibition* on war certainly could not be enforced *with war*. But if not war, then what? Economic sanctions had been illegal under the Old World Order; only war was legal. Now that war was illegal, maybe sanctions could take its place as a legal tool for punishing states? As the world hurtled toward disaster in the 1930s, philosophers, lawyers, and statesmen struggled to answer these questions, to figure out what would fill the vacuum left by the outlawry of war. Their failure to achieve consensus as to how to respond to illegal behavior—if not with war—created chaos and paralysis, thwarting the possibility of a coordinated, and thus effective, response to the growing Axis threat.

It was not until the Second World War ended that a complete world order premised on the outlawry of war—what we call the "New World Order"—finally came into view. That New World Order, the one in which we now live, is a photo negative of the old one. The Old World Order had rules governing conquest, criminal liability, gunboat diplomacy, and neutrality. The New World Order has rules for all these, too, except they are precisely the opposite. In the New World Order, aggressive wars are illegal. And because aggressive wars are illegal, states no longer have the right to conquer other states; waging an aggressive war is a grave crime; gunboat diplomacy is no longer legitimate; and economic sanctions are not only legal, but the standard way in which international law is enforced.

The New World Order is not simply the law. States actually obey it. There have been breaches, of course—for example Russian president Vladimir Putin's brazen annexation of the Crimea in 2014. But the disparity between the world before and after the Peace Pact is extraordinary. Russia's seizure of Crimea is the first significant territorial seizure of its kind in decades. Indeed, we will show that in the century before 1928, states seized territory equal to eleven Crimeas a year on average. The likelihood that a state will suffer a conquest has fallen from *once in a lifetime to once or twice a millennium*.

Our data do not merely show that the international order changed dramatically after the Second World War. Coupled with the historical evidence, they enable us to draw an even more startling conclusion: The transformation in the way that states relate to one another began earlier, in 1928, set in motion by the Pact. Of course, the Pact was not the *only* factor responsible for this transformation. The Pact repealed the core principle of the Old World Order, but it did not replace it with a new set of institutions. It would therefore take more than the Pact alone to successfully transform the legal order and change state behavior. But the Pact's outlawry of war was a crucial—and overlooked—trigger. It sparked a series of events that would lead to the construction of a new global order.

The prohibition on war has affected when and how often states go to war, but it has also changed how they relate to each other in times of peace. In the New World Order, the only legitimate way for one sovereign state to get another sovereign state to do what it wants is by offering to cooperate in ways that benefit both. The end of war as a legal mechanism for resolving disputes has thus resulted in the rise of unprecedented trade cooperation and has helped propel the creation of thousands of international agreements on everything from coffee growing to tax collection to criminal law. The latest edition of the United Nations Treaty Series includes hundreds of thousands of international agreements filling over 2,800 volumes. Through these agreements, even the smallest states can gain access to nearly every other state in the world using cooperation rather than war.

There is much to celebrate about the New World Order and the decline in interstate war it helped precipitate. But the switch from the Old World Order to the New has had unexpected consequences, not all of them positive. In the Old World Order, where war was legal, a sovereign nation that did not have well-functioning state institutions was at risk of losing territory to a sovereign nation that did. In the New World Order, military aggression is illegal, allowing even weak states to survive. But a world in which weak states can survive is also a world in which weak states can become failed states. Failed states all too often collapse into civil war and humanitarian catastrophe, and they serve as breeding grounds for insurgencies and terrorism. The decline of interstate war and territorial aggression precipitated by the New World Order has thus led to a corresponding increase in failed states and intrastate war. That, too, is the result of changes set in motion by the Peace Pact of 1928.

Historians and international relation theorists have traditionally referred to the modern international order as the "Westphalian order." It is named after Westphalia, the northwestern region of Germany in which two peace treaties were signed concluding the Thirty Years War (1618–1648), the bloodiest of the European religious wars, which, by most estimates, killed a third of the German population.[22] According to these scholars, the Westphalian peace treaties instituted the modern order of sovereign states. In this system, states are authorized to treat their citizens as they see fit. They are sovereign within their geographic territory, answering to no external power.[23]

This book does not begin in 1648 with the treaties of Westphalia but rather forty years earlier with the work of the Dutch lawyer and philosopher Hugo Grotius (1583–1645). We start here for two reasons. First, as scholars now acknowledge, the treaties of Westphalia had little to do with the international system. Their aim was not to impose the principle of sovereignty on the states of Europe. Their focus was local—to reorder the internal constitution of the Holy Roman Empire and thus end the religious and political conflict between Catholics and Protestants in Germany.[24]

Second, we begin with Grotius because he is generally considered to be the "Father of International Law." Even more important (and less well understood), he is the preeminent philosopher of war. One of the main arguments of this book is that the defining feature of an international system is how it regulates armed conflict. Grotius was the most creative and articulate exponent of the idea that states are permitted to wage war against each other in order to enforce their legal rights. He was, in other words, a seminal theorist of the Old World Order.

Once we look at the international system through the lens of war, we will see that the system has fundamentally changed. States are no longer permitted to enforce their legal rights through the resort to arms whenever they feel aggrieved. We locate the source of this transformation in 1928—with the signing of the Paris Peace Pact. Beginning then, we aim to show that there has been a tectonic shift—a transformation from what we have called the Old World Order to the New World Order.

Grotius did not invent the Old World Order. Though he was enormously influential, he was describing practices and systematizing ideas that had been present in Western culture and politics for centuries. But he was, and is, the most articulate exponent of the logic of the Old World Order, and for that reason we use his trenchant, if to modern eyes often troubling, defense as the entryway into its brutal rationale. The Old World Order came fully into its own over the course of the seventeenth century as Grotius was writing about it. And, if we are right, it came to an end on August 27, 1928.

Though we examine a rich trove of data and describe sometimes unfamiliar events, this book is, at its core, a work of intellectual history. It charts the long attempt to address perhaps the most important question about war: When is it legitimate? When is one group of human beings allowed to kill members of another group of human beings?

In tracing how leaders and thinkers have grappled with these questions, we focus on what we believe are key moments in the last several centuries when their answers have changed. We track these changes through the work and lives of two groups of men (they were almost all men). The first we call the "Interventionists." The Interventionists argued that war was a legitimate method for enforcing rights in the absence of a world government. They were led by Grotius, who saw the Old World Order as a system and constructed an intellectual foundation for a legal order built on war. Nishi Amane (1829–1897) followed Grotius's lead, seeking to understand the Western system of international law and bringing the Grotian vision to Japan, where he transformed a once isolated nation into a mirror image of the Western imperial powers. Carl Schmitt (1888–1985) anticipated the transformation that would result from the outlawry of war, and in his role as one of the most powerful legal minds of the Third Reich did all he could to prevent it. Sayyid Qutb (1906–1966), an Egyptian Interventionist disenchanted with the excesses of the West and the increasing secularism of his country, politicized radical Islamic thought, setting a course toward what is today the Islamic State.

The second group, which we call the "Internationalists," maintained that war was a barbaric way to resolve disputes and that the best way to resolve controversies was through international institutions. The Internationalists were led by Salmon O. Levinson (1865–1941) and James T. Shotwell (1874–1965), rivals who nonetheless shared a vision of a world in which war was outlawed. Levinson organized a social movement behind that vision, and he and Shotwell, in different ways and with different emphases, persuaded the U.S. government to make that idea a reality. Sumner Welles (1892–1961), a rigid, lonely State Department bureaucrat, was forced to resign after news spread that he had propositioned a male railway worker, but not before he succeeded in creating the Internationalist framework for what would become the United Nations. Hersch Lauterpacht (1897–1960), a Jew whose family was murdered in the Holocaust, would become for the Internationalists what Grotius was for the Interventionists. He recognized that the rules of the international system were shifting and put them together to form a new world order based on the illegitimacy, rather than legitimacy, of war. These historically and geographically disparate men did not invent their ideas about war *ex nihilo*. Each in his own way built on the work of those who came before him. But each one introduced remarkable innovations that transformed world history.

A key theme of this book, then, is that *ideas matter*, and people with ideas matter. In that respect, the book is both a history of ideas about war and a history of how these ideas found their way into practice. It is a story of how ideas emerged, clashed, and evolved. It is a story, too, of how ideas became embedded in institutions that restructured human relations, and in the process reshaped the world.

Finally, this book is an effort to reflect on our own generation's place in this still unfolding tale. It is now easy to take the Peace Pact's historic achievements for granted. War has been outlawed for nearly a century, and the result has been a period of unprecedented peace and cooperation between states. But we can't assume that this peace and cooperation will remain. The rules have changed before, and if we forget the lessons of the past, they could change again.

The Old World Order—the world in which war was a permissible way to address wrongs—was bloody, brutal, and unjust. Millions fought and died before it was defeated. This book asks readers to take a hard look at the world that Aristide Briand, Frank Kellogg, and the others who gathered in that sweltering Paris room in 1928 brought to an end. It also asks them to think about the world that the Pact painfully but successfully brought into existence—and how we can preserve and improve it for future generations.

PART I

OLD WORLD ORDER

ONE

HUGO THE GREAT

On the night of February 24, 1603, three Dutch ships reached the mouth of the Johor River off the Strait of Singapore. They dropped anchor in the olive-green waters and waited. The next morning, the men woke to a wondrous sight: The Portuguese great-ship *Santa Catarina* had arrived during the night and was moored right beside them.[1]

The *Santa Catarina* was a gigantic carrack, a U-shaped boat with towering fore- and aft-castles, designed to be invulnerable to smaller ships. It rode high in the water, allowing for a daunting number of cannons as well as ample room for cargo. To give a sense of scale, the *Victoria*, the carrack in which Magellan circumnavigated the world, weighed 85 tons.[2] The *Santa Catarina* weighed 1,500.[3] It was able to transport nearly a thousand people: seven hundred soldiers, one hundred women and children (some were probably family members, others captured natives to be sold as slaves), and assorted crew.[4]

At eight in the morning, the captain of the fleet, Jacob van Heemskerck, ordered his crew to attack, instructing them to fire only at the carrack's mainsails. It was important to avoid puncturing its hull, he warned, "lest we destroy our booty by means of our own cannonades."[5] The attack was one-sided. The *Santa Catarina* was nearly three times larger than any of Van Heemskerck's ships, but its enormous size made it cumbersome to maneuver. It also had too many people and the confusion on deck made coordination impossible. Nor was the crew practiced in naval warfare. The Portuguese did not choose their bombardiers on the basis of skill or experience; they auctioned the positions off to the highest bidders. What was a great way to raise money turned out to be a lousy way to keep it.[6]

The battle was over by six-thirty in the evening. The *Santa Catarina*'s sails were in tatters, and the ship was in danger of crashing into the shallow rocks on the eastern shore of Singapore Island. The Portuguese captain, Sebastiano Serrao, surrendered to Van Heemskerck, thereby setting into motion a series of events that would change the world.

GOOD PRIZE

By the time Van Heemskerck returned to the Netherlands in 1604, the United Amsterdam Company, the trading corporation that had sent him to the East Indies, no longer existed. It had been acquired by the newly formed Dutch East India Company. The supreme legislative body of the Dutch Republic, the States-General, had granted the Dutch East India Company a monopoly to avoid damaging competition among Dutch traders. Having towed the *Santa Catarina* all the way back from Singapore—twelve thousand nautical miles—Van Heemskerck delivered it to his new employer in Amsterdam.[7]

Following standard procedure, the Dutch East India Company and Van Heemskerck filed a lawsuit before the Amsterdam Admiralty Board to secure rights to the ship and its cargo.[8] The suit alleged the following facts: The company "had sent a fleet of eight ships to the East Indies under the command of [Jacob van Heemskerck] in order to trade with the inhabitants in the usual fashion."[9] When Van Heemskerck arrived in the Indies, however, he discovered that the Portuguese government had designed an extensive terror campaign to drive out the Dutch, who were threatening Portugal's monopoly over the Asian spice trade. The commander of the mission, Captain André Furtado de Mendonça, had led an armada of warships to Bantam in Java in an effort "to destroy all Dutch ships and their crews."[10] He had also punished the natives who had granted the Dutch "access to their harbors and markets," by attacking them as well.[11] His mission laid waste to Ambon, one of the largest of the Spice Islands (today the Maluku Islands in Indonesia), and "brutally tyrannized the poor inhabitants."[12] Van Heemskerck also discovered that the Portuguese in Macao, China, had murdered seventeen sailors from another Dutch expedition. One of the men who stayed behind from Van Heemskerck's previous voyage to set up trading posts in the Spice Islands "was captured by the Portuguese and quartered alive by means of four galleys."[13]

Outraged by these atrocities, Van Heemskerck and his crew prepared to retaliate against the Portuguese. After spending months looking for a carrack to capture, they found one on the morning of February 25, 1603, conveniently moored beside them. And not just any carrack, but the treasure ship *Santa Catarina*.[14]

After the lawsuit was filed, the Admiralty Board sent out notices summoning all claimants to contest the seizure and they repeated the process every fortnight for the next six weeks. Nobody responded, of course: The Portuguese owners of the *Santa Catarina* were halfway around the world and never saw the notices. On September 9, 1604, the Admiralty Board issued its opinion declaring the seizure to be "good prize" and ordering it to be "auctioned off in its entirety and the proceeds to be divided among the plaintiffs."[15]

News of the *Santa Catarina*'s capture spread quickly and the auction of its cargo attracted interest from all over Europe. At the public sale in Amsterdam, merchants marveled at the legendary riches of Ming Dynasty China. The ship's bounty included over seventy tons of gold, over a thousand bales of raw Chinese silk, chests filled with colored damask, atlas (a type of polished silk), taffetas, large quantities of gold thread, robes and bed canopies spun with gold, silk bedcovers and bedspreads, sixty tons of porcelain dishes, substantial amounts of sugar, spices, gum, and musk (a crucial ingredient in perfume), wooden beds and boxes, some lavishly adorned in gold, and a bejeweled throne, which one awestruck observer described as a "wonder."[16]

The expedition yielded a staggering profit. Proceeds of the auction amounted to 3.5 million guilders, or 37.5 metric tons of silver. In English currency, it converted to £300,000—more than 60 percent of the average annual expenditures of the English government at that time.[17] The Dutch East India Company awarded Van Heemskerck 1 percent of the sale and the crew split 3 percent. The company kept the rest.[18]

HUGO GROTIUS, CORPORATE LAWYER

Even though they had won the case, the company directors were nevertheless concerned. Their shareholders complained about the seizure. They had invested in a trading company, they protested, not a freebooting operation. The decision of the Admiralty Board did little to quell the criticism, for its reasoning was a jumble.[19] To address these worries, and perhaps to clear the way for future captures of this kind, the directors sought a lawyer who could offer a better public defense of Van Heemskerck's actions.[20] The assignment was offered to an ambitious and talented young man named Hugo Grotius.[21]

Grotius was an inspired choice. Born in Delft, Holland, on Easter Sunday 1583, Grotius—the family name in Dutch is de Groot (literally, "the Great"), but he preferred the Latinized "Grotius"—was a renowned child prodigy. When only eight years old, he wrote such expert Latin verse that one of his poems was presented to Prince Maurice, the military leader of the Dutch Republic, as a gift.[22] At eleven, he matriculated at State College (soon to be Leiden University). His professors there were so impressed that one of them composed a poem comparing the adolescent Grotius to his country's most famous man of letters, Erasmus. "Am I deceived?" the professor gushed. "Or was our Erasmus even so great?"[23] At age fifteen, Grotius accompanied a diplomatic mission to the French court. According to legend, Henry IV of France was so overwhelmed by Grotius's erudition that he dubbed him "the Miracle of Holland" and presented him with a gold pendant bearing the royal likeness.[24] Grotius stayed in Paris for five more months and received a doctorate in law from the University of Orléans.[25]

He was licensed to practice law shortly after returning to Holland. A silverpoint drawing by the Dutch engraver Jacques de Gheyn commemorates the event.[26] The caption states that Grotius is fifteen, but he looks no more than twelve. De Gheyn was clearly aiming to capture his subject's legendary precocity, depicting his youthful face with a conspicuously furrowed brow, but the effect is more comic than dramatic.[27] Grotius's friend Daniel Heinsius later noted that Hugo never had a childhood. "Others were men after a long time, but Grotius was born a man."[28]

A portrait painted only a few months later shows a different person. Jan van Ravesteyn's circular panel depicts a handsome teenager, elfin in appearance, with rosy cheeks and a hint of a smile. He is clean-shaven, still too young for the fashionable Van Dyke beard he would later grow. Posed in partial profile, he is relaxed, full of hope and promise. But like so many others before and after him, Grotius would soon discover that practicing law can be frustrating and disappointing. "You know not, my worthy Heinsius," the young lawyer wrote to his friend, "how much time the ungrateful practice robs me of. In no case has the fruit repaid the cost of the work done."[29] Grotius described himself as a "*vulturiolus togatus*," a vulture in a gown.[30] He would have preferred to spend his time on literary pursuits. In this area, too, Grotius distinguished himself at an early age. At eighteen, he completed a biblical play, *Adam the Exile*, which became a critical hit and helped inspire the great English poet John Milton to write *Paradise Lost*. Milton considered Grotius one of his heroes.[31]

In 1601, Grotius was named official historian for the State of Holland. The eighteen-year-old was chosen over Dominicus Baudius, a prominent scholar more than twice his age who, after losing to Grotius, was appointed Extraordinary Professor of Rhetoric at Leiden.[32] Baudius probably did not object to finishing second to Grotius. In a letter written five years later, Baudius confessed how he had been so intimidated when the Miracle of Holland unexpectedly showed up at one of his lectures that he got lockjaw.[33] Afterward, he begged Grotius's forgiveness for having given such a poor performance.

Hugo the Great was a rising star in Dutch public life, with powerful friends and an even more powerful mind. The Dutch East India Company would be well served by hiring this illustrious and connected polymath. And Grotius would be well served, too. Grotius was nothing if not ambitious and a high-profile case would increase his public standing and accelerate his political career.[34]

Grotius had a personal stake in the case as well. The maiden name of his paternal grandmother was Elselinge van Heemskerck.[35] In justifying the capture of the *Santa Catarina*, Grotius was not only defending a powerful trading company—he was defending his own cousin.

PIRATES AND SOLDIERS

To satisfy the anxieties of their shareholders, the directors of the Dutch East India Company probably expected Grotius to write a short pamphlet pleading the company's case.[36] The favorable opinion of the Admiralty Board was only a few pages long. Surely Grotius would not need much more space? The case, however, turned out to be far more complicated than the brief and embarrassing Admiralty Board opinion suggested. Once he untangled the issues, Grotius knew that a short pamphlet defending the seizure—and setting the stage for more like it—would not do.[37] In the end, Grotius spent the next two years composing a lengthy treatise on the laws of war, totaling 163 folios of neatly written, concise Latin. The English translation runs just shy of five hundred pages.

The legal case turned on an apparently simple question: Was Van Heemskerck a pirate? After all, he attacked a foreign ship that had done him no harm; and after overpowering it, he plundered its treasure and kidnapped its passengers. Isn't this *exactly* what pirates do? The stakes here were high: If Van Heemskerck was a pirate, then the riches he transported from Singapore, and which the Dutch East India Company sold at an astounding profit, had in fact been stolen goods.

The legality of Van Heemskerck's actions would have been easily settled had he been a soldier fighting in a naval battle. Soldiers in war were permitted to attack enemy ships and seize their cargo as prizes. But Van Heemskerck was no soldier: He was a private merchant working for a trading company. And though the Dutch Republic was indeed at war, it was at war with Spain, not Portugal.[38] Furthermore, its conflict with Spain was a *civil* war. Beginning in 1568, the Protestant northern provinces of the Netherlands had rebelled against their Catholic overlord,

King Philip II of Spain. The Dutch Republic, as the breakaway provinces would later be called, declared itself an independent nation, but no other European state had acknowledged it. Indeed, England and France, the republic's two closest allies, refused to recognize its representatives as full ambassadors in their courts.[39] To justify the capture and defend his cousin, then, Grotius had to square a legal circle. He had to explain how Van Heemskerck was not engaged in piracy when he attacked and seized the *Santa Catarina*.[40]

Grotius's solution to this dilemma was radical: Van Heemskerck had the same legal powers as a soldier at war because he was, in fact, *at war*. Though he was not fighting with the authorization of a sovereign nation, he did not need one. This employee of a trading company could wage war on his own authority.

To defend this outlandish idea, Grotius knew that he had a lot of work to do. He had to rethink the legal foundation of war and rebuild it from the ground up.

WHAT WAR IS GOOD FOR

In his classic 1970 protest song, Edwin Starr asks, "War—what is it good for?" then belts out the answer to his own question, "Absolutely nothing!" Most would still agree with the sentiment, even if not with its categorical sweep. The modern attitude is to regard wars as uncontroversially bad, moral catastrophes to be avoided at almost all costs. We recognize that some wars may be just—even necessary—but they are to be entered only in a narrow range of cases, such as repelling military aggression or preventing humanitarian disasters.

Grotius would have given a different answer to Starr's question. He would have said that war is good for many things. It is good for defending lives and territory, of course. But it is also good for collecting debts. If loans are not repaid, war is a morally permissible way for collecting what is owed. War is also good for restitution: If property is taken without permission, it may be recovered by force of arms. War is also good for securing compensation. If an injury has not been repaired, the military may be used to collect reparations. War is also useful for punishing criminals. If someone has engaged in egregious wrongdoing and is evading justice, war may be used to achieve retribution.[41]

For Grotius, then, war is a morally acceptable way to prevent or remedy the violation of rights. Though it does not go particularly well to music, Grotius expressed this idea in his defense of Van Heemskerck as follows: "Armed execution against an armed adversary is designated by the term 'war.' A war is said to be 'just' if it consists in the execution of a right, and 'unjust' if it consists in the execution of an injury."[42]

In setting out this conception of war, Grotius was drawing on a long tradition in Western moral thought often called "just war theory," whose contributors include the Roman orator Cicero, one of the great Fathers of the Western Church, Augustine of Hippo, and the leading scholastic theologian, Thomas Aquinas.[43] These thinkers differed on many aspects of the right of arms and just conduct in battle, but they (and many others) all agreed that war was a morally legitimate activity. Just war theorists were not pacifists and believed that wars could be waged justly. They also agreed on the basic function of war, which is to respond to threatened or actual wrongs when no peaceful option remains.[44] If the enemy has not violated or threatened to violate any rights, states may not wage war. Battles for glory, riches, or sheer animus are unjust wars, indistinguishable from mass killing and robbery sprees.

Grotius accepted this traditional conception of war and drew from it several important conclusions. Because the function of both warfare and litigation is to right wrongs, Grotius claimed that the reasons to wage war are identical to those that prompt lawsuits. The subject matter, he wrote, "is the same in warfare and in judicial trials."[45] The *casus belli*—the justified causes of war—are what lawyers today characterize as "causes of action," namely, those violations that may be remedied by a court. These causes include not only self-defense and the punishment of crimes, but also matters of a completely commercial nature, such as the collection of "debts arising from a contract" and "defence of one's property . . . which makes it permissible not only to offer resistance but also to dispossess others."[46]

Grotius drew another conclusion from the just war tradition: Because the function of war is to right wrongs, property seized in a just war belongs to the captor. Prize, booty, and conquest are merely the recovery of goods already due the attacker: "[W]ar is just for the very reason that it tends toward the attainment of rights; and in seizing prize or booty, we are attaining through war that which is rightfully ours." Grotius also argued that those who wage a war whose injustice is "clearly evident" do not have the same rights. They are not entitled to "the things captured in that war" because they are not attaining through war what is rightfully theirs.[47]

Going to war to recover property may seem shocking, but what else are victims of injustice supposed to do? When courts are available, victims are obligated to go to them for redress. But "ordinary remedies do not serve in an extraordinary situation," Grotius argued, and "when one recourse fails, we turn to another."[48] Thus, if courts are unavailable—for example, because the parties are sovereign states and recognize no higher authority—then the injured party is entitled to redress by any means possible. Having been wronged, the victim has the right to go to war precisely because he *cannot* go to court.

Grotius not only deployed the traditional conception of war as a substitute for courts, but he took the idea one step further. He explained why the basic principle of just war theory was true: War is a substitute for courts, Grotius argued, *because courts are the original substitutes for war.*

According to Grotius, all human beings are born with the right to defend their life and property, enforce their agreements, and punish crimes with violence. This right of "private war," as Grotius called it, was conferred on all individuals by the moral law, or to use Grotius's terminology again, by the "law of nature."[49] Private war is the natural and primordial response to injustice. But, he continued, a world in which everyone has the right of private war proved to be extremely dangerous. Thus, individuals decided to band together and form governments with effective legal systems—leaving what later philosophers would call the "state of nature" and entering the "social contract." Through the social contract, people transferred their natural right of private war to the state and consented to use its courts as a way to protect their lives and property, enforce their agreements, and punish wrongdoing. They decided to replace private war with public courts.[50]

On this account, states are not the only ones who have the right of war. Individuals have this right as well.[51] The reason why citizens are not

entitled to use violence within the jurisdiction of the state—why vigilan-
tism is illegal—is that they have transferred their right of private war to
sovereign authorities. When aggrieved, they must appeal to the state for
help. But the transfer does not cover all forms of violence. It does not apply
in political vacuums, such as the high seas, where sovereigns have no legal
powers of enforcement.

This account of private war, not coincidentally, allowed Grotius to formulate a defense of his client. Van Heemskerck was permitted to attack the
Santa Catarina off the coast of Singapore because he was outside the state
whose jurisdiction he consented to obey. Van Heemskerck was not a vigi-
lante, therefore, but the leader of a private war on the high seas.

Grotius's defense of Van Heemskerck, however, was not yet complete.
To show that Van Heemskerck was not a pirate, Grotius had to show that
his private war was just—that he was actually righting wrongs. But when
Van Heemskerck attacked the *Santa Catarina*, what wrongs was he righting?

HEEMSKERCK'S PRIVATE WAR

The first part of Grotius's defense is an abstract work of moral theory. As
he explained in his introduction, his ambition was to ground the laws of
war, and his defense of Van Heemskerck, in "the inmost heart of philosophy."[52] He wrote in a dispassionate, methodical, almost mathematical style.
Beginning with general principles about moral rights and obligations, he
derived specific conclusions about the proper conduct for, and in, war.
Grotius knew the text was tough going. He apologized for the "tedium"
of the presentation, but hoped that the "accuracy of the arguments" would
make up for it.[53]

In the second half of his defense, where Grotius laid out the facts
of Van Heemskerck's case, the tone changed dramatically.[54] No one expected Grotius to be evenhanded, of course, but what he produced was
a vicious screed against the Portuguese.[55] Grotius sought to expose what
he called "the instances of unparalleled treachery, the mangling of women
and children belonging to the households of native potentates, the disturbance of [East Indian] kingdoms through the poisonous activities of the
Portuguese and the abominable cruelty displayed toward both subject and

allied peoples."[56] The Portuguese are filled with "uncontrollable hatred" and "an insane greed for gain," their "madness (for no other term will describe their attitude) flamed out with incredible force against the Dutch," a "savagery . . . that far exceeds the bounds customarily observed between enemies."[57] The Portuguese are "men of bad faith, assassins, poisoners, and betrayers," their cruelty "characteristically Iberian."[58]

To substantiate these accusations, Grotius cited a letter found by Van Heemskerck's men aboard a captured Portuguese frigate. The dispatch described a Dutch expedition to the Chinese town of Macao in September 1601.[59] Having never been to China, the Dutch commander of the mission sent a small boat with eleven aboard to investigate. The Portuguese, who had established a large concession in neighboring Canton, lured the boat to shore waving white truce flags and arrested the sailors as they landed.[60] When the first party did not return, a slightly larger contingent was sent and these sailors were also arrested. The Portuguese threw the captives in a cave and tortured them. The letter reported that seventeen were hanged on the orders of the Portuguese magistrate, though Grotius alleged that only six were actually strung up, while the remaining men were led to shore at midnight in iron fetters and "weighted with rocks, they were rolled into the sea."[61]

These atrocities, Grotius claimed, were meant to deter the Dutch from trading in the East Indies. "Our chief crime lay in the fact that, instead of being crushed by want, we vied with the Portuguese in seeking those benefits to which nature has given all men free access." And since there were no courts in which the Dutch could prosecute the Portuguese for these offenses, Van Heemskerck was meting out the punishment they deserved.[62] His private war, therefore, was just.

Grotius not only produced an ingenious defense of Van Heemskerck's attack on the *Santa Catarina*. He also supplied the Dutch East India Company with something even more valuable: a legal justification to continue this belligerent behavior. While on the high seas, or anywhere outside the effective control of a court, company employees could use deadly force against the Portuguese, English, French, or anyone else who threatened to wrong them. As long as they were preventing or righting a wrong, they would not be pirates—they would be waging a just private war.

WHY RIGHT CAN'T MAKE RIGHTS

Grotius spent two years working on his defense of Van Heemskerck and revised it for two more.[63] Nonetheless, it appears he never gave his five-hundred-page tome a title, instead referring to it as "*de rebus Indicis opusculum*," that is, "my little work on Indian affairs."[64] He also never published it as a whole. Only a single chapter was printed in his lifetime.

Scholars have debated why Grotius held on to his manuscript. The leading theory is that Grotius had taken so long composing his defense that the Dutch East India Company no longer needed it. The shareholder controversy petered out with time.[65] But there may have been another reason: Grotius may have noticed that the work he had written contained a serious defect. His defense managed to justify Van Heemskerck's capture of the *Santa Catarina* and, indeed, the Dutch East India Company's violent strategy in the Indies. But it also threatened to damage the very trading system upon which his client's business depended.

Recall Grotius's argument about the rights of booty and conquest: Those who fight in a just war have the right to keep what they seize because they are attaining through war what is owed to them. But those who fight in manifestly unjust wars, he also argued, have no such right because they are not attaining through war what is owed to them. Denying the rights of war to the unjust might seem like a good idea—perhaps even a painfully obvious one. It seems clearly wrong for states (or individuals) to be able to wage unjust wars and keep their plunder. Might does not make Right. But, on reflection, restricting the rights of war to the just side is a bad idea. It is an *especially* terrible idea if you work for a global trading company in early modern Europe.

To see why, bear in mind that there were very few institutions that could peacefully resolve disputes between states in the seventeenth century. There were tribunals, known as "prize courts," which heard maritime claims between nationals of different countries. When a ship captured an enemy vessel, the owners would bring a condemnation proceeding in prize court to establish their right to sell what the ship had seized. The Amsterdam Admiralty Board that ruled on Van Heemskerck's capture of the Santa

Catarina was such a court.[66] There were also ad hoc tribunals formed by mutual consent of states to resolve particular controversies.[67]

The Old World Order, however, was missing general institutions that could resolve the bulk of international disputes. There was no United Nations Security Council, no World Trade Organization, no organizations of commercial arbitration. The pope was the only person who had played such a role in Western Europe, but he had long lost whatever supranational political power he possessed.[68] Even before the Protestant Reformation, when the Roman pontiff was at the height of his influence, he held no sway over Eastern Orthodox rulers, or the Islamic world. Similarly, the Ottoman caliph claimed authority over all Islam, but that power was restricted to Sunnis. The Safavid Empire held supreme authority in Shiite Persia. And the caliph possessed little real power over the Mamluk kings in Egypt, tribal leaders in Mesopotamia and Arabia, or the Mughals in Afghanistan and India. The Qing Dynasty ruled China, but not Japan, which was the province of the Tokugawa Shogunate.[69] And no one held sway over the petty kingdoms of the Indies, which played a central role in the spice trade.

That the early modern world did not have an effective ruler or general court system to resolve disputes created a serious problem for states and their chartered trading companies: How were most international disputes to be resolved?

Grotius's answer in his defense of Van Heemskerck had been simple: war. But this solution, Grotius may have realized, did not really eliminate the underlying problem—it merely shifted it onto traders. Using war to right wrongs when there are no effective courts to choose the just side meant traders now bore the burden of deciding which party was in the right. Whenever a trading company, like the Dutch East India Company, bought goods that were captured in war, it could not assume that the seller had the right to them. The seller, after all, might have been the aggressor and, therefore, no better than a pirate. Indeed, anyone buying from the Dutch East India Company would have the same concern: The Dutch East India Company may have seized the goods in an unjust war, or bought them from sellers who seized the goods in an unjust war. Knowing this risk, trading companies would be hesitant to buy goods seized in war—and others would be reluctant to buy from them in turn. At the very least, the goods would be heavily discounted to account for the risk that they had been stolen—perhaps so much so that it would make no sense to buy them in the first place.

The problem of legal uncertainty didn't merely affect goods seized in war. It affected *all* goods in the stream of commerce. In a world in which victims could wage war to right wrongs, and markets were global, traders need only worry that goods *might* have been procured in an unjust war for the contagion of uncertainty to creep into the transaction. And when goods came from India, Singapore, the Spice Islands, China, Japan, or, for that matter, New York, Massachusetts, Canada, Cuba, or Brazil, no one could ever be sure that the seller had the right to the goods he was selling.

Wait a minute, you might say. This is not a problem. If I buy something—say, a car—at market price at a reputable dealer and it turns out to be stolen, the original owner cannot take it back from me. I am what lawyers call a "good faith" purchaser. The absence of a clean chain of title at the time of my purchase does not eliminate my right to the car. The person whose car was stolen can go after the seller, but not after me.

Unfortunately for Grotius, the European laws of property were not so forgiving in the seventeenth century. European courts still followed the basic rule of Roman law—*nemo dat quod non habet* ("one cannot give that which one does not have")—which provided that thieves cannot transfer legal title.[70] No matter how many different hands through which property passed, how innocent those transactions, how many years had passed between the theft and later deals, if the property had been stolen at some point, no subsequent sales were valid.[71] Theft left, as it were, an indelible stain on goods. The original owner always had the right to reclaim his property and did not even have to compensate the innocent person who bought it.

One indication of how fastidious merchants were about clean title is the institution of prize courts. Merchants brought proceedings in prize court because a verdict of "good prize" established good title. The ruling of the Amsterdam Admiralty Board in favor of the Dutch East India Company enabled the company to sell its goods at auction and keep the proceeds.

While Europe had prize courts that awarded clean title for goods seized at sea, there were no similar ones for territorial warfare—there were no "booty" or "conquest" courts for the land. Title to goods captured on land, or sovereignty over territory seized during military conquest, could not be adjudicated and certified by a court. As it happens, the Dutch East India Company's business model came ashore not long after Grotius penned his defense of Van Heemskerck. In 1612, the company began shipping settlers to the East Indies and, by the end of the decade, it started to conquer native territories. The Dutch West India Company was established in 1621 and charged with "the peopling of those fruitful and unsettled parts."[72] The first families arrived on Manhattan Island in 1624.

Grotius's theory of war would have wrought havoc on the emerging global economy. A world in which clean title was essential to commerce could not also be a world in which clean title was only acquired in a just war. For this requirement would have placed intolerable demands on traders. It would have required them to know the provenance of all goods and whether they had been acquired in a just war. And they would have to do so in the absence of any courts with the power to resolve ambiguities or disputes. What trader would risk his money under these circumstances?

Grotius's brilliant defense of Van Heemskerck may have attempted to legitimate private wars by trading corporations, but if the theory had been adopted in practice, it would have caused enormous chaos for these very companies. Grotius's recognition of this fatal flaw may have been the reason the manuscript languished in his drawer. Before Grotius could publish his theory of war, he would first have to fix it.

DOWNFALL

There are just so many times one can engage in risky behavior without getting burned. And in seventeenth-century Europe, there were few activities more dangerous than naval battles and confessional politics. Our heroes' luck was about to run out.

Van Heemskerck was the first to come up short. The *Santa Catarina* incident made him a rich man and earned him a promotion.[73] Prince Maurice appointed him admiral of the Dutch navy and gave him command of a fleet to destroy the Spanish armada at Gibraltar.

The mission succeeded. In April 1607, the Dutch fleet obliterated the armada and sent every galleon to the bottom of the Bay of Gibraltar, though Admiral Van Heemskerck did not live to see his victory.[74] His armor presently on display at the Rijksmuseum in Amsterdam reveals how he was killed. The metal suit is conspicuously missing the left cuisse, the thigh piece: A Spanish cannonball ripped into his left leg at the hip and he bled to death.[75]

Grotius composed a long epicedium—a funeral ode—in honor of his fallen cousin.[76] The poem celebrates Van Heemskerck's short but event-filled life, beginning with his failed attempt to reach the Indies by sailing through the Arctic Ocean and getting stuck on the ice for a bleak eight-month winter: "I myself remember how I heard from you about your journey to the far North where in the polar night you sought the sunlight." The poem also wonders how the rajas Van Heemskerck encountered on his journeys to the Spice Islands and Singapore would react to his death: "Who will bring the message of this funeral to the Indies? The princes will mourn you, Heemskerck; they had expected you to go there in order to chase away the Portuguese and to make free trade possible." The ode ends by declaring that his countrymen would not grieve for their hero, knowing how happy he was to die in a battle against their enemy: "Much more pleasant for you will be the moaning with which the Spanish mothers lament their sons."[77]

Van Heemskerck's victory at Gibraltar led to a temporary armistice between Spain and the Dutch Republic.[78] The armistice was the occasion for vigorous negotiations over the terms of a more durable truce.

Grotius played no direct role in the negotiations, but he continued to work for the Dutch East India Company. The directors of the company worried about the insistent demands of the Spanish Empire for the Dutch to cease trading in the Indies. To bolster the Dutch company's negotiating position, Grotius revised Chapter Twelve of the defense of his now deceased cousin as a separate pamphlet and called it *Mare Liberum* ("The Free Sea"). The pamphlet argued that navigation and trade on the high seas is a natural right that cannot be taken away by any power. Because the purpose of the work had changed, Grotius carefully deleted incendiary references to Portuguese atrocities and the right of private war that had been the cornerstones of his original manuscript.

The Dutch position on trade in the Indies ultimately prevailed. In the final truce agreement, signed in 1609, Spain agreed to treat the Dutch Republic as an independent nation and gave up its demand that the Dutch cease trading in the Indies for twelve years.[79] The Dutch East India Company's trading interests were now secure.[80]

Grotius spent the next decade as the faithful servant of the Dutch East India Company.[81] He continued to lobby on its behalf and acted as one of the main Dutch negotiators in diplomatic disputes involving Spain, France, and England.[82] By some accounts, he was a more talented scholar than diplomat. George Abbot, the Archbishop of Canterbury, described the first meeting between Grotius and King James of England: "At his first coming to the King, by reason of his good *Latine* tongue, he was *so tedious* and full of *tittle tattle* that the King's Judgment was of him *that he was some Pedant, full of Words and of no great Judgment.*"[83] The king wasn't the only person to regard Grotius as a gasbag and bore. At another dinner, Grotius bloviated to such an extent that his host sat dumbfounded and wondered "what a Man he had there, who never being in the Place or Company before, *could overwhelme them so with Talk for so long a time.*"[84]

Grotius seems to have suffered from the occupational hazard of the child prodigy: when the pearls pouring from your mouth dazzle everyone, you may never learn to shut up and let someone else have a turn. The wunderkind had grown into an enfant terrible. Archbishop Abbot portrayed Grotius as someone who "did imagine that every Man was bound to hear him so long as he would talk."[85] But it is a testament to Grotius's brilliance that, despite his overbearing narcissism and Latin logorrhea, his political career continued to advance. In 1607, he was selected to be the advocate-fiscal (the equivalent of the modern-day attorney general) for the states of Holland and Zeeland, and six years later was appointed the pensionary (general counsel) of Rotterdam and a member of the States-General.[86] Grotius also became involved in the Arminian movement, a liberal form of Calvinism that denied the orthodox doctrine of predestination and preached religious toleration.[87]

This open-mindedness, however, was his undoing. In 1618, Prince Maurice and Calvinist hardliners arrested Grotius and his patron, Johan van Oldenbarnevelt, the grand pensionary of Holland. Both men were

convicted of heresy and treason in a show trial. Oldenbarnevelt was be-
headed, but Grotius was spared, receiving the more lenient sentence of life
imprisonment.[88]

THE LAW OF WAR AND PEACE

Grotius was sent to serve his sentence at Loevenstein Castle in the central
province of Gelderland. With its moat and high walls, the fortress was an
ideal place to hold political prisoners and religious leaders. Soon after Grotius arrived, his wife and two children, ages six and eight, joined him, for
their house and all their possessions had been seized and they had no other
place to live.[89] Together they shared two rooms, each just over ten paces
across, with small barred windows.

Grotius used one of the two rooms as a study, where he continued his
work. He used the time well, writing a defense of his religious views and
a treatise on Dutch jurisprudence. He also continued his earlier research
on the laws of war. Though able to work and accompanied by his family,
Grotius was unsurprisingly desperate to escape. For a man used to holding
forth at court and enjoying the adulation of other scholars, the isolation
was suffocating. And imprisonment in the damp castle was taking its toll
on his health.

Grotius's extensive library had been confiscated as part of the treason
conviction, so his friends lent him books.[90] These books were delivered
in large chests, and when Grotius was finished with them, they were returned in these chests, along with his dirty laundry. After twenty months
of examining books and wash, the guards had stopped checking the chests'
contents. This gave Grotius and his wife a ridiculous but brilliant idea: He
could take the place of the books inside a chest on its return trip, escaping
the prison.

With his wife's help, Grotius began practicing lying quietly inside the
chest until he could remain inside without moving long enough for the
chest to be delivered far from the castle. In 1621, he climbed into a chest,
with his head resting on a Bible but without shoes on his feet, for there
was no room. The ruse worked, at least initially. Unaware that Grotius was
wedged within, the guards allowed the chest to be carried out of prison.

At one point, however, the bearers noticed the trunk's unusual weight and suspected that the prisoner might be inside. "I'll fetch a drill and drill into his arse until the crap runs out," a guard said. But Elsje, his chambermaid, replied: "Then you'll need a drill that goes all the way to his room."[91] Persuaded by her quick response, the guards continued on their way.

Delivered to the home of a friend, Grotius emerged from the chest, embraced the loyal friend, and left out the back door dressed as a bricklayer, bound for Paris.[92] When his escape was discovered, his wife and children were kept under close confinement, but because there was no basis for keeping them, they were soon released and allowed to rejoin him abroad.

Grotius spent several years in Paris preparing a new treatise on the laws of war.[93] He rushed to finish it so that it could be sold at the Frankfurt book fair in 1625, under the title *De Jure Belli ac Pacis Libri Tres* or "The Law of War and Peace in Three Books." It was a hit and quickly became *the* textbook on the laws of war. By the eighteenth century, *The Law of War and Peace* had gone through fifty editions in Latin alone.[94]

Grotius attempted to reduce all the laws of war to a single treatise.[95] It covered an astonishing range of topics—the definition, permissibility, and causes of war; delineation of state boundaries; common use of land, rivers, and seas; procedures for making treaties; rights of burial and diplomacy; division of booty; use of hostages; right of conquest; proper treatment of prisoners of war; prohibitions on rape, assassination, and use of poison in battle; duties of allies; responsibilities of neutrals; making of truces; and negotiation of peace treaties.

The encyclopedic coverage of the treatise was matched only by its philosophical ambition. Grotius plumbed deeper than any thinker before him in an effort to justify war. Because he treated war as a permissible response to the violation of rights, he audaciously attempted to catalogue every right that any person could possess. Grotius wanted to know what rights people could have, in other words, because he wanted to know when they could go to war over them.[96]

One innovation that made Grotius's work so modern was that, unlike other Protestant thinkers, he did not limit his moral focus to Christians. He wanted to discover the rights of *all* people, irrespective of race, creed, or religion—not just Protestants and Catholics, but Jews, Muslims,

Hindus, Buddhists, barbarians, and savages as well—and for that he looked to the law of nature.

The law of nature, according to Grotius, is remarkably egalitarian: It confers the same basic rights on everyone. He claimed, for example, that all human beings have the right to acquire and sell property. The natural right of private property is "universal" and "whatever each had thus taken for his own needs another could not take from him except by an unjust act."[97] The legal implications of this position were enormous. It meant that Christians were not only forbidden from taking property from non-Christians, but that non-Christians would have a just cause of war against Christians for doing so.

Grotius made the same claims about contracts and treaties. All human beings are able to create binding contracts and every nation can enter valid treaties. "[N]othing is so in harmony with the good faith of mankind as that persons should keep the agreements which they have made with one another."[98]

It is tempting to see Grotius as a courageous critic of bigotry and racism, even an early champion of the idea of human rights. No doubt Grotius's sterling reputation today is due, at least in part, to these progressive passages. But before we get too impressed, we should recognize how congenial these enlightened ideas were to his client's commercial interests. After all, if heathens could own property, they could sell it to the Dutch. More importantly and insidiously, if heathens could enter valid contracts and treaties, then the Dutch East India Company could negotiate exclusive trading deals with native rulers of the Indies.[99] Since these treaties would be valid, they would be enforceable not only against the natives themselves, but against other European countries as well.

For all of Grotius's talk about the freedom of the seas and the right to trade, he helped negotiate monopolistic trading agreements with East Indian nations and pressed these legal claims against the Dutch East India Company's European competitors. The hypocrisy did not go unnoticed. During trade negotiations with England's East India Company, the English were stunned to hear the author of *The Free Sea* deny them the right to trade freely. In one of his position papers insisting on Portuguese-style monopolies for the Dutch East India Company, Grotius wrote: "We think it very honest to defend oppressed people." An English delegate scrawled in the margins, "against their wills."[100]

MIGHT IS RIGHT

The moral world Grotius describes in his 1625 treatise, *The Law of War and Peace*, is teeming with rights. Individuals have rights; states have rights; native peoples have rights; trading companies have rights. But though moral, this world is not peaceful. For among the entitlements that Grotius recognizes is the right to wage war to defend all these other rights.

Grotius's earlier defense of Van Heemskerck remained tucked away, but he relied on it heavily as he wrote his new treatise. Like the earlier manuscript, *The Law of War and Peace* is an unabashed defense of the morality of war. Grotius argued that the law of nature permits individuals and states to use force to prosecute their rights. Indeed, *any* right that could be enforced by courts could also be enforced by war if courts were unavailable. "It is evident that the sources from which wars arise are as numerous as those from which lawsuits spring."[101]

By the time he wrote *The Law of War and Peace*, however, Grotius understood that if war was to play its role as an enforcer of rights, it had to do so in a way that did not scramble the system of property rights and create debilitating legal uncertainty for merchants. And he had the solution to that problem—a way to fix the flaw in his earlier defense of Van Heemskerck.

Grotius's solution to this problem was also radical: If traders could never be sure which side has the just case, *then the law should not require them to figure it out.* The laws of war, in other words, should allow traders to take physical control over goods and territory as legal ownership. Possession in war would always be ten-tenths of the law. That would allow traders to remain neutral about disputes while also vigorously engaging in commerce.

Let's call Grotius's solution the "Might is Right" Principle. The Might is Right Principle states that success creates legal rights in war. Applied to the case of booty, for example, the principle requires that title transfers when property is seized in war. Soldiers become the rightful owners of

booty not because they were engaged in a just war, but because they succeeded in taking valuables from the other side. The Might is Right Principle also applies to conquests. If a state is able to wrest territory from
another state, it acquires sovereignty and has the right to rule its inhabitants. Those not engaged in the fight do not need to know the legal details
of the dispute. They can let war be the judge.

Grotius expressed the Might is Right Principle as follows:

> [K]ings and peoples who undertake war wish that their reasons for so
> doing should be believed to be just, and that, on the other hand, those
> who bear arms against them are doing wrong. Now since each party
> wished this to be believed, and it was not safe for those who desired to
> preserve peace to intervene, *peoples at peace were unable to do better than to
> accept the outcome as right*.[102]

That is, because each belligerent would claim that it had justice on its
side, nonbelligerents could do no better than to "accept the outcome as
right." The Might is Right Principle would allow them simply to treat the
winner as the legitimate rights holder. "By the law of nations not merely
he who wages war for a just cause, but in a public war also any one at all
becomes owner, without limit or restriction, of what he has taken from the
enemy," Grotius proclaimed. "[B]oth the possessor of such booty, and those
who hold their title from him, are to be protected in their possession by
all nations."[103]

Treating Might as Right would not only benefit trading companies.
It would also prevent local conflicts from escalating into global conflagra-
tions, for the belligerents would have no right to wage new wars to recover
goods lost in old battles. "[N]either slaves nor things taken in war are restored with peace," Grotius wrote. "To controvert this principle would in
truth be to make wars to spring up from wars."[104]

THE PECULIAR EFFECTS OF WAR

Grotius was not the first to propose the Might is Right Principle. The
idea had been suggested two centuries earlier by the Italian lawyer

Raphael Fulgosius. Fulgosius observed with puzzlement that the Roman law of booty and slavery did not distinguish between just and unjust wars.[105] "How is it," Fulgosius asked, "that the one who wages an unjust war acquires the ownership of things he captures through his unjust action?" Fulgosius responded: "as it was uncertain which side waged war rightfully, and as there was no common judge above the parties by whom this could be ascertained in terms of civil law, the nations with the best of reason decided that war would be judge of the matter."[106] In 1582, the Flemish-born judge advocate general for the Spanish army, Balthazar Ayala, agreed with Fulgosius and accepted a version of the Might is Right Principle in his treatise, *The Rights and Duties of War and Military Strategy*, though he gave no explanation for it.[107]

In a sense, the world also accepted the Might is Right Principle. In war, soldiers grabbed what they could. After battles, the victors quickly combed the landscape for valuables and stripped coats, shoes, muskets, swords, jewelry, and money from the fallen. As Victor Hugo later observed, "The dawn which follows a battle always rises on naked corpses."[108] The English word "robe," for example, derives from "rob," garments being common objects looted from the battlefield.[109] Booty taking was the normal way that soldiers profited from war; indeed, armies tolerated this distasteful behavior because it saved them from having to pay their soldiers much of a salary.[110] In turn, states that won wars took territory as conquest. To be sure, just war theorists were adamant that the unjust side did not have the moral right to booty and conquest. From a practical perspective, however, these admonitions did not much matter. Booty and conquests were recognized as a matter of course.

In his original defense of Van Heemskerck, Grotius cited Fulgosius and Ayala, but only to reject their views.[111] He denied that the laws of war accorded the same rights to both sides. Grotius made one concession to reality: Soldiers acting in good faith and having reasonable grounds for believing in their cause could keep what they took, even if they found out afterward that they were wrong. But if their side was clearly unjust, Might was not Right and the victors could not legally keep or sell what they had seized. As Grotius wrote then, rewarding injustice was "lacking any rational basis" and would "incite men to wrongdoing."[112]

By the time Grotius wrote *The Law of War and Peace*, however, he had reversed course, apparently realizing that rewarding injustice had a rational basis. After all, treating Might as Right would protect merchants from the legal chaos that war would otherwise unleash.[113] Grotius also conceded that the world followed the Might is Right Principle. The principle "met with the approval of nations," he explained, precisely because it was rational.[114] To be sure, adding this principle to his theory of war created perverse consequences. After all, Grotius followed the just war tradition, which limited wars of conquest, and the taking of prize and booty, to the restoration or protection of justice. Only victims and their allies were permitted to resort to arms. Yet he now granted *everyone* the legal right to keep what they took, even wrongdoers who took territory and property from the victims themselves. Recognizing this perversity, he referred to such outcomes as *peculiares effectus*—the "peculiar legal consequences"—of war.

Grotius sought to limit the likelihood of abuse by granting these peculiar powers only to some wars—what he called "formal" wars.[115] Formal wars are state-on-state conflicts that commence with formal declarations of war, such as the War of the Spanish Succession, Seven Years War, Franco-Prussian War, the First and Second World Wars. In formal wars, Might is Right. All other conflicts, such as Van Heemskerck's attack on the *Santa Catarina*, are informal wars where Might is not necessarily Right. In this revised theory, the Dutch East India's legal claim depended solely on the fact that Van Heemskerck seized the *Santa Catarina*'s cargo at sea and his seizure was blessed by a prize court. Had the same seizure occurred on land, the Dutch East India Company could have been required to return the vast riches to Portugal. Indeed, unless he had a just cause, Van Heemskerck and the Dutch East India Company would have had no more legal claim to the *Santa Catarina* than a pirate.

It is likely no coincidence that Grotius's new theory favored sovereigns and their chartered trading companies. After Van Heemskerck's victory at Gibraltar and the subsequent truce with Spain, European states began to recognize the Dutch Republic as an independent, sovereign nation. Grotius probably expected his pro-Dutch writings would put him in good stead back home and persuade his political enemies to forgive him. He actually returned incognito for a few months in 1631, when the second edition of his treatise was published, to test the waters. Grotius discovered that he was still not welcome, and probably never would be. The celebrated prodigy of the Dutch Republic fled once again, exiled from his country during its Golden Age, the glorious period of Rembrandt, Vermeer, Huygens, and Descartes. He would die in 1645, after being injured in a shipwreck off the coast of Eastern Pomerania, a broken and lonely outcast.[116]

THE FATHER OF INTERNATIONAL LAW

Hugo Grotius was twenty-three years old when he completed his defense of Jacob van Heemskerck. It was a brilliant beginning to a brilliant career: His writings would be recognized as classics and remain part of the Western canon. Grotius was once known to all educated westerners and revered as one of the greatest western minds.

The Law of War and Peace would become the foundation for all future treatises on international law. The leading international scholar of the second half of the seventeenth century, the German lawyer and philosopher Samuel von Pufendorf, cited Grotius's views hundreds of times in his magnum opus, Eight Books on the Law of Nature and Nations. In some cases, he simply adopted them. The complete entry on the right to kill in war reads: "How far in particular many peoples commonly extend the license of war on the persons of the enemies is shown in detail by Grotius."[117] The preeminent international law scholar of the eighteenth century, the Swiss lawyer and diplomat Emer de Vattel, cited "that great man" Grotius in his main work, The Law of Nations, more than any other authority.[118]

Grotius's influence was likewise strong among the Founding Fathers of the American Revolution. George Washington, like most educated English gentlemen of his day, owned a copy of The Law of War and Peace.[119] James Madison declared that Grotius "is not unjustly considered . . . the father of the modern code of nations."[120] During a fight over the ratification of a treaty, John Adams scoured the half-built city of Washington, D.C., for international law treatises and found what he was looking for in Vattel. But he wrote to his son Thomas in Philadelphia, "I wish you would look into

Grotius & Puffendorf [*sic*] among the rules for the interpretation of treaties, & send me extracts of the law upon this point."[121]

Even today, lawyers and diplomats celebrate Grotius and consider him the "Father of International Law."[122] His name graces societies, journals, and professorships and his image adorns grand public monuments. A marble relief of Grotius hangs over a gallery door to the House Chamber in the United States Capitol, alongside those of Moses, Hammurabi, and Thomas Jefferson. Grotius's standing is even honored in the breach. The late United States senator Daniel Patrick Moynihan once described the contempt for international law held by many in the Reagan Administration by saying that "Real men did not cite Grotius."[123]

Grotius did not invent international law, of course.[124] He explicitly relied on a long tradition of just war theory and, in most instances, he described prevailing state practice. His great achievement was melding these ideas and rules together into a coherent system that formed the basis by which global commerce and international relations were governed for centuries—what we have called the Old World Order. The core idea that animated the Old World Order, as he explained it, is simple but powerful: War is a legitimate method for sovereigns, and their chartered trading companies, to enforce rights against one another. The right to wage war, to conquer and seize booty, to destroy anything that is necessary to win all derives from this basic function of war.

Grotius was a humanist scholar, Latin poet, and Protestant theologian—but he was also an attorney for a trading company, and he approached the laws of war through the lens of a corporate lawyer. His project was to enable his client, and his country, to advance their interests in the absence of courts that could resolve disputes. He designed his theory of war to enable the beginnings of a globalizing world, where states and trading companies set out all over the earth in search of goods to buy and sell. And he came to realize that, for this purpose, the rights of war could not depend on the justice of the war waged. A world in which war was a legitimate means of law enforcement was one in which Might had to be Right.

Grotius's achievement extended beyond developing a systematic approach to war that worked for merchants and their state sponsors. Perhaps even more importantly, he provided war with a firm moral foundation. The moral and legal right of war, he explained, always derived from the same place—the natural rights of individuals.[125] Public wars, no less than private ones, are just only when they are fought on the basis, and in the name, of the moral entitlements ceded to them by their citizens. States have no right to use violence except as bestowed upon them by the social contract. Indeed, the right of public war is nothing but the amalgamation and distillation of all the rights of private war.[126]

By grounding the right of war, and indeed all of politics, in the natural rights of individuals, Grotius captured the emerging spirit of the times. Like Jacob van Heemskerck, he was a man of a new age. Grotius wrote during the transition between the medieval world and the Enlightenment, in which humanity's self-conception underwent a fundamental change. The neatly ordered, hierarchical view of the ancient cosmos had begun to fray, and a different conception of the world, one more materialistic and individualistic, was forming to replace it.[127]

In this newer conception, the cosmos cleaves into two spheres—the physical and the moral. The physical realm is a desacralized space, devoid of spirit, where particles bounce around in a void obeying the mindless, mechanical laws of physics. The moral realm remains hierarchical as before, but the order of precedence is inverted, with the individual emerging as the most significant moral being. Regardless of birth, all men have the natural right to determine the course of their lives, to acquire property, to enter agreements, and to protect these rights through the use of force. Top-down authority is legitimate only when authorized from the bottom up. On this understanding of politics, which philosophers eventually called "liberalism," sovereigns rule by grace of their subjects, rather than the other way around.

God exists in this bifurcated universe, having created matter and the laws of physics, but His status has been diminished. The physical world is a clockwork cosmos operating for all eternity without the need of divine intervention. And though God created man, He created man with Reason, a faculty that itself bestows sovereignty. As Grotius claimed in his infamous "*etiamsi daremus*" passage, human beings would still have moral rights "even if we should concede [*etiamsi daremus*] that which cannot be conceded without the utmost wickedness: that there is no God, or that the affairs of men are of no concern to Him."[128] God was irrelevant for morality or politics, for man was sovereign by virtue of his rational will and capable of constructing his political world through the exercise of that will, through his consent to the social contract.

The emergence of the Old World Order, therefore, was not merely a change that merchants could benefit from—it was a change they could believe in. In the new liberal conception of politics, God and the aristocracy had been demoted and the individual elevated in their place. All of humanity had achieved noble, even divine, status, for the right to war ultimately derived from human will.

When Jacob van Heemskerck attacked the *Santa Catarina* off the coast of Singapore in 1603, he drew Hugo the Great into his legendary career as an international lawyer. It was Grotius who showed his employer, and every state in the world, how they could do business across the globe in the absence of a universal sovereign who could police the system. They did not need a world government to enforce their rights—all they needed was war.

TWO

MANIFESTOS OF WAR

The American literary critic Edmund Wilson had advice for historians of war: Pay more attention to sea slugs. Wilson described a nature film in which this marine invertebrate gobbles "up small organisms through a large orifice at one end of its body; confronted with another sea slug of an only slightly lesser size, it ingurgitates that, too." Wilson believed that wars are fought in a similar fashion, "by the same instincts as the voracity of the sea slug."[1]

Many historians seem instinctively to follow Wilson's advice. Their accounts routinely portray warring sovereigns as moved by ravenous greed or naked self-interest. For example, historians usually describe James Polk, the U.S. president who presided over the Mexican-American War, as a rabid expansionist who coveted Texas, Oregon, and California for the material advantages they each offered. Texas would be a breeding ground for slaves; San Francisco, an ideal port on the Pacific; and the intervening land, with its fertile soil and temperate climate, a breadbasket with which to feed the growing nation. In order to avail himself of these various benefits, the story goes, Polk invaded Mexico in 1846. Over the course of two years, the

United States army killed tens of thousands of Mexican soldiers to conquer 500,000 square miles of Mexican territory. By decisively defeating Mexico, Polk added what is now California, Nevada, Utah, Arizona, and the western parts of New Mexico, Colorado, and Wyoming to the United States and confirmed its sovereignty over Texas.[2]

Sometimes the motives to wage war are described as defensive, rather than expansive. Historians tell us that Louis XIV launched the War of the Reunions in 1683 and the Nine Years War in 1688 to create a *cordon sanitaire*—a series of buffer zones—around his eastern flank to protect France from the Holy Roman Empire.[3] At other times, we are told that sovereigns are moved by the desire for glory. Thus, historians have recounted how, in the next century, the Prussian ruler Frederick the Great sought the rich lands of neighboring Silesia for his kingdom and the prestige they would bring.[4] The invasion of Silesia of 1740 was a brazen act of aggression that burnished Frederick's reputation as a bold military leader and a "great" monarch.

By focusing on the ulterior motives that sovereigns had, or may have had, for waging war, historical narratives like these foster the impression that sovereigns functioned, if not like sea slugs, at least like gangsters. They conjure up images of heads of state simply threatening their neighbors with brute force: "*I want your territory. Give it to me or else.*" But a more careful look at the history of war shows that sovereigns have always been extraordinarily careful to distinguish themselves from criminals. When a gunman demands your money, he doesn't try to justify his demand. He doesn't claim that *he is entitled* to the money. He doesn't say that you should give him your money because it is really his money, or because you owe it to him, or because God wants you to hand it over, or because it isn't fair that he has less money than you do. He simply says: "Your money or your life."

But war waged by sovereigns is different: The decision to go to war always requires justification. Waging war entails more than following through on a threat, or the ingurgitation of territory: Waging war always entails the assertion of a *right*. In the Old World Order, heads of states went to extraordinary lengths to justify the wars they waged. And though their notions of justice were different from ours, sovereigns rarely, if ever, went to war unless they could assert that their cause was in some way just.

WAR FOR UNPAID BILLS

The Mexican-American War is a textbook example of how sovereigns of the Old World Order entered into armed conflict with each other—and, in particular, how they established their legal right to wage war.

Though President Polk wanted the land owned by Mexico, he did not simply threaten to invade unless the Mexican government handed it over.[5] In that respect, Polk did not act like a gangster. He made a *legal* claim for the territory.

His legal justification for the war looked back to 1821, when Mexico secured its independence from Spain. The years following independence brought deep instability. Mexico went through thirty-five administrations in thirty-four years. U.S. citizens conducting business there were subject to illegal confiscations of property and physical assaults by government officials and made numerous claims against Mexico for compensation.[6] U.S. diplomats collected these complaints and presented them to the Mexican government.

The claims were many and varied.[7] Several involved ships, which were then the primary mode of transportation between the United States and Mexico. In one typical case, the owner of the brig *Paragon* of New York claimed that his ship had been maliciously fired upon by the Mexican schooner *Tampico* in the summer of 1834, as she made her way to Vera Cruz.[8] Many of the other claims concerned unpaid debts or improperly seized property.[9]

In early 1837, President Andrew Jackson threatened war unless Mexico satisfied these claims. His successor, Martin Van Buren, issued a similar warning later that year.[10] Faced with the threat of war, Mexico eventually agreed to arbitration. A treaty signed in 1839 empowered a panel of four arbitrators, composed of two Americans and two Mexicans, to decide the validity of these claims.[11] In the event of a tie, the deciding vote would be cast by the King of Prussia's representative.[12]

The panel considered fifty-four claims totaling $6.2 million worth of injuries and awarded the United States roughly $2 million in damages.[13] Unfortunately, the cost of near-constant revolution had depleted Mexico's treasury and it could not satisfy those awards. The United States thus offered to accept Mexican territory in lieu of cash. In 1842, Daniel Webster, secretary of state for President Tyler, wrote to his ambassador, instructing him to "sound the Mexican Govt. upon the subject of a cession of the Territory upon the Pacific, in satisfaction of those claims, or some of them."[14] Mexico refused.

With the land-for-debt plan off the table, the United States negotiated a second agreement in which Mexico agreed to pay the existing award in quarterly installments in gold or silver coins over the course of five years.[15] After four installments, Mexico defaulted again.[16]

To recoup the remainder of the award, Polk revived the aborted plan to accept territory in lieu of cash. He sent his emissary John Slidell down south with instructions to offer to relinquish these claims if Mexico agreed to establish the Rio Grande as the new border of Texas. He also offered to throw in $5 million for part of New Mexico, $20 million for land that included Monterey or San Francisco, and $25 million for all of California.[17] In order to induce Mexico to accept his offer, Polk also issued a threat. He ordered General Zachary Taylor to advance his troops to the edge of the Rio Grande.

In the end, Slidell never managed to deliver the offer, for the Mexican president refused to meet with him.[18] Shortly thereafter, the Mexican army attacked General Taylor's scouting team, which was conducting reconnaissance along the Rio Grande, killing or wounding sixteen soldiers and capturing the rest. Polk asked Congress for a declaration of war and Congress obliged.[19]

Because Polk approached Congress immediately after the attack on Taylor's troops, it has generally been assumed that the main justification for the war was self-defense. Indeed, in his appeal to Congress, President Polk charged Mexico with having "shed American blood upon the American soil."[20] Polk's war message, however, focused first and foremost on the issue of unpaid debts. He led with this issue and cited it as the primary justification of the war. He explained how "the redress of wrongs of our citizens naturally and inseparably blended itself with the question of boundary."[21] Polk presented the attack on Taylor's scouting party as the last straw in a long series of wrongs perpetrated by Mexico against the United States of America.[22]

Polk was not the only one to cite unpaid debts as the central justification for war. James Westcott of Florida bellowed from the Senate floor: "We negotiated a treaty with her, by which she engaged to indemnify our citizens. . . . Has she done so? No, sir! No sir! . . . She ought in justice to pay that amount, and this Government should compel her to pay it."[23]

Polk remained adamant that the war was entirely justified by the unpaid debts throughout the conflict.[24] In his 1846 State of the Union address, Polk described the long history of American grievances, the public appeals, international treaties and arbitration panels, including the dollar amounts of damages awarded and still outstanding: $2,026,139.68.[25] He repeated these claims at his next State of the Union address, in 1847.[26]

By emphasizing the need to recover damages and unpaid debts, Polk's purpose was to show that his country was not acting like a gang of bandits. The United States had made repeated complaints of wrongdoing against the Mexican government, signed an arbitration treaty to resolve these claims, won many favorable rulings for its citizens, negotiated a treaty for the payments of damages, negotiated another treaty following the Mexican default, and offered to accept territory in lieu of cash.[27] It was only after nearly two decades of frustrating negotiations that the United States went to war.[28]

BLOODY CONSTRAINT

War may appear to epitomize the absence of law and order, but in the Old World Order, war *was* law and order. As such, each stage was carefully regulated. Grotius detailed these rules in the seventeenth century but, by that time, they were far from new.[29] They belonged to a lengthy tradition that stretched back more than two millennia.

During the Roman Republic, a priest would approach the border of any territory Rome intended to attack wearing a wool veil. Once there, he would announce a legal grievance, called the *clarigatio*.[30] If the other side ignored the *clarigatio* for thirty-three days, the Senate could authorize war. War would officially commence when the priest returned to the border and, in the presence of three military-age men, threw an iron-tipped spear over the line.[31] As their empire expanded overseas, Rome had to alter the process, for no priest could fling his spear over the ocean. In the revamped system, a priest would take a prisoner from the soon-to-be enemy's territory and force him to buy a small plot of land on the *Campus Martius*, the field of Mars, just outside the ancient city walls of Rome. When the prisoner proved unable to meet the priest's demands, the priest could then throw the spear into "foreign soil," thereby starting the war, and still be home for supper.[32]

Sovereigns in medieval and early modern Europe introduced variations to the protocols: priests with woolen veils and spears were replaced by heralds accompanied by trumpeters. The immunity and safe passage of heralds were absolute; they were benign figures who did not fight.[33] During the Battle of Agincourt in 1415, French and English heralds stood together on a hill overlooking the battlefield and watched as their respective countrymen hacked each other to death.[34] Afterward, the French herald declared the English army the victor.

Because a war could not start until the herald had delivered his message, heralds were not always welcome.[35] When the French herald carrying the colors of the duchy of Alençon arrived in Brussels in 1635 to present a declaration of war to the Spanish ruler Don Fernando, known as the Cardinal-Infante, he discovered that the Cardinal-Infante refused to grant him an audience. To fulfill his mission, the French herald tossed a copy of the declaration of war from his horse into the middle of an angry crowd. The Spanish herald, however, urged those gathered not to touch the paper lest doing so count as accepting the declaration and thus starting the war. The French herald then raced to the border where he nailed two additional copies to a post and notified the mayor of a nearby village about the postings.[36] The declaration, which complained about the false imprisonment of a prince, read:

> The herald of arms of France under the title of Alençon lets it be known
> to all concerned that he came to the Netherlands to find there the

Cardinal-Infante of Spain, . . . as he holds a sovereign prince prisoner who was not at war with him, against the dignity of the Empire and against the law of nations, His Majesty [the King of France] declares that he will get redress for this offense through the use of arms.[37]

States eventually dispensed with the fanfare for the more efficient process in which they relied on diplomats to convey their grievances. In Shakespeare's *Henry V*, the Duke of Exeter, Henry's ambassador and special envoy, claims that Henry is entitled to rule France and demands that the French king abdicate his throne:[38]

> *He wills you, in the name of God Almighty,*
> *That you divest yourself, and lay apart*
> *The borrow'd glories that by gift of heaven,*
> *By law of nature and of nations, 'long*
> *To him and to his heirs; namely, the crown*

When the king asks what happens if he ignores this demand, Exeter replies: "Bloody constraint"—by which he meant, *war*.*

---

*The rules did provide an alternative to an ultimatum: so long as a state made its grievances known to the other side with a reasonable time to respond, the state could attack and declare war simultaneously. Grotius, *DJB*, 3.3.13; Emer de Vattel, *The Law of Nations; or, Principles of the Law of Nature, Applied to the Conduct and Affairs of Nations and Sovereigns*, trans. Joseph Chitty (Philadelphia: T & J. W. Johnson & Co., Law Booksellers, 1867 [1758]), 3.4.60; Henry Wheaton, *Elements of International Law: With a Sketch of the History of the Science* (Philadelphia: Carey, Lea & Blanchard, 1836), 213. Because giving advance notice of an attack to the enemy is usually bad strategy, the alternative procedure became the common approach. When an Anglo-French consortium considered building a railway tunnel under the English Channel in 1881 and the British military was concerned that the tunnel could be used to launch a surprise assault, the military commissioned a study to determine whether states typically gave prior warning before they attacked. The author of the study reported that they did not. Of the 177 wars surveyed from 1700 to 1882, there were only ten instances where war had been declared beforehand. John Frederick Maurice, *Hostilities Without Declarations of War* (London: W. Clowes & Sons, 1883).

THE FRENCH ARE ROOSTERS

In the Old World Order, sovereigns not only issued short declarations of war stating their demands—usually a page or so—they also published longer documents that laid out their case in detail.[39] These documents were known as "war manifestos" because they made "manifest" the legal reasons a sovereign invoked as justifications for waging war.

War manifestos were valued for their literary flair as well as their persuasive force. Heads of state enlisted esteemed writers and scholars as well as experienced lawyers to draft them. The English military and political leader Oliver Cromwell commissioned John Milton, the great epic poet, to write *A Manifesto of the Lord Protector of the Commonwealth* in 1655 when he ordered the invasion of the Spanish possessions in the Caribbean.[40] In 1703, the Holy Roman Emperor Leopold I employed Gottfried Leibniz, the rationalist philosopher, co-inventor of calculus, and a trained lawyer, to compose the *Manifesto for the Defense of the Rights of Charles III*, which defended the empire's involvement in the War of the Spanish Succession.

Consider the very first published war manifesto printed in 1492, a copy of which we obtained from the Yale University's Beinecke Rare Books Library. Written on behalf of Maximilian I (1459–1519), soon to become the Holy Roman Emperor, the document is eight pages long and made of fine parchment. Unlike many of the later manifestos we found, which are pamphlet sized, this manuscript is larger, with its pages approximately the size of standard notebook paper. The printing is clear but the typeface betrays the transitional nature of the document. Many of the Latin words are abbreviated, following the medieval practice of using scribal shorthand to reduce the labor of copying manuscripts.[41]

Modern-day readers will have difficulty understanding the document. The manifesto begins as follows: "Since there is no one who would not know that the French are roosters."[42] The problem is not simply that most won't get the joke—"*gallus*" means "a Gaul" (i.e., a French person) but also "a rooster" in Latin—or don't know enough about fifteenth-century history to appreciate why the French are being called roosters, or even what it means to be called a rooster. Most puzzling is that Maximilian claimed the right to wage war against the French king, Charles VIII, because Charles stole Maximilian's wife.

In 1491, Charles invaded Brittany. When Anne, the Duchess of Brittany, surrendered, Charles demanded that she marry him. Unfortunately, not only was Charles notoriously unappealing—the portraitist Francesco Mantegna confided that the thought of this "tiny, hunchbacked man," with "big, bulging eyes," a "large hooknose," and "a few scanty hairs on his head," gave him nightmares—but Anne was also already married to Maximilian. She nevertheless felt compelled to renounce her marriage to Maximilian and marry the French king.[43] Three days later, Charles and Anne were secretly engaged and on December 6, 1491, they were publicly wed in the Langeais Castle of Touraine.

Unsurprisingly, Maximilian was furious. He decided to attack Charles on the battlefield and in the court of public opinion. Availing himself of the new media of the day, the printing press, Maximilian published a manifesto setting out his just cause for war.

The manifesto is a long, acid-soaked diatribe against Charles. The opening insult about the French being roosters is a reference to their king: Charles is the rooster claiming Anne of Brittany as one of his many hens. The manifesto proceeds to accuse the French king of feeding the "gullible people" "fictitious lies" full of "inane trifles and boastings" and preferring these "treacheries" to the "power and vigor of just war."[44] Charles "surpasses the name of the fornicator and of the rapist and of the adulterer."[45] The manifesto concludes that Charles's crimes were so heinous that Maximilian had no choice but to go to war.

To use a more modern example, President Polk's war message to Congress in 1846 was understood to be a manifesto, though the United States stopped using this term after 1812, presumably because it sounded too European.[46] In this message, Polk justified the Mexican-American War by setting out his nation's just cause, namely, the collection of debts.

Why did sovereigns bother to explain their reasons for war? Why not just go to war? War manifestos served several purposes. They looked and functioned a lot like complaints in lawsuits today—although, as Maximilian's manifesto demonstrates, they usually displayed more panache. Like a complaint, a manifesto laid out the injured party's claim against the alleged injurer. And just as a complaint is a demand for an award of damages, so, too, was the manifesto.

By making the reasons for war manifest, manifestos sought to make clear that the war in question was just. As Vattel explained, "War is at present published and declared by manifestos. These pieces never fail to contain the justificatory reasons, good or bad, on which the party grounds his right to take up arms." He added: even "[t]he least scrupulous sovereign would wish to be thought just, equitable, and a lover of peace."[47]

Manifestos sometimes led to peaceful settlements, as can be traced by looking at what might be called "counter-manifestos." If the manifesto is the equivalent of a complaint by a plaintiff in a lawsuit, the counter-manifesto is the equivalent of the answer that the defendant files in response. And just as an answer can lead to settlement, by clarifying the terms of dispute, a counter-manifesto allowed states to resolve the underlying disagreement. Instead of resorting to war, one side might, for example, offer an apology or compensation.

During the Nootka Crisis of 1790, Spain captured several British ships it claimed were encroaching on its sovereign territory in the Pacific Northwest. Great Britain issued a manifesto, in the form of the king's message to both houses of Parliament, threatening war over the seizure.[48] In a series of counter-manifestos, Spain slowly gave ground.[49] While it denied that Britain had the right to trade directly with Spanish America, and asserted its right to use force to protect its claims, it nevertheless agreed to return the ships. The crisis was eventually diffused.

When counter-manifestos did not lead to settlement, they remained as rebuttals to the justifications for war offered by the other sovereign—as well as a statement of any counter-claims. One notable example, the 1672 counter-manifesto written by the States-General of the Netherlands, is split into two columns. The left column—titled, English Declaration—reprints the English declaration of war against the Dutch; the right column—titled, ANSWER—contains a point-by-point rebuttal of each English accusation. The left column, for instance, repeated an English allegation that it was intervening in the West Indies for the purposes of freeing slaves from Dutch sugar plantations—"to give liberty to all of our subjects in that colony"—and the right column replied that the true reason was to cripple Dutch trade and "by all possible means to destroy our Colony."[50]

Manifestos were meant to be distributed widely, to reach the population that would be called on to pay for and fight in the war. Their audiences also included foreign neutral powers, allies, the enemy, and their elites. As the technology of distributing the written word changed, so, too, did the means of distributing manifestos. Medieval manifestos were hand-copied and delivered throughout the countryside, where they were often read aloud to gathered crowds. In 1340, King Edward III of England ordered that his justification for his war with France "be fixed upon church doors, and other public places, whereby the manifest notice thereof may come to all men."[51] But with the advent of the printing press and increasing literacy rates, manifestos were printed and eventually sold as pamphlets to the European public.[52] Some surviving manifestos still have their price tags. Louis XV's Declaration of War on Spain of 1719, with accompanying manifesto, was sold for an affordable six pence.[53] In the eighteenth century, with the proliferation of newspapers, manifestos migrated there as features of the daily press.[54]

The style of manifestos differed according to the political strategy of the sovereign, the nature of the dispute, and the writer. Some were vicious and personal; others, dispassionate and clinical. The most legally rigorous and compelling were often extremely tedious. Leibniz's long manifesto has all the charm of a lawyer's motion to dismiss. His point was that the French had exerted undue influence over the dying King of Spain by forcing him to change his will, but this is how he explained it:

> It was with this in view that the partisans of France at the court of Madrid drew up a will in the name of the late king, when he was near his end, in which, in article XVII, they made him interpret the Treaty of the Pyrenees and the contract of marriage with Queen Maria Theresa, together with the renunciation which is inserted therein, in a manner contrary to everything that had always been understood; as if the aim of this renunciation was nothing but the stopping of the union of the two crowns under one head.[55]

States continued to issue war manifestos into the nineteenth and twentieth centuries, though the term "manifesto" became less common. Regardless of what they were called, sovereigns were always anxious to distinguish themselves from gangsters by providing reasons that made reference to their *right* to use force. As Gustavus Aldophus, the King of Sweden, began his manifesto: "When we come to the business of war, the first question to be proposed is, whether it be just or no."[56]

"JUST" CAUSES

Even though sovereigns took war manifestos very seriously, we might wonder whether *we* should. Should we not be suspicious of these documents, which after all were propaganda used by sovereigns to sell wars to their subjects?

Of course, it would be naive to assume that every manifesto is an accurate statement of why sovereigns decided to wage war. Some are; some aren't. It is hard to know what lies in the hearts of those who send men off to battle. But the value of war manifestos has little to do with what they may or may not reveal about the inner lives of sovereigns. Manifestos matter *precisely because they are propaganda*. The function of propaganda is to persuade. We can therefore tell what reasons people usually found persuasive by examining the reasons that propaganda offered to persuade them.

Even though war manifestos are invaluable resources for understanding war in the Old World Order, very few studies of them exist, and none are in English.[57] Manifestos have been neglected by historians in part because they are so hard to find. The surviving copies are scattered throughout the libraries of the world and published in many different languages. In order to learn more about the legal claims sovereigns made when going to war, we compiled our own collection of manifestos. Our compilation contains more than 400 manifestos starting from the late fifteenth century to the Second World War and in languages as varied as Latin, English, French, German, Ottoman Turkish, Dutch, Portuguese, and Classical Chinese. This collection offers a glimpse into an alien world—one in which war was made for reasons that today would be deemed utterly absurd but which were then deemed entirely legitimate.[58]

Maximilian's manifesto, for example, justifies a war against France because Charles stole his wife—though, admittedly, it is the only document in our collection that alleges wife stealing. The other manifestos charge their enemies with less salacious forms of wrongdoing and usually with more than one type. These include self-defense (69 percent of manifestos), enforcing treaty obligations (47 percent), obtaining compensation for tortious injuries (42 percent), violations of the laws of war or law of nations (35 percent), stopping those who would disrupt the balance of power (33 percent), enforcement of succession laws and other hereditary rights (30 percent), protection of trade interests (19 percent), humanitarian considerations (17 percent), protecting the religious liberty of one's people (15 percent), protection of diplomatic relations (14 percent), defending the "true religion" (13 percent), seeking independence (6 percent), collection of debts (4 percent), and defending missionaries (1 percent).[59]

That self-defense was the leading reason given for war is not surprising, but many of the other justifications bespeak a world dramatically different from our own. Rectifying tortious injuries, collecting debts, protecting trade interests, and defending religious interests of various kinds: not one of these would be regarded as a remotely acceptable reason for launching a war today. But there are surprising similarities as well. We tend to think of humanitarian intervention, such as NATO's 1999 bombing campaign to protect Kosovar Albanians, as a recent invention. But as the above list indicates, a full 17 percent of the manifestos we examined from the late fifteenth through the mid twentieth centuries included humanitarian justifications.[60] Milton, for example, claimed that the war with Spain was justified in part by the brutality of the conquistadors. Warships should be "employed in avenging the blood of the English, as well as that of the poor Indians, which in those places has been so unjustly, so cruelly, and so often shed by the hands of the Spaniards."[61] Teddy Roosevelt defended the U.S. invasion of Cuba on the ground that "there are occasional crimes committed on so vast a scale and of such peculiar horror as to make us doubt whether it is not our manifest duty to endeavor at least to show our disapproval of the deed and our sympathy with those who have suffered by it."[62]

The best strategy to bear in mind when reading manifestos is the old lawyerly adage: "When the law is on your side, pound the law; when the facts are on your side, pound the facts; when neither is on your side, pound the table." When sovereigns had good arguments, they made them clearly. When they had evidence to back up their claims, they were specific and detailed. When sovereigns had neither, it was obvious. They performed the rhetorical equivalent of pounding the table by deploying random insults and red herrings. But what *all* the manifestos did—regardless of merit—was to defend their actions as justified responses to wrongs. Wars could not be entered for any reason whatsoever. They had to be made in the name of justice.

ENFORCING THE LAW OF NATIONS

The manifestos demonstrate one additional, essential feature of the Old World Order: Violations of international law were not merely a cause for complaint. They were a just cause for war. A full 47 percent of manifestos in our collection cite a broken treaty obligation as a justification for war, and 35 percent reference the laws of war or law of nations. In addition, a number cite violations of rights protected by customary international law, including self-defense (69 percent), trade interests (19 percent), and diplomatic relations (14 percent).

The Framers of the U.S. Constitution understood this well. They were close students of Vattel,[63] who followed Grotius in claiming that a breach of the law of nations was a just cause for war.[64] Indeed, the Framers built their new constitution around this concern. At the Constitutional Convention, James Madison declared that any plan for a new national government must "prevent those violations of the law of nations & of Treaties which if not prevented must involve us in the calamaties of foreign wars."[65] For this reason, the new constitution declared treaties to be "the supreme law of the land" and judges in every state would be required to enforce them, *even if* it meant overriding their own constitutions or laws.[66] The Framers were concerned that violating treaties that the national government made would invite lawful military responses.

In the modern era, it is not uncommon for observers to wonder whether international law is really law when there are no police to enforce it (a problem to which we will return in Chapter Sixteen).[67] Few recognize that this problem is so vexing in part because it is so new. During the Old World Order, international law did not need police. International law was backed by the very real threat of war.

CONQUEST

Anyone who has studied history at pretty much any level knows that conquests have caused the map of the world to be redrawn countless times. Consider the following very short list of prominent examples from European history: Julius Caesar, who famously said *"veni, vidi, vici"* ("I came, I saw, I conquered") after the Battle of Zela in 47 BC, completed the Roman conquest of Gaul in 58 BC. Then the Visigoths conquered the City of Rome in AD 410, prompting Saint Jerome to lament: "My sobs stop me from dictating these words. Behold, the city that conquered the world has been conquered in its turn."[68] Pepin the Short, King of the Franks, conquered the Italian lands of the Lombards and donated them to the pope as the new "Papal States" in 756. Charlemagne conquered the Saxons of Northern Germany and was crowned "Roman Emperor" by the pope in 800. William, Duke of Normandy, conquered England in 1066. Mehmet the Great finally destroyed the Roman Empire when he conquered Constantinople in 1453. Ferdinand and Isabella completed the *Reconquista* of Spain from the Moors by annexing Granada in 1492. Oliver Cromwell and his New Model Army conquered Ireland in the middle of the seventeenth century. A few years later, Charles X of Sweden conquered half of Denmark-Norway by sending his army from Jutland to Zealand over the ice during an especially cold winter in the March Across the Belts of 1658. Louis XIV, whose motto was the Caesarian *"ut vidi, vici"* ("as I saw, I conquered") seized Strasbourg, now one of three capitals of the European Union (along with Luxembourg and Brussels) and the home to the European Parliament and the European Court of Human Rights, but then a city that strategically lay on the border of France and the Holy Roman Empire, in 1681. Peter the Great conquered part of Sweden upon which he built the new Russian capital, St. Petersburg, in 1703. Frederick the Great of Prussia conquered Silesia in 1740. Napoleon conquered Spain, Italy, the Netherlands, and a good part of Central Europe in the Napoleonic Wars during the first decade of the nineteenth century. And Germany, led by Kaiser Wilhelm I and Otto von Bismarck, recaptured Strasbourg in the Franco-Prussian War in 1871, only to lose it again to France in the First World War, regain it in 1940, and lose it for good after the Second World War. And so on.

Conquest was so prevalent in the Old World Order precisely because war served as an indispensable tool of justice. Any sovereign who had demanded satisfaction for the violation of a right and failed to receive it was *legally permitted to seek redress through force*. The function of manifestos was to explain the legal basis of the war being waged. What sovereigns were entitled to redress through war depended on which rights were at issue. Since many of the rights over which wars were waged involved disputes *over* territory, it was only natural that victims should be entitled *to* territory. Thus, by sanctioning the use of violence to enforce rights, the Old World Order legitimated the practice of conquest.

Conquest entailed the seizure and control of territory in war.[69] Moreover, what a sovereign militarily won, it legally got to keep.[70] Conquest thus functioned as compensation for whatever injury had supposedly justified the war in the first place. In the Old World Order, when territory was captured in war, the captors automatically inherited all of the legal rights of the previous sovereign.[71] The conqueror stood, as it were, in the shoes of the vanquished; the new ruler could now do anything that the old ruler had been able to do. Similarly, the new sovereign became the owner of any property that had belonged to the old sovereign.

Perhaps most valuable to the conqueror was control over the conquered legal system. As the new sovereign, a conqueror could appoint its own governors, administrators, and judges and thus control the rules that regulated the life of the community. By co-opting the bureaucracy of the state, the conqueror was able to tax the population, impose import and export duties, and sell licenses to engage in commercial activities. In the late sixteenth century, the Estado da Índia, the Portuguese state in India, generated most of its revenue from licensing the right to trade in Asia, not from buying and selling spices.[72] Sovereignty also brought manpower, including the right to conscript men to fight in future wars. Territory wasn't simply land—it was land inhabited by potential soldiers who could bolster existing armies for future conquests.

Conquest differed from occupation—as it does today.[73] In conquest, the conqueror claims sovereignty: that is, the supreme authority to rule the vanquished population on a permanent basis. Occupiers do not. They claim certain powers to govern—namely, those that are strictly necessary to maintain law and order—but their authority is temporary and bounded. During the Franco-Prussian War of 1870–1871, German forces invaded Paris and exercised control over the population. But Germany did not conquer France, or even Paris. The Arc de Triomphe did not become the Triumphbogen, Parisians were not forced to swear allegiance to the Kaiser, and the Prussian Civil Code did not replace the Napoleonic Code. Germany merely occupied the city without asserting sovereignty over it.

Conquest also differed from surrender.[74] In surrender, one side agrees to lay down its arms, usually under certain conditions. Those conditions could be more favorable than conquest—for example, they might take the form of cash payments. But they could also be less favorable. Those in a strong military position could even demand unconditional surrender. As far as we know, no state in the Old World Order agreed to such a demand, and for obvious reasons: "After the surrender," Grotius wrote, "there is nothing that the vanquished may not have to suffer."[75]

It is hard to think of a legal right that has a longer or more illustrious pedigree than conquest. Cyrus the Great, who ruled the Persian Empire in the sixth century BC, admonished his court not to feel guilty about their imperial prerogatives: "It is an eternal law the wide world over, that when a city is taken in war, the citizens, their persons, and all their property fall into the hands of the conquerors. It is not by injustice, therefore, that you hold what you have taken, rather it is through your own human kindness that the citizens are allowed to keep whatever they do retain."[76]

When he wrote *The Law of War and Peace*, Grotius built on this tradition, incorporating conquest into his theory of war as compensation for wrongs that could be satisfied in no other way. He certainly did not invent the legal right of conquest. It is not even clear that the right of conquest was "invented," if by this we mean deliberately created by someone or some group. Like most of international law, or as it was called during the early modern era the "law of nations," its rules developed over time, as customary practices among sovereigns and statesmen who accepted them as binding.[77]

In *The Law of War and Peace*, Grotius not only collected many of the rules of conquest that had been written down in digests of Roman and canon law, but he shaped them according to his theory of war. He emphasized that a state is permitted to conquer another state *only* to prevent or redress the violation of a right. The fact that a neighboring state has better land is not a valid reason to take it. "The desire to change abode, in order that by abandoning swamps and wildernesses a more fruitful soil may be acquired, does not afford a just cause of war."[78] Nor can a state conquer another state simply because it believes that the people would be better off under new management. "[E]ven if something is advantageous for any one, the right is not forthwith conferred upon me to impose this upon him by force."[79] Neither are theological differences nor bad character valid causes of war. Grotius deemed it "shameless" to conquer territory "even though the occupant may be wicked, may hold wrong views about God, or may be dull of wit."[80]

President Polk, therefore, was following the Grotian rules when he justified his decision to wage war on Mexico. He emphasized Mexico's failure to pay its debts, rather than California's desirable access to the Pacific or the fertility of its soil, because the United States had the right to collect those debts. And in a just war, rights are all that matter.

BY THE SWORD

Europeans brought the Old World Order to the New World. They came as conquerors and claimed sovereignty over the indigenous peoples in accordance with the law of (their) nations.

The Spanish conquistadors were the first to arrive and they subdued much of the hemisphere with breathtaking savagery.[81] The official justification for the massacre, enslavement, and domination of the Aztecs, Incas, and other native peoples was humanitarian intervention.[82] Francisco de Vitoria, Spain's leading theologian of the sixteenth century, argued that wars waged "in lawful defence of the innocent from unjust death" are permissible, and listed "human sacrifice practiced on innocent people or the killing of condemned criminals for cannibalism" as justifying military intervention.[83] Vitoria chose his examples carefully, for it was widely believed that these practices were rampant throughout the New World. Others, like Alberico Gentili, another sixteenth-century authority on the laws of war, agreed that military intervention was justified by savagery, though not in order to protect the innocent. War was to punish the guilty. "The cause of the Spaniards is just when they make war on the Indians who practised abominable lewdness even with beasts, and who eat human flesh slaying men for that purpose. For such sins are contrary to human nature."[84] Grotius agreed with Gentili.[85] Though bad deeds were not normally just causes for war, these particular deeds were so heinous that punitive war was justified.

The United States justified its sovereignty on the basis of conquest. In the Supreme Court case of *Johnson v. M'Intosh*, decided in 1823, Chief Justice John Marshall ruled that the sovereignty of the United States was "maintained and established as far west as the river Mississippi, *by the sword*."[86] The Supreme Court is one of the "Courts of the conqueror" and "[c]onquest gives a title which [it] cannot deny."[87] As far as the Indian tribes are concerned, the chief justice did not mince words. Though they had the right to use the land they once owned, they were nevertheless conquered peoples and mere tenants, who had to accept the superior power of the United States. "[The Indians] were admitted to be the rightful occupants of the soil, with a legal as well as just claim to retain possession of it, and to use it according to their own discretion," Marshall wrote, "but their rights to complete sovereignty, as independent nations, were necessarily diminished."[88]

Thomas Jefferson also argued for American independence based on the right of conquest. In 1774, he published a pamphlet declaring that the colonists were entitled to revolt because *they* were the ones who had conquered the land, not the British. "America was conquered, and her settlements made, and firmly established, at the expence of individuals, and not of the British public. Their own blood was spilt in acquiring lands for their settlement."[89]

To acquire Indian land, settlers usually purchased it. Famously, or infamously, the Dutch settlers paid $24 worth of trinkets to the Lenape tribe for the island of Manhattan. British colonists followed the same practice in their founding of New England. In 1629, the Massachusetts Bay Company

ordered its colonists that "[i]f any of the Savages pretend Right of Inheritance to all or any Part of the Lands graunted in our Pattent . . . purchase
their Tytle, that we may avoyde the least Scruple of Intrusion."[90] Though
those who sold their land did not appreciate the consequences of the sale
or its value, it does appear that the colonists did purchase most of the land
they settled. As one scholar puts it, "[C]ontrary to the common belief that
the Indians were ruthlessly deprived of their land, almost every part of
[Massachusetts] that came to be inhabited by the whites was purchased
from the Indians, except the areas that were either acquired by conquest or,
like Salem and Boston, never claimed by the Indians, because of depopulation by epidemics."[91]

This pattern, "purchases punctuated by rare conquests," was the standard way in which land was acquired from Native Americans across the
continent.[92] Felix Cohen, the founder of the field of Federal Indian Law
in the United States, estimated that, by 1947, the federal government had
paid over $800 million for the right to Indian lands.[93] As the commissioner
of Indian affairs reported in 1872, "[e]xcept only in the case of the Indians
in Minnesota, after the outbreak of 1862, the United States government
has never extinguished an Indian title as by right of conquest; and in this
latter case the Government provided the Indians another reservation, besides giving them the proceeds of the sales of the lands vacated by them in
Minnesota."[94]

While most Indian land was purchased, these transactions were hardly
fair. In 1763, King George III proclaimed that only the Crown could buy
Indian land. The U.S. Supreme Court later ruled in *Johnson v. M'Intosh*
that by virtue of its conquest, this exclusive right to purchase passed to
the United States government. This created what is called a monopsony—
one buyer with many sellers. With no competitors to outbid the United
States, the government was free to lowball Indian tribes and drive down
land prices. But the legal predicament of the Indian tribes was crueler still:
The United States government was not only able to dictate land prices, it
could threaten to go to war unless it got them. Given the "choice" between
selling their land and being raided by the cavalry, most elected to sell.

In a few notable instances, when Indians refused to sell their land, they
suffered the consequences. When gold was discovered in the Black Hills of

MANIFESTOS OF WAR   51

South Dakota in 1874, the United States government tried to persuade the Sioux Indians to sell the land. And when the Sioux rebuffed these offers, the United States ordered the Seventh Cavalry to remove them. However, the incompetence of their commander, Lieutenant Colonel George Armstrong Custer, led to the company's slaughter at the hands of Sitting Bull and Crazy Horse in the Battle of the Little Bighorn. Congress responded to one of the worst military defeats in American history by cutting off the Indians' food supply. Faced with starvation, the Sioux surrendered and signed a treaty ceding the Black Hills to the United States.[95]

Under the rules of the Old World Order, agreements such as these were fully enforceable. An agreement between sovereigns made under duress was still an agreement—and violating such an agreement was a just cause for war. In the Old World Order, states were empowered to practice what today we call by the derogatory term "gunboat diplomacy." Though gunboats were often used to coerce agreements from weaker states—the Dutch Republic established its empire in the seventeenth century by using warships of the Dutch East India Company to extract exclusive trading agreements from East Indian potentates—ground forces were used as well.[96] Thus, King Stanislaw August and the Polish legislature (known as the Sejm) agreed in 1773 to cede 30 percent of Polish territory and half of its population to Austria, Prussia, and Russia when these states threatened war otherwise.[97] As the historian of Poland Norman Davies described the macabre act of self-mutilation, "the victim not only gave his assent for the operation; he was persuaded to wield the knife himself."[98]

Though the term "gunboat diplomacy" is often used whenever one state makes a military threat against another state, we use the term more narrowly to refer to its use or threat of violence to negotiate agreements: The more powerful state threatens to unleash its military on the weaker unless it agrees to unfavorable terms. As distinct from contracts in domestic settings that are undermined by coercion, treaties in the Old World Order signed with menacing gunboats in the harbor, or troops amassed on the border, were legally valid.[99]

The Old World Order accepted the legitimacy of gunboat diplomacy because it accepted the legitimacy of war. It would be absurd, after all, to give a state the right to use force to gain compensation for a wrong but not give it the right to *threaten* to use force to gain the same compensation. Indeed, the horrors of battle were such that a threat was sometimes all that was needed.

WHO OWNS CALIFORNIA?

On January 12, 1847, a commandant of the Mexican army signed the Articles of Capitulation at Campo de Cahuenga in Los Angeles, right across from the current address of Universal Studios in North Hollywood.[100] The United States had defeated Mexico and conquered California. This story of violent acquisition and subjugation is not secret, behind-closed-doors diplomatic history. The conquest of California was openly admitted and indeed celebrated, most of all by the President of the United States. In his State of the Union address of 1848, President Polk praised the skill, diligence, and courage of the military in their "conquest of the Californias."[101] The United States saw California, it came to California, and it conquered California.

President Polk did not hide the truth and felt no shame in seizing Mexican territory because the United States was following the rules that existed at the time, and had existed for centuries. The United States fought to collect unpaid debts—a just cause of war in the Old World Order. It then took conquered territory as compensation for the injuries its citizens had suffered, as well as reimbursement for the cost of waging the war. Far from being a tale of a rogue imperial power molesting a weaker neighbor, the story he presented is a triumphal one, a proud history of a war fought in accordance with international law and just war theory.

When we look more closely, this story unfortunately is missing several crucial facts. In the years preceding the outbreak of the Mexican-American War, the southern boundary of the Mexican state of Tejas was the Nueces River. When Texas declared independence from Mexico in 1836, it claimed that the boundary lay south of the Nueces, at the Rio Grande. Texans justified this claim by citing the Treaty of Velasco, signed the same year, by the Mexican General Santa Anna while he was being held prisoner at the conclusion of the Battle of San Jacinto. Santa Anna agreed to withdraw his troops south of the Rio Grande and, in return, Texas would withdraw its troops to five leagues north. Texans believed that this agreement reset the border further south and, when the United States annexed Texas, it took this view as well.[102] This legal position, however, was absurd. As a young congressman from Illinois named Abraham Lincoln pointed out, if the treaty had shifted the border from the Nueces River to the Rio Grande, "it contains the singular features [sic] of stipulating that Texas shall not go within five leagues of her own boundary."[103]

If Lincoln was right, and the treaty did not actually change the border between Texas and Mexico, then Polk sent Taylor and his men into Mexican territory when he sent them to the edge of the Rio Grande in 1846! Though the debts were real, Polk's moving plea to avenge "American blood shed upon American soil" was based on either a lie or a terrible mistake.

But it turns out that none of these complications matter. In fact, even if Polk had been lying about the real legal cause of the war—Mexico's unpaid debts—that would not change the legal status of the conquest. For as we have seen, in the Old World Order, Might was Right. Winning in war meant winning in law. California became part of the United States simply because the United States Army was victorious in a formal war. As the Secretary of War William Marcy explained to the new governor of California, General Stephen Watts Kearny, "Under the law of nations, the power conquering a territory or country has a right to establish a civil government within the same, as a means of securing the conquest."[104]

But if states can get what they want, no matter what, even when they act for unjust causes, what was the point of the whole charade of claiming justice? Why did sovereigns make such an effort to list their just causes for going to war in elaborate manifestos that they painstakingly distributed as far and wide as possible? And why did Grotius spill so much ink on the "just causes" of war if it really did not matter, in the end, whether the war was launched for just reasons or not?

There are four related reasons. First, it would be a mistake to think that unjust wars were costless. Even in nondemocratic states, waging war requires marshaling the resources of the nation. Bad reasons for war can undermine the war effort; it can also hurt sovereigns' legitimacy at home and embolden their opponents.

Of course, sovereigns made do with bad reasons when they had no other choice. In defending his marriage to Anne, Charles VIII made the best arguments he could, and though in the end he got the girl, he was publicly humiliated by the pope. The papal bull annulling Anne's previous marriage to Maximilian scolded the couple for their recklessness in marrying before receiving a dispensation and warned others not to repeat their mistake.[105] No rule can stop someone who is intent on breaking it, but it can make the offender pay dearly nonetheless. Sovereigns live by the law, so they can die—or at least be badly injured—by it as well.

Second, the justice of a war might not have mattered for legal rights in war, but many believed that it mattered for their souls in the afterlife. To wage an unjust war was to engage in a mass slaughter of innocent people and thus to commit mortal sin. In a world in which religion was almost universally accepted, the threat of eternal damnation was reason enough to worry about just causes.

Third, even if belligerents didn't care about the justice of their wars, their allies did. The obligation of a state to comply with its pledge to render military assistance to another state was conditional on the legality of the conflict in question. In legal terms, the *casus foederis*—the event that triggers the duty to aid an ally—always depended on the *casus belli*—the event that justifies the war itself. As Grotius wrote about mutual assistance treaties, "such agreements cannot be stretched to include wars for which no just cause exists."[106] Manifestos presented the case that a state's war was just so as to make it difficult for allies to wriggle out of their treaty obligations.

The last response goes to the heart of the Old World Order. The Old World Order rewarded conquests made for unjust causes, as well as for just ones, *because there was no other choice*.

The manifestos issued by sovereigns may have functioned like a complaint in a lawsuit, but there was no world court to weigh the evidence and arguments on both sides and render a decision on who was truly in the wrong. After all, sovereigns, by definition, do not recognize any higher authority. As a result, there was no neutral, impartial procedure for distinguishing bad reasons from good ones. One side would boldly trumpet the justice of its cause, whereas the other would bitterly decry the hypocrisy and villainy of the whole enterprise. The most that a state could do was to offer the best arguments in its favor.

In a world where states are sovereign and war is legal, it is impossible to adjudicate between just and unjust wars. Once the Grotian legal order allowed victims to use force to redress their injuries (or those of their citizens), there was no choice but to permit aggressors to profit from their wrongs as well. For penalizing those with unjust causes would jeopardize the entire global economy.

In the Old World Order, with its commitment to the Might is Right Principle, abuse was not only possible—it was inevitable. But in the absence of global courts, if war is legal, Might must be Right, even if it is wrong.

THREE

LICENSE TO KILL

The settlers called it the "Ghost Dance," and it terrified them. The Indian ritual began with a solemn song. In unison, the celebrants raised their hands to the west and chanted about the return of their ancestors: "The father says so; The father says so; You shall see your kindred—*E'yayo'*!"[1] Once the song ended, everyone wept.

The mood shifted when the group joined hands and circled a sacred tree. The dancers accelerated until they whirled as fast as they could, their feet kicking up dust and their rhythmic chants turning into shrieks. Decorum gave way to pandemonium as hysteria swept the crowd. Some dancers were euphoric, pulsating and screaming in spiritual ecstasy; others were abject, trembling and howling from overwhelming grief. One by one, they broke from the spinning ring and wandered about as if possessed, then toppled over and writhed in the dirt.

A spectator described a woman who staggered away from the dance, "her hair flying over her face, which was purple, looking as if the blood would burst through; her hands and arms moving wildly; every breath a pant and a groan; and she fell on her back, and went down like a log.

I stepped up to her as she lay there motionless, but with every muscle twitching and quivering. She seemed to be perfectly unconscious."[2] Others imagined themselves transformed into animals, "stepping high and pawing the air in a frightful manner."[3] Even while delirious, the dancers tried not to trample those underfoot, until they, too, succumbed. When the last one collapsed, the dancers slowly regained their senses, gathered in a circle, and discussed their encounter with the ghosts.

The Ghost Dance was created by a Pauite shaman from Nevada known as Wovoka in 1889. Wovoka claimed to be the incarnation of Christ, who had come to earth two thousand years before to save the white men, only to be scorned and crucified by them. Now he was returning to rescue the red men instead. He heralded the imminent resurrection of their ancestors and claimed that his dance would enable the living to commune with the dead—the "ghosts." He also promised that the dance would sweep evil from the land, cure disease, restore the buffalo and game to the plains, and reestablish the rule of the tribes.

Wovoka did not preach violence, but as the Ghost Dance spread across the West, it developed a menacing edge. Some performed it as a war dance, or so it appeared to skittish settlers. When the Sioux joined hands, they chanted ominous verses: "Father, I come; Mother, I come; Brother, I come; Father, give us back our arrows."[4] The Sioux also wore sacred garments—white sheets called "ghost shirts" that were trimmed with blue stripes and decorated with birds and other animals. They believed that the ghost shirts were powerful enough to stop bullets.[5]

Like other forms of millenarianism, the Ghost Dance movement was born of great desperation. In addition to the cultural disintegration that befell all Indian tribes as they were herded onto reservations, the Sioux in 1889 were starving to death. With whites settling their former hunting grounds and driving its once plentiful game to extinction, repeated crop failures devastated the Sioux population. Making matters worse, the federal Bureau of Indian Affairs failed to deliver the food and clothing rations pledged as part of the peace treaties that the Sioux had been compelled to sign. Even General Nelson A. Miles, the commanding officer sent by Washington to investigate the Ghost Dance disturbances, conceded that the Sioux had ample cause for complaint. "They claimed that the government had not fulfilled its treaties and had failed to make large enough appropriations for their support; that they had suffered for want of food, and the evidence of this is beyond question and sufficient to satisfy any unprejudiced intelligent mind."[6]

The Sioux expected the Ghost Dance to deliver the Messiah. It brought the Seventh Cavalry instead. On the morning of December 29, 1890, soldiers from the same company Custer commanded at Little Bighorn arrived at Wounded Knee Creek in the Pine Ridge Reservation of South Dakota with the intention of disarming a band of Miniconjou Sioux. When a soldier attempted the take the rifle of a deaf tribesman named Black Coyote, a struggle ensued and a shot rang out. In the confusion, the commanding officer ordered his troops to open fire. They cut down scores during the initial volley and slaughtered several hundred more soon after. Soldiers on horseback hunted men, women, and children for hours.

As the news of the massacre at Wounded Knee reached the Rosebud Reservation twenty miles away, the Brulé Sioux feared that they were next. They danced the Ghost Dance as they waited for the soldiers. Lieutenant Edward "Ned" Casey, with his men, was on his way, but he was not looking for a fight. Hoping to avoid another calamity, the officer sought to defuse the tense situation through calm diplomacy.

Lieutenant Casey was the consummate soldier. Hailing from a long line of military men, the West Point graduate and forty-year-old veteran of the Indian wars was liked and respected by the members of the tribes with whom he worked. He commanded an elite band of Cheyenne scouts who affectionately called him "Big Nose."

As Casey made his way up the White Clay Creek to No Water on January 9, 1891, he encountered a group of forty Brulé Sioux. Casey asked the men whether it would be possible to meet with the chiefs at their camp. A messenger left with the query and another one returned with the answer: The chiefs thought it unwise to approach No Water, for the ghost dancers were agitated and would likely attack.

As the message was being delivered, a twenty-year-old Brulé named Tasunka Ota (known as Plenty Horses)[7] slowly edged away from the group. He stood a few feet back from the lieutenant as he calmly removed the Winchester from his blanket. When Casey agreed to take the chiefs' advice and head back to Pine Ridge, Plenty Horses raised the rifle to his shoulders and, for no discernible reason, pulled the trigger. The bullet ripped through Casey's skull and exited below his right eye. He fell dead from his horse.[8]

THE TRIAL OF PLENTY HORSES

Newspapers around the country reported the killing. A Sioux Indian, they wrote, had treacherously gunned down a gallant American officer from behind. Casey's killing outraged General Miles. Aside from the sheer senselessness of the deed, Miles knew the victim well. He also knew Casey's brother and had served under his father in the Civil War.[9] The general ordered Plenty Horses arrested and transferred to the civilian authorities to be tried for murder.

The trial began on Friday morning, April 24, 1891, at the Sioux Falls Masonic Temple, the building used when federal judges came to town. Interest was so great that the *New York World* sent a reporter to cover the proceedings. According to the correspondent, the spectators in the packed courtroom had already made up their mind: "A white man has been murdered by an Indian. The Indian must be hanged."[10]

Throughout his trial, Plenty Horses appeared detached and confused. Though he had spent several years in a Pennsylvania boarding school as a teenager and had been fluent in English, he had found no occasion to use the white man's language when he returned to the reservation and had lost his facility with it. Plenty Horses sat impassively wearing the drab wool blanket issued to him by the United States government, neither acknowledging nor reacting to the events in the packed courtroom. He was unable to defend himself, but his plight attracted the attention of two talented lawyers, who represented him *pro bono*.

Evidence and testimony presented during the first three days of the trial established two facts: First, Plenty Horses killed Ned Casey with a gunshot to the head and, second, the Sioux believed that they were at war with the United States. The defense argued that the second fact absolved Plenty Horses of responsibility for the first fact. Since the enemy killed Casey in a war, the killing was not murder.

The judges instructed the jury accordingly. They said that if the jury thought a war existed between the United States and the Sioux, it should acquit Plenty Horses of all charges. On the other hand, if the jury did not believe that a war was being waged, it had to select which type of homicide Plenty Horses had committed: murder if the killing was premeditated, manslaughter if done in the heat of passion.

The jury deliberated into the night and the following day. After twenty-three ballots, the group of local farmers was hung: six voted for murder, six for manslaughter. The judge declared a mistrial. Showing just how little he understood about his predicament, Plenty Horses seemed heartened by this development. "I thought last night that they would hang me sure. But now I feel it will not be so."[11] Hoping to avoid another deadlock in the retrial, the prosecutor sought a witness from General Miles's staff to testify that no war existed at the time of the killing. The prosecutor was stunned by the response. "My boy, it was a war," Miles is reported to have said. "You do not suppose that I am going to reduce my campaign to a dress-parade affair?"[12] Miles had evidently changed his mind since he ordered that Plenty Horses be charged for murder—he was now denying the basic assumption upon which the prosecution rested.

Miles had good grounds for the about-face. When Plenty Horses was first captured, Miles held him at Fort Meade as a prisoner of war.[13] The army report about the incident also described Casey as engaged in a scouting expedition for the army. But aside from honor and evidence, there was another factor that pushed Miles in the new direction: Wounded Knee. He must have realized that if the massacre wasn't merely a misfortune of war, it was mass murder. Surely Miles did not want to expose his men—indeed, himself—to criminal liability.

The defense's star witness in the second trial was Captain Frank Baldwin, a member of Miles's staff and two-time Congressional Medal of Honor recipient. He told the court that a war did in fact exist between the United States and the Sioux, testimony so credible that the prosecution did not seek to contest it. "Wait a moment, gentlemen," Judge Oliver Shiras interjected. "If you have both concluded the presentation of testimony, I have something to say to the jury. . . . [I]t clearly appears that on the day when Lieutenant Casey met his death there existed in and about the Pine Ridge Agency a condition of actual warfare between the Army of the United States there assembled under the command of Major General Nelson Miles and the Indian troops occupying the camp on No Water and in its vicinity."[14] Since the existence of a war had been established beyond a reasonable doubt, the defendant—an Indian warrior—had to be acquitted. The judge condemned Plenty Horses's behavior, but also recognized that in these special circumstances the law barred his prosecution. The jury acquitted on the spot, the trial ended, and Plenty Horses left a free man.

KILLING IN WAR

In 1953, Ian Fleming created an entertainment franchise around the character of James Bond, Agent 007 of the British Secret Service. Fleming dazzled his readers with tales of the glamorous world of international espionage. As an elite British spy, Bond was amply provided with the perks of his profession—high-tech weapons, trips to exotic locations, dry martinis, not to mention stunning associates. But there was one benefit that no other British employer could match. The double zero in his title designated that Bond had a "license to kill." According to British law, Bond could not be prosecuted for killing Dr. No, Goldfinger, Blofeld, Scaramanga, or any of their gigantic, metal-teethed minions. He was judge, jury, and executioner, all in a tailored tuxedo.

007's legal powers, however, were nothing compared to Plenty Horses. Bond may have had a license to kill under British law, but—unlike Plenty Horses—he was not protected by the international laws of war. After all, he was not a soldier, nor was the United Kingdom at war. As a result, although Bond could not have been charged for murder in Britain, he could still have been tried in any other court in the world. If the Soviets had caught Bond, they could have prosecuted him for murdering the legions of KGB agents he slayed over his long book and movie career, let alone for spying. By contrast, Plenty Horses was acquitted in a *U.S.* court for killing a *U.S.* soldier. Plenty Horses did not even have a good reason for killing Lieutenant Casey. But in the Old World Order, every soldier had the license to kill a soldier of the opposing force. It wasn't simply the law of the land—it was the law of the world. As Grotius wrote, the law of nations decreed that if a soldier "happens to be caught in another's territory [he] cannot for that reason be punished as a murderer or a thief."[15]

The soldier's license to kill in war is an ancient right. Indeed, it is of such antiquity that it is almost impossible to find an explicit statement of it before Grotius. The right seems to have been so obvious that it went without saying. Even Plenty Horses understood that killing in war was not murder. He told a reporter, "I do not deny that Lieutenant Casey came to his death at my hands. . . . He was killed, yes; but not murdered." The reason was simple. "We were at war with the whites," Plenty Horses explained.[16]

A soldier's license to kill in the Old World Order is notable for a number of reasons. First, as we have seen, self-defense was not the only just cause of war. Soldiers had the legal right to kill others not simply to defend the realm from the Barbarians at the Gate, but also to satisfy debts, collect damage awards, enforce hereditary rights of their monarch, or punish wife stealing. At least James Bond was trying to stop evil geniuses from terrorizing the world, not collecting unpaid bills. More important, the license to kill applied in the absence of any justification whatsoever. Soldiers enjoyed an absolute immunity from prosecution *even if their side was waging an unjust war*. Thus, not only were Sioux warriors such as Plenty Horses immune from prosecution, but so were the soldiers of the Seventh Calvary. In the words of Grotius: "it is permitted to harm an enemy both in his person and in his property; that is, it is permissible not merely for him who wages war for a just cause . . . but for either side indiscriminantly."[17]

Grotius was not only the first to formulate the license to kill, he also formalized it using the "declaration" of war. As with the right of conquest and booty, which applied only when a public war had been declared, soldiers enjoyed immunity from prosecution only when their sovereigns declared a state of war. When their sovereigns failed to follow proper legal form, their men suffered the consequences.

On December 21, 1602, Charles Emmanuel, the aggressive Duke of Savoy, sought to conquer the city of Geneva, which was then an independent republic. Instead of issuing an ultimatum or simply declaring war, Charles plotted to take the city by surprise when everyone was asleep. Choosing the longest and darkest night of the year, and using ladders painted black, he assembled two thousand soldiers outside the city gates at ten in the evening. As the soldiers scaled the city walls, however, the plan fell apart. Not only was a sentry alerted, but the petard set to blow up the gate malfunctioned. The Savoyard soldiers who made it over the outer fortification were trapped in the space between it and the inner city wall. The battle was over an hour later with thirteen men captured.[18]

Instead of slaying these men on the spot or holding them for ransom, the Savoyards were hung as common thieves, their heads severed and displayed atop poles on the ramparts facing Savoy.[19] According to Geneva's chief magistrate, the captives got off lightly. Because it was peacetime, these men were not combatants (*gens de guerre*) and could have been "broken on the wheel," a method of torture in which the executioner lashes the condemned to a wagon wheel and shatters each limb with the strike of a cudgel.[20]

International opinion agreed with the decision. According to Vattel: "The inhabitants of Geneva, after defeating the famous attempt to take their city by ladder, caused all the prisoners whom they took from the Savoyards on that occasion to be hanged up as robbers, who had come to attack them without cause and without a declaration of war. Nor were the Genevese censured for this proceeding, which would have been detested in a formal war."[21] The Duke of Savoy's mistake was not that he waged an unjust war—it was that he failed to wage a war at all.

MIRACULOUS POWERS

The license to kill in wartime is among the strangest rules ever recognized by human beings. Mass murder is morally monstrous and obviously criminal. But, somehow, when the slaughter took place after a formal declaration of war, it suddenly became legal.

Even stranger, soldiers did not merely have the license to kill in war. They also had the license to trespass, break and enter, steal, assault, maim, kidnap, extort, destroy property, and commit arson—indeed, they invariably had a general license to perform acts that would be crimes if committed in peacetime. Thanks to this general license, a declaration of war operated like the ultimate get-out-of-jail-free card. When a sovereign state formally declared war, what was once criminal suddenly became legal. (There are some notable exceptions—so-called war crimes—but more on this later.) From where did sovereigns get such a miraculous power?

The Salamancan theologian Francisco de Vitoria offered the traditional justification for the right of soldiers to kill in war. In his lectures on the Spanish conquest of the Americas, later published as *On the Law of War*, Vitoria claimed that soldiers suffered from "invincible ignorance," that is, from ignorance that could not reasonably be cured. Because soldiers were not members of the king's council, they were not privy to the information necessary to determine whether their sovereign was acting justly. Hence, Vitoria concluded, "the subjects on both sides are justified in fighting."[22]

If this were true, then soldiers would be exonerated, but the king and his council would not, for they surely do not suffer from invincible ingorance. But it turns out that *they too* were protected by the laws of war. In the Old World Order, heads of state and their advisers also got away with murder.

THE EMPEROR IN EXILE

In the early morning of New Year's Day 1814, Napoleon Bonaparte retired to his study and asked not to be disturbed.[23] Shortly thereafter, a tall man wearing a red suit appeared and asked to see the emperor. His attendant, Count Molé, refused. "I must speak to him," the visitor insisted. "Tell him that it is the Red Man who wants to see him and he will admit me." When Molé inquired, Napoleon answered, "Let him in."

Molé pressed his ear against the door of the study to eavesdrop on the conversation. "This is my third appearance before you," the Red Man began. "The first time we met was in Egypt, at the battle of the Pyramids. The second, after the battle of Wagram. I then granted you four years more, to terminate the conquest of Europe, or to make a general peace; threatening you that, if you did not perform one of those two things, I would withdraw my protection from you. Now I am come, for the third and last time, to warn you that you have now but three months to complete the execution of your designs." Napoleon begged for more time, but was rebuffed. On his way out, the Red Man warned again: "Three months, no longer."

This preposterous story about Napoleon selling his soul to the Devil was one of many such reports that circulated the streets of Paris and London. Another version, represented in a popular etching, had him swaddled in the shape of an Egyptian sarcophagus cradled in the loving arms of his father, Beelzebub. The attraction of these stories derived from the implausibility of Napoleon's achievements, whose invincibility seemed, at least to his detractors, unnatural. Napoleon appeared able to win battles at will and vanquish every coalition that formed to stop him. He defeated and dissolved the Holy Roman Empire, the thousand-year-old realm founded by Charlemagne, and convinced the pope to crown him emperor, just as Charlemagne had. Most incredible, he managed to conquer almost all of Europe, with only Britain, Russia, Scandinavia, and the Ottoman Empire remaining beyond his grasp.

Tall tales of dark forces were not only testaments to the awe that Napoleon inspired; they spoke to the revulsion as well. His enemies thought of him as evil incarnate. The British press called him the "Corsican Ogre" and the "Mediterranean Mulatto." The Spanish war manifesto described Napoleon as "*un monstre nourri de sang humain*," a monster fed on human blood.[24] For eleven long years, he terrorized Europe, marching his Grande Armée across the continent, chewing it up as he went along. It is hard to know how many lives were lost, but estimates range from four to seven million dead, homicide on a scale not seen in Europe for nearly two centuries and not seen again until the First World War. But Napoleon did not seem overly concerned with the number of young conscripts he sent to their deaths. According to Prince Metternich, the Austrian foreign minister, Napoleon remarked: "I grew up on the battlefield. A man like me does not give a shit about the lives of a million men."[25]

Yet when Napoleon was defeated at the Battle of Leipzig in 1813 and ousted from the French throne in 1814, the Allies did not prosecute him. They offered him generous terms of peace in the Treaty of Fontainebleau. While Napoleon renounced his sovereignty over France, Italy, and other countries, the Allies permitted him to retain his imperial title. They also tactfully described his banishment to Elba, announcing that the tiny Mediterranean island had been "adopted by his Majesty the Emperor Napoleon, for the place of his residence." France had sliced off a bit of herself and donated the sliver to Napoleon as "a separate principality, which shall be possessed by him in all sovereignty and property." The treaty also guaranteed him two million francs a year to run the island.

Being demoted from the Emperor of France to the Emperor of Elba was undoubtedly humiliating. All the same, getting a country to rule, even if a puny one, hardly seems adequate penance for butchering so many. Strictly speaking, though, exile was not a punishment, for Napoleon had committed no crime. Like his soldiers, Napoleon was licensed to kill. Furthermore, as a sovereign, he had the right to resort to arms—to plan, declare, and wage war. Elba, therefore, was not a prison. It was more like a sanitarium, sealed off from the rest of Europe to protect it from the Corsican contagion. An even more accurate analogy might be to a maximum security asylum for the dangerously insane. To his enemies, Napoleon had such an insatiable thirst for blood and power that he had to be removed from civilized society before he could strike again.[26]

Indeed, the Allies had no choice but to give him a sovereign country of some kind. With the war over, Napoleon lost his status as a prisoner of war and had to be released. But the Allies could not let him stay in France as he posed too great a danger to the newly restored Bourbon king. Nor did they have the authority to detain him on foreign soil against his will. There was only one remaining option: give him his own kingdom and then forbid him from coming back to theirs.

Napoleon disembarked on Elba on May 4, 1814 and, with his characteristic hyperactivity, went to work.[27] In between playing with his pet monkey, Jénar, and rearranging the drapes in the little imperial palace, he reformed the island's public administration, reorganized its defense, paved roads, built bridges, and constructed irrigation systems.[28] The fountain he installed outside Poggio still functions two hundred years later. Napoleon even rebuilt the latrines in the capital of Portoferraio because they smelled.[29] But he grew bored of the tiny principality—he lacked "Elba room," the British would later pun—and set sail for France.[30] Landing at Cannes and marching one thousand miles back to Paris, he assumed the throne and assembled his forces to strike again.[31]

The Allies, then convening in Vienna to reestablish the order shattered by twenty years of constant warfare, were scandalized by this breach of the treaty.[32] They issued a declaration branding Napoleon "an enemy and disturber of the tranquillity of the world." By escaping Elba and taking control of France, thus violating the Treaty of Fontainebleau, an honorable settlement that he had signed and swore to uphold, Napoleon Bonaparte had "deprived himself of the protection of the law" and "rendered himself liable to public vengeance."[33] By marking Napoleon an outlaw, the Allies declared him a man who could be killed on sight.[34]

Yet, even after his decisive defeat by the Duke of Wellington and Marshal Blücher at the Battle of Waterloo in which fifty thousand men were slaughtered, his life was spared. At eight in the morning on Saturday, July 15, 1815, Napoleon surrendered to Captain Frederick Lewis Maitland of the British navy.[35] Humbly removing his bicorne hat and revealing his graying, thinning hair, he threw himself on British mercy: "I come on board your ship to place myself under the protection of the laws of England."[36] Napoleon was hoping for asylum in Britain. He would have settled for safe passage to the United States. He was sent instead to the ends of the earth.

INDEFINITE DETENTION

Napoleon said nothing when he saw his new home from the deck of HMS *Northumberland*. St. Helena was a forbidding, impregnable fortress-island. Its basalt outcroppings, formed eons ago by volcanic eruptions, were rimmed with imposing battlements. The crags in its rocky face were studded with cannons.[37]

Not that anyone would try to rescue him, even if they could penetrate the island defenses. St. Helena is among the remotest places in the world. The closest other land, Ascension Island, is seven hundred miles away.[38] His new home was forty-four hundred miles from Europe. It had taken the *Northumberland* nearly three months to reach St. Helena. Even today, the island lacks an airport, ATMs, businesses that accept credit cards, cell phone towers, or high-speed Internet.[39]

Security considerations favored St. Helena. Not only was there no escape, but the island was so far off the grid that Napoleon would languish in obscurity until he was forgotten. But legal concerns loomed large as well. Lord Liverpool, the British prime minister, confided to Castlereagh, his foreign minister, that detaining Napoleon in England would be awkward. "We are all decidedly of opinion that it would not answer to confine him in this country. Very nice legal questions might arise upon the subject which would be particularly embarrassing."[40]

Shipping Napoleon off to St. Helena made British lawyers cringe.[41] Lord Chancellor Eldon, the British counterpart of the American attorney general, could not contrive a legal theory that would sanction it. For the island was a Crown territory, under the management of Britain's East India Company. If detaining Napoleon in England was illegal, it would be illegal in St. Helena as well. In theory, Britain could give the island to Napoleon, but this option was not realistic. Unlike Elba, which was strategically insignificant, St. Helena was a valuable asset, serving as a vital replenishing station for British ships en route to and from the Indies.

Lord Eldon came up with several options. The first was to declare Napoleon a French rebel and treat his deportation to St. Helena as a punishment for treason. The problem with this proposal, however, was obvious. If Napoleon were a French rebel, France should punish him, not Britain. There was also the issue of Napoleon's citizenship. According to the Treaty of Fontainebleau, he was the Sovereign of Elba, an independent nation. Napoleon, therefore, could not be a French rebel because, from the perspective of the law, he was not even French.

Another suggestion was to treat Napoleon's escape from Elba and attack on the Allies as an act of piracy. Since piracy is a crime, the Allies would have grounds to punish Napoleon. Unfortunately, this proposal was also a nonstarter. While pirates can commit crimes, they cannot wage war. But the British Parliament had recognized the hostilities as a war—that was the basis for funding the Battle of Waterloo. And since waging war was not a crime, Napoleon could not be punished for waging it.

Eldon's best attempt was to claim that the Allies had not been at war with France, but with Napoleon and his associates. Thus, the British could continue to treat Napoleon as an enemy simply by refusing to make peace with him. They could imprison him indefinitely, in other words, by extending the war forever. Eldon was not happy with this alternative either. Though the workaround was clever, it was, as the British say, too clever by half. There was no getting past the glaring fact that Napoleon *had* surrendered. How could Britain continue the war when the enemy had already thrown up his hands?

Despite Eldon's misgivings—or perhaps because of them—Parliament enacted a special law that empowered the government to keep Napoleon in its custody, in a weak and transparent attempt to justify a violation of the law of nations. "Whereas it is necessary for the Preservation of the Tranquillity of *Europe*, and for the general Safety, that *Napoleon Buonaparte* should be detained," the statute read, "it shall and may be lawful for His Majesty, his Heirs and Successors, to detain and keep the said *Napoleon Buonaparte* in the Custody of such Person or Persons in such Place within his Majesty's Dominions, and under such Restrictions . . . as to His Majesty his heirs and successors, shall from time to time seem fit."[42]

Though we might be tempted to excuse the British government, it is important to note that it brought this problem upon itself. Napoleon was able to escape Elba because Britain assigned only one ship to guard the island, which then proceeded to abandon its post. The British captain explained this dereliction of duty by claiming that he had an appointment in Italy with his ear doctor, though more likely he went to see his mistress.[43] Exiling Napoleon to St. Helena could easily have been avoided.

This violation of the law of nations had its costs, making a martyr out of Napoleon and thereby keeping the Bonapartist flame alive. Several decades after Napoleon's exile, his nephew and heir, Louis-Napoleon Bonaparte, became the first popularly elected president of France. Louis-Napoleon served a second term as well, this time holding on to his office through a coup d'état. In a homage to his uncle, he assumed the throne as self-proclaimed "Emperor Napoleon III" on the anniversary of the first Napoleon's coronation.

THE MORAL MAGIC OF WAR

Vitoria's justification for the license to kill in war might have had some validity for soldiers, for they could have pleaded ignorance. They were just following orders. But sovereigns like Napoleon could not offer the same excuse because they were the ones making the decision to wage war.

Grotius provided the first convincing explanation for the license to kill in war that applied to both sovereigns and soldiers. His argument began with the victims. Why, Grotius asked, does the just side have the license to kill? Because, he answered, they are the *just* side—they are trying to vindicate rights and are permitted to do whatever is necessary to correct injustice. "[W]e are understood to have a right to those things which are necessary for the purpose of securing a right."[44] If someone takes your property, you are justified in taking it back. If you cannot get that property back, you are justified in taking property from the thief that is worth the same as what was taken from you.[45] If the person resists this taking, then you can respond to his resistance. If the conflict escalates, you may use deadly force to counteract deadly force. "[I]f otherwise I cannot save my life," Grotius wrote, "I may use any degree of violence to ward off him who assails it."[46]

Having established the license to kill of the just side, Grotius moved on to the hard part, namely, establishing the same license for the unjust side. How can a sovereign's declaration of an unjust war possibly license his own morally monstrous behavior, and those of his soldiers?

Grotius's answer is the same he gave for the right of conquest and booty: the laws of war protect the unjust aggressors because that is the only practical way to protect the just ones. For if the license to kill only applied to the just, they would live in constant fear that outsiders would mistake them for the unjust and treat them as common criminals. Extending protections to all belligerents eliminates the insecurity that would afflict those fighting for a just cause—that is, victims trying to vindicate their rights— and it would avoid the possibility of injustice that would result from such mistaken prosecutions.

To be sure, the fear of prosecution would not be a serious problem if there were a relatively mechanical way of determining whether a particular war was just. If there were such a simple procedure, victims could be confident that their actions would be judged permissible by most everyone. Unfortunately, this is not the case. "Even in a lawful war," Grotius wrote, "it can hardly be adequately known from external indications what is the just limit of [defensive war], or recovering what is one's own, or of inflicting punishments."[47] Once again, outsiders usually do not have enough information about the legality of the conflict to tell whether a war is just and which actions are necessary to vindicate their rights.

Uncertainty about the justice of wars was not just a problem of information; it was also a problem of expertise. In the Old World Order, any legitimate cause of action was a just cause for war. Wars were legal disputes that were fought on the battlefield because they could not be resolved in a court. The justice of a war, therefore, could only be determined by resolving complex legal issues, such as questions of dynastic succession, testamentary inheritance, navigation rights, debt obligations, tortious responsibility, and treaty interpretation. If courts would struggle to comprehend such issues, surely combatants and bystanders would too.

And so the safest solution, according to Grotius, was blanket immunity. Because outsiders to the conflict couldn't accurately distinguish just from unjust wars, they couldn't reliably prosecute only those who fought in unjust wars either. Some courts would prosecute some belligerents; other courts would prosecute others. The inconsistency and unpredictability of criminal prosecutions would make crossing the border very dangerous for anyone who had ever fought in a war. The only solution to this problem was to let everyone off.[48]

WAR CRIMES

That sovereigns and soldiers could not be punished for waging war did not mean that they could not be punished at all for what they did during war. The Old World Order did have rules—but not against waging war. Its rules were about waging war in the right way. Properly declaring war was the first legal obligation. The second was to adhere to particular rules of combat. Violation of these rules constituted "war crimes," and those who committed them were criminally liable.

Grotius recognized three kinds of war crimes: the use of poison, treacherous assassination, and rape.[49] These offenses constituted exceptions to the license to kill. Moreover, these exceptions applied to *all* wars—just as well as unjust. By the common consent of nations, these actions were never acceptable, no matter the reason. This indifference to purpose was simply the flip side of the license to kill. Soldiers who respected the laws of war could not be punished for fighting in an unjust conflict, but soldiers who violated the laws of war could be punished even if they were fighting in a just conflict. A war criminal was not someone who harmed the enemy for the wrong reason. He was someone who harmed the enemy *in the wrong way* and, in so doing, lost his license to kill.

From a contemporary perspective, Grotius's list of war crimes is remarkable, not so much for what it contains—the use of poison (think chemical weapons), treacherous killing, and sexual assault are still grave violations of the laws of war—but for what it does not. Grotius saw enslavement of those captured as completely legal: "all without exception who have been captured in a formal public war become slaves from the time when they are brought within the lines."[50] Torture, too: "There is no suffering which may not be inflicted with impunity upon such slaves, no action which may not be ordered, or be forced by torture."[51] Likewise execution of prisoners: "So far as the law of nations is concerned, the right of killing such slaves, that is, captives taken in war, is not precluded at any time."[52] Pillage and devastation, ditto: "the law of nations has permitted the destruction and plunder of the property of enemies."[53] Most astonishing of all, Grotius did not regard as a war crime the paradigmatic breach of our age—the intentional killing of unarmed civilians: "[T]he slaughter even of infants and of women is made with impunity."[54]

Grotius certainly did not think that soldiers were legally *permitted* to massacre civilians whenever they liked. Soldiers were only legally allowed to do what was necessary to enforce rights that the enemy had infringed. Since killing women and children usually did not advance the goal of enforcing rights, there was no legal justification for killing them. Nevertheless, soldiers could not be punished for these brutalities.[55] Senseless violence was technically illegal, but it was not criminally prosecutable—it could be "made with impunity." The early modern laws of war, therefore, produced odd consequences. Raping and slaying women were both illegal, but only rape was a war crime.

These rules were barbaric, but Grotius was not particularly inhumane for his time. Samuel von Pufendorf thought that he could add nothing to Grotius's definitive discussion of the rules of proper combat.[56] Cornelius van Bynkershoek, the Dutch jurist and judge, made Grotius and Pufendorf look like weak-kneed bleeding hearts. War was "by its very nature so general that it cannot be waged within set limits."[57] According to Van

Bynkershoek, even poisonings and the hanging of prisoners were legitimate according to the laws of war.[58]

GOD WITH US

On the first day of May 1631, the Protestant city of Magdeburg was besieged by the Catholic forces of the Holy Roman Emperor. The city held out for weeks, hoping for the relief armies to arrive, and was on the verge of surrender when the soldiers stormed the walls. Count Pappenheim, who led the siege, had provided large quantities of wine to the soldiers to bolster their courage. Once inside the fortress, the drunken soldiers went berserk.[59] "And then there was nothing but murder, burning, plundering, torment, and beatings," reported a member of the city council.[60] In accordance with the Grotian rules of booty taking, everything that wasn't bolted down was whisked away.

Jürgen Ackermann, a captain under Pappenheim's command, recounted his own looting. He began by seizing another soldier's ax and used it to snap off the hinge of the front door of a house. The homeowner, who was waiting on the other side with a leveled gun, fired at Ackermann but missed, hitting another man instead. The owner raced upstairs and bolted the iron door behind him. Once the soldiers finished ransacking the first floor, they grabbed a servant and threatened to kill him unless he divulged the hiding place of his master's valuables. "He said yes, he knew of good booty, whereupon he led us into a chamber, helped to move a bedstead, and there was a vault, out which we hauled an iron chest." The chest was carried from the house, but not before the owner reemerged from the upstairs and shot a second soldier. Ackermann and his men now had the chest, but it was locked. The soldiers resorted to brute force, chopping away at the chest with their ax, eventually hacking a hole large enough to pull objects out. "Then we groped through the hole, one after another as one does in a lucky dip," Ackerman reported. "Among other things I got some good silver and gold dishes and a pretty gold chain with a valuable jewel." The haul was so great that Ackermann set himself up as a landowner with his spoils.[61]

When the city had been stripped bare, the carnage did not end. Fueled by alcohol, adrenaline, and rage that there was nothing left to loot, the soldiers continued their rampage. "Finally, however, when everything had been given out and there was nothing left to take, then the misery really began," the council member continued. "For then the soldiers began to beat, frighten, and threaten to shoot, skewer, hang, etc., the people."[62] A few houses were set on fire, and an inferno ensued when one of them, an apothecary containing gunpowder, ignited. Those not consumed by the flames or murdered by the soldiers suffocated to death hiding in their basements. One thousand seven hundred out of 1,900 buildings were destroyed and, according to the census taken the following year, only 449 people could be found in this once thriving and majestic city.[63] In his message to the emperor, Count Pappenheim celebrated his victory: "I believe that over twenty thousand souls were lost. . . . All of our soldiers became rich. God with us."[64]

Where in the world would Pappenheim get the idea that God approved of the slaughter of women and children? From the Bible, of course. The Book of Numbers, for example, recounts the war against the Midianites. "The LORD said to Moses, 'Take vengeance on the *Midianites* for the Israelites.'"[65] Moses complied, sending twelve thousand Israelites and Phineas the Priest into battle, along with holy articles of the Sanctuary. The military operation was successful. "They fought against Midian, as the LORD commanded Moses, and killed every man."[66] The five kings of Midian—Evi, Rekem, Zur, Hur, and Reba—and their High Priest—Baal, the son of Peor—were summarily executed. The soldiers pillaged, looted, and, when they left, burned the cities to the ground. The only survivors were the women and children, all of whom had been taken as prisoners.

When the report of the campaign came in, Moses was in disbelief. He berated his officers, asking: "Have you allowed all the women to live??"[67] God had sent the Israelites to battle in order to punish the Midianites. The Midianite women had prostituted themselves with the Israelite men and lured them into idolatry. Sparing the women, therefore, defeated the whole point of the war. He ordered his officers to finish the job. "Now kill all the boys. And kill every woman who has slept with a man, but save for yourselves every girl who has never slept with a man."[68]

In the Hebrew Bible, it was often a war crime *not* to kill civilians. Thus, King Saul of Israel was rebuked for not having slain "men and women, children and infants" when he spared King Agag of Amalek.[69] The Amalekites had ambushed the Israelites during their exodus from Egypt and Saul was sent to exterminate their descendants. Saul's mercy was misguided because he failed to cleanse the land of evil, to "blot out the name of Amalek from under heaven."[70] Saul's failure was a terrible wrong—a wrong so grievous, in fact, that God Himself confessed error for having chosen Saul as king. In order to make up for Saul's misguided mercy, the Prophet Samuel proceeded to chop Agag, a chained prisoner of war, to pieces in the temple at Gilgal.[71]

THE PRINCIPLE OF DISTINCTION

Fortunately for the civilians of Europe, the biblical model of war was finally repudiated. By the middle of the eighteenth century, European armies had come to recognize a "Principle of Distinction," the doctrine central to modern humanitarian law, which distinguishes between soldiers and civilians and protects the latter from the former. "At present, war is carried on by regular troops," Emer de Vattel explained in 1758, "the people, the peasants, the citizens, take no part in it, and generally have nothing to fear from the sword of the enemy."[72] The laws of war now decreed that combatant could only attack combatant. Civilians, those who did not take part in the conflict, were not lawful targets.[73]

To target civilians had become a serious violation of the law of nations. According to Vattel: "If, sometimes, the furious and ungovernable soldier carries his brutality so far as to violate female chastity, or to massacre women, children, and old men, the officers lament those excesses: they exert their utmost efforts to put a stop to them; and a prudent and humane general even punishes them whenever he can."[74] What had previously been merely lamentable became criminal thanks to the new Principle of Distinction.

Why armies spared civilians at this point is a matter much debated among historians. Some attribute the new rules to moral progress—either as part of the humanitarian revolution of the Enlightenment, which began to regard all human life as valuable, or the specific desire not to revisit the horrors of previous wars.[75] Others situate these developments in the

political milieu of eighteenth-century Europe—either because the aristocracy dominated the army and regarded wars as duels governed by the rules
of chivalry,[76] or because monarchs dominated the armies and treated wars
as formal legal procedures governed by the dignified rules of the courtroom.[77]

While Vattel strained credulity when he claimed that civilians had
"*nothing* to fear from the sword of the enemy"—unarmed civilians are
never safe from armed soldiers in wartime—it was undeniable that their
lot had vastly improved.[78] The radical depopulation of cities and villages so
characteristic of the wars of the sixteenth and seventeenth centuries ceased
by the middle of the eighteenth century, as the inhabitants no longer had to
flee from gangs of undisciplined soldiers who raided their homes, raped the
women, and killed for sport. In fact, Adam Smith reported that the Dutch
peasants eagerly awaited foreign troops because military occupation created a market for their goods, which they could now sell at inflated prices.[79]

The nineteenth and twentieth centuries were far less kind to civilians.
The wars of the French Revolution and the subsequent Napoleonic Wars,
the Indian wars, the colonial wars in Africa, and the Second World War
were appalling disasters for noncombatants. But even when these massacres happened, the civilized world did not excuse them as the inevitable
pity of war. Though General Miles maintained the events at Wounded
Knee took place during a war, thus allowing Plenty Horses to be acquitted,
many recoiled at the senseless slaughter.[80] Plenty Horses had shot a soldier,
but Miles's men had slaughtered unarmed men, women, and children, thus
violating the distinction between soldier and civilian.[81]

While the Principle of Distinction provided civilians with relief, it did
come at a price. For in order to gain the protection from attack, civilians
had to relinquish their own right to use force. According to the new rules,
only soldiers had the right to kill other soldiers. Civilians could not be attacked, but neither could they attack, and those who did were treated as
criminals. "[E]ven after a declaration of war between two nations, if the
peasants of themselves commit any hostilities, the enemy shows them no
mercy, but hangs them up as he would so many robbers or banditti."[82]
The names given to civilians who participated in hostilities changed over
time: from "robbers," "banditti," "brigands," to "partisans," "*franc tireurs*,"

"bushwhackers," then to "guerrillas," "irregulars," "freedom fighters," "insurgents," and finally to "civilians directly participating in hostilities," "unlawful enemy combatants," and, of course, "terrorists."

The Principle of Distinction thus involved a great trade-off. Civilians gained legal protection from being killed but they lost their license to kill. The underlying logic of the trade was simple. If civilians did not have the legal right to kill, they would not be a threat to soldiers. And if they were not a threat to soldiers, soldiers would not have the legal right to attack them.

The introduction of the Principle of Distinction had a civilizing effect on war, reducing the horrors visited on civilians who had little to do with the fight. Even so, the core rules of war remained the same. A soldier fighting in a war had a license to kill. What in ordinary life was murder for which he could be tried and hung was now simply the performance of his soldierly duty—one for which he was immune regardless of whether the war in which he fought was just. As long as he followed the rules.

REPRISALS

The Principle of Distinction was the first curtailment of Grotius's blanket immunity for those waging war. In the next century, it was followed by a flood of new legal regulations placing stricter controls on a soldier's license to kill. International treaties protected the wounded and medical personnel (First Geneva Convention, 1864);[83] prohibited the use of fragmenting, explosive, and incendiary small arms ammunition (St. Petersburg Declaration, 1874);[84] banned explosives from balloons, asphyxiating gas, and dum-dum bullets (First Hague Convention, 1899);[85] and proscribed pillage, the execution of surrendering soldiers and prisoners of war, and forcing civilians to swear an allegiance to a foreign power (Second Hague Convention, 1907).[86]

These rules were all to the good, a harbinger of new legal and moral understandings. Nevertheless, they created problems of their own—the most pressing of which was the problem of enforcement. In the Old World Order, after all, war was the way that states righted wrongs. But how were states to right wrongs if they were already at war?

To solve this problem, armies developed a procedure known as the "reprisal." In a reprisal, one army punished another for violating the rules by violating the rules in return. Thus, when Spanish guerrillas shot at a French column as it marched through the Sil valley in 1808, the commanding officer, General Loison, sent raiding parties out to torch the countryside. "Never before can so terrible a storm have hit this previous peaceful valley," Loison reported. "Its people go out and watch its destruction from afar; those we were able to find, we killed."[87]

Or consider the problem of land mines or, as they used to be called, "torpedoes." In order to sweep captured land of torpedoes, which were deemed illegal by many authorities once territory had been captured, General William Tecumseh Sherman ordered his soldiers to drag Southerners across suspected minefields by long ropes. "Now if torpedoes are found in the possession of an enemy to our rear," Sherman instructed General James Steedman at Chattanooga, "you may cause them to be put on the ground, and tested by wagon loads of prisoners, or if need be, by citizens implicated in their use."[88]

Indeed, many of the familiar laws of war arose from this tit-for-tat process. At the beginning of the Eighty Years War, the Duke of Alva treated the Dutch as rebels and ordered their hanging.[89] The Dutch responded by hanging Spanish captives. By 1599, both sides agreed to a "cuartel general," a treaty stipulating ransom rates for soldiers of different ranks, ranging from 7.5 guilders for the rank and file to 1,000 guilders for lieutenant colonels. As for entertainment and accommodations, the agreement provided: "[G]entlemen of higher quality shall be treated as they themselves state and desire."[90] This cartel was reissued several times during the war and soon thereafter was copied by other European nations.[91]

Some states eliminated ransom, with its needless money shuffling, and replaced it with a system of prisoner exchanges. A 1703 agreement between France and the United Provinces set out a conversion table specifying that a sergeant was worth two rank-and-file soldiers, a captain twelve soldiers, a colonel forty-eight, and a brigadier seventy.[92] These agreements were enforced through reprisals: Breach of the cartel by one side led to breach by the other.[93]

By the mid-eighteenth century, it dawned on armies that executing prisoners was counterproductive. Prisoners were worth more alive because they could be exchanged for one's own captive comrades. It was not long before killing prisoners was forbidden—and subject to reprisal—even without prior agreement.[94] As Vattel declared with a chilling matter-of-factness, "If the hostile general has, without any just reason, caused some prisoners to be hanged, we hang an equal number of his people, and of the same rank—notifying to him that we will continue thus to retaliate, for the purpose of obliging him to observe the laws of war."[95] Armies could kill those who surrendered in order to enforce other laws of war as well: "There is, however, one case in which we may refuse to spare the life of an enemy who surrenders," Vattel wrote. "It is, when that enemy has been guilty of some enormous breach of the law of nations, and particularly when he has violated the laws of war."[96]

Though everyone accepted the legitimacy of reprisals, no one liked them. The great international lawyer of the early twentieth century Lassa Oppenheim called them a "terrible means."[97] J. M. Spaight, another authority on the laws of war, described reprisals as the "very saddest of all the necessities of war."[98] Numerous attempts were made to rid warfare of this revolting practice—during the Brussels Conference in 1874 and Hague Conferences in 1899 and 1907—but every effort failed.[99]

Reprisals were detested for the obvious reason that they were indiscriminate. "It is a dreadful extremity," Vattel lamented, "to condemn a prisoner to atone, by a miserable death, for his general's crime."[100] As an instance of collective punishment, reprisals were unquestionably unfair. Then again, war is unfair. In war, people are made to pay for the wrongs of their state. Indeed, the Old World Order was built on the idea of collective responsibility. Reprisals were simply a special case of the general injustice of the Old World Order, where collective responsibility forced the innocent to give up their property, their security, and their lives because of the wrongdoing of others.

Reprisals were tolerated because of their civilizing effects. After bemoaning their barbarity, Oppenheim went on to defend them: "Reprisals cannot be dispensed with, because without them illegitimate acts of warfare would be innumerable."[101] Brutality was used to counteract brutality.[102] In this perverse way, war became more civilized—up to a point. Even when the rules of proper warfare were followed scrupulously—when prisoners of war were spared, poison gas was kept in its tanks, civilians were left unmolested, false flags of surrender were not raised—war was still an orgy of death and destruction. The rules of war relieved only a small fraction of the misery, suffering, and horror. They barely changed the true nature of the Old World Order: All this—all the death and destruction; all the misery, suffering, and horror—could be inflicted with perfect impunity.

THOU MAY KILL

Perhaps the most basic rule of communal life is "Thou shall not kill." In the Old World Order, however, the most basic rule was "Thou *may* kill—if at war." We now know why. Those who live in the same political community have courts to hear their case. For this reason, victims are not permitted to enforce the law themselves. They must go to a judge. In the Old World Order, however, different sovereigns did not acknowledge a common authority to resolve their disputes. For this reason, victims were granted the right to enforce the law if they had no other choice. They could be the judge (and jury and executioner), and they could do whatever they deemed necessary to right perceived wrongs. As the Old World Order matured, the rules of warfare became somewhat more civil. But the underlying logic remained constant. Soldiers and sovereigns had a license to kill. They had that license regardless of whether the war was just. And they could do almost anything—within increasingly constricted but nonetheless shockingly permissive bounds—to exercise that license.

Grotius managed to construct a parallel legal universe—a system of rules that were absurd in times of peace, but indispensable in times of war. They were indispensable because they answered the thorny question raised by the Grotian perspective: Why were soldiers and sovereigns not criminals when the wars they fought turned out to lack a legal basis? Grotius's answer was that they had to be treated *as if* the wars they fought always had a legal basis. Soldiers and sovereigns were not criminals because outsiders to the conflict were incapable of knowing enough of the facts or the law to judge otherwise. They could legally kill (and do much else that would be illegal in times of peace) because outsiders couldn't and shouldn't take sides. The license to kill was thus granted in the name of neutrality, the duty of those not party to a conflict to stay out of it. Indeed, the Old World Order took neutrality so seriously that it extended this idea to its logical—and ludicrous—conclusion.

FOUR

CITIZEN GENÊT GOES TO WASHINGTON

The British prime minister Edward Heath once defined a diplomat as someone who thinks twice before saying nothing. By this definition, Edmond-Charles Genêt was no diplomat. He was brash and outspoken, careless in his choice of words, and incapable of nuance. He better fit the definition of a blowhard—someone whose mouth is not on speaking terms with his brain. Yet Genêt *was* a diplomat. In 1792, he was appointed the French minister to the United States.[1]

At the time, France was in desperate shape. In its fervor to spread the blessings of the Revolution to the rest of Europe, it waged war on most of it.[2] France had declared war on Austria in April 1792 and Prussia had allied with Austria. The following February, France declared war on Great Britain and Holland, and a month later, on Spain and Portugal. Overextended and surrounded, the revolutionary government sent the bumbling Genêt to persuade the United States to join the European war that it had foolishly started and was currently losing.

Fortunately for Genêt, the United States was sympathetic to his message. Memory of France's support of the American Revolution was fresh in the minds of the erstwhile colonists. Like its former benefactor, the United States had just liberated itself from a European monarchy and embarked on a daring experiment in self-government. Together France and the United States formed, in the words of the Ministry's instructions to Genêt, a new "Empire de la Liberté."[3] Americans saw the French Revolution through the lens of their own struggle for independence—those storming the Bastille were charging along the path blazed by George Washington, Thomas Jefferson, and Benjamin Franklin. French revolutionaries were happy to concede the point. The Marquis de Lafayette sent Washington the key to the Bastille, for as Thomas Paine explained, "That the principles of America opened the Bastille is not to be doubted; and therefore the key comes to the right place."[4]

Unfortunately for Genêt, while idealism suggested one course of action, prudence counseled quite another. The United States could not afford to become embroiled in a European war. Its army was insignificant, its navy nonexistent. It barely had a functioning government. Its only real source of income was import duties from British trade. Waging war against Britain, let alone its many allies, would have been financial and military suicide.

Genêt's task was a mission impossible. Perhaps a master diplomat could have eked out a semblance of victory. As events would make clear, Genêt was no master diplomat.

ASSISTANCE JUST SHORT OF WAR

Edmond-Charles Genêt was born in Versailles on January 8, 1763, the only son of five children. Though his family was bourgeois, it had strong connections to the nobility. His eldest sister was the First Lady of Marie Antoinette's Bedchamber, a sort of personal assistant who arranged the queen's social calendar and paid her bills. Edmond's father was the head of the Bureau of Interpretation and schooled his son in various European languages. The son turned out to be a linguistic prodigy, mastering English, French, Swedish, Italian, German, Latin, and Hebrew by the age of twelve. With the help of his tutor, he translated a Swedish biography of the sixteenth-century King Eric XIV into French—a feat that so impressed

Eric's descendant, the present King of Sweden, that he gave Edmond a gold medallion as a gift.[5]

Edmond grew into a dashing young man with polished manners and sparkling wit. He was also a talented singer who performed for the ladies at court. With the queen's help, Edmond broke into the diplomatic corps as the secretary of the French embassy in St. Petersburg, arriving there in 1788. But he was an ardent republican and after four years at his post, Empress Catherine banished him. He returned to Paris in September 1792, just as the Revolution began its radical phase.[6]

News of his expulsion for excessive revolutionary zeal endeared Genêt to the Girondins, the hawkish party of the French National Convention. When these hawks shattered the peace and plunged the country into a bloody confrontation with most of the crowned heads of Europe, they realized that they needed assistance. The plan was to send Genêt to the United States where he would persuade France's fellow republic to join its noble cause.[7]

The Girondins understood that the United States might refuse to enter the war.[8] In that case, they expected assistance just short of war.[9] The French Foreign Ministry instructed Genêt to ask the United States to expedite the repayment of the debt owed to France that was incurred during the Revolutionary War. He would then use the funds to buy American supplies for the war effort back home.[10] Next, the ministry instructed Genêt to undermine the Spanish and British Empires by assembling teams of American adventurers to infiltrate Spanish-held Florida and Louisiana and the British colony of Canada, where they would foment rebellion.[11] Finally, Genêt came armed with a thick stack of three hundred blank *letters of marque* (special letters authorizing private sailors to attack and capture foreign vessels) that he would use to assemble a fleet of "privateers"—a veritable private navy of American sailors—to prey on British shipping.[12]

On February 7, 1793, Genêt set out in the forty-four-gun frigate *Embuscade* for Philadelphia, then the capital of the United States. Adverse winds blew the ship off course, forcing it to land in Charleston, South Carolina, two months later. To Genêt's delight, a boisterous throng of well-wishers met him at the pier. Local dignitaries and the state governor also received Genêt and offered him their unlimited assistance.[13]

Proper protocol would have called for Genêt to head straight to Philadelphia, present his credentials to the administration, and clear his plans with the president. Genêt, however, was not one for protocol. He regarded diplomatic conventions as vestiges of aristocratic politesse, archaic mannerisms unbecoming of democrats. Though benefiting much from the *ancien régime*, Genêt now distanced himself from its decadence and used the unpretentious title of "Citoyen," or Citizen.[14]

Citizen Genêt remained in Charleston, where he went to work. He liberally dispersed his *letters of marque* at the bustling waterfront, commissioning four ships of privateers and rechristening them the *Républicain*, *Anti-George*, *Sans Culotte*, and *Patriote Genêt*. He empowered local French consuls to act as prize courts, thus bypassing the American judicial system. He also assembled bands of adventurers to overthrow British and Spanish colonial rule. Having completed this phase of his mission, Genêt traveled overland to Philadelphia so that he could bask in the adulation of the crowds along the way, a detour that took him twenty-eight days to complete.[15]

Given his leisurely pace, news of Genêt's exploits preceded his arrival on May 16. George Hammond, the British ambassador, had complained to Thomas Jefferson, the secretary of state, about the commissions and outfitting of privateers in Charleston. He was especially galled by the *Embuscade*'s recent seizing of the *Grange* as a prize of war.[16] The British ship was undiplomatically hauled into Philadelphia harbor by the French ambassador's frigate to the cheers of the crowd.[17] Hammond wrote to Jefferson that he "can entertain no doubt that the executive government of the United States will consider this infringement on its neutrality."[18]

Jefferson was among the staunchest supporters of France in America, his Francophilia verging on fanaticism. Serving as the American ambassador in Paris, he witnessed the inception of the Revolution and was profoundly moved by its success.[19] The influence and appreciation was mutual—the French "Declaration of the Rights of Man" drew upon Jefferson's own "Declaration of Independence."[20] But even Jefferson had to agree with the British ambassador that Genêt's actions were illegal. The United States was a neutral country and could not allow its ports to be used by one nation against another. Writing to Genêt on June 5, he asserted "the duty of a neutral nation to prohibit such as would injure one of the warring powers" and expected him to make reparations for this offense against "the laws of the land, of which the law of nations makes an integral part."[21]

This response stunned Genêt. Not only did he regard Jefferson as a fellow republican and steadfast friend of France, he was convinced that he had done nothing wrong.[22] To the contrary, he was sure that the United States was reneging on its commitments, charging it with acting in "defiance of treaties that bind the French and the Americans."[23]

Genêt was referring to the Treaty of Alliance of 1778, the agreement the United States signed in order to secure France's assistance in its revolution against Britain. The treaty was such a powerful symbol of Franco-American friendship that the inkwell used to sign it would be preserved and used 150 years later to sign the Paris Peace Pact. One of the clauses of the treaty, Article 24, declared that the Americans and the French would exclude each other's enemies from their ports for the purposes of arming privateers.[24] According to Genêt, since the treaty prohibited France's enemies from using American ports, it implicitly permitted France to use them in their place.[25]

Jefferson, however, was not persuaded. In a follow-up letter of June 17, he reminded Genêt that Article 24 did not explicitly give the French permission to use American ports.[26] It only denied France's enemies the right to do so. Since the United States was a neutral country, it could not show favoritism—it could not give France benefits that it denied France's enemies, such as Britain.

Genêt exploded when he received Jefferson's letter. He conceded that Jefferson's interpretation was "ingenious," but scolded him for its deceit. The secretary of state was using verbal tricks "to justify or excuse infractions committed on positive treaties."[27] Alexander Hamilton and Henry Knox, the secretaries of treasury and war, were outraged by the tone of Genêt's letter, claiming it to be "the most offensive paper perhaps that ever was offered by a foreign minister to a friendly power."[28] Genêt's tone also shocked Jefferson. He confided to James Madison, another staunch partisan of France, that Genêt was harming their cause and *"will sink the republican interest if they do not abandon him."*[29]

There is no question that Genêt acted like a clod, offending friends

and enemies at every turn. But while his style was indefensible, his position was more comprehensible. Indeed, it is tempting to regard Genêt as
the victim in the whole affair and see his anger toward Jefferson as not
merely an understandable response but an entirely justified one. If France's
enemies were explicitly prohibited from outfitting in American ports, isn't
it natural to infer that France itself *was* permitted?

In truth, Jefferson's interpretation was the far better one. As Genêt
should have realized, the rules of the Old World Order prohibited neutral states from playing favorites in war. According to these rules, neutrals
had a "duty of impartiality"—they were forbidden from favoring one side
over another.[30] To show partiality was to forfeit neutrality and become a
co-belligerent. From the legal point of view, it was no different from sending in ground troops.

It is true that the prohibition on discrimination in the Old World
Order did not apply to preexisting treaties.[31] A state was permitted to help
a belligerent if they had agreed to do so before the war began, because the
assistance would have been supplied to fulfill a treaty obligation, not to
help a victim. The prohibition on discrimination, in other words, barred
nonbelligerents from penalizing one side for waging an unjust war—the
same logic that gave soldiers and sovereigns a license to kill.[32]

But the Treaty of 1778 between France and the United States did not
trigger this exception. As Jefferson recognized and Genêt failed to grasp,
the prohibition on aiding France's enemies had to be read in light of the
existing rules of neutrality. Neutrality entailed *strict impartiality*. If Britain
could not use American ports to outfit privateers, then the law of nations
would not allow France to use them in this way either. To prove his point
about "what that law and usage is," Jefferson quoted long sections of Vattel
in the original French and then concluded that his country had no choice
but to deny France the use of American ports.[33]

Genêt was furious that Jefferson would "bring forward aphorisms of
Vattel" to justify his interpretation of the treaty.[34] One wonders, though,
how else Jefferson would support his interpretation other than by citing
the leading authority of the day. Indeed, the French envoy's unfamiliarity
with international law stunned Jefferson. The law of nations constituted
the ground rules of diplomatic practice. "His ignorance of every thing

written on the subject is astonishing," Jefferson wrote to James Madison. "I think he has never read a book of any sort in that branch of science."[35]

Genêt failed to understand that the duty of impartiality was taken so seriously in the Old World Order that statesmen were skittish about even giving the *appearance* of partisanship. Indeed, when Jefferson castigated Genêt for using American ports on June 5, he tried to soften his letter with a concluding expression of goodwill. "The assurance conveyed in your letter of the friendship and attachment of your nation gives very sincere pleasure and is as sincerely returned on the part of our country," Jefferson wrote. "That these may continue long and firm, no one more ardently wishes."[36] The attorney general, however, deemed these anodyne sentiments too sympathetic to France. "Were I to speak for myself, as an individual, I should assent with equal cordiality to the last clause. But," he continued, "I can't help believing, that it would accord better with a neutral situation, to omit the reciprocation of affection."[37] Jefferson struck the entire paragraph.

Because the Old World Order had different rules about discrimination, the original instructions given to Genêt by the Foreign Ministry made little sense. France wanted assistance just short of war when such assistance did not exist. Any unequal support provided by the United States to France would have been a *casus belli*, an act of belligerency warranting a military response. The Girondins should have realized that the United States government could not let its territory be used as a recruiting ground for a rebel army to foment insurrections. To aid France this way would have been an act of war against Britain and Spain.

Nor could the United States advance the money it owed on its war debt. Even if the United States could scrounge up the remaining $3 million, paying off the debt prematurely would have violated its duty of impartiality and compromised its neutrality.[38] Genêt had run up against something more powerful than his incompetency—the rules of the Old World Order.

TWO AND TWO MAKE FIVE

Despite this—and despite Jefferson's blunt order to stop—Genêt did not relent. In addition to organizing seditious expeditions to Kentucky, he outfitted another privateer in Philadelphia harbor, renaming it *La Petite Démocrate*, boosting its guns from four to fourteen, and recruiting a crew of 120, including some American citizens. It was a sign of the U.S. government's feebleness that it took a month to discover such outright defiance in the heart of the nation's capital.[39]

When word reached President Washington, he ordered an investigation. And when the investigation confirmed the report, Alexander Dallas, the Pennsylvania secretary of state, directed Genêt not to let *La Petite Démocrate* leave the harbor. Even though he and Genêt were on friendly terms, Genêt became incensed, asserting his right to outfit prizes in American ports and send them to sea, which he proceeded to do. But then he made a threat that was brazen even for him. He told Dallas that he would "appeal from the President to the People."[40]

Washington lost all patience. He could not permit the French ambassador to bully him with his own electorate. Genêt had to go. Jefferson assembled a long list of Genêt's peccadillos with supporting documentation and sent the packet to the French government requesting his recall. The French government was happy to comply. Not only was it still hoping for help from the United States, but Genêt was a member of the Girondins, a party that had been ousted by the even more radical Jacobin faction, led by Maximilien Robespierre. To justify the recall, the Jacobins accused Genêt of being a British agent insufficiently loyal to France.[41]

Genêt was not so foolish as to return to France at the height of the Terror. He stayed in the United States and soon married the daughter of George Clinton, the governor of New York. Genêt retired from public life and settled down as a gentleman farmer along the Hudson River three miles from Albany.[42] In his spare time, he dreamed up new inventions, such as a cigar-shaped hydrogen balloon with stabilizers and rudders, detailed in a book he published in 1832.[43]

It may come as no surprise that Genêt's inventions were hopeless, based as they were on a complete ignorance of the laws of physics. "I have looked, in vain, for a single fact, tending to prove the correctness of these assumptions," one reviewer of his book wrote; "they stand . . . in the same predicament with the assertion that, two and two make five."[44]

RIGHTS AND DUTIES OF NEUTRALITY

According to some scholars, classical Greece and Rome did not recognize neutrality in war.[45] Ancient states were either allies or enemies—there was no in-between. These scholars have pointed out, for example, that Greek and Latin had no word for "neutrality." *Amici* and *socii* connote allies, rather than neutrals. Whether or not ancient international law recognized neutrality in war, the Old World Order certainly did. Indeed, by the eighteenth century states developed a rich and detailed set of rules to regulate the behavior of those who wished to stay out of the fight, many of which were set out in legal treatises by distinguished authorities such as Vattel and later codified in the fifth Hague Convention of 1907.[46]

These rules did not simply say that states had the choice to be neutral; they conferred many valuable rights as well. The most important was that no state could be forced into fighting alongside another, provided of course that it had not agreed to a military alliance beforehand. Further, the territory of a neutral state was inviolable. Enemies could fight in each other's lands or on the high seas, but neutral ground was off limits. Recruiting soldiers on neutral territory was also prohibited, which is why Genêt's activities constituted a serious violation of the United States' sovereignty.

The benefits didn't end there. Neutrals also had the right to conduct business with belligerents—trading did not compromise neutrality. Thus, Britain could not, and did not, complain about the United States selling its goods to France, even though France and its colonies would have starved without American produce. By ensuring the right of neutrals to trade with belligerents, the Old World Order minimized the economic disruption of war. Economies would not grind to a halt when hostilities broke out. The world would remain open for business.

With rights, however, came responsibilities. The Citizen Genêt affair showed that neutrals were expected to be strictly impartial: They were prohibited from discriminating between warring sides unless there was an explicit agreement otherwise. As Vattel stated, "[A] neutral and impartial nation must not refuse to one of the parties, on account of his present quarrel, what she grants to the other."[47] Jefferson quoted this precise passage in his June 17 letter to Genêt.

The duty of impartiality was more than a technical legal rule. It embodied Grotius's bedrock argument—the argument that granted a license to kill—that no one outside a conflict could judge the justice of a war. Nor did the duty of impartiality simply prohibit overt fighting by nonbelligerents. By requiring neutrals to treat belligerents equally, it precluded the possibility of economic sanctions. Trading with one side to the exclusion of the other transformed a neutral—"a common friend of both parties," in legal parlance—into a co-belligerent, an ally of the trading partner. Vattel was explicit about the forfeiture of neutrality. "But to refuse any of those things to one of the parties purely because he is at war with the other, and because she wishes to favor the latter, would be departing from the line of strict neutrality."[48] Even though no shots were fired, discrimination in trade was an act of war that licensed the other side to respond with shots of its own.[49]

Indeed, the historical record shows that by the end of the eighteenth century the rule of strict impartiality was strictly followed. The authors of the leading contemporary study of economic sanctions note, with some puzzlement, that "[o]nly after World War I was extensive attention given to the notion that economic sanctions might substitute for armed hostilities as a stand-alone policy." [50]

This comment gives the impression that the late arrival of economic sanctions resulted from the failure of imagination, as though restricting trade by neutrals was a new form of statecraft that had to be dreamed up before it could be implemented. But the late arrival of economic sanctions is perfectly explicable: Economic sanctions were not imposed by nonbelligerents because the Old World Order did not permit them. For a neutral to impose trade sanctions on a belligerent would have been a violation of its duty of impartiality, a wrong that licensed war. What makes no sense today made impeccable sense in the Old World Order.

To some states, the rigors of neutrality were a straitjacket, severely limiting their freedom to help their friends—unless they were willing to go to war. To others, however, these demands were enormously liberating. For the law gave them what they wanted most: an excuse. Refusing to assist one side was not a statement about the justice of that side's cause—it was simply obeying the rules. Thus Jefferson could deny Genêt's request by spouting

Vattel. From the perspective of his cash-strapped, militarily weak government, the legal barrier against lending its ports for outfitting privateers or accelerating the repayment of debt was not a vexing limitation, but a great relief. What the Grotian philosophy had taken away—the ability to aid an ally without going to war—it had also given: the ability to remain at peace and to trade with both sides of the conflict.

CODA I

On the Fourth of July 1899, the United States contingent to the First Hague Convention on the Laws of War commemorated Independence Day by celebrating the life of Hugo Grotius. The State Department commissioned the crown jeweler in Berlin to fabricate a large silver wreath for Grotius's tomb: a large garland of frosted silver, one side of oak, with acorns in silver gilt, and on the other of laurel, with berries, also in silver gilt. The stems at the base were held together by a large silver ribbon and bow with an inscription on blue enamel. The plaque read:

TO THE MEMORY OF HUGO GROTIUS

In Reverence and Gratitude
From the United States of America
on the occasion of the International Peace Conference of The Hague

July 4th, 1899

The celebration took place in the New Church in Delft where Grotius is buried. The proceedings began with the choir's rendition of Mendelssohn's "How Lovely Are the Messengers That Bring Us Good Tidings of Peace." In his tribute to Grotius, Andrew Dickson White, the leader of the American group and organizer of the event, said of *The Law of War and Peace*: "Of all works not claiming divine inspiration, that book, written by a man proscribed and hated both for his politics and his religion, has proved the greatest blessing of humanity. More than any other it has prevented unmerited suffering, misery, and sorrow; more than any other it has ennobled the military profession; more than any other it has promoted the blessings of peace and diminished the horrors of war."[1]

Read in light of Grotius's advocacy in the *Santa Catarina* case, his extensive lobbying efforts on behalf of the Dutch East India Company, and his philosophical construction of the Old World Order, White's description of *The Law of War and Peace* is absurd. White made Grotius sound like a humanitarian pacifist, when he was the chief spokesman, if not architect, of the right of trading companies and sovereign states to wage war around the globe.[2]

There were internationalist writers who understood Grotius's work. Kant called Grotius a "sorry comforter" of warmongers.[3] Rousseau thought that Grotius "could not be more favorable to Tyrants" and saw no difference between him and Thomas Hobbes, who thought that there were no rules of justice that governed war.[4] These Internationalists appreciated Grotius's message because they saw its impact—how often it had, in Kant's words, been "quoted in justification of military aggression."[5]

But their voices have long been drowned out by those, like the attendees at the ceremony in Delft, who celebrate Grotius's contributions to peace and international law. Not only is Grotius still revered as the "Father of International Law," he is the patron saint of the "Peace Palace"—the name of the building that houses the International Court of Justice. Its library possesses the world's greatest collection of Grotiana.

Grotius has been misunderstood for so long in part because of a historical accident: His defense of Van Heemskerck was lost for several centuries. Grotius never prepared the manuscript for publication, and the handwritten sheaves were left in a pile of old letters and other materials and passed down through his descendants. When the last male Cornet de Groot died, his belongings were sold off to the public. The bookseller Martin Nijhoff auctioned the papers in 1864. Simon Vissering, a law professor at Leiden University, recognized the significance of the manuscript and conjectured that it was the original source for *The Free Sea*.[6] The manuscript was published in 1868, but only in Latin. It would not be translated into English until 1950.[7]

The defense of Van Heemskerck is, in many key respects, a rough draft of Grotius's later, widely read work. But it lacks the diplomatic artifice and thus exposes Grotius's true aim. As the great Dutch historian Robert Fruin put it, the goal was "[n]ot, as he assured us, to set bounds to warfare in general, but on the contrary to vindicate the trade of his compatriots with the Indies and the capturing of Portuguese monopolists."[8]

Without access to his earlier work, generations of scholars interpreted Grotius through an internationalist lens. When reading the work in this way, it is possible to find many passages that *sound* pacific. Grotius's admirers cite the famous passage from the beginning of *The Law of War and Peace*: "Throughout the Christian world I observed a lack of restraint in relation to war, such as even barbarous nations should be ashamed of; I observed that men rush to arms for slight causes, or no cause at all, and that when arms have once been taken up there is no longer any respect for law, divine or human."[9] The standard assumption is that Grotius was referring to the Thirty Years War, which began in 1618 and would devastate Europe.[10] The aim of *The Law of War and Peace*, on this benign reading, was to reduce the number of wars and to render the remaining conflicts more humane and less destructive.

While Grotius wrote *The Law of War and Peace* during the Thirty Years War, Grotius did not know that it was the *Thirty Years* War. He composed the famous passage toward the beginning of the conflict, when it was only the Five, or Six, Years War, long before France or Sweden entered the conflict. Grotius was probably not referring to the confessional battles between Protestants and Catholics in Germany. His preoccupation was the imperial struggles between Europeans in the East Indies. Indeed, the book's aim becomes clear in the next (often overlooked) passage: "Confronted with such utter ruthlessness many men, who are the very furthest from being bad men, have come to the point of forbidding all use of arms to the Christian."[11] Grotius was worried, in other words, that the colonial conflicts in the East Indies were giving war a bad name and that the pacifists would win the political battle to end them.

One aspect of Grotius's work deserves celebration. Grotius did not merely seek to legitimate just wars—he also sought to delegitimate another kind of war, ones that seek to cleanse territory of evil or contagion, which might be called "hygienic wars." In these conflicts, killing is not normally a means to the end of remedying a wrong. Killing is the end itself. Many holy wars, such as those described in the Hebrew Bible and waged during the medieval Crusades, were hygienic. They were bloody wars of annihilation, seeking to rid sacred lands of infidels. Perhaps because he was a Protestant who was born and raised in the midst of a terrible confessional conflict, Grotius denied the legitimacy of hygienic wars. He rejected the idea that religious differences were just causes of war.[12]

But Grotius's aim was not to end war. He was an Interventionist who was adamant that just wars were acceptable to wage, even if other sorts of wars, such as hygienic ones, were not. Grotius did not reject war or seek to make the world safe for peace. Rather, the signal contribution of the "Father of International Law" was to make the world safe for war.

Though he insisted that war could only be waged for justice, Grotius also understood that in an international order of sovereign states, there are many versions of justice. The stability of legal rights upon which global commerce and international cooperation depends would be undermined by the multiplicity of opinions over the justice of particular conflicts. The only possible way to allow victims to vindicate their rights through war is to allow nonvictims to gain legal rights from war, too. When Might is Right, multiple views on justice no longer matter, and all those who are engaged in war, victims and nonvictims alike, have a license to kill.

Grotius did not invent conquest, criminal immunity for waging war, gunboat diplomacy, or the idea of neutrality as impartiality. He was building on the intuitions and works of those who came before him and articulated similar thoughts. In some cases, he was describing what had been the practice for decades, if not centuries. And yet Grotius saw more than any other that the rules were intertwined and formed a complex system, and he articulated more clearly than any other the brutal logic of that system. Once war was legal, Grotius understood, there was no alternative to a world where Might made Right.

The logical structure of the international order that Grotius described might look something like the figure below. The diagram not only highlights the parts—the individual rules of war and peace—but also the way in which they fit together into a system. Once states have a privilege to use force to enforce their rights, a range of legal rules inevitably follows.

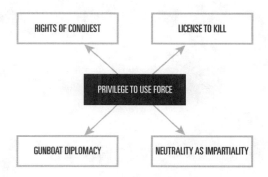

Those who gathered in Delft in 1899 thus honored a thinker who stood for much of what they reviled and had fought to change. Hugo Grotius was not the great apostle of peace. He was the great apologist of war.[13] As the leading Interventionist, he recast the mass killing of human beings as a justified moral and legal procedure. He also provided states with a new framework and language for legitimating wars. Rulers could now deny that they were fighting for their own rights. They could declare instead that they were fighting for the natural rights of their citizens. In waging war, they were just doing the job delegated to them by the governed.

The theory that Hugo the Great constructed was a work of formidable intellectual power, even beauty. It was also the legal framework that, just a few years after the Delft celebration, sanctioned a war whose moral absurdity no rational person could condone. The war that began in 1914 was the terrible culmination of the Old World Order. It would leave millions dead, millions displaced, and the world's leaders in despair. And it would prompt another corporate lawyer to rethink the theory that had justified so much suffering and rebuild a very different world order—one in which war was not only irrational, but illegal.

PART II

TRANSFORMATION

FIVE

THE WAR TO END WAR

It was the last Sunday morning of June 1914 in Sarajevo, when a thin, sickly, nineteen-year-old Bosnian Serb named Gavrilo Prinčip pointed his semiautomatic pistol at the Archduke Franz Ferdinand and fired two rounds. The first bullet pierced the door of the archduke's motorcar and struck his wife, Sophie, in the stomach—the second bullet hit the archduke in the neck, punctured his jugular vein, and lodged in his spine. By 11 a.m., the heir apparent to the Hapsburg throne and his wife were dead.

Following the Grotian script, Austria-Hungary issued an ultimatum: Unless Serbia met ten conditions aimed at suppressing the "subversive movement" behind the assassinations, there would be war.[1] Serbia acceded to all but the second part of the sixth condition, which insisted that Austria-Hungary participate directly in the investigation of the assassination. This demand was unacceptable, Serbia explained, because its constitution did not permit a foreign power to participate in an internal investigation.[2]

Nine and a half out of ten was not good enough. On July 28, 1914, Franz Joseph, the Emperor of Austria-Hungary and octogenarian uncle of Franz Ferdinand, declared war on Serbia. Because "Serbia has rejected the just and moderate demands of my Government," Franz Joseph explained in his manifesto accompanying the declaration, "I must proceed by force of arms to secure those indispensable pledges which alone can insure tranquility to my States within and lasting peace without."[3]

A chain reaction ensued. Russia sided with Serbia and began to mobilize its military forces. Germany regarded Russia's mobilization as tantamount to declaring war.[4] It issued a forty-eight-page manifesto, sold in pamphlet form for 40 pfennigs, entitled *How Russia Betrayed Germany's Confidence and Thereby Caused the European War and How the Franco-German Conflict Might Have Been Avoided*.[5] Russia responded to Germany's declaration of war with a counter-manifesto arguing that it was *Germany* that had ignored Russia's attempts at "well-intentioned" mediation, and it was *Germany* that was attacking Russia.[6] War with Russia also meant war with France, due to the Franco-Russian Alliance Military Convention.[7] Germany, therefore, declared war on France when France refused to declare its neutrality.

Because France's border was heavily fortified, Germany asked Belgium for the right of passage to outflank French defenses. Belgium refused, citing the 1839 Treaty of London, in which the European powers—including Great Britain—had recognized and guaranteed the independence and neutrality of Belgium. Germany invaded Belgium anyway, betting that Great Britain would not go to war over a mere "scrap of paper."[8] But the bet went bad. Great Britain declared war on Germany the day of the invasion.[9]

Austria-Hungary joined in by declaring war on Great Britain and France. Great Britain and France responded in kind. Many of the Eurasian states soon picked sides. The Ottoman Empire and Bulgaria allied with Germany and Austria-Hungary; Italy and Japan with France, Russia, and Great Britain.[10] Manifestos and counter-manifestos pointed to an overlapping web of wrongs and counter-wrongs that gave legal license and public justification to wage war. With no country willing to relent—and pent-up grudges, jealousies, and ambitions fueling the fire—the continent collapsed into war.

The United States attempted to stay out of the escalating mess. In an address to Congress upon the outbreak of the war in Europe, President Woodrow Wilson declared that the country would remain neutral.[11]

Indeed, many Americans saw an opportunity. With its European competitors at war, the United States could expand into new markets. But Wilson understood the rules of the Old World Order. He cautioned the public that the country could enjoy the rights of neutrality only so long as it observed its responsibilities: "The United States must be neutral in fact, as well as in name, during these days that are to try men's souls. We must be impartial in thought, as well as action, must put a curb upon our sentiments, as well as upon every transaction that might be construed as a preference of one party to the struggle before another."[12] Any sign of partiality, however slight, could draw the country into the European inferno.

Impartiality would not be easy. Tension between the U.S. and Germany began to mount in 1915, when a German U-boat torpedoed a British passenger liner, the RMS *Lusitania*, without warning.[13] President Wilson had just finished lunch and was preparing to go golfing when he first learned of the disaster.[14] The report included no mention of casualties. Just before eight that evening, news arrived that many passengers had likely died. At ten, Wilson learned the worst: As many as a thousand passengers had lost their lives. Americans were certain to be among them.[15]

Wilson struggled to remain impassive. His antiwar secretary of state, William Jennings Bryan, delivered a carefully worded note to the German ambassador seeking a "clear and full understanding as to the grave situation which has resulted." Shortly thereafter, Wilson composed a second, more confrontational, note. "Men, women, and children were sent to their death in circumstances unparalleled in modern warfare," he wrote, then demanded that Germany respect the rights of neutrals. Bryan resigned rather than send it. Endless diplomatic wrangling ensued. By April 1916, angered by continued German dissembling, Wilson threatened war.[16]

In May, Germany finally agreed to respect the rights of neutral nations, stating that it had "now decided to make a further concession, adapting methods of submarine war to the interests of neutrals."[17] It was a great victory for Wilson, who proceeded to campaign for reelection in 1916 on the slogan "He kept us out of war."[18] Less than two weeks before his second inaugural address, however, Wilson learned of a coded telegram sent by the German foreign secretary, Arthur Zimmermann, offering Mexico the opportunity to reverse its calamitous defeat by the United States in 1848.

"Make war together, make peace together," the telegram proposed.[19] The "understanding on our part is to reconquer the lost territory in Texas, New Mexico, and Arizona."[20] When the telegraph hit the papers a week later, the United States found it increasingly difficult to remain impartial in deed, much less in thought.

Germany's resumption of unrestricted submarine warfare—firing on neutral ships without warning—in February 1917 undid the fragile accord. A month after assuming his second term, the president went before a joint session of Congress to ask for a declaration of war. In a speech that echoed *The Free Sea*, Grotius's justification of the use of war to secure freedom of the seas,* Wilson argued that it was no longer enough "to assert our neutral rights with arms, our right to use the seas against unlawful interference, our right to keep our people safe against unlawful violence."[21] It was time to enforce those rights with war.

The "Great War" was a true Grotian war—launched to right wrongs, both real and imagined. In the fight for justice, belligerents wrought destruction on an unprecedented, unimaginable scale. They left eight million combatants dead;[22] seven million permanently disabled; another fifteen million wounded. By one estimate, roughly 3.5 percent of the European population died because of the war.[23]

Recognizing the war would be a terrible one, Wilson had promised that it would also be the last one, the "War to End All Wars."[24] But when the war came to a close, it was far from clear how to secure the hard-won peace, let alone end all wars.

---

*The introductory note to a version of *The Free Sea* reprinted on the eve of the war by the Carnegie Endowment for International Peace explicitly draws the connection: "the expression 'Freedom of the Seas' has been on the lips alike of belligerent and neutral, and it seems as advisable as it is timely to issue—for the first time in English—the famous Latin tractate of Grotius proclaiming, explaining, and in no small measure making the 'freedom of the seas.'" Hugo Grotius, *The Freedom of the Seas or the Right Which Belongs to the Dutch to Take Part in East Indian Trade*, trans. Ralph Van Derman Magoffin (New York: Oxford University Press, 1916), v.

HOW TO ENFORCE THE PEACE

In January 1919, the representatives of almost forty countries descended on Paris to wrangle over territory and compensation.[25] The Paris Peace Conference, like the war, was guided by the rules of the Old World Order. Great Britain and France insisted on crippling reparations from Germany, and borders across Europe, Asia, and Africa were redrawn to reward the winners at the expense of the losers.

But how to secure the peace? Wilson's solution was a new organization that would regulate international affairs—in the words of his Fourteen Points peace program, a "general association of nations" that would afford "mutual guarantees of political independence and territorial integrity to great and small states alike."[26] It would be called the "League of Nations."

The document outlining the new League—the "Covenant of the League of Nations"—sought to secure the peace through a compulsory system of dispute resolution. Instead of proceeding to war, the Covenant required member states to submit their disputes to the League, either to an arbitral tribunal agreed to by the parties, the new Permanent Court of International Justice, or an "enquiry" by the League Council.[27] States were obligated to wait until one of these bodies reached a judgment. If a state won the dispute, and the loser complied with the judgment, the winner could not go to war. But if a state lost and did not want to comply with the judgment, it could resort to war provided it waited three months before doing so.

The Covenant not only established a new system of dispute resolution, it created a new mechanism to compel states to use it. Articles 10 and 16 stated that members that went to war in contravention of the Covenant would face sanctions determined by the Council—including not only trade and financial sanctions but military sanctions as well. The League would *enforce* its Covenant—with war, if necessary.

Upon his return to the United States, President Wilson embarked on an ambitious and punishing tour across the United States to promote American membership in the League, traveling eight thousand miles in twenty-two days. "My clients are the children; my clients are the next generation," he declared in his last major address. "They do not know what promises and bonds I undertook when I ordered the armies of the United States to the soil of France, but I know, and I intend to redeem my pledges to the children; they shall not be sent upon a similar errand."[28]

As critics would later complain, the problem with the League was not that it tried to do too much to secure the peace—it was that it tried to do too little. Though it curtailed the individual right of war, the reduction was modest. Even if the tribunal rejected states' claims, they could go to war after three months. And to enforce these modest limitations on the right of war, the League could impose a *duty* of war. According to Article 16, a majority of states in the League Council had power to order member states to take up arms in defense of the Covenant. To solve the problem of war, the League's answer seems to have been . . . more war.

War as a legal institution had been so central to international relations that even a bloodbath that devastated millions of lives, and wasted billions of dollars, could not shake it loose. The League of Nations did not herald the end of the Old World Order. The League was its reprieve.

AN UNLIKELY REVOLUTIONARY

Salmon Levinson was an unlikely revolutionary. A successful corporate lawyer in Chicago, he made his name as the go-to man for major financial reorganizations.[29] His many high-profile clients included Westinghouse; the St. Louis and San Francisco Railroad; and Sears, Roebuck and Company.

Salmon's business experience ran deep. His grandparents and father emigrated from Germany to escape political unrest in 1848, when his father was eighteen. Salmon's father found work as a tailor in Noblesville, Indiana. Over time, his shop became one of the most successful clothing stores in the city. Even before Salmon was in his teens, he opened the store every morning at 6:30 and worked with his father until it was time for class. He attended the University of Chicago after being rejected by Yale, likely a victim of restrictive quotas on Jewish enrollment. Not one to give up, he was allowed to transfer to Yale for his senior year after passing a battery of tests designed to keep him out. After graduating, he returned to Chicago to practice law.[30]

Though he would become a leading Internationalist, Salmon showed little interest in international affairs for most of his career. He was the son and grandson of Jewish German immigrants, but Europe and its affairs did not much concern him. As he continued to build his successful law practice, his letters to friends and colleagues mentioned matters beyond the country's shores no more than a handful of times before 1914.[31] He was the perfect corporate lawyer—hardworking, calm under pressure, and allergic to wasteful fights. His only political involvement was the occasional campaign contribution.

In August 1914, the New York Stock Exchange closed in the face of an almost unprecedented sell-off—only the third time it had done so in history.[32] The senselessness of it all angered Levinson. He also complained about the crippling rise in interest rates and Wilson's decision to "tax[ ] us in every conceivable way as if we ourselves were at war."[33]

But it was only after he read an exchange in *The New York Times* between German émigré and New York financier Jacob Schiff and Harvard president emeritus Charles W. Eliot that he decided to do something about it. Schiff blamed the war on England, alleging that she "is unwilling to stop short of crushing Germany," while Eliot maintained that Germany had shown itself unwilling to compromise, setting up the choice between "world empire or utter downfall."[34] Levinson decided that if he could use his negotiating skills to get these leading intellectuals to agree on a plan to bring the war in Europe to an end, perhaps there was "a chance in a million of something coming of it."[35] He became convinced that international relations were not much different from industrial relations: In both cases, one had to coax the parties to act rationally, to persuade them not to make a bad situation even worse.[36]

He used his extensive network to secure introductions, managing to meet with both Schiff and Eliot several times—flattering and cajoling one and then the other into overcoming their mutual dislike and agreeing to meet to find a compromise. The stakes were not just intellectual for Levinson. He had two fighting-age sons.[37] But events soon overtook his efforts. The German army's military victories, coupled with the sinking of the *Lusitania*, ended his hopes of compromise. "The torpedo that destroyed the Lusitania," he later wrote, "knocked the bottom out of our peace plans and my optimism in that line is laid up for repairs."[38] Within two years, his sons—and the nation—were fighting in Europe.

Levinson's endeavor to find common ground between Schiff and Eliot, though fruitless, would have a lasting impact. In his correspondence with Schiff, he had begun to develop a simple but profound idea. "The real disease of the world is the legality and availability of war," he wrote in August 1917, "as the Court of first and last resort to protect criminal nations in their greed of aggression. Morally we are all accessories before the fact by recognizing and sanctioning wars as lawful."[39] He concluded, "We should have, not as now, laws *of* war, but laws *against* war; just as there are no laws *of* murder or *of* poisoning, but laws against them."[40]

Over the course of the next year, Levinson developed his thoughts into a memo that he circulated to close friends. Among them was John Dewey, a professor of philosophy at Columbia University. Dewey and Levinson had met years earlier through their spouses. Levinson's wife had been Dewey's student, as well as a classmate and intimate friend of Dewey's wife at the University of Michigan. The two couples had become close before Dewey and his wife decamped to New York.[41]

Like Levinson, Dewey was not a wild-eyed radical. Famously pragmatic, he radiated sober moderation. Indeed, the two men looked almost like brothers. Both had gray hair parted down the middle, neatly trimmed mustaches, and wire-rimmed glasses. Like Levinson, Dewey was conspicuously unpretentious. According to James Tufts, who worked as an instructor under Dewey at Michigan, "As a man he is simple, modest, utterly devoid of any affectation or self-consciousness, and makes many friends and no enemies."[42] Dewey's modesty was all the more remarkable because he was a great philosopher, perhaps one of the greatest thinkers America has ever produced. Dewey defined public intellectualism in the early twentieth century: He founded an experimental elementary school to test his ideas about educational reform and wrote nearly two hundred essays for *The New Republic* (the progressive magazine founded in 1914). And he would become Levinson's most important intellectual mentor over the course of the next decade as Levinson worked to overturn the Old World Order.

THE LEGAL STATUS OF WAR

Levinson's salvo, "The Legal Status of War," appeared in *The New Republic* in 1918. Levinson had not intended to enter the public fray. He had sent what he called his "memo" to Dewey, asking Dewey to consider publishing the ideas as his own. Dewey instead forwarded the memo to his friends at *The New Republic*. They published it under Levinson's name.[43]

"Suppose the world at peace," the article began.[44] "Abruptly Germany declares war upon France and invades her territories without even disguising the intention of annexation or even of reducing her neighbor to vassalage." "What," he asked, "happens legally?" The answer: It is henceforth a "legal war," with "other nations as much bound to neutrality and the observance of the rules laid down by international law as if the war were a benign enterprise." This "primary fact," he pointed out, is often ignored: "the civilized world puts all wars, as soon as they are initiated, upon the same plane of legality, without any regard to their origin and objectives." Even the League, he explained, "does not propose to declare war illegal; it proposes simply to refine those regulations under which war is legal."

The only real way to bring an end to war was what Levinson called "[t]he outlawing of war."[45] He acknowledged that "[w]ar, though made illegal, might still conceivably occur." But, he explained, "it would be branded as a crime and the force of the world would be organized to deal with the criminal." Levinson drew the analogy to dueling. For centuries, efforts were made to moderate duels through "codes," which became increasingly more elaborate and more "humane"—not unlike the Hague Conventions regulating the humane conduct of war. Like the Hague Conventions, the codes assumed the legality of the enterprise. Dueling was eventually declared illegal, and—as he later elaborated—"dueling is now extinct because it is plain murder under our laws." So, too, should efforts to regulate war be abandoned and war instead declared illegal.

Levinson's idea, outlawing war, was unlike any other peace plan then under discussion. All the plans to date—proposals for disarmament, the League of Nations, and countless variations—assumed the legality of war. They varied only in the ways in which they sought to direct its use, their designers working to shape institutions and incentives to make recourse to war as rare as possible. Those who had endeavored to secure the peace had not even thought to question the legality of war. It took someone new to international law and politics to propose an idea directly at odds with the international system.

But ideas are not likely to change the world as long as they stay in the pages of *The New Republic*. The public would need to be engaged. And even that would not be enough: proposals would go nowhere without politically savvy advocates.

The evolution of outlawry from an idea to a movement to a plan and finally to a treaty began with a phone call to Levinson from Philander C. Knox, the junior senator from Pennsylvania. Both men had voiced public support for the League while it was under negotiation. Levinson had even gone so far as to hold mass meetings in Chicago to drum up popular support.[46] But that support evaporated when he saw the text of the Covenant negotiated by Wilson. Knox, too, was dismayed. The day after it was made public, he invited Levinson to New York to discuss the new idea of outlawry. The two men met over three consecutive days in February.[47]

The first task was to defeat the League.[48] Levinson—in one of many undated memos to himself that he was in the habit of writing (perhaps meant as a draft of an article or letter)—explained his opposition to the League by likening it to antiquated practices of medieval hygiene:

> Recently I heard a man cite a statement from a book on sanitation in the middle ages to the effect that in the days before bath tubs had been invented perfumes were used very profusely, and that when bath tubs came in, perfumes very largely went out. Now, our international experts are sold on perfumes, so to speak. They think to get rid of war's menace by stifling its stench somewhat. No matter how poor a perfume is put on the market, they never fail to embrace it eagerly nor to give it the most flattering advance notices, especially if it has been bottled in a certain town in Switzerland.[49]

The League Charter negotiated by Wilson was just more perfume masking the rankness of war. Outlawry would be the cleansing bath. "To outlaw war means to abolish this now lawful institution by smashing its legal props and branding it a crime."[50]

Knox had more immediate concerns: He, and many of his fellow Republicans in the Senate, worried that membership in the League not only assumed the legality of war, but would draw the United States into one. Their fears focused in particular on provisions of the proposed Covenant—particularly Articles 10 and 16—that appeared to require members to come to one another's aid in the event of an act of aggression.[51] Senator Henry Cabot Lodge, then chairman of the Senate Foreign Relations Committee, objected to participating in an organization that might draw the United States into "internal conflicts in other countries, no matter what those conflicts may be."[52] Lodge had proposed adopting the Covenant with reservations meant to clarify that the United States would not go to war without congressional approval.[53] Wilson had dismissed the proposal as an attempt to undermine the agreement he had so carefully crafted. He lost Lodge's support and, though he did not realize it at the time, probably any hope of gaining Senate approval.[54]

Levinson, Knox, and Lodge were joined by Republican senator William E. Borah of Idaho. Once called the "perfect isolationist,"[55] Borah led the "Irreconcilables" in the Senate—a group of Republican senators unbendingly opposed to the League.[56] He was known to enjoy riding horseback, and his opponents joked that he was so contrarian, it was amazing that he would go in the same direction as his horse.[57]

Borah was a formidable adversary. Widely recognized as one of the Senate's great orators, he honed his advocacy skills during a career as a criminal lawyer and special prosecutor. When he rose to speak on the day of the vote on the Treaty of Versailles, as the treaty ending the war and creating the League was now known, he emphasized the danger posed by the requirement that member states use force to enforce the League's decisions: "You cannot yoke a government whose fundamental maxim is that of liberty to a government whose first law is that of force and hope to preserve the former," Borah thundered. "[Y]ou may still delude yourself, as others have done in the past, with appearances and symbols, but when you shall have committed this Republic to a scheme of world control based upon force," he warned, "you will have soon destroyed the atmosphere of freedom, of confidence in the self-governing capacity of the masses, in which alone a democracy may thrive."[58] The speech, which one contemporary pronounced "one of the Senate's oratorical master-pieces," moved Lodge to tears.[59]

In his own speech in support of the Treaty, President Wilson asked the Senate Foreign Relations Committee: "Dare we reject it and break the heart of the world?" The Senate took the dare.[60] The vote spelled the end not only for the treaty but for its greatest champion as well. The president had spent months in Europe negotiating the treaty and had stumped throughout the nation seeking to rally Americans to its cause. Its defeat left him battered, ill, and alone. Wilson would not be able to keep his promise to make the last war the *last* war. History was destined to repeat itself, he feared, without a strong international institution led by America to prevent it. Shortly after the vote Wilson suffered a stroke and fell into a decline from which he never recovered. In the campaign to succeed him, Warren Harding ran against Wilson's political agenda, a strategy that won him thirty-seven of forty-eight states. His legacy in tatters, Wilson died less than three years after leaving office.[61] Three months after co-sponsoring legislation to enter a separate peace with Germany without joining the Treaty of Versailles, Knox, too, passed away.[62] But not before helping to launch the plan to outlaw war.

A PLAN TO OUTLAW WAR

With the League defeated, the next step for Levinson and his allies was to devise a plan for peace based on outlawry. In 1919, Levinson and Knox worked together on a pamphlet—entitled *Plan to Outlaw War*—that would explain outlawry to the members of Congress and the public.[63]

Before issuing the plan, Knox showed a copy to Borah, a member of the Senate Foreign Relations Committee and soon to be chairman.[64] Borah had not only proven an implacable foe of the League, he would be one of only two Republicans in the Senate to vote against the separate peace treaty with Germany, claiming that it was merely an "instrument so framed as to bring the United States into the League of Nations some time in the future."[65] He was not an obvious ally for those seeking a global treaty to outlaw war.

But Borah knew he was gaining a reputation as a man who was against everything, and for nothing. He harbored presidential ambitions and was eager for a plan for peace that he could support.[66] Levinson—ever the clever negotiator—spoke to Borah's anxiety and ambition. "Great as your rising fame is," he wrote to Borah, "there seems to be a general criticism you are always in the opposition and that you have done nothing really constructive."[67] Outlawry would offer him a positive—but uncompromising— approach that he could champion.[68]

By Levinson's account, the three men spent an entire afternoon in Knox's office poring over the plan that Levinson had drafted at Knox's behest.[69] Later published on Christmas 1921 as a pamphlet by the newly created American Committee for the Outlawry of War (founded and largely funded by Levinson),[70] it called for a conference of "all civilized nations" to declare, in part:

1. The further use of war as an institution for the settlement of international disputes shall be abolished.
2. War between nations shall be declared to be a public crime, punishable by the law of nations.
3. War shall be defined in the code and the right of defense against actual or imminent attack shall be preserved.
4. All annexations, exactions or seizures, by force, duress or fraud, shall be null and void.[71]

Levinson's friend John Dewey wrote a foreword to this anti-war manifesto, explaining that the outlawry plan does more than any other "for concentrating all the moral forces of the world against modern war, that abomination of abominations."[72]

To start a nationwide movement, Levinson sent his pamphlets to anyone of influence. He had fifty thousand copies made and had the "type held for more"—100,000, "possibly more."[73] The number of printed copies topped 200,000 within a month,[74] and 350,000 by the end of April.[75] Chambers of Commerce, lawyers, men's and women's clubs, universities, colleges, libraries, ministers, superintendents of schools, leading manufacturers, labor organizations, and farmers throughout Idaho, Montana,

Oregon, Washington, California, and Arizona all received copies.[76] He blanketed Senator Borah's mailing list.[77] He sent out 20,000 alone under Senator Arthur Capper's name to "farmers and country merchants."[78]

Levinson and his American Committee for the Outlawry of War also tapped into an already robust peace movement made up of hundreds of loosely coordinated groups. Jane Addams, a Chicagoan like Levinson, had founded the Women's International League for Peace in 1919 and served as its first president. The Women's League organized chapters not only in Washington, D.C., and New York, but across the country, providing a nationwide network for events in support of outlawry.[79]

After Knox's death in 1921, Borah agreed to take over the political leadership of the outlawry movement.[80] As the plan to outlaw war gained momentum, pressure built on supporters to answer the question that they had thus far avoided: How to enforce the law? Borah opposed any mechanism that would require force. And, indeed, the idea of enforcing a law against war with war was anathema to most of those who had opposed the League. As they saw it, the international institutions meant to secure the peace would lead to war.

"When Borah actively took up the cudgel," Levinson later recounted, "he kept after me to solve the problem of force in international relations, which was perhaps the most difficult thing that I have had to do in this entire venture."[81] Levinson was anxious for Borah to introduce a resolution to outlaw war in the Senate, but Borah was reluctant to do so as long as he was unsure of how it would be enforced.[82]

The outlawry pamphlet called for disputes to be settled by a court with jurisdiction over international disputes. But the pamphlet had conveniently avoided the obvious next question: How would the decrees of this court be enforced? Levinson had concluded that any kind of sanctions by one nation against another would be tantamount to war—as the Old World Order regarded them. Surely the same would be true of efforts to enforce a court decision.

In a private exchange of memos and letters, Levinson and Borah considered whether the solution might be to levy criminal sanctions against individuals. "With war made a crime," Levinson observed, "governments can not employ conscription because the boys cannot be conscripted to commit murder."[83] Borah agreed.[84] But this solution created its own problems. Some outlawry advocates worried that if a world court were empowered to punish officials such as the President of the United States, the court would have the power of a "super-state."[85] But if it could not enforce its judgments, would its pronouncements have any meaning at all?

After wrestling with the dilemma, Levinson concluded that all laws rest to some degree on the willingness of those bound by them to obey: "the very basis of government is not force but what might be called the habit of obeying laws."[86] But, then again, states are not people. Could states develop a "habit" of obeying the law? The answer, Levinson suggested, was to go through the people themselves. In an article entitled "Can Peace Be Enforced?" he argued that citizens will internalize pacific norms by their participation in the outlawry of war. Each nation would hold a plebiscite whereby the people would "condemn and outlaw the war system." Once they have done so, they shall "handle and punish their own war criminals."[87]

This position bore the clear hallmarks of Levinson's years of conversation with Dewey. Dewey was a progressive reformer who had long maintained the flexibility of human nature. While basic instincts are fixed, Dewey argued that the way these instincts are channeled, and habits of thought and action shaped, depends on social structures, such as legal institutions and public education. Human nature can thus be altered by changing these background social structures. In *Human Nature and Conduct*, published in 1922, Dewey criticized those who thought war inevitable because human nature was, at bottom, bellicose. They believe that war is "so grounded in immutable human nature that effort to change [it] is foolish."[88] But, Dewey argued, the same was said of slavery, yet it was abolished. Human nature is not doomed to immoral conduct. Just as society chose freedom over slavery, it could be made to prize peace over war.

OUTLAWRY "WITH TEETH"

Not far from Dewey's office in the Philosophy Department of Columbia University, a friend and colleague was developing a different vision for enforcing the peace. James Thomson Shotwell was a professor in Columbia's

History Department and a former managing editor of the *Encyclopaedia Britannica*.[89] Born to American Quaker parents and raised in Ontario, Shotwell came to the United States in 1898 to write his dissertation at Columbia on the history of the Eucharist in the medieval church. His department hired him as an instructor in 1903. He became a full professor in 1908.

In 1917, President Wilson named Shotwell to "The Inquiry," a group of more than one hundred academics assembled to assist him in peace negotiations. Shotwell was also one of twenty-one members selected to accompany Wilson on his transatlantic voyage to the Paris Peace Conference.[90] A journalist described these advisers as a "desperate crew of college professors, in horn-rimmed glasses carrying textbooks, encyclopedias, maps, charts, graphs, statistics, and all sorts of literary crowbars with which to pry up the boundaries of Europe and move them around in the interests of justice."[91]

Shotwell did not do much prying up of boundaries. He played only a small role in the negotiations—focusing primarily on the proposed International Labor Organization.[92] A photograph of The Inquiry taken at Versailles shows the mustachioed Shotwell standing in the back row, a full head shorter than his fellow medieval historian on his right and the economics professor on his left. It wasn't a bad reflection of his influence in his first foray onto the international stage.

Shotwell, however, was undeterred. He would emerge from Versailles with a new calling. Having seen history in the making, it was hard to go back to studying and teaching dusty medieval history. He took a leave from Columbia University and accepted a job as chief editor of a comprehensive modern history of war that would eventually involve two hundred collaborators working on 150 volumes covering fifteen countries. He saw the project as a way to help the public understand war and its costs.[93]

But Shotwell did not stop there. He wanted to shape history, not merely write about it. In the spring of 1923, he trained his attention on the proposals for disarmament being debated at the League and in Washington.[94] The leading proposal called for allocating military personnel and armament quotas among the leading states. Shotwell found the idea misguided. Peace could not be established "merely by insisting upon idealistic attitudes."[95] He convened a group of scholars and public intellectuals at the Columbia University Club to examine the draft treaty on disarmament.[96] The opening words of the treaty declared: "aggressive war is an international crime." Shotwell told the group that this provision was likely to prove empty rhetoric without a working definition of aggression—which the treaty failed to provide. But no one had been able to figure out how to define aggression without sweeping in too much or too little.

As the evening unfolded, an idea occurred to Shotwell: If a substantive definition of aggression was impossible, why not turn to a procedural one? States could be required to bring their disputes to a court and to accept its decision in good faith. Those that refused would be considered the aggressor. He excitedly explained it to those gathered, and together they began drafting the text of a new treaty on the back of a menu card.[97]

The document that emerged in 1924 came to be called "the American plan." The plan conceived and drafted by a group of Americans found its audience in an organization the United States had spurned, the League of Nations. By negotiating with the League, Shotwell and his collaborators risked prosecution under the Logan Act, which made it a felony for U.S. citizens to negotiate with foreign governments having disputes or controversies with the United States.[98] But when Secretary of State Charles Evans Hughes suggested to Shotwell that he was committing a crime, Shotwell cheekily replied that he could not violate the Logan Act because the administration had not recognized the League. He could not, after all, be prosecuted for negotiating with an organization that did not exist. By Shotwell's own account, the secretary burst out laughing and said, "You have me there!"[99]

To sell his new plan, Shotwell claimed the mantle of "outlawry." "It is the first attempt of which I am cognizant," he explained to the press, "to prepare a treaty that could actually give us an outlawry of war."[100] Though early on he courted Levinson, hoping to secure his support for his plan,[101] Shotwell could not resist criticizing outlawry as Levinson had proposed it—that is, without "forceful sanction."[102] He contrasted Levinson's outlawry with what he called his "practical plan"—one that not only outlawed war but also provided machinery for enforcement. The proposed treaty that emerged from the American plan at the League, known as the "Geneva Protocol," adopted outlawry but put the idea into a "new setting."

Not only would aggression "be deemed forbidden by international law,"[103] but the Permanent Court of International Justice would also have jurisdiction to hear disputes over aggression. Its power did not simply rest on the goodwill of its participants, but it would be backed up by a new system of harsh financial sanctions. Shotwell presented his proposal as outlawry, but with teeth.

The proposal did not provide for a collective military response to enforce the peace, which would have alienated Borah, then chair of the Senate Foreign Relations Committee. Instead, the aggressor would be cut off from all commercial interactions and lose all rights afford them by international law. States could not afford to ignore the court, Shotwell later explained, for they would almost certainly have ships at sea. "Will they be received in any port with the world in league against them?"[104] The aggressor would become a pariah.*

As Shotwell launched a campaign on behalf of the Protocol,[105] Levinson boiled in rage back in Chicago at the appropriation of the movement he had nurtured. When asked for his opinion of the Protocol by William Hard, a leading political journalist, Levinson made clear in a telegram that outlawry with teeth was not outlawry at all: It "conforms to diplomatic orthodoxy by using soft glove of Outlawry promise to conceal its iron hand of world control by force."[106]

On October 2, 1924, forty-seven member states of the League approved the Protocol. Less than a month later, however, elections in the United Kingdom led to the defeat of the Labour Party by the Conservative Party, and the new government set about reexamining the Protocol. An advisory committee to the new prime minister prepared a report detailing likely effects. The committee warned that the peace-enforcing sanctions might put the United Kingdom on a collision course with the United

---

*Shotwell's proposal bears a striking resemblance to his early research on the history of the Eucharist. In his doctoral dissertation, he argued that control over the sacraments was the main way that the early Church controlled its flock. "Its enactments against sin and evil would have remained mere moral censures, mere rhetorical denunciations, if it had not been able to attach a penalty to them." James T. Shotwell, *A Study in the History of the Eucharist* (London: Eyre and Spottiswoode, 1905), 2. Excommunication was the penalty—the Church's "teeth."

States.[107] The Geneva Protocol solved one problem very cleverly—the problem of defining aggression—by providing that any state that resorted to war without first submitting to the international dispute settlement machinery was an aggressor.[108] But in solving this problem, Shotwell and his allies created a new one.[109] Under the Protocol, League members would "have the obligation of preventing all financial commercial or personal intercourse between the nationals of the State against whom the sanctions were directed, and those of a nation like the United States of America, which is not a member of the League."[110] Yet, as neutrals, the United States and other states not party to the League Covenant had the legal right to carry on trade with all parties to a conflict. Parties to the Protocol, then, might be required to interfere with the legal rights of neutral states, thus committing a legal wrong against them. What's more, for those states that had not joined the League and therefore would not be party to the Protocol, *war was still a perfectly legal response.*

The Protocol thus threatened not only to awaken the dormant sanctions regime under the League, but to expand it.[111] This was, the committee noted, "a position fraught with the gravest danger."[112] In a world in which sanctions were still a cause for war, outlawry backed by sanctions did not offer an end to war but simply a new path to it. Once the United Kingdom made clear it had no intention of ratifying the Protocol,[113] support in the League crumbled.

The fight over the Protocol exposed tensions between the two main factions in the peace movement. A long-standing friend of Shotwell, Dewey had been reluctant to jeopardize a camaraderie forged when the two marched together in a suffragette parade down Fifth Avenue. But as their disagreements grew sharper, the friendship frayed. Their relationship never recovered from Dewey's decision to write a foreword to a volume on outlawry in which he declared his alliance with Levinson: "I am glad of the opportunity to ally myself in any possible way with the movement which he has so convincingly shown to be the only way to get rid of the curse of the war-system."[114]

"IN MUCH MORE DIPLOMATIC TERMS"

Disappointed but undaunted by the defeat of the Protocol, Shotwell redoubled his efforts. Again, his path ran through Europe—this time through France and the foreign minister, Aristide Briand, who had just won the Nobel Prize for Peace, together with German foreign minister Gustav Stresemann, for his work on the 1925 Locarno Treaties: a series of interlocking treaties aimed at keeping the peace in Europe.[115]

In March 1927, Shotwell wrote to Arthur Fontaine, whom he had met at the 1919 Paris Peace Conference, where they had served together on a commission.[116] In his letter, Shotwell pointed out that France was increasingly viewed by those in the United States as hostile to disarmament—a perception encouraged by German propaganda and given weight by the French government's refusal to join the United States, Great Britain, and Japan in a naval disarmament conference to be held in Geneva that summer. He argued that "the only way to recapture American opinion is by some signal action of outstanding importance." He suggested that the occasion for a bold move "is at hand in the tenth anniversary of America's entrance into the war on April 6, 1917."[117] Fontaine passed the letter along to the French cabinet. Within the week, Briand invited Shotwell to discuss the proposal in his office. At the end of the discussion on March 22, Briand asked Shotwell to draft a memorandum to serve as a basis of negotiations. For once cautious about violating the Logan Act—this time by advising a foreign government how to negotiate with his own country—Shotwell proposed instead that he outline a draft of a public address on the topic.[118]

Although he did not find the outlawry proposal of Levinson and Borah practical, Shotwell used the terminology of outlawry in his draft message, believing it would appeal to the public.[119] He explained to Briand that it "represented a formula which had attained a definite place in the thinking of large sections of the Middle West through the advocacy of the inventor of the phrase, Salmon O. Levinson, and the acceptance of it by Senator William E. Borah."[120] The draft then unpacked the meaning of outlawry: "By this is meant that the signatories to such an engagement would renounce . . . the use of war as an instrument of national policy, an institution for the carrying out or enforcement of national purposes."[121] The phrasing was a clever twist on Carl von Clausewitz's famous claim that "war is an instrument of policy."[122] Shotwell did not mention sanctions, knowing that doing so would be a poison pill for the United States.[123] His failure with the Geneva Protocol had taught him to be shrewder, to cloak his intentions "in much more diplomatic terms."[124]

Briand saw that Shotwell's proposal was the next best alternative to the agreement he had sought. The United States had rebuffed his efforts to draw it into collective security arrangements with its European allies. But could it refuse a nonaggression pact, particularly one dressed in language drawn from a grassroots movement whose most prominent public face was the chair of the Senate Foreign Relations Committee? If France could not bind the United States to come to its aid, at least it could neutralize the threat that it would find itself on the opposite side of a future military conflict from the emerging superpower.

"—— PACIFISTS"

On the ten-year anniversary of the United States' entry into the First World War, Briand delivered what he and Shotwell hoped would be a historic address. In a draft that closely followed the memorandum prepared by Shotwell,[125] he called for an agreement between France and the United States for the "'outlawry of war,' to use an American expression." Briand also adopted Shotwell's gloss on the expression, the "renunciation of war as an instrument of national policy."[126]

The proposal was met with indifference in the United States. It was printed on page five of *The New York Times*, page twelve of the *Chicago Herald-Tribune*, and page four of *The Washington Post*, and ignored by the *Chicago Daily Tribune* and the *Los Angeles Times*.[127] The newspapers were far more concerned at the time with the prohibition on alcohol than the one on war. Shotwell arrived home from a lengthy sea voyage to discover that Briand's proposal had already been forgotten. He set to work, persuading Nicholas Murray Butler, president of Columbia University, to support the proposal and *The New York Times* to carry Butler's endorsement. On April 25, 1927, Secretary of State Frank Kellogg opened the paper and found

Briand's proposal, accompanied by a letter by Butler (that Shotwell later claimed to have largely written).[128]

On his desk at the Department of State, Kellogg had a keyboard with buttons that would summon various officials. On mornings when he read something irritating in the paper, "he would strike the keyboard like a piano concertmaster, all fingers at once, and summon everybody he could think of."[129] On the morning of April 25, chances are good that officials from all over the Department scurried to his office.[130] Kellogg fumed at the impudence of Butler and the French foreign minister—going to the newspapers rather than making the proposal to him directly. In a meeting soon after with a mutual friend of Butler's, Kellogg displayed his "doctor's degree in invectives and profanity." He called Butler and his allies a "set of — — fools," and accused them of making "impractical suggestions which didn't mean anything, never would mean anything and would have no effect whatever except temporarily to embarrass him." He added that "if there was anything in the world he hated, it was these — — pacifists."[131]

Years later, when his ire had died down, Kellogg described his reaction more dispassionately: "I explained to a great many people that it was not customary for me to answer informal speeches made by Ministers of Foreign Affairs of other countries and that if Mr. Briand wished to make such a proposition to the United States, it would receive very careful and sympathetic consideration."[132] Briand did just that in June, proposing a treaty between France and the United States containing two articles. The first provided that the parties "in the name of the French people and the people of the United States of America . . . condemn recourse to war and that they renounce it respectively as an instrument of their national policy towards each other." The second stated that the settlement of any disputes would be "by pacific means."[133]

Kellogg sat on the proposal for months. He later claimed the long wait was due to the president's absence from Washington, which had made it impossible to discuss the matter with him.[134] In truth, Kellogg had little interest in the proposal. Was there really a danger, he thought, of the United States going to war with France? He saw Briand's proposal for what it likely was—an effort to rope the United States into an alliance with France.[135]

The advocates of a peace treaty, however, would not relent. On this point, Shotwell and Levinson were in rare agreement.[136] It was an opportunity to achieve what they had each been working toward for close to a decade. Levinson wrote Kellogg in June and, at Kellogg's "kindly suggestion," offered a draft form of a treaty between the United States and France. Levinson kept the treaty "perfectly simple" to "avoid the influence of European complications or subtle indirections."[137] He enclosed the draft *Outlawry of War* pamphlet, which proposed a multilateral conference to outlaw war on a global scale.[138]

The two corresponded on and off over the next several months, with Levinson offering effusive praise and occasional suggestions, and Kellogg issuing short but courteous replies.[139] Levinson encouraged Kellogg to resist efforts to limit the pact to aggressive wars or to add reservations preserving the right to self-defense (which he regarded as implicit).[140] "When people get it through their heads that war has been and is used as a 'court'—as a lawful method of settling disputes, they will then see that the right of self-defense is irrelevant to the question of abolishing the institution of war as it is inherent and ineradicable as a naked right."[141]

Levinson's renewed emphasis on the legal status of war—and the absence of any direct mention of war as a crime—may have been influenced by his friend Dewey's advice earlier that year: "It occurred to me," Dewey wrote to Levinson, "that the statement of our case might be simpler if you left out everything about war being made a crime; and stuck simply to taking it out from under the present protection of law. The reason is simply a talking point; the moment you speak of crime, they retort that crimes have to be opposed and punished. The mental association of crime, criminal police and punishment is very fixed."[142] It was advice Levinson apparently heard, as he rarely mentioned criminalizing war thereafter.

With their goal so close at hand, Levinson and his allies unleashed a barrage of editorials, letters, resolutions, and public meetings in support of outlawry. Not content to limit his efforts to the United States, Levinson spread the message of outlawry in Europe as well. He hired an agent to "buttonhole statesmen and their secretaries from London to Paris to Berlin to Geneva."[143] He sent them voluminous outlawry literature, wrote them letters, and gave away copies of *The Outlawry of War: A Constructive Policy for World Peace*, a book written by the editor of *The Christian Century* magazine, Charles Clayton Morrison, with a foreword by John Dewey.[144] Briand and Kellogg may have been ambivalent about the treaty that would forever be linked with their names, but the "— — pacifists" were not.

TOUCHÉ

After several months, Kellogg unhappily concluded that he could not remain silent about Briand's proposal. What to do? The proposal put him in an impossible position. Accept it, and be drawn into the European system of alliances the United States had carefully avoided. Reject it, and not only be attacked by Butler, Shotwell, and their Internationalist allies, but also be suspected of harboring militaristic intentions. After reflecting, he adopted a brilliant solution: He would suggest opening Briand's agreement up to every country in the world, turning Briand's bilateral pact into a multilateral one. Although Levinson had advocated just such a treaty for years, including in correspondence with Kellogg, Kellogg later claimed the idea as his own: "I prepared a note proposing a multi-lateral treaty to be signed by the principal powers and open to the adhesion of all the nations of the world. This was the first suggestion of such a treaty."[145]

Kellogg drafted a note to the French ambassador to the United States, Paul Claudel, deflecting the proposed bilateral arrangement, noting that the friendship between France and the United States "happily is not dependent upon the existence of any formal engagement." He then turned the proposal around: "it has occurred to me that the two Governments, instead of contenting themselves with a bilateral declaration of the nature suggested by M. Briand, might make a more signal contribution to world peace by joining in an effort to obtain the adherence of all the principal powers of the world to a declaration renouncing war as an instrument of national policy."[146]

With these words, Kellogg evaded Briand's trap. Indeed, it is possible that Kellogg initially embraced the idea of a multilateral treaty not out of a desire to outlaw war, but to put an end to the bilateral treaty without outright rejecting it. After all, he suspected that France, which had hoped to draw the United States into a de facto alliance, would be much less enthusiastic about an agreement open to all states on the same terms.

At first, it seemed Kellogg was right. Upon receiving word of Kellogg's response, Briand was inclined to drop the matter altogether. Not only would a global treaty fail to create a special bond between the U.S. and France, but it also threatened to upset the delicate system of alliances France had constructed to shield itself from harm. An agreement open to all nations would undermine the Locarno Treaties with Belgium, Germany, Great Britain, and Italy, as well as bilateral pacts with Poland, Czechoslovakia, Romania, and Yugoslavia. The treaties required states to go to war to protect one another in the event of an attack. But with the new treaty, France might find itself obligated to make war and prohibited from doing so at the same time. Worse still, the new treaty might dissuade its allies from coming to the defense of France in case of attack. Rather than strengthen France's position in Europe, then, a multilateral treaty threatened to undermine it. But how could the man who had just won the Nobel Peace Prize for the Locarno Treaties refuse a treaty to renounce war among all nations, much less one that repeated the operative clauses of his proposed treaty almost verbatim? Kellogg had not only sprung himself from a trap, but dropped Briand right into one just as vexing.[147]

Likely not aware of the diplomatic jousting, Levinson praised the president and Kellogg. "If I have at times lacked faith in the international views of the administration," he wrote the president, "let me now record my unstinted admiration and gratitude for the genius of common sense that epitomizes your present stand. I sincerely believe the Kellogg proposal in response to the Briand offer will mark the greatest milestone in the history of world peace."[148] Privately, however, he griped to Dewey that Kellogg's answer had not used the term "outlawry." "Evidently Shotwell and his followers have put enough pressure on him so as to deprive us of the honor of having that word used."[149]

Though Kellogg did not use Levinson's word, his response brought Levinson's dream closer to realization than it had ever been before. The Geneva Protocol had used the outlawry language, but it had threatened to require parties to violate the neutral rights of nonparties, increasing the risk of war in the name of ending it. Briand's draft treaty—which Kellogg proposed opening to all the nations of the world—contained no such requirement. While the absence of sanctions may have made the proposal appear weaker, it actually made it much more powerful. By being explicit about the implications of outlawry, earlier proposals provoked a clash between states seeking to bring an end to the Old World Order and those still adhering to it. This draft avoided that by outlawing war—renouncing it as an instrument of national policy—and leaving the consequences of renunciation for another day. If, that is, Kellogg and Briand could come to an agreement.

A PLAN TAKES SHAPE

For the next few months, Kellogg and his assistant secretary of state William Castle negotiated with French ambassador Paul Claudel, who spoke on behalf of Briand. As talks unfolded, Castle wrote in his diary that it was "more and more evident" that Briand had made his bilateral suggestion "for political reasons solely and that he has now got a bad case of cold feet. They will be positively frozen when we drive him into the open and make him do something, or refuse to do something."[150]

The negotiators had to decide what, precisely, the pact should prohibit. Should it just prohibit "aggressive war," leaving states free to engage in "defensive wars"? Should it preserve the right to self-defense? These were issues over which Levinson and Shotwell had long sparred, without agreement or resolution. Levinson had always insisted on outlawing all war, whereas Shotwell had pressed for banning only "aggressive war." Shotwell thought it a distinction without a difference, as Levinson allowed for self-defense and thus, in Shotwell's view, for defensive war.

Kellogg, however, agreed with Levinson that any express reference to aggressive or defensive war was unnecessary and, indeed, counterproductive.[151] He, too, regarded the right to self-defense as given, and therefore resisted efforts to reserve that right in the treaty. As he testified before the Senate Foreign Relations Committee, "It seemed to me incomprehensible that anybody could say that any nation would sign a treaty which could be construed as taking away the right of self-defense if a country was attacked. That is an inherent right of every sovereign, as it is of every individual, and it is implicit in every treaty." He continued, "I said it was not necessary to make any definition of 'aggressor' or 'self-defense.' I do not think it can be done, anyway, accurately."[152]

Another issue of contention was how the prohibition on war would be enforced. Unlike the League Covenant, the proposed treaty did not allow states to go to war to enforce the peace. And unlike the Geneva Protocol, it did not provide for severe financial sanctions. But how then would it be enforced? The prominent journalist Walter Lippmann complained that a treaty without sanctions would be worthless. "I do not believe that the peace of the world can be or will be advanced by renunciation," he wrote, "but only by common action whenever the peace of the world is threatened."[153] Levinson fumed in a telegram to Borah, "With Lippmann a treaty to go to war is good without sanctions to enforce it while a treaty not to go to war is worthless unless it has sanctions. What price logic."[154]

Logical or not, the criticism required an answer. The advocates of the treaty to outlaw war came to a startlingly simple but effective one: If a state broke the multilateral treaty, the other parties "would be released and could take such action as they saw fit as to the belligerent nations."[155] The crucial difference between the new treaty and the League Covenant or the Geneva Protocol was that it would not *require* states to respond in any particular way, to impose sanctions, military or economic, against parties or nonparties. States would be released from their obligation not to resort to war against a state that itself resorted to war.[156]

While talks were ongoing, Levinson met with Kellogg. As Levinson recounted by letter to Borah, Kellogg was irritated by the many questions over how best to frame the prohibition on war. Kellogg paced the room, and "seemed to be obsessed with the idea that France was unreasonable, making impossible conditions." Levinson was troubled by his reaction, noting that what so upset Kellogg struck him as "mere questions of phraseology." "[M]y dear Borah," he closed the letter, "you still have an enormous job on your hands taking care of the situation in the interest of world peace."[157]

Less than a week later, Kellogg sent France a suggested draft treaty that looked remarkably like the early drafts of the original bilateral arrangement.[158] Over the course of the next several months, Kellogg resisted efforts to add additional clauses, caveats, and exceptions, intent on keeping the text simple. The draft as finally adopted contained only two substantive articles:

> Article I. The High Contracting Parties solemnly declare in the names of their respective peoples that they condemn recourse to war for the solution of international controversies, and renounce it, as an instrument of national policy in their relations with one another.

> Article II. The High Contracting Parties agree that the settlement or solution of all disputes or conflicts of whatever nature or of whatever origin they may be, which may arise among them, shall never be sought except by pacific means.

Once Kellogg and his counterparts agreed on the text, they turned to the question of where the treaty would be signed. The U.S. ambassador to Italy encouraged Kellogg to go to Europe for the ceremony.[159] Holding the ceremony in Paris would allow all the foreign ministers to be present, whereas an American signing ceremony would be more sparsely attended. Kellogg agreed, but insisted that the text be finalized beforehand.[160] The ceremony would be a "solemn and impressive occasion," with the treaty signed "only by high officials."[161]

On August 27, 1928, the representatives of fifteen nations gathered together in Paris to sign this renunciation of war. The dignitaries assembled in the Salle de l'Horloge, the camera lights heating the air as the ministers sat one by one to affirm their country's commitment to peace before escaping to the fresh air of the gardens of the Quai d'Orsay—the relief evident on their faces as they posed for pictures. Levinson celebrated from afar, cabling Borah: "The first realization of our dream comes true today and forecasts the destruction of the infamous war system."[162]

On his trip home on the USS *Detroit*, Kellogg received a "Navy Despatch" from the U.S. embassy in Paris summarizing the flood of positive press. The *Baltimore Sun* declared, "Praise should not be withheld from Secretary Kellogg author of the Covenant for the splendid diplomacy." The *New York Herald Tribune* gushed that "Americans can be proud of the bearing of Mr. Kellogg throughout this historic episode[.] [H]is modesty and sincerity have played an important role in dignifying this gathering of the nations in the cause of peace." *The Washington Star* declared "this should be a day of rejoicing among the nations of the world."[163]

With Senator Borah's vigorous support, the treaty met little resistance in the Senate. On January 16, 1929, the General Treaty for the Renunciation of War (later known as the Paris Peace Pact, the Briand-Kellogg Pact, and the Kellogg-Briand Pact) passed with a vote of 85 to 1, with only Wisconsin Republican John J. Blaine voting against.[164] The president ratified it the next day. By July 24, 1929, all the signatory powers had formally ratified the Pact, and it entered into effect.

"I HAVE FORGOTTEN HIS FIRST NAME"

The closer the Pact came to fruition, the more Kellogg warmed to it. Now that it was law, he saw an opportunity to secure his place in history.[165] While publicly feigning disinterest, he launched a full-scale campaign for the Nobel Peace Prize shortly after the agreement was signed.[166] He charged his assistant, William Beck, with conducting systematic outreach to dozens of leaders to solicit letters in support of his Nobel nomination, even offering to pay for their telegrams to the committee.[167] What followed was an intense drive to seek endorsements among the leading members of society. Kellogg also corresponded personally with a number of close friends and associates, asking them to drum up additional letters of support.[168]

At the same time, Kellogg sought to consign Levinson, who had also been nominated for the Prize, to oblivion.[169] When Kellogg learned in December 1929 that Levinson was in contention, he wrote to the ambassador of Norway, who was actively involved in Nobel Committee matters. "A campaign was being carried out for a man by the name of Levinson in Chicago—I have forgotten his first name—who claims to be the originator of the idea." Kellogg went on to claim that Levinson "never had anything to do with the negotiation of the Treaty" and that while he may have sent documents to the State Department, he had never seen them nor had anything to do with Levinson. "Levinson is a persistent, bumptious, conceited man," he added, "who evidently thinks that he is the first man in the world who ever thought of outlawing war." "I am not going to lower myself by starting a campaign," he assured the ambassador.[170] A year later, Kellogg was awarded the Nobel Peace Prize.

Kellogg had written Levinson out of the story, but the Chicago lawyer—and the New York historian against whom he had sometimes struggled—had triumphed. The agreement would be known in the United States as the Kellogg-Briand Pact, but it embodied the Levinson-Shotwell vision of a world where military might no longer made legal right. It was a vision that would continue to gain adherents. Within a few short years of Kellogg's acceptance of the Nobel Prize, nearly every country in the world had ratified the agreement. War was, to use Levinson's word, outlawed.

SIX

THINGS FALL APART

On Saturday, September 19, 1931, at 5 p.m., the sixty-fifth session of the Council of the League of Nations opened in Geneva. Seated around a large horseshoe table, the Council addressed a few mundane administrative matters before turning to the representatives of Japan and China. The Japanese representative, Yoshizawa Kenkichi,[1] speaking in French, reported on a "collision" that had occurred between Japanese and Chinese troops in Mukden, China, near the South Manchuria Railway the previous night. Yoshizawa seemed embarrassed by the violence, and confused about what had transpired, but assured the Council that his government would provide more information and "would do everything possible to relieve the situation."[2]

His Chinese counterpart, Dr. Sao-Ke Alfred Sze, also spoke briefly, though in English. He "would not conceal from the Council that he had been greatly disturbed by the news from Manchuria." He, too, had no information beyond that in the press reports, but he promised to keep the Council apprised. The president of the Council expressed "sincere hopes for a prompt settlement of the question."[3]

It soon became clear that the shape of the table would bring no luck to the Council. At its next meeting three days later, Sze read aloud two telegrams received from Nanking the night before. "Kirin Changchun Railway seized," the first cable began. "Yingkow, Antung, Changchun, Fushun and many other towns have been seized by Japanese who have cut all telegraph, telephone and wireless, hence difficult for Government to get complete news." The second message, sent the same day, reported that the city of Changchun "is feared now half in ruins. . . . Approximate casualties among Chinese soldiers and civilians estimated 600 while over 1,000 now under detention by Japanese military. Entire region Wanpaoshan has been occupied by Japanese troops."[4] The staccato rhythm of the cables only reinforced the sense of confusion on the ground.

Yoshizawa responded to Sze's alarming news: "The Chinese representative has alleged that the incident took place without provocation on the part of the Chinese troops. That is a mere affirmation and we cannot accept it without clear proof." To the contrary, he claimed, Chinese troops were responsible, for they had blown up Japan's railway tracks at Mukden: "Hence it was as a result of this act of destruction—such acts are unhappily frequent in those parts—that the small Japanese garrison force was obliged to take up arms."[5]

Debate over the expanding Japanese occupation of Manchuria lasted weeks. At the eighth meeting on the matter on October 13, with Aristide Briand serving his first day as president of the Council, Sze nearly lost his composure. "I am speaking under the stress of great emotion," he confessed, before reading a statement prepared in advance for fear of using "intemperate" words. Sze first noted Japan's refusal to withdraw its troops back to the railway zone, as it had promised, and its continued acts of "occupation, aggression, and violence."[6] He went on to declare: "The Covenant and the Pact of Paris are our two sheet-anchors, to which we have moored our ship of State and with the help of which we believe we shall ride out this storm." The Covenant and Pact were supposed to protect China, he said, but not only China. They are "also the corner-stones of the worldwide edifice of peace . . . and, if they crumble, the edifice collapses." These events stood as "the first great test" of the Pact and the League. If they failed, Sze asked, wouldn't each state conclude that it "must rely on its own armed forces, and on those alone? . . . However remote and irrelevant this disturbance in the Far East may seem to the West . . . the web of fate binds us all together."[7]

Briand concluded the acrimonious meeting by acknowledging the difficulty of stopping the emerging war and the danger it posed to the international order. He proclaimed that the Council would nevertheless perform its duty "with the necessary firmness when it has obtained full information as to the causes and extent of the dispute."[8] Briand did not acknowledge what was clear to all around the table: The Pact that bore his name was about to face its first great test.

THE OLD WORLD ORDER COMES TO ASIA

Japan first came into contact with the Old World Order in the early 1850s. Innovations in shipbuilding technology rendered cross-oceanic voyages reliable and economical. A steamship could make the journey from the West Coast of the United States to Japan in a breathtaking eighteen days.[9] The world was on the brink of a global trade revolution, and the United States was eager to open up relations with the East.

With the successful conclusion of the Mexican-American War in 1848, the United States had acquired California and, with it, an immense Pacific coastline. A turn toward Asia was the next logical step.[10] The United States had already gained a foothold in China in the early 1840s, when it joined several other countries in forcing open five Chinese ports to foreign trade.[11] Yet resentment festered on both sides, with the Chinese balking at unequal and unfairly imposed treaty terms and Western powers irritated by the failure of the Chinese government, then embroiled in a civil war, to follow through on its treaty commitments.[12]

China's neighbor, Japan, thus offered several benefits. It was not only a potentially valuable trading partner, but gaining access to its ports would also strengthen the U.S. position in the entire region. The United States naval depot was located in Hong Kong, then under British control. Great Britain had forced China to cede the port of Hong Kong "in perpetuity" as a price of peace in the First Opium War—a war waged to ensure a continued market for its East India Company's opium in China.[13] Townsend

Harris, who later served as the first American Consul General to Japan, described Hong Kong as "one of the worst spots in the whole East" to locate the depot, not least because "the whole of the supplies for our Eastern squadron, are in the hands of our great political and commercial rival." [14]

But it was not only the need for a better foothold in Asia that led the United States to Japan. As more American fishermen and whalers entered the Pacific, more became shipwrecked off the coast of Japan. Under its policy of isolation, Japan confiscated their possessions and effectively imprisoned them until the sailors could be transferred to one of the few foreign ships permitted to visit the country. Japan's extreme isolationism was not just a lost opportunity; it was actively harming U.S. citizens—giving Congress another reason to act. [15]

GUNBOAT DIPLOMACY

In 1852, Congress charged Commodore Matthew Perry with leading an expedition to Japan to secure a treaty of amity and commerce. Although he would turn fifty-nine during the expedition, Perry retained a full head of brown hair and cut an imposing figure, prompting his men to refer to him as "Ursa Major" (after the constellation also known as the Great Bear) behind his back. Some considered him "imperious," "harsh," and "too rigid," and he was given to bursts of anger. [16] He had just a few years earlier helped lead the United States Navy to victory in the Mexican-American War. He was now determined to open Japan to the West. [17]

Since the 1600s, Japan had been closed to foreign commerce, with the primary exception of very limited trade with the Chinese and Dutch through the port of Nagasaki. [18] Townsend Harris described the Japanese attitude as follows: "Shut up by their system of exclusion, they have heard little, and perhaps have cared less, about the events, that have convulsed other Nations, during the last two hundred and fifty years, it is not therefore to be wondered at, that many of them should be opposed to any alteration, of a system, which has secured their tranquility and happiness for so long a time." [19] Perry's clerk, John Sewall, put it more colorfully: "Japan was a somewhat supercilious dame, and had hotly resented such overtures before." [20]

Perry brought four imposing ships to render his intentions unmistakable. "America had reason to demand a hearing," Sewall explained, "and her fleet made it possible to get it."[21] Perry's squadron consisted of two steam frigates and two sloops of war.[22] The flagship, the *Mississippi*, was a sentimental favorite, for Perry had commanded the Mexican Gulf Squadron from its deck a half decade earlier.[23] The immense black ships inspired awe as they belched smoke and moved against the wind.[24] When the ships first pulled within sight of land, those on shore were terrified: "In all directions were seen mothers flying with children in their arms and men with mothers on their backs."[25]

The ships set to anchor just off the coast of Uraga, twenty-seven miles from Edo (modern-day Tokyo). Numerous boats surrounded them.[26] A local official informed Perry that Japanese law forbade any exchange with foreigners anywhere but Nagasaki. Perry, in turn, told the official that he "had come purposely to Uraga, it being near to Edo" for the purpose of delivering a letter from the president of the United States to the emperor of Japan and that "if the Japanese government did not appoint a suitable person to receive the documents addressed to the emperor, I would go on shore with a sufficient force and deliver them, whatever the consequences may be."[27] If the boats surrounding his ships were not removed in fifteen minutes, "he should be obliged to open his batteries and sink them."[28] He would wait three days for an answer from Edo, but no more.[29]

Perry then directed several "well manned and armed" boats to survey the harbor and bay of Uraga. When the Japanese governor informed him that Japanese laws forbade such surveys, Perry replied that American laws commanded them "and that we were as much bound to obey the American as he was the Japanese laws."[30] He then sent the *Mississippi* closer to Edo "than any foreign vessel had ever before ventured." He refused to meet any envoy "until the reply from Edo was received." Perry's journal makes clear his motives: "I had purposely sent *Mississippi* and the boats on this service, being satisfied that the very circumstance of approaching nearer to Edo with a powerful ship would alarm the authorities and induce them to give a more favorable answer to my demands."[31] When his movements provoked consternation from local officials, Perry explained that unless he obtained the agreement he sought, he would return in the spring with a larger force nearer to Edo "which would make our communications with that city more convenient."[32] After further delays, Perry issued an explicit threat: "If this friendly letter of the President to the Emperor is not received and duly replied to, he shall consider his country insulted and will not hold himself accountable for the consequences."[33]

How could Perry justify this blatant threat of force? After all, didn't each state have the right to refuse to trade, as long as they did not violate principles of neutrality? Yes, states could refuse to trade particular goods or with particular nations, but under the Old World Order they were not entitled to refuse to trade altogether. As Grotius explained, "Every nation is free to travel to every other nation, and to trade with it."[34] God made no country self-sufficient—no place supplies all the "necessaries of life" and "some nations excel in one art and others in another." In this way, God had made clear that "He wished human friendships to be engendered by mutual needs and resources, lest individuals deeming themselves entirely sufficient unto themselves should for that very reason be rendered unsociable."[35] Hence every country is obliged to engage in *some* trade. Any country refusing *all* trade is rejecting God's plan. Townsend Harris's later explanation to the Japanese reflected this view precisely: "No nation has the right to refuse to hold intercourse with others."[36]

In the Old World Order, moreover, gunboat diplomacy of the kind Perry threatened was routine. After all—as the East Indian potentates learned in the seventeenth century and the Sioux Indians learned in the nineteenth—it was not only permissible to go to war and to keep what one conquered, it was permissible to *threaten* to go to war to obtain a binding agreement. Perry understood this idea well, and he had no intention of standing down until he had delivered his country's demands.

The Japanese relented, agreeing to send an emissary to receive the letter from the president in Uraga "in opposition to the Japanese law," as the note acknowledging receipt put it.[37] After delivering his letter in a grand ceremony that was held in a building erected just for the purpose of this exchange, Perry decided to depart and return in the spring for his answer. Leaving now, he reasoned, would give the Japanese time for deliberation and provide him an opportunity to return with overwhelming force. He was also running low on provisions and was worried that the Japanese would wait him out until he had to leave.[38]

With characteristic flourish, Perry offered two parting "gifts": a white flag and a letter explaining that if the Japanese chose war over the proposed treaty, "victory will naturally be ours and you shall by no means overcome us." If at that point they desired reconciliation, he counseled, "you should put up the white flag that we have recently presented to you, and we would accordingly stop firing and conclude peace with you, turning our battleships aside."[39]

As promised, Perry returned in February 1854, this time with seven ships. Wrangling over the location for negotiations ensued. The Japanese wanted the meetings to take place in Uraga, but Perry insisted on a point closer to Edo. Perry later explained his "unreasonable obstinacy" as an attempt to set a tone for the negotiations to come: "I was convinced that if I receded in the least from the position first assumed by me, it would be considered by the Japanese an advantage gained."[40]

When the Japanese proved just as obstinate, Perry ordered his squadron to move within sight of Edo—so close that the ships could hear the striking of the city bells at night.[41] By Perry's account, the Japanese responded by suggesting a meeting place on shore close to where the boats were anchored—near, but not in, Edo.[42] Perry then prepared for another exchange of "gifts." Along with gallons of whiskey, he brought various valuables meant to showcase Western technology and learning. The gift manifest includes a long list of gifts for "the Emperor," including a miniature steam engine, two telegraph sets, a series of U.S. Coast Guard Survey Charts, a small armory of Hall rifles, Maynard muskets, pistols, and books ranging from the full nine-volume set of Audubon's *Birds* to a *Catalogue of New York State Library and of Post Offices*.[43] For "Abe, prince of Ise, first councilor," he presented two books: George Wilkins Kendall and Carl Nebel's *The War Between the United States and Mexico Illustrated*, and Roswell Sabine Ripley's *History of the War in Mexico*.[44] Ripley's account detailed some of Perry's own heroic exploits, including his capture of the towns of Tuspan and Tabasco.[45] The message was obvious: Agree to our offer of friendship or we'll wage war. Perry was an envoy of the United States, but he was also the envoy of the Grotian legal order.

With his ships moored "in a line abreast . . . covering with their heavy guns an extent of shore of five miles," Perry entered another special building constructed by the Japanese for the event.[46] Within days, he had secured a treaty that met nearly all his demands. As captain's clerk Sewall put it, "It cannot be said that Japan ever really yearned to be 'opened' any more than an oyster does; yet when the time came, she yielded as gracefully as any oyster I ever had the pleasure of meeting."[47] The treaty opened three ports to the United States. If American ships wrecked on the coast of Japan, their crews and cargo would be carried to one of these ports and they would be "free as in other countries."[48] Additional details would be worked out in a subsequent agreement.

Perry may not have realized it, but he was introducing Japan to the Old World Order—and the Japanese would prove to be outstanding pupils.

"WHAT KIND OF THING IS THE LAW OF NATIONS?"

A couple of years later, Townsend Harris arrived in Japan to serve as the first general consul assigned by the United States to Japan.[49] On his arrival in 1856, he was just over fifty years of age, with sweeping white hair, a carefully trimmed beard, and a slightly upturned mustache. He was robust, but repeated illness during his lengthy stay in Japan would whittle his frame until he was dangerously thin.

The Japanese were unprepared for his arrival. Edo lay in rubble, having months earlier suffered a devastating earthquake. The Japanese insisted his arrival was premature—the treaty, after all, required mutual agreement before the exchange of consuls.[50] Harris insisted that the opposite was true—the treaty allowed the United States to send a consul to Japan to negotiate a commercial treaty. They were both right. The Japanese and English texts of the agreement—both translated from the original Dutch in which the agreement had been negotiated—differed on this point. Backed by the implicit threat of force, the English version prevailed.[51]

Predictably, Harris proceeded to negotiate an agreement that favored the United States.[52] The treaty permitted Americans (and later others) to live under the laws of their own country and be subject to their courts even while on Japanese soil. It required the Japanese government to collect tariffs at specified rates that could not be changed for at least five years.[53] Coins would be traded without any duty—a decision that would lead Japan to hemorrhage gold currency. In return, Harris gave up little. The agreement allowed Japan to send diplomatic agents to reside and travel freely in the United States and promised to render "friendly assistance" to Japanese vessels that American ships might meet on the high seas.[54]

During the negotiations, there was a telling, even poignant, exchange between Townsend Harris and several Japanese dignitaries. One of the dignitaries asked, "What kind of thing is the law of nations?" Harris replied, "To give a full answer to this question would require the space of a large book."[55] He went on to explain the rules regarding the treatment of diplomats. But when it came to an education in the law of nations, Perry's gunboats had already offered a powerful introduction to the subject.[56]

The negotiations unleashed intense struggles among elites inside Japan. Harris was almost entirely oblivious, at least initially.[57] Unlike Perry, he knew enough not to insist on negotiating with the emperor. Though he was the head of state and appointed the shōgun, the emperor was largely a symbolic figure, much like the present Queen of England.[58] Harris negotiated instead with representatives of the Tokugawa Shogunate—the feudal military government in Edo headed by the shōgun and run by the military command office. Unlike the emperor, the shōgun held effective power. He was not, however, all powerful. Much local governance was ceded to feudal lords, or daimyō, who alternated their residence between their domains and Edo. As it turned out, the daimyō were not happy with the treaty that Harris had negotiated with the shōgun's representatives—as much for being left out of the negotiation as for the agreement's inequitable terms. The emperor's advisers, initially intent on proceeding with the treaty, agreed under pressure not to present the treaty to the emperor until the daimyō had approved it.[59]

Harris, unaware of the intense struggle among the various centers of Japanese power, regarded the delays with growing anger and frustration. Late in the negotiations, he fell ill with a "very dangerous nervous fever."[60] The shōgun sent two of the best imperial physicians. When the physicians informed the shōgun that Harris's case was hopeless, Harris later reported, they received "orders to cure me, and that, if I died, they would themselves be in peril"—a response he took as a touching sign of the "kindly disposition" of the Japanese.[61]

When well enough to resume negotiations, Harris made sharper arguments.[62] The shōgun's chief minister, Hotta Masayoshi, requested a two-month delay before the formal signing of the treaty (during which time he presumably hoped to obtain the emperor's approval). In response, Harris "threatened to proceed to Kyōto to enter into negotiations with what he was now convinced was the real Sovereign power in Japan"—meaning the emperor.[63] Hotta reported on the impasse and was stripped of his position.

On July 3, 1858, an American steamship arrived carrying the news that China—in the midst of the Second Opium War—had agreed to demands by the United States, Britain, France, and Russia to open more ports, legalize the import of opium, establish a customs service with foreign inspection, and establish diplomatic relations. The next day Harris wrote a letter to Hotta, apparently unaware that he had been sacked, warning that Japan would be the new object of the West's attention. A British fleet of thirty or forty vessels could be expected "at any hour," soon followed by the French.[64] If the treaty already negotiated were concluded before they arrived, Harris offered to serve as "friendly mediator" to encourage the British and French to peacefully accept the same terms.[65]

The decision of how to respond fell on Hotta's replacement, Ii Naosuke—an ambitious official who was intensely loyal to the shogunate. Having learned enough about the "law of nations" to know that the alternative to the treaty was war, Ii decided to sign the treaty without the emperor's approval.[66] He later endorsed similar treaties with the British, French, Dutch, and Russians.[67] They were even less subtle than the Americans in threatening force to obtain the terms they wanted. According to Harris, the British representative, James Bruce, the 8th Earl of Elgin and High Commissioner and Plenipotentiary in China and the Far East, informed the Japanese commissioners that if they delayed agreeing to a draft treaty, "he should go away, and soon return at the head of a fleet of fifty ships, and that he should then not only demand what he now asked, but should also require the Japanese to give to all British subjects the right to travel in any or all parts of the Japanese Empire and also that the Japanese should be free to adopt the Christian faith, if they saw fit."[68]

Though he likely saved his country from invasion, Ii would pay for his actions. Less than twenty months after the treaty was signed with the

Americans, the forty-four-year-old Ii, accompanied by fifty or sixty samurai bodyguards, was set upon by a band of eighteen young imperial loyalist rōnin—masterless warriors. The bodyguards, whose swords were covered by bulky raingear to protect the ornamental work in their hilts from the falling snow, were slow to react. Three or four of the rōnin tore open the door to Ii's palanquin, dragged him out, and sliced off his head.[69]

DISCOVERING GROTIUS

Perry's expedition and the events that followed sparked an intense interest in the question: "What kind of thing is the law of nations?" But in 1860s Japan it was not easy to answer, for not a single Japanese scholar or statesman had studied international law. Japanese leaders needed their own Grotius. The found him in a scholar, philosopher, and statesman named Nishi Amane.

Like Grotius, Nishi would become a philosopher and leading international lawyer. Indeed, today he is known in Japan as the father of modern philosophy, having coined the Japanese word for philosophy (*tetsugaku*).[70] The son of a minor samurai who served as the personal physician of the local daimyō, Nishi spent his early village life receiving a traditional Confucian education. When he completed his studies, his daimyō sent Nishi to teach in Edo.[71] He received his orders on March 10, 1853, just four months before Perry's first expedition arrived. He discovered a city brimming with energy. Among the most fascinating people he encountered were the "Dutch doctors"—Japanese court and clan physicians who could read Dutch and knew something of Western thought. Nishi taught Confucianism during the day, but studied Dutch in his spare time.[72]

Perry's arrival in July plunged the city into political turmoil. Nishi decided that learning Dutch in his spare time was not enough, telling friends, "I cannot after all neglect Western learning."[73] Because his daimyō had ordered him to teach Confucianism, the only way he could devote his time to learning about the West was to relinquish all ties to his clan. This would make him a rōnin. Cutting himself off from his clan was no longer grounds for capital punishment, as it once had been. But it would still lead to exile from his daimyō's lands, his childhood home.

He decided to throw himself into studying Dutch despite the consequences. He also learned a bit of English, then a language hardly known in the country. In a few short years, he was one of the leading Dutch linguists in the country—a sign both of his aptitude and of his country's meager knowledge of foreign languages.[74] Nishi's growing proficiency coincided with the Tokugawa Shogunate's decision to learn as much as it could from the outside world. In the wake of Perry's visit, the government's once small translation office grew into a research institute, Bansho Shirabesho— Institute for the Investigation of Barbarian Books—which became the center of Western studies in Japan.[75] Nishi was appointed an instructor in the school, joining an urgent effort to translate Western texts and concepts.[76]

It soon became clear, however, that studying books alone would not lead to true understanding. It would be necessary to study the ideas and language in the countries where they originated. The government began to make plans to send scholars to the United States to gather the knowledge it desperately needed.

Nishi and his close colleague at the Institute for the Investigation of Barbarian Books, Tsuda Mamichi, had been plotting a trip abroad since 1858. They gained tentative approval to study in the United States in 1861, but the American Civil War made safe travel in the country impossible. Instead, they were granted leave to board a ship bound for Japan's longtime trading partner, Holland. Together with five men from the Warship Navigation Institute, two medical students, and seven craftsmen, Nishi and Tsuda would be the first Japanese men sent by the government to study in Europe.[77]

On July 14, 1862, the group set off.[78] After months of voyage, a shipwreck off the coast of Sumatra, and several planned stops, they arrived in Holland almost a year after they had set out.[79] Nishi and Tsuda were initially put in the charge of Johann Joseph Hoffmann, a professor of Chinese and Japanese at Leiden. Eight days after he arrived, Nishi wrote out his plan of study, which included "statistics, law, economics, politics and diplomacy."[80] He also indicated that he wished to learn "those subjects within the realm of philosophy."[81]

A photograph of Nishi survives from his time in Leiden. Posing with eight other Japanese students, the photo, taken in 1865, shows Nishi dressed as a proper Dutch man, in a morning coat, button-down vest, bow tie, light slacks, and polished boots. He is clean-shaven, with long, curly hair parted on the side. His arms are folded over his chest and his face bears an impatient, almost defiant, look.[82]

Hoffmann first had his students perfect their Dutch, under the direction of a local high school principal. Within a couple of months, the two were sent to Professor Simon Vissering of Leiden University. Vissering would serve as their tutor until their return voyage in December 1865.[83] He devised a five-part course in natural law, international law, constitutional law, economics, and statistics. Every Thursday and Friday night for two years, the three met for a private lecture. Nishi and Tsuda took copious notes, carefully recording this knowledge not simply for themselves but for their entire country.[84]

The university put the Japanese scholars under Vissering's care largely because the Dutch professor was a polymath, whose knowledge of the social sciences and humanities was extensive enough to cover the wide-ranging curriculum. But the assignment would have an impact no one anticipated. Vissering was at that very moment playing a pivotal role in the history of international law: He had discovered the long lost manuscript of Grotius's defense of Jacob van Heemskerck in 1864. Thus, while Nishi and Tsuda were studying international law, their tutor studied Grotius. But Vissering wasn't merely studying Grotian theory. He was immersed in a detailed analysis of Grotius's most militant tract. The defense of Van Heemskerck was the treatise that shocked Dutch scholars and disabused them of the common view that Grotius was an early antiwar humanitarian. The lost manuscript was a call for the Dutch to attack the Portuguese. In its bellicosity, the book laid out the intellectual blueprint of the Old World Order. It was the original source of the theory of natural rights and the social contract, the modern justification of the just war. As Nishi had come to Holland to learn the underlying logic of the Western rules of international law, he could not have picked a better teacher than Vissering.

Through Vissering, Nishi and Tsuda discovered Grotius. They would have discovered not only the mature scholar of his later years, but also the young lawyer who justified the seizure of a Portuguese ship the occupants of which had done nothing to the Dutch who seized them. It was this Grotius they would bring home to Japan.

TRANSLATING INTERNATIONAL LAW

In 1866, Nishi and Tsuda returned to Japan. Almost immediately, the Tokugawa Shogunate made Nishi an official adviser on European affairs. His first duty was to translate his notes of Vissering's lectures. He turned them into a compilation, entitled *Fisuserinku-shi Bankoku Kōhō* (literally, "Vissering's International Law"), published in Japan in 1868, the same year that Grotius's defense of van Heemskerck was published in Holland. (Tsuda, meanwhile, wrote *Taisei kokuhō ron* ["Lectures on National Law," sometimes also translated, "On Western Law"].[85]) In the introduction to his book, Nishi explains its provenance: "My notes of Professor Vissering's teachings are the basis for this book. Professor Vissering is a scholar holding a teaching position at Leiden University, in Holland, where he was also my teacher."[86]

Vissering's International Law was not the first text on international law in Japan. A Chinese translation of Henry Wheaton's *Elements of International Law* had been translated into Japanese and printed as *Bankoku Kōhō Yakugi*.[87] As one might expect from a translation of a translation, however, the Japanese version was largely incomprehensible. Even if a perfect translation had been possible, the treatise would have created more confusion than illumination. For the original English version of Wheaton's text was perplexing as a stand-alone document. The Japanese translation was based on the sixth edition, and new editions were not simple rewrites of the original. Rather, increasingly lengthy glosses and footnotes were added to each version to explain how each rule had been refined, elaborated, or rejected. By the sixth edition, reading the Wheaton treatise was like studying sediment layers. Where a practice or understanding had changed, the additions often contradicted the text to which they were appended. Nishi diplomatically described the Wheaton text in the introduction to his own book: "[I]t is for people already competent in matters of law."[88]

The task of introducing international law to a Japanese audience required much more than translating the sentences of existing texts. The concepts the texts represented were so foreign that there were often no existing Japanese words that captured their meaning. Indeed, Nishi drew on a method of translation known as *kanbun kundokutai* that was initially used by Japanese scholars to read Chinese texts. He combined existing Chinese characters in new ways to render Western terms that had no natural analogs in Japan—in language or lived experience.[89]

Even the idea of what was "law" was contested. The term "international law" was translated in Japanese as *bankoku kōhō*, "the public law of all countries."* But some Japanese scholars objected to the use of *hō* for "law" in "international law." *Hō* meant common standards or models of behavior—"those regulations, orders, and penal reprisals established and upheld through the power and authority of the absolute ruler."[90] But to many Japanese, the behavior of Western states they had witnessed under this so-called international law was not a common standard or model of behavior and was not upheld by a sovereign power. How, then, could it deserve to be called *hō*? Understandably, they saw Western "international law" as unpredictable and inconsistent, reflecting the value of "might," not "law."[91]

NISHI'S *BANKOKU KŌHŌ*

Nishi set out, then, to render Western international law comprehensible to his countrymen—not simply by translating a text but by communicating an alien worldview of states and how they were to interact with one another.

The text reflects Hugo Grotius's masterwork: Its table of contents almost perfectly mirrors *The Law of War and Peace* (with one major difference, which we will discuss shortly). However, unlike Grotius's work, which is cluttered with classical erudition, Nishi's text stripped the rules of Western international law down to their basics. He modestly described the book as "meant for beginners" and "a reference tool, or . . . an aid for examinations."[92] As Nishi knew well, everyone in Japan, from students to high-level government officials, was a beginner.

But if the aim of his work was different from Grotius's, the underlying theory was the same. The first chapter explained that Western international

---

*The term *bankoku kōhō* literally means "the law of ten-thousand countries." The expression was first used in translating Wheaton's *Elements of International Law* and was then borrowed by Nishi.

law, and its conception of war, was first developed by Grotius: "Positive law is only one part of Western public law, but it too is based on natural law, so there is nothing in Western public law that does not originate from natural law. The articles of natural law were first clearly discussed by the Dutch Hugo de Groot (Grotius is his Latin name). He wrote the famous work *De Jure Belli ac Pacis* [*The Law of War and Peace*] which was published in 1625."[93] And, indeed, much of the rest of the work reads almost as though it were lifted straight from Grotius. Explaining the rules of war, Nishi's text states: "According to the rules of natural law, if a man suffers an injury [*kutsujoku*, literally "his rights are damaged"], then he can resist this, protect himself, and seek reparations in order to compensate for the damage. According to natural law, this right is inherent. In Western public law, the right to war is based on the above rule."[94] War, however, is "the last resort. One cannot deploy an army in order to protect one's right, or to regain one's right, unless one has exhausted all other methods, with no result."[95]

Drawing explicitly from Grotius, *Vissering's International Law* explains the main structural—and seemingly paradoxical—feature of the Old World Order, namely, that Might made Right. Only those who had been wronged were legally permitted to go to war, but states were legally empowered to keep what they seized in a war even if they had not truly been wronged. This paradoxical result is necessary because there is no entity with the power to say who wronged whom: "When war between two countries is declared, it is extremely difficult to say whose rights were first violated, and who was the party that perpetrated the injury."[96] To solve this problem, Western states treated the outcome of all declared wars as decisive— whichever state won was right: "That is why in Western public law . . . two sovereign countries engaged in war are both correct."[97] That was not to say that there were no rules. Nishi devoted much of his work to explaining the intricate technical legal procedures that had to be followed by states, including the various ways in which states could declare war, triggering the special legal consequences that flowed from formal war.[98]

Grounding international law on the natural rights of the individual also established the equality of Japan with the West. If all individuals have the same natural rights, and states derive their rights from the individuals from which they are comprised, all states are equal.[99]

For all the similarities between Grotius's work and Nishi's text, there was one major structural difference. *The Law of War and Peace* was three books, but *Vissering's International Law* had four. The extra book focused on diplomatic practice. Having been isolated for several centuries, Japan did not understand even the basic rules of diplomacy. The country lacked rules for granting diplomats authority to negotiate on behalf of the nation and for formally approving treaties. Ii, caught between a court unwilling to present a treaty to the emperor and a negotiating partner willing to wage war, had been a victim of this failure. Nishi intended to give the government the tools it would need to avoid repeating such mistakes.[100] The book ends with a chapter entitled "Etiquette at Sea," a reminder that Nishi's studies had been set in motion by the arrival of Perry's black ships.

Nishi's influence was not limited to words on the page. After completing his book on international law, Nishi, like Grotius before him, helped shape his country's foreign policy. Nishi became a valued adviser to the government on foreign affairs.[101] In the waning years of the Tokugawa Shogunate, he even served as private tutor to the shōgun. As the political climate shifted against the shogunate, the government called on Nishi to draft a new constitution—one that would restore formal imperial rule but quietly retain actual power in the shogunate.[102] But the effort was doomed. The Meiji Restoration, as the revolution came to be known, forced the shōgun from power in 1868, replacing him with the fifteen-year-old Emperor Meiji, who had become emperor upon his father's death less than a year earlier.

Even after the revolution, Nishi never drifted far from the center of power. The ex-shōgun's family established a military school and invited Nishi to run it.[103] The success of the school gained the attention of the new government in Tokyo, as Edo was renamed in 1868, and Nishi joined the Meiji government. For sixteen years, he worked in the highest ranks of the military bureaucracy, counseling Japan on what it meant to be a "civilized" state that followed the law of nations.

During the early Meiji era, Nishi helped devise nearly all of the most important army and navy regulations,[104] including the first Military Criminal Code in 1872 and the first Conscription Act in 1873.[105] He was the principal author of the 1878 Admonition to Soldiers (*Gunjin kunkai*), which enumerated the rules for proper military conduct, and the 1882 Imperial Rescript to Soldiers and Sailors (*Gunjin chokuyu*), which laid out the moral basis for military behavior.[106] Nishi also drafted the handbook, *Doppō*—"Soldiers' Rules"—carried by all soldiers serving the Imperial house.[107]

Nishi was guided throughout his work by a stark vision of world history. In the Netherlands he had studied Kant's *Perpetual Peace*, which persuaded him that the world would ultimately arrive at peace though a universal republic—but not until "10,000 years in the future at the earliest."[108] That eventual enlightenment could only be reached, he argued, through the use of power. "Both the history of Japan and the West show that there is no instance where the union of two or more countries was accomplished by negotiations, by virtue of a religion, on the basis of some theory or by legislation. No, it is through none of these; but through power alone." To remain independent, then, Japan had to arm: "If you have an independent nation you will certainly find a government, if you have a government you will surely find military strength and for military strength you must have armaments."[109]

In 1871, Nishi served as a private tutor on Western history and philosophy to the then teenaged emperor. The emperor would soon lead the country to its first wars in over two centuries. His grandson, Hirohito, would continue the tradition.[110]

THE PUPIL BECOMES THE TUTOR

The more Japan learned about the Western legal order, the more it recognized both opportunities and threats. Viewing the world through the Grotian lens, Japan's leadership came to see Korea as a danger. Its nearest neighbor was, as a German military adviser would put it, a "dagger pointed at the heart of Japan."[111]

Korea was a threat not because of its strength, but because of its weakness. As a poorly defended tributary state of China—a country that had repeatedly lost its own battles with the West—Korea was alluring prey for aggressive Western nations. As Nishi Amane would later explain, defending one's borders "is like riding in a third-class train; at first there is adequate space but as more passengers enter there is no place for them to sit. . . . The logic of necessity requires the people to plant both feet firmly and expand their elbows into any opening that may occur for, unless this is done, others will close the opening."[112] He and his fellow government officials were determined not to let the Korean opening close.

The Japanese had learned that they could not attack without a just cause. But how would they find one? Korea was almost as insular as Japan had been. It was therefore unlikely to offer a cause for war. The Korean monarchy *had* succeeded in insulting the Japanese emperor by refusing to recognize his restoration in 1868. As a tributary state of China, Korea recognized only China's emperor as the "son of heaven." But an insult was not enough. Saigō Takamori, a proponent of the restoration, offered to provoke a member of the Korean court to kill him, which would probably suffice. But others worried his plan was too risky.[113]

Japan instead followed the course charted by Commodore Perry. In 1875, it sent one of its new Dutch-built warships, the *Un'yo*, to "survey" the Korean coast. When the ship entered the waters around Ganghwa Island seeking water and firewood, it faced rifle and artillery fire. Japan took the response as legal grounds to invade the island, slaughter the Korean soldiers stationed on it, and reduce many buildings to rubble.[114]

Now that it had a just cause for war, Japan sent two warships and three troop transports carrying eight hundred men to an anchorage twenty miles from Seoul. The envoys aboard the ships demanded that Korea compensate Japan by opening trade relations. The Korean government had no choice but to concede. In 1876, Japan and Korea entered a Treaty of Amity, the Korean government's first.[115] At the elaborate signing ceremony, Japan presented Korea with a set of gifts that mirrored those presented by Perry two decades earlier. There was no white flag, but there were several items of Western technology—a cannon, six-shooter, pocket watch, barometer, and compass.[116]

The treaty, too, looked remarkably like the unequal treaties that the West had forced Japan to sign with the West a few years earlier. The Treaty of Ganghwa Island opened three Korean ports to Japanese trade, provided for the exchange of envoys and permanent diplomatic missions, promised aid to shipwrecked ships, permitted Japanese merchants to engage in unhindered trade, and guaranteed the Japanese living in Korea the right of extraterritoriality—the right to live under Japanese law. It also imposed specified tariff rates.[117] During negotiations, the Koreans expressed puzzlement over the rules of international law.[118] The Japanese diplomats explained that the treaty "relies on the precedent of customary exchange among nations and is based on the just ways of the world."[119] The pupil had become the tutor.

There was one key difference between the unequal treaties Japan accepted and the one it forced on Korea. The first provision of the treaty stated that Korea was "an independent state enjoying the same sovereign rights as does Japan."[120] This might seem a puzzling provision to place at the beginning of a treaty that was coerced. But it was there for a specific reason—the Japanese wanted to sever Korea's ties to China, which had long exercised tributary control over the peninsula.[121]

TAKING THE DAGGER

Unable to prevent the treaty—and in no position to fend off Western incursions into Korea—China responded by pitting "barbarian" against "barbarian." If it could not keep foreigners out, it would let them *all* in. In this way, every state would have a stake in keeping any other state—including Japan—from seizing control of Korea. China therefore encouraged the Korean court to enter a series of trade treaties with the Americans, British, and Germans in the early 1880s.[122] The strategy, however, backfired. To the Japanese, now conversant in Western international law and military strategy, the strategic concessions highlighted the Korean Peninsula's weakness and vulnerability.

That vulnerability would become intolerable. In 1884, tensions between China and Japan reached a new pitch when the Japanese supported a coup attempt in Korea—one that China helped put down. To avert full-out war, Japan and China concluded the 1885 Convention of Tientsin. They both agreed to withdraw forces from the Korean Peninsula and not to move troops back without giving the other advance written notice.[123] A decade later, in 1894, the Korean monarchy, threatened by a peasant revolt, requested assistance from China. China sent a force of nearly three thousand to help defeat the rebels.[124]

Alarmed by the arrival of troops, the Japanese government worried that China would use the opening to strengthen its hold on Korea once again—or, worse, that the Western powers would see an opportunity for conquest. If Korea remained "backward" and "uncivilized," it would be "inviting prey for foreign predators."[125]

Japan became determined to take the dagger into its own hands.[126] It declared that by bringing troops into Korea, China had violated its obligations under the Convention of Tientsin, a violation that gave Japan just cause for war. In 1894, Japan launched what would later become known as "the first Sino-Japanese War" to wrest control of Korea away from China. In his declaration of war, Nishi's former student, Emperor Meiji, proclaimed that the country would operate within the Western legal order: "We hereby declare war against China, and we command each and all our competent authorities . . . to carry on hostilities by sea and by land against China, with all the means at their disposal, consistently with the Law of Nations."[127]

The war was over almost as soon as it began. In a decisive victory that marked its emergence as a formidable military power, Japan took control of the peninsula, ending centuries of Chinese domination.[128] As the price of peace, Japan demanded not only all of Korea but also the Liaodong Peninsula in southeast Manchuria, then under tenuous Chinese control. "We are the conquerors and you the conquered," the Japanese representative explained to a balking Chinese delegation.[129] China had little choice but to concede to nearly all the demands and sign the 1895 Treaty of Shimonoseki.[130]

GANBARU

The European powers were not happy that Japan had proven such an astute pupil. They feared that Japan would disturb the balance of power in the Far East and interfere with the Open Door Policy, which gave them easy access to China. Still, they had few options.[131] Japan, after all, had played by the rules of the Old World Order. It had conquered Korea and won the Liaodong Peninsula. The West therefore came up with a creative Grotian alternative: Japan would forgo its territorial claims to southeast Manchuria in exchange for monetary compensation from China, which the Western powers would quietly finance.[132] In return for the financing, China would grant Russia a twenty-five-year lease in southern Manchuria along with the right to build a railway from the ports of Dairen (Dalian) and Port Arthur (Lushun)—giving Russia access to a warm-water port on the Pacific that it had long sought. The deal was confirmed in a series of agreements in 1896.[133]

Increased monetary compensation was not the only incentive the West offered Japan. The Japanese diplomats knew the three powers would intervene militarily if Japan did not agree to the deal. Though Japan had given them no just cause for war, its officials worried that one would nevertheless be "found." If that happened, all the gains Japan had made in the war would be lost, for it could never hold out against their combined might. At the moment it was poised to take its place as an equal of the Western powers, Japan relearned a basic Grotian lesson. As Foreign Minister Mutsu put it, "diplomacy shorn of military support will not succeed, however legitimate its aims might be."[134] The Japanese public's dismay over the concession soon gave way to a *ganbaru* attitude or "grim determination to do better next time."[135] Japan would have to focus on building its military strength if it was ever to be taken seriously by the Western powers.[136]

The *ganbaru* attitude would soon pay off. Japan began to regard the growing Russian presence in the region as an intolerable threat. In 1904, after failing to receive diplomatic assurances that Russia would not interfere in Korea, Japan launched an attack on Port Arthur, the termination point of the South Manchuria Railway.[137] In the final and decisive Battle of Tsushima, the Japanese destroyed two thirds of the Russian fleet and, with it, Russia's ambitions to become a leading naval power. In the peace negotiations that followed, Japan insisted on taking back much of what it had earlier given up. In the 1905 Treaty of Portsmouth, Russia agreed not to interfere with Japan's actions in Korea. Russia and Japan both agreed to evacuate southern Manchuria, which was restored to China with several important exceptions: Japan retained control over the Liaodong Peninsula and its strategic ports of Port Arthur and Dalian, as well as the newly built rail system leading through Manchuria.[138]

Three years later, Takahashi Sakuyé stood before an audience in the Hall of the Long Island Historical Society in Brooklyn at a celebration of the 325th anniversary of the birth of Hugo Grotius. A professor of international law, Takahashi had served as a legal adviser for the Japanese Ministry of Foreign Affairs during both the Russo-Japanese War and Sino-Japanese Wars.[139] The title of his talk was "Influence of Hugo Grotius in the East." "About forty years ago not even a single Japanese subject perhaps had any knowledge of the modern International Law," he explained.[140] Since that time, "Japan has had many hard experiences in international affairs, and for that hardship, I dare say, Japan ought to be very grateful, as that hardship pushed her to study International Law and to become a good pupil to Grotius."[141]

THE PACT'S FIRST TEST

As the 1930s began, having won two wars in succession, Japan was now in the strange but lucrative position of controlling a Russian-built railway running through Chinese Manchuria. Over the course of the two and a half decades that followed Japan's victory over Russia, the newly dubbed Japanese South Manchuria Railway became an enormous corporate conglomerate. The company not only ran an extensive railway system in Manchuria, but it also owned coal mines, electric power plants, and steel mills. Much like the Dutch East India Company, the railway came to function almost as a sovereign state—with schools, libraries, hospitals, utilities, farming, and industrial production.[142]

The success and expansion of the railway fed growing tensions between Japan and China. The Japanese had tallied hundreds of provocative incidents in Manchuria in which the Chinese had attacked or harassed Japanese subjects living in the region. One event began after Korean immigrants cut an irrigation ditch across the lands of Chinese farmers outside the small Manchurian village of Wanpaoshan. The Chinese farmers retaliated by driving the Koreans away and filling in most of the ditch.

Japanese consular police based in nearby Changchun—the first station of the South Manchuria Railway—intervened on behalf of the Koreans (who were, after all, now subjects of Japan), and the Chinese farmers backed down. Sensationalized and often inaccurate accounts of the incident published in Japanese and Korean newspapers sparked anti-Chinese riots throughout Korea, leading to the death of over one hundred Chinese immigrants.[143] In response, anti-Japanese incidents broke out across China, further inflaming anger and resentment against China in Japan. Both sides were on edge. Like much of the world, China and Japan were facing hard economic times—in Japan, conditions among the peasantry were becoming desperate.[144]

Tensions worsened after what Japanese newspapers called the "Nakamura butchery case."[145] Early in June 1931, a Japanese army officer named Nakamura Shintarō and a small group of companions, dressed as civilians and carrying new passports to conceal their identities, were traveling in a militarily sensitive region of Manchuria. They made several stops along the Chinese Eastern Railway, taking extensive notes. Their activities attracted the attention of a local warlord, who had the group arrested. Nakamura claimed to be an agricultural expert, but he was found carrying a military map, narcotics, weapons, and surveying instruments. Suspecting Nakamura of engaging in espionage, the Chinese executed him. They cremated the body, in an attempt to cover up the deed.[146]

When news of Nakamura's death emerged, the Japanese public and army were furious. It mattered little to them that Nakamura was almost certainly a spy, gathering information Japan would need to invade northwest Manchuria. Some of Nakamura's fellow officers demanded retribution for the killing of their colleague. It was time, they argued, to take back the rest of Manchuria.[147]

Tokyo would not sanction the bold action—perhaps recognizing the tenuous legal position of one state having been caught sending a spy into militarily sensitive regions of another sovereign state. It instead allowed popular anger against the Chinese to build. When news arrived of Chinese plans to begin construction of a rival railway through Manchuria—a railway that when completed might threaten Japanese dominance in the region—the Japanese population and army were thirsting for vengeance.[148]

The young Japanese military officers assigned to guard the South Manchuria Railway in early fall 1931 knew that their government did not sanction a takeover of Manchuria. They were assigned to patrol the sixty-two-meter-wide strips of land on either side of the railway tracks while China built a competing railway that would make their work largely irrelevant. But the government in Tokyo could not expect them to ignore a direct attack. The young officers devised a plan: On the night of September 18, they set a charge along the railway they had been assigned to protect. They probably acted with the tacit blessing of several of their superiors, including the commander-in-chief of the Kwantung Army in Manchuria, General Honjō Shigeru, who would later commit seppuku (ritual suicide) rather than testify about these and other events before the postwar Tokyo war crimes tribunal at which he had been indicted.[149]

The government in Tokyo had dispatched an officer, Tatekawa, to keep the troops in line. The evening Tatekawa arrived, the young officers blew up a thirty-one-inch section of the railway. Even as news arrived in Geneva and the world's representatives began to react, a cascade of events had begun that would quickly lead to the entire occupation of Manchuria.[150] Although the government in Tokyo had not planned the attack, it allowed its military to extend control from the south to the north, eventually forming an "independent state"—a Japanese puppet government—called "Manchukuo."[151]

"JAPAN STANDS READY TO BE CRUCIFIED!"

As events unfolded, the League of Nations received conflicting accounts. The Japanese representative, Yoshizawa Kenkichi, claimed that Japan's railway had been unlawfully attacked by Chinese brigands and its troops were merely taking "measures of legitimate defense."[152] The Chinese representative, Dr. Sao-Ke Alfred Sze, responded that Japan had engaged in a blatant violation of the Pact and the Covenant.[153]

Unable to determine the truth, the League decided to send a commission to investigate, led by Victor Alexander George Robert Bulwer-Lytton, second earl of Lytton. The commission spent six weeks in Manchuria in the spring of 1932 piecing together what had transpired. Members of the commission interviewed participants on both sides of the conflict and traced the course of military operations. Their investigation revealed that Japan had been the aggressor.[154]

The Lytton Commission report, filed in October 1932, concluded that the military operations of the Japanese troops on the night of September 18, 1931, "cannot be regarded as measures of legitimate self-defense," but in an effort to soften the blow, it did not exclude the possibility that "the officers on the spot may have thought they were acting in self-defence." It also concluded that the "state" of Manchukuo "cannot be considered to have been called into existence by a genuine and spontaneous independence movement."

The Commission recognized that its findings would be explosive and that Japan would not receive them well. The new head of the Japanese delegation, Matsuoka Shuzo, was a hardliner on Manchuria who had spent much of the previous decade working for the South Manchuria Railway, first as a director, then as vice president.[155] Matsuoka had dedicated his energies to increasing the area controlled by the railway by forging alliances with various Chinese warlords. Now that such valuable territory had been won, he was not about to return it to China.

Matsuoka was not provincial. Born in Japan but raised in Portland, Oregon, where he graduated from the University of Oregon Law School and converted to Christianity, Matsuoka spoke English fluently and understood Western culture.[156] Yet he had a brusque manner and was prone to using inflammatory, even offensive, rhetoric. On December 8, 1932, in response to the Lytton Report, he compared the attack on Japan to the Passion of Christ. "We Japanese feel that we are now put on trial. Some of the people in Europe and America may wish even to crucify Japan in the Twentieth Century. Gentlemen, Japan stands ready to be crucified!" Through the shrill shouting of "We are right! We are right!" Matsuoka threatened to withdraw from the League.

The Great Powers were willing to make a deal with Matsuoka, but the Small Powers balked.[157] In December 1932, the Irish Free State, Czechoslovakia, Spain, and Sweden introduced a condemnation of Japan.[158] Like China, they were tethering their futures to the "sheet-anchors" of the Pact and the League. Accepting Japan's actions would leave them as defenseless as China. This could prove the undoing of the tenuous postwar peace.

The final report on the situation in Manchuria by the League's Lytton Commission tried to walk a fine line, giving a full account of the facts, but stopping short of branding Japan the aggressor. When the report of the commission was put up for a vote on February 23, 1933, the resulting roll call was forty-two in favor, one opposed.[159] The dissenting vote was of course Japan's, which was not counted in the official tally.[160] The League of Nations had unanimously sided with China.

After the vote concluded, Matsuoka approached the rostrum and announced that his country would no longer continue cooperating with the League over Manchuria. After professing his country's sincere desire for securing peace in the Far East, he declared: "Japan, however, finds it impossible to accept the report adopted by the Assembly."[161] He left the dais. As he walked down the aisle, he removed his glasses and used them to beckon his associates to leave as well. The Japanese delegation followed Matsuoka out the door.

In the cloakroom, Matsuoka nervously took out a cigar, clipped the end, struck a match and put it to the tip. Given the drama of his exit and the whirring of movie cameras catching the events on film, he failed to notice that the cigar did not light. He puffed hard as he emerged from the building and entered a bright limousine with a flag of the Rising Sun on its radiator cap.[162] Japan left the League of Nations, never to return. Those who remained were left to wonder if the Pact would survive the great tests to come.

SEVEN

THE SANCTIONS OF PEACE

Psychologists call the tendency of witnesses to describe reality in multiple, often contradictory, ways the "Rashomon Effect." The phenomenon takes its name from Akira Kurosawa's classic film *Rashomon*, which relates four different versions of two events: a sexual encounter that may have been rape and a samurai's death that may have been murder. Viewers never learn which version is correct.

States also experience the Rashomon Effect. Japan, for example, did not think that it had renounced the rules of the Old World Order on August 27, 1928. Its signing of the "No-War Pact," as the Paris Peace Pact was known in Japan, was regarded as a diplomatic gesture, a noble proclamation affirming the aspiration of all civilized nations to seek peace. Indeed, Japanese officials considered it a sign of how far their nation had come that it was included among the fifteen countries at the grand ceremony in Paris.

Japan was wrong in believing that "No War" did not mean "No War." And it was wrong in a way that obviously served its own interests. Japan had finally emerged as a military power, and it was poised to become a dominant, if not *the* dominant, regional power in Asia.

But as in *Rashomon*, maybe Japan's view wasn't so unreasonable. After all, Japan was still new to the Old World Order. It had only been sixty years since Nishi Amane returned from Grotius's birthplace to write the first textbook on international law. Now that Japan had dutifully learned "What kind of thing is the law of nations?" it would have been hard to imagine that the system was open to debate, much less radical change.

A few cautious officials had argued against signing. But Hirohito's teacher of diplomacy and international law, Tachi Sakutarō, downplayed the Pact's intent and significance. He advised the emperor that the treaty permitted self-defense and thus would not prevent Japan from protecting its interests in the region.[1]

Tachi pointed to statements by Western nations to support his interpretation. In correspondence with the United States, Great Britain stated that it would join the new Pact only on the "understanding" that it would not limit Britain's "freedom of action" relating to "certain regions of which the welfare and integrity constitute a special and vital interest for our peace and safety"—namely, the vast territory that constituted the British Empire.[2] France also required public assurances that it could defend territory within its own imperial orbit.[3]

In testimony before the U.S. Senate, Kellogg explained that the treaty would not interfere with the right of self-defense. He even said it would not disturb the Monroe Doctrine—which prohibited European intervention in the Western Hemisphere.[4] These assurances persuaded the Japanese Foreign Ministry that the concept of self-defense in the Pact was, as an internal memo put it, "elastic enough to rationalize future Japanese actions in China."[5]

That, it would turn out, was a terrible miscalculation—one that Japan would realize too late. Japan had failed to appreciate the critical difference between the past and the future. *Past* conquests would be protected, but *future* conquests would not.

Indeed, the Pact appealed to the West because it promised to secure and protect previous conquests, thus securing Western nations' place at the head of the international legal order indefinitely. The British Empire of 1928 encircled the globe, covering nearly 31 million square kilometers. The French Empire was smaller but still immense, stretching over

12.5 million square kilometers.[6] Together, the United Kingdom and the United States controlled three quarters of all the mineral resources in the world.[7] The Peace Pact would protect this territory from reconquest, securing the vast empires at the moment they had begun to weaken—and competitors had begun to emerge.

The British were brazenly candid about their intentions during the negotiation of the treaty. Yes, Britain reserved the right to freedom of action where it had a "special and vital interest"—but these were interests in *existing* colonies, not future ones. Indeed, the British revised the preamble to include among the initial signatories "all parts of the British Empire which are not separate members of the League of Nations"—to make explicit that they, too, would gain the protection of the Pact.[8]

When the League unanimously approved the Lytton Commission report that condemned Japan's aggression in Manchuria, Japan was thunderstruck. The Japanese Foreign Office issued a statement accusing the Assembly of "[p]rejudiced thoughts."[9] The commander-in-chief of the Kwantung Army declared, "We remain convinced that our actions were unquestionably in conformity with what has always been approved by International Law and by the accepted usages of nations."[10] Those across Japanese elite society—leaders of opposing political parties, the House of Peers, the Privy Council, and nearly every newspaper—decried the report and the conclusions it reached.[11] The reactions shared a common sense of outrage and frustration—frustration that the commission did not credit Japanese claims to be acting in self-defense, frustration that it had almost laughed off Japanese claims of the "independence" of Manchukuo, and, unspoken but perhaps worst of all, frustration that just as Japan had learned to use the rules of the Old World Order to its advantage, those rules had changed.[12]

PARALYSIS

Japan's intransigence, meanwhile, incapacitated the League. Decisive action was needed to restore the status quo, but it was not forthcoming. This paralysis might seem puzzling since it was precisely the requirement of mandatory military enforcement that had kept the United States from joining the League in the first place. Salmon Levinson and his allies had opposed U.S. ratification of the League Covenant because it not merely allowed member states to go to war to enforce the Covenant but could have even *compelled* them to do so. Had Levinson been wrong?

No, for Levinson's opposition to the League came before the Pact existed. By the time of the Manchurian invasion, however, the majority of League members had joined the Pact and thus renounced war as an instrument of national policy.[13] The widespread adoption of the Pact had created a real problem for the organization. Levinson and his allies were not the only ones to notice that the League and the outlawry of war imposed conflicting legal obligations. As the committee appointed by the League Council to examine the matter put it, "The League Covenant, under some of its articles, reserves the right to go to war."[14] But the Pact prohibited the resort to war—perhaps even wars that would be approved by the Covenant.[15] Belgium reflected the consensus view when it stated that revising the Covenant was necessary "both from a moral and from a juridical standpoint."[16] Even before Japan's invasion, it was clear that something would have to change.

But what? Simply tacking the Pact to the League Covenant would not be enough, League members agreed, for that would leave "undesirable contradictions."[17] The Covenant stipulated that states could not go to war for a period of three months after the resolution of a dispute, but there was no limit on the right to go to war afterward. The Pact, by contrast, prohibited wars unless in self-defense. Incorporating the Pact into the Covenant would mean that League member states would be permitted and forbidden to go to war—by the same document.

The German representative suggested that "all the provisions of the Covenant relating to the prohibition of resort to war . . . would have to be re-examined."[18] Many joined Germany in endorsing this approach, and a committee was appointed to recommend appropriate revisions.

The committee first proposed to eliminate the right to wage war after the three-month cooling-off period. Under no circumstances would members be able to "resort to war for the solution of their dispute."[19] The committee's next suggestion was to revoke the right of member states to wage war if the League Council's report did not have unanimous support.

Instead, the League Council should "examine the procedure best suited to meet the case and recommend it to the parties."[20] The commitments to wage war to enforce the League's pronouncements that had so worried Levinson and Borah would be stripped from the Covenant to bring it into harmony with the Pact.

Yet many on the committee recognized that stripping the offending provisions would not be enough. Simply deleting sections of the Covenant would mangle it. The committee explained that the Covenant had an "organic character" that had to be maintained.[21] The League of Nations was devised as a complete system. If one part—the resort to war—was removed, the committee concluded, some other way to resolve disputes would need to take its place.

The chief candidate for the replacement was a requirement that states submit to pacific settlement of disputes. But many states worried that simply requiring pacific settlement—without more—would fail. The Austrian delegate pointed out, as Borah had pressed Levinson several years earlier, that without recourse to war there would be no way to enforce a judgment in a dispute against a recalcitrant state.[22] The French delegate raised a similar concern: "The Pact of Paris having suppressed the threat of war, there must be substituted measures of collective action" to enforce Council decisions and arbitral awards.[23] Yet the delegate stopped short of describing what those measures of collective action might be.[24]

For a time, it seemed that disarmament of major military powers would be the solution. Deprived of arms, a state would be less likely to flout the Pact's prohibition on resort to war. This approach appealed to the majority of League members, most of whom declared their support for the proposed amendments to the Covenant on the condition that a separate Convention for the Reduction of Armaments be adopted.

Yet hopes for a comprehensive agreement on disarmament would evaporate when the Nazis seized power in Germany. In January 1933, Adolf Hitler became chancellor. He withdrew Germany from the amendment negotiations and in October withdrew it from the League itself.[25] After years of debates, the proposed amendments to the Covenant were referred to a special committee—then, as now, a euphemism for the circular file.

THE "SANCTIONS OF PEACE"

With the League paralyzed, American leaders debated how to respond to Japan's flagrant violation of a treaty that bore an American statesman's name.[26] The question fell to a man who epitomized the East Coast establishment that had long benefited from and supported the rules of the Old World Order, Henry Stimson. Born to a wealthy New York family in 1867, Stimson attended Phillips Academy Andover, received his bachelor's degree from Yale, where he joined the elite secret society Skull and Bones, and was awarded a law degree from Harvard. He was an avid outdoorsman, went foxhunting nearly every Saturday from September to March, and patronized private clubs, frequenting the exclusive Century Association when in Manhattan and the Metropolitan Club when in Washington.[27]

Stimson began his career by working in a law firm run by Elihu Root, who served as secretary of state and secretary of war under Theodore Roosevelt. Under Root's influence, Stimson became a strong advocate of American expansion. He cheered the United States' temporary occupation of Cuba and permanent seizure of Puerto Rico, Guam, and the Philippine Islands in the 1898 Spanish-American War, though he rejected incorporating them as states because of their "inferior" populations. And he supported the 1904 Roosevelt Corollary to the Monroe Doctrine, under which the U.S. would intervene to ensure that other nations in the Western Hemisphere fulfilled their obligations to international creditors so that European powers would have no cause for waging wars of conquest in the region.[28]

From 1911 to 1913, Stimson served as secretary of war, during which time he carried out plans to modernize the military first outlined by Root. When the U.S. entered the First World War, he joined the men he once led, volunteering for the army and serving as an artillery officer in France, reaching the rank of colonel. He looked the part. Trim and fit, he had a "military bearing and a horseman's posture," always wore a nicely tailored suit and tie in public, and sported a tidy mustache.[29] "He was a man of such total uprightness," his law partner remarked, "that everyone with whom he worked had nothing but confidence in him."[30] Stimson was also famously censorious. He and his wife did not entertain divorced people.[31]

In 1929, Stimson accepted an appointment from President Herbert

Hoover to become secretary of state. Within a few short months of taking office, he prepared to preside at the Washington ceremonies proclaiming the entry into force of the Paris Peace Pact scheduled for July 24, 1929.[32] As the date approached, it seemed fighting was about to erupt between Russia and China in Manchuria. Stimson appealed to the countries to refrain from violence, reminding them of their new treaty obligations under the Pact.[33] The Russian commissar's reply relieved Stimson: "Our signature of the Kellogg Pact was not just a diplomatic gesture. . . . [W]e shall not fight unless our country is invaded."[34] At the ceremony, President Hoover was able to congratulate "the entire world" on the coming into force of the treaty pledging "to obtain by pacific means alone the settlement of international disputes."[35]

While Stimson staved off hostilities on the eve of the ceremony, he could not stop them. After Japan's invasion of Manchuria, Stimson hoped the situation would resolve itself. He informed the U.S. ambassador to Japan that he was "making every effort to save Japan's face and to give them time to settle this by themselves with China," though cautioned that "they must settle it mighty quick."[36] The watchful waiting came to a sudden end, however, when in October 1931 Japanese planes dropped some eighty bombs on the city of Chinchow in southern Manchuria. The town was a significant distance from the railroad zone. The likely target was the Chinese Provincial Government, which had relocated from Mukden to Chinchow.[37] Stimson discovered that his policy of "playing no favorites" was playing out badly.[38]

It was difficult to get President Hoover to pay attention to the crisis in Manchuria, saddled as he was with the arduous task of leading the country through the depths of the Great Depression.[39] But the president was clear about one matter: He did not want to be drawn into aggressive action in the Far East.[40] Besides his fear of foreign entanglement, Hoover remained concerned that any action would provoke the isolationists and the Hearst newspapers that supported them. Hoover would agree only to "moral pressures"—diplomatic exhortations—repeatedly ruling out both economic and military sanctions as "roads to war."[41]

As the war dragged on and Japan continued to expand its reach into northern Manchuria, it became clear that moral sanctions had no effect.

The League began to discuss the possibility of economic sanctions. In a show of support for this course, Stimson persuaded Hoover to send a U.S. delegate to a joint session with the League "centered on the subject of the Kellogg-Briand Pact."[42] But when the British foreign secretary inquired whether the United States would join an embargo, Stimson answered that the United States would not. In a carefully calculated show of support, however, Hoover authorized Stimson to make clear that the American fleet would do nothing to interfere with an embargo by the League. In addition, he permitted Stimson to share that, given the sympathies of the American public, "there might be a private embargo put on here by voluntary action in refusing to trade with Japan."[43]

Hoover's caution was understandable, and not only for political reasons. Under the Old World Order, putting in place the kind of economic sanctions Britain was suggesting would violate a neutral state's legal duty of impartiality. Indeed, it would be an act of war. For the U.S., which had an unemployment rate of 25 percent and a generally isolationist electorate, such action was unthinkable.

But Stimson was beginning to regard sanctions not as a road to war, but as a road to peace.[44] He had not come to the idea on his own. Two years earlier, he had read an article by Levinson, who had been one of his classmates at Yale. They had fallen out of touch but had come back into contact in April 1929, soon after Stimson became secretary of state.[45] Stimson sent a personal telegram inviting Levinson to the White House ceremony to celebrate the entry into force of the Pact.[46] Their early correspondence focused on the proposal for the United States to join the Permanent Court of International Justice. Stimson hoped that Levinson might help persuade Senator Borah, whom he feared would lead the opposition to the court as he had to the League a decade earlier.[47]

In January 1930, however, Stimson wrote on another matter: "The Editor of the Christain [sic] Century has sent me your article on 'Sanctions of Peace' and I have read it with very great interest. It is a thoughtful and stimulating article. As you know, I have already been thinking of some of the points you suggest, and the authorities you cite are most interesting."[48]

In the article that Stimson mentioned, Levinson addressed the vexing question he had long resisted: How could a Peace Pact be enforced? [49] For the first time, Levinson openly acknowledged that eliminating war was not enough. Something would need to take its place. The solution he now proposed was to replace the "sanctions of force" with the "sanctions of peace."

What were these "sanctions of peace"? The key, according to Levinson, was to deny an illegal conquest any legal effect: "If it is unlawful to wage war, conquests by war should furnish no legal title." That refusal to give war legal effect, he argued, would serve as a real sanction, for it would mean that "[n]ever again can a nation bent upon conquest acquire indefeasible title to anything."[50] As he put it in a letter to a friend when he was working out the idea, a nation could no longer "establish right, justice or title by brute strength."[51] Yes, the aggressor could still take a city by force, "but it would not, as a matter of law, be *his* city."[52]

THE STIMSON DOCTRINE

Now, nearly two years after reading his classmate's article, Stimson faced the dilemma of how to respond to Japan's invasion of Manchuria. By December 1931, it was clear that the League was no longer considering military or economic sanctions but was instead moving toward establishing an independent commission—what would become the Lytton Commission. Yet Stimson was still thinking about Levinson's proposal. A boycott would probably require military might to enforce. "Sanctions of peace," however, would require no military action. The United States would just refuse to recognize the conquest.

Knowing that what he contemplated was unprecedented and might be met with skepticism in the White House, Stimson drafted two different sets of notes to be sent to China and Japan. The first stated that the United States would not recognize any new agreements that interfered with its commercial rights under the Open Door Policy in China. The second was a broader declaration of intent not to recognize *any* change in legal rights, citing Japan's violations of the Pact. Hoover agreed with Stimson's recommendation to take the second approach.[53]

On January 8, 1932, the United States delivered simultaneous diplomatic notes to the governments of China and Japan.[54] The notes proclaimed a policy of nonrecognition—what would later come to be called the Stimson Doctrine. Stimson wrote, "[T]he American Government . . . does not intend to recognize any situation, treaty or agreement which may be brought about by means contrary to the covenants and obligations of the Pact of Paris of August 27, 1928."[55]

On August 8, 1932, Stimson gave a speech for the Council on Foreign Relations entitled: "The Pact of Paris: Three Years of Development." Stimson stood before an audience at the opulent Ritz-Carlton Hotel in New York City with a microphone nearby, transmitting his words via the National Broadcasting Company to the entire nation.

"Four years ago," he began, "the United States joined with France in the initiation of the . . . so-called Briand-Kellogg Pact for the Renunciation of War. . . . Scarcely had its ratification been announced on July 24, 1929, when it became subjected to the first of a series of difficult challenges which are still going on." In light of these challenges, he proposed to take stock of where the Pact then stood "and the part which we may hope that it eventually will play in the affairs of the world."

Sounding like his old classmate Levinson, he continued: "During the centuries which had elapsed since the beginnings of international law, a large part of that law had been a development of principles based upon the existence of war." In such a world, states were required to remain neutral— "to maintain impartiality between two belligerents." War was, after all, "a legal situation out of which these rights and obligations grow." International law thus forbade neutral states from taking sides.

Yet, Stimson continued, the world had outlawed war in 1929. Now those who made war were "lawbreakers," and war was no longer only of legal concern to those directly involved. It was now of legal concern to all states connected with the treaty. These nations, "bound together by a new viewpoint towards war," were obliged to act, Stimson declared, even when a conflict occurs in "far-off Manchuria."

Stimson acknowledged that in this new world, the action of a single state alone—even one as powerful as the United States—would have little effect. But he maintained that the sanctions of peace had great collective weight: "Moral disapproval, when it becomes the disapproval of the whole world, takes on a significance hitherto unknown in international law."[56]

Stimson's speech was well received. A letter from future Supreme

Court justice Felix Frankfurter praised its articulation of a new approach to enforcing international law: "The Kellogg-Briand Treaty was the child of a new world, and . . . has been growing up and through steady evolution is attaining its own maturity."[57]

Before Stimson's "child" could reach maturity, however, President Hoover was defeated by Franklin Roosevelt and Stimson was forced to leave office. Stimson's successor at the State Department, Cordell Hull, was cooler to the Stimson Doctrine. He worried that it would drag the United States into war when the country could least afford it.

Yet, even as the United States retreated from the doctrine, the League embraced it.[58] The members of the League had spent the last few years debating how to reconcile the Covenant with the Pact's prohibition on the sanctions of war. Through Levinson's sanctions of peace, Stimson offered them a way out of the impasse.

THE CHANGING LAW OF NEUTRALITY

In February 1933, with the Stimson Doctrine in mind, the League cautioned that it was "incumbent upon the Members of the League not to recognise any situation, treaty or agreement which might be brought about by means contrary to the Covenant of the League of Nations or to the Pact of Paris."[59] Member states would be forbidden from recognizing the existence of territorial conquests. From the perspective of the League of Nations, "Manchukuo" did not exist.

The secretary general of the League sent a letter to all member states laying out the broad and draconian recommendations of the committee that had considered the matter. The committee encouraged members not to recognize the regime "either *de jure* or *de facto*"—in law or in fact. Manchukuo was therefore not to be permitted to accede to international conventions or to participate in international commissions and associations. Member states were discouraged from recognizing Manchukuo currency or passports. The letter reminded member states that Manchukuo was not a member of the Universal Postal Union and therefore postal service to and from Manchuria had been suspended. It finally suggested that members notify their citizens of "the special risks attendant upon the acceptance of concessions or appointments in Manchuria," though these were not forbidden.[60]

It would be hard to overemphasize the importance of the League's acceptance of the Stimson Doctrine.[61] By February 1933, the vast majority of states had joined the League—including the defeated Central Powers of Austria, Germany, Turkey, and Bulgaria.* By accepting the Stimson Doctrine, a policy proposed by the nonmember United States, the members of the League had renounced the most ancient right of sovereignty: the right of conquest. For the first time in international relations, Might would no longer make Right.

Japan was the outlier. On the verge of leaving the League, it abstained during the vote. This dissent reflected Japan's *Rashomon* view of the Pact. In accepting the Stimson Doctrine, the League affirmed the Pact's revolutionary rejection of the fundamental legal principle of the Old World Order. A system once based on the legality of war as a remedial tool would have to be reorganized around the outlawry of war. Since war was now illegal, the fruits of war could not be recognized. Japan, which saw the Pact as protecting the basic logic of the Old World Order that it had so painfully learned and from which it now hoped to profit, could not accept a doctrine premised on its destruction.

The Stimson Doctrine was the first step in dismantling the Old World Order and constructing a new system of law. Like a thread that hangs from a sweater, the League tugged on the strand until the fabric began to unravel. And though the unraveling would not happen all at once, there would be no way to stop it once it began.

The thread led first to conquest, then to the law of neutrality. Recall that neutral states were under a strict duty of impartiality—no outsider to the conflict could treat insiders differently from one another. Strict impartiality was the only option in a world in which war was legal and no party could definitively judge who was right. For if everyone were permitted to choose sides based on their own particular interpretation, chaos would

---

*Argentina would rejoin the League in late 1933 after a twelve-year hiatus. The USSR, Afghanistan, and Ecuador would join in 1934 and Mexico in 1937. When they joined, they were bound by the rules of the League.

ensue. As Stimson noted in his speech, the law of neutrality attempted to "narrow and confine" the destructive effects of war—creating "oases of safety for life and property in a world which still recognized and legalized the destruction of human life and property."

If the law of neutrality depended on the legality of war, however, it could not continue unchanged with the outlawry of war. Stimson suggested as much in his 1932 speech, though he never said it outright. In imposing economic sanctions on Japan—a course precluded in the Old World Order—the United States had charted a course away from prior understandings of what neutrality legally required.

Others, however, were more explicit. A number of scholars began to note that the law of neutrality had shifted. A lengthy book by a scholar of international law on war and neutrality published in 1937 began with the text of the Pact, explaining that "this Treaty . . . substantially abolished the law of neutrality."[62]

Not everyone was willing to embrace the revolution. Stimson's doctrine not only threatened to discard centuries of established law. It also threatened to upend most of the existing scholarship about that law— and plenty of legal academics were willing to challenge *that*. John Bassett Moore, a scholar who had penned an exhaustive eight-volume codification of international law known as *Moore's Digest*, was a vocal critic.[63] Throughout the 1930s, he and his protégé, Yale Law School professor Edwin Borchard, opposed efforts to revise U.S. neutrality legislation to accord with Stimson's vision.[64] They complained that Stimson had based his radical interpretation on two small articles in the Pact that said nothing at all about neutrality or sanctions or any of the other subsidiary rules of international law that the doctrine's advocates suggested had been undone. That was not how international law worked, they charged; there needed to be debates, conferences, detailed commentaries. You couldn't just yank a thread from a delicate fabric.[65]

Despite this resistance, Stimson's view continued to gain adherents, especially outside the United States. In 1934, an international assemblage of scholars in Budapest concluded a report on the "Effect of the Briand-Kellogg Pact of Paris in International Law."[66] In addition to accepting the Stimson Doctrine, it concluded that the law of neutrality ceased to protect

After Vasco da Gama reached India in 1498, Portugal dominated the Asian spice trade. A century later, Dutch merchants (shown here returning from the East Indies in 1599) began to challenge the lucrative monopoly. The Portuguese retaliated by harassing natives who did business with the Dutch and by killing and torturing Dutch traders.

In 1601, Jacob van Heemskerck led a fleet of ships to the East Indies on a trading expedition. When he arrived, he learned about the Portuguese terror campaign and decided to respond.

Van Heemskerck attacked the Portuguese carrack *Santa Catarina* (shown here at center in the only known contemporary depiction) on February 25, 1603, off the coast of Singapore. He seized the ship and hauled it to Amsterdam. To defend the valuable seizure, the Dutch East India Company hired a young lawyer named Hugo Grotius.

Left: Grotius, shown here at sixteen, worked as a lawyer but hated the job. Nevertheless the challenge of defending Van Heemskerck's seizure fascinated him, and he spent more than two years writing a five-hundred-page treatise. *Right:* Though Grotius, portrayed here at age forty-eight, never published his defense of Van Heemskerck, it became the starting point for his greatest work, *The Law of War and Peace*, in which he argued that war is a legitimate tool for enforcing legal rights.

Grotius's power in Dutch politics grew until he was convicted of heresy and sentenced to life imprisonment in 1618. He was held in Loevenstein castle, accompanied by his wife and children. He escaped after three years by hiding in a chest carried out of his cell by unsuspecting guards.

From at least the fifteenth century, sovereigns who went to war published "manifestos" setting out their "just causes." The first known war manifesto was written for Maximilian I, soon to be the Holy Roman Emperor, to defend his resort to arms against Charles VIII on the grounds that the French king stole his wife, Anne of Brittany. The first line declares "there is no one who would not know that the French are roosters."

According to Grotius's theory of "just war," conquest and booty-taking were both perfectly legal as long as the war was fought for a "just cause." In a series of drawings entitled *Miseries and Misfortunes of War*, Jacques Callot conveyed the horrors of booty-taking.

In 1631, the Catholic forces of the Holy Roman Emperor sacked the Protestant city of Magdeburg after it refused to surrender to a siege. In his message to the emperor, Count Pappenheim celebrated the victory: "I believe that over twenty thousand souls were lost . . . All of our soldiers became rich. God with us."

Left: In 1793, the French revolutionary government sent Edmond-Charles Genêt to convince the United States to support France in its war with Great Britain. A dashing man with polished manners and sparkling wit, he was also brash and outspoken. Even Thomas Jefferson, who was sympathetic to the French cause, became impatient with his efforts to draw the United States into war. *Right:* To many, Napoleon's military prowess was unnatural. An etching from 1814 shows Napoleon swaddled and cradled in the loving arms of his father, Beelzebub. Nevertheless, even after his defeat at Leipzig and ouster from the throne, the Allies did not prosecute Napoleon for waging war because waging war was not illegal. Instead, they sought to rid themselves of "the Devil's Darling" by giving him the Island of Elba to rule as sovereign.

After his escape from Elba and subsequent defeat at the Battle of Waterloo, Napoleon surrendered on July 14, 1815. He was exiled yet again, this time to the remote South Atlantic island of Saint Helena, where he died in 1821.

The United States went to war against Mexico in 1846 with a "just cause": Mexico had failed to pay its debts to the United States. At the close of the war, the United States seized much of what is now the American Southwest to settle the books.

Tasunka Ota (known as Plenty Horses) was put on trial in 1891 for killing Lieutenant Edward Casey in cold blood. He was acquitted when the judges determined that war existed between the United States and the Indian tribes, and he was therefore licensed to kill.

In 1853, Commodore Matthew Calbraith Perry led a U.S. expedition to Japan, which had been largely closed to trade with the West since the 1600s. Perry told Japanese officials that if they did not deliver a letter to the emperor offering a treaty of friendship, he and his men would deliver it "whatever the consequences may be."

This Japanese woodblock print depicts the American steamship commanded by Perry. Most Japanese had never before seen a ship that belched smoke and moved against the wind. The terrifying sight sent "mothers flying with children in their arms and men with mothers on their backs."

After the opening of Japan by the United States, the Japanese government sent a delegation of students to Holland to learn Western ideas. Nishi Amane, sitting at far right, and Tsuda Mamichi, behind him, were studying international law with Dutch scholar Simon Vissering when Vissering discovered Grotius's long-forgotten defense of Van Heemskerck.

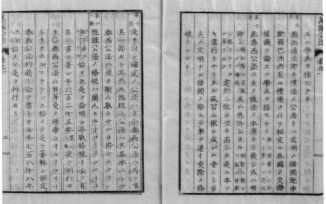

18

After he returned from the Netherlands, Nishi wrote *Fïsuserinku-shi Bankoku kōhō* to introduce Western international law to a Japanese audience. He modeled his text on Hugo Grotius's masterwork, *The Law of War and Peace*.

19

Nishi became a leading scholar at the "Institute for the Investigation of Barbarian Books," before joining the Meiji government. He devised nearly all of the most important Japanese military regulations, wrote the rules of warfare carried by all Japanese soldiers, and served as private tutor to the then teenaged emperor, who would lead his country to its first wars in over two centuries.

20

In 1875, Japan sent one of its new Dutch-built warships, the *Un'yo* (depicted in this wood-block print) to "survey" the Korean coast. When Korean soldiers opened fire, Japan took the response as a "just cause" for war. It then forced Korea to accept a "treaty of friendship" much like the one it had signed with the United States two decades earlier.

21

In 1917, Salmon Levinson, a corporate lawyer in Chicago, began to develop a simple but profound idea: "We should have, not as now, laws of war, but laws against war; just as there are no laws of murder or of poisoning, but laws against them."

When he began to develop his idea of outlawing war, Levinson wrote to his friend John Dewey, by many accounts the greatest American philosopher of his generation. Dewey encouraged and assisted Levinson as he refined his proposals.

The Women's International League for Peace and Freedom, led by Jane Addams, held large public rallies against war throughout the 1920s, many of them coordinated with Levinson's American Committee for the Outlawry of War.

24

25

Top: James T. Shotwell (standing second from right), here with a group of experts who accompanied President Woodrow Wilson at the Paris Peace Conference after the First World War, shared Levinson's outlawry dream. But Shotwell argued that it would not work without enforcement. *Bottom:* Shotwell gave a lecture in Berlin on the outlawry of war on March 1, 1927. The lecture unnerved the German law professor Carl Schmitt (not shown). He worried that the ideas would lead to disaster for Germany. Shortly after the lecture, Shotwell traveled to France and met with Foreign Minister Aristide Briand to set in motion the very process Schmitt feared.

26

In 1927, Briand (left) became the first foreign leader to propose a treaty to outlaw war—though his initial proposal was made only to the United States. When the treaty was circulated to all countries, German Foreign Minister Gustav Stresemann (right) convinced the German cabinet to sign on. Though no pacifist, he was certain that trade, not war, was the way to restore Germany's rightful place in the world.

27 Briand spoke before the signing of the Peace Pact on August 27, 1928, in the Salle de l'Horloge, the "Clock Room," inside the French Foreign Ministry. Blazing klieg-lights set up to film the ceremony turned the room into an oven. Dignitaries spent the hour mopping their faces with handkerchiefs.

28

Briand, U.S. ambassador to France Myron T. Herrick, and U.S. Secretary of State Frank B. Kellogg met in the French Foreign Office before the signing ceremony.

29
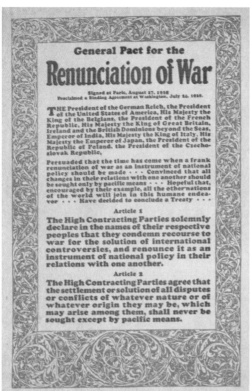

The "General Pact for the Renunciation of War," also known as the Peace Pact and the Kellogg-Briand Pact, included only two substantive articles. The key provisions were so short they fit on a postcard, thousands of which were produced to advertise the Pact.

30

As U.S. Secretary of State Henry Stimson looks on, the Japanese ambassador to the United States, Katsuji Debuchi, ratifies the Peace Pact on July 24, 1929. The Japanese invasion of Manchuria just over two years later would prove the first major test of the Pact.

Kellogg (left) and Stimson (right) leaving the State Department on July 25, 1929, the day after the Peace Pact was celebrated at the White House. Whereas Kellogg had done all he could to exclude Levinson from receiving any credit for the Peace Pact—and campaigned against him for the Nobel Peace Prize—Stimson, a Yale classmate of Levinson's, invited him to the ceremony. Stimson also drew on Levinson's work as he considered how to enforce the Pact.

In September 1931, young Japanese officers set an explosion on the Japanese-owned South Manchuria Railway, then blamed it on "Chinese saboteurs." Japan responded to the "attack" by invading Chinese Manchuria. Here the Lytton Commission, sent by the League of Nations, inspects the thirty-one-inch section of track damaged during the incident.

The Lytton Commission prepared a series of maps as part of its report. This one shows the "Spot of Explosion (alleged)" on the Japanese-controlled railway. It then traces the path Japanese troops (shown in blue) took through the nearby Chinese barracks, the path of the fleeing Chinese soldiers (in red), and the brief exchange of fire between the two.

34

U.S. Undersecretary of State Sumner Welles (left) with George Kennan, attaché at the U.S. embassy in Berlin. Welles was in the midst of a European tour, where he met with Hitler and his foreign minister, Joachim von Ribbentrop. Hitler was wary of Welles, referring to him as "the cunning fox."

Secretary of State Cordell Hull and Welles (right) arriving at the White House for a meeting with President Franklin Delano Roosevelt on May 10, 1940. Hull resented Roosevelt's close relationship with Welles, who had known First Lady Eleanor Roosevelt since childhood.

35

36

Roosevelt and U.K. Prime Minister Winston Churchill chatting on August 10, 1941, on the quarterdeck of HMS *Prince of Wales*. The two leaders and their closest advisers were drafting the Atlantic Charter, a joint declaration of war aims, grounded in the Pact's rejection of aggressive war. Welles stands in the background between the two world leaders.

37

~~Secret~~

P-I.O. Document 99
October 28, 1942.

Not to be removed from the
State Department building

PROVISIONAL OUTLINE

of

INTERNATIONAL ORGANIZATION

(prepared by J.T.S., August 31, 1942)

This sketch of a possible organization is both
provisional and incomplete. It is offered as a basis for discussion in order to ascertain whether it offers a method of
approach to the problem which justifies further elaboration.

Although the method differs from that followed
in the drafting of the Covenant, the aim is to construct a
stronger, not a weaker, organization than in the League of
Nations. The necessity for this is admitted by all thoughtful
observers, and even has had strong endorsement in the enemy
states.

The cover page of the first draft of what would become the United Nations Charter, prepared by "J.T.S." for the "Subcommittee on International Organization" at the State Department, which Welles quietly convened in February 1942. The first section of the draft
repeated the Peace Pact almost verbatim.

38

James T. Shotwell, the "J.T.S." of Document 99, saw the drafting of a new international
agreement as an opportunity to reaffirm the Pact but with "teeth."

39

At a conference held in 1944 at the mansion and gardens of Dumbarton Oaks, the United States introduced a draft Charter of the United Nations for consideration. U.K. Under-Secretary for Foreign Affairs Sir Alexander Cadogan (front left) led the U.K. delegation; Ambassador Wellington Koo (at center, in sunglasses) the Chinese delegation; and U.S. Undersecretary of State Edward R. Stettinius Jr. (front right) the U.S. delegation. Because the Soviets would not meet with the Chinese, they left before Wellington Koo arrived.

40

Left: From right to left: Roosevelt (in jeep), Churchill, Soviet Foreign Minister Vyacheslav Molotov, and Stettinius listen to the Russian national anthem after their arrival at the airport for the Yalta Conference in early 1945. There, the Allies worked out the final details of the new United Nations. The president, wasted by the arduous journey, died three months after returning to the United States. *Right:* Churchill pulls out a new cigar as Stalin smiles at the Yalta Conference. Andrei Gromyko later wrote that while Roosevelt reacted to Stalin's remarks calmly during the conference, Churchill could not hide his irritation. His cigars gave him away: "He smoked far more of them when he was tense or excited. The number of his cigar stubs was in direct proportion to the stresses of the meeting."

states that had violated the Pact. Neutrals were now allowed to discriminate between belligerents, including selling munitions to victims, providing them with financial assistance, and refusing to allow aggressors the
right to visit and search their vessels.[67]

Quincy Wright, the most prolific American scholar on neutrality at the
time, pointed to the Budapest articles as evidence that giving the president
the power to enact an arms embargo against an aggressor did not violate
the international law of neutrality.[68] Wright acknowledged, however, that
abandoning traditional neutrality would not be easy. As he bluntly put it,
"neutrality was profitable." By remaining neutral, the United States had in
the past been able to "raise, manufacture, and ship provisions, goods, and
munitions for cash to both belligerents at war prices."[69] Giving up traditional neutrality would mean saying good-bye to all of that.

The United States Congress was unwilling to take such a drastic
step.[70] Instead, an uneasy compromise emerged in 1935—one that fit with
Moore's and Borchard's view of neutrality law but that also allowed the
country to stop supporting aggressor states. The solution was what Moore
had called in 1933 "a comprehensive, non-partisan embargo" on arms to all
states engaged in warfare.[71] As Borchard had asked rhetorically, "Why not
make it a part of the statutes of the United States that in time of a foreign
war, civil or international, no munitions of war shall be shipped from the
United States to any belligerent engaged in war? The ban must apply to all
the belligerents."[72]

Wright would later speculate that the attraction of the new policy
stemmed less from an interpretation of international law and more from
practical imperatives. Many nations were now short on cash and therefore had begun to purchase goods on credit. Their mounting debts could
force America to take sides to protect its largest debtors from defeat. A
mandatory embargo on both sides might alleviate this problem, by preventing the sale of arms to those at war.[73] In 1935, Congress adopted the
universal arms embargo on belligerents—a policy it renewed in successive Neutrality Acts in 1936 and 1937.[74] That balancing act would soon
prove untenable, however, and the nation that had risen to power as the
first world order began to give way to the second would be forced, finally,
to choose between the two.

COLLISION OF THE OLD AND NEW WORLD ORDERS

In late 1934, the Dubats—armed irregular bands of Somalis employed by the Italian Regio Corpo Truppe Coloniali (Royal Corps of Colonial Troops)—clashed with the Ethiopian militia on the border between Ethiopia and Eritrea, an Italian colony. When the fighting died down, 107 Ethiopians and 50 Italians and Somalis were dead. Ethiopian emperor Haile Selassie charged Italy with aggression. Italy responded to the accusation by demanding an apology. A few days later, it followed that demand with a call for financial and strategic compensation.

Ethiopia appealed to the League of Nations to arbitrate the dispute. But shortly after the League exonerated both parties of wrongdoing, Italian soldiers from Eritrea invaded Ethiopia. Four days after the invasion, the League of Nations declared Italy the aggressor. But League members were not prepared to adopt the formal policy of nonrecognition they had adopted in Manchuria. It was far from clear that the nonrecognition of Manchukuo had produced any positive effect. Japan still occupied the region and showed no signs of relenting. If anything, the Stimson Doctrine had driven Japan further from compromise.[75]

Indeed, by 1935, it had become clear that cutting off Manchukuo was nearly impossible. Once the sanctions were in place, mail was unable to travel on the Trans-Siberian route, which passed through Manchuria, and had to take the longer, slower route through the Suez Canal. By 1935, China, the state with the most to gain from the nonrecognition of the conquest of Manchuria, had decided it was impractical to cut off Manchukuo entirely.[76] China came up with a series of work-arounds that would allow it and other nations to do limited business with Manchuria without recognizing Japan's conquest. China lifted its embargo on postal service into and out of Manchuria, but continued to refuse to recognize stamps issued by the government of Manchukuo or transfer mail on which the word "Manchukuo" appeared.[77] It also began narrow cooperation on customs matters and railway passage. The problem, it turned out, wasn't that Levinson's sanctions of peace were too weak. It was that they were too powerful. Nonrecognition meant not just cutting off Manchukuo from the world, but cutting the world off from Manchukuo.

The experience with Manchukuo left League members reluctant to wield the weapon of nonrecognition against Italy. Adding to that reluctance was Italy's proximity. For League members in Europe, the latest lawbreaker was not in far-off East Asia. It was one thing to cut off a land with which they had little trade. It was another to cut off a core member of the European economy.

The League also knew that any effort to pressure Italy by excluding it from global commerce would be blunted by the states that stood outside the League—including the United States, Japan, and Germany. Some of the largest economies in the world would not be part of the sanctions regime and, therefore, would be free to supply Italy without limit.[78]

The League thus settled on a more measured approach. It would allow members to recognize the conquest of Ethiopia but would require them to institute piecemeal economic sanctions. In November 1935, the League adopted four separate sets of sanctions, banning the sale of arms to both countries, prohibiting financial transactions with and imports from Italy, and restricting exports of war matériel to Italy or its colonies.[79]

What was perhaps most notable about this new sanctions regime was what it left out: It did not prohibit exports of oil to Italy, without which the country would have found it impossible to continue to wage war. As a British diplomat later put it, the sanctions were "a series of half-way measures, measures intensely exasperating to the Italians without being effective."[80]

The United States' response was even more lackluster. The Emperor of Ethiopia called on the United States to take action under the Pact. Secretary of State Cordell Hull responded that, with the matter before the League, the U.S. government "did not feel that [it] could properly or usefully take action."[81] U.S. newspapers interpreted this response as an abandonment of the Pact. Hull had no choice but to issue a statement reiterating U.S. support: "The Pact of Paris is no less binding now than when it was entered into by the 63 nations that are parties to it."[82] The administration would, of course, follow the Stimson Doctrine and refuse to recognize the conquest of Ethiopia by Italy. It would also initiate what Secretary Hull termed a "moral embargo," in which Americans would be encouraged to boycott Italian goods.[83] But the United States refused all invitations by the League to impose comprehensive economic sanctions on Italy fearing that doing so would invite attacks by powerful isolationist forces. The president slapped an arms embargo on both countries, as required by the Neutrality Act.[84] But these modest sanctions had little effect.

On May 5, 1936, Italy captured the capital of Addis Ababa. The representatives gathered at the League that July concluded that the sanctions had become pointless. Indeed, they had become counterproductive. With the capture of the capital, as Chile's representative Rivas Vicuña put it, "[s]anctions no longer have any object, and they affect, not only the country against which they have been enforced, but also the countries applying them."[85] The League dropped all sanctions, and Italy merged Ethiopia with its colonies in Somaliland and Eritrea to create the unified colony of Italian East Africa. The Emperor of Ethiopia, then living in the United Kingdom, wrote to castigate the League, reminding it of its pledge "not to recognize any territorial acquisition brought about by force." He warned: "The disastrous consequences of a policy of ignoring promises are making themselves felt in Europe, threatening to bring about a general war which would drench the world with blood."[86]

BRINK OF AN ABYSS

On July 7, 1937, the Japanese carried out military training exercises to the southwest of Beijing without giving the local Chinese authorities notice. Fearing an attack was under way, the Chinese troops fired several ineffectual shots. The Japanese returned fire. After a Japanese soldier was presumed dead—he had become lost looking to relieve himself and failed to report back in time for roll call—the conflict escalated into full-scale fighting. A fragile cease-fire fell apart, and Japan began a march into China.[87]

Wellington Koo, the new Chinese representative to the League, implored the League to take action: "The lives of four hundred and fifty million people are at stake; the civilisation and the security of the whole world are in the balance."[88] Although it was clear that Japan had engaged in gross violations of the Pact and Covenant, the League failed to act. Cowed by the collapse of sanctions in Italy and still suffering the effects of the global depression, its members were unwilling to put in place even the weakest of collective sanctions. Timid resolutions inviting states to consider giving individual assistance to China assuaged a few consciences, but did little to help the Chinese.[89]

The ensuing conflict was among the most brutal the world had yet seen. The Japanese army cut a swath of horror as it advanced from Shanghai to the capital of Nanking. One journalist embedded with Japanese forces remarked, "The reason that the [10th Army] is advancing to Nanking quite rapidly is due to the tacit consent among the officers and men that they could loot and rape as they wish."[90] Knowing that the fall of Nanking was only a matter of time, Chinese leader Chiang Kai-shek fled, taking with him most of his troops and leaving the city nearly defenseless. In the six weeks after they captured the city, Japanese troops engaged in widespread rape and looting and killed more than 200,000 people.[91]

Gloom pervaded the League's 100th session in early 1938, just over a month after the fall of Nanking. The French foreign minister acknowledged that "The League is reproached—no doubt because too much was expected of it."[92] Wellington Koo declared, "During the nearly two decades of its existence the League of Nations has never found its prestige and authority at such a low ebb as it finds them to-day."[93]

ROOSEVELT'S QUARANTINE

Yet if the League's authority was in decline, the new understanding of neutrality that the Pact embodied was on the rise. As war spread in Asia and Africa, Secretary of State Hull began to reconsider his earlier dismissal of economic sanctions. The spiraling violence posed a significant threat to world peace, and the League had proven incapable of preventing escalation of the violence. At the same time, deep-seated isolationism among the American public limited Roosevelt's ability to take action, threatening to render the international system lawless. Hull decided the time had come for the president to make a speech to counteract the growing trend toward isolationism and assert his support for economic sanctions to stop the slide toward world war.[94]

On October 5, 1937, President Roosevelt took the lectern in Chicago— the "heart of isolationism" and Salmon Levinson's hometown.[95] "The high aspirations expressed in the Briand-Kellogg Peace Pact and the hopes for peace thus raised," he began, "have of late given away to a haunting fear of calamity." Roosevelt proposed to address the military problem with a medical solution. "When an epidemic of physical disease starts to spread, the community approves and joins in a quarantine of the patients in order to protect the health of the community against the spread of the disease."[96] The president's solution was isolation: Peaceful nations would cut communications with aggressors and refuse to cooperate with them in any way.

At first, the speech met with positive reviews. But the proposal to end traditional neutrality had its vocal critics. A few days after the speech, questions began to emerge about what a "quarantine" would mean.[97] Many remained unconvinced that the obligations of neutrality had changed. They feared that the quarantine was war by another name. It was clear to the administration that the country was not yet ready to change its stance on neutrality; it would continue to adhere to its "neutral" embargo on all belligerents to a conflict.[98]

Thus stood U.S. law on September 1, 1939, as German tanks rolled into Poland, beginning Europe's descent into brutal war for the second time in three decades. But now the "compromise" neutrality legislation placed Roosevelt in an impossible position. When Britain and France declared war on Germany two days later, the Neutrality Acts required him to impose an arms embargo on America's most important European allies when they most needed help. The effect of the embargo was devastating because both Britain and France had placed large armament orders with the United States before the outbreak of the war—orders that now had to be frozen.[99] The neutrality legislation, Roosevelt came to believe, was having the opposite effect of what was intended. Far from keeping the United States out of war, the embargo would lead it into war. If Britain, France, and their allies could not count on the enormous resources of the United States, after all, they would make easier targets. And if Britain and France fell, it would be impossible for the United States to avoid being drawn into the conflict. As Hull put it in his memoir, "if Germany won there was every likelihood that we should soon have to fight."[100]

EMBRACING THE NEW NEUTRALITY

Even with German forces laying siege to Warsaw, opposition to any change in U.S. domestic law of neutrality remained staunch. Senator Borah and several of his colleagues launched a national radio campaign against a change in the neutrality laws that sparked a flood of some one million pro-embargo telegrams, letters, and postcards into congressional offices. Some senators received four thousand messages a day.[101] The success of the campaign reaffirmed what Roosevelt already knew: A complete repeal of the Neutrality Acts was impossible.

There were not many signs that the tide of public opinion had turned. Even though 80 percent of the public favored the Allies in the war, 70 percent wanted the United States to continue to show impartiality in its exports to belligerents, for fear that any sign of favoritism would drag the country into war.[102] So Roosevelt sought and won the next best thing: a repeal of the mandatory arms embargo with a "cash and carry" provision.[103] This new proviso required that arms be sold only for cash and be carried away by the seller. Although on its face the revised Neutrality Act treated all states equally, "cash and carry" favored the nation with the strongest navy—because it could not only transport more, but also defend itself on the open sea. And the country with the strongest navy was Great Britain.

There was at least one person who understood precisely what Roosevelt meant to do—Roosevelt's own secretary of war, Harry Hines Woodring—and he wasn't happy about it. Woodring was the former governor of Kansas and, like most Midwestern politicians of his time, he stood behind the twin pillars of neutrality and nonintervention. Favoring one side in the fight, he warned, would lead to war, regardless of what Roosevelt (or international legal scholars) said. As time wore on, Woodring repeatedly pressed back against Roosevelt's efforts to aid the Allies in Europe. When the president proposed selling surplus arms to Sweden for resale to Finland, Woodring warned that it would violate neutrality, forcing the president to abandon the idea. Woodring also opposed plans to sell military equipment to Britain and France. He backed down only after the president ordered him to go along or resign.[104]

Even as Woodring expressed discomfort, others pushed for quicker action. Speaking in New Haven on June 18, 1940, Henry Stimson described the crisis in Europe as "probably the greatest" in American history (a devoted alumnus, he was in town for the Yale University commencement). The stakes were dire, he declared: "America today is standing at the parting of two ways: In this moment of world peril she can cling to the dreams of a mistaken fiction of neutrality no longer applicable to her interests or her safety." The better choice, the only choice, according to Stimson, was to embrace the new understanding of neutrality, to "repeal the provisions of our ill-starred so-called neutrality venture which have acted as a shackle to our true interests for over five years." Freed from the constraints of impartiality, he argued, "America can frankly realize that now as for many years past our own safety depends in part upon the continuance of British sea power"—which meant, of course, generously aiding Britain.[105]

Reading about the speech in the newspaper, Roosevelt decided that Stimson was the man he needed at the War Department.[106] He asked Woodring to resign that day.[107] Woodring complied, but took a public swipe at the president on his way out: "I trust you will advise those who would provoke belligerency," his letter of resignation warned, "that they do so with the knowledge that we are not prepared for a major conflict."[108]

Stimson's nomination came as a surprise to everyone.[109] He had, after all, served the president that Roosevelt had defeated, and he was a stalwart Republican—a seventy-two-year-old stalwart Republican. But he was also a steady hand at a dangerous time. And Roosevelt knew he could trust him: Stimson had worked with Roosevelt during the transition from the Hoover administration. Tapping a Republican also signaled Roosevelt's desire to remove partisan politics from the War Department.[110] He further reinforced the message with an announcement the same day that Colonel Frank Knox, the 1936 Republican vice presidential candidate, would be named secretary of the navy.

Although the appointments met widespread acclaim and easy Senate approval, some saw darker motives in the president's decision to reach across the aisle. Opponents of the nominations worried that "with Knox and Stimson in the Cabinet, the nation is more likely to get into war."[111] Others celebrated the appointments for the same reason. The *Daily Mirror*, along with other British papers, could hardly contain their excitement, gleefully declaring "Hitler Haters Join United States Cabinet."[112]

With Stimson in office and the war spreading in Europe, the administration began pushing the bounds of traditional neutrality even more aggressively. On September 2, 1940, the United States transferred fifty retired destroyers to the United Kingdom in exchange for the rights to establish bases on British-controlled territory. In an opinion that strained credulity, Attorney General Robert H. Jackson argued that the Neutrality Act did not bar the deal because the act did not apply to "over-age destroyers, which were not built, armed, equipped as, or converted into, vessels of war with the intent that they should enter the service of a belligerent."[113]

After a crushing victory in the 1940 election, the administration dispensed with this fiction and embraced the new neutrality. The Lend-Lease Act, which Roosevelt signed in March 1941, allowed the United States to discriminate between belligerent nations when it sold, lent, or disposed of supplies.[114] And discriminate it did. In the first ninety days after the act was passed, the U.S. allocated $4.25 billion to procure the authorized aid to the Allies, immediately made available two million gross tons of cargo ships and oil tankers to carry the aid, and began training seven thousand British pilots.[115]

NO OTHER RECOURSE

The United States began to act on the new theory of neutrality not only in Europe but in Asia as well. In 1941, Japan invaded southern Indochina and threatened British Malaya, North Borneo, and Brunei. That July, the U.S. responded by freezing Japanese assets in the United States and by embargoing oil and gasoline exports to Japan.[116] The embargo dealt Japan a devastating blow. More than 80 percent of its oil came from the United States. When Roosevelt persuaded the British and Dutch to join the oil embargo, Japan was completely cut off from the international oil markets. With no indigenous supply of oil, Japan would soon run out.

It seemed yet another cruel twist to Japanese leaders. Just as their nation was poised to claim its rightful place in a world governed by rules it had struggled to learn, the Americans and the Europeans had changed those rules. Conquest was no longer permitted (though holding on to and defending land conquered before 1928 was). Nonbelligerents were now permitted to impose crippling economic sanctions on belligerents. Any military response would be regarded as illegal aggression under the Pact of Paris, a Pact that many in Japan—including those close to Emperor Hirohito—regarded as little more than words on a page.[117]

The Japanese navy began pushing for an early war with the United States. The longer Japan waited, the navy argued, the lower oil supplies would become and the weaker Japan would grow. Japan needed to strike before it became too incapacitated. The emperor, doubting that Japan could win a war with the United States, resisted. But his mind began to change as the embargo dragged on and the situation grew more desperate.[118] On November 26, 1941, Secretary Hull presented the Japanese ambassador with a note that called for the complete withdrawal of all Japanese troops from French Indochina and China.[119] Although not explicit in the note, Japan assumed that Hull's reference to "China" included Manchukuo.

Unknown to Hull, the strike force that would attack Pearl Harbor had already set out for Hawaii, though it remained close enough to recall. Japanese prime minister Tojo Hideki regarded Hull's note as evidence that war was inevitable, describing it as an "ultimatum to Japan": Withdraw from China—including Manchukuo—or face the consequences. After reviewing the note with his advisers, Hirohito agreed. He approved the attack on Pearl Harbor, and with it the decision to wage war against United States, Britain, and the Netherlands.[120] The next day, the Japanese fleet received the signal "*Niitakayama Nobore*" (literally "climb Mount Niitaka"): Proceed with the attack.[121]

The emperor began to craft a declaration of war. Its wording reveals a leader caught in the throes of the Old World Order. The declaration began by blaming the United States and Britain for taking sides in Japan's dispute with China: "Both America and Britain, giving support to the Chungking regime, have aggravated the disturbances in East Asia." Of the sanctions: "They have obstructed by every means Our peaceful commerce and finally resorted to a direct severance of economic relations, menacing gravely the existence of Our Empire." The declaration concluded that this situation "would, if left unchecked, not only nullify Our Empire's efforts of many years for the sake of the stabilization of East Asia, but also endanger the very existence of Our nation."[122]

The day before Hull delivered his note to the Japanese, Stimson wrote in his diary, "[Roosevelt] brought up the event that we are likely to be attacked perhaps next Monday, for the Japanese are notorious for making an attack without warning, and the question was what we should do. The question was how we should maneuver them into the position of firing the first shot without allowing too much danger to ourselves."[123] He would soon learn no more maneuvering would be necessary. The first shot was on its way.

It is tempting to regard the Japanese attack on Pearl Harbor as a lawless act for which there can be no justification or excuse. For Americans, December 7 remains "a date which will live in infamy," in the words of President Roosevelt. But the devastating strike on the United States was not lawless. Japan was simply following the law of nations that U.S. Commodore Matthew Perry's black ships had introduced in 1854. What Japan failed to recognize, however, was that those rules had been renounced in 1928. The United States itself had only recently come to terms with the complete transformation in the legal order initiated by the Pact—it finally embraced the new understanding of neutrality with the passage of the Lend-Lease Act in March 1941, only six months before Pearl Harbor.

That the Japanese understood the law differently than the United States is most apparent from a note the Japanese Ambassador hand delivered to Secretary Hull at the U.S. Department of State on December 7, 1941, mere minutes after Hull learned of the Japanese attack on Pearl Harbor.[124] The memorandum, which the Japanese published three days later, reads much like an Old World Order manifesto. It details the many perceived wrongs done to Japan by the United States. It complains of U.S. support for the Chinese and the U.S. insistence on Japanese withdrawal from China. Though it never mentions the Paris Peace Pact directly, the memorandum rejects the American view of the changes brought about by the Pact. It complains that "[w]hereas the American government, under the principles it rigidly upholds, objects to settle international issues through military pressure, it is exercising in conjunction with Great Britain and other nations pressure by economic power." This economic pressure, the

Japanese Foreign Ministry argued, "should be condemned, as it is at times more inhumane than military pressure."[125]

The war that resulted would become a contest between two competing visions of the world: between one that saw the Pact as a piece of paper and one that saw it as a new legal reality; between one that clung to the right of conquest and one that rejected it; between one that held on to the belief that neutrality required impartiality and one that regarded the "sanctions of peace" as an essential tool of law enforcement; between one that condemned economic sanctions and one that condemned military force. It would be a war, in short, between the Old World Order and the New.

EIGHT

FIELD MARSHAL IN THE WAR OF BRAINS

On a warm spring day in 1942, Walter Lippmann called on Sumner Welles at his office in the massive State, War, and Navy Building just west of the White House. As the most influential newspaper columnist in America, Lippmann enjoyed unparalleled access to those in power. He came to discuss a matter of signal importance. Even though the war had just started, he implored the undersecretary of state to plan for its end.

Lippmann spoke from experience. He was among the original members of The Inquiry, the secret group hastily organized by President Wilson to provide technical assistance to the victors after the First World War. In Paris, Lippmann witnessed firsthand the fatal mistake of delay. The delegates gathered at the Peace Conference made unsound decisions, he believed, because they did not have sufficient time for study. Their problems were compounded by fraying unity. Once the war ended, the triumphant states began to grab as much as they could rather than taking time to lay the foundations for peace. Lippmann fretted that the world was about to make the same mistake.[1]

Welles offered a measured reply. The position of the president, secretary of state, and Senate Foreign Relations Committee, he explained, was that there would be no agreement on territorial adjustments or political settlements until after the war. What he did not disclose to Lippmann, however, was his strong opposition to the official wait-and-see policy. Secretly he agreed with Lippmann. Indeed, at that moment, he was studying the records of the 1919 Paris Peace Conference. The more he read, he later recounted, "the more I was convinced that our wisest course would be to try to work out with our allies now, before V-Day, as detailed an agreement as possible." As a result, he had for many months been carrying out just the kind of planning Lippmann was pleading with him to conduct.

The challenge as Welles saw it was stark. As long as the war raged, "our armed strength, our material resources, the moral authority of President Roosevelt and, even more perhaps, our allies' need of us, would give us infinitely greater leverage now than we could have after the victory was won." Victory would inevitably unleash "exaggerated forms of selfish nationalism" that would fuel a scramble over the spoils. The frenzy could be even worse than after the last world war, for the United States would not just be negotiating with France and Great Britain. The Soviets would be at the front of the line, and Welles had little confidence in the "inherent altruism of the Politburo's foreign policy."[2]

Welles understood that the collapse of the international order had done more than put the security of the world at risk. It had called into question the ideals for which the Allies had stood. This time they needed a postwar vision that could withstand the challenges to these ideals—one that would not place the world at the mercy of a few uncooperative states. Turning that vision into reality, Welles believed, would require the creation of a new world organization, one that would put the prohibition on war at its core and enlist the Great Powers to restrain any state that dared to disobey. But in the dark days of 1942, with Germany at its height in Europe and Japan tightening its grip on Asia, a new, unifying world organization seemed a distant goal.

THE FIELD MARSHAL IN THE WAR OF BRAINS

Welles had been thinking about the end of the war even before the United States entered it. Six months before the Japanese assault on Pearl Harbor, Welles—then serving as acting secretary of state due to Cordell Hull's illness—gave a speech that propelled him from obscurity to acclaim.

The occasion was the laying of the cornerstone for the new wing of the Norwegian legation in Washington. The expansion of the embassy was an act of defiance, for Norway had been overrun by the Nazis the previous year. After Crown Princess Martha raised the Norwegian flag and led the crowd in Norway's national anthem with her rich soprano voice, Welles spoke.[3]

He began by saying what everyone then knew—the world would not know peace until Hitler's government had been "finally, and utterly, destroyed." But what then? Would the end of war mean only "a return to ruined homes, to the graves of slaughtered wives and children, to poverty and want, to social upheaval and economic chaos"?

He called on "free governments of peace-loving nations everywhere" to begin to plan for the peace. At the end of the last war, he reminded the audience, a president gave his life in the struggle to achieve "the vision of an ordered world governed by law." That experiment had failed, "in part because of the blind selfishness of men here in the United States." Despite this failure, he was confident that the victors would realize the "great ideal of an association of nations through which the freedom, the happiness, and the security of all peoples may be achieved."[4]

The speech was broadcast to Europe in twenty-five languages.[5] The *South China Morning Post* described it as "the most specific announcement yet made by a high administration official on the post-war aims of the United States Government."[6] *The New York Times* went a step further, calling it the most specific declaration on peace aims "by the spokesman of any government since the war began."[7] The *St. Louis Post-Dispatch* described Welles as the first American or Briton to "put on the drawing board a 'V' that looks toward victory at the peace table, as well as on the battlefield."[8] Asked about Welles's speech in the House of Commons a week later, British foreign secretary Anthony Eden declared his government's "cordial agreement," and expressed hopes that there would soon be another meeting of governments of the Allied powers "at which we can begin the examination of postwar problems."[9]

Time featured Welles on its front cover the following week, describing the "unknown gentleman" as the "field marshal" in the "War of Brains" against the Axis. The story, entitled "Diplomat's Diplomat," breathlessly characterized Welles as having "a firm hold on every one of the diplomatic virtues: he is absolutely precise, imperturbable, accurate, honest, sophisticated, thorough, cultured, traveled, financially established . . . is one of the few U.S. men who can carry a stick with assurance, is a linguist of idiomatic excellence, never forgets names, never leaves so-necessary little things undone."[10]

Not a story was written about Welles that did not mention his formal manner. Born into wealthy New York society, he attended a fashionable cadet corps for boys before attending the elite private boarding school Groton at the age of eleven, followed by Harvard College.[11] Even as an adult, he never lost the military bearing he learned as a young cadet. He stood six feet three inches "plumb-line-straight, ramrod-stiff." A Central American minister described him as looking like a "tall glass of distilled ice water."[12] Reporter Blair Bolles put it more harshly: "He was brought up in . . . cold-fish ways . . . went to the cold-fish schools . . . entered a cold-fish calling. . . . He is as reserved as a box at the opera. . . . Even his blond mustache looks cold."[13]

Hull never liked Welles, but it was not just because of his formal bearing. Hull would not admit it, but he envied Welles's access to the president and first lady. When Welles and Eleanor Roosevelt were growing up, their two families were close. When she married Franklin in 1905, she invited twelve-year-old Sumner to serve as a page.[14] As a young man, Welles had joined the diplomatic service, a position that took him first briefly to Tokyo, then to Argentina, where he learned Spanish and began developing an expertise in the region. Welles went on to serve in the State Department as chief of the Division of Latin American Affairs. His swift rise through the departmental ranks was derailed, however, after he divorced his first wife and married Mathilde Scott Townsend, the recently divorced wife of Senator Peter Gerry. Leaving his wife to marry a senator's ex-wife might not have been enough to get Welles sacked, but Gerry was also a good friend of President Calvin Coolidge. Under pressure from his superiors, Welles resigned from the State Department in 1925, his chance of achieving diplomatic greatness seemingly gone.[15]

Welles devoted his involuntary retirement to writing what even *Time* magazine's celebratory article called a "ponderous, lifeless, two-volume work" on the history of the Dominican Republic. The lifelessness, however, masked a careful indictment of American foreign policy in the Western Hemisphere. The book criticized the United States' penchant for using brute force where diplomatic negotiations would have worked just as well. It urged instead "the stimulation of commercial ties, the interchange of experts, the sharing of the responsibility of keeping the Hemispheric peace."[16]

Welles and Roosevelt came back into contact just as Roosevelt was contemplating running for governor of New York. In 1923, Welles visited Roosevelt at his home in New York, where he was struck by how Roosevelt, who had suffered a polio attack two years earlier, had changed: "It was exactly as if all the trivialities in life had been burned [out] in him."[17]

The two men began an exchange of ideas about Latin America, and Welles's insights helped Roosevelt develop his policy for the region.[18] The conversation became more focused in 1928, when Roosevelt supported Alfred E. Smith in his bid for the presidency and Smith, in turn, endorsed Roosevelt to replace him as governor of New York. During that period, Welles produced a twenty-six-page speech offering a detailed critique of the GOP's policy on Latin America that he shared with Eleanor. She pronounced it "one of the best things" she had ever read on the subject, solidifying what would become a lifelong collaboration.[19] A decade later, Welles's ideas would form the foundation of the Good Neighbor Policy announced by Roosevelt in his first inaugural address.[20] The policy represented nothing less than a full-throated rejection of the long-held American right to intervene in the affairs of its southern neighbors—a right that had been exercised in thousands of interventions both large and small. Roosevelt reaffirmed this rejection a few months later, declaring, "The definite policy of the United States from now on is one opposed to armed intervention."[21]

After Roosevelt's election as president, a rehabilitated Welles was appointed undersecretary of state at Roosevelt's insistence, beating out Hull's favored candidate, R. Walton Moore. As a longtime friend of the president, Welles had influence and access that went far beyond his official station. He visited regularly with the president and first lady. Between April 1933 and March 1945, his name appears four hundred times in the presidential White House calendar—a number that does not include informal visits that occurred outside the While House.[22] While Hull, too, visited the White House frequently, his visits were almost always limited to formal occasions, such as welcoming foreign officials, and nearly always as part of a group. Unlike Welles, Hull rarely had time alone with the president.

For all the flood of press attention that followed Welles's 1941 Norway speech on the postwar peace, it may have been easy to forget how much Welles left unsaid. He called for an international organization, but said nothing about what it would look like or how, exactly, it would avoid the mistakes of the League. As one newspaper put it, "Mr. Welles has made only a few pencil scratches on the sketching paper."[23]

Welles did not fill out the sketch because he did not yet know how. He knew the League had been a terrible failure. He saw the Peace Pact as a misguided waste. Writing at the tail end of the Second World War, Welles would look back and—like many who didn't yet recognize its revolutionary implications—blame the Pact for giving "the delusion of a great body of the American people that the mere formulation of a wish is equivalent to positive action." Welles thought the Pact had been taken by millions of Americans as "justification for the refusal of their government to take part in the League of Nations," forgetting, for the moment, that the Pact post-dated the defeat of the League in the U.S. by a decade. To Welles, the Pact embodied the isolationist thinking in the country—when in fact the isolationist thinking in the country made achieving its vision all but impossible.[24] But Welles was surely correct in the conclusion he drew from his unflattering portrait: Any new international organization could not repeat such mistakes.

THE ATLANTIC CHARTER

President Roosevelt, however, was not yet convinced a new international organization was necessary to secure the peace—and Welles knew it. According to Welles, FDR often said "first things must come first," and "[i]n the summer of 1941, the 'first thing' was . . . for the Axis to be defeated."[25] Afterward, there would be plenty of time to design a world organization for keeping the peace. Roosevelt was convinced, moreover, that no organization would be effective until, in Welles's words, "some policemen armed with the necessary force" undertook "an extended cleaning-up job."[26]

That an undersecretary of state would give a speech calling for a major foreign policy initiative that he knew his president did not support is unthinkable today. But in 1941, an undersecretary of state like Welles could write his own speech without White House vetting—and hope the president would come around to his view.

It would take time. Roosevelt continued to hold his first-things-first view even as he made plans to meet with Winston Churchill later in the summer of 1941. Roosevelt had been communicating with Churchill since he became prime minister in 1940, but the two had not yet met in person. The meeting would take place in secret at Placentia Bay, off the coast of Newfoundland, where the United States was building a new naval base, having recently traded destroyers to Britain for that privilege. The first gathering took place aboard the president's ship, the USS *Augusta*, on August 9, 1941.

Both leaders arrived accompanied by advisers. President Roosevelt's team included Harry Hopkins. Best known today for the role he played in designing and implementing the New Deal, Hopkins had stepped down as secretary of commerce and was acting as Roosevelt's close personal adviser and unofficial emissary to Churchill. Hopkins was the chief architect and administrator of the Lend-Lease program, and he knew Churchill better than anyone else in the U.S. government. He might have known Roosevelt best, too, for he was effectively living at the White House at the time.[27]

The president admired and trusted Hopkins for perhaps another reason: Hopkins, too, was suffering from an acute and chronic illness. In the late 1930s, stomach cancer began to kill him. He would later spend much of the final wartime conference at Yalta in bed.[28] Yet despite his illness, his zest for life endeared him to Roosevelt. The president's physician, however, was less pleased, once declaring, "Our biggest job is to keep Harry from ever feeling completely well. When he thinks he's restored to health he goes out on the town—and from there to the Mayo Clinic."[29]

Hopkins was a doer, not a thinker; a fixer, not a visionary. He was adept at moving things along once the course had been set, but he did not have the power to look past the horizon, to solve not just the problem at hand, but to anticipate those that would follow. That was Welles's job.

Welles had led the State Department's efforts on postwar planning, which would have been reason enough to include him. But that was not the only reason. When FDR's son asked him why he had brought Welles instead of Cordell Hull, FDR answered: "One, I trust him. Two, he doesn't argue with me. Three, he gets things done."[30]

Churchill's key adviser on the trip was Sir Alexander Cadogan. As permanent undersecretary for foreign affairs, Cadogan was Welles's British counterpart. Though initially not fond of Welles, he warmed to him over the course of their negotiations. Cadogan wrote in his diary on the second day of the conference that Welles "improves upon acquaintance, but it is a pity that he swallowed a ramrod in his youth."[31]

Roosevelt had called this secret meeting for one purpose: a joint declaration of war aims.[32] This goal may seem perplexing, given that the United States had not yet entered the war—and would not declare war until after the attack on Pearl Harbor four months later. The decision to join with a belligerent power in making a declaration of war aims was, as Churchill later put it, "astonishing."[33] But by this point, the United States had made its loyalties clear. Thanks to the cash and carry provision inserted into the Neutrality Act in 1939, Roosevelt had been able to provide substantial support to Britain. Additional support came through the Lend-Lease program (largely orchestrated by Hopkins). It had proven a lifeline for Britain.

But this lifeline was a political liability for Roosevelt. Americans feared that providing matériel to the Allies put the country at risk of being pulled into the war. For a nation so accustomed to the idea that economic favoritism was an act of war, it was difficult not to worry. Knowing he had brought the country closer to a confrontation with the Axis, Roosevelt wanted to issue a public statement making clear what was at stake. Indeed, he hoped that a joint statement with Churchill could "affect the whole movement of United States opinion,"[34] encouraging Americans to take greater risks in support of the Allies.

The first night of the meeting, Churchill set to work on a joint declaration of principles to guide the two countries, as Roosevelt put it, "along the same road."[35] The next morning, Cadogan handed Welles the papers containing Churchill's draft of what would become the Atlantic Charter. The first half, Welles would later write, "glowed with Churchill's genius," but the latter half was, he thought, "too vague or too sweeping." Welles and Roosevelt shut themselves in Roosevelt's cabin and began, together, to revise the draft, after which Welles and Cadogan hashed out the final language.[36]

The result was a remarkable document. It began by restating the principles of the Stimson Doctrine—there would be no conquest; the two countries would "seek no aggrandizement, territorial or other." Moreover, there would be "no territorial changes that do not accord with the freely expressed wishes of the peoples concerned." The Charter looked ahead to a time "after the final destruction of the Nazi tyranny"—a remarkable statement for a neutral in the war—and declared the two states' "hope to see established a peace which will afford to all nations the means of dwelling in safety within their own boundaries."

The Charter closed with a final paragraph added by Roosevelt and Welles. It declared that "all the nations of the world . . . must come to the abandonment of the use of force." Churchill's draft had endorsed the creation of "an international organization," but Roosevelt was still not ready to do so. The new draft called instead for disarmament, "pending the establishment of a wider and permanent system of general security."[37]

DECLARATION OF THE UNITED NATIONS

On December 22, 1941, just over two weeks after Japan's attack on Pearl Harbor brought the United States into the war, Churchill arrived in Washington for his first state visit. He stayed at the White House for three weeks, turning his room, located on the second floor across from Harry Hopkins's, into a temporary command headquarters for the British Empire. The once quiet hallway that had been used to store Christmas presents became a bustling thoroughfare of British staff officers and secretaries, carrying battered red leather dispatch cases.[38]

Now that the U.S. had entered the conflict on the side of the Allies, Roosevelt proposed they prepare a joint statement of war aims. It would be based on the Atlantic Charter but open to signature by all the nations then at war with Germany, Italy, or Japan. He also came up with a new phrase to describe the signatories, some of whom, after all, were not located on the Atlantic: the "United Nations."[39]

On New Year's Day 1942, the Atlantic Charter went from a binational declaration to a global manifesto of the New World Order. Roosevelt, Churchill, Maxim Litvinov of the USSR, and T. V. Soong of China gathered in the president's study to sign the new "Declaration of the United Nations," leaving the State Department to gather the signatures of the twenty-two other countries named in the document.[40] By signing, the new Allies subscribed to the "common program of purposes and principles" embodied in the Atlantic Charter—the rejection of war and territorial aggrandizement foremost among them. It was the first time the term "United Nations" had been used in an official document.[41]

The Axis powers stood for the Old World Order. Germany, Japan, and Italy had each rejected the principles of the Peace Pact—Japan by invading Manchuria and continuing into China, French Indochina, British Malaya, Indonesia, and Singapore; Italy by invading Ethiopia, Greece, Yugoslavia, and North Africa; and Germany by seeking to gain control of nearly all of Europe. Each had a reason to resent the Allies and their efforts to outlaw war. The Axis powers had largely missed out on the colonial land grab. Japan only began to participate in international affairs in the 1860s, and it was more than a generation before it was prepared to project military force outside its own borders, too late to successfully participate in the empire-building scramble. Both Germany and Italy finally achieved unification in the same year—1871. They joined the land grab soon after, but were never as successful as France, Spain, Portugal, Britain, and the Netherlands, which built extensive empires. Without the authority to wage war and conquer new territory, the Axis powers saw little possibility of ever achieving equality.

The Axis had set out its own declaration of war aims in the Tripartite Pact of 1940. Though these same states had signed the Peace Pact, they now saw it as an obstacle to gaining their "proper place."[42] Together they announced their agreement to "establish and maintain a new order of things"—under which Germany and Italy would "establish . . . a new order in Europe" and Japan "a new order in greater East Asia."[43] These "new orders" were already being established in the old-fashioned way—through ruthless and brutal wars of conquest.

The war was no longer about who would control what territory. It was about what rules would govern when the war was over.

PLANNING FOR PEACE

The grand declarations had been made, but the difficult work of implementing them still lay ahead. Hull and Welles convened an Advisory Committee on Post-War Foreign Policy in the Department of State.[44] After consulting with the committee, Welles pressed the president to convene an international group to plan for peace. Welles later credited Mrs. Roosevelt with the idea—noting that she had first suggested convening an international group "continuously to plan for future peace" in 1939. But it was likely that the idea was not hers alone. Welles and Mrs. Roosevelt had become close friends. Welles was her closest confidant working in the State Department, and they would undoubtedly have long discussed such plans. For his own part, Welles had argued for international conferences since at least 1937—first to keep the peace and then, when war broke out, to forge it.[45]

The president dismissed the idea. The war, after all, was going badly for the Allies. It was clear that victory would turn on the Soviets' capacity to hold off the German onslaught. The Joint Chiefs warned that any negotiations over peace would run into the Soviets' territorial demands—demands that the United States could not refuse without risking the alliance, perhaps even sending Soviet leader Joseph Stalin back into the embrace of Hitler, who must have realized his mistake by then. Yet buckling to the Soviets' demands was not an option either, for it would reveal the Allies to be pushovers. The best option, Roosevelt concluded, was to let the war run its course before convening an international group to plan for peace.[46]

The president did like the idea, however, of a secret American planning process overseen by Welles. As Harley Notter, a State Department bureaucrat who became involved in the planning process, later recalled, "The President desired to be able later to reach in his basket and to find there whatever he needed in regard to postwar foreign policy." That would leave him free "to devote himself wholly to ways and means of winning the war."[47]

Welles quietly formed the Special Subcommittee on International Organization at the State Department.[48] To staff it, he picked men with a range of expertise and experience inside and outside government. The group included Isaiah Bowman, the former head of The Inquiry, which had sought to reinvent global governance after the First World War. Bowman was generally regarded as the world's leading expert on exploring, mapping, and conceiving physical space.[49] He had written a comprehensive book on the intertwining of politics and territory he termed "political geography."[50] He was also a vicious and vocal anti-Semite.

Bowman was thus surely unhappy about another of Welles's picks, White House lawyer Benjamin V. Cohen. Cohen had advised the president on the changing law of neutrality, and had helped clear the way for the transfer of "over-age" destroyers to Great Britain in exchange for British bases.[51] He was "known for his slouching posture, sloppy dress, absentminded table manners—and for a skill at drafting legislation that was generally reckoned the best in the United States."[52] Green Hackworth, the legal adviser to the U.S. Department of State, joined the committee as the chief legal officer of the department. Also from the State Department came Leo Pasvolsky, a short, rotund, hardworking "one-man think tank."[53]

The final member of Welles's team was James T. Shotwell, Bowman's colleague from The Inquiry and the ghostwriter of the Peace Pact.[54] Following his diplomatic triumph with the Pact, Shotwell had returned to Columbia University. Now approaching seventy and recently retired from teaching, he bore little resemblance to the slim man in the photograph taken at the 1919 Paris Peace Conference. He was stout with deep lines in his face and baggy folds of skin giving him multiple chins. He liked to joke that he looked just like Aristide Briand.[55]

Shotwell was eager for the opportunity to correct what he saw as the mistakes of the past. After the group's first meeting on February 12, 1942, he sent a memorandum to Welles outlining the principles, functions, and shape of a new international organization.[56] The twenty-three-page document was sweeping in scope and organized around the "major interests of mankind: Security, welfare, justice, and provision for the advancement of culture." Security, of course, came first. Shotwell took direct aim at his old adversaries in the outlawry movement—Levinson, Borah, and Dewey— though he never mentioned them by name. He explained that those who had argued against collective security arrangements before the war had been proven wrong. It was finally time for "an international organization 'with teeth in it.'"[57] While not knowing precisely how to achieve peace, he went on, "we know at least some of the ways in which it cannot be achieved. We know that it is not enough to attempt to get rid of war by denunciation of its evils."[58]

Shotwell had the beginnings of a solution: write the Pact into a new treaty—and then build an enforcement structure up around it. Doing so would fulfill the promise made in 1928. It was this kind of enforcement structure, Shotwell explained, that "was in Briand's mind when he proposed the negotiations with the United States and in his final speech on the occasion of the signature in Paris when he said, 'We have proclaimed peace . . . now we must organize it.'"[59] Shotwell had good claim to know what was in Briand's mind, for he had written the first draft of Briand's proposal to Kellogg. Clearly, Shotwell had lost none of his brashness.

To show how it might be done, Shotwell produced a draft treaty. He distributed the first version, characterized as a proposed revision to the League Charter, to the team on August 21, 1942.[60] Shotwell was far from subtle about his effort to treat the Pact as a starting point. He placed the Pact at the start of his preliminary draft.[61] Article 1 repeated the Pact verbatim. Article 2 provided that "[t]he United Nations, in order to strengthen and safeguard the peace of nations as set forth in the General Pact for the Renunciation of war, agree to cooperate in the establishment of the necessary instrumentalities for its effective maintenance."[62] What followed was an outline of nearly every essential institutional component of the modern-day United Nations. Ten days later he circulated a more detailed draft, now entitled "Provisional Outline of International Organization."[63] This new draft interlaced proposed text with explanatory discussion. Often referred to in later documents as "Doc. 99," it would remain the touchstone for the team's deliberations. Indeed—though later historians would largely miss both Welles's and Shotwell's pivotal role—it would prove to be the first draft of what would become the United Nations Charter.*

The United Nations was a fundamental departure from the League of Nations. As under the League, there would be an International Court of Justice, which would help prevent "the violation of international legal obligations by force and violence."[64] But the organization would back up the peaceful resolution of disputes *with force*. It would secure the peace and provide "a permanent machinery for security and disarmament." Shotwell emphasized that "the ultimate problem of disarmament is the elimination of war by the substitution of other techniques for the settlement of international controversies."[65] He reemphasized that "[i]t was generally recognized that the weakness both of the Kellogg-Briand Pact and the League of Nations lay in the absence of an adequate organization of international police action." The new organization would have to fill this crucial gap. It would need the capacity not only to condemn illegal action, but the power to stop it.[66]

The other members of the team were wary of such naked reliance on the Peace Pact, worrying that "[i]t would be politically and psychologically unwise to attempt to revive an instrument which had given rise to much fallacious thinking about the problems of peace and was now generally discredited."[67] They wished to focus instead on the institutional structures missing from the Pact.

---

*As far as we are aware, no one has previously made the connection between Shotwell and the first draft of the United Nations Charter. The draft was not signed, but it was initialed "J.T.S.," which we believe stands for James Thomas Shotwell. Shotwell was the only person on the subcommittee with these initials. The ideas in the draft, moreover, embody the views expressed in a memorandum to Welles three weeks earlier with the same initials, this time accompanied by a cover letter from Shotwell. Letter from James T. Shotwell to Sumner Welles, July 30, 1942, box 192, folder 8 SWP FDRL; "Preliminary Memorandum on International Organization," July 28, 1942, box 192, folder 8 SWP FDRL.

Yet even those not enamored with the optics of repeating the Pact verbatim still considered it the starting point for the new organization. The team even went so far as to consider forcing every single state that was party to the Pact into involuntary and irrevocable membership in the new organization. As the minutes of an early meeting explained, the group "believed that the Kellogg Peace Pact, since it had not been renounced by any state, might be used as a basis for inaugurating automatic membership."[68] After considerable debate, the drafters decided to make membership voluntary instead and offer it, at least initially, only to those who had signed the "United Nations Declaration," which had incorporated the principles of the Peace Pact.[69] The United Nations would be a new and improved Pact, not a continuation of it.

By December, the subcommittee revised Shotwell's draft into a "Draft Constitution of International Organization."[70] The draft contained a foundational principle that would remain intact as the draft wound its way through the State Department, then the White House, and finally a series of international conferences: the prohibition on war.[71] The agreement was devoted to making that commitment as effective as possible.

Welles, however, would not remain to see it through. Three years earlier, on September 16, 1940, Welles traveled by train with the president and nearly the entire cabinet to Jasper, Alabama, to represent the Department of State at a funeral in place of Cordell Hull.[72] Weary, he began drinking in the dining car. Around 4 a.m., he staggered to his compartment and rang for a porter. John Stone, an African American veteran of the Pullman service, responded and later reported that Welles offered him money for "immoral acts." Stone refused and returned to the dining car, where he recounted the incident to his fellow porters. They responded to Welles's subsequent calls and reported "indirect" advances. Word reached the dining car manager and conductor, and, eventually, the president of the railway company, Ernest E. Norris.

In an unfortunate coincidence for Welles, Norris was good friends with State Department counselor R. Walton Moore—the man who had been passed over for undersecretary of state in favor of Welles. Moore, who was terminally ill, made plans to share the incriminating affidavits with the diplomat William Christian Bullitt, Jr., a determined opponent of

Welles's. A quarter century later, Bullitt's daughter would find the affidavits hidden in the floorboards of Bullitt's home, along with instructions that they be turned over after Moore's death to Bullitt "for his use."[73] Though he didn't hand the documents over until after he died, Moore arranged for Bullitt to view them and allowed him to take copious notes. Two years after the incident took place, incriminating evidence in hand, Bullitt pressed to have Welles sacked, enlisting Hull, who delighted in the opportunity to rid himself of his rival.

Roosevelt refused. Bullitt then committed an act of betrayal for which he would never be forgiven: He informed Senator Owen Brewster, a Republican opponent of Roosevelt's, who threatened to hold hearings on the matter—which would have destroyed Welles along with Roosevelt's political agenda. On September 30, 1943, Roosevelt reluctantly accepted Welles's resignation.

Bullitt would pay for his betrayal. Roosevelt encouraged him to run for mayor of Philadelphia, then secretly told Democratic leaders in the city to "Cut his throat." After his resounding defeat, Bullitt enlisted Hull to seek a diplomatic post for him. The president leaned back, paused, and then replied, "That's right, Cordell. What about Liberia? I hear that's available."[74]

Following Welles's departure, the Subcommittee on International Organization disbanded. Welles would no longer be a part of postwar planning and negotiations, but his handiwork was clear. When the foreign ministers agreed to establish a general peacekeeping organization "at the earliest practicable date,"[75] the United States was ready. Most of the members of the subcommittee reconvened to put together a final draft proposal.[76]

The subcommittee presented the proposal, dubbed a "Plan for the Establishment of an International Organization for the Maintenance of International Peace and Security,"[77] to the president in December 1943. After meeting with Hull and several members of the group at the White House in February 1944, he initialed the draft "OK FDR." The U.S. plan—the plan that Shotwell had crafted but would never be properly credited for, the plan that Welles had initiated and shepherded to conclusion but would never get to implement—was now official.[78]

"YOU REAP WHAT YOU HAVE SOWN"

On a blazing hot August day in 1944, the British, American, and Soviet delegates gathered at the Dumbarton Oaks mansion in the heart of the Georgetown neighborhood of Washington, D.C. The gate to the gardens adjacent to the mansion read *Quod Severis Metes*—"You reap what you have sown."

All three nations had submitted proposals, but the American one—a more detailed version of the Welles team's plan from December 1943—became the "basic frame of reference" for the conference.[79] A key agreement came early. The members decided that states would be prohibited from using force against one another. The new Charter would require "avoidance of the threat or use of force in any manner inconsistent with" the purposes of the organization.[80] The British representative, Sir Alexander Cadogan, explained that "in view of the uncertainty of the meaning of the word 'aggression,'" it was advisable to use "broader and more inclusive language" such as that proposed by the Americans.[81] The Chinese delegation later asked whether the agreement allowed states to use force unilaterally. The answer was no: "except in cases of self-defense, no unilateral use of force could be undertaken without the approval of the council."[82] There could be no doubt that the outlawry of war remained the law of the civilized world: All offensive uses of military force would be covered by the prohibition.

The next issue was how to enforce this prohibition. The basic structure of the organization proposed by the Americans—including a General Assembly, Executive Council (renamed the "Security Council"), and International Court of Justice—was accepted by the other delegations. But two issues proved intractable and, indeed, threatened to derail the entire project. The first was representation in the General Assembly. The parties agreed that each member of the United Nations would have one vote. But the Soviet ambassador, Andrei Gromyko, proposed that each of the sixteen republics of the Soviet Union be given individual membership.[83] Worried that if it leaked, the proposal would destroy domestic support for the international organization, the Americans took to referring to it as "the X matter."[84] Roosevelt sent an urgent telegram to Stalin, warning that "to raise this question at any stage before the final establishment and entry into its functions of the international organization would very definitely imperil the whole project." Stalin refused to budge.[85]

But there was a second, even more serious issue: Gromyko also insisted that the permanent members of the Council should each have an absolute veto over *all* matters—even over matters in which they were directly involved. The U.S. and U.K. maintained the opposite: Permanent members should not have a veto, especially not on matters in which they were directly involved. Leo Pasvolsky, speaking for the American contingent, barely contained his frustration. The American group felt "so confident that this country will not wish to use force on a unilateral basis," he declared, "that it is willing to recommend that the United States should put itself on the same plane as all other nations of the world in regard to the settling of disputes." Moreover, "if the United States were ever to conclude that it was not willing to listen to the Council in the event of a dispute in which it might be involved such a conclusion would be practically tantamount to a decision that the United States was ready to go to war with all the rest of the world."[86]

President Roosevelt invited Gromyko to an intimate one-on-one meeting early in the morning in the president's White House bedroom.[87] There, Roosevelt explained that it was a long-standing American understanding that parties to a dispute should not be involved in deciding it. He traced the development of "this . . . American concept of fair play back to the days of our founding fathers." The Soviet proposal that members of the Council be permitted to vote in cases in which they had an interest would never gain the support of the U.S. Senate.[88] Gromyko still would not move. Even an urgent telegram from the president to Stalin failed to produce any concessions.[89]

After two months of negotiations and almost three years of preparations, it seemed possible that the entire exercise had been for naught.[90] Edward Stettinius, who had replaced Welles as undersecretary of state, wrote in his diary, "This brings the whole conference to a climax. We are deadlocked . . . and the success of the whole undertaking lies in the balance on this one point."[91]

Three options remained: conclude the conference and declare the parties were unable to reach an agreement; publish the document they had already drafted containing all those matters on which they had agreed and reserve the issue of voting to a general conference of the United Nations; or, third, publish the document already drafted but plan another meeting of the Great Powers to address the voting issue ahead of any general conference. Everyone agreed the first would be a disaster. Gromyko ruled out the second. The Soviet government, he declared, would never agree to attend a general United Nations conference until an agreement had been reached with the other Great Powers on voting in the Council and the X matter.[92] "You can't have an international organization without us. We can't have one without you. And there has to be unanimity between us and the other powerful states. The moment this principle of unanimity breaks down there is war," he proclaimed.[93]

The delegates settled on the third approach. At the close of the conference, the delegates issued a draft of a proposed agreement on an international organization. That document contained nearly every element of what would become the United Nations Charter. But in the section that would have described the voting rules, the draft simply stated: "(NOTE— The question of voting procedure in the Security Council is still under consideration.)"[94]

NINE

OPERATION ARGONAUT

On January 22, 1945, just two days after delivering his fourth inaugural address, President Franklin Delano Roosevelt set off on a journey. Late in the evening, the president and his entourage began their trip by train from Washington. The president's private car, built for him after the start of the war, had bulletproof windows, armor-plated sides, and a reinforced concrete floor. When the train arrived in Newport News, Virginia, in the early morning hours, the Secret Service bundled the group on board the USS *Quincy* before daylight.[1]

At 8:30 a.m., the ship embarked on a four-thousand-mile ocean voyage from the East Coast of the United States to Malta, one that took the convoy through U-boat-infested waters. German submarines had been spotted by radar between Casablanca and Gibraltar. Planes followed the convoy throughout the trip, along with eight destroyers and nine cruisers, but they offered uncertain protection against the underwater menace that had devastated the British navy.

Dangerous and exhausting as the ocean trip was, it may have been the easiest part of the journey. From Malta, the U.S. team, followed by the British, flew seven grueling hours to Saki in Crimea. The aircraft that ferried the president was fitted with an elevator to allow him easier access. The plane had been so heavily guarded that the few who knew about it called it the "Sacred Cow." Six fighter planes accompanied the Sacred Cow to ward off enemy attacks. But the Germans were not the only concern. The president's men also worried about Soviet antiaircraft batteries, for the Soviets were known to "shoot first and identify later." [2]

The final leg of the journey was perhaps the least pleasant of all—eighty miles over rough and winding roads to the Livadia Palace, near the small town of Yalta, overlooking the Black Sea on the southern tip of Crimea.[3] Soviet troops guarded the entire way from Saki to Yalta. Many of them were young girls, their fathers and brothers having fallen in battle or still off fighting on the front.[4]

For anyone, the trip would have been a terrible risk. For a sitting wartime president—one whose "worn, wasted" appearance worried his advisers—it threatened to be a suicide mission.[5] Although the White House physician publicly celebrated the president's good health at the time of the election—proclaiming him "in excellent shape"—those close to him knew better.[6]

Roosevelt was no fool. He knew the risks. But he decided they were worth taking. Stalin had just turned the tide on the German onslaught. He agreed to meet and discuss a potential postwar peace, but he refused to leave the Soviet Union so long as his troops fought on the Eastern front.[7] If they were to finalize the arrangements for a new international organization, Roosevelt and Churchill would have to come to him. And Roosevelt was convinced that the meeting was necessary. As he put it to Stalin, "the three of us, and only the three of us, can find the solution to the still unresolved questions."[8] With his usual rhetorical flourish, Churchill dubbed the meeting "Operation Argonaut."[9]

Though he agreed to attend, Churchill bemoaned the choice of Yalta as the site of the conference, noting that "if we had spent ten years on research we could not have found a worse place."[10] His complaints were not unwarranted. The seas near Yalta were icebound at this time of year, necessitating the arduous journey from Malta. And while the lavish homes of the Russian elite appeared intact from afar, on closer inspection they were revealed to be burnt, roofless hulls, stripped by retreating German troops.

Stalin—dubbed "Uncle Joe" or "U.J." for short by Roosevelt and Churchill in their extensive correspondence before the conference— had demanded they meet at Yalta. In a telegram to Roosevelt, however, Churchill had declared the Black Sea port "out of the question."[11] To avoid meeting there, Churchill and Roosevelt had even considered encouraging Turkey to declare war on Germany so that Russian ships could more easily leave the Black Sea via the Turkish Straits to bring Stalin to meet them at Malta, Athens, or Cyprus.[12] But Stalin refused.[13]

Perhaps no spot in the world offered such a stark reminder of the costs of the wars Russia had fought over the past century. The ruin brought by the recent German occupation could be seen all around, but the scars of earlier wars ran deep. The ground had been consecrated again and again by Russian blood. In the mid-nineteenth century, an alliance of France, Britain, and the Ottoman Empire had wrested significant portions of the Crimean Peninsula from Russia, territory it would take a generation to regain. And during the Russian Revolution of 1917, Crimea repeatedly changed hands, each shift producing fresh slaughter.

The Soviet Union now stood on the brink of victory—but at a terrible cost. The number of military dead and missing would reach nearly nine million.[14] At least as many Soviet civilians died due to military activity or war-related famine and disease. U.S. and U.K. losses—awful as they were— paled in comparison. Both would estimate fatalities at just over 400,000 by war's end.[15] The location, then, served as a reminder to the American and British guests that the Allies could plan for peace only because of one country's incomparable sacrifices. But it served, too, as a reminder to Stalin of the perils of war—not only for his country, but for his government and, indeed, himself.

Having won the battle of wills over the conference's location, Stalin had faced the near-impossible task of preparing Yalta for the arrival of hundreds of visitors. The Soviets ruthlessly marshaled exhausted local workers and terrorized prisoners of war in a frenzied effort to prepare the palace for the historic meeting.[16] Despite these extraordinary efforts, discomforts abounded—chief among them an acute shortage of bathrooms and an abundance of bedbugs.[17] Two sanitary squads from the Americans were marshaled to spray DDT everywhere.[18] Churchill had his own solution: fend off the bugs with "an adequate supply of whiskey."[19]

The discomforts, however, presented trivial challenges compared with the vexing issues that brought them together. Still unresolved were the two most explosive issues at the Dumbarton Oaks conference: the X matter and the voting procedures for the Security Council.[20] Nor were the voting rules for the new international organization the only topics of concern. The war, after all, had not yet been won. At the first meeting, the discussion focused on fighting the war, not keeping the peace. After President Roosevelt opened the gathering by expressing his gratitude to Stalin for hosting,[21] the session focused on the recent Soviet offensives. The Soviets made clear their wish that the Allies speed the advance of troops on the Western Front, to release some of the pressure in the east.[22] Surrounded by the devastation the war had wrought on the Soviet Union, Roosevelt and Churchill agreed.

The imperatives of winning the war led Roosevelt to make concessions that the Americans would later regret. Roosevelt's chief strategic goal, aside from reaching an agreement on the new United Nations, was to gain a commitment from Stalin to enter the war against Japan.[23] Thus far the Soviets had avoided the Asian theater. Roosevelt feared that without Soviet support, the battle against Japan would drag on for months, if not years. The United States had made progress developing a nuclear bomb, but the weapon remained unproven. The American president was willing to pay a hefty price to obtain Soviet assistance in Japan, including cession of the Kuril Islands and portions of Manchuria and the southern half of Sakhalin Island lost by Russia to Japan in the 1904–1905 war.[24]

Stalin, meanwhile, worried about renewed German aggression. Indeed, he was determined to do everything to ensure that Germany would never again pose a threat to the Soviet Union. The United Nations was a piece—a crucial piece—of a broader plan: First, disable Germany. Carve it up into several zones of occupation (with as large an area as possible for the Soviets) and extract crippling reparations.[25] Second, create physical barriers along his country's western flank. Stalin demanded that the Allies hand over a portion of Poland. Since Poland had been the thoroughfare used by Germany to attack twice in thirty years, Stalin viewed these territorial concessions as "not only a question of honor for Russia, but one of life and death."[26]

Last was the United Nations. The Charter would draw the Great Powers into an ongoing alliance and reduce the chance that war would once again engulf his country or—worse—leave it isolated. For a country that did not have any stable alliances, such protection was invaluable. But an absolute veto on any action that body could take was also essential. Without it, Stalin could not be sure that the organization he was helping to create would not turn against him.[27] The Eastern shield could change into a Western sword.

The conference ranged back and forth across these topics, with each party jousting to obtain the upper hand, only to lose it the next day. They began on Sunday, February 4. After spending most of the morning and afternoon discussing plans for the war, conversation at dinner turned to the United Nations veto, though obliquely. The formal topic was the "voice of smaller powers in postwar peace organization." As reported in extensive minutes taken of the meetings, Stalin reiterated his position that it was "ridiculous to believe that Albania would have an equal voice with the three Great Powers who had won the war and were present at this dinner." He complained that "some of the liberated countries seemed to believe that the Great Powers had been forced to shed their blood in order to liberate them and that they were now scolding these Great Powers for failure to take into consideration the rights of these small powers." He would never agree to "having any action of any of the Great Powers submitted to the judgment of the small powers."[28]

Gromyko later wrote that while Roosevelt reacted to Stalin's remarks calmly during the conference, Churchill could not hide his irritation. His cigars gave him away: "He smoked far more of them when he was tense or excited. The number of his cigar stubs was in direct proportion to the stresses of the meeting."[29]

When Stalin finished speaking, Churchill replied that there was "no question of the small powers dictating to the big powers but that the great nations of the world should discharge their moral responsibility and leadership and should exercise their power with moderation and great respect for the rights of the smaller nations."³⁰ A member of the American delegation, Charles Bohlen—Roosevelt's interpreter at the meeting, who was also responsible for taking the minutes—added that the American people would never accept a deal that shortchanged the smaller states. In response, Andrei Vishinsky, later described by a British diplomat as a "cringing toadie only too anxious to obey His Master's Voice even before it had expressed his wishes,"³¹ barked that the "American people should learn to obey their leaders." Bohlen commented that he would "like to see him undertake to tell that to the American people." Vishinsky retorted that "he would be glad to do so."³²

After the president and Stalin retired for the evening, with little progress having been made, Churchill met with Anthony Eden, the British foreign minister, and Edward Stettinius, the American secretary of state. He admitted to them that he had come to believe that there was no choice but to fold on the veto. "[E]verything depended on the unity of the three Great Powers. Without that the world would be subjected to inestimable catastrophe and anything that preserved that unity would have his vote." Eden disagreed, arguing that the Allies would lose the support of the small nations, as well as the British people.³³ When Churchill left, Stettinius, Eden, Ambassador Averell Harriman, and Bohlen all agreed that no progress had been made on the crucial question of the veto. In fact, the issue had advanced but in the wrong direction: The British prime minister seemed to have flipped to the position of the Soviet general secretary. Eden worried that his boss simply did not understand the stakes of the question.³⁴

The next day's discussion turned to the postwar treatment of Germany, whose defeat appeared imminent. The three powers had earlier agreed that the country would be divided into zones of occupation, but much else remained unsettled—including the boundaries of the zones and the permanence of the divisions. Stalin referred repeatedly to the "dismemberment" of Germany, while Churchill and Roosevelt were careful to describe the occupation zones as merely "temporary."³⁵

Stalin was in little mood to compromise on the third day, when President Roosevelt proposed that they return to the matters left open at Dumbarton Oaks—the Security Council voting procedures, especially the veto, and the X matter. Roosevelt felt strongly, he said, that "all the nations of the world shared a common desire to see the elimination of war for at least fifty years."[36] To ensure this aim, they would have to resolve the question of voting in the Security Council. Roosevelt then turned the floor over to Stettinius to outline what the American delegation regarded as a compromise proposal to try to break the deadlock: Decisions of the Security Council that would authorize the use of force or impose sanctions would require seven votes out of eleven—the two-thirds majority that Stalin had advocated. In addition, the five permanent members—the Soviet Union, U.S., U.K., China, and France—could veto any substantive decision, but not mere procedural matters. In a face-saving move, for decisions of the Security Council that would not authorize the use of force or impose sanctions, the permanent members party to the dispute should refrain from exercising their vetoes—they should, as the draft put it, "abstain from voting."[37] Last, the permanent members could not prevent debate from occurring in the Security Council, even if they could prevent it from taking action.

Churchill voiced support for the proposal. Stalin did not reject the compromise, but he did not embrace it either. As Churchill later recounted, Stalin feared that although the three leaders were united now, in ten years they would no longer be in power. A new generation might forget what they had been through together. "The greatest danger," Stalin warned, "is conflict among ourselves." "Therefore," he counseled, "we must now think how to secure our unity in the future, and how to guarantee that the three Great Powers (and possibly China and France) will maintain a united front."[38] As long as the unity could be preserved, he argued, "there was little danger of the renewal of German aggression."[39]

After studying the proposal, Stalin decided that it gave him what he needed: the ability to prevent the Great Powers from using the machinery of the United Nations to take action against the Soviet Union. Two days after it was first brought to the group, Stalin agreed to the American compromise proposal.[40] Stalin, however, wanted something in return. Though he dropped his demand made at Dumbarton Oaks on the X matter, he still wanted three, or at least two, Soviet republics admitted into the General Assembly.[41] The republics of Ukraine, White Russia (today part of Belarus), and Lithuania had suffered more in the war than most states, he argued, and they deserved a voice in the new world organization that the blood of their people had made possible. On this claim Stalin had a point. Ukraine had lost 15 percent of its population, and Belarus almost one fifth—and not just fighters; everyone had suffered.[42] Eventually, the three leaders reached a compromise: None of the Soviet republics would be invited to the final United Nations Conference, but if Ukraine and White Russia were proposed by the Soviets for membership in the organization, the British and American representatives would support their admission.[43]

In the end, the agreement forged among the three leaders did not give either side all they wanted, but it gave them enough. The American delegation knew that the decision to allow the Soviets an absolute veto over most United Nations decisions would require the most explaining at home, even though the Charter gave the United States the identical power. As Welles later explained in his public defense of the Charter, the veto was the price paid for bringing the Soviets into the organization. "Can any objective observer . . . seriously maintain that in light of conditions as they existed in 1945 was it not far better to obtain a United Nations of which Russia would be a member from the outset . . . than to risk having no United Nations at all by refusing compromise?" Moreover, the compromise was not one-sided: The Soviets conceded that the veto would not preclude the Security Council's consideration of a dispute, even one involving a Great Power. "The compromise formula, therefore, made it possible for the Security Council to ventilate publicly all future controversies in which Russia or any other great power might be involved."[44] The compromise on the admission of Ukraine and Belarus (as the White Russia republic became known) was of little practical importance but was "psychologically wise," allowing the Soviet Union to join an organization in which it "could count upon only a small handful of thick and thin adherents" and was therefore likely to be outnumbered on nearly every matter of substance.[45]

AN END TO THE BEGINNING OF ALL WARS

At the close of the conference, the American delegation returned to the United States in mid-February 1945, confident that they had secured an agreement that would give rise to a United Nations organization. Roosevelt, already unwell, had been ravaged by the journey. Those who saw him noted how thin and fatigued he looked. Visiting him not long after his return, Treasury Secretary Henry Morgenthau reported, "I was terribly shocked when I saw him, and I found that he had aged terrifically and looked very haggard."[46]

But Roosevelt had plans. He told his wife that he intended to go to San Francisco in late April to be present at the final conference that would give birth to the new United Nations. He wanted her to come hear him speak and then join him on a trip to England, where Churchill had promised that the British people would give him "the greatest reception ever accorded to any human being since Lord Nelson made his triumphant return to London."[47]

But first, he needed a rest. He decided to retire to his cottage in Warm Springs, Georgia. It was the place he went when he wanted to get away from the rigors of Washington and the press of political demands. Though he rested, he was far from idle. Still a wartime president, he had visitors, answered letters, and wrote speeches. It was there that, on April 11, he penned a message for a radio address he was scheduled to deliver in a nationwide radio broadcast a few days later:

> The work, my friends, is peace, more than an end of this war—an end
> to the beginning of all wars, yes, an end, forever, to this impractical,
> unrealistic settlement of the differences between governments by the
> mass killing of peoples.[48]

He would never deliver these lines. The afternoon after he wrote them, he sat in the living room of his cottage, signing documents, pausing occasionally to talk with friends and the artist preparing a portrait of him. He put his hand to his head and slumped backward. Minutes later, he was dead of a massive cerebral hemorrhage.[49]

Eleanor Roosevelt, learning of his death, cabled her four sons—all on active service: "He did his job to the end as he would want you to do. Bless you all and all our love. Mother."

Later that month, the conference that Roosevelt had planned to attend opened in San Francisco. Representatives of fifty nations—all of whom had been allied with the U.S., U.K., and USSR, and had signed the United Nations Declaration during the war—were present.

James Shotwell was at the conference as well, representing the Carnegie Endowment, one of forty-two nongovernmental groups invited. Though Welles was not there, his ideas were in evidence. Not only had he germinated the document that came to be the United Nations Charter, but his 1944 book, *The Time for Decision*, which sold a half-million copies, educated the American public on the goals of the organization and helped gain easy adoption of the United Nations Charter by the U.S. Senate.[50] He also joined the American Broadcasting Company as "Advisor on the Peace," providing expert on-air commentary and overseeing the "Sumner Welles Peace Forum," a series of four radio broadcasts in which he and other experts discussed the San Francisco Conference.[51] His onetime nemesis Cordell Hull was also absent from the conference, too ill to attend. Hull would later receive the 1945 Nobel Peace Prize for his contributions to the new organization.[52]

Newly sworn-in President Harry Truman opened the conference with an address, delivered by cable: "We who have lived through the torture and the tragedy of two world conflicts must realize the magnitude of the problem before us. . . . We still have a choice between the alternatives: The continuation of international chaos, or the establishment of a world organization for the enforcement of peace." Those gathered in San Francisco, he declared, had one goal: "We must provide the machinery which will make future peace not only possible but certain."[53]

As Truman's words make clear, the conference was far from a mere formality. All but the Great Powers had yet to approve the terms of the agreement. And to reach a consensus, several amendments would need to be made to the text. Indeed, at one point it appeared that plans for the organization might again break down over the voting procedure in the Security Council. As predicted, the smaller states rebelled over the inequities. There was, moreover, considerable debate over the precise meaning of the voting compromise at Yalta—for example, whether the deal indeed allowed the permanent members to keep issues off the agenda or only to prohibit enforcement action.[54] Nonetheless, the text that would develop, and that would win the votes of all fifty states, was identical in its broad outlines and even in most particulars to that which emerged from Yalta.

Perhaps the most striking point about the conference, given the long history of the role of war in international law, is that not a single state voiced disagreement with the prohibition on the "threat or use of force"— embodied in Article 2(4) of the new United Nations Charter. The reason for the silence was that the matter had been settled. After all, nearly every state in attendance had ratified the Peace Pact and pledged in the United Nations Declaration to "come to the abandonment of the use of force."

In the twenty-two-volume record of the San Francisco conference containing well over ten thousand pages, a scant handful are devoted to Article 2(4). These few pages are, nonetheless, revealing. Some of the smaller states hoped that the Great Powers would promise to respond to illegal uses of force—transforming the Charter from a nonaggression pact into a global mutual defense treaty. A proposal by New Zealand, for example, would have provided that "All members of the Organization undertake collectively to resist every act of aggression against any member."[55] The delegate from Panama, too, proposed an amendment that would impose a positive obligation on states to respond to aggression.[56] The American delegates maintained that the existing language, with minor phrasing modifications, was sufficient. After all, "the larger nations too were faced with the threat of extinction if aggression were not resisted."[57] The proposals, moreover, were "reminiscent of certain features of the Covenant which had made that document unacceptable to the United States."[58]

The message was clear: The United States would never agree to a text that would obligate it to play world policeman—or that would permit the Soviets, British, Chinese, and the French to do the same. The proposal that all members agree to resist aggression against any member would "mean the use of European forces in the Western Hemisphere and forces from the Americas in many parts of the world, which would not be acceptable to many nations"—including the United States.[59] On paper it might seem to strengthen the prohibition on war, but in practice it would doom it. As Welles later put it, such a guarantee of world peace would lead to its own destruction: The police power approach necessarily assumed "the right to carve up the world into four zones of great power influence." "How long," he asked, "would it have been before the most powerful of them would have sought to assert that right without interference from its partners?"[60] Yes, failing to respond to illegal uses of force was a danger. But allowing states to take up arms whenever they perceived a violation of international prohibitions on force was more dangerous still.

The opponents of mandatory enforcement prevailed.[61] There would be no affirmative obligation to respond to aggression; that would be left to states acting in self-defense and to the Security Council, which could only take action collectively.[62]

On June 26, 1945, all fifty nations signed the United Nations Charter. The United Nations organization was now born, but the war was not yet over. Germany had surrendered during the conference—on May 8, 1945— but Japan continued to fight. Faithful to his pledge at Yalta, Stalin massed more than a million troops along the Soviet border with Manchuria. The Soviet invasion, launched on August 9, 1945, coincided with America dropping the second nuclear bomb on Nagasaki, a few days after having detonated the first over Hiroshima. Japan ceased fighting roughly a week later and surrendered on September 2. The war had come to an end.[63]

From the start of the Second World War, the Allies had made clear that they fought for more than their own safety, more than the rights of those conquered, more than the defeat of Hitler and his allies and their vile ideas. They fought, as Churchill, Roosevelt, and Welles had put it in the 1941 Atlantic Charter, for the principle that "all the nations of the world . . . must come to the abandonment of the use of force." When the Allies won the war, they did more than defeat Germany, Japan, and Italy. They defeated the Old World Order.

The United Nations was the embodiment of the New World Order. Made as war still raged, it was forged out of difficult choices. But these were not ill-considered choices. Those who made them knew the stakes, understood the costs, and did the best they could to bring "an end to the beginning of all wars." A great American president risked his life to make the agreement possible, and the agreement is, fundamentally, an American document—conceived by Americans, negotiated by Americans, and made possible by Americans. Like the American Constitution, the United

Nations Charter was idealistic and pragmatic at once. It was meant not to solve all possible international problems but to solve a particular one—the scourge of interstate war.

The prohibition on war was not limited to the Charter. The Allies supervised the drafting of new constitutions for each of the Axis powers and enshrined the prohibition on war into each state's own governing documents. Article 26 of Germany's Basic Law provided that "Acts tending to and undertaken with intent to disturb the peaceful relations between nations, especially to prepare for a war of aggression, shall be unconstitutional. They shall be made a criminal offense."[64] Article 9 of Japan's new constitution provided that "the Japanese people forever renounce war as a sovereign right of the nation and the threat or use of force as a means of settling international disputes."[65] Article 11 of the Italian constitution provided that Italy "rejects war as an instrument of aggression against the freedom of other peoples and as a means for settling international disputes."[66]

The world had begun to meet Briand's call not only to proclaim the peace, but to organize it. Organizing the peace required more, however, than reiterating the prohibition on war, more even than creating a global institution that could collectively respond to threats to international peace and security. If waging aggressive war had indeed been illegal since 1928, then it had to be possible to hold those who had waged it responsible.

TEN

FRIEND AND ENEMY

Nuremberg, Germany, April 3, 1947, 3:45 in the afternoon. A fifty-eight-year-old law professor waited in Room 166 at the Palace of Justice for the interrogation to begin.[1] Short but distinguished looking, the professor was clean-cut with chiseled features and expressive eyes, his symmetrical face marred only by a protruding lipoma—a benign, fatty tumor—on the left side of his forehead.

According to a report compiled by the Allies, the professor is Carl Schmitt, Germany's leading political scientist and one of the world's greatest political writers, "a man of near-genius rating."[2] Schmitt is not only "one of those rare scholars who combined learning with imagination," but one who can use this "book knowledge with a realistic sense of what is possible in politics."[3] Despite these immense talents, or perhaps because of them, the report recommended his prosecution as a war criminal. "Carl Schmitt is one of the intellectual props of the Hitler state who has actively prepared and promoted the acts of aggression committed by the latter."[4] Another report, recommending the confiscation of Schmitt's library, concluded: "I hardly know of any individual person who has contributed more for the defense of the Nazi regime than Carl Schmitt."[5]

Schmitt was convinced that there was a conspiracy against him, and he was sure who its leaders were. "I have fallen into the hands of this mighty American empire," he wrote in his diary. "I was curious about my new masters. But I have until this very day, five long years, not yet once spoken with an American, but only with German Jews."[6] His persecutors were the *Juden* and the Americans their pawns. "A peculiar master of the world, these poor modern Yankees, with their ancient Jews."[7]

Schmitt's interrogator that afternoon was, indeed, a Jew. His name was Robert Kempner, a German Jewish lawyer who served in the early 1930s as the chief counsel for the Prussian police. Kempner was a tough, and somewhat unscrupulous, prosecutor. He was not above threatening to turn uncooperative witnesses over to the Soviets. His colleagues did not like him. They found him uncouth and difficult.[8]

Kempner knew Schmitt, or at least knew of him. In 1932, Schmitt was a key participant in a case that caused Kempner to lose his job and then flee Germany. But Kempner, who returned to prosecute Nazi war criminals, was not there to talk about his past. He wanted to talk about the Peace Pact.

Kempner began the interrogation by informing the prisoner that he had the right to remain silent.[9] Schmitt said that he was happy to cooperate but wanted to know the charge. "I will tell you what I am interested in," Kempner answered, "your participation, direct or indirect, in the planning of wars of aggression."[10]

"Planning wars of aggression is a new and very broad concept," Schmitt responded.[11]

Kempner suspected that Schmitt was playing dumb. "I take it for granted that, as a professor of public law, you know exactly what a war of aggression is."[12]

He certainly did. For the professor was the world expert on the subject. He had been writing about it longer than any other scholar. He was also the main opponent of this "new and very broad concept." For years, Schmitt had been warning that criminalizing wars of aggression would lead to disaster, not only for Germany, but for the world. When Friedrich Flick, the wealthy industrialist, feared he would be prosecuted by the Allies in 1945, he retained Schmitt to write an expert legal opinion on the crime of aggression. That opinion likely formed the basis for the Nazi defense at the Nuremberg tribunal held at the same complex in which Schmitt was now being detained.

Schmitt lost that case. And he was in danger of losing again, this time with his own life on the line.

FRIENDS AND ENEMIES

Twenty years before sitting in a Nuremberg interrogation room, Schmitt sat in a lecture hall at the Hochschule für Politik (Graduate School for Politics) in Berlin.[13] The lecturer was James Shotwell, who had been invited as part of a program launched by the German government to restore relations with American universities. The publicized lecture, held on March 1, 1927, celebrated this new era of goodwill between the former enemies. The chief justice of the German Supreme Court presided. Also in attendance were the chancellor of the Reich, Wilhem Marx; the prime minister of Prussia, Otto Braun; members of his cabinet; and the heads of the War Ministry and General Staff, clad in full military regalia bearing side arms.[14]

By 1927, Shotwell had lost the fight in the League of Nations over the Geneva Protocol. But from this defeat he learned an important lesson: start by outlawing war; worry about enforcement later. So he used his lecture to lay out the basic proposal of the outlawry movement. "[W]e are at the greatest turning point in human history," Shotwell declared. "The intelligence which has won so many triumphs over our material environment is now at grips with the human problem." The only solution to this most human of problems—the problem of war—is to ensure that "all war but defense be outlawed."[15] Three weeks later, Shotwell would make the same proposal in Paris to Aristide Briand, who would embrace it, making it the foundation of his proposed treaty between France and the United States.

Shotwell's lecture unnerved Schmitt. He regarded the speech as "one of the most important for Germany's destiny" and wanted to respond.[16] On May 10, 1927, as Shotwell's outlawry proposal was gaining momentum among the Great Powers, Schmitt delivered one of the most famous lectures of the twentieth century. In his counteroffensive, entitled "The Concept of the Political," he warned Germany of impending disaster. Outlawry of war was a trick and the world was falling for it.

Schmitt denounced outlawry in the same building in which Shotwell had proposed it. It is absurd, Schmitt claimed in his lecture at the Hochschule für Politik, for states to renounce war. As nice as it sounded—and it was dangerous in no small part because it sounded so nice—outlawry is an impossibility. To think that war can be outlawed is to misunderstand politics. Politics presupposes the very possibility of war. A state that outlaws war outlaws itself.

This claim sounds just like the sort of crude militarism one would expect from a Nazi. But Schmitt was not a Nazi at this point and, although he would later join the party, he was no ideologue of National Socialism. His objection was not founded in a glorification of violence, but rather on a dark, but deep, vision of politics.

According to Schmitt, the world of politics (or as he calls it, following the German, "the Political") is not defined by its subject. Political disputes can break out over any issue. What defines the Political is its intensity: The more intense the struggle, the more political the dispute. "The political," Schmitt wrote, "is the most intense and extreme antagonism."[17]

Because political disputes are intense, they are dangerous. The most extreme disputes, and hence the most dangerous, are those organized according to what Schmitt called the "friend-enemy" distinction.[18] Friends and enemies are engaged in a struggle of survival: Friends protect their friends, but they try to kill their enemies.

Schmitt emphasized that friends need not hate their enemies. Nor need they regard them as evil. What makes the enemy *the enemy* is simply that conflicts with them are so great as to become existential: For whatever reason, the enemy threatens one's way of life and must be eliminated. "The friend, enemy and combat concepts receive their real meaning precisely because they refer to the real possibility of physical killing."[19] Of course, people usually hate their enemies. They tend to think they are immoral, sinful, or ugly. Enemies use these moral and aesthetic evaluations to increase antagonism and make the task of killing one another that much easier.[20]

According to Schmitt, the defining task of the state is to regulate political disputes, to ensure that intense conflicts, the ones that threaten the community's way of life, are resolved. *In extremis*, states distinguish friend from enemy and deploy the most political of all weapons—war. "The state as the decisive political entity possesses an enormous power: the possibility of waging war and thereby publicly disposing of the lives of men."[21] Indeed, the right of war endows the state with an almost God-like power: "the right to demand from its own members the readiness to die and unhesitatingly to kill enemies."[22]

Schmitt was no militarist.[23] He denied that the purpose of the state is to wage war. "War is neither the aim nor the purpose nor even the very content of politics."[24] But states must always be prepared to go to war, because there are some conflicts—conflicts that threaten the state's very existence—that only war can resolve. Thus, the awful prospect of homicide looms over all political action. It must serve as an option—a drastic option, but still an option.[25]

Because the function of the state is to regulate political conflicts, Schmitt concluded, it is impossible for the state to outlaw war. If a state were to try, it would prevent itself from distinguishing friend from enemy. That would end politics and, in turn, the state as well, *for the state is by definition the entity that resolves intense conflicts by any means necessary*. Schmitt explained: "A people which exists in the sphere of the political cannot in case of need renounce the right to determine by itself the friend-and-enemy distinction. . . . Were this distinction to vanish then political life would vanish altogether."[26] In Schmitt's view, Shotwell was not proposing that Germany outlaw war—Shotwell was asking Germany, and every other state that listened to him, to commit suicide.

"HE WHO FIGHTS WITH MONSTERS"

All fiction, they say, is autobiography. It is less of a cliché, though no less true, that philosophical writing is also autobiographical. Philosophers have pretensions of discovering abstract and timeless truths about the human condition, but they cannot help but draw on their own personal and parochial experiences. Schmitt's theory of politics is typical: Intense conflict defined his life and distinguishing between friend and foe was his principal obsession—one critical to his own survival through the intense turmoil that marked the turn of the century.

Schmitt was born on July 11, 1888, in Plettenberg, a small German town nestled in the lush mountain forests of Westphalia.[27] His family was Catholic, with strong ties to the Church. Three of his great-uncles were priests. When he was young, Carl's mother expected him to enter the clergy as well.[28] His relatives were on the front lines of the *Kulturkampf*, Bismarck's long battle to wrest power from the Catholic Church. The bitterness of the struggle seared the Schmitt collective memory and, though Bismarck would eventually surrender, the family never lost its siege mentality.

Carl was raised in a predominantly Protestant town, one whose sectarian divide was so palpable and raw that violence often erupted between rival denominations. Plettenberg may have been predominantly Protestant, but it was a town in the Catholic Rhineland, which was in turn a region of the Protestant Reich. Germany itself was sandwiched between Catholic France and Orthodox Russia. Schmitt therefore spent his formative years at the center of a series of confessional Matryoshka dolls. For him, the wars of religion that ravaged Germany did not end in 1648. They simply went underground, threatening to erupt as though the Peace of Westphalia had never been concluded.

Carl's humble origins also alienated him from the ruling, upper-class Protestant elite. Rejecting his father's advice to enter a trade, he matriculated at the prestigious Humboldt University in Berlin, an unusual move for a young man of his background.[29] He excelled in school, but he never felt accepted. "I was an obscure young man of modest origins," he later wrote, "standing wholly in the dark, I looked from the darkness into a brightly lit room."[30] In 1915, he married the flamboyant Pavla Dorotić, a Viennese dancer who claimed descent from Croatian nobility. Schmitt seems to have been taken as much by her alleged pedigree as by her beauty. Schmitt began using her maiden name in his publications, signing his articles as "Carl Schmitt-Dorotić."[31]

Cari, as he called her, was the incarnation of friend *and* enemy. The two were in love, but her behavior toward him was erratic and often abusive.

Schmitt could never quite figure out whose side she was on. Carl later discovered, to his great sorrow, that Cari was an impostor, an older woman of common descent, who had fabricated her life story. After seven miserable years of marriage, a period during which he "felt like a madman in Hell," Schmitt was granted a divorce.[32]

Schmitt saw himself as a member of a beleaguered minority, a lower-class Catholic among the ruling Protestant elite. But he was also a German, and like his fellow countrymen, he was living through the humiliation and immiseration of Germany's defeat in the First World War. Outside a small few in the military high command, no one expected to lose the war. The country's defeat was a shock, leading many to conclude that the country had been undermined from within.

Fueling the Germans' anger was the punitive peace settlement. According to the galling "Versailles Diktat," Germany had to relinquish the territory it had won from Russia at Brest-Litovsk in 1918, the land it had conquered from France in the Franco-Prussian War in 1871, and all of its overseas colonies. It committed to pay crushing financial reparations. It accepted responsibility for the *entire* war. The Allies indicted the Kaiser, forcing him to remain in exile in the Netherlands. They capped the German army at 100,000 men, prohibited rearmament, and mandated that the Rhineland be demilitarized. When Germany later refused to pay reparations, the French reinvaded the Ruhr valley, precipitating a crisis that culminated in the hyperinflation of 1923. In this economic nightmare, prices climbed several times a day, day after day.[33] Life savings vanished in a matter of hours and paper money was so worthless that it was burned for heat. In November 1923, the German government was forced to print 100 trillion mark notes, though at the prevailing exchange rate, each bill was worth little more than $20 U.S.[34]

Even once the economy calmed down, normalcy did not return. Germany was riven by deep, sometimes uncontrollable, conflict. In 1928, no fewer than forty-one parties contested the election.[35] Political violence was rampant. Parties had their own paramilitaries that fought each other in the streets after they lost in the Reichstag. The Nazis had two of these groups: the Sturmabteilung (SA), the brown-shirted storm troopers, and the Schutzstaffel (SS), the black-shirted security personnel. Germans not only felt besieged, but they were unsure who was besieging them. Was the enemy Bolshevism, liberalism, America, France, "the cursed Republic," the Catholic Church, trade unions, or, perhaps, the Jews?

Schmitt, however, denied that his theory of politics was parochial, the understandable reaction of a German living through tumultuous times. War, he maintained, was the ever-present subtext of politics, a permanent feature of the human condition. "Nothing can escape this logical conclusion of the political," he claimed.[36] Pacifism might seem an exception but, Schmitt argued, this is an illusion. For if pacifists felt strongly about pacifism—if they were really committed to ending war—*then they would go to war to stop war*.[37]

Indeed, when the second edition of Schmitt's lecture was published in 1932, the Peace Pact had been signed. Schmitt used the occasion to call the Pact out as a dangerous sham. Contrary to its packaging, he argued, the Pact did not outlaw war. Rather, it created a new set of enemies, namely, those who would violate the Pact. "The solemn declaration of outlawing war does not abolish the friend-enemy distinction, but, on the contrary, opens new possibilities by giving an international *hostis* [enemy] declaration new content and new vigor."[38]

If outlawing war is impossible, Schmitt asked, why did the world try to do it? Schmitt's answer was simple: Outlawry is a weapon. The proponents of the Pact were not selflessly motivated by a pious desire to stop killing. They designed it as a trap to neutralize their adversaries. "That wars are waged in the name of humanity . . . has an especially intensive political meaning. When a state fights its political enemy in the name of humanity, it is not a war for the sake of humanity, but a war wherein a particular state seeks to usurp a universal concept against its military opponent."[39] Outlawry, therefore, is worse than absurd—it is dishonest, hypocritical, sneaky. It is a Trojan Horse built by Germany's enemies for world domination. "[W]hoever invokes humanity," he sneered, in equal parts disgust and admiration, "wants to cheat."[40]

Properly understood, he explained, the Peace Pact would not end war: It would create a new kind of war, one between those who use military force and those wielding other forms of influence, such as economic or cultural power. Wars will still be waged, but they won't be called "wars" anymore—they will be cloaked in the terminology of criminal justice and camouflaged by the idioms of humanitarian intervention: "executions, sanctions, punitive expeditions, pacifications, protection of treaties, international police, and measures to assure peace."[41] And "enemies" will continue to exist, but they won't be called by that name either—an enemy will be branded "a disturber of peace" and "an outlaw of humanity."[42]

Worse still, when wars are cast as police actions against criminals, all restraints will fall away. Those who fight wars in the name of "humanity" will regard the enemy as less than human. Dehumanized, the enemy will be denied the legal protections that all humans deserve. Even the victors will be transformed by outlawry. The wars of the future will become holy wars, crusades, savage battles of annihilation fought to the bitter end, with terrible destruction left in their wake. This worry was best expressed by Schmitt's predecessor, the German philosopher Friedrich Nietzsche: "He who fights with monsters should look to it that he himself does not become a monster."[43]

STRESEMANN'S PLAN

Schmitt played the role of Cassandra, prophet of doom, foretelling the impending destruction of his country. And like Cassandra, Schmitt was cursed to be ignored. For Germany not only signed the Pact, but rushed to do so. When Frank Kellogg circulated his draft outlawry proposal to the Great Powers in April 1928, Gustav Stresemann convinced the German cabinet to sign on. The German foreign minister announced his country's willingness to join the Pact that very day, thereby becoming the first nation to join the United States and France.[44] When the Peace Pact was signed, Stresemann sat at the center table in the Salle de L'Horloge next to Briand and Kellogg.

Stresemann was no pacifist. He was an ardent nationalist and monarchist. Taking a hard line in the First World War, Stresemann urged Germany to conquer lands in the east and west and wage unrestricted U-boat warfare against the United States. He stuck by the high command until the very end, only to be shattered by the news of its abrupt capitulation.[45] But the shocking conclusion to the war convinced him that Germany could not compete militarily with the other world powers. Trade, not war, was the way to restore Germany's rightful place in the world. His country's best option was global economic engagement, forming strong financial connections with the United States and trade relations with the United Kingdom.

For Germany, signing the Pact was a calculated overture, signaling to the United States its rejection of militarism and commitment to economic cooperation. Stresemann understood his country's near-total dependence on the new superpower. Given its large trade deficit, American loans were all that was keeping the German economy afloat. Stresemann also hoped that the United States would use its influence with the Allies to reduce the war reparations imposed at Versailles. In Stresemann's plan, the two issues were linked: The United States would continue to loan money to Germany only if it could protect Germany's ability to repay these loans; but Germany could only repay its loans if the United States could convince France and Britain to reduce the intense burden of reparations.

Indeed, the invitation to Shotwell to deliver a lecture in Berlin was part of Germany's rapprochement with the United States.[46] Stresemann did not attend Shotwell's lecture—he was attending a session of the League of Nations at the time—but they did meet when Shotwell traveled through Geneva on his way to meet Briand in Paris. They had a pleasant chat. Outlawry did not come up. "We just talked nonsense and had a jolly time together," Shotwell reported.[47] Outlawry did not come up because Shotwell did not want it to: He feared that Stresemann would accept his proposal, thereby dissuading the Americans from signing on. Shotwell knew that the United States would never follow Germany's lead. To succeed, it would have to be the other way around.[48]

Stresemann was able to continue his conciliatory approach toward the United States because the strategy had been working. In 1924, the American banker John Dawes convinced the Europeans to lower the reparations amount demanded from Germany.[49] With the Dawes Plan in place, American banks were keen to loan money to German industries. Economic conditions improved dramatically. Under Stresemann's leadership, the back of hyperinflation was broken. The unemployment rate also fell, dropping from 18 percent in 1926 to 8.6 percent in 1928, better than Britain's rate of 10.8 percent.[50] During the federal elections of May 1928, the Nazi party made a disastrous showing, pulling a barely detectable 2.6 percent of the vote and electing only twelve delegates to the Reichstag (though two of the newly elected delegates were Joseph Goebbels and Hermann Göring). Sales of *Mein Kampf* were so weak that the publisher advised Hitler to hold off publishing his second book, written largely as an attack on Stresemann's internationalism.[51]

The Germany that signed the Peace Pact, therefore, was not the same Germany that would just a few years later plunge Europe back into war. Germany in 1928 was a constitutional democracy—the "Weimar Republic"—basking in the glow of its "Golden Years," an era of stability and prosperity that produced one of the greatest outpourings of creative genius the world has ever seen. Weimar created Expressionism in film, Art Deco in design, Bauhaus in architecture, modernism in literature, quantum mechanics in physics, logical positivism in philosophy, Pilates in exercise. It has long been a great mystery how a culture that produced an Albert Einstein, Max Planck, Bertholt Brecht, Walter Gropius, Walter Benjamin, Thomas Mann, and Fritz Lang could also spawn a Heinrich Himmler, Hermann Göring, Rudolf Hess, and Joseph Goebbels. But in August 1928, this was not yet a riddle and optimism was still possible.

The Golden Years of Weimar were soon over. The finale was ugly. For Stresemann's plan of economic entanglement with the United States, though undoubtedly shrewd, was also a gamble. If the American economy happened to go down, it would take the German economy down even further—which it proceeded to do. When the U.S. stock market crashed on October 29, 1929, American banks called in their loans. Without foreign capital, Germany could neither finance its economic recovery nor make reparation payments. Bank runs led to the collapse of the German financial system. Whether any politician could have saved Germany from the ensuing calamity is doubtful, but if anyone could, it would have been Stresemann. The foreign minister for seven consecutive administrations, he was the only political figure with the stature to stabilize the country when the hurricane hit. But the fifty-one-year-old Stresemann suffered a series of strokes and died on October 3, 1929, just three weeks before Black Tuesday, when the financial props holding Germany up gave way. With the economy in free fall, Hitler had a disaster he could exploit, and with Stresemann gone, there was no one who could stop him.

THE DECLINE OF WEIMAR AND
THE RISE OF SCHMITT

For most of the 1920s, Schmitt taught public law at the University of Bonn, located in the capital city of the Catholic Rhineland. In 1926, he married a Serbian woman, Duška Todorović, who was the translator in the divorce proceedings with his first wife, Cari.[52] Though she was fifteen years his junior, their marriage appears to have been more successful than his first.

During this period, Schmitt published a highly regarded study of dictatorships and several incisive critiques of parliamentary democracies.[53] Later, he wrote a monumental study of the Weimar Constitution, as well as *The Concept of the Political*, his broadside against Shotwell.[54]

On the strength of this scholarship, Schmitt was offered a chair in constitutional law at the Handelshochschule, the School of Business Administration in Berlin, in 1927. Schmitt accepted the offer. He had grown tired of the sleepy town of Bonn and wanted to experience the "joys of the big city."[55] He was also seeking a fresh start. Schmitt could not convince the Catholic Church to recognize the dissolution of his marriage to Cari, and when he married Duška, he was excommunicated. A cloud of scandal hovered over the newlyweds in the provincial city.

Years later, Schmitt would claim that his move to Berlin was motivated by scholarship, writing that he could "become familiar with the object of my discipline, namely, the state, at close range."[56] If so, he got his wish. For a year after arriving in Germany's capital, the global financial crisis hit. As the government struggled to cope with unemployment levels not seen since the hyperinflation crisis, he witnessed firsthand a constitutional system under extreme pressure.

In response to severe budget shortfalls, the conservative cabinet proposed an austerity budget. It slashed unemployment insurance, halted social works projects, and increased taxes. Because the measures were so painful and so evenly spread, the Reichstag would not approve the government's budget. Both sides dug in, leading to a political standstill.

Several members of the government saw in Schmitt a legal scholar who could justify their attempt to end the crisis and pass their budget. In his academic writings, Schmitt had extolled the virtues of dictatorship during emergencies to reestablish normalcy. Indeed, he argued, Article 48 of the Weimar Constitution conferred dictatorial powers on the president of the Reich to restore "public security and order."[57] Schmitt was adamant that courts could not play this stabilizing role because, unlike the president, judges were not elected and could not be trusted to act for the German people. And though members of parliament were elected, Schmitt argued that parliaments are irrational institutions. Governed by fragile coalitions and prone to bitter infighting, parliaments are ineffective and unreliable in times of crisis.[58]

In September 1930, the government commissioned Schmitt to write a *Gutachten*—an expert legal opinion—legitimating the government's plan to seize power from the Reichstag. In this *Gutachten*, Schmitt not only argued that the president, Paul von Hindenburg, had the power to enact the budget as an emergency measure under Article 48 of the Weimar Constitution, but also to dissolve the Reichstag if it rejected his assertion of emergency power.[59] Schmitt went even further. He claimed that, under Article 48, the president could implement the government's budget in the interim before new elections were held. In the months between the dissolution of the old Reichstag and the election of a new one, Hindenburg would in effect be a dictator, acting as the sole, supreme legislative power in the Reich.[60]

The selection of Schmitt was no fluke. He lobbied hard for the assignment. In addition to sending the president's chief of staff his writings that supported the government's position, Schmitt also befriended several confidants of Colonel Kurt von Schleicher.[61] Schleicher was the true power behind the government, a charming, witty, and gifted tactician.[62] He recognized Schmitt's political value and commissioned the *Gutachten*.

With Schmitt's legal justification in hand, Schleicher set the plan in motion. When the government's budget failed in the Reichstag, Hindenburg enacted it under Article 48. When the Reichstag rejected this exercise of emergency powers, Hindenburg dissolved the parliament, called for new elections, and reenacted the budget, again under Article 48.

Schleicher thought that the German people wanted strong leadership and would reward this bold assertion of power. This turned out to be a titanic miscalculation. The middle class blamed the government for the worsening economy and punished it at the ballot box. On September 14,

1930, the Nazi party achieved a spectacular victory, increasing its representation from 12 to 107.[63] Hitler had risen from the political grave, leading the second largest party in the Reichstag. Schmitt had shown Schleicher how to pick the lock of the Weimar Constitution. The barbarians flooded through the open gates.

THE PRUSSIAN COUP

The Nazis were committed to the destruction of the republic and, therefore, had no intention of cooperating with the government. Following Schmitt's legal advice, the president bypassed the gridlocked Reichstag and governed by emergency decree. What Schmitt had advocated as a temporary expedient to break a parliamentary deadlock became the new normal. The political system was permanently suspended in a state of exception. Freed from parliamentary control, the government doubled down on its austerity program, which only served to dampen demand further and drive unemployment to an astounding 40 percent of the entire labor force by the beginning of 1932.[64]

As the misery deepened, Nazi power grew. In April of 1932, the Nazis garnered 36.3 percent of the vote in the Prussian elections, hugely outperforming their dismal 1.8 percent of 1928. More impressive and ominous still, the SA had grown to over 400,000 storm troopers, four times larger than the German army.

As the Reich government hemorrhaged support to the Nazis from the right, Schleicher sought to neutralize the opposition from the left. Prussia was the last stronghold of the socialists. Schleicher decided to oust them. This massive power grab would come to be known as the *Preussenschlag*— in English, the "strike against Prussia," or in semi-French, the "Prussian Coup." Schleicher planned to justify the coup in the way he justified everything: by invoking the emergency powers of Article 48. The socialist government of Prussia, he would claim, was no longer able to control the political violence raging between the Nazis and the communists.

On July 20, 1932, Hindenburg declared a state of emergency and placed the control of the Prussian government in the hands of the new chancellor, the ultraconservative aristocrat Franz von Papen. As the new

Reich commissar for Prussia, Papen ordered the imperial army into the streets of Berlin. Hopelessly outgunned, the Prussian police stood down. The socialists decided not to call out their own paramilitary group to fight back. They called their lawyers instead, who promptly filed a lawsuit against the Reich government to have the coup declared unconstitutional.

The argument for the case, *Prussia v. Reich*, took place in Leipzig in October 1932. Schleicher asked Schmitt to represent the government in the legal proceedings, a task for which he received a large legal fee and an audience with Hindenburg.[65] After six long, tense days of argument involving the best legal minds in Germany, the court issued a split decision.[66] Though the Reich could appoint Papen as commissar to run Prussia temporarily, it was unconstitutional to deprive the Prussian government the right to rule the state permanently. The Reich would have to restore Prussian rule. Schmitt, upset that he did not score a complete victory, raged against the "triumphant cries of the Jewish press."[67]

No one was happy with the result.[68] The left understood that even temporary control meant permanent damage. Goebbels later joked that Papen had purged the Prussian government of socialists so thoroughly that when the Nazis took power, there was nothing left for them to do.[69] And the left never forgave Schmitt for his role in its defeat. For those like Franz Neumann, Schmitt was its antihero. Neumann, a Jewish labor lawyer who worked with the socialists in Prussia, had been friends with Schmitt. For several years, he attended Schmitt's seminars at the Handelshochschule.[70] When Göring assumed command of Prussia, he had Neumann arrested, though Neumann managed to escape from prison to the United States. While teaching at the New School for Social Research, a haven for German Jewish émigrés in New York City, Neumann wrote the leading analysis of the Nazi State entitled *Behemoth*, published in 1941. Schmitt is depicted in the book as one of the main villains, the "ideologist" of the conservative attacks on Weimar, whose theory was a "sham" and "deliberate maneuver" to end parliamentary democracy.[71] With the Prussian coup, Neumann concluded, "the last hope of resistance against the National Socialists seemed to have vanished."[72]

The Weimar Republic was falling apart. So, it seems, was Schmitt. Racked by anxiety and depression, he drank to excess, kept mistresses, and frequented prostitutes. He was plagued by nightmares and wild mood swings.[73]

Schmitt's prominence did lead to a new job prospect: a professorship at the University of Cologne.[74] The chair was a step up, but Schmitt was not sure he wanted to leave Berlin. He decided to seek the position after learning that the only way to get a better position in Berlin was first to go to Cologne. But to get to Cologne, he would have to overcome a giant hurdle first.

SCHMITT V. KELSEN

In 1934, Roscoe Pound, the dean of the Harvard Law School, hailed him as "unquestionably the leading jurist of the time. His disciples are devoted and full of enthusiasm in every land. His ideas are discussed in all languages."[75] Two years later, Pound invited him to Harvard's 300th anniversary celebration, where he received an honorary degree, along with the psychoanalyst Carl Jung and philosopher Rudolf Carnap.[76] Sixty-five years later, the judge and novelist Bernhard Schlink concurred with Pound's judgment, going so far as to award him the title of "Best Lawyer of the Millennium" in *The New York Times*.[77]

Pound and Schlink were not talking about Carl Schmitt. They were praising his enemy: Hans Kelsen. Kelsen represented everything that Schmitt hated. But he was the most important professor at Cologne and Schmitt needed his vote.

Hans Kelsen was born in 1881 into a Jewish, middle-class family with deep roots in the Galician shtetl.[78] His German-speaking father grew up in Prague, but moved his family to Vienna when Hans was three, by which point they were secular and determined to assimilate into Viennese culture. Hans was sent to the state gymnasium to receive a traditional humanistic education. Philosophy fascinated him, but he chose law for the sake of practicality, becoming an assistant professor at the University of Vienna in 1911. Kelsen was a staunch agnostic, but nevertheless converted to Catholicism and, a few years later, to Protestantism. Though cosmopolitan, fin de siècle Vienna was also a hotbed of anti-Semitism. Being Jewish was a professional liability.

Kelsen did not belong to a party, believing that scholars should be above partisan politics. Nevertheless, he had strong sympathies for the Social Democrats and was an ardent supporter of parliamentary, liberal democracies. He also participated in many progressive causes, including the women's rights movement. A friend of Sigmund Freud's, Kelsen also attended the "Wednesday Group" where the basic outlines of psychoanalytical theory were debated and developed.[79]

During the war, Kelsen served as the legal adviser to the Austrian minister of defense, specializing in international law and the laws of war. When the war ended, the new leader of Austria tapped Kelsen to help draft the Austrian Constitution and then appointed him to the Constitutional Court he designed. Kelsen served for a decade until he was removed over a controversy involving the validity of marriage dispensations. The Austrian Catholic party attacked Kelsen for his support of the rights of couples to remarry.

Soon after, the faculty board of Cologne, headed by the mayor of Cologne (and future chancellor of West Germany), Konrad Adenauer, invited Kelsen to join its law school.[80] By then, Kelsen had become the target of anti-Semitic attacks in Vienna and was eager to leave Austria. He accepted the offer at Cologne.

The following year, Kelsen wrote a scathing review of Schmitt's book on dictatorships.[81] Schmitt's assertion that the Reich president could be trusted with dictatorial powers was absurd, he argued. The president, after all, was a member of a political party and elected by its supporters. Why would anyone expect a politician to be impartial in a crisis? To the contrary, only courts could be trusted to be fair precisely because they were not elected to office. Kelsen predicted that Schmitt's excessive reliance on Article 48 of the Weimar Constitution would ultimately spell the end of parliamentary democracy.[82]

But when Schmitt's appointment came up in the Cologne faculty in May of 1932, Kelsen voted in favor.[83] Kelsen could not deny Schmitt's brilliance. Fairness, he felt, dictated that he support the appointment.

As the dean of the law faculty, Kelsen's job was to negotiate the offer with Schmitt. The two met in Kelsen's office on October 22. Hans Mayer, the German literary scholar who was writing his dissertation with Kelsen at the time, later described the meeting: "[Schmitt] paid a visit to Kelsen in Cologne, campaigned to work with him, and offered—despite the obvious scholarly differences—the best of friendship between the two great figures of a mediocre faculty: Hans Kelsen and Carl Schmitt. Kelsen was a good fellow, and wanted to believe what he heard."[84] The negotiations, however, must have been awkward: Not only were Schmitt and Kelsen on opposite sides of the Prussian coup case, but Schmitt insisted that his salary and benefits be no lower than Kelsen's.[85]

Kelsen soldiered on with his decanal responsibilities, and Schmitt accepted the appointment. Kelsen even wrote Schmitt a letter expressing his "great joy" at hearing Schmitt's decision.[86] The joy would not last.

TAKEOVER

On December 3, 1932, Franz von Papen was dismissed as chancellor of the German government and Schleicher took his place. Schmitt probably expected that the elevation of his advisee would increase his own influence, but it had the opposite effect. Facing the task of governing a country on the verge of collapse, Schleicher concluded that he could no longer rule by emergency decree alone and resolved to form a coalition government after all. Schmitt was now dispensable and, indeed, was dispensed with.[87]

When Schleicher failed to cobble together a majority coalition, he convinced Hindenburg to appoint Hitler as the next chancellor. In his final, and fatal, error, Schleicher thought he could box Hitler in by stacking the cabinet with non-Nazis. Hitler was handed the chancellorship, effective January 30, 1933. Undaunted by being outnumbered, he requested that Hermann Göring be made Papen's assistant in administering the Prussian government. Göring—the brilliant, charismatic sociopath—began demolishing the Weimar Republic from within.

Göring's first act as Reich commissar to the Prussian Interior Ministry was to fire twenty-two out of twenty-three police chiefs and replace them with SA officers. In his speech to the reconstituted police force, Göring explained the new system: "In the future, there will be one man with the power and responsibility in Prussia and that man is myself. . . . I know of only two types of people: those with us and those against us."[88] Göring impressed Schmitt when they met in April. Schmitt liked his dynamism and decisiveness, saying that he was "maybe the right type for these times."[89] By contrast, "the stupid, ludicrous Hitler" disgusted him.[90] When he saw Hitler give a speech for the first time, Schmitt described the famed beer hall agitator as "a raging bull in the ring."[91]

Having fired the police chiefs, Göring went after the prosecutors. Robert Kempner, the chief of the legal division, had been a fierce opponent of the Nazis and advocated for their prosecution as members of a criminal terrorist organization. He should have been fired for his political unreliability, but an old friend transferred him to another ministry, where he checked the levels of Berlin's waterways. He held on until September, when he was finally dismissed.[92]

On April 7, Hitler dismantled the civil service. The Law for the Restoration of the Profession of Civil Servants decreed that civil servants not of Aryan descent or who were politically unreliable were to be fired. Because university professors in Germany were classified as civil servants, many Jewish, Marxist, and socialist professors lost their tenure. Law departments were badly affected. By 1937, 22 percent of all law professors were fired. The sub-discipline of international law fared even worse, with 34 percent of all faculty members dismissed.[93]

When the Education Ministry asked the University of Cologne for a list of law professors to be dismissed, there was only one name on it: Hans Kelsen. Kelsen discovered the decision from the newspaper after returning from a lecture tour in Sweden.[94] The law dean who replaced him was outraged by the dismissal and composed a long petition of protest. The petition pointed out that Kelsen had never been politically active, served in the war as a legal adviser, and was a decorated military officer. Kelsen's removal would constitute an enormous loss for the university and would damage Germany's international reputation.[95] Every single member of the faculty signed the petition but one: Carl Schmitt.

According to Hans Mayer, Schmitt was the culprit behind Kelsen's dismissal. "At the beginning of the Spring Semester" Schmitt showed up in Cologne, and "the first thing he did was demanded the immediate dismissal of the Jew and Marxist Hans Kelsen. Which was done."[96] Whether or not Mayer's report is accurate, Schmitt went out of his way to support the expulsions. "The new regulations concerning civil servants, doctors and lawyers purge public life of non-Aryan foreign elements," Schmitt wrote in the Nazi paper of Cologne. "We are once again learning to discriminate. Above all, we are learning to discriminate between friend and foe."[97]

In hindsight, and at the risk of blaming the victim, it is baffling that Kelsen trusted Schmitt. After all, no one fit Schmitt's definition of the enemy—"the other, the stranger . . . existentially something different and alien"—better than Kelsen.[98] He was an assimilated Jew, a pretend Protestant (formerly a pretend Catholic), liberal parliamentarian democrat with strong socialist sympathies, stalwart believer in courts as guardians of constitutions, fierce critic of Schmitt's proposals, and the more prominent scholar to boot. Nor was Schmitt's problematic personality a secret. Adenauer warned the faculty that Schmitt was a "difficult character who could destroy harmonious relations among colleagues on the faculty."[99] Kelsen knew of these admonitions—and he knew Schmitt's work as well as anyone—but he had relished the thought of having a worthy intellectual rival on the faculty.[100] Kelsen not only fit Schmitt's definition of the enemy, but his caricature of the liberal: someone incapable of discriminating friend from foe.

Unsurprisingly, the petition did not engage the sympathies of the new personnel in the Education Ministry. On September 11, Kelsen was notified of his involuntary retirement, effective January 1, 1934. In the new game of academic musical chairs, Hermann Jahrreiss, a young international law professor from Leipzig, took Kelsen's place.

New opportunities would also open for Schmitt. This obscure man of modest origins was finally poised to step out of the dark and enter the brightly lit room.

THEORIST FOR THE THIRD REICH

In a candid interview to the foreign press in 1938, Adolf Hitler expressed his attitude toward intellectuals. "Unfortunately, one needs them. Otherwise, one might—I don't know—wipe them out or something. But, unfortunately, one needs them."[101]

When Hitler came to power on January 30, 1933, Schmitt had to decide whether to be one of those intellectuals that the new regime needed. He held back for several months, unsure. Schmitt was not a Nazi sympathizer. He had been in Schleicher's camp and fought hard to prevent the Nazis from gaining power. As late as July of 1932, Schmitt was on record as stating that voting for the Nazis was "acting foolishly" and described the party as an "ideologically and politically immature movement."[102]

Schmitt soon realized that his past opposition to the Nazi party made collaboration all the more imperative. The universities were being purged of politically unreliable professors. He would be one of them unless he proved otherwise. Schmitt also thought that he could influence the direction of the regime, acting as a conservative counterweight to the "politically immature" movement. Thus, on April 27, 1933, he stood in a long queue outside the Cologne offices of the National Socialist Party and became its 2,098,860th member.[103]

Fear undoubtedly figured into Schmitt's decision to collaborate. By nature, Schmitt was an anxious person.[104] But one did not have to be paranoid to fear the Nazis. Schmitt's university job was at risk, but so was his wife, Duška. As a Serbian, she was not considered an Aryan and was therefore vulnerable to the new legalized racism. Schmitt could have resigned his position. To do so, though, would have meant losing his pension as well as his job, for under German law, civil servants who resigned their posts were not entitled to retirement benefits.[105]

While Schmitt had much to lose, he also had much to gain. The Nazis were willing not only to forgive past indiscretions, but also to reward intellectuals whose prestige they could exploit. Once Schmitt struck his Faustian bargain, the perks followed.

On July 31, Göring appointed Schmitt a member of the Staatsrat, a council to advise him on matters of state. The council had no formal power and stopped meeting after 1936. The position, however, did come with a large honorarium, guaranteed for life, a privilege that, Göring decreed, could not be waived. It was a telling sign of Schmitt's prodigious insecurity that he regarded this corrupt sinecure as the greatest honor of his career and, until 1945, signed his letters as "Carl Schmitt, Staatsrat."[106]

The University of Berlin offered Schmitt a chair in public law, perhaps the most prestigious legal academic posting in Germany. The position had been created especially for him, given his friendship with Hans Frank, the minister of Bavaria and Hitler's personal legal adviser.[107] The Academy of German Law, the new Nazi legal organization, awarded Schmitt a seat on its governing board, as well as the directorship of its academic branch.

The quid, of course, came with a quo. To fulfill his part of the deal, Schmitt began penning explicit *apologia* for the regime. Notable was his justification of a legally dubious execution—the beheading of Marinus van der Lubbe. Van der Lubbe, a dimwitted Dutch anarchist, set fire to the Reichstag in 1933. Göring wanted the death penalty imposed, but the law did not provide for it. A new law therefore was promptly passed—the so-called *Lex Lubbe*—which retroactively rendered political arson a capital offense. Schmitt wrote a strong defense of this ex post facto legislation.[108]

Unfortunately for Schmitt, his success also elicited jealousy among his rivals, and they began a vicious campaign to bring him down. They pointed out that Schmitt was critical of the Nazis before they came to power. He had many Jewish friends and students. He was a Catholic. There was no evidence of Nazi ideology—no anti-Semitism or racism—in his pre-1933 writings.

Because these attacks were accurate—even Hannah Arendt, the Jewish author of *The Origins of Totalitarianism*, later conceded that Schmitt was not a good Nazi—he decided to double down on his support for the regime.[109] In his most infamous work, Schmitt defended the legality of the Night of Long Knives, the bloody purge of June 30, 1934, when Hitler ordered the murders of hundreds of his political opponents. One of these victims was Kurt von Schleicher. On that night, the SS burst into Schleicher's home and gunned him down. When his wife discovered his bleeding body, she was shot as well. Given his past associations with Schleicher, Schmitt feared the same fate. Since no jurist would defend the assassinations, Schmitt saw his opening. Relying on his theory of dictatorship and the right of the dictator to violate the law to save it, he lent his considerable prestige as a scholar to Hitler and wrote these words that will live in legal infamy: "The Führer protects the law from its worst abuse when in the moment of danger he, by his domain as Führer and as the supreme judicial authority, directly creates law."[110]

Schmitt was a man stuck in moral quicksand: The more he struggled, the deeper he sank. In truth, Schmitt was his own worst enemy. His anxiety and ambition fed off each other, trapping him in a vicious spiral of sticks and carrots. Fear led to collaboration; collaboration led to perks; perks led to jealousy; and jealousy led to yet more fear.

The mounting terror crescendoed in farce. In 1936, Schmitt organized a conference on "The Jewish Spirit in German Law," whose aim was to ferret out Jewish influence from German jurisprudence. As part of this intellectual pogrom, Schmitt called for bibliographies of Jewish authors to be compiled and their books segregated in a special part in the library—the "Judaica" section—where they would not infect German minds.[111] He also recommended a revision of scholarly practice: Henceforth, Jewish authors must be cited as "Jews." This was only fair, he noted, because the Jewish scholars did not cite German scholars. "I only need to remind you of the audacity of the Vienna School of the Jew Kelsen who only quoted each other with the opinion of others ignored, for us Germans an incomprehensible cruelty and impudence."[112] Kelsen and his followers' crime appears to have been that they did not footnote Schmitt enough. He then proceeded to call all Jews "parasites" because they can only mimic the thought patterns of better nations. Schmitt concluded his talk by quoting Hitler's *Mein Kampf.* "'While fighting the Jew,' our Führer once said, 'I do the Lord's work.'" When the proceedings were published, Schmitt sent a copy to Himmler, adding that the legal profession still had more purifying to do.[113]

Schmitt discovered, however, that he could not outcrazy the Nazis. Nazis distrusted intellectuals, Arendt once observed, for no other reason than they were not charlatans.[114] Attacks on Schmitt's loyalty were published in the SS paper, *Das Schwarze Korps* (the Black Corps). He feared for his life. The attacks were finally halted by Göring, who did not contest the allegations, but refused to allow the SS to assail his Staatsrat.[115]

Schmitt had learned a painful lesson. Being a Nazi may be bad, but being a halfhearted one is worse. Failed Nazis have few friends and many enemies. Indeed, in a breathtaking display of self-pity, he claimed that the true victims of the Nazis were those, like him, with party "membership numbers over two million."[116] *Everyone* despised their opportunism and celebrated their defeat.

Schmitt did not realize that his fall had given him one last chance to save himself. It was only 1936 and Hitler's tyranny was still confined to Germany. Schmitt had done nothing to associate himself with Hitler's foreign policy. Yet.

THE END OF NEUTRALITY

The 4th Annual Conference of the Academy of German Law began on Saturday, April 23, 1937, in Munich. Hans Frank, the academy's president, opened the conference with Konstantin von Neurath, Germany's foreign minister. The next day, the attendees toured the construction site of the "House of German Justice," which was to be the academy's home and Frank's headquarters. The building, a superb example of fascist architecture, is a large, symmetrical fortress. It radiates power and unity. Frank described it as the "National Socialist ideal set in stone."[117]

On Friday, at the close of the conference, Schmitt delivered a report entitled "The Turn to the Discriminating Concept of War." He aimed to summarize recent changes occurring in international law, beginning with Japan's invasion of Manchuria in 1931. The world was becoming more violent and the rules regulating this violence were changing as well. "[O]ld orders are unravelling," he warned.[118]

Schmitt reported that French and English lawyers were beginning to discriminate between just and unjust wars. States that waged wars deemed just were being subject to favorable treatment, whereas states that waged wars deemed unjust were being penalized through economic sanctions and other discriminatory treatment. Neutrality was fading.

Schmitt focused on the League of Nations' attempt to impose sanctions on Italy for its invasion of Ethiopia. He called this action "pathognomic," namely, a symptom so indicative of a disease that a definitive diagnosis can be made. The disease was the outlawry of war. The willingness to impose sanctions showed that war was no longer being regarded as a sovereign prerogative. Aggressive war now illegal, bystanders were no longer required to remain neutral. Because Italy was acting unjustly, members of the League claimed a new right to punish it.

Schmitt had an uncanny ability to spot the enemy and identified him in the report. His name was Hersch Lauterpacht, a professor of international law at the London School of Economics. Lauterpacht was not English, but an *Ostjude*—an Eastern European Jew—who had studied with Kelsen in Vienna.[119] Indeed, Lauterpacht considered Kelsen among his heroes and kept his picture on the wall of his study, alongside one of Arnold McNair, his mentor at the LSE, and an engraving of Grotius.[120] Schmitt might even have known about this relationship: He mentioned in his report that Lauterpacht was a native of Galicia, Kelsen's ancestral home.

McNair selected Lauterpacht for the prestigious task of revising the premier treatise on international law of its day, Lassa Oppenheim's *International Law*. In the 1935 edition, Lauterpacht added twenty pages on the Peace Pact. In the preface, he justified this major revision by saying that the Pact had "effected a fundamental change in the system of International Law."[121] In particular, Lauterpacht claimed, the old principle of neutrality had to be abandoned. Under the Pact, "the outbreak of war is no longer an event concerning the belligerent alone."[122] Rather, it is the concern of the entire world. "The guilty belligerents, by breaking the [Pact], violate the rights of all other signatories, who, by way of reprisals, may choose to subject him to measures of discrimination, for instance . . . by actively prohibiting some or all exports into his territory."[123] In essence, Lauterpacht was granting legal permission to those not part of the League, such as the United States, to impose economic sanctions on nations deemed to be aggressors. Soon he would give the same advice to the United States in a much more direct and explicit form.

Schmitt's prediction was coming true: The Pact was a revolutionary document and the rules were changing right under Germany's nose. This revolution presented two distinct dangers, Schmitt cautioned. The first was the peril of legal uncertainty. Different states were playing by different rules. Some accepted the legality of war, while others did not: "war and yet no war at the same time; anarchy; and chaos in international law."[124] The second danger was more treacherous: further movement away from the Might is Right principle and toward the discriminatory concept of war. Ever the prophet of doom, Schmitt forewarned of an eventual union between the League and the Pact, the creation of a worldwide organization dedicated to the outlawry of war. Such an organization would not rid the world of war, of course. It would be a secret weapon for global domination.

Any attempt "to turn the League of Nations into an even more 'effective' organization," Schmitt predicted, would be "one that gears itself more towards the event of war."[125] The result would be disastrous, not only for this organization's enemies—who would be treated as subhumans not entitled to the protections usually granted to "enemies" in war—but for all of humanity, because the war would be fought in the name of humanity and thus would show no restraint. It would be a return to hygienic war.[126]

GROSSRAUM

A war of hygiene was indeed imminent, though not the one Schmitt predicted. Five days after Schmitt delivered his report, Hitler called a secret meeting of his top advisers. The audience stunned, Hitler announced his policy of *Lebensraum* (literally, "Living Space"). Germany was simply not large enough, Hitler said—"[t]he German racial community . . . constituted a tightly packed racial core," describing his countrymen as though they were tinned sardines.[127] Germany had to expand. Their first steps would be to take Austria and Czechoslovakia and, with Germany's eastern flank protected, France would be next.

Lebensraum itself was not a secret. Hitler could not have been clearer about his intentions in *Mein Kampf.* "National Socialists must hold unflinchingly to our aim in foreign policy, namely, *to secure for the German people the land and soil to which they are entitled on this earth.*"[128] Nor was he coy about where Germany would get most of this land. "If we speak of soil in Europe today, we can primarily have in mind only *Russia* and her vassal border states."[129] It was not the policy itself, but its timing, that surprised his advisers. They worried that Germany was not yet prepared for these wars of expansion.

Hitler had a starkly different vision for Germany than did Stresemann. Instead of integration into the global economy, Hitler planned to use war in order to accumulate as much territory as possible. *Lebensraum* was based on a pre-modern, almost feudal, conception of economics: the wealth of nations as determined by area of farmland rather than volume of trade. But Hitler's plan was built on a crackpot racial theory as well. On his demented worldview, the German people were entitled to Eastern lands because they were superior to Slavs. Just as humans used animals for their own purposes, Aryans have conquered inferior races to achieve their cultural greatness.

Though clearly an anti-Semite, Schmitt did not subscribe to the Nazi version of "scientific racism." He did not think that Jews belong to a lower life form that must be enslaved, exiled, or eradicated. When Hitler began to execute his plan—annexing Austria and conquering Czechoslovakia—Schmitt scrambled to justify, or at least describe, Hitler's new aggressive foreign policy in his own terms. At a speech given at the University of Kiel on April 1, 1939, he set out a new alternative: the theory of the *Grossraum*—literally, "Great Space."

The inspiration for Schmitt's *Grossraum* theory was the Monroe Doctrine. Just as the Americans had prevented European nations from intervening in the Western Hemisphere, Germany had the legal right to exclude intruders from its own part of the world. Central Europe was Germany's "Great Space," its sphere of influence protected from outside interference. Schmitt not only co-opted an American doctrine for Germany's use, but sought the moral upper hand by recasting the emerging Western alliance as the new "Holy Alliance" and Germany as the savior of weaker states. Schmitt was also careful to describe the *Grossraum* as a political doctrine, not a racial one: It asserted the right of a Great Power to protect its friends against their common enemies.

Schmitt's speech on the *Grossraum* and the new "German Monroe Doctrine" was reported in the British press. The *Daily Mail*, in fine tabloid style, commented not only on his proposal, but on his appearance. "Herr Hitler's 'key' man in this policy is Professor Carl Schmitt, middle-aged and handsome, who is the leading international lawyer in Germany."[130] Word had gotten back to Hitler as well, who liked Schmitt's idea—so much that he claimed it for himself.

Hitler trotted out "his" idea in the Reichstag speech on April 28, 1939, responding to FDR's letter seeking assurances that Germany would seek no more territory in Europe. Hitler rhetorically asked the American president how he would feel if Germany asked for the same assurances. "In this event Mr. Roosevelt would, I must admit, have every right to refer to the Monroe Doctrine and to decline to comply with such a request as an interference in the internal affairs of the American Continent." Hitler was simply asserting the same right for his country. "We Germans support a similar doctrine for Europe—and, above all, for the territory and interests of the Greater German Reich." The next day, Hans Frank called Schmitt on the phone and advised him to remain silent about the idea's true provenance, explaining that "the Führer prided himself on his originality."[131]

Hitler used Schmitt's idea again when Sumner Welles, the not-yet-famous undersecretary of state, visited Germany the next year on a fact-finding mission.[132] Hitler was wary of Welles—he referred to him as "the cunning fox"—and instructed his advisers that "as far as possible Mr. Sumner Welles be allowed to do the talking."[133] He also drew up a talking points memo. His advisers were to say that "[j]ust as on the basis of the Monroe Doctrine the United States would firmly reject any interference by European governments in Mexican affairs, for example, Germany regards the Eastern European area as her sphere of interest."[134]

Göring had nicknamed Joachim von Ribbentrop "Germany's number one parrot." The foreign minister's meeting with Welles on March 1, 1940, demonstrated why. As Welles later recounted, Ribbentrop "received me at the door, glacially, and without the semblance of a smile or a word of greeting."[135] After Welles asked whether there was any chance for a lasting peace, Ribbentrop proceeded to launch into a two-hour monologue. "The Minister, who is a good looking man of some fifty years with notably haggard features and grey hair, sat with his arms extended on the sides of his chair and his eyes continuously closed. He evidently envisioned himself as the Delphic Oracle."[136] More likely, he had his eyes shut because he was reciting Hitler's instructions from memory. Ribbentrop parroted over and over that "Germany must have her 'Monroe Doctrine' in Central Europe."[137]

Ribbentrop was lecturing the wrong person. In his scholarly study on the Dominican Republic Welles had authored during his exile from government following his divorce, Welles had argued that the United States "should keep in our own back yard and stop claiming rights for ourselves that we denied to other sovereign States," as *The New York Times* later summarized it.[138] Drawing on his extensive diplomatic experience in Latin America, he had also helped conceive Roosevelt's Good Neighbor Policy, which was effectively a rejection of a muscular Monroe Doctrine.[139]

Once Ribbentrop finished speaking, Welles explained that "the Minister was laboring under a misapprehension as to the nature of that policy."[140] Though the United States may have used the Monroe Doctrine as an instrument of political control in the past, it no longer views it in this way now. "At this moment, I was glad to say, a new relationship existed in the Western Hemisphere."[141]

Hitler deployed Schmitt's Monroe Doctrine idea the next day when he met Welles, and he repeated it in other venues as well.[142] Schmitt had regained his influence. But, as always, success brought vulnerability. The attacks on Schmitt resumed. Unwilling to go through another ordeal, Schmitt withdrew to his study and refrained from commenting publicly on matters of contemporary concern. He would not resurface until May 1945.

ELEVEN

"GOD SAVE US FROM PROFESSORS!"

Dismissed from Cologne in 1933, Kelsen moved to Geneva, where he managed to secure a teaching position at its Graduate Institute. But in 1936 he decided to return to his birthplace, Prague, accepting a chair in international law at the German University. He left his wife and two daughters in Switzerland because he knew the move was risky. Fascism was on the rise in Czechoslovakia, but Kelsen believed that he could help shore up the progressive defenses in the last holdout of democracy in the region.[1]

Kelsen was a tiny man, standing five feet two and a half inches, and of slight build. Bespectacled, balding, and middle-aged, he looked like exactly what he was—an Austrian law professor, almost straight out of Central Casting. His physical bravery was bolstered by an almost naive optimism in the power of reason. Kelsen believed that giving lectures on international law at a university would counteract the irrational forces of militant nationalism.

Predictably, Kelsen's plan went poorly from the start.[2] His inaugural lecture on October 22, 1936, was attended by a large group of students—too large in fact. Most of them, it turns out, were not there to hear the great man speak. They were there to prevent others from hearing him speak. When Kelsen began his lecture, the majority of the crowd stood up and left. The few who remained were beaten and dragged from the room. As a result of this debacle, the Education Ministry shut the university down for three weeks. When it reopened, Kelsen needed police protection. He gave up his quixotic mission at the beginning of 1938 and returned to Geneva.

But Kelsen could not outrun European fascism. When its escalation in Geneva threatened to shutter the Graduate Institute, Kelsen began his quest to find a permanent position in the United States. His many abject letters to Roscoe Pound, dean of Harvard Law School, reveal his desperation. In 1938, he wrote that "the development of political events in this unhappy Europe has now—for the third time—resulted in much suffering for me."[3] After pleading with Pound to write to schools and institutions on his behalf, his note ends with an apology: "As I know how busy you are, it is not easy for me to ask so much from you."[4]

Pound spent the next several years heroically writing to law schools, foundations, and libraries all over the country on Kelsen's behalf. Unfortunately, nothing materialized. The president of Harvard, James Conant, informed Pound that the university had no money for Kelsen, though its budgetary problems did not prevent the Government Department from hiring Heinrich Brüning, the former chancellor of Weimar, as a tenured professor the same year.[5] Other universities complained of budgetary shortfalls due to declining wartime enrollments or hiring policies that gave preference to American candidates.[6] Pound did manage to create temporary employment for Kelsen during the academic years 1940–1942 through the Oliver Wendell Holmes Lectureship at the Harvard Law School. But when the two-year stint ended, Kelsen was unemployed once again.

"THE FORK-KNIFE BUSINESS"

Having left Vienna much earlier than his teacher, Hersch Lauterpacht fared far better. Though barely able to speak a word of English when he stepped off the boat at the British seaport of Grimsby in 1923, Lauterpacht's career progressed so quickly that he was elected to the Whewell Chair in International Law at Cambridge University in 1937. When the war broke out, the Carnegie Endowment offered Lauterpacht a fellowship to lecture on international law throughout the United States.

Carnegie had set up a grueling schedule for Lauterpacht in the fall of 1940, one that took him over six thousand miles to fifteen universities in two months. His letters to his wife are filled with complaints about his health, the weather, lack of money, the discomfort of train travel, and "the fork and knife business," the mystifying American practice of cutting food with both knife and fork, placing the knife down, and transferring the fork to the right hand before putting the cut food in one's mouth.[7] By the end of this exhausting ordeal, he began to think that his efforts would not amount to anything. "All this, of course, is sheer waste of time and energy."[8]

But the time had not been wasted. In the course of traveling the country and debating questions of neutrality with American isolationists, he honed his arguments and developed a sharper picture of how the Peace Pact had changed the rules of international law. This maturation would be invaluable when he called on the attorney general of the United States, Robert Jackson, at the end of December. At their meeting, Jackson asked Lauterpacht for legal advice on the international law of neutrality. The president had pledged to the Allies that the United States would provide "all assistance short of war." But many international lawyers maintained that supplying war matériel to Britain would be a violation of American neutrality and hence an act of war under international law. Jackson told Lauterpacht that he did not simply want a narrow, technical legal justification for what would become the Lend-Lease Act. "What is wanted is a philosophy, in terms of international law, of our policy of all aid to the Allies short of war."[9]

Holing himself up in a Washington hotel room for nearly two weeks, Lauterpacht wrote Jackson a long memo on neutrality. He had argued in his 1935 revision of *Oppenheim's International Law* that the Pact had altered international law. But he was now ready to take the next step. By legally prohibiting war as a method for enforcing rights, the Pact legally permitted neutral states to discriminate between aggressors and victims. "The effect of the [Pact] was to render unlawful wars undertaken in violation of its provisions," he wrote. "In consequence, the [Pact] destroyed the historical and juridical foundations of the doctrine of neutrality conceived as an attitude of absolute impartiality."[10]

Jackson used Lauterpacht's memo as the basis for his celebrated speech in front of the Inter-American Bar Association in Havana on March 27, 1941, in which he claimed that the Pact legally authorized the Lend-Lease Act. In fact, he simply cut-and-pasted the main paragraphs straight out of Lauterpacht's memo. But Jackson did more than parrot Lauterpacht's memo. With the apparent zeal of a convert, he concluded his speech with a stirring call to use the Pact as the foundation for a new world order. "The principle that war as an instrument of national policy is outlawed must be the starting point in any plan of international reconstruction. And one of the promising directions for legal development is to supply whatever we may of sanction to make renunciation of war a living principle of our society."[11]

In an account composed more than a decade later, Jackson recounted that this view of the Pact was shared by the president and his inner circle. The Peace Pact, he reported, "left no vestige of legal right for [a state] to resort to a war of aggression. From the beginning, Roosevelt, Hull, Welles, Stimson and I had been in agreement that Hitler's war . . . was an illegal one, and that other powers were under no obligation to remain indifferent."[12] "This view," Jackson went on to say, "had been too often discussed and too fully agreed to need repetition within the official circle."[13]

Did Lauterpacht convert Jackson to the cause of outlawry? Or did he merely hand the attorney general a politically convenient *Gutachten*, an expert opinion from a reputable authority, the sort of legal justification that Schmitt routinely provided Schleicher to answer his critics in the Reichstag? In truth, it was probably a little of both: Jackson obviously wanted the result he got, but getting this answer from such an eminent authority, an answer that made excellent legal sense, strengthened his conviction and resolve. Jackson never backed down from his view that the Pact had transformed the law of the world. He would be a vocal proponent of this idea even after the Lend-Lease controversy was resolved, even after he became an associate justice of the United States Supreme Court, and, most momentously, when he was appointed the chief prosecutor for the United States at the International Military Tribunal at Nuremberg.

"WHAT WE MUST DO WITH THE WAR CRIMINALS"

In the fifth edition of *Oppenheim's International Law*, published in 1935, Lauterpacht admonished scholars not to get out too far in front of statesmen. International law had to change through state practice, "by common action of States themselves, and not by jurists engaged in drawing logical consequences from the [Pact]."[14] The outlawry of war was revolutionary and provided a fresh foundation upon which a new world order could be built, but states had to build that order themselves. Scholars could not do so simply by writing treatises from the comfort of their academic offices.

Still, scholars could nudge statesmen along. They could deduce implications from the Pact, propose them for consideration, and hope for the best. Having succeeded in changing Robert Jackson's mind on neutrality during the Lend-Lease debate of 1941, Lauterpacht took the next step down the road of building a new order. He began to toy with the idea of criminal prosecutions for waging aggressive war. After all, if the Pact changed the rights of belligerents against neutrals, shouldn't the Pact also have changed the rights of victims against belligerents as well? If the United States could penalize Germany for invading Poland, couldn't *Poland* penalize Germany for invading Poland? When Lauterpacht returned from the United States, he would write a famous memo for the "Cambridge Group"—a collection of scholars who met at Cambridge University to discuss the legality of war crimes prosecutions. In it, he set out the case for the next step in the revolution begun by the Pact.

This memo, written in July 1942, is best known for its rejection of the "Superior Orders" defense. Lauterpacht had argued that it was no longer acceptable for soldiers to defend the commission of atrocities by claiming that they were "only following orders." Defendants at Nuremberg would try to justify their conduct in this way—thus earning the plea its moniker as the "Nuremberg Defense"—but the Tribunal would reject it and accept Lauterpacht's position instead. But in the memo Lauterpacht also claimed that the Pact could be used to prosecute the Axis leaders for waging aggressive war. "The law of any international society worthy of that name must reject with reprobation the view that between nations there can be no aggression calling for punishment, and it must consider the responsibility for the premeditated violation of the General Treaty for the Renunciation of War as lying within the sphere of criminal law."[15]

Lauterpacht wasn't the first to make this suggestion.[16] Another Jewish law professor beat him to it. Like Hersch Lauterpacht, René Cassin believed in the promise of peace through international law. As a young man fighting for France in 1916, Cassin was shot twice in the stomach and, though he narrowly survived, the bullets caused so much internal damage that he lived in pain for the rest of his long life.[17] This traumatic experience fostered in him, quite literally, a visceral hatred of war. Later appointed the French delegate to the League of Nations from 1924 to 1938, he fled with Charles de Gaulle to London after the Nazis overran France.

On November 14, 1941, in the bleakest days of the war, Cassin addressed the first meeting of the Cambridge Group and asserted that waging aggressive war was now a crime under international law: "But as far as the criminal character of war in itself is concerned we are not, as in 1914, without legislation. . . . On August 27th, 1928, the Briand-Kellogg Pact was signed—Germany being a party thereto—solemnly renouncing war as an instrument of national policy."[18] Cassin followed with a warning to his colleagues about the perils of timidity. The hard lesson learned by the League was that allowing states to break the rules merely encourages them to continue.[19]

By the beginning of 1943, Senator Elbert Thomas, the reigning expert on international law in the United States Senate, advanced a similar proposal. In an article entitled "What We Must Do with the War Criminals," in the February issue of *The American Magazine*, immediately above a skin cream ad informing readers that "men in the service want Noxzema," he set out his plan for the Axis leaders: Hitler, Mussolini, and Tojo.

Senator Thomas explained how international law had changed during the interwar period. "We did not hang the Kaiser: everyone knows that. He lived to a rich old age in sumptuous mock royalty, attended by his courtiers and protected by his guards." While this impunity was unjust, it was legal, "for at that time war was a commonly accepted instrument of national endeavor, and had been so recognized for centuries." The Axis leaders, however, could no longer find protection in the laws of war. "The Kellogg-Briand Pact changed all that. When the great powers signed that agreement renouncing war as an instrument of national policy, war in that instant became an act of outlawry, a crime against society, against the whole human family."[20]

Senator Thomas did not call for the heads of the Axis leaders, though sparing them was no act of mercy. "I should be unalterably opposed to it, not because I think it is unjust, but because I think it is inadequate." Instead, "the victorious United Nations should select isolated islands and set them up as No Man's Lands under control of the Inter-Allied Peace Council." The arrangement should be as spartan as possible, both incommodious and conducive to excruciating introspection. "We should build no villas for these men. . . . No ship should ever be permitted to touch the shores of these islands, and the only contact of the exiles with the world should be international sentries forever patrolling their shores."[21]

At this point in the war, however, these thinkers were ahead of their governments. As late as October 8, 1942, Sumner Welles would not even say whether the Allies intended to prosecute *Hitler* for wartime atrocities. *The New York Times* reported that when Welles was "asked whether Reichfuehrer Adolf Hitler would be one of [those prosecuted], he countered that he would leave that to the judgment of his questioners."[22] In October 1943, Churchill, Roosevelt, and Stalin committed in their Moscow Declaration to "pursue them to the uttermost ends of the earth," but the "them" to which they were referring were traditional war criminals—"those German officers and men and members of the Nazi party who have been responsible for or have taken a consenting part in the above atrocities, massacres and executions."[23] There was no mention of prosecuting the Axis leaders for waging aggressive war.[24]

In 1943, the Allies were far more concerned with victory than with its legal consequences. While Japan had lost the military initiative in the waters off Midway Island and Germany in the Stalingrad snow—Italy never had any initiative to lose—the Axis powers still maintained their grip over most of the Eurasian landmass, and the Allies had yet to figure out how to breach the Atlantic Wall. Moreover, war crimes were still ongoing, and the Allies hoped to deter more from being committed through their warnings. But the war itself could not be unstarted. Its criminality was an academic question, at least at this point, which is why academics were the principal ones discussing it.

Aside from prematurity, there were several other serious political problems with prosecuting the Axis leaders. The catastrophe of Versailles loomed large. No one could forget the festering resentment created by attributing war guilt to an entire nation. Litigating the causes of war in open court would also provide the Axis leaders an immense soapbox from which to broadcast their propaganda to the world, much as Hitler had done with great effectiveness during his trial for the Beer Hall Putsch in 1923. There was also the risk of drawing attention away from the traditional war crimes, which were undeniably horrific. Why muddy the moral waters with novel legal theories when there were so many other villains to prosecute in open-and-shut cases?[25]

There were numerous legal problems with criminal prosecution for aggression as well, and international lawyers were split on them. The most difficult was the so-called retroactivity problem: The Axis leaders could be punished for waging an aggressive war only if there was a preexisting law that made waging aggressive war a crime. No civilized legal system imposes criminal punishment—let alone the death penalty—ex post facto.[26]

Historical precedents that seemed encouraging turned out, on closer inspection, to confirm the novelty of prosecuting heads of state for waging aggressive war.[27] While Napoleon had been exiled to Elba after his defeat at the Battle of Leipzig, his banishment was not a form of criminal punishment. The exile was a desperate attempt at civil confinement. Since the victors could not make Napoleon their prisoner, for he had committed no crime, they instead made him an emperor of his own country and barred him from traveling to theirs. His exile to St. Helena was indeed a punishment, but not for the crime of waging aggressive war, but instead on the tenuous legal ground that his escape from Elba was a violation of the terms of his surrender as embodied in the Treaty of Fontainebleau.[28]

Slightly more promising was the indictment of Kaiser Wilhelm II in the Treaty of Versailles. Article 227 reads: "The Allied and Associated Powers publicly arraign William II of Hohenzollern, formerly German Emperor, for a supreme offence against international morality and the sanctity of treaties."[29] But a careful reading shows that the charge was not for a *legal* violation. The treaty states that Wilhelm had committed an offense against "international morality" and the "sanctity of treaties." Reinforcing that there was no law to apply, the treaty directs the future tribunal to be guided "by the highest motives of international policy."[30] The legal impropriety of the treaty was so glaring that the Netherlands government, which had granted Wilhelm asylum after he abdicated his throne and slipped across the Dutch border a day before Germany surrendered, would not release him to the Allies.[31]

The challenge, then, was to figure out how to prosecute the Axis leaders for waging aggressive war without violating the principle forbidding ex post facto punishment.

A SOLUTION

Of course, there was one answer to the ex post facto problem. Punishing the Axis leaders might be unjust, but so would not punishing them. Indeed, having them escape accountability would be the greater injustice. Who would feel that Hitler was wronged if he were put to death? Surely, his moral culpability was so great that it outweighed any injustice done by convicting him of a new crime.

The problem with this easy answer is that it was too easy. It sounded like Carl Schmitt's defense of the *Lex Lubbe*. Hadn't he argued that Van der Lubbe's crime of burning down the Reichstag was so evil that justice demanded retroactive legislation? Didn't he urge the Nazis to replace the ancient legal principle *nullum crimen sine lege*—no crime without law—with a new principle *nullum crimen sine poena*—no crime without punishment?[32] In punishing the Nazi leadership, the Americans did not want to become like them. Lawyers had to develop arguments that distinguished the Anglo-American approach to law from the National Socialist one.[33]

The first breakthrough did not come from a British or American scholar, but from a Czech lawyer, Bohuslav Ečer.[34] Ečer had been an opponent of the Nazi party in Czechoslovakia and fled to Paris when the Nazis invaded his country. As the Nazis pivoted to France, Ečer fled to Britain, where he participated in the London International Assembly, a working group similar to the one that met in Cambridge.[35] Ečer agreed that the Peace Pact rendered aggressive war illegal. But that did not make waging aggressive war *criminal* or *punishable*. For the violation of the law to be a criminal violation, the law must contemplate a public prosecution in which the prosecutor condemns the defendants and seeks to punish them for their transgressions. Criminal codes, therefore, have a distinctive form: They contain detailed definitions of offenses and clearly state the punishments for each violation. But the Pact looked nothing like the criminal code. It did not define a crime of aggression, nor did it set out punishments for its violation. Indeed, it makes no mention of sanctions at all. It states that the signatories renounce the recourse to war and condemn its use as a solution to international controversies. Ečer recognized, therefore, that attempting to treat the Peace Pact as a criminal statute was a dead end.

But Ečer thought that there was another way to interpret the Peace Pact.[36] Instead of treating it as a criminal statute, one could read it as a constitutional principle. By outlawing war, the Pact repealed the core principle of the Old World Order. War was no longer a lawful way to enforce rights. Only self-defense would be a just cause. The old Grotian rules no longer made any sense. They had lost their reason for being.

The Peace Pact, then, did not convert aggressive war into a separate crime. It merely removed the legal protections that aggressors enjoyed when war was a legitimate method for resolving disputes between states. States could now pierce the legal veil of war and expose its underlying criminality. Unjustified killing on the battlefield would now be seen and treated the same as its off-the-battlefield counterpart, namely, as murder. The Nazis, therefore, were prosecutable according to ordinary criminal law.[37]

Ečer first set out his solution to the retroactivity problem in a memo dated October 10, 1942, to the London Assembly.[38] Ečer made the same argument in an even crisper form the following year: "As soon as international law, as law of a higher order, deprived aggressive warfare of its legality, it was seen in its original, true likeness: a chain of forbidden crimes punishable by the heaviest penalties in the criminal law of the countries affected." Ečer concluded with this rhetorical question, which captured the power of the argument: "Whose legal conscience will be troubled when the international court sends the authors of this war as accomplices in mass murder, arson, robbery, etc. . . . to the only place where the national court sends those guilty of murder, namely to the scaffold?"[39]

SUMMARY EXECUTIONS

Ečer had come up with an inspired solution to the retroactivity problem. But there were several obstacles to overcome. First was transmission. How was the legal theory of an exiled law professor supposed to get to the politicians in charge? Unlike Lauterpacht and Schmitt, Ečer did not have the ear of those in power. But there was an even more difficult problem to be solved before aggressive war could be criminalized. For it wasn't clear that the Allies wanted to put the Axis leadership on trial. Many were against it. They demanded justice that would be simple and primal, a process short and decisive, a reckoning swift and terrible. They wanted mass summary executions.

In the United States, the lead agitator was the secretary of the treasury, Henry Morgenthau, Jr. Morgenthau had developed a postwar plan to neuter Germany for at least a century. To ensure that Germany would not rise again, the plan called for the total obliteration of German industry. The Allies would strip and loot all of its useful machinery, shutter its mines, deport those with technical skills, and smash everything else. They would hit hardest the Ruhr river valley of the Rhineland, Schmitt's family home. "Here lies the heart of German industrial power, the cauldron of wars. This area should not only be stripped of all presently existing industries but so weakened and controlled that it cannot in the foreseeable future become an industrial area."[40] Morgenthau also urged the president to skip trials for the Axis war criminals and proceed directly to the executions.[41]

Henry Stimson attributed the unhinged fury behind this plan to its author's ethnicity. Morgenthau was in the grip of "Semitism gone wild for vengeance."[42] At one point, Morgenthau advocated "the entire elimination of every member of the Nazi Party."[43] When informed that there were perhaps thirteen million members, he responded that he thought there were only five million.[44] Though no other official suggested such lunacy, Morgenthau was not alone in his thirst for vengeance. Cordell Hull, the Episcopalian secretary of state whose wife was half-Jewish, told Morgenthau, "The reason that I got along so well with the Russians was when I went to Moscow, the first thing I told them I would do was to bring up all these people before a drumhead court martial, and I would shoot them before sunset, and from that day I got along with the Russians beautifully."[45] When Stimson objected to Morgenthau's plan in a cabinet meeting, insisting that legal procedures had to be followed, Morgenthau reported Hull's response: "Hull doesn't want to wait; he just wants to shoot them all at dawn."[46]

The president initially sided with Morgenthau. When Roosevelt met with Churchill in September 1944 in Quebec, Morgenthau was the only U.S. cabinet secretary invited.[47] To his delight, Morgenthau discovered that Churchill agreed with him. Unlike Morgenthau, however, Churchill understood that the optics were awful and tried to put a softer face on the plan. He christened it "Pastoralization": the Allies were merely "converting Germany into a country primarily agricultural and pastoral in its character."[48] Churchill also favored summary executions, though only for the leadership—the fifty to one hundred Major War Criminals.[49] He wanted to establish courts of inquiry "not for the purpose of determining the guilt or innocence of the accused but merely to establish the fact of identification." Once identified, the accused should be "shot to death within six hours and without reference to higher authority."[50] Churchill did not want trials. Trials produce surprises—and sometimes end in acquittals.

Stimson was flabbergasted. In a memo written after the Quebec Conference, he warned the president that Carthaginian peaces merely perpetuate hostilities. "Such methods, in my opinion, do not prevent war; they tend to breed war."[51] He denounced summary executions.[52] Convening drumhead courts-martial would not only betray American values, but would also squander the opportunity to build an authoritative record of Nazi crimes.[53] "It is primarily by the thorough apprehension, investigation, and trial of all the Nazi leaders and instruments of the Nazi system of terrorism, such as the Gestapo, with punishment delivered as promptly, swiftly and severely as possible, that we can demonstrate the abhorrence which the world has for such a system and bring home to the German people our determination to extirpate it and all its fruits forever."[54] These desperate pleas for judiciousness went unheeded. Roosevelt stuck with Morgenthau.[55]

It seemed like Friedrich Nietzsche and Carl Schmitt had been right all along: Those who fight monsters become monsters themselves. To punish Germany for its aggression, the Allies intended to impoverish an entire nation for many generations; for its racism and genocide, the Allies planned to engage in massive, systematic ethnic cleansing; for the execution of prisoners, the Allies wanted to shoot hundreds, maybe thousands or tens of thousands, with no due process.

But Nietzsche and Schmitt had not been right. For when the news of the plan leaked, the press was merciless. *Time*'s reaction was typical. It ran a piece entitled "The Policy of Hate," which lampooned Morgenthau's plan as being "just barely above the level of 'sterilize all Germans.' "[56] No one was fooled by the euphemism. "Pastoralization" suggested a peaceful process and bucolic outcome, but it was obvious that the proposal to flatten a large part of Central Europe and transform it into a vast meadow would have resulted in the forcible deportation of millions of civilians and probably mass starvation as well. Nazi propagandists made the most of the news. The *Völkische Beobachter*, the official mouthpiece of the Nazi party, ran a screaming headline: "ROOSEVELT AND CHURCHILL AGREE TO JEWISH MURDER PLAN!"[57]

The president realized his blunder and disavowed it. According to Stimson, Roosevelt tried to shift the blame, saying that "Morgenthau pulled a 'boner.' "[58] Pastoralization was so toxic, in fact, that it tainted the provisions for summary execution of the Nazi leadership, which were popular with the public. A Gallup poll taken ten days after Göring was captured reported that only 4 percent of respondents wanted to try him in court. Fifty-six percent opted for "hang, shoot, execute, decapitation, capital punishment," while 15 percent wanted to "kill him slowly, torture him to death, hard work and starve to death, cut into pieces."[59]

That even Nazi leaders are entitled to due process of law was not a fashionable position. The American public did not want war crimes tribunals— nor did the United States or British governments. Even some Nazis did not want them. Robert Ley, the leader of the German Labor Front, told the psychologist Gustave Gilbert at Nuremberg, "Stand us against a wall and shoot us!— All well and good—you are victors. But why should I be brought before a Tribunal like a c-, c-, c-, like a c-, c-, c-?" When Gilbert supplied the word "criminal," Ley responded: "Yes, I can't even get the word out."[60] The next day Ley hung himself from the toilet pipe in his cell.

Perhaps the only major political figure who agreed with Henry Stimson was Joseph Stalin. Stalin was a passionate advocate for trials—not the real kind, of course, but show ones. He knew that show trials are great propaganda and was confident that Andrei Vishinsky, the veteran prosecutor of the Great Purges of the 1930s, could reprise those performances.

Stalin not only supported war crime trials—he wanted to try the Axis leadership for the crime of aggression. The Soviet legal scholar A. N. Trainin expressed Stalin's view in a 1944 book entitled *Hitlerite Responsibility Under the Criminal Law*. "[T]he Soviet view," Trainin reported, is "that the launching of an aggressive war is today a crime in international law."[61] Trainin, a talented lawyer, introduced an elegant distinction. He described aggression not as a crime of war, but as a crime against peace. Aggressors do not only violate the rights of their victims—they upset the peaceful world order.[62]

Stimson and Stalin made for an odd couple, but both appreciated the power of law. They understood better than most the enormous legitimacy that legal processes bestow on the outcomes they produce. And they appreciated the damage that an international trial could inflict on the institution of aggressive war. Here, though, the agreement ended. For unlike Stimson, who respected legal processes, Stalin exploited them. Stalinist trials were only for show. They never had surprise endings.

Nor did Stalin care whether crimes against the peace were actual crimes under international law. Stimson, however, needed to be persuaded with good legal arguments. Stimson *wanted* to be persuaded, but he still *required* convincing. Stimson would get the requisite confirmation, but it did not come from an eminent scholar such as Lauterpacht, Ečer, or Trainin, but from his friend, neighbor, and law partner, William Chanler.

WILLIAM CHANLER

William Chamberlain Chanler was a bona fide member of the New York aristocracy.[63] He could trace his roots to the first director-general of the New Netherlands Colony, Peter Stuyvesant, and the fur trader turned New

York City real estate mogul John Jacob Astor, Sr., his great-grandfather. His father, Lewis Stuyvesant Chanler, was one of the "Astor Orphans," the group of ten children who were left the Astor fortune when their parents met untimely deaths.[64] After his graduation from Harvard Law School, William Chanler entered law practice with Winthrop, Stimson, Putnam and Roberts, a white-shoe Wall Street firm with strong internationalist leanings. It had been established by Elihu Root, secretary of state in Theodore Roosevelt's administration and founding president of the American Society of International Law. For many years, Henry Stimson was one of its lead partners.[65]

Like other Wall Street lawyers and financiers of that era, Chanler possessed a strong sense of noblesse oblige and civic virtue. Thus, when the United States entered the war, the forty-seven-year-old Chanler rushed to enlist. An experienced lawyer, Chanler was appointed chief military officer for the Allied Military Government for North Africa, Sicily, and then southern Italy. He drafted many of the occupation laws for the military government.[66] He was also the first member of the United States government to try to indict a sitting head of state for violating the Peace Pact.

Even though Benito Mussolini joined the Pact on Italy's behalf, he never took it seriously, announcing to his Chamber of Deputies with characteristic bluster: "We signed the Kellogg Pact. I defined it as sublime. In reality, it is so sublime that it might be called transcendental."[67] His audience laughed. They understood their leader's message: The Pact is so otherworldly as to be meaningless. It was an ethereal gesture, a piety backed by nothing. For how could a piece of paper constrain Il Duce's will? The League's feeble reaction to his invasion of Ethiopia confirmed its impotence. But Mussolini did not get the last laugh. For he failed to appreciate that the Pact would become effective over time, as nations realized the costs of inaction and learned how to use it. Nor did he grasp how transcendental his own army had become.

Clarity came at five o'clock in the afternoon of July 25, 1943, when he pulled his Alfa Romeo into the driveway of the Royal Palace of Victor Emmanuel III, the King of Italy. Mussolini regarded the five-foot-tall monarch not only as his friend but also as a figurehead. The king therefore stunned Mussolini when he called the fascist dictator "the most hated man in Italy" and placed him under arrest.[68] Thinking that he might trade Mussolini to the Allies, the king had him whisked away to the Campo Imperatore, an isolated ski resort high in the Apennine Mountains. Chanler recognized the opportunity Mussolini's capture presented and, along with another colleague, drew up an indictment charging him with multiple counts of violating the Pact: the first count for the invasion of Ethiopia in 1935, and the others for invading England, France, Greece, and Yugoslavia.[69]

Unfortunately, the indictment Chanler drafted quickly became moot. On September 12, 1943, Mussolini was rescued in a daring raid ordered by Hitler himself, who had consulted occultists to divine his friend's whereabouts.[70] The mission was led by Otto Skorzeny, the six foot three Austrian commando, known alternatively as "Scarface," for the many dueling wounds on his left cheek, and the "most dangerous man in Europe," for his skill in special operations.[71] He overwhelmed Mussolini's well-armed captors with a squadron of gliders and paratroopers. Upon landing in the isolated mountainside resort, Skorzeny raced up the stairs of the building where Mussolini was held and shouted "Duce, the Führer has sent me to set you free!" Mussolini replied, "I knew that my friend would not forsake me!"[72] Mussolini was carried off to a warm reunion with Hitler. He eventually returned to Italy as the leader of Italian Socialist Republic, a tiny puppet state of Nazi Germany off Lake Garda.

Even though Chanler did not succeed in indicting Mussolini, he was able to draw on the same legal theories when he returned to Washington in 1944. The occasion was a deadlock in the United Nations War Crimes Commission, the successor institution to the London Assembly, over the question of aggressive war. Sir Arnold McNair, Lauterpacht's mentor, had taken the position that waging aggressive war was not a crime under international law, with Bohuslav Ečer disagreeing.[73] Fearing that McNair might prevail, Stimson instructed the United States representative to stall for time while the United States government researched the issue.[74] Chanler composed a long memo to Stimson, dated November 30, setting out the legal theory he had first devised a year earlier in Italy.

Chanler's idea was nearly identical to Ečer's. The Peace Pact did not create a new international crime of aggression—it simply removed any immunity that the aggressor had when waging war was legal. Aggressors were no longer lawful combatants, but common criminals.[75] Anticipating the defense "that the acts charged were lawful acts of war," Chanler responded that such a "defense is not valid because the defendants having violated the Kellogg Pact are not lawful belligerents."[76]

Despite the remarkable similarity in approaches, Chanler claims he did not get his idea from Ečer, though at least one of Ečer's memos had been floating around the U.S. War Department at the time.[77] In a letter written a decade later, Chanler claimed that he "based the theory at that time on Feilchenfeld's Fifth Edition of *Oppenheim*, which had a footnote spelling the theory out very clearly."[78] Chanler's recollection, unfortunately, is faulty. For Hersch Lauterpacht, not Ernst Feilchenfeld, was the editor of the fifth edition of *Oppenheim*. Nor is it obvious which footnote Chanler had in mind.* It is possible that Lauterpacht was the original inspiration for Chanler, but how remains unclear.

Despite his strong desire to prosecute the Axis leaders for the crime of aggression, Stimson was not convinced by his friend's memo. He described Chanler's argument as "thought-provoking," but it made him nervous. In a cover memo to his deputy Jack McCloy, Stimson opined that Chanler's views were "a little in advance of the progress of international thought." Nevertheless, it "well deserves a look-over by you and your committee."[79]

Look it over they did, but they, too, were nervous. The skeptical memos written in response did not directly address Chanler's arguments, but it is not hard to see what bothered its authors.[80] Not only was Chanler's

---

*Chanler claimed that this footnote was "recanted" in "Feilchenfeld's Sixth Edition." Not only did Lauterpacht, not Feilchenfeld, revise *Oppenheim*'s sixth edition, but the only relevant footnote that appears in the fifth edition, but not in the sixth, is the following: "It might be argued that a war undertaken in breach of the Pact would be an unlawful act, and as such incapable of producing results otherwise associated with the outbreak of war." This footnote suggests that those who violate the Pact would not enjoy immunity from prosecution, but it hardly counts as "spelling out the theory very clearly." And it would be an exaggeration to say that dropping this footnote in the sixth edition amounts to recanting. It is possible that Chanler was referring to the paragraph on the Peace Pact that appeared in Lauterpacht's private memo for the Cambridge Group in 1942, but had been excised when it was published in 1944. See Hersch Lauterpacht, "The Law of Nations and the Punishment of War Crimes," *British Yearbook of International Law* 21 (1944): 58–95.

theory novel, but to military lawyers it had dangerous implications. For if the Axis leaders were unlawful belligerents—if they were no different, as Chanler said, than guerrilla fighters such as Pancho Villa, the legendary Mexican revolutionary—they would not be protected by the laws of war.[81] They would not be entitled to the protections granted lawful belligerents, and their actions in war would be punishable by death. Much worse, the same might be said of Axis soldiers. And if the Allies took such a line, the Axis would take it, too. They would claim *the Allies* to be the aggressors. The laws of war would break down, with each side asserting that the other had violated the Peace Pact. Each would treat the other as guerrillas, not protected soldiers, and executable on sight.

Chanler was not about to surrender. He sought to outflank his skeptics. The scion of an aristocratic family, he had been raised with a keen understanding of social networks and how the right access can slice through Gordian knots of bureaucracies. Chanler knew he needed an "in" with the president and found one in John Boettiger. Boettiger was a colleague of Chanler's at the Pentagon who also happened to be married to Anna Roosevelt, the president's daughter and confidante. When Boettiger went up to Hyde Park to spend the holidays with his in-laws, Chanler composed a short, half-page cover letter to his memo and asked his friend to deliver it to the president.[82] Nothing is known about what happened in the interim. But on January 3, 1945, the president initialed Chanler's cover memo and composed the following note to the new secretary of state, Edward Stettinius: "Please send me a brief report on the status of the proceedings before the War Crimes Commission, and particularly the attitude of the U.S. Representative on offenses to be brought against Hitler and the chief Nazi war criminals. The charges should include an indictment for waging aggressive war, in violation of the Kellogg Pact."[83]

The Stimson faction was now ascendant and began to plan the prosecution of the Axis leaders for violating the Peace Pact.

THE APPOINTMENT OF ROBERT JACKSON

Three months after he signed off on Chanler's memo, the president died. The next day Attorney General Francis Biddle asked Robert Jackson, now an associate justice of the Supreme Court, to speak about the president to his former staff. In his tribute before a packed audience in the Great Hall of the Department of Justice, Jackson compared the overwhelming military might that Roosevelt commanded with his even greater moral authority.[4] "No Alexander, or Caesar, or Hannibal, or Napoleon, or Hitler ever commanded such an aggregation of physical force. . . . But it was the moral forces and spiritual aspirations of mankind that he really typified, and they never were so passionately concentrated around a single person."[85] Jackson controlled himself until he broke at the end. Barely able to finish, he managed to eke out how glad he was that the president had lived to "see that his efforts have led our country to the very threshold of victory" and that he was on his way "to the Peace which shall have no end."[86]

After this speech, Jackson set out for the Hotel Carlton, where the American Society of International Law was holding its annual meeting. Speaking to the assembled lawyers, Jackson announced that he was joining those who held an "inveterate belief that international law is an existing and indestructible reality . . . in a timely and resolute confession of faith." The main topic of the talk was the question of war crimes tribunals. On this issue, Jackson was noncommittal. As a justice of the Supreme Court, he could not take sides in any political debate. He stressed, however, that if trials were held, they must be real trials. "Farcical judicial trials conducted by us will destroy confidence in the judicial process." While Jackson made clear that he was not supporting trials over summary execution, he dropped hints about his true sympathies: "Of course, if good faith trials are sought, that is another matter. I am not so troubled as some seem to be over problems of jurisdiction of war criminals or of finding existing and recognized law by which standards of guilt may be determined."[87]

Jackson must have known that the new administration would interpret this public speech, one reprinted in the Sunday edition of *The Washington Post*, as a serious expression of interest. The overture was noted.[88] Two weeks later, Samuel Rosenman, the administration official in charge of war crimes policy, approached Jackson to see whether he was indeed interested in being appointed chief prosecutor for the United States.

Chanler claims that he forwarded Jackson's name to Stimson and, through Boettiger, to the new president, Harry Truman. "I strongly urged the designation of Justice Jackson, both in private conversation with Colonel Stimson and, through my associate in the Civil Affairs Division, John Boettiger, 'at the highest level,' as we used to say in the Pentagon."[89]

Jackson's selection is unsurprising, for he was the most natural person for the position. The new administration was aware that Jackson viewed the Peace Pact as a revolutionary document, one that fundamentally altered the laws of neutrality and of war.[90] It also knew that Jackson was an able public servant. He had held almost every top legal office in the government: general counsel to the Bureau of Internal Revenue, solicitor general, attorney general, and now Supreme Court justice. Especially relevant for a war crimes prosecutor, Jackson was an experienced trial attorney. Like Harry Truman, who had been a small-town judge before entering politics, but unlike William Chanler, who was born into privilege, Robert Jackson was a self-made man. Jackson began as a country lawyer in Jamestown, New York, having once tried a case in a barn and litigated another over the paternity of a Holstein-Jersey mixed breed cow.[91] He was the last Supreme Court justice who did not graduate from law school. He did not even attend college. Despite his lack of formal higher education, Jackson was a gifted writer and eloquent speaker, one who sprinkled his prose with learned references gleaned from his extensive reading. He was short and stocky, with a widow's peak and an almost porcine face, yet he dressed elegantly, usually in a three-piece suit, replete with stuffed handkerchief and pocket watch.

By nature Jackson was a man of action and was frustrated by the strict confines of the judicial office. He told President Truman that he felt like he "was not doing anything that promoted the war effort and not much that seemed to be very important in contrast with the great issues at stake in the world."[92] Moreover, the war crimes trial was shaping up to be the trial of the century, if not of history. At the time he was offered the position, the five lead defendants were Adolf Hitler, Benito Mussolini, Heinrich Himmler, Joseph Goebbels, and Hermann Göring.[93] To prosecute these fiends was an offer that no lawyer could refuse. He accepted the position on April 29.

Within a few days, however, the first four defendants were no longer able to stand trial. On April 28, partisans captured Mussolini and his mistress on their way to Switzerland. They placed them against a stone wall and mowed them down with machine guns. Their bodies were strung up by their heels at an Esso gas station in Milan, then later cut down and defiled by a mob.[94] Hearing the news about Mussolini, Hitler decided that there was only one way to avoid a similar fate. On April 30, he and Eva Braun, whose marriage was less than forty hours old, killed themselves, he by gunshot to the head, she by ingesting hydrogen cyanide, the potency of which Hitler had first tested on his dog Blondi. The following day, Goebbels and his wife also committed suicide, but not before poisoning all six of their children while they slept.[95] Himmler survived the longest, until May 8, when he was captured by Allied troops and bit into a cyanide capsule.

Fortunately for Jackson, other creatures of the Nazi bestiary were still alive. Göring surrendered to the Americans on May 9, in part to escape the death sentence imposed when he offered to assume control of the Reich while Hitler was still alive. Göring was also under the delusion that he could talk his way out of trouble, asking repeatedly for an audience with General Dwight Eisenhower. He wasn't the only delusional one. On June 14, Joachim von Ribbentrop was discovered in a Hamburg apartment, lying in a bed wearing pink and white pajamas. He later informed his interrogators that he was on a mission for the "dead Führer." When asked whether he thought that Hitler was in fact dead, Ribbentrop replied: "I am quite certain he is, but it is possible that I am wrong."[96] Germany's parrot had gone cuckoo.

TRÈS FRAGILE

When President Roosevelt died on April 12, the survivors of the recently liberated Buchenwald raised a black flag in his honor at the entrance way.[97] A few days later, General George Patton ordered residents from the neighboring city of Weimar on a forced tour of the camp.[98] The first sight they encountered was a display of parchment with engraved drawings. As they got closer, they realized that these pieces of canvas were large sections of human flesh with elaborate tattoos. The specimens had been assembled for a German doctor writing a treatise on tattoos, and for the commandant's wife, who fancied skin art and would single out prisoners with unusual markings for her collection. Those visitors who had not yet fainted were led past the squalid barracks packed with thousands of sick and dying prisoners. They passed others who, though strong enough to walk, shuffled around the grounds like zombies with no aim or purpose. They were then led into the laboratories where Nazi doctors experimented on the inmates, ghoulish rooms lined with jars of body parts, internal organs, and shrunken heads. They observed patients barely alive who had been injected with typhus to develop a serum to cure Germans. The death rate in this room was 98 percent. The next lab was the pediatric wing. The German visitors saw a nine-year-old boy, a Jew from Budapest, who had been jabbed with several doses of typhus. He was still chipper. When asked where his parents were, he answered: "My father was killed and my mother was burned to death." They were then led to Barrack 58, where the sickest inmates were taken. Appropriately enough, the crematorium was next door. It was a one-story, red-brick building with a red-tile roof. In front of the building was a stack of naked, emaciated corpses. The crematorium was equipped with souped-up baking ovens designed to turn the corpses into fine powder. As if this were not hideous enough, the basement of the building contained a torture chamber. Victims had to stand on a low stool and place a noose around their necks, at which point the next victim in line was forced to kick out that stool from under them.[99]

This story was reported on the front page of *The New York Times* on April 18, 1945. In the days that followed, the newspapers filled with other tales of the atrocities committed by the Nazis. But even as the nightmarish news from the other camps—Bergen-Belsen, Auschwitz, Treblinka, Dachau, Theresienstadt—flooded the American press, those in charge of American war crimes policy fixated on the crime of aggression. To them, the main subject of the upcoming war trial was not the Holocaust—it was the war. According to Stimson, the war crimes planners rallied around the idea of "a big trial in which we can prove the whole Nazi conspiracy to wage a totalitarian war of aggression violating in its progress all of the regular rules which limit needless cruelty and destruction."[100]

Stimson did not even want to include charges related to the Holocaust. He was not being insensitive or anti-Semitic. He did not think the Allies had the legal authority to prosecute such deeds, abominations though they were. "I have great difficulty in finding any means whereby military commissions may try and convict those responsible for excesses committed within Germany both before and during the war which have no relation to the conduct of the war."[101] On Stimson's view, these atrocities were not crimes that could be prosecuted by an international tribunal. Jackson managed to shoehorn the Holocaust into the upcoming trial, but only by linking it to the war. "The reason that this program of extermination of Jews and destruction of the rights of minorities becomes an international concern is this: it was part of a plan for making an illegal war."[102] In Jackson's view, the Nazis could be prosecuted for the Holocaust only because it was part of an aggressive war waged in violation of the Peace Pact.

Jackson's commitments were apparent from the moment he assumed the office of chief prosecutor. When he revised the draft charter that the Americans hoped would be approved at the upcoming conference in London, he made sure that the crime of waging aggressive war was up front. He redrafted the list of charges:

a. Violation of the customs and rules of warfare.

b. Invasion by force or threat of force of other countries in violation of international law or treaties.

c. Initiation of war in violation of international law or treaties.

d. Launching a war of aggression.

e. Recourse to war as an instrument of national policy or for the solution of international controversies.[103]

The massive redundancy in the charges shows how adamant Jackson was that the upcoming trial be about violations of the Pact.

He took the same line in his public report to President Truman, dated June 6, 1945, the one year anniversary of D-Day. "[T]he crime of making unjustifiable war," Jackson declared, is "the crime which comprehends all lesser crimes."[104] And the legal justification he offered for this approach was none other than the Ečer-Chanler theory. "War necessarily is a calculated series of killings, of destructions of property, of oppressions."[105] The Old World Order had thrown "a mantle of protection around acts which otherwise would be crimes, when committed in pursuit of legitimate warfare."[106] The Peace Pact had removed that mantle of protection. The New

World Order, Jackson concluded, "has abolished the defense that those who incite or wage it are engaged in legitimate business."[107]

By taking such a public stance, Jackson had created a predicament. The proposed war crimes tribunal was not intended to be an American affair. It was envisioned as an international court, a concerted effort by the Allies to punish the Axis war criminals. But when the Allies had converged on London at the end of June to hammer out the rules for the upcoming trial, they could agree on very little. The French delegation was hostile to Jackson's approach. The French representative, André Gros, was insistent that there was no crime of aggression in international law. If the Allies went through with Jackson's plan, critics would rightly claim that the aggression charge was merely "a creation by four people who are just four individuals," nothing more than "ex post facto legislation."[108]

Jackson had suspected that the French were not sympathetic during the earlier San Francisco conference when a professor of international law, Jules Basdevant, described the charge of aggression as "*très fragile.*" Jackson could not believe that the French would resist his approach, having been the repeated victims of German aggression over the course of modern history. "God save us from professors!" he fumed in his diary.[109]

In truth, professors saved Jackson. Hersch Lauterpacht served as an informal adviser to Jackson during the negotiations in London. Jackson twice traveled to Cambridge during July for consultation, especially on the legal issue of aggression. Jackson also followed Lauterpacht's advice on how to organize the charges, which had been arranged haphazardly. Lauterpacht suggested three neat categories: (1) Crimes against the Peace; (2) War Crimes; and (3) Crimes against Humanity. This organization was so intuitive that it became the template for the upcoming trial.[110]

Jackson also leaned on Lauterpacht's advice about Lend-Lease during his negotiations with the French. He argued that the criminalization of aggression was consistent with the changes in the rules of neutrality that the Pact had wrought. As Lauterpacht had argued in his 1941 memo for Jackson on the eve of his Havana speech, the Pact inaugurated a revolution in international law and the upcoming trials would simply recognize and extend this revolution. "If that is wrong," Jackson told the French, "then we have been wrong in a good many things in the policy of the United States which helped the countries under attack before we entered the war."[111]

Jackson, of course, did not think the United States was wrong. He justified his Havana speech in support of the Lend-Lease Act by reference to the sixth edition of *Oppenheim*. "And I notice that the latest issue of Oppenheim on International Law, just out, says that my Havana speech, which some of you have read, was a sound view of international law, although it was criticized in my own country at the time."[112] Jackson never let on that there was a simple reason for the agreement: The author of the Havana speech and of the most recent edition of *Oppenheim* was one and the same, namely, Hersch Lauterpacht. Indeed, Lauterpacht had handed Jackson the latest edition of *Oppenheim*, which included the Havana speech reference, just two weeks earlier.

Jackson even intimated that the Allies were ungrateful in not supporting his proposal when he had gone out on a limb to support them during the Lend-Lease debate. "[T]he justification was made by the Secretary of State [Cordell Hull], by the Secretary of War, Mr. Stimson, by myself as Attorney General, that this war was illegal from the outset and hence we were not doing an illegal thing in extending aid to peoples who were unjustly and unlawfully attacked. . . . We want this group of [Allied] nations to stand up and say . . . that launching a war of aggression is a crime and that no political or economic situation can justify it."[113]

But Lauterpacht was not the only professor to help Jackson. Another academic consultant to the delegation identified a terrible flaw in the American proposal, one that, if undetected, could have undermined it all. Not being international lawyers, Jackson and his team did not notice their massive blunder. But Hans Kelsen did, and he showed them how to fix it before it was too late.

THE RETURN OF HANS KELSEN

In 1942, after his two-year lectureship at Harvard was over, Kelsen had to find a new job. No law school in the United States was willing, or was in a position, to hire him. Kelsen managed to secure a position at the University of California at Berkeley, but only in the Political Science Department and only for one year. At the last moment, the school extended his term for a second year because Berkeley had opened a new school of military government and needed someone to teach courses on German government and National Socialism. The program of the new military school changed a year later, however, and Kelsen's expertise was no longer necessary.[114]

Facing penury, the sixty-three-year-old former justice of the Austrian Supreme Court and the world's most prominent legal thinker was reduced to writing Roscoe Pound for a job working "as a research associate, or in a library."[115] Even this Pound could not help him secure.[116] Finally, the State Department offered Kelsen employment as a consultant at the Foreign Economic Administration in its Bureau of Areas, Liberated Areas Branch. Given his expertise in international law and, particularly, the Austrian constitutional system that he had helped design, his work centered on the legal status of Austria and Germany after the war.[117]

Kelsen later moved to the Judge Advocate General's office, working under General John Weir on war crimes issues. In two trips to Washington, one in July and one in September of 1945, he composed eight memos on the crime of aggression.[118] The most important of these memos was the one he drafted in July, in which he identified a critical mistake that Jackson's team had made in its proposed draft agreement on the war crimes prosecutions. Kelsen zeroed in on the offending provision: "The Tribunal shall be bound by this declaration of the Signatories that the following acts are criminal violations of International Law."[119] The untrained eye would not spot the problem, but Kelsen could see the disaster in the offing.

In his memo, Kelsen explained a fundamental difference between domestic and international law. Domestic law is built on the principle of individual responsibility, which is to say that those who commit wrongs without justifications or excuses are sanctioned for their actions.[120] Murderers and their accomplices are punished for their murders, no one else is.

In contrast to domestic law, international law operates according to the principle of collective responsibility.[121] Only murderers and their accomplices can be held liable for murder, but any member of the state can be held liable for the violation of their state's legal obligations. If Germany violates international law, *any German* is responsible, regardless of whether it is his or her fault. International law, therefore, embodies a primitive morality—Kelsen went so far as to call international law a "primitive" legal system, for it imposes liability on the innocent as well as the guilty.[122]

Once one sees that international law accepts the principle of collective responsibility, the fault in the American draft becomes glaring. Requiring the Tribunal to declare acts of waging aggressive war to be "criminal violations of International Law" would be useless to the prosecution. For the prosecution wanted to impose individual responsibility on the defendants, but international law only imposes collective responsibility.[123] The only consequence that follows from Göring and Ribbentrop waging aggressive war was that their victims were permitted to wage war against Germany in retaliation. But the Tribunal would not be able to say that Göring and Ribbentrop themselves could be punished as a result.

Kelsen, however, suggested a fix. Since the Allies had to enter into an agreement with each other to form an international tribunal, they should insert a provision on individual responsibility. He even drafted the language to be inserted, namely, that any person who violates "international law forbidding the use of force . . . may be held individually responsible for these acts . . . and brought to trial and punishment before the court."[124]

Kelsen conceded that this provision would create new law.[125] That was its point—to enable the Allies to prosecute specific individuals. In that sense, the law would be ex post facto. But, Kelsen pointed out, this retroactivity would be innocuous. For retroactive legislation is unjust when it surprises defendants, but here there would be no element of unfair surprise. The Axis leaders could not claim that they were unaware of the illegality of their actions. The Peace Pact forbade the waging of war—and their countries had signed the Pact just a few years earlier. Nor would the leaders' deaths be unpredictable as a legal matter. The Axis leaders, after all, were German and, under international law, every citizen was responsible for their state's violation of international law. Since Germany had violated the Peace Pact, *all Germans* were liable for its violation. Göring knew the risks. He was well aware that the Allies could drop a bomb on him as a result of his country's violation of the law—what complaint could he then have if they decided to hang him from a gibbet instead?[126]

Indeed, any law that rendered the Axis leaders individually responsible for waging aggressive war would be an improvement over the then current system of collective responsibility. For such a system is not merely terribly inefficient—it is morally perverse. It holds the entire nation responsible for the crimes of the few *and* protects the guilty few from prosecution. A law imposing individual responsibility on the authors of the war would rectify this injustice. It would place blame where it morally belonged.[127]

Jackson saw Kelsen's point. Across the top of the memo, he wrote: "Hans Kelsen is worried over the absence of any international law on the subject of individual responsibility. He thinks a definite declaration is essential. I think it may be desirable. . . . I think it may be worth including to stop the argument about whether the law does so provide."[128] During the negotiations in London, Jackson insisted that the Charter include individual responsibility for the defendants.[129] It was included. Article Six of the Charter of the International Military Tribunal reads: "The following acts, or any of them, are crimes coming within the jurisdiction of the Tribunal *for which there shall be individual responsibility*: (a) CRIMES AGAINST PEACE: . . . ."[130]

Kelsen not only forestalled the possibility that the Tribunal would find criminality but no individual responsibility. He also gave the prosecution a powerful new argument for holding the Axis leaders individually responsible for waging aggressive war. They could now say that the Charter was targeting the right people.

THE RETURN OF CARL SCHMITT

As Kelsen was working on the crime of aggression, his nemesis was toiling away on the same issue, but to the opposite conclusion. At the end of May 1945, a representative of the industrial tycoon Friedrich Flick approached Carl Schmitt for legal help.[131] Flick had read in the American military newspaper *Stars and Stripes* that Jackson was not content to pursue the political and military leaders of Germany. He wanted to prosecute major industrialists as well. Since Flick was a key financial supporter of the Nazi party and the leading matériel supplier to the German war effort, as well as an exploiter of slave labor from the camps to produce these funds and supplies, he feared that he would be a target of prosecution.

Needing the money, and believing in the cause, Schmitt accepted the assignment. Over the course of three months, as the Allies began their military occupation of Germany, Schmitt dictated a long *Gutachten* to his secretary in his Berlin apartment entitled "The International Crime of Aggression and the Principle '*Nullum crimen, nulla poena sine lege.*'"[132] In this legal memo, Schmitt made a vigorous case that Jackson's approach to aggression was legally illegitimate.

Much of the memo is conventional, setting forth arguments that any competent lawyer would make. Schmitt pointed out that the Peace Pact does not have the appearance of a criminal statute.[133] It does not define the crime of aggression, specify the punishment for its commission, or establish a court for its prosecution. The Pact is "without definition, without sanction, and without organization."[134] Schmitt also described the legislative history of the Pact, particularly how Kellogg and Borah denied that the Pact had any criminal sanctions associated with it and how no one had ever pointed out the possibility of prosecution until now.[135]

Schmitt conceded that the Pact could be read as creating a new crime of aggression. He had warned of precisely this possibility almost twenty years earlier, after Shotwell's lecture proposed outlawry. But he claimed that the promise of the Pact—the creation of a new world order built around the outlawry of war—had not materialized. It remained "a project and a postulate," not a "practical reality."[136] In this part of the memo, Schmitt's understanding of international law, an understanding rivaled by very few then or now, reveals itself.

Schmitt offered two main arguments for his claim that the Pact remained an unrealized promise. The first concerned the political realities of the interwar years. In order for a new order based on the outlawry of war to supplant the old one, three developments had to take place. "All efforts towards the abolition of war," Schmitt wrote, "immediately ran into the connection of the three great concrete problems, which represented more political problems than juridical problems: security, disarmament, and peaceful change."[137] No state could forfeit its legal right to go to war unless there was an effective system of collective security, a reduction in armaments, and a peaceful way to revise the draconian measures of the Versailles treaty. But the League of Nations was a failure, European nations had not disarmed, and the Stresemann policy of peaceful revision perished with the 1929 stock market crash. If war were truly outlawed, something else had to replace it. Nothing had.

Schmitt's second objection was a reprise of his earlier claim about the discriminatory concept of war. Recall that, in 1937, Schmitt complained about authors such as Lauterpacht who were claiming that the Pact enabled states to discriminate between belligerents. The imposition of sanctions by the League on Italy and the suggested change in the nature of neutrality were not only unprecedented developments, but dangerous. In this new postwar memo, Schmitt flipped the argument around. With the benefit of hindsight, he argued, the predicted revolution in international law had not occurred by the time that the war began. League members may have labeled Italy an aggressor and called for states to adopt sanctions on Italy but the states had not followed through. In fact, they ended up effectively recognizing its conquest of Ethiopia. The United States, Switzerland, Spain, and Sweden, had declared their neutrality in the unfolding European war in 1939.

Nor did the Pact change the *jus in bello*, the rights in war. If war were outlawed, Schmitt argued, the just side should have more rights than the unjust one. But the rules relating to the treatment of soldiers, prisoners, the wounded, and civilians remained nondiscriminatory. Just and unjust warriors alike were prohibited from engaging in the same types of behavior. This was evidence that the Pact had not revolutionized the law of war, as its proponents had hoped.

Schmitt finished the assignment on August 25, 1945. But within four days, the memo was moot. For when the Allies released the list of the Major War Criminals on August 29, Flick's name was missing. It appears that the Allies had been unsure whether to prosecute Flick or do business with him instead. They finally decided that Flick was more valuable to them as a rebuilder of Germany than as a major war criminal, at least for the time being.[138]

Because Flick was not prosecuted for waging aggressive war, scholars have assumed that Schmitt's memo was never used.[139] But this is almost certainly not the whole story. Scholars have missed that Schmitt delivered his memo to Flick's criminal defense attorney, Rudolf Dix.[140] That Dix received the memo is apparent from Schmitt's diary. Recording Dix's reaction, Schmitt wrote: "At the time, Dix called my memo of the summer of 1945 a 'homework assignment for a seminar in international law.'"[141]

While it is impossible to say for sure what happened, piecing together Schmitt's writings, known personal connections, and the underlying legal arguments reveals the following picture: Dix had invited Schmitt to be on Flick's legal team. Dix was not an international lawyer—he was a domestic criminal attorney—and needed an expert on the laws of war. Schmitt, in contrast, was the most prominent international lawyer in Germany. He was the leading expert on, and critic of, the crime of aggression. He had written and lectured on the subject for almost twenty years. Schmitt had another advantage: He had perhaps the largest private legal library in Berlin. Containing approximately five thousand volumes, it was later requisitioned by the Allies for the occupation government to be used as its law library. Schmitt also had experience in court. He was famous for his role in the Prussian coup case. He would have been the natural person to join the legal team.

Schmitt thought that his memo would be submitted to the International Military Tribunal. Though the *Gutachten* was written in German, Schmitt appended a one-page note written in English, presumably directed to the American judges. Schmitt was emphatic in the note that he did not object to the prosecution of the Nazis for the Holocaust. "It goes without saying that—at the end of this second world war—mankind is obliged to pass a sentence upon Hitler's and his accomplices' '*scelus infandum*.'"[142] *Scelus infandum*—literally, "unspeakable crime"—is the term he used to describe the Nazi genocide of the Jews. Schmitt was adamant that the Holocaust, as well as the war crimes perpetuated by the Gestapo and the SS, had to be punished. "This sentence must be solemn in its form and striking in its effect."[143] Schmitt's main concern, however, was to ensure that the moral abominations of Nazism not be conflated with the waging of war. The Holocaust and war crimes should be prosecuted, but war itself must not.[144]

The memo on which he had labored would never see a courtroom, and not only because Flick was never indicted. The memo may have been deeply informed but it was not suitable for submission to a court—a point

Dix did not spare Schmitt from hearing. Schmitt was no doubt insulted by Dix's dismissal of it as a "homework assignment," perhaps even humiliated. But Dix was correct. The memo was excessively academic, even pedantic. From a rhetorical point of view, it was a disaster. While it might move scholars, it was unlikely to influence a court. Nor did Schmitt's comments on the *scelus infandum* help either. After all, Flick's brazen exploitation of slave labor from the concentration camps implicated him in Nazi atrocities. Dix did not need a lawyer on his team who thought his client was guilty of an unspeakable crime.

It is possible that Dix threw Schmitt off the legal team at this point, or he might have refused to use Schmitt's memo and let the matter drop. Regardless, the United States took Carl Schmitt off Dix's hands. For in September, Schmitt was himself arrested by OMGUS, the Office of Military Government of the United States.

What, then, happened to the memo? Many have assumed that Schmitt filed the document away in his personal papers, not to be seen again until after his death, when a German scholar unearthed and published it in 1994. But that is unlikely. For when Flick was left off the list of Major War Criminals, Dix was free to find another client to represent. And he did find a new defendant: Hjalmar Schacht, the former Reich finance minister. The Allies had decided that instead of prosecuting Flick for the crime of aggressive war, they would pursue Schacht instead. And when they did, Dix had his defense in hand.

TWELVE

NAZI CIRCUS TOWN

"It was an unforgettable experience," Hersch Lauterpacht wrote to his wife, Rachel, "to see, for the first time in history, a sovereign State in the dock."[1] Lauterpacht was present in Nuremberg on November 21, 1945, when Robert Jackson delivered his opening speech at the International Military Tribunal. He was sitting with the British prosecution team, fifteen yards from the defendants. While it thrilled Lauterpacht to witness the former leaders of Nazi Germany humbled before a court and made to answer for their crimes, it must also have been awful to sit so close to the men responsible for the near-annihilation of his people.

The trial took place at the Justizgebäude, the Palace of Justice, in Nuremberg, a site Jackson settled on for lack of alternatives. Most major German cities, and many of the minor ones, had been obliterated by bombings. Berlin was a moonscape, and Nuremberg was nearly as desolate. According to Allied analysis, 91 percent of the city had been reduced to ruin.[2] The stench of rotting flesh buried beneath the rubble was everywhere.[3] The water was undrinkable.[4] Miraculously, though, a large courthouse on the western outskirts of Nuremberg remained standing. The Palace of

Justice was heavily damaged by five direct bomb hits but it was repairable. Even more remarkably, the courthouse connected to a large, working jail that could house the defendants. The Grand Hotel suitable for housing dignitaries was also intact. A courtroom, jail, and a hotel, Jackson quipped, "[t]hat . . . was precision bombing."[5]

Aside from practicality, Nuremberg had symbolic significance. The city was the site of the annual rallies of the Nazi party. Zeppelin Field, featured prominently in Leni Riefenstahl's 1935 film, *The Triumph of the Will*, had been designed partly by one of the defendants, Albert Speer, and was only a short distance from the courthouse. Nuremberg was also where the Reichstag deprived Jews of their civil rights, where Hermann Göring, another defendant, proclaimed the infamous "Nuremberg Laws." Nuremberg was so emblematic of the Third Reich that some army maps labeled it "Nazi Circus Town."[6]

In light of the damage and the size of the proceedings, the courtroom had to be renovated. A dock for the defendants was built on the left side of the courtroom, in front of an elevator that transported the prisoners from the basement of the connecting jail. The defendants sat in two rows on plain wooden benches in the order that they appeared in the indictment. Seven "snowdrops"—military guards so named for their white helmets—stood behind the defendants, with truncheons and pistols in white holsters. The defense attorneys sat in front of the dock, enabling them to confer with their clients.

Facing the defendants was the International Military Tribunal. It was composed of four judges, one from each of the prosecuting powers, with four alternates, all eight sitting in one row. Lord Justice Lawrence from Great Britain presided. Next to Lawrence was the American judge, Francis Biddle. Biddle had been appointed by Truman to the Tribunal as consolation for having been sacked as attorney general. Rebecca West, reporting for *The New Yorker*, described Biddle as "a highly intelligent swan, occasionally flexing down to commune with a smaller waterfowl."[7] She did not mention that she was romantically involved with Biddle at the time. Behind the judges were the windows of the courtroom, but thick green drapes covered them. They were usually drawn to allow the proceedings to be filmed.

The prosecution occupied the center of the room. Each nation had its own table: French, Russian, American, and British teams, arranged left to right. The podium used by the lawyers to address the courtroom was sandwiched between the defense tables and the judges. It faced the witness box at the front of the room, to the right, and a bank of eight translators providing simultaneous translations behind glass walls, to the left. The press and visitors sat in the rear on two hundred red plush chairs requisitioned from a theater.[8] A balcony gallery held an additional 150 spectators.

The focus of the trial, both visually and morally, was the dock. And the main attraction in the dock was Hermann Göring. Göring, the highest-ranking Nazi survivor, was awarded the place of honor—the corner seat in the front. He usually wore a pale blue Luftwaffe tunic, shorn of his medals, languidly reclining during the proceedings with his right arm draped on the balustrade. He exuded unrepentant arrogance, his face alternating between smirk and scowl.

Many were surprised when they saw Göring in the courtroom. The newsreels had shown him to be obese, his five-foot-ten frame lugging around almost two hundred and eighty pounds.[9] He dressed flamboyantly, adorned with medals and jewelry. He sometimes wore lipstick and rouge with painted fingernails and toenails.[10] With his mischievous grin, he resembled a comic book villain. Rebecca West thought that when in good spirits, he looked like "a madam in a brothel."[11] At their first meeting, Colonel Burton Andrus, the commandant of the prison, described Göring as a "simpering slob."[12] Göring not only arrived with sixteen matching, monogrammed suitcases filled with baubles, outfits, and cash, but one of those bags was filled with paracodeine, a synthetic form of morphine, close to twenty thousand pills (he had more but flushed them down the toilet before he was caught).[13] He possessed almost the entire world's supply of the drug. But Göring was weaned off narcotics and put on a diet. By the time the trial began, he had lost seventy pounds. Those who expected to see a bloated drug addict were disappointed.

It was hard to know who Göring held in greater contempt: the prosecution or his fellow defendants. Göring had to bear sitting next to Rudolf Hess, once deputy führer and third-ranking member of the Nazi party. He thought Hess insane, which he almost certainly was. In 1941 Hess flew from Germany and parachuted into Scotland, by himself and without warning. His mission was to convince Churchill to join the Nazi effort against the Soviets. When this mission failed, he spent the rest of the war in a British prison. Göring explained the predicament this stunt presented for the Reich: "Do you think it was a pleasure for us to have to state publicly that one of our leading figures was crazy?"[14]

Next to Hess was Ribbentrop. Göring, of course, had no regard for Germany's number one parrot. When Göring asked Hitler why he appointed Ribbentrop, who up to that point had little political experience, Hitler said that Ribbentrop knows all the diplomats. "Yes," Göring replied, "but the difficulty is that they know Ribbentrop."[15]

The next seat down was Wilhelm Keitel, commander of the Wehrmacht, the German armed forces. Keitel was known in the army as the consummate yes-man—a sycophant whose favorite words were *"Jawohl, mein Führer!"*[16] After Keitel was Alfred Rosenberg, the oppressively dull and dull-witted "philosopher" of National Socialism. Rosenberg was the author of *The Myth of the Twentieth Century*, a racist tract filled with so much pseudoscience about Aryan superiority that even Hitler deemed it incomprehensible. A few places down sat Julius Streicher, a short, squat, bald-shaven sadist, a pariah even among the defendants.[17] West pegged him as a "dirty old man of the sort that gives trouble in parks."[18] He was the publisher of *Der Stürmer*, an anti-Semitic newspaper deemed so outrageous that, for a short time, it was banned even in Nazi Germany. Streicher was also the *Gauleiter* (regional party leader) of Franconia, a region that included his native Nuremberg, but was fired, unsurprisingly, when he published a rumor about how Göring's daughter Edda had been conceived in a test tube due to Göring's impotence. Streicher tested lowest among the defendants on his IQ test at 106.

Not all of the twenty one defendants were that pathetic. Schacht, who sat at the very end of the first row, scored an impressive 143 on his IQ test. Though he was an early supporter of National Socialism, he participated in the failed July 20 assassination plot on Hitler's life and spent the final year of the war in concentration camps, lastly in Dachau. Göring despised Schacht for turning traitor.[19] Göring began the trial on good terms with Albert Speer, Hitler's architect and later minister of armaments, who sat in the second row behind Streicher. Göring admired Speer, once telling Hitler that, next to Hitler, Speer was the greatest man Germany possessed.[20] But Göring turned on him when, during the trial, Speer accepted responsibility for his actions. This admission of culpability defied Göring's demand that the defendants present a unified front of innocence to the Tribunal. Speer thought that Göring was not fighting for his life, but for his place in history. Göring told the other defendants that "within fifty years his remains would be laid in a marble sarcophagus and he would be celebrated by the German people as a national hero and martyr."[21]

"THE PACT OF PARIS IS THE LAW OF NATIONS. THIS TRIBUNAL WILL DECLARE IT."

On November 20, the Trial of the Century opened neither with a bang nor a whimper, but with a drone. The Tribunal insisted that the long indictment containing the detailed charges against the defendants be read in its entirety. The intoning was so tedious that the junior prosecutors handled it. During the lunch recess, Ribbentrop asked Dr. Gustave Gilbert, "Why all this fuss about breaking treaties? Did you ever read about the history of the British Empire? Why, it's full of broken treaties, oppression of minorities, mass murder, aggressive wars, and everything."[22]

The next morning the Tribunal responded to a joint motion of all the defendants challenging its jurisdiction. Waging aggressive war, they objected, was not a crime when committed and thus the Tribunal was conducting an ex post facto inquiry. The Tribunal tabled the decision for the time being, but allowed that "they may be heard at a later stage."[23]

Next came the entering of pleas, all of which were "Not Guilty." With preliminaries having been settled, Robert Jackson, wearing a morning coat and striped trousers, approached the lectern to present the opening argument for the United States. Jackson considered the speech "the most important task of my life." By all accounts, it was a spellbinder.

Jackson began by noting that the proceeding was the "first trial in history for crimes against the peace of the world." Civilization, he said, could not tolerate these crimes being ignored "because it cannot survive their being repeated." And then he delivered the most famous line of the trial, a paean to the rule of law: "That four great nations, flushed with victory and stung with injury stay the hand of vengeance and voluntarily submit their captive enemies to the judgment of the law is one of the most significant tributes that Power ever has paid to Reason."[24]

Jackson's aim in his opening address was to set out the case for Count One of the indictment, which charged the defendants with a conspiracy to wage aggressive war. He presented the history of the Nazi party—from 1921, when Hitler became its supreme leader or "führer," to his appointment as chancellor in January 1933, to his capture of absolute power a few months later, to his crushing of the labor movement, the repression of the Church, and, finally, the persecution of the Jews—as all part of a plan to wage aggressive war. "This war did not just happen," Jackson claimed, "it was planned and prepared for over a long period of time and with no small skill and cunning." Domestic terrorism was a matter of international concern, he argued, because it was the manner by which the Nazi party controlled the German people for belligerent purposes. "[P]ersecution was a step in the preparation for aggressive warfare that the offense becomes one of international consequence. To remove every moderating influence among the German people and to put its population on a total war footing, the conspirators devised and carried out a systematic and relentless repression of all Christian sects and churches."[25]

During the lunch recess, Göring expressed shock over Jackson's accusations regarding the Nazi campaign against the Catholic Church. He did not deny their accuracy. He thought that Jackson was not entitled to make them. "But that was our right! We were a sovereign state and that was strictly our business."[26]

After lunch, Jackson continued by listing various atrocities committed by the Nazis—the execution of captured soldiers, targeting of civilians, the horrors of the concentration camps. Gruesome details filled the speech. In one particularly lurid passage, Jackson described the medical experiments performed on Jews. "At Dachau, the reports of the 'doctor' in charge show that victims were immersed in cold water until their body temperature was reduced to 28 degrees centigrade (82.4 degrees Fahrenheit), when they all died immediately." Doctors then figured out how to use warm water to resuscitate their subjects. The last experiment in the series was "rewarming with animal heat." Jackson explained: "The victim, all but frozen to death, was surrounded with bodies of living women until he revived and responded to his environment by having sexual intercourse. Here Nazi degeneracy reached its nadir."[27]

He concluded his speech by defending the prosecution of the defendants for waging aggressive war. Predictably, he focused on the charge of retroactivity. He responded with the Ečer-Chanler theory. "War inevitably is a course of killings, assaults, deprivations of liberty, and destruction of property. . . . The very minimum legal consequence of the treaties making aggressive wars illegal is to strip those who incite or wage them of every defense the law ever gave, and to leave war-makers subject to judgment by the usually accepted principles of the law of crimes."[28]

Jackson presented a version of Kelsen's theory as well, in a section justifying individual responsibility for the defendants. As Kelsen had explained to Jackson in his memo, collective responsibility through war is the standard remedy in international law. "An International Law which operates only on states can be enforced only by war because the most practicable method of coercing a state in [sic] warfare." However, it would make little sense to enforce the prohibition on war through war. Only by substituting individual punishment could international law end this scourge. "This principle of personal liability is a necessary as well as logical one if international law is to render real help to the maintenance of peace."[29]

Jackson concluded by invoking civilization once again and its expectations for the Tribunal. "Civilization . . . does not expect that you can make war impossible. It does expect that your juridical action will put the forces of international law, its precepts, its prohibitions and, most of all, its sanctions, on the side of peace."[30]

HANDSOME HARTLEY

Truth be told, Jackson's speech was more of a rhetorical triumph than a legal one. The legal arguments were not crisply rendered. They seemed rushed. The responsibility for presenting the detailed legal case for aggressive war fell to the British prosecutor, Hartley Shawcross.

Shawcross was an unlikely choice. He was not an international lawyer. Nor was he a well-known public figure. In fact, he won his very first election only a few months before the trial began. Clement Attlee, who defeated Winston Churchill in the July elections, surprised the British establishment when he appointed this obscure backbencher attorney general. Though Shawcross was a respected barrister, he was probably chosen in part for his appearance. He was known as "the best looking man in English public life."[31]

Lauterpacht was the legal adviser to the British delegation, but did not see a draft of Shawcross's speech until he was on his way back to England. What he read horrified him. "Just as I was leaving Nuremberg, I was shown the British case which the Attorney-General was to put next Monday, December 3, and I saw immediately that it was bad to the point of being ridiculous."[32] Lauterpacht does not describe its failings, but given the difficult legal issues surrounding the crime of aggression, it is likely that Shawcross's analysis was poorly reasoned and presented. To his credit, Shawcross agreed with Lauterpacht and allowed him to redraft the speech. Lauterpacht toiled for five days and produced a completely new draft for Shawcross to give in court.[33]

As delivered by Shawcross, the opening legal argument emphasized the radical nature of the Pact. He called it "that most fundamental, that truly revolutionary enactment in modern international law, namely, the General Treaty for the Renunciation of War of 27 August 1928, the Pact of Paris, the Kellogg-Briand Pact." Shawcross then read aloud its two provisions. The Pact, he went on to say, "abolished war as a legally permissible means of enforcing the law or of changing it. The right of war was no longer of the essence of sovereignty." Though Shawcross took these, and many other passages, verbatim from Lauterpacht's draft, he also added his own rhetorical touches, stating his case as a barrister would: "The Pact of Paris is the law of nations. This Tribunal will declare it. The world must enforce it."[34]

Having established that the Pact rendered war illegal, Shawcross's speech got to the hard part: showing that the Pact rendered war criminally punishable as well. But he did not rely on the Ečer-Chanler theory to do so. In contrast to Jackson, he may have understood the dangerous implications that such an account would have on the law of war. Instead, Lauterpacht's draft—again delivered nearly verbatim by Shawcross—relied on his teacher's theory. As Kelsen had taught, classical international law was built upon the principle of collective responsibility. States that violated the law were traditionally sanctioned through war. [35] But the practice of collective responsibility is a primitive form of morality that states ought to reject: "[T]he conscience shrinks from the rigors of collective punishment, which may fall upon the guilty and the innocent alike." Singling out the leaders of a state and holding them individually responsible for the violations of the law they ordered would represent a moral advance, for the punishment would lie with the truly guilty rather than being inflicted on their subjects. "Above all, much hardship can be obviated by making the punishment fall upon the individuals who were themselves directly responsible for the criminal conduct of their state." The charter of the Tribunal does just that: It substitutes individual responsibility for collective responsibility. "It is a salutary legal rule that persons who, in violation of the law, plunge their own and other countries into an aggressive war should do so with a halter around their necks."[36]

The charter of the Tribunal may have created a new law of individual responsibility, but that is all for the good, Shawcross summed up. "If this be an innovation, it is an innovation which we are prepared to defend and to justify."[37]

"CITADEL OF BOREDOM"

Though the mills of the gods grind slowly, Longfellow wrote, they grind exceedingly small. He might have added that to watch the grinding is exceedingly boring. Rebecca West described the Nuremberg courtroom as a "citadel of boredom."[38] The prosecution teams built their case largely on documentary evidence—mountains of it—and the introduction, authentication, and translation of these documents took forever. "Every person attending it is in the grip of extreme tedium."[39] Even the judges were bored to distraction. When an attractive secretary entered the courtroom, the presiding Judge Geoffrey Lawrence passed her a note: "How are you doing Pops—bored as we are?"[40]

The trial had a few intense days. On November 29, the U.S. prosecution presented its case for the crime of waging aggressive war. At one point, the prosecution read out the transcript of how Göring orchestrated the takeover of Austria on a telephone call with Ribbentrop. The presentation was not having the desired effect. Göring, Hess, and Ribbentrop were cackling in the dock.

In the afternoon, the good cheer vanished. The prosecution presented two hours of footage from the concentration camps. The images were beyond anyone's imagination. The film began with a group of people being burned alive in a barn. It just got worse from there. Everyone was shocked, including the defendants. Göring drooped in his chair, not watching the screen; Hans Frank, the "Butcher of Poland," fought back tears; Rosenberg fidgeted in his seat; Hans Fritzsche was in agony; Walther Funk cried; even the defense attorneys muttered "for God's sake— terrible."[41] After the movie was over, Judge Lawrence stormed out of the courtroom without adjourning the proceedings. Later that night, another defendant, General Alfred Jodl, wrote a letter to his wife: "This disgrace, however, besmirches everything."[42] Göring was also in a foul mood. "It was such a good afternoon, too, until they showed that film. . . . [I]t just spoiled everything."[43]

The evidence that Nazi Germany had waged an aggressive war was overwhelming and irrefutable. Whether certain defendants, such as Franz von Papen or Hjalmar Schacht, had participated in the conspiracy was debatable, but for others, such as Göring, Keitel, and Jodl, the accusations were undeniable. The emotional power of the films and testimony from camp survivors and guards devastated their case. The defendants' only hope was to convince the Tribunal of the injustice of a conviction. They had to show that the Peace Pact had not criminalized war in 1928. This task fell to an obscure professor of international law, Kelsen's successor at the University of Cologne, Hermann Jahrreiss.

VENTRILOQUISM

Most defendants found their lawyers by picking from a list provided by the Americans. Not Julius Streicher. He thought that the names "looked like those of Jews" and insisted on an anti-Semitic attorney.[44] He asked for Hanns Marx, a local Nuremberg lawyer and former Nazi party member.

His request was granted.[45] Alfred Jodl wanted to know whether he should get an expert in criminal law or international law. He was told that he probably needed both.[46]

His wife, Luise, found the criminal lawyer. She made a personal appeal to Herbert Wechsler, an assistant to Francis Biddle, to contact a family friend. Could he ask Franz Exner at the University of Munich for help to defend her husband? Wechsler replied that he knew him. Exner had visited Columbia Law School before the war, where Wechsler was a faculty member. He agreed to have Exner tracked down. When found, Exner accepted the job.[47]

Jahrreiss was looking for employment at the same time, for the University of Cologne, where he had worked since replacing Kelsen in 1937, would not let him teach.[48] Though Jahrreiss had not joined the Nazi party,[49] he was an active member of the Academy of German Law, the Nazi legal organization founded by Frank and on whose board Schmitt sat.[50] Jahrreiss had become a follower of Schmitt's ideas. When the war broke out, he wrote two favorable commentaries on Schmitt's theory of the *Grossraum* in which he supported Schmitt's call for the establishment of a German "great space" over continental Europe.[51] These articles haunted him after the war. An internal university committee in charge of denazification barred him from teaching. Jahrreiss went searching for work and contacted Exner, an old colleague from Leipzig. Since Exner had no experience in international law, he invited Jahrreiss to join the Jodl team.

Jodl was proud that two law professors were defending him. The law professors were proud of themselves, too, as indicated by their decision to wear their violet academic robes in the courtroom. Since Jodl's wife spoke English, Wechsler arranged for Luise to join the legal team as their secretary. A handsome woman, she would inspire the character later played by Marlene Dietrich in the Hollywood film *Judgment at Nuremberg*.[52]

Counsel for the accused selected Jahrreiss to present their collective defense on the issue of retroactivity.[53] On July 4, 1946, he took to the lectern to make the case. His arguments followed the exact lines that Schmitt had set out in the *Gutachten* written for Flick. Jahrreiss began by making all the arguments that a competent lawyer would offer: The Pact did not resemble a criminal statute, the signatories did not think that it would be enforced through the criminal law, and the Pact was subject to so many reservations as to make it useless as a criminal prohibition.

But Jahrreiss went beyond these basic objections and presented the same sophisticated arguments Schmitt had conjured up in his *Gutachten*. First, he argued that the Pact could not deliver on its promise of a new world order because the political institutions that would make that order possible—collective security, disarmament, and revision of the Versailles treaty—had not materialized. The League of Nations had been a failure; the great nations had not disarmed, and the Allies would not soften the harsh peace settlement.[54]

Having argued that the political environment would not support a new legal order, Jahrreiss then asked, as Schmitt had, whether there was evidence in 1939 that the law had in fact changed. To answer this question, Jahrreiss proceeded just as Schmitt had: If the Pact had changed the law, Jahrreiss argued, then the discriminatory conception of war would have emerged in the practice of states. In particular, there would have been changes in the (1) laws of war, (2) duties of neutrality, and (3) recognition of conquest.[55]

(1) Do the international laws of war—which, after all, spring from the right to wage war freely and from the duel-like character of war and certainly from the equality of the belligerents before the law—apply for the qualification of the acts of the belligerent powers against one another?

(2) Is it possible, or indeed permissible, that neutrality should still exist in such a war?

(3) Can the result of the war, assuming that the aggressor is victorious, be valid under law, especially when compressed into the form of a treaty, or must not the community of states deprive the aggressor of the spoils of his victory by a policy of nonrecognition?

To each question, Jahrreiss argued that the law had not changed by the start of the war. No nation had ever suggested that the laws of war applied only to those fighting a just war and not to the other side. Nor did nonbelligerents, such as the United States, renounce their neutrality in 1939. Finally, while the United States did follow the Stimson Doctrine, many other countries, including England and France, persisted in recognizing the validity of territorial conquests.

Jahrreiss came to the same conclusion as Schmitt. The laws set out in the charter of the Tribunal punishing individuals for waging aggressive war are "new—revolutionarily new. The laws regarding war and peace between states provided no room for them and could not do so. Thus they are criminal laws with retroactive force."[56]

Jahrreiss impressed the prosecution. Nuremberg prosecutor Telford Taylor commented that "the defendants could hardly have had a better spokesman."[57] Taylor did not realize that he was praising the man spouting Schmitt's ideas. For while there is no way to know for sure, it is likely that Jahrreiss's speech was based on Schmitt's *Gutachten*.[58] First, Dix had Schmitt's memo—or, at the very least, had read it—and his client, whom Jahrreiss was representing in his collective defense, was facing the death penalty for the charge of waging aggressive war. It would have been malpractice for Dix not to give Schmitt's expert memo to Jahrreiss, or at least to convey its main arguments. Second, Jahrreiss was a Schmittian—he respected Schmitt's theory of international law. He would not have ignored Schmitt's ideas on the topic he was charged with handling. Third, the arguments that Jahrreiss presented were identical to the sophisticated arguments that Schmitt had set out in his memo.

Given this evidence, it appears that the Nuremberg Trial was the scene of one of the greatest acts of ventriloquism in legal history. Hersch Lauterpacht had essentially written Shawcross's opening speech. Carl Schmitt had written the basis of Jahrreiss's response. These two antagonists—a Jew and a Nazi—were debating the legal effect of the Pact through courtroom lawyers.

Lauterpacht got the last word, for he composed Shawcross's legal response, delivered on July 26, 1946. Lauterpacht began the rebuttal by scoffing at the idea that the Pact made aggressive war illegal, but not criminal. How could the prohibition on *mass homicide* not be understood as a crime? "[T]here is no difference between illegality and criminality in a breach of law involving the deaths of millions and a direct attack on the very foundations of civilized life."[59]

Lauterpacht then savaged Jahrreiss's argument about the League's failure to enforce the Pact. Does a crime cease to be a crime just because the criminal got away with it?[60] That the League failed means that better enforcement mechanisms were necessary—it did not relieve states of their obligations. "It may be that the policemen did not act as effectively as one could have wished them to act. But that was a failure of the policeman, not of the law."[61]

Lauterpacht was also scathing about Jahrreiss's claims about neutrality. "The fact that the United States declared its neutrality in 1939 was cited as an example of the collapse of the system as if the United States had been under any legal obligation to act otherwise."[62] The Pact *permitted* neutrals to take discriminatory action against aggressors, but it certainly did not *require* them to do so.

According to Lauterpacht, Jahrreiss failed to appreciate that the Pact had indeed changed the law in radical ways. For the League did impose sanctions on Japan and Italy, an unprecedented renunciation of traditional neutrality.[63] While the League did not follow through, it acted as though it was legally permitted to do so. "[T]he reluctance of the peace-loving states to take arms against the blackmail and the bullying which was directed against them" was a failure of political will, not of legal right.[64] They had the legal right to punish states for waging aggressive wars because these states, through their leaders, had committed crimes.

He sarcastically asked how much these leaders cared about state sovereignty when they launched their aggressive campaigns. He even took aim at Schmitt himself. "It is strange to see the accused who in their capacity as the German Government overran most of the states of Europe, who trampled brutally upon their sovereign independence, and who with boastful and swaggering cynicism made the sovereignty of the conquered states subservient *to the new conception of the 'Grossraumordnung'*—it is strange to see these defendants appealing to the mystic virtues of the sanctity of state sovereignty."[65] *Grossraumordnung* was the theory that Schmitt developed in 1939, the one that Hitler appropriated for himself, the one that had so influenced Jahrreiss, and the one that nearly became the law of the world.

THE VERDICT

On October 1, 1946, the International Military Tribunal handed down its verdicts. It sentenced twelve of the defendants to death by hanging (Göring, Ribbentrop, Keitel, Ernst Kaltenbrunner, Rosenberg, Frank, Frick, Streicher, Fritz Sauckel, Jodl, Arthur Seyss-Inquart, Martin Bormann in absentia), seven to terms of imprisonment ranging from ten years to life (Admiral Karl Dönitz, Funk, Hess, Admiral Erich Raeder, Baldur von Schirach, Speer, Konstantin von Neurath), and three were acquitted (Schacht, Papen, Fritzsche).

In its judgment, the Tribunal justified the charter's provision criminalizing aggressive war by referring to the Peace Pact. Its justifications for using the Pact as a foundation for individual criminal punishment, however, were disappointing, even shocking. For the Tribunal did not accept, or even mention, the Ečer-Chanler theory. It did not accept, or even mention, the Kelsen theory. Its principal argument was the very one that the prosecution team had tried to avoid making: the theory that Schmitt offered to justify the *Lex Lubbe* in which it is permissible to punish evil acts even if they were not legally crimes when committed. "To assert that it is unjust to punish those who in defiance of treaties and assurances have attacked neighbouring states without warning is obviously untrue," the Tribunal wrote, "for in such circumstances the attacker must know that he is doing wrong, and so far from it being unjust to punish him, *it would be unjust if his wrong were allowed to go unpunished*."[66]

The Tribunal mumbled some more sentences about the uniqueness of international law—how it does not have a legislature and how international agreements such "as the Pact have to deal with general principles of law, and not with administrative matters of procedure." "This law is not static," it wrote, "but by continual adaptation follows the needs of a changing world."[67] True enough, but why does any of this entitle the Tribunal to send men to their deaths?

In its brevity and failure to take more seriously the arguments made before it, the Tribunal missed an opportunity to justify the basis for its decision. It left the impression that its decision was legally unfounded and politically motivated, an act of victor's justice. That it did so is all the more unfortunate because the Tribunal had excellent arguments available. Some of the greatest legal minds of the time had devoted themselves to crafting the arguments on both sides of the cases—not just Jackson but Ečer, Lauterpacht, Kelsen, and, yes, Schmitt. They had treated the issue with seriousness. By passing over these arguments, the Tribunal failed to do what was necessary to vindicate its decision. Indeed, those who read only the opinion of the Tribunal severed from the arguments presented before it—as nearly everyone still does today—have no way of knowing that such arguments were ever made. They might reasonably conclude, as so many have, that the Tribunal offered the best case it could for the decision it had made, and that the case was weak, or even unjustifiable.

There is some indication that the Tribunal was uncomfortable with its own decision. For it decreed that no defendant would get the death penalty simply for waging aggressive war.[68] Only those who committed war crimes or crimes against humanity would be hanged. The Tribunal also acquitted five out of twenty-three defendants for waging aggressive war. Schacht, for example, was cleared for his role in rearmament, for it could not be proven beyond a reasonable doubt that he intended to rearm for the purpose of waging aggressive war, as opposed to providing a strong defense against the aggression of others.

The Tribunal rejected the prosecution's argument that the domestic terror campaign before the war constituted the crime of aggressive war. Nevertheless, it did punish those who participated in the Holocaust in the occupied territories after the war began. "[I]nsofar as the inhumane acts charged in the Indictment, and committed after the beginning of the war, did not constitute war crimes, they were all committed in execution of, or in connection with, the aggressive war, and therefore constituted crimes against humanity."[69] Thus, although no one was executed solely for waging an aggressive war, the legal justification for the execution of the Major War Criminals ultimately stemmed from the Peace Pact. The crimes against humanity committed during the Holocaust, though not war crimes, were committed in execution of an aggressive war. As such, they could be punished—with death.

CARL AND KARL

An enemy need not hate his adversary, Schmitt had argued in *The Concept of the Political*. He simply must see his foe as an existential threat, a mortal danger to eliminate.[70] This attitude described Schmitt's main enemy after the war, Karl Loewenstein. Loewenstein admired Schmitt, followed his scholarly work, and even corresponded with him. He also fought harder than anyone to have him arrested when the war was over.

Karl Loewenstein was born to a Jewish family in Munich, three years after Schmitt.[71] He practiced law throughout the 1920s, while also publishing prolifically. He and Schmitt exchanged scholarly offprints and cited each other in their publications. Loewenstein managed to secure a teaching position at the University of Munich in 1931, but lost it two years later when Jewish civil servants were dismissed by the Nazis. He fled to the United States, where he worked for two years at the Yale Law School before securing a permanent position teaching government at Amherst College. Loewenstein published many articles on Nazi law and, given his expertise, joined the occupation government in Berlin as a legal adviser in 1945.

One of Loewenstein's first missions upon arriving in Germany was to arrest Carl Schmitt. His plane touched down in Berlin on August 7 and by the 13th there is a longhand notation in his diary, "Conf. with [indecipherable] about Carl Schmitt."[72] The next day there is a typed entry: "wrote memo about the arrest of Carl Schmitt-."[73] The day after, August 15, he tried to have Schmitt arrested, but with no success. "Nobody seems inteested [*sic*] to assume jurisdiction. One bureau refers to another."[74] He tried again the next day, heading over to the Public Safety Office. "Found litt [*sic*] interest."[75]

Loewenstein did not give up. On September 13, he had a conference with two men about "the investigation of Carl Schmitt." He also "studied various materials about Schmitt."[76] On September 26, the military government arrested Carl Schmitt without charges.[77] Eight days later Loewenstein went to Schmitt's apartment and advised the impounding of his enormous book collection for the use by the occupation authorities.[78]

Loewenstein completed a memo on Schmitt in the middle of November. His arrest report read, as the literary theorist Werner Sollors observed, almost like a letter of recommendation.[79] It described Schmitt as "the foremost political scientist," "a man of near-genius rating," who "possesses not only a vast and by no means sterile erudition," "drawing from an immense store of factual information," and "one of those rare scholars who combine learning with imagination." Loewenstein went on to say, however, that Schmitt "abused his gifts for evil purposes." His defense of the political assassinations during the Night of the Long Knives legitimated Hitler's illegal actions to the rest of the world. And his theory of the *Grossraum* "provided the regime with the theoretical foundations of its drive for world power."[80]

Schmitt wasn't only influential in Germany, Loewenstein added. He had a worldwide reputation as the chief ideologist for totalitarian and fascist regimes, especially influential in France, Spain, and Latin America. "Hardly any contemporary writer can claim for himself to have influenced his time to such an extent as has Carl Schmitt."[81]

Loewenstein did not simply want to punish Schmitt for his sins. He wanted to protect Germany, and the world, from his ideas. His danger consisted in his genius, in his ability to make the irrational seem rational.

WITNESS TO THE END

Schmitt spent a year in different internment camps. During his imprisonment, he feared for his life. The events he prophesized two decades earlier in a Berlin lecture hall had come to pass. The enemies of Germany had used the Pact to prosecute its leaders. And these enemies were now after the herald.

But he also feared for civilization. At some point in 1946, in captivity, he typed out a eulogy for the legal order that had just expired. Like so much of Schmitt's work, it manages to be both moving and repulsive. It seems sincere while also self-serving. It is filled with undeniable brilliance, astonishing erudition, and manifest absurdity.

Schmitt's main lament is the criminalization of war. The outlawry of war was being used as a weapon of war, but its deadly role was being concealed. "One sits in court," Schmitt wrote, "without ceasing to be the enemy."[82] In the name of peace, criminal trials like Nuremberg dramatically increase the stakes, turning military battles into moral crusades. And those deemed the enemies of humanity were losing their human rights. "The establishment of revolutionary tribunals and world courts will not diminish the terror but escalate it."[83]

Schmitt appealed to "the crucified God," one who "died the death of a slave by crucifixion, which was imposed on him by a foreign conqueror."[84] And as he prayed in his cell, he had a mystical experience. "Sometimes the doors of our capture open all of the sudden and a secret passage presents itself."[85] Schmitt imagined himself with the great figures of modern political philosophy, the creators of the *ius publicum europaeum*, European Public Law, the Old World Order. He communed with these Interventionists in his thoughts, even without his confiscated books. "Contacts and conversations emerge, whose power move [*sic*] mountains of entire libraries."[86] He talked with Vitoria, Gentili, and Grotius. "I love them. They belong to our camp."[87] But he identified most with the political theorists Jean Bodin and Thomas Hobbes, who preached the virtues of the absolute state. "These two figures from the religious civil wars became living, contemporary people to me. They are brothers to me and we became, transcending centuries, a family."[88]

These men constructed a legal order as an antidote to the bloody wars of religion. And with this era now over, "the legal terror of bloody civil wars" will reign again.[89] "I am the last representative of *ius publicum Europaeum*, its last teacher and scientist in its existential sense, and also witness its end."[90]

REARREST

Schmitt was cleared in August 1946 and returned to his home on October 10.[91] But on March 16, 1947, he was rearrested, transported to Nuremberg, and kept in solitary confinement at the Palace of Justice. Schmitt appears not to have known why he was arrested. His wife, Duška, wrote to Hermann Jahrreiss to ask him for an explanation, though no reply has been found.[92]

Military records indicate that Robert Kempner requested Schmitt's transfer to Nuremberg.[93] But whether the idea to pursue Schmitt was Kempner's is unclear.[94] It might have come from Loewenstein, who left Germany in September 1946, but maintained an active correspondence with Kempner.[95] Kempner was also friends with Franz Neumann, who had just completed *Behemoth*, his study of Nazi Germany in which he assigned Schmitt a large role in the fall of Weimar and the justification of Hitler's aggressive wars. In 1945, Neumann took a leave from teaching at the New School for Social Research and worked for Justice Jackson at Nuremberg, in charge of evidence collection. Another possibility is the man who actually rearrested Schmitt: Ossip Flechtheim. Flechtheim had been a doctoral student at Cologne in 1933. He asked Schmitt to be his doctoral supervisor, but Schmitt turned him down. Flechtheim assumed that he was rejected because he was a Jew, but Flechtheim was also a communist and Schmitt would not have wanted to supervise a communist. Flechtheim went on to study with Kelsen in Geneva, and then as a research assistant of Franz Neumann in New York.[96]

Loewenstein, Kempner, Neumann, and Flechtheim were Jews and had ample reason to hate Schmitt.[97] They had been traumatized, each in their own way, by this man and they likely bore him a grudge. But this was no mere vendetta. Each sincerely believed that Schmitt should be prosecuted as a war criminal.[98]

Schmitt arrived at Nuremberg two weeks later. Kempner interrogated him in the Palace of Justice on four occasions.[99] Based on the transcripts of these interrogations, Kempner seemed most interested in Schmitt's theory of the *Grossraum*. He was convinced that his writings justified Hitler's wars of aggression.

The first interrogation took place on April 3 and it was tense. "Did you not provide the ideological foundation for those kinds of things?" Kempner asked. "No," Schmitt replied. "Could your writings be so interpreted?" Kempner then asked. "I do not think so—not by anyone who has read them," Schmitt answered.[100]

Kempner did not believe that Schmitt was telling the truth. After all, Schmitt was "one of the leading jurists of the Third Reich." Schmitt responded with equal disbelief: "Someone who in 1936 was publicly defamed in *Das Schwarze Korps* cannot be described in that fashion."[101]

Kempner asked Schmitt to justify his claim in writing, prefacing his request with the intention to hold intellectuals responsible. "We are of the opinion that the executing agencies in the administration, the economy and the military are not more important than the men who conceived the theory and the plans for the entire affair. Maybe you would like to write down what you have to say. To what extent did you provide the theoretical foundation for Hitlerian *Grossraum* policy?"[102]

In his long response, Schmitt distinguished his theory of the *Grossraum* from Hitler's policy of *Lebensraum*. *Grossraum*, according to Schmitt, is not a biological, racial theory. It did not claim the right of Germany to conquer other nations based on racial superiority. As Schmitt pointed out, his theory was condemned by hard-core Nazis as *"unvölkisch"*—that is, "not racial."[103]

In the ultimate irony, Schmitt sought refuge in the Nuremberg decision, citing the outcomes as "precedents for the evaluation and judgment of my conduct."[104] According to the Tribunal, those not part of the intimate war-planning sessions could not be held responsible for planning or preparing an aggressive war. "What was ultimately said of Fritzsche could well also be said of me," Schmitt pleaded. "'He was never considered important enough to be drawn into the planning discussions which led to wars of aggression.'"[105]

Kempner appeared convinced by Schmitt's arguments and agreed to release him. At the end of their last session on April 28, which was cordial, Kempner asked Schmitt about his collaboration with the regime.[106]

KEMPNER: Are you not ashamed that you wrote these kinds of things
          at that time?

SCHMITT: Today, of course. I do not consider it appropriate to con-
          tinue to rummage around in the disgrace we suffered at that
          time.

KEMPNER: I do not want to rummage around.

SCHMITT: Without question, it was unspeakable. There are no words
          to describe it.*

*Carl Schmitt was barred from teaching at the University of Berlin, though he received
his pension. After his release from the Nuremberg prison in 1947, he returned to his
hometown of Plettenberg, where he received many visitors on pilgrimages and influenced a new generation of scholars. He died there in 1985, age ninety-six. Schmitt's
nemesis, Hans Kelsen, was finally hired as a full professor at the University of California, Berkeley, in the Political Science Department in 1945. He was honored by many
universities for his groundbreaking legal scholarship. He died in 1973, age ninety-one.
Austria honored him with a stamp bearing his likeness, calling him "A Father of the
Constitution." Kelsen's replacement at the University of Cologne, Hermann Jahrreiss,
resumed teaching there in 1948 and eventually became the rector of the university.
When Jahrreiss died in 1992, age ninety-nine, *Der Spiegel* wrote that his defense at
Nuremberg "made German legal history." "Gestorben, Hermann Jahrreiss," *Der Spiegel*,
November 2, 1992.

CODA II

With the possible exception of Robert Jackson, no one can claim more credit for or left a greater mark on Nuremberg than Hersch Lauterpacht. From his early call to criminalize wars of aggression, to his framing of the charges in the indictments, to his drafting of the British speeches setting out the prosecution's theory of the case, the International Military Tribunal followed Lauterpacht's plan. Yet after the opening arguments, he fled the historic proceedings and left his plan to be executed by others.

Given how much he had invested over many years to bring the Tribunal to life, Lauterpacht's decision to leave when he did may seem strange. But the atrocities meticulously recounted during the trial were not mere legal abstractions for this Galician Jew. Among those innumerable victims for whom Jackson spoke was Lauterpacht's entire family. His mother, father, sister, and brother were all murdered in the Holocaust. So were his grandparents, brother- and sister-in-law, uncles, aunts, cousins—almost his whole extended family was wiped out. As the trial opened, he held out hope that a niece had survived (he later discovered that she had).[1] Lauterpacht never committed his feelings to paper beyond the simple letter to his wife, quoted earlier, in which he wrote of the "unforgettable experience" seeing "a sovereign State in the dock."[2] After he returned home, however, his son reported that "he used to cry out awfully in his sleep at the recollection of the bestialities he had heard described."[3] Most likely, it was too painful for him to be present during the testimony. He followed the trial through secondhand reports.

Lauterpacht retreated from bombed-out Nuremberg to bucolic Cambridge. He was, as he put it, "glad to be free of Nuremberg for a spell."[4] In the seclusion of his office, he began to compose what he would later refer to as one of his greatest works.[5] The three-hundred-year anniversary of the death of Hugo Grotius was approaching, and he was determined to revisit the work of the man who was, in his estimation, "one of the greatest international figures of his age—a prodigy, almost a miracle of learning . . . the acknowledged greatest exponent of the Law of Nations."[6]

Lauterpacht did not write a hagiography. Far from it. The first half of the article is a damning record of the many shortcomings of Grotius's work. *The Law of War and Peace* was, he contended, a "somewhat superficial, hasty, and pretentious production."[7] The first half of Grotius's masterwork was devoted to matters that, "to all appearance, have no connection with international law."[8] This focus was necessitated, Lauterpacht explained, by Grotius's account of international law, in which "the main cause of a just war is a threatened or actual violation of a legal right or the refusal of reparation."[9] Hence, "it was necessary to give an account of the substantive law which may be affected by a breach of legal duty."[10] The work also had a "patchy character," he explained, because Grotius had made substantial use of a largely unpublished defense of Jacob van Heemskerck, which he had written years earlier in connection with a case in which he appeared as counsel for the Dutch East India Company.[11]

But it was not only poorly done, at least to modern eyes. It was brutal. Grotius's work "seems to elevate that 'lack of restraint in relation to war, such as even barbarous races should be ashamed of' to the dignity of a rule of the Law of Nations."[12] In the Grotian worldview, "[t]he Law of Nations gives the right to kill or injure all those who are in the territory of the enemy. . . . Captives taken in war may be killed. So can those who surrender but whose surrender is not accepted. . . . In general, by the Law of Nations anything is permissible as against an enemy."[13] Destruction, pillage, enslavement—all were justified. Hence Grotius's work, far from tempering war, lends support to "the inhuman conduct of warfare by conceding to it the character of law."[14]

Given this barbarity, Lauterpacht asks, how can Grotius be so celebrated? The answer, Lauterpacht concludes, is simple: "the teaching of Grotius has become identified with the progression of international law to a true *system* of law both in its legal and in its ethical content."[15]

Grotius described international law not only as a system, Lauterpacht explained, but as a system with certain key features. These features endured even as the rules themselves changed. Though *The Law of War and Peace* no longer offered any "assistance in the search for a legal rule which we may assume an international court would now apply in a case before it," it was a guide to the function, to the role, and to the "persistent problems" of international law.[16] These contributions were still relevant—indeed, timeless.

Lauterpacht understood the horrors to which the Grotian legal system could lead as well as anyone. After all, his family had been slaughtered during the last gasps of the world order Grotius had systematized. But he saw and appreciated the genius behind Grotius's work nonetheless. "Grotius," Lauterpacht explained, "conceives of the totality of the relations between States as governed by law."[17]

The three-hundred-year anniversary of Grotius's death marked a key moment in the world of international law. With the surrender by the Axis powers, the opening of the United Nations, and the unfolding trials at Nuremberg—the Old World Order that Grotius had inaugurated met a decisive end. With the conclusion of the Old World Order, Lauterpacht saw the possibility of a new beginning and an opportunity to lay claim to Grotius as the patron saint of international law—not because the rules Grotius espoused were good or right or moral, but because Grotius understood that international law, to function, must form a complete system.

Lauterpacht knew that his generation had to lay claim to that tradition. In appropriating it, though, he would transform it. Lauterpacht had already done much to describe this transformation. But there was still more to be worked out. Now that threats of force were illegal, what would become of gunboat diplomacy? And if force could not be used to enforce a treaty, how would treaties be enforced? How would any international law—including the prohibition on conquest—be enforced? The Security Council could not respond to every minor infraction.

Lauterpacht was not alone in trying to discover the answers to these questions. The United Nations Charter anticipated that such issues might emerge and gave the General Assembly the power to initiate studies and make recommendations to encourage "the progressive development of international law and its codification."[18] Lauterpacht would soon be appointed to the newly formed International Law Commission whose charge from the U.N. General Assembly was nothing less than working out the new rules of the international system.

THE DEMISE OF GUNBOAT DIPLOMACY

Lauterpacht accepted his election to the International Law Commission. He thought it would offer "a great opportunity to do a thing of enduring value."[19] His hopes soon ran into political realities. The work was taxing and working with the other members frustrating. "They are an ignorant lot," he wrote to his wife, Rachel. "Sometimes I think that they appreciate what I am doing. Sometimes it seems that they are angry at being treated like members of my seminar. However, members of my class are much better."[20] Toward the end of his first session, Lauterpacht was selected as the rapporteur on the Law of Treaties for the commission. And, much to his relief, he was left to work on his own in producing the commission's report. Over the course of nine months, he produced a masterful, comprehensive seventy-page *Report on the Law of Treaties*.

In many respects, the report was a restatement of existing law, identifying those enduring elements of treaty law that had survived the massive transformation of the Pact and the Charter. But parts of the report were groundbreaking—replacing black with white and white with black. Perhaps the most striking example was Article 12—entitled "Absence of compulsion," which invalidated treaties imposed as a result of threat or use of force.[21]

This position was revolutionary. Just over two decades earlier, in a book published in 1927, a year before the Pact was signed, Lauterpacht had recognized that gunboat diplomacy, though deplorable, was legally effective: "The special structure of international law deprives the conception of a treaty of one of the essential elements of contract, namely, of the requirement of a free declaration of will."[22] Traditional international law had not regarded coercion as vitiating the validity of treaties for a simple reason: War was legal. "If war was permitted as an institution, it followed that the law was bound to recognize the results of successful use of force thus used."[23]

Now writing for the International Law Commission and its member states, Lauterpacht explained that these foundational rules had changed: "In the General Treaty for the Renunciation of War of 27 August 1928 (Pact of Paris) the Parties renounced recourse to war as an instrument of national policy in their relations with one another."[24] As a result, "war could no longer be resorted to either as a legal remedy or as an instrument for changing the law."[25] As a result of this "fundamental change in the legal structure of international society,"[26] agreements could no longer be coerced.[27]

The turnaround by the most authoritative body in the world on international law set off a scuffle between states. There were, after all, hundreds—if not thousands—of such treaties. Were they still valid? Predictably, states that had stared down gun barrels were eager to declare those treaties invalid, while states who had pointed the guns warned of the destabilizing effects of such declarations. The U.S. government—home of Commodore Matthew Perry—argued that "the validity of a large number of treaties, notably peace treaties, would be thrown into question."[28] The International Law Commission agreed. The rules had changed in 1928, but that did not render earlier treaties invalid. The old treaties would stand.[29]

The complete inversion of the rules in so short a time puzzled many in Japan. At a deposition in connection with the Tokyo War Trials held in 1946, Kanji Ishiwara, the mastermind behind the invasion of Manchuria, complained:

> Haven't you heard of Perry? Don't you know anything about your own country's history? . . . Tokugawa Japan believed in isolation; it didn't want to have anything to do with other countries, and had its doors

locked tightly. Then came along Perry from your country in his black ships to open those doors; he aimed his guns at Japan and warned that "If you don't deal with us, look out out for these; open your doors and negotiate with other countries too." And then when Japan did open its doors and tried dealing with other countries, it learned that all those countries were a fearfully aggressive lot. And so for its own defense it took your own country as its teacher and set about learning about how to be aggressive. You might say we became your disciples. Why don't you subpoena Perry from the other world and try *him* as a war criminal.[30]

But even if Commodore Perry could have been raised from the dead, he could not have been tried as a war criminal. For when he steamed his black ships into Edo Bay and threatened to unleash his cannons unless Japan agreed to trade with the United States, aggressive war was not yet a crime.

HERSCH THE GREAT

The emissaries who signed the Peace Pact in 1928 had no inkling of the chaos they would unleash. Their goal of outlawing war was glorious. Yet, little did they realize it was also perilous, for they were removing the linchpin of the international system. By eliminating war as a tool for solving international disputes, they left the remaining rules of the system suspended. It did not take long for the entire international legal order to fall to pieces.

The crisis of the interwar period was the predictable result. The delegates had made a grave mistake. They had rejected a world in which war was the tool for resolving disputes and righting wrongs, but they had not yet considered what would take its place. War may have been terrible, but it served an essential function in a world of sovereign states. How could a system of sovereign states exist without it? It would take a brilliant mind to answer this question, one that could build a new legal system grounded not in war but in its opposite—the new prohibition on war. The world needed a new Grotius to develop the New World Order.

Hersch Lauterpacht was too modest to claim this mantle for himself, but his modesty should not preclude us from draping him in it. Whereas

Grotius is the father of the Old World Order, Lauterpacht is the father of the New World Order. He labored for a decade to understand the changes that the Peace Pact had wrought in international law. Then, beginning in 1940, he began putting the four pillars of the new system into place.

In his work with Jackson, he helped establish that neutrality did not require impartiality. States could, and increasingly did, place economic sanctions on aggressors and other wrongdoers, while offering more favorable terms to those they regarded as in the right. In 1945, he helped establish the principle that those who waged aggressive war could be put in the dock. In 1947, he completed the leading study of state recognition in which he wrote that conquest was illegal and states not only were prohibited from using force to establish territorial control but also from recognizing the actions of those who did.[31] And in 1949, he enshrined the principle that a coerced agreement was no agreement at all. In each case, he grounded the new principles—which in many instances were reversals of his own deeply held positions—on the change wrought in the system of international law by the 1928 Peace Pact.

The New World Order that Lauterpacht helped elaborate was, as we put it at the opening of the book, a photo negative of the Old World Order. Grotius's system had rules governing conquest, criminal liability, gunboat diplomacy, and neutrality. As we can see in the figure below, Lauterpacht's rules were the same as Grotius's except in one simple respect: They were the opposite.

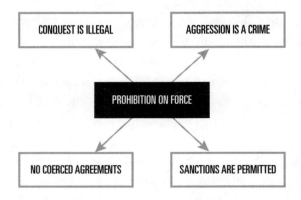

With the new legal order now established, Lauterpacht left the commission and accepted an appointment as a judge on the International Court of Justice.[32] He was chosen for the position despite lingering anti-Semitic opposition. He served with great distinction, though he remained a scholar at heart. As his son put it, "[H]e did not accept comfortably what he saw as the presumption of others who might question his drafts in areas of law, or in modes of presentation, where he felt that his knowledge and experience exceeded theirs."[33] Even while working as a judge, he continued his scholarly work, writing a book and several articles alongside his judicial opinions. He passed away in 1960, after a battle with cancer and series of heart attacks, at the age of sixty-two—the same age as Grotius when he died in 1645.[34]

The legacy of Hersch Lauterpacht was nothing less than a system of rules embodying the idea that war is an illegitimate tool for establishing or enforcing legal rights. Now, there would only be one way for states to get what they wanted from other states—they had to offer those states something that they wanted in return. Compulsion by war was over. The era of global cooperation had begun.

PART III

NEW WORLD ORDER

THIRTEEN

THE END OF CONQUEST

The revolution began on a cold November evening as twenty students milled about Kiev's central plaza and awaited the promised crowd. More trickled in over the next few hours, slowly responding to the call via Facebook and Twitter to gather in Maidan Nezalezhnosti—Independence Square. A man helping to lead the protest against pro-Russian president Viktor Yanukovych spoke to a gathering crowd through a bullhorn: "Ukraine should be part of Europe. No one—not even those in the highest offices—should have the right to take away the wishes of the majority of Ukrainians for European integration," he blared. A woman wearing a blue and yellow ribbon in colors matching the European Union and Ukrainian flags waved by the protesters spoke next. She reassured the small crowd in the Maidan that more would come. "This is only beginning. We may get several hundred, even a thousand tonight, but tomorrow there will be ten thousand; after that will be a hundred thousand and then a million. This is our only chance to save this country!"[1]

Indeed, within a few days, twenty thousand people had joined the demonstrations. Blue and yellow ribbons, a symbol of the growing movement, were everywhere. After Yanukovych ignored the protesters' complaints and signed a trade deal with Russian president Vladimir Putin, the protests boiled over into riots. The club-swinging security police sent to disperse the crowds only made them bigger. On February 20, 2014, the "Euromaidan" protesters, now more than a million strong, exploded in fury when snipers began picking off demonstrators from buildings that lined the square. In the face of such brutality, activists vowed armed resistance if President Yanukovych did not step down. Fearing for their lives, Yanukovych and other leading members of his administration fled the country.

When jubilant activists stormed the president's abandoned residence, they discovered the outrageous excesses of Yanukovych's kleptocracy: gaudy chandelier-filled rooms reminiscent of Versailles, a private cinema with leather recliners, a lakeside bathhouse complete with hot tub, a private floating restaurant, a flock of ostriches, ornamental duck houses, gold-plated bathroom fixtures, a golf course, a helicopter pad, an aircraft hangar, bronze and marble statues galore, and bottles of brandy with the ousted president's face on the label.[2]

Still, not everyone was celebrating. Even as gawking activists explored the abandoned palace, opposition to the newly formed government was brewing in the eastern part of the country, where support for close ties with Russia ran highest. In Crimea, which the Russian Black Sea fleet had called home since the time of Catherine the Great, fierce agitation by pro-Russian demonstrators soon began. But the local counter-protesters were not alone. On February 27, unidentified troops believed (and later confirmed) to be Russian special forces seized the buildings that housed the Supreme Council of Crimea and the Council of Ministers, raising the Russian flag in a portent of what was to come.[3] Within days "little green men"—countless professional soldiers in green camouflage but no identifying insignia—had occupied strategic points throughout the Crimean Peninsula.

The Crimean parliament hastily organized a referendum on independence under the watchful eyes of growing numbers of still unidentified soldiers. Ukraine's Constitutional Court declared the planned referendum unconstitutional,[4] but it went forward nonetheless. To no one's surprise, the vote overwhelmingly favored independence. On March 17, the Supreme Council of Crimea declared the Republic of Crimea an independent nation. The republic then renounced its independence and requested admission into Russia.[5] Russian president Vladimir Putin granted the request.[6] The world responded with disbelief, followed by anger. Yet no country would use force to reverse the fait accompli.

On April 17, Putin acknowledged what the world already knew to be true: Russia had intervened in Crimea. Putin declared that the purpose of the invasion was "to ensure proper conditions for the people of Crimea to be able to freely express their will."[7]

These events seem to suggest that the outlawry of war was a failure. The signing of the Peace Pact was supposed to mark a new era. Conquest, once essential to establishing legal rights, had become a wrong—and in some cases a crime. But with a few lies and legal fictions, the Russian military flouted this legal prohibition, conquering a large portion of a sovereign state in the heart of Europe. Indeed, in a supreme irony, the territory Russia conquered, Crimea, was the very place in which the Allies of the Second World War finalized the agreement that became the United Nations Charter—the document that President Franklin Roosevelt had proclaimed would mark the "end of the beginning of all wars."

But Roosevelt's prophecy was not a false one. Yes, Putin violated the rules of the New World Order. But stark violations of this sort are far more the exception than the rule. If we view the annexation of Crimea in broader historical perspective, what is most remarkable is not that it happened. What is most remarkable is that events like it happen so rarely.

A BIRD'S-EYE VIEW

To see how unusual Russia's invasion of Crimea is, we need to step back from the current headlines to look at how state behavior has changed over the long sweep of time. How common are cases of territorial acquisition during military conflict? More important, how has their frequency changed since the outlawry of war? To answer these questions, it's not enough to cite a few high-profile examples (the temptation to cherry-pick is just too strong). We have to look at all known cases for a long period both before and after the 1928 Peace Pact.

Fortunately, a loose team of political scientists has assembled comprehensive data to help them study war. The resulting project, with the intentionally clinical name "Correlates of War," hosts datasets on everything from "militarized interstate disputes" to "world religion data" to "bilateral trade." Most relevant here, it includes extensive data on "territorial change"—a record of every single territorial exchange between states from 1816 to 2014, totaling over eight hundred entries.[8] The dataset tracks which country won the territory, which lost it, the area of the territory transferred, the size of the population in that territory, and whether there was military conflict at the time of the transfer. It is the best dataset of military conflict ever developed.

Even the best datasets are imperfect, however, and "Correlates of War" is no exception.[9] Information on events that occurred over a century ago is not always reliable. For example, it is difficult to determine how many people and how much territory was transferred when the United Kingdom won Butwal and surrounding areas from Nepal at the close of the Anglo-Gorkha War in 1816. The "Correlates of War" dataset contains no estimate of population transfers due to this conflict, and it lists a territorial transfer of one square kilometer—certainly a vast underestimate. This problem is most pronounced in the early years covered by the dataset, about which precise information is more difficult to obtain.[10] (This actually makes it harder for us to prove our argument that the seizure of territory through military conflict has declined, since it artificially depresses the number and size of conquests in the pre-Pact years of the data.) In short, the dataset offers a birds'-eye view: sweeping and thus invaluable for our purposes but also lacking nuance in some cases, especially as we peer further back in time.

While we began with the "Correlates of War" data, we did not stop there. We narrowed down the dataset by looking at cases of territorial change that took place during a militarized conflict. This process eliminated hundreds of territorial transfers that took place peacefully, not as a result of a military campaign. To this, we added any instance that the "Correlates of War" project had coded as a "conquest" (cases where the transfer "took place with a bare minimum of force and no organized military resistance was encountered"). This sifting of the data produced a net total of 254 instances of territorial change that were possible conquests.

We then burrowed into these 254 cases with the help of eighteen brilliant Yale Law students who worked with us over the course of more than a year, investigating whether the intervention was carried out by, or with the approval of, a multinational organization (such as the United Nations, NATO, and the League of Nations); whether the state that gained territory occupied rather than conquered it (that is, did not claim sovereignty); and, last, whether the territorial change was the result of independence. If any of these were true, we did not consider the territorial change a conquest. Hence dissolution of a state is not a conquest if the state dissolves into independent units (for example, the breakup of the Soviet Union in 1991), but it does if the territory is seized by another state or states (for example, much of what was taken from the Ottoman Empire). We similarly excluded territorial changes from "conquest" when it was simply a reversal of an earlier unrecognized seizure of the same territory—that is, when state A took back territory that state B had seized but sovereignty had never transferred because other states had never recognized it. For example, China's seizure of Manchuria from Japan in 1945 is not recorded as a conquest because the initial seizure of Manchuria by Japan in 1931 was not broadly recognized by other states. China, in other words, was not conquering Japanese territory but merely regaining what the international community had considered to be Chinese territory all along.*

Enough about the data. What do our 254 cases of territorial change tell us? They tell us something that is at once striking and surprising: Conquest, once common, has nearly disappeared. Even more unexpected, the switch point is that now familiar year when the world came together to outlaw war, 1928.

ONCE IN A LIFETIME TO ONCE OR TWICE A MILLENNIUM

From the time the data start in 1816 until the Peace Pact opened for signature in 1928, there was, on average, approximately one conquest every ten months (1.21 conquests per year). Put another way, the average state

*For those who want to look at the underlying data, our dataset is posted online at www.theinternationalistsbook.com.

during this period had a 1.33 percent chance of being the victim of conquest in any given year.[11] Those may seem like pretty good odds. They are not: A state with a 1.33 percent annual chance of conquest can expect to lose territory in a conquest once in an ordinary human lifetime.[12]

And these conquests were not small. The average amount of territory conquered during this period was 295,486 square kilometers per year. That is roughly *eleven* Crimeas per year for more than a hundred years.[13]

As staggering as these numbers are, they are consistent with the legal order that Grotius helped construct—and that governed state behavior for hundreds of years. War was *the* mechanism for solving disagreements between states. When disputes arose, as they often did, states went to war seeking compensation. This compensation often came in the form of land.

At first, little changed when the Old World Order came to a close. During the two decades after the Pact went into effect, 1929–1948, the average annual number of conquests remained fairly constant—at 1.15 per year, or one every ten months. The average annual amount of territory conquered during the twenty years following the ratification of the Peace Pact was 240,739 square kilometers—not so different from the 295,486 square kilometers per year in the preceding 113 years. Because more of the conquered territory was held by states rather than nonstate entities, the average state during this period had a 1.8 percent chance of being the victim of conquest in any given year, as compared to a 1.33 percent chance in the prior period.

Not until the end of the Second World War—which reaffirmed, consolidated, and institutionalized the transformation that began in 1928—do we see a clear decline in conquests in our data. And it was a steep decline indeed: When the chaos had settled and the United Nations had begun to meet, the average number of conquests per year fell dramatically—to .26 per year, or one every four years (3.9 to be exact). The average size of the territory conquered declined as well, to a mere 14,950 square kilometers per year. Given the increased number of states over this period, the likelihood that any individual state would suffer a conquest in an average year plummeted from 1.33 percent a year to .17 percent from 1949 on. Remember our estimate that an average state before 1928 could expect one conquest in a human lifespan? After 1948, the chance an average state would suffer a conquest fell from once in a lifetime to *once or twice a millennium*.[14]

"IT WOULD NOT . . . BE *HIS* CITY"

Thus far, the story told by our data doesn't seem all that favorable to pinpointing 1928 as an important moment in the transformation of the international legal order. If we look simply at the frequency of conquest, the outlawry of war seems no more than a speed bump on the well-traveled road to conquest. Not until 1948, after a war in which seventy million people died, did the frequency of conquest decisively fall—a reflection of the new international institutions created after 1945 and, perhaps, the concurrent emergence of nuclear weapons. If 1928 was a speed bump, the Second World War was the stop sign.

But that is not the whole story. Yes, it took the Second World War to end conquest. But when it did, something startling took place. Conquest didn't just stop. Prior conquest of an immense amount of territory was *reversed*. That is, a huge expanse of land that had been seized by the close of the war was returned to the states that had originally held it. But here's the even more startling fact: The land returned was not simply territory seized after the formal beginning of the Second World War in 1939. Instead, the reversals went back to a particular year that predated the war by more than a decade. That year was 1928.

Recall that in advocating for the Peace Pact, Salmon Levinson had promised that a nation could no longer "establish right, justice or title by brute strength."[15] Yes, the aggressor could still take a city by force, "but it would not, as a matter of law, be *his* city."[16]

Levinson proved right: If we examine the conquest numbers again, but separate out those recognized by a majority of countries from those that were not, the picture shifts: Territory continued to be conquered in the period between 1928 and 1949, but the majority of those transfers, beginning with Japan's seizure of Manchuria, *were not recognized by most states*. The change in the legal rules did not prevent states from seizing land, but possession was no longer sufficient to establish legal rights. Other states, knowing that the seizures were now illegal, rejected them as illegitimate. In doing so, they reaffirmed the break with the past represented by the Pact.

But James Shotwell, Levinson's rival in the outlawry movement, proved right, too. Outlawry rendered transfers brought about through force illegitimate. But with "no teeth" behind outlawry—no mechanism to force states to release illegitimate seizures—there was no way to undo them. Yes, economic sanctions reduced the benefits a state could gain from conquered land—as Japan discovered in Manchuria. But the system of international economic sanctions outside of war was in its infancy in the early decades after 1928, and the tools needed to make it a powerful instrument of statecraft were yet to be invented. When the nations of the world signed the Peace Pact outlawing war, they took the first step toward transforming the legal order. But it would take more than simply rejecting the Old World Order to make a new one. The project of the Internationalists remained incomplete.

Levinson's prediction would nonetheless prove prophetic. At the close of the Second World War, forceful transfers that had been made after the Peace Pact were reversed. Might still produced *military* victories. But it could no longer provide lasting *legal* victories. And the failure of the Axis challenge ensured that these illegal territorial seizures would not stand. As a result, the conquests between 1928 and 1949 left almost no long-term imprint on the distribution of territory across states. Indeed, only a single one of the unrecognized transfers during this period—the Chinese claim to Taiwan in 1945—remained in place after 1948. Even this seizure remained effective only a short time—in 1949, the fleeing nationalist army declared Taiwan an independent state (a declaration China still does not recognize, leaving Taiwan in legal limbo today).

Figure 1 illustrates the point. It divides the total amount of conquered territory per year, as defined above, into four categories: (1) Transfers recognized by a majority of other states that were "sticky"—that is, not later reversed (we count a transfer as having reversed if the same or nearly the same territory returned to the state that lost it).[17] (2) Transfers that were recognized by a majority of other states but where the territory later transferred back (sometimes decades later). (3) Transfers not recognized by a majority of other states but that were nonetheless sticky. (4) Transfers that were not recognized by a majority of other states and later reversed.

In the early 1800s, the amount of territory seized ranged between 810,000 and 1.77 million square kilometers a decade. After a brief slowdown in the 1850s and 1860s, that number shot up to between 5.9 million and 8.8 million square kilometers a decade for the rest of the century—a good deal of it caused by the European scramble for Africa.

The pace of conquest slowed in the early 1900s, but only relative to the acquisitiveness of the late 1800s. Military seizure of land remained both common and legally sanctioned. This was true during the continuing colonization of Africa by the United Kingdom and France. It was true when an emergent Japan launched aggressions against Korea and Russia. And it was true during the First World War, which ended with the forced dissolution and transfer of territory from the defeated Central Powers.

After the war, the Ottoman Empire collapsed, and its territory divided among many states, with its successor, Turkey, retaining only a fraction of the empire's prewar territory. The Austro-Hungarian empire, too, was dissolved. Its successor states—Austria and Hungary—also lost substantial territory to Italy, Poland, Czechoslovakia, Romania, and the Kingdom of Serbs, Croats, and Slovenes. Germany lost territory to Belgium, France, Poland, and Portugal. Bulgaria lost territory to Greece and the Kingdom of Serbs, Croats, and Slovenes. Romania received Bessarabia and Bukovina

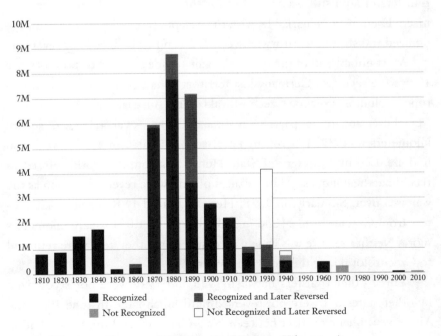

Figure 1: Territory Conquered Per Decade (in Square Kilometers)

from Russia, as payment on a promise by the Allies to induce its support in the war. Then, in 1920, post-revolutionary Russia went on the offensive. It succeeded in seizing Azerbaijan, Georgia, and Armenia, consolidating them into the Transcaucasian Soviet Federated Socialist Republic, a republic of the newly formed Soviet Union, in 1922. Meanwhile, the Polish-Soviet war ended with a peace treaty at Riga in March 1921 that divided disputed territory in Byelorussia (Belarus) and Western Ukraine between Poland and the Soviet Union.[18]

Nearly all of these transfers were recognized by other states. And while some were later reversed, most of these reversals did not occur until well into the twentieth century. Russia's seizure of Tajikistan in 1868, for example, was not reversed until the unraveling of the USSR in 1991. Similarly, the U.K.'s seizure of present-day Nigeria in 1885 was not reversed until 1960.[19] Throughout the nineteenth and early twentieth centuries, land that was seized was generally recognized as legally obtained and retained by the conquering state. Might, after all, made Right.

Then, in 1931, states began to refuse to recognize conquests. Forceful transfers of land still occurred, but for the first time they went unrecognized. Even more remarkable, with the exception of Taiwan, all the unrecognized transfers of territory between 1928 and 1949 were later reversed.

Most notably, all of the territorial gains made by the Axis powers since 1928 were reversed. Germany lost territory it had gained throughout Europe, including Poland, Czechoslovakia, and Austria. Japan's seizures of Manchuria and other parts of mainland China—over 1,304,292 square kilometers in 1932, 173,960 in 1933, and 1,500,000 in 1937—were also undone. Led by Secretary of State Henry Stimson, the world refused to recognize the conquests. The seizures of land were reversed as soon as the war was over. Similarly, in 1938, Hungary seized 11,826 square kilometers from Czechoslovakia, and in 1939, it seized 11,094 square kilometers more. Neither seizure was widely recognized, and they, too, were returned to Czechoslovakia at the close of the war.

Three other transfers between 1928 and 1949 were not recognized by other states but were not reversed until much later. In June 1940, the Molotov-Ribbentrop Pact between Nazi Germany and the Soviet Union awarded the Soviet Union control of Estonia, Lithuania, and Latvia. Many states, including the United States, refused to recognize the transfer. In a forceful statement drafted by Sumner Welles, who as acting secretary of state worked closely with FDR in crafting the response,[20] the United States issued what became known as the "Welles Declaration" on July 23, 1940. In an echo of Stimson's notes to China and Japan after the Japanese invasion of Manchuria, the letter condemned the "predatory activities . . . carried on by the use of force or by the threat of force" and refused to recognize the legitimacy of Soviet control over the states. Welles continued, "These principles constitute the very foundations upon which the existing relationship between the twenty-one sovereign republics of the New World rests."[21] The U.S. maintained that position for more than five decades— until the eventual release of the Baltic states from Soviet control in 1991.[22]

Italy's seizure of Ethiopia in 1935 did not spark the same condemnation, though it, too, was eventually reversed. Despite great consternation in the League of Nations after Italy's takeover of Ethiopia, the League ultimately failed to take effective action, precipitating the collapse of the institution. Japan recognized Italy's seizure in November 1936 in exchange for Italy's recognition of Japan's occupation of Manchuria. France and Britain followed in 1938. Six countries continued to object, including the United States, which never recognized the transfer.[23] After the war ended, the illegal seizure was undone and Ethiopia regained its independence from Italy.

In short, while territory continued to be seized after the Peace Pact went into effect, the Pact meant that transfers of control over territory did not, except in rare cases, translate into legal rights over that territory. *Might was no longer Right*.

STICKY CONQUESTS

One way to see how much the world changed after the Peace Pact is to examine those conquests that stuck. Sticky conquests, recall, are those territorial changes wrought by military conflict that remain in place, reshaping the global map.

Figure 2 shows how much territory changed hands between states because of sticky conquests in our now familiar eras: 1816–1928 (before the Peace Pact), 1929–1948 (between the Pact and the end of the peace process

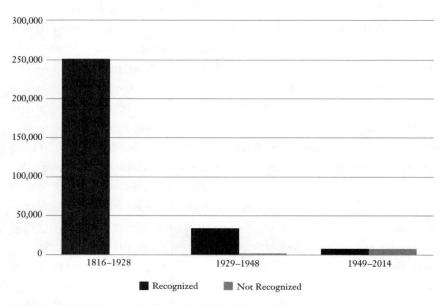

Figure 2: Sticky Conquests (Average Square Kilometers Per Year).

for the Second World War*), and 1949–2014 (after the Second World War). The message is clear. Conquests made after 1928 were much less likely to stick than those of the prior era. To put it more precisely, between 1816–1928 and 1929–1948, the average amount of land that was permanently seized each year declined by 86 percent. After 1948, it fell another 59 percent. Together, these dramatic declines brought the total amount of land that was acquired through sticky conquest to 6 percent of its original level.

*We extend the middle period through 1948, because the postwar territorial transfers did not wrap up until then. The Paris Peace Treaties between the Allied powers and most of the Axis powers were signed on February 10, 1947, but did not enter into force until September 15, 1947. The treaties provided the parties an additional year to meet many of the treaty obligations. The peace treaty with Japan was not signed until September 8, 1951 (and entered into force on April 28, 1952), but the territories seized by Japan during the war had all been returned by that point. The Potsdam Agreement, promulgated on August 2, 1945, specified the initial terms under which the Allies would govern Germany. The Federal Republic of Germany became an independent state in May 1949, but the postwar territorial transfers had already been settled.

In other words, for every 100 square kilometers taken through sticky conquests before 1929, just 6 square kilometers were thus obtained after 1948.

These numbers reflect the very different world orders that prevailed at the end of the two great wars of the twentieth century. The First and the Second World Wars were both horrific conflicts originating in Europe. But what happened in their wake reflected the legal transformation that occurred between. In contrast to the end of the First World War (and most wars before it), the losing states of the Second World War were not carved up and parceled out to the victors. Germany and Japan, both of which unconditionally surrendered, were occupied, but not for the purpose of establishing territorial claims.

As Figure 2 shows, the amount of territory seized in sticky conquests was dramatically lower in the period between 1928 and 1949, but such conquests did not disappear altogether. At the close of the Second World War, Germany, Italy, and Japan did lose some territory they had held before 1928. But the amounts did not begin to approach those of previous wars. In 1945, the Allies made Germany cede territory in its east to Poland. This land—referred to in Polish as "Ziemie Odzyskane," or "Regained Lands," because it was once part of the traditional Polish homeland—was ceded to Poland in significant part to make up for the loss of the Polish territory of Kresy to the Soviets in 1945 after Roosevelt and Churchill capitulated to Stalin's demands at Yalta.

As for Italy, its biggest losses were not conquests but instead the liberation of prior colonial holdings—particularly Libya, Somaliland, and Eritrea, which were put under Allied administration. However, it suffered some noncolonial losses as well. The 1947 Paris Treaty of Peace contained a small border adjustment with France that gave Italy's northern neighbor the towns of Tenda (Tende) and Birga (La Brigue). Italy lost the long-contested Dodecanese islands to Greece, part of the Free Territory of Trieste and the Island of Pelagosa to Yugoslavia, and Saseno Island (Sazan, as it is known in Albania) to now independent Albania. Even taken together, however, these losses were small: Italy's noncolonial losses totaled just over 7,000 square kilometers—a small sliver of what was forfeited by those vanquished in the First World War.

Japan, meanwhile, lost its colony of Korea, which it had held since

1910 and which became an independent state under joint U.S. and Soviet administration. Japan also withdrew its claims to a number of islands in the South China Sea (claims that had long been contested by its neighbors).

Japan and Italy were far from alone in losing their colonial holdings, of course. Shortly after the war, France relinquished its claims to Syria. As the mandate that had been granted to the United Kingdom expired, Israel declared its independence—the first of what would soon become a tidal wave of such declarations by former colonies.

Most telling of all from a historical perspective, the United States, United Kingdom, and France—three of the four leading Allied powers— took no new territory after the war (aside from the aforementioned minor adjustment of the border between France and Italy). Consistent with their pledge in the Atlantic Charter to resist territorial aggrandizement, they won the war yet took no land. [24] When the war was over, they vacated the land they had liberated from the Axis powers, transferring power to local governmental authorities. The Allies not only transferred authority back to the states that they had liberated, but they also transferred authority over the defeated powers back to the defeated powers. * In the Old World Order, this was not how winners behaved.

The only ally to gain any significant territory after the war was the Soviet Union. More than twenty million of the nation's citizens had died in the course of the war, and Stalin insisted on several territorial gains as the price of peace—many, but not all, of them in areas previously contested. These included part of East Prussia previously held by Germany along with part of Poland, the southern part of the island of Sakhalin from Japan (which it had lost to Japan in 1905), Bessarabia and Northern Bukovina from Romania (some of which Romania had won from Russia in 1920), and border territories from Finland (some of which had been ceded by Russia in 1917). These concessions to Stalin were seen by the other Allied powers as regrettable deviations from accepted law, not precedents to be followed in the future.

---

*The Allies established the Allied Military Government for Occcupied Territories in Germany, Italy, Austria, and Japan, transferring authority to local civilian government in each country by the mid-1950s.

Aside from these postwar transfers, the only other recognized transfers of territory in the period from 1929 to 1948 not later reversed were the result of border disputes over territory that had been brewing since before 1928. For the most part, these were modest: Saudi Arabia seized a small portion of previously disputed territory from Yemen in 1934 in an area where the border between the two countries had not been delineated during decolonization (the area is recorded in the "Correlates of War" dataset as comprising a single square kilometer). In 1935, the Chaco War between Paraguay and Bolivia over land that had been in dispute ever since Spanish decolonization of the region in the early nineteenth century also left an uncertain border. After a cease-fire and international mediation, Paraguay gained control over the majority of the contested territory. And, last, in 1942, Peru gained previously disputed border territory, known as "the Oriente," from Ecuador—a dispute that also arose from ambiguities in the borders between Spain's former colonies. In all three cases, the territory had been disputed for years—a point to which we will return.*

MAPPING A NEW WORLD ORDER

We can see this transformation not just by looking at the numbers but also by examining maps of the world. A map of 1910 shows a sprawling Ottoman Empire and immense Austria-Hungary; Germany is much larger than it is today; Africa is a patchwork of colonial empires.

The map of 1928—after the upheaval of the First World War and before the ratification of the Peace Pact—shows a different world. The

---

*If anything, figures 1 and 2 understate the transformation that took place in 1928. The "Correlates of War" database on which we relied does not record any transfer of land that occurs during a war until the war is over. This makes a good deal of sense, since the toing-and-froing on the battlefield could lead to an endless number of territorial transfer events that last only a short while. But this makes it impossible to tell whether the losers gave up the winners' territory or the winners gave up the losers' territory. At the end of the First World War, the losers gave up the territory they had won. When Germany signed the Armistice in November 1918, it occupied vast areas of Allied territory. By contrast, at the end of the Second World War, the victorious Allies occupied much of Axis territory—a gain they almost entirely released. This difference is not reflected in the figures.

Austro-Hungarian Empire had been severed into pieces. Germany, too, lost immense amounts of territory. The Ottoman Empire, meanwhile, was obliterated, with just a small portion of what had once been the territory governed by the Ottoman regime now designated the new state of Turkey.

If you look at a comparable map of 1950, it does not look terribly different from the map of 1928. The overall picture is one of continuity. This map looks familiar to the modern eye. Indeed, the basic outlines have changed little in more than a half century. The most significant change, which we will discuss in more detail in the next chapter, has been the fracturing of larger units into smaller ones. But the outlines are otherwise almost entirely the same.

The contrast with the previous global conflagration is even starker when comparing land lost with lives lost. Even though the Second World War destroyed four times as many lives as the first (approximately seventy million versus fifteen million), the amount of territory transferred was radically less. The First World War reshaped Europe; the Second made only small shifts on the margins, principally between the Soviet Union, on the one hand, and Poland and Germany, on the other. The spoils of war went way down even as the costs of war went way up—the opposite of what would have been expected in a Grotian world.

What the maps cannot show is that the change in the practice of conquest was not just quantitative—the dwindling of territorial changes through military conflict to near-zero—but also qualitative. For the conquests that did occur after the start of the New World Order bear little resemblance to the seizures that Grotius had so brilliantly justified as legitimate legal behavior. They did not result from the classic wars of aggression that defined conquest for thousands of years. In every case, they arose from a civil war, the messy process of decolonization, or some combination of the two.

That was the case with Taiwan. In 1949, upon losing the internal struggle against the communists led by Mao Zedong, Chiang Kai-shek fled to the island and proclaimed the Republic of China, establishing it as an entity separate from mainland China. A dozen years later, Benin forced Portugal to vacate the small colonial city of Ouidah in 1961. Similarly, in the same year, India seized the Portuguese colony of Goa from Portugal, after

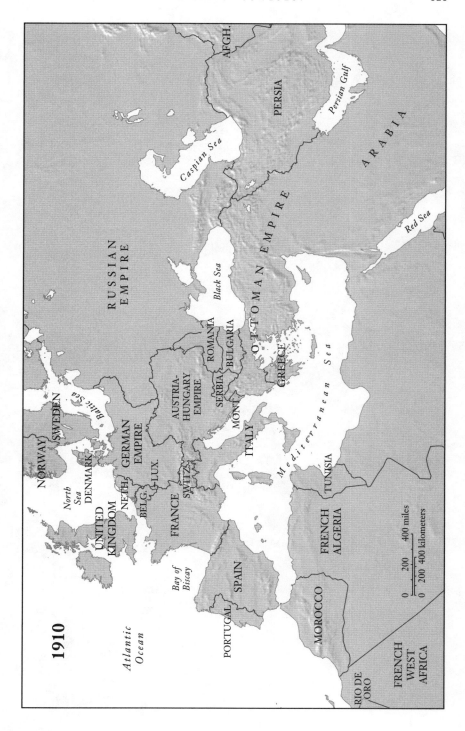

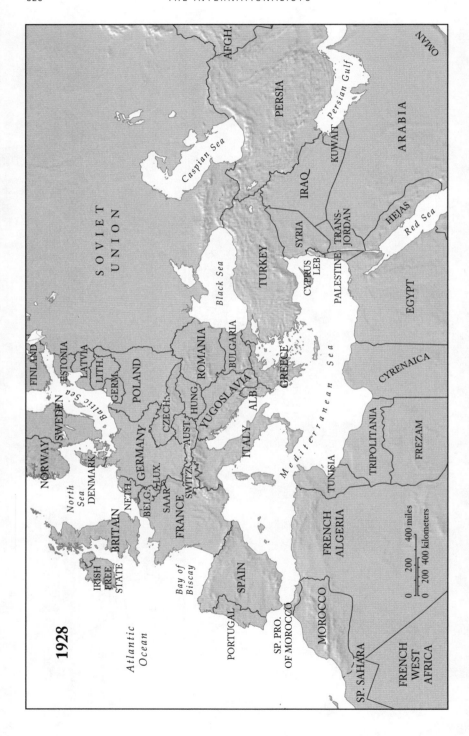

1928

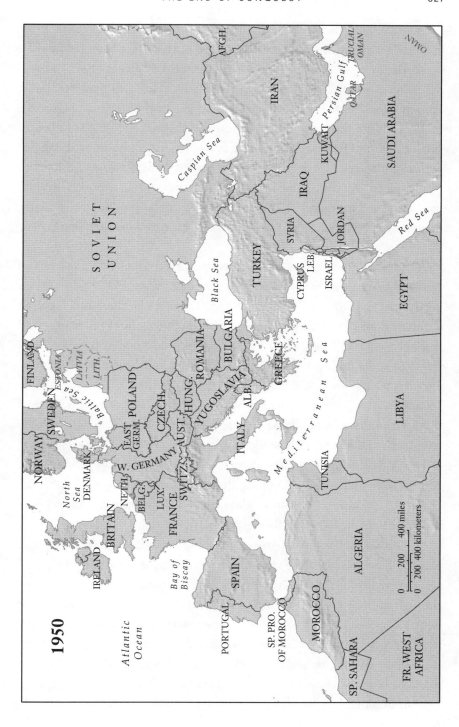

1950

SOVIET UNION

FINLAND
NORWAY
SWEDEN
ESTONIA
LATVIA
LITH.
Baltic Sea
NORTH
Sea
IRELAND
BRITAIN
DENMARK
NETH.
BELG.
LUX.
EAST GERM.
POLAND
CZECH.
W. GERMANY
SWITZ.
AUST. HUNG.
FRANCE
Bay of Biscay
Atlantic Ocean
PORTUGAL
SPAIN
SP. PRO. OF MOROCCO
MOROCCO
SP. SAHARA
FR. WEST AFRICA
ALGERIA
TUNISIA
ITALY
ALB.
YUGOSLAVIA
ROMANIA
BULGARIA
GREECE
Black Sea
Mediterranean Sea
LIBYA
EGYPT
TURKEY
CYPRUS
LEB.
ISRAEL
SYRIA
JORDAN
LEB.
CAspian Sea
AFGH.
IRAN
IRAQ
KUWAIT
Persian Gulf
QATAR
TRUCIAL OMAN
SAUDI ARABIA
Red Sea
OMAN

0   200   400 miles
0   200   400 kilometers

Portugal refused demands to grant the territory independence. In 1963, Indonesia asserted control over West Papua, which had been held by the Netherlands even after Indonesia won its independence in 1949 (indeed, the transfer of West Papua, which is 412,781 square kilometers, almost entirely accounts for the recognized conquest in the 1960s in Figure 1). In 1971, in the war over Bangladeshi independence, Pakistan won back a small amount of territory from India, even as it lost the entirety of Bangladesh to independence. In 2004, Yemen gained some territory from Saudi Arabia when the two countries signed a treaty settling a border dispute that had raged for decades. And in 2008, Cameroon won 665 square kilometers from Nigeria when the two settled their own long-standing border dispute.[25]

These lasting transfers of territory were all recognized by the rest of the world. Yet there have been sticky conquests since 1928 that have not been so recognized—ten of them, in fact. These sticky conquests involved a tiny amount of territory compared with the huge chunks of land seized through such conquests before 1929. They include transfers between Pakistan and India during the war over Kashmir; China's seizure of the Yijiangshan Islands from Taiwan in 1955; Israel's seizure of control of East Jerusalem from Jordan during the Six Day War in 1967; Libya's seizure of the Aouzou Strip from Chad in 1973; the defeat of the Republic of Vietnam by the Democratic Republic of Vietnam in 1975; Indonesia's seizure of East Timor from Portuguese colonial control in 1976; Egypt's seizure of control from Sudan in 2000 of long-disputed border territory; and Russia's seizure of Crimea in 2014. In an eleventh case, Jordan seized control over the West Bank in 1949, but this seizure was reversed.

These were all events of great significance to those involved. Still, they plainly do not make for the vivid narrative of conquest that the Old World Order provided. And that is the point. In surveying the territories taken through military conflict in the New World Order—a border adjustment here, a disputed island there—the observer risks missing the forest for the trees, or more accurately failing to see that the forest *has so few trees*. Reading a litany of conquests since 1948 may be tedious, but a comparable list from the last several decades of the Old World Order would be a true slog. Instead of a number of cases that can be counted on two or three hands, that list would have encompassed over a hundred cases with far greater territory at stake.

The woods of the Old World Order were deep and dark, nothing like the light bramble of the New World Order. Moreover, these ancient growth forests were populated by mighty sequoias, such as Egypt's conquest of Darfur in 1874 (2.65 million square kilometers), the conquest of Sudan by the United Kingdom in 1899 (2.51 million square kilometers), and Italy's conquest of Turkey in 1912 (1.05 million square kilometers). The largest conquest of the New World Order—the seizure by Indonesia of West Papua from the Netherlands in 1963 (412,781 square kilometers)—would not even make the top twenty of the Old World Order.

War is never minor, and many of these conquests visited horrors on the populations of the territories involved. Although the transfer of West Papua to Indonesia did not involve lengthy military conflict, the next two largest transfers, Vietnam and Kashmir, involved conflicts that went on for years and caused terrible destruction and suffering (and, in the case of Kashmir, still remains unsettled). Without minimizing this pain and distress, the broad perspective provided by our data makes clear that these conquests were, in historical terms, both relatively rare and comparatively small. From our bird's-eye view, it is possible to see what observers on the ground too often miss: that what was once frighteningly common is now thankfully infrequent, because what was once seen as the embodiment of international law is now understood as its repudiation.

We should be clear about what our data show and do not show. They show that conquest, once the rule, has become the exception. But they reveal nothing about whether strong states use or threaten force to dominate weaker ones without actually conquering them. Indeed, we can point to cases when states have used their militaries to exert significant pressure on—and, occasionally, domination over—other states. True puppet governments (such as the Polish Committee of National Liberation, established by the Soviets, or Manchukuo, established by the Japanese) are rare and have generally been rejected as illegitimate by the international community. But in several cases, states have forced a change in regime, or prevented one. Most famously, the CIA orchestrated a coup to remove Mohammad Mossadegh and reinstall the Shah of Iran in 1953, the Soviet

Union crushed the Hungarian Revolution in 1956 and invaded Czechoslovakia in 1968. Much more recently, the United States invaded Iraq in 2003, toppled Sadaam Hussein, and installed the Coalition Provisional Authority to govern the country. But what's most notable about these "nonconquests" is how ineffective and unstable they usually are. Exerting influence indirectly is inefficient and expensive. What's more, influence often wanes as soon as the threat disappears. Shaky coercion and sticky conquests are not the same.

CONQUEST'S END

We have argued that the transformation to a world in which conquest is exceptional was set in motion by the Peace Pact of 1928. The data strongly support our claim, showing that few conquests have stuck since the Pact went into effect. This did not happen because the Peace Pact suddenly caused all nations to play by a new set of rules. The Pact declared a break with the Old World Order, but it would take years for the new legal order that would replace it to take shape.

That the tumultuous events discussed at length in Part II of this book resulted at least in part from the Pact is evident from what those involved said. After the Japanese invasion of Manchuria in 1931, for example, Secretary of State Henry Stimson declared that the United States "does not intend to recognize any situation, treaty, or agreement which may be brought about by means contrary to the covenants and obligations of the Pact of Paris of August 27, 1928."[26] His later speech, which became the touchstone of the Stimson Doctrine—nonrecognition of international territorial changes executed by force—was entitled "The Pact of Paris—Three Years of Development." The League of Nations followed the United States' lead by declaring that it is "incumbent upon the Members of the League not to recognize any situation, treaty or agreement which might be brought about by means contrary to the Covenant of the League of Nations or to the Pact of Paris."[27] Though the Atlantic Charter, and the subsequent Declaration of the United Nations (signed by forty-seven countries), did not specifically reference the Peace Pact, it premised its rejection of conquest

Carl Schmitt, speaking in 1930, was a leading defender of the German government's plan to seize power from the Reichstag.

Left: In 1930, the Jewish law professor Hans Kelsen fled anti-Semitism in Vienna and moved to the University of Cologne. Kelsen voted in favor of an appointment for Schmitt, with whom he disagreed but whose brilliance he recognized. Schmitt repaid his generosity by engineering Kelsen's dismissal a year later when the Nazis came to power. *Right:* A report compiled by the Allies after the war described Schmitt as Germany's leading political scientist and one of the world's greatest political writers, "a man of near-genius rating." The report also called for his prosecution as a war criminal.

This index card shows the history of Schmitt's internment by the United States Military Government at the Palace of Justice in Nuremberg (arrested March 20, 1947, released on May 6, 1947).

SCHMITT, Carl   Berlin-Schlachtensee
                                 Kaiserstuhlstr. 19
"A" Def.

Leading Nazi Propagandist
in field of International law
& Nazi theories.

Req. of Trans. 17.3.47   KEMPNER

(Called Berlin MG 19.3.47)

20.3.47: arrested in Berlin
30.3.47: Nuremberg
6. May - Left for witness house
13. May 47 - Sent to Combs for Repment

The dock at the International Military Tribunal in Nuremberg (center row, left to right: Hermann Göring, Rudolf Hess, Joachim von Ribbentrop, Wilhelm Keitel, Ernst Kaltenbrunner). Hermann Jahrreiss, who replaced Kelsen at the University of Cologne and presented the defense for the German prisoners, is in the lower right corner, wearing violet academic robes.

Robert Jackson, chief prosecutor at Nuremberg. Despite his lack of formal higher education—he never attended college and did not graduate law school—he was a gifted writer and eloquent speaker. By all accounts, his opening statement at Nuremberg was a spellbinder.

Legal scholar Hersch Lauterpacht recognized the revolutionary nature of the Peace Pact and was central in rethinking the laws of war and peace. In 1941, he helped Jackson, then U.S. attorney general, defend the Lend-Lease program by explaining that the Pact now allowed states to assist the victims of an illegal war. He also helped the prosecution team at Nuremberg establish the crime of aggression.

MEMBERS OF THE BRITISH PROSECUTING BODY AT NUREMBERG: IN THE CENTRE OF THE FRONT ROW IS THE ATTORNEY-GENERAL, SIR HARTLEY SHAWCROSS,

THE WAR CRIMINALS VASTLY AMUSED DURING THE HEARING OF EVIDENCE AGAINST THEM; GÖRING SEEMS TO HAVE BEEN THE "LAUGH-LEADER" IN THIS INSTANCE.

These photographs, together with Captain de Grineau's drawing, provide interesting contrasts of the trial of the war criminals at Nuremberg. The attitude of the prisoners on the occasion when Göring initiated a loud laugh at the evidence was vastly changed when they were confronted with the horrors of their concentration camps during the showing of atrocity films in the court-room. Nor were they amused by the evidence of General Erwin Lahousen, one-time Deputy to Admiral Canaris, Chief of German Intelligence, whose revelations aroused Göring at least to a state of fury and gesticulation.

During the Nuremberg trial, Lauterpacht sent a newspaper clipping to his wife showing the British prosecution team alongside the major Nazi war criminals: "In case you do not recognize your husband," he wrote in an accompanying letter, "he is on p. 633, in the bottom left hand picture, seated in the extreme left. You never expected your husband to be photographed with Goering."

9

On January 10, 1946, the first meeting of the United Nations General Assembly opened in the Methodist Central Hall at Westminster in London. The hall, which served as an air raid shelter during the Blitz, had miraculously emerged unscathed. Above the dais hung a golden map of the world from a north polar perspective—an image that would soon become the official symbol of the United Nations.

10

Under the U.N. Charter, states may use armed force in self-defense or if authorized by the Security Council. After Iraq invaded neighboring Kuwait in 1990, the Security Council voted to adopt Resolution 678. Acting under this authority, the United States and coalition forces expelled Iraq from Kuwait.

On June 30, 1948, a member of the British Army hauled down the Union Jack for the last time in Palestine. When the British Mandate over Palestine expired with no designated successor, the resulting legal vacuum made it impossible to resolve the ensuing conflict without the consent of all involved—leading to decades of fighting.

Today, international law is no longer enforced with war. Instead, it relies on "outcasting," in which a group denies rule-breakers the benefits of cooperation. When Turkey invaded Cyprus in 1974, it displaced approximately 160,000 Greek Cypriots (shown here searching for relatives). More than two decades later, one of the displaced, Titina Loizidou, sued for compensation in the European Court of Human Rights and won. Turkey refused to pay but capitulated after the Council of Europe threatened to outcast it.

Outcasting can work against the most powerful states. When running for president in 2000, George W. Bush promised to protect jobs in the steel industry. Once elected, he boosted steel tariffs. Several countries filed a complaint in the World Trade Organization, which found the tariffs illegal and authorized equivalent tariffs against swing state industries. Bush ended the steel tariffs shortly thereafter.

Ukrainians seeking closer relations with Europe began protesting in November 2013. Demonstrations, which spread across the country, led to the ouster of Ukrainian president Victor Yanukovych, who had close ties to Russia. Russia responded by sending unidentified gunmen into Crimea, including these in Simferopol Airport. Europe and the United States imposed sanctions, and Russian GDP shrank by 3.4 percent in 2015.

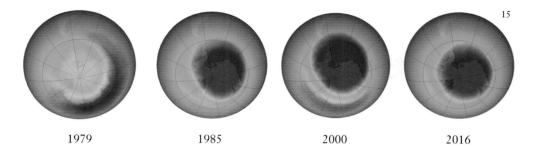

| 1979 | 1985 | 2000 | 2016 |

By the 1980s, chlorofluorocarbons from aerosols and Styrofoam production began to tear a hole in the ozone layer, which protects the Earth from harmful ultraviolet radiation. The 1987 Montreal Protocol on Substances That Deplete the Ozone Layer used outcasting to encourage states to reduce their consumption of ozone-depleting substances. As a result, the ozone hole, which reached its maximum size in 2000, has shrunk by 4 million square kilometers.

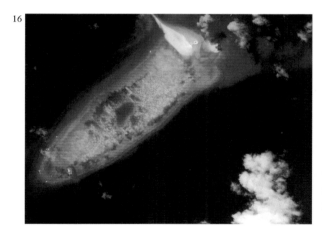

16

Islands are one of the remaining sources of territorial conflict in the modern era, because the legal sovereign is often unclear. Nowhere is this more true than in the South China Sea. In 2014, in a bid to assert sovereignty over the contested Fiery Cross Reef, China began to turn the reef into a large artificial island. The white bloom is dredged sand dumped on the reef.

By September 2015 Fiery Cross Reef had been transformed into an island containing an almost ten-thousand-foot runway, antiaircraft weapons, and a missile-defense system. No country has recognized Chinese claims over the reef.

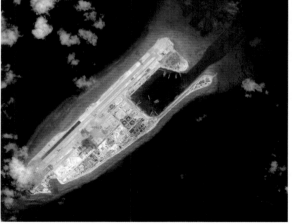

17

19

Left: Sayyid Qutb (right) came to the United States in 1948 to study at Colorado State College of Education. Qutb was appalled at the moral decadence, racism, and vacuity he encountered. "There has been a Ph.D. dissertation about the best way to clean dishes, which seems more important to them than the Bible or religion." *Right:* After returning to Egypt, Qutb became a leader of Islamic extremist thought. He wrote his most influential work, *Milestones*, while imprisoned. In it, he argued that the war with the West has always been a battle of ideas between those who recognize that only God possesses sovereignty and those who impute it to man.

20

Left: Abu Bakr al-Baghdadi, the self-declared caliph of the Islamic State, gave his first public address on Ramadan in 2014. Qutb's worldview permeated his message. Baghdadi called all Muslims to join the Islamic State—a state defined by belief, not ethnicity, nationality, or international law. *Right:* In 2014, the Islamic State released a video in which a follower declares that his group will eliminate all state borders. Standing at an overrun border post between Iraq and Syria, he raises his right index finger in the air, a gesture that alludes not only to the "oneness" of God, but also to the rejection of any legitimate source of authority but God—including every modern state.

as a mode of territorial acquisition both in the principle of self-determination and "the abandonment of the use of force."[28]

But more important than what states said is *what they did*. And what they did was invest in the vision of the Internationalists, who fought to outlaw war through the Pact, and worked over the course of two decades to make the promise of the Pact a reality. Once the war was over, the Allies reaffirmed and reinforced the Pact's principles. The new United Nations Charter placed the prohibition on the "use of force" at its core and created an institutional structure to maintain international peace and security.

State behavior did not change the moment the Pact was signed. Nor was the change that followed inevitable. Indeed, much of this book has been devoted to showing how contested the transformation from the Old to the New World Order was. The outlawry revolution would have failed had the Allies not won the war, reversed nearly every single conquest made since 1928, and enshrined the prohibition on war and territorial conquest in the United Nations Charter.

That the Pact was not sufficient by itself should come as no surprise. When seeking change, it is simply not enough to pass a law and expect everyone to comply. No political endeavor escapes the need to make laws binding through governmental power. Legal revolutions do not end with the passing of a law. They begin with them.

So it has been from the beginning of American history. It took the Revolutionary War to make the independence declared in 1776 a reality, and not one but two attempts at creating a constitution to ensure it would last. It took the Civil War to give full force to the emancipation of the slaves, and over a century for the Thirteenth, Fourteenth, and Fifteenth Amendments to the United States Constitution to end state-enforced racial discrimination. Similarly, the Americans with Disabilities Act, the Social Security Act, and the Clean Water Act did not achieve their ambitious goals overnight. It took years, indeed decades, of dedicated effort to turn these legal reforms into meaningful change: more equal access for persons with disabilities, increased standards of living, cleaner water—in short, all the profound promises the new laws embodied.

Countless other changes occurred after 1945, of course, and many

thoughtful analysts have offered theories to explain the relatively peaceful postwar order—including the advent of nuclear weapons, the spread
of democracy, and more robust global trade. While each of these changes
likely played a role in creating and sustaining postwar peace, each leaves
crucial aspects of the shift unexplained. None of these explanations offers
a convincing answer to a basic question raised by our data: Why did most
of the borders after the Second World War snap back to the lines that had
existed when the Peace Pact was signed? After all, in previous wars, it was
rare for the winners to return territory to the losers without at least exact-
ing a price. Part of the reason is that the winners had just fought a war in
which the rallying cry was the rejection of territorial aggrandizement by
force. That rallying cry was rooted in the Pact.

Indeed, the phenomenon highlighted by our data did not occur in isolation. The Allies did not simply return land they won by force. They also
prosecuted Axis leaders for waging a war of aggression. They also rejected
gunboat diplomacy. They also altered the rules of neutrality giving states
the right to impose economic sanctions against aggressors. And they also
built a network of institutions that replaced war as a way to acquire power
with free trade and global cooperation.

This shared internationalist commitment also helps explain why, after
the war, nuclear weapons were used to keep the peace rather than to establish territorial dominance. The threat of nuclear attack has *never* been
used for territorial aggrandizement, not even against a state too small or
inconsequential for other nuclear states to care who controls it. The rule
against conquest prohibits it. And powerful states can usually be counted
on to police that rule even when they are not directly affected (as Saddam
Hussein learned after he invaded Kuwait in 1991).[29]

The spread of democracy, too, has played a role in reducing the inci-
dence of interstate violence (though in what situations and by how much
remains a matter of intense scholarly debate).[30] But this is true at least in
part because democratic leaders must justify their reasons for going to war,
and conquest no longer "counts" as a legitimate reason. It *used to* count.
Sovereigns proudly declared their just causes for war in elaborate manifestos. President Polk celebrated the conquest of Mexican territory and

justified it by claiming that the U.S. Army was collecting unpaid debts. After 1928, however, such wars were no longer considered just. Instead, democratic leaders feel compelled to make reference to a much more limited set of reasons for war that are legally permissible—most commonly self-defense.

Last, some might claim that conquest has declined because it is unprofitable. Waging war has always been very expensive, but the costs of trading have precipitously declined and the value of mobile resources, such as knowledge and technology, has increased. From a purely economic point of view, conquest no longer pays. Perhaps. But even if conquest is no longer profitable, this explanation does not account for why this is so. Surely a major reason why conquest no longer pays is that wars of conquest are illegal. States cannot fully enjoy the fruits of their victories now that conquests are not recognized by other states. Moreover, as we will explain at greater length in the next chapter, the rise of global free trade was at least as much a consequence as a cause of the outlawry of war. The end of conquest helped unleash greater economic cooperation by making it safe to trade even when the other side might do better in the bargain. That, in turn, helped generate more trade. In this way, global trade and the outlawry of war reinforced each other. With aggressive war illegal, trade flourished, and as trade flourished, aggressive war became more costly and peace more valuable. Finally, the "territory is less valuable" account would only explain why states prefer trade and technology to war. It would not explain why conquests, when attempted, are no longer *recognized* by other states.

Each of these explanations is at least partially correct. Nuclear weapons, democracy, and free trade have all contributed to the decline in conquest. But though correct, these explanations are nevertheless incomplete. They work only because they assume an idea that they never make explicit, namely, that Might no longer makes Right. The missing element in all of these explanations, in other words, is the outlawry of war that began with the Peace Pact.

THE END OF INTERSTATE WAR

The outlawry of war not only led to the end of conquest. It precipitated the end of international war itself. Many have noticed that international wars—that is, wars between states—are now rare (more on wars *inside* states later). Scholars who observe these changes are sometimes called "declinists."[31] Declinists note, for example, that the major powers of the world have not fought a war against each other directly since the Second World War.[32] Over the last several decades, the total number of conflicts has dropped by 40 percent.[33] The deadliest, those that kill at least 1,000 people, have declined even further—by half.[34]

Several declinists argue that the decline in war has led to a decline in war deaths. Proving this claim, however, is difficult. Unfortunately, the available historical data on war deaths are much less complete and reliable than the data on territorial change.[35] Combining data and narrative history, Steven Pinker concludes that though wars have become more deadly, they are less frequent, yielding fewer war-related deaths overall.[36]

The decline in interstate war is so widely accepted and well documented as to have almost become conventional wisdom.[37] There is far less agreement, however, on its *cause*. Pinker points to a gradual evolution in human empathy, self-control, morality, and reason—the "better angels of our nature." Many political scientists point instead to the reasons discussed above for the decline of conquest—the invention of nuclear weapons, the spread of democracy, the rise of global trade.

What these accounts miss, however, is the decision to outlaw war in 1928. Outlawing war did not immediately stop interstate war, as the Second World War makes all too clear. But it helped set in motion a series of events that would eventually lead to an unprecedented period of peace between states. The legal prohibition on war operated as a direct constraint on states committed to the Peace Pact. But it did not constrain all states—some disputed the meaning of the Pact and others simply ignored it. Those states discovered that violating the law eventually brought consequences: Their illegal conquests would no longer be recognized and would be reversed as soon as possible. Indeed, the reversal of nearly all the post-Pact conquests at the end of the Second World War established that states could take the territory of other states, but they could not benefit from it if they did. And they would never be entirely secure in their ownership. If states could not keep what they took in war, then what was the point of going to war in the first place?

For hundreds of years, war shaped and reshaped the world's borders, moving the lines back and forth, causing states to grow and shrink. It created and destroyed empires. It generated new countries out of the ashes. It ravaged populations, razed property, decimated lives, destroyed livelihoods. And it was accepted not just as unavoidable but as the appropriate legal means of resolving disputes.

After 1928, that changed. For the first time in history, states refused to recognize conquests. Once the Second World War had ended, all but one of the unrecognized conquests were reversed. And after 1948, conquests and international wars dwindled to a small fraction of what they had once been.

In short, the Peace Pact formed the background of rules and assumptions against which the rest of the new system operated. As states adapted to the transformed legal order, their adaptations helped reinforce those new rules and became *reasons of their own* for playing by them. The Pact did not bring about the end of conquest and interstate war on its own; no treaty, no law could have. But it was a necessary start, the beginning of the end of the Old World Order.

FOURTEEN

WAR NO LONGER
MAKES STATES

The United Nations Headquarters is located on the former site of a slaughterhouse. The eighteen-acre complex on the East River of Manhattan is dominated by a thirty-seven-floor glass and steel tower with a modern, international aesthetic, meant to reflect a sense of "newness" and an optimistic vision of the world's nations working together as one. The lightness of this utopian structure is offset by the opaque heft of the concrete General Assembly building. The contrast between the buildings betrays the warring designs of the two architects for the site, selected by an architectural committee that, in typical U.N. fashion, was unable to choose between them.

Entering the complex is like entering another world. As visitors file past a phalanx of flags of all the member nations,[1] they may not realize that they are leaving the United States and passing into international territory, where U.S. officials have no special powers. As the U.N.'s own website puts it, "No federal, state or local officer or official of the United States, whether administrative, judicial, military or police, may enter UN Headquarters, except with the consent of and under conditions agreed to by the Secretary-General of the Organization."[2] The U.N. even has its own police, firefighters, and post office.

The highlight of a visit to the United Nations complex is the General Assembly hall. The enormous chamber has none of the colonial charm of the halls of the United States Congress. The General Assembly is a futuristic space that bears a strong resemblance to the Galactic Senate from *Star Wars*. Onstage in the front of the hall sits a large dais and, behind the dais, an immense brightly lit gold-leafed background bearing the United Nations insignia—a map of the world centered on the North Pole, surrounded by a wreath of olive leaves.

When the United Nations building was being designed, the architects debated how many seats to include in the General Assembly meeting hall. Oscar Schachter, one of the senior legal counselors at the U.N. Headquarters and leading international law scholar, advised them to include room for an additional twenty members beyond the current fifty-one. That seemed like more than enough.[3]

Today, the United Nations has 193 members—almost four times the number at the time of its founding and three times as many as Schachter predicted. Nearly all the seats once dedicated to the audience are now taken by the new states. The latest renovation in 2014 made additional room so as to accommodate 204 members.[4]

Schachter could be forgiven for his mistake. At the time the architects consulted him, the number of states in the world was just over sixty, and the number had remained steady for decades, with only a gradual increase during the preceding century. That the number of members of the United Nations would go much above seventy, even if every state in the world were admitted, seemed implausible.

Unfortunately for Schachter, and the architects who relied on his advice, the past was not prologue. For the international order was undergoing a revolution. At the end of the 1940s, the number of states was already at seventy-five. By 1960, it hit 107. The explosion in the number of states can be seen in Figure 3. Because nearly the entire earth's mass was controlled by states in 1945, the increase in the number of states after this date came from the division of existing states. As the number of states climbed, the average size of states fell.

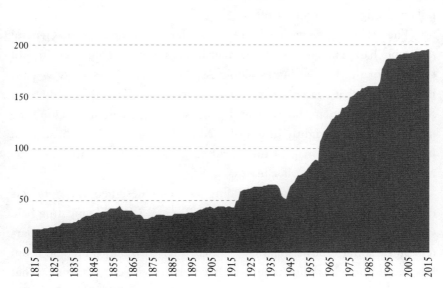

Figure 3: Number of States in the World[5]

How and why did the number of countries in the world grow so rapidly in the span of seventy years? Why did states begin to fracture in the 1940s? The answer, again, starts with the outlawry of war. To see why, we have to return to the dawn of the Old World Order—with the rise of the modern state.

WHEN WAR MADE STATES AND VICE VERSA

The modern state is a recent invention.[6] As late as the sixteenth century, there were few, if any, entities that would be recognizable as states. There were myriad principalities, bishoprics, free cities, and urban leagues. And, of course, there were empires, which exercised loose control over vast territories. But these entities did not meet the minimal definition of a state offered by Max Weber, a foundational theorist of the state: "a human community that (successfully) claims the monopoly of the legitimate use of physical force within a given territory."[7]

In the 1990s, Charles Tilly offered a simple but powerful explanation for why states emerged: "War made states, and vice versa."[8] Beginning in the seventeenth century, Tilly argued, states began to exercise a monopoly on violence—making it "criminal, unpopular, and impractical for most of their citizens to bear arms."[9] This centralization of the legitimate use of force in the state had the effect, Tilly argued, of creating durable state structures: To wage war, one needed an army. And to raise and maintain an army, one needed arms, munitions, transportation, roads, barracks, supply depots, and a system of military recruitment and training.

Above all, to run a military, monarchs needed money—lots of it. Military innovation in premodern Europe, particularly the development of gunpowder weapons and mass armies, made war expensive. Only entities with significant capital and a sizable population could afford to wage war effectively. "From the late seventeenth century onward," Tilly argued, "budgets, debts, and taxes arose to the rhythm of war."[10] No one designed the principal components of states. Instead, they formed "more or less as inadvertent by-products of efforts to carry out more immediate tasks, especially the creation and support of armed force."[11]

One need not accept all elements of Tilly's argument to find his central insight—that war helped propel the creation of the modern state and state structures—persuasive. War required both men and money and monarchs needed compliant populations to get both.[12] Tilly rightly noted that no monarch could "make war without securing the acquiescence of nearly all of his subject population, and the active cooperation of at least a crucial few."[13] The need for a supportive, or at least acquiescent, population was, indeed, one of the reasons that sovereigns crafted beautifully written war manifestos to win the hearts and minds of the population—a population that had to pay taxes to finance the army and supply their sons, husbands, and fathers to fight. The sovereign needed, moreover, to build effective state institutions that could keep the war machine going. Even if the population supported the sovereign's plans, men and material had to be organized effectively to win wars.

A sovereign who did this job poorly would be vulnerable. In a world where states could wage war and seize territory even over a small grievance, a sovereign that did not have a well-functioning military would not stay a sovereign for long. As states came into contact with one another, successful states were more likely to win more territory, growing larger in the process, while weaker states shrank and even disappeared altogether in a kind of Darwinian survival of the fittest.

But it was not only war that led to consolidation of territory into larger political units. In the sixteenth and seventeenth centuries, the emergence of global markets coincided with the rise of the powerful and influential economic theory of mercantilism. According to mercantilist thought, which held sway in much of Western Europe, economic growth was a zero-sum game.[14] As Voltaire put it: "It is clear that one country can only gain if another country loses."[15]

The government's charge, then, was to manage the economy to augment state power at the expense of rivals. The only way to assure free and open trade with a territory was to control it. Mercantilist states—including most of the leading European powers—adopted economic policies aimed at producing a positive balance of trade through high tariffs and quotas. To export more than the country imported would, mercantilist leaders thought, lead to an accumulation of currency and precious metals and, hence, power.

Sovereign policies designed to keep money, precious metals, and raw materials within their control drove states to conquer territories nearby and—increasingly—overseas. Africa and the Americas were newly accessible to Europeans thanks to technological advances in navigation, shipping technology, and mapping. Those lands were often controlled by tribes or other entities that European powers did not consider to be sovereign states. The formal requirements of war were therefore frequently discarded and the land treated as *terra nullius*—no man's land, with no just cause for war required.

The colonies served as sources of raw materials and markets for finished goods. Portugal, Spain, France, the Netherlands, Denmark, Sweden, and—above all—the United Kingdom fanned out across the globe, seeking to establish colonial footholds as far and wide as possible. Mercantilism encouraged states to make war to expand territorial control and market size, while war, by expanding the markets under unified sovereign control, helped sustain mercantilism. These forces fed each other, encouraging greater amalgamation of territory under sovereign control.

And, indeed, beginning in the sixteenth century, states began to consolidate into fewer, larger entities. At the close of the fifteenth century, in Europe there were somewhere on the order of "200 states, would-be states, statelets, and statelike organizations."[16] By the early 1900s, competition and consolidation had cut that number down to roughly twenty. The rest of the world experienced a similar dynamic. States became bigger and less numerous over the course of the eighteenth century as control over territory consolidated in the hands of those most successful at conquest.[17] All that would soon change.

WAR NO LONGER MAKES STATES

The change in the legal rules operated like a sudden shock to the system. The Old World Order had rewarded states capable of seizing and holding territory. The New World Order removed these powerful pressures and replaced them with a different logic of international competition. Like an environmental disaster that wipes out all the predators in the ecosystem, the outlawry of war fundamentally altered the balance of power in the world. And by transforming that balance of power, it also *transformed states themselves*.[18]

With the outlawry of war, the forces that favored larger states and empires were undermined and even reversed. States no longer had to be big simply to survive. The threat of conquest—and the pressure it placed on states to grow so they could field larger and better-equipped militaries— receded. The prohibition on war and territorial conquest, backed by the promise of nonrecognition and even possible Security Council action to reverse illegal seizures, meant that vulnerable states could nonetheless thrive.[19] The meek, once under constant threat, were now able to hold their ground.

Colonies, too, were also immune from new conquest. In the Old World Order, if a colony managed to gain independence from its imperial overlord, it exposed itself to takeover by another power. Some vulnerable territories acquiesced in the establishment of protectorates that would permit them some measure of self-governance for this reason. In a world where conquest was common, a colonial "protectorate" offered the subjugated state security against would-be conquerors. During the scramble for Africa, for instance, local leaders frequently agreed to the creation of protectorates as a defensive move to prevent more aggressive assertions of authority. With the outlawry of war, however, colonies no longer had to worry that they would be reconquered if they became independent. In a world where aggressive war was illegal, protectorates offered little that an independent state could not obtain on its own.

FREE TRADE UNLEASHED

By the time war was outlawed, mercantilist thought, which favored exports over imports and encouraged states to accumulate vast territory, had long been discredited. In his 1776 classic work, *An Inquiry into the Nature and Causes of the Wealth of Nations*, Adam Smith demonstrated that specialization in production allows for economies of scale, improving efficiency and growth.[20] In 1817, David Ricardo showed that countries could gain from trade even if one was more efficient at producing *all* traded goods—what mattered was their *comparative* advantage.[21]

These revolutionary ideas swept the Western world. And yet growth in global trade was sluggish. From the end of the eighteenth century, when Adam Smith first launched his famous critique of mercantilism, until the early twentieth, global trade rose from just under 10 percent of global GDP to just over 20 percent.[22]

This tepid response is puzzling. If states were aware that they could do better by trading, why didn't they? One explanation is domestic politics: Powerful industries within the state typically want protection from outside competition and are often able to exert pressure on political leaders to enact protectionist policies. But another explanation for why states traded so little—even once they realized it was economically beneficial—is that they feared their trading partners.

Gains from trade, after all, are almost never equal. Both sides gain, but one side usually gets more than the other. Whether England or Portugal does relatively better when they trade cloth and wine depends on a wide array of factors, including the gains from specialization, the responsiveness (what economists call "elasticity") of demand and supply, exchange rates, transportation costs, competition for labor, the terms of trade, and the level and amount of the increase in productive efficiency. Thus even though both states generally benefit from increased trade (that is, both enjoy "absolute" gains), those benefits are never identical—"relative" gains will vary. Portugal and England will be reluctant to trade, because each is afraid of making the other relatively better off and placing itself in a disadvantageous position if they go to war.

This insight—that states care more about relative than absolute gains—is a central tenet of one of the most influential theories of international relations known as Realism.[23] Realists argue that states must constantly be on guard against relative losses of power. States therefore cannot engage in true cooperation of any kind, for cooperation will yield uneven gains, leaving one partner relatively worse off. And since war and trade are more likely to take place between neighboring countries,[24] states have a distinct disincentive to trade.

Realism's chief critics have argued that Realists have the priority backward: States privilege absolute, not relative, gains.[25] They maintain that even in an anarchic system, certain forms of cooperation are possible. To support their claim, these critics point to the array of international institutions that emerged after the Second World War. The European Union, NATO, World Bank, International Monetary Fund, the World Trade Organization, and a host of other complex organizations demonstrate that—contrary to Realist expectations—cooperation among states is not only possible, but real.

But Realism's critics have always had a hard time explaining *why* relative gains don't matter as much as absolute gains.[25] And they have had an even harder time explaining why international cooperation has been so much more robust in recent decades than it was for the three centuries previous. The answer—and the reason why Realists are largely right about prior centuries but wrong about the present era—is that war has been outlawed. The claim that states prioritize relative gains was a pretty good description of the world when Might was Right, but it is a pretty bad description of our current world, in which it is not. In a world without war, states are no longer fixated on getting ahead of the competition. They can focus on whether they are better off with trade than without it, and in most cases they are better off with it.

The sum of world exports and imports as a share of world GDP rose from a low of 10 percent at the close of the Second World War to roughly 60 percent today.[26] The change in the law was not the only reason global free trade boomed at this moment. Improved financial and transportation technology also played an important role, as did the declining dependence of governments on tariffs for revenue. But many of these forces had long been building. The outlawry of war in 1928—and the broader legal transformation that it unleashed—made it safer to trade. With conquest no longer a threat, states did not have to fear that their trading partners would turn on them and go to war.

COOPERATION INSTEAD OF CONQUEST

The rise of free trade meant that states no longer needed to control territory to access markets. States that once maintained enormous empires to extract resources through privileged trading relationships could now gain the benefits of trade without the costs of controlling far-flung territories. Yes, they would have to share the market with others, but others would also have to share with them.[27] Raw commodities, once obtained by colonization and extraction, now could be acquired through simple exchange.

Trade was not the only area in which states could gain the advantages of size through cooperation. International organizations focusing on a wide range of activities emerged in the postwar era. These include the World Bank, founded in 1944 to provide loans to developing countries; the North Atlantic Treaty Organization, a military alliance formed in 1949 encompassing twenty-eight member states including the United States and much of Western Europe; and the World Health Organization, founded in 1948 to direct and coordinate a global array of public health programs. But they also include smaller, less well-known institutions such as the International Coffee Organization, which provides assistance to coffee growers around the world; the International Olive Oil Council, which does much the same for olive oil producers; and the International Whaling Commission, which was founded to "provide for the proper conservation of whale stocks and thus make possible the orderly development of the whaling industry."[28]

By offering a way to cooperate with each other, these international organizations allow states to reap many of the benefits of being big, even if they themselves are quite small—not only in trade but on other dimensions. Through this growing array of international institutions, states could gain access to resources that once came only with territorial control. Bigger used to be better. Now many of the benefits of being large could be obtained through cooperation with other states instead.

In the Old World Order, only large, expanding states thrived. In the New World Order, states became freer to choose the size that fit their national aspirations. They could choose to be small without jeopardizing their existence or their ability to gain from larger cooperative ventures.

What they could not always choose, however, was which populations remained part of their national political community. For the last great change brought about by the outlawry of war was growing demands of people within states for states of their own. With conquest an ever-present danger (or, for those doing the conquest, a tempting opportunity), the Old World Order had created powerful centripetal forces. The New World Order replaced them with centrifugal forces, and none pulled harder than the pressure for decolonization unleashed by conquest's collapse.

MERDEKA

The Atlantic Charter, issued by Roosevelt and Churchill as a statement of principles for which their countries would fight, promised to "respect the right of all peoples to choose the form of government under which they will live."[29] Along with the prohibition on territorial aggrandizement through force and support for free trade, the commitment to self-determination was reaffirmed in the Declaration of the United Nations and in the United Nations Charter itself, which included among the new organization's three purposes "the development of friendly relations among nations based on respect for the principle for equal rights and self-determination of peoples."[30]

When the Second World War came to a close, the tension between the rhetoric of self-determination and the reality of colonization became difficult to maintain. An account by a member of the British 23rd Indian

Division—known as "The Fighting Cock" for the insignia on the uniforms of the men within it—shows how the colonized turned the colonizers' ideals against them. During the war, the Japanese had seized control of Indonesia from the Dutch. When the Japanese surrendered in early September 1945, the Fighting Cock went to Java to accept a transfer of authority to Allied forces. In Singapore, en route to Java, an advance party met a "cheerful Dutchman who assumed that he and his countrymen were coming back to the peaceful reoccupation of their Empire."[31] But the Indonesians had a different idea. To greet the returning imperialists, they covered carriages and vehicles with graffiti declaring: "Atlantic Charter means freedom from Dutch Imperialism." "Indonesia for Indonesians." And, simply, "*Merdeka*"—Freedom.[32] The armed resistance did not abate until the United Nations recognized the country's independence in 1949.

Indonesia was not alone. With the war won, it was difficult to square the ideals for which the Allies had fought with the realities of empire. In a world where slavery was illegal and both individual and national self-determination were increasingly recognized as basic human rights, it was morally untenable for states to possess and rule over colonies. People in colonized states had their own national identities—and they demanded the same rights to rule themselves claimed by their rulers. These impulses to self-determination were in many cases reinforced by the Soviet Union and United States, which offered support for nationalist movements in Greece, Vietnam, Iran, Indonesia, Algeria, Lebanon, Congo, Cuba, Colombia, Thailand, Yemen, Ethiopia, Peru, and Afghanistan, as the superpowers competed with each other for influence.[33]

The desire for self-determination was not new, of course. People have yearned to govern themselves for far longer than war has been outlawed. But the rise of self-determination as a principle uniting the Allies against the Axis meant empires were all but impossible to sustain once the war was won. Equally important—and far less recognized—the major features of the global system that had once made it dangerous or impracticable to act on the desire for self-governance had been eliminated. The outlawry of war, the end of conquest, and the rise of global free trade meant that smaller entities could now not only survive but thrive. Self-determination was not only morally required in the New World Order, but it was practically realistic as well.

A WORLD TRANSFORMED

And so, after 1945, the number of states exploded. Two key forms of state birth—decolonization and the fracturing of larger states into smaller ones—led to the rapid increase in United Nations members that so defied the initial expectations of those who built the General Assembly Hall. The 1940s through the 1970s witnessed the largest wave of decolonization the world had ever seen. The British Empire collapsed and with it huge swaths of the world became independent, including Transjordan (now Jordan), India, Burma (now Myanmar), Ceylon (now Sri Lanka), Eritrea, parts of Egypt, Sudan, the Federation of Malaya (now Malaysia), Ghana, Rhodesia (present-day Zimbabwe), Northern Rhodesia, Zambia, Malawi, Malta, Mauritius, and Swaziland. France, too, released its grip over Syria, Laos, Libya, Tunisia, Morocco, Cambodia, Vietnam, Guinea, Dahomey (now Benin), Upper Volta (present-day Burkina Faso), Cameroon, Chad, Republic of the Congo, Côte d'Ivoire, Gabon, the Mali Federation (present-day Mali and Senegal), Mauritania, Niger, Togo, the Central African Republic, and Madagascar. Belgium, Italy, Spain, and the United States relinquished their smaller holdings. Between 1945 and 1960, three dozen new states in Asia and Africa achieved independence.

New states also emerged through fracturing of larger geographically contiguous states into smaller ones—a trend that gained momentum just as the wave of decolonization began to dissipate. In 1958, Egypt and Syria created the United Arab Republic, which split again in 1961. In 1965, Singapore was established as a sovereign state independent of Malaysia. Bangladesh split from Pakistan in 1971, which itself had split from India in 1947. In the 1990s, the Soviet Union, Czechoslovakia, and Yugoslavia all disintegrated, producing tens of smaller sub-states.

Yemen divided in two and then reunited again (and is presently in danger of dividing once again). Eritrea broke from Ethiopia, also in the early 1990s. And most recent of all, in 2011, Sudan split into Sudan and South Sudan.

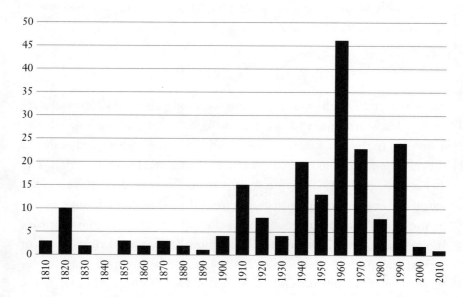

Figure 4: Independences Per Decade[34]

Drawing again on the Correlates of War database employed in the last chapter, it is possible to map the number of "independences" that occurred each decade. Here "independence" does not necessarily mean colonial independence. Instead, it refers to the process by which territory that had been part of one state broke away and became its own free-standing state—for example, when South Sudan became a state separate from Sudan. As Figure 4 shows, although there had been state births all through the 1800s and early 1900s, the number of "independences" jumped in the 1940s and stayed high throughout most of the second half of the twentieth century, falling off only in the beginning of the twenty-first.

To see where all these new states came from, we mapped the transformation in states' reach and character over the course of the nineteenth and twentieth centuries by looking at the control of territory. Because there is no existing database that accurately records the size of states over this period, we combined the "Correlates of War" territorial transfer dataset with the World Bank's data on the present-day size of states. We worked backward, applying the gains and losses of territory year by year to estimate the size of each country at any point in time. For example, the present-day size of the United Kingdom is 243,930 square kilometers. Working backward, we added 1,084 square kilometers in 1997, which corresponds to the transfer of sovereignty of Hong Kong from the U.K. to China. The U.K. then remains at 245,014 square kilometers from 1997 until 1984, the year in which Brunei gained independence, when we added 5,270 square kilometers to the U.K. total, and so on all the way back to 1816. At that time, the U.K. and its empire was a staggering 21,384,864 square kilometers, more than two times the size of present-day China and eighty-eight times the U.K.'s present size.

We then started moving forward in time. Looking at the ten largest states in 1816 and the territories they controlled—the United States, the Netherlands, Portugal, China, France, Spain, Russia/USSR, Turkey/Ottoman Empire, Belgium, and the United Kingdom—we traced their development through the present. All territorial transfers to states that became independent after 1816 are included in the graph as "independences." Meanwhile, all other territory—territory held by states that existed in 1816 but that were not among the ten largest, territory held by states that came into existence after 1816 through forced dissolution (as distinct from independence), and territory that was not in the state system in 1816 but later was incorporated into it—is in the "other" category.[35]

The picture that emerges in Figure 5 is striking: Only one of the ten largest states in 1816—China—is roughly as big today as it was then. The Ottoman Empire (today Turkey) gradually lost territory before collapsing at the close of the First World War. Portugal, once a great empire, shriveled with the loss of the colony of Brazil in the 1830s. Spain, too, collapsed in size when it lost control of its American territories. Russia/USSR held steady until it contracted with the breakup of the Soviet Union in 1991. The United States started small but ballooned through a variety of significant acquisitions, the Louisiana Purchase, the Mexican-American War, and the purchase of Alaska chief among them. Perhaps most remarkable, the United Kingdom and France grew over the course of the nineteenth century and early twentieth century. They then began to shrink, with the rapid decolonization that began with the release of Canada and Australia by the U.K. in 1931 and accelerated in the 1950s and 1960s. Belgium and the Netherlands lost territory at the same time, also due to decolonization.

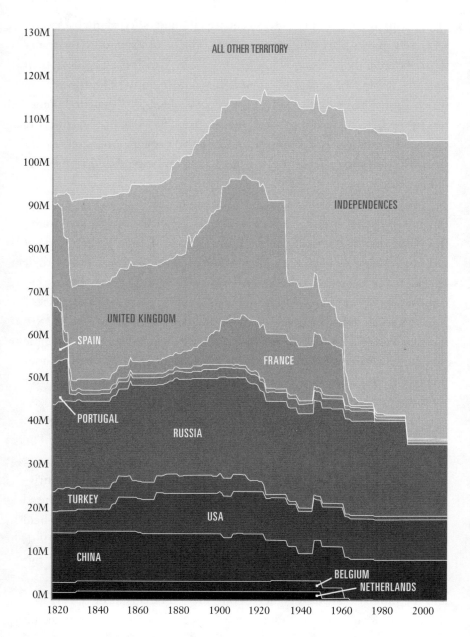

Figure 5: Share of Territory Controlled by States (in Square Kilometers)

As the biggest states shrank, the newest proliferated. Indeed, what is perhaps most remarkable in the figure is the growing swaths of territory created by the fracturing of the Great Powers. By 2014, states that became independent after 1816 covered more than half of the world.

The outlawry of war brought an end to the pressures that once produced bigger and stronger states. Instead, it allowed smaller and weaker states to survive and even thrive. With the end of conquest, states no longer faced the constant threat of attack, and those too small or ineffective to defend themselves could expect, if not success, at least survival. In many ways, this was—and is—an overwhelmingly positive change. But it has not been without its costs.

FIFTEEN

WHY IS THERE STILL SO MUCH CONFLICT?

The decision to outlaw war changed the world. Wars between states are now rare. Conquest has become the exception, not the rule. But if this is true, why have so many missed the remarkable success of the outlawry of war?

At least part of the reason is that the postwar world has been far from peaceful. India and Pakistan have fought over the region of Kashmir off and on since 1947. Since 1948, conflict involving Israel has led to three interstate wars and several intifadas. War raged in Korea from 1950 to 1953 and in Vietnam from 1955 to 1975. Genocidal conflicts erupted in Yugoslavia (now the former Yugoslavia) and Rwanda in the 1990s, and civil war ravaged Sudan for more than two decades. In 2014, the United States and China began playing a high-stakes game of chicken over islands in the South China Sea and many fear a war with China in the near future. And in 2015 alone, high-fatality civil wars continued in Nigeria, South Sudan, Yemen, Syria, Iraq, Afghanistan, Pakistan, Somalia, and Ukraine.[1]

Why, if war has been outlawed, is there still so much conflict?

The answer is that these conflicts are not prohibited by the Pact.

Indeed, they are the predictable consequences of it. Even though the Peace Pact was extraordinarily—many thought foolishly—ambitious, it was nonetheless limited in its scope. It outlawed territorial aggression by one state against another. The United Nations Charter followed its example, prohibiting "the threat or use of force against the territorial integrity or political independence of any state." This prohibition has been remarkably effective, as the decline in conquest and interstate war shows. But the prohibition on the use of force by one state against the territory of another has allowed two sources of conflict to simmer—one *between* states and one *within* them.

UNCERTAIN SOVEREIGNTY

International law prohibits aggression against the territory of another state. But what if it is not clear which state, precisely, a particular piece of territory belongs to? Then *every* state that thinks it has a claim to the territory will view any *other* state's incursion as a violation—and its own efforts to respond as legitimate self-defense.

In the Old World Order, a state could resolve such ambiguities by seizing the territory. But in the New World Order, conquest is prohibited. That's good if sovereignty is clear and the boundary lines broadly accepted. But if sovereignty is disputed and the lines hazy, the legal situation gets complicated very quickly.

We can analogize sovereignty in the New World Order to homeownership. If you want to own a house you admire, you cannot just take it by force. If you go to the house and throw the owner out, you don't acquire title to it. The owner will call the police, who will arrest you for breaking and entering. But even if there were no police, no one who knew what you had done would touch the property. No bank would accept the house as collateral for a loan. No one would purchase it. Friends might not even visit.

Instead, to acquire the right to property, you have to buy it from (or have it gifted to you by) the true owner. Only he can convey it. If you want to purchase the house, your lawyer will conduct what is known as a "title search." She will determine whether the seller bought the house from the true owner and whether he bought it from the true owner before that, and so on. Title searches can be laborious because they might require tracing real estate transactions over decades, even centuries.

Eventually, all title searches bottom out at what lawyers call the "root of title": the first true owner of the property. In the United States, root title is established by a land grant from the United States government. If you can prove that the current possessor bought the land from someone who bought the land from someone who bought the land—and so on—from the first true owner, you will have established a chain of title. Many jurisdictions let you stop before reaching the first link in the chain. They may allow you to stop at a specific date—say, 1930.

State sovereignty is not that different. As ownership to property can be established by following a chain of title, so, too, can sovereignty be established by following a chain of sovereignty. Under the Old World Order, this process was easy: Whoever seized the land and claimed sovereignty over it *had* sovereignty over it. Conquests restarted chains of sovereignty with the conquering state becoming the new root sovereign—it was like a consensual purchase of a home, only much worse for the previous owners. But in the New World Order, conquest is no longer recognized. Merely occupying a territory does not establish sovereignty any more than occupying a house establishes ownership.

But how is the root of sovereignty established in the New World Order? The answer is provided by the Peace Pact: *The true sovereign is the state that had sovereignty in 1928.* As we saw in the last chapter, when war was outlawed and territorial aggrandizement prohibited, state borders hardened—lines on maps once written in pencil were traced over in permanent marker. Sovereignty became rooted. Military victories no longer established legal sovereignty, as Japan learned in 1931. A state now had to be able to show the political equivalent of title.

Many places in the world have a simple chain of sovereignty and thus pose no problems for those trying to figure out who they belong to. Unfortunately, however, not all places: There are a number of territories where sovereignty was not well established in 1928, when the permanent marker was laid down. Those territories continue to be sources of international conflict.

BLURRY LINES AND BOTCHED HANDOFFS

Perhaps the most enduring source of ongoing conflict in the postwar era is clumsy decolonization. When empires crumbled after the Second World War, they left vast uncertainty in their wake. Two of the biggest sources of that uncertainty are "blurry lines" and "botched handoffs."

Blurry lines resulted from the sloppiness with which imperial powers delineated borders between colonial holdings. Because colonial holdings often served as mere administrative divisions, imperial mapmakers tended to draw imprecise boundaries. When these colonies became independent, the blurry lines on imperial maps became the borders of newly sovereign states. Conflicting and careless historical records provided no easy answer as to which new state had a verifiable claim to the territory in 1928—and therefore which state had the claim to the territory after independence.

The only legal way to resolve disputes over border territory post-1928 is by securing the agreement of the contesting states. But that can take decades. Indeed, some of the border disputes that emerged after decolonization have raged for close to a century. It was not until 2012 that Vietnam and Cambodia settled a border dispute that first erupted after the French withdrew in 1954. And conflict is still ongoing between Egypt and Sudan over Bir Tawil, an eight-hundred-square-mile piece of territory that both countries have claimed since the United Kingdom withdrew in 1956. That territory remains a "no-man's-land"—land claimed by both that can be developed by neither.

A second problem created by clumsy decolonization arises from what we call botched handoffs. Imperial powers often did not take enough care to identify the new sovereign of the territory they were vacating—or failed to complete the transfer in full. It would be as if you sold your house to several different people, or handed over the keys before finishing the paperwork. As you happily drive off in your moving truck, you are leaving chaos behind.

Perhaps the most infamous example of a botched handoff is former British Palestine. To trace the chain of sovereignty, we need to begin in the years before the territorial lines solidified—that is, before 1928. After the First World War, through a series of machinations the closing chapter of this book will trace, Great Britain took control of Palestine. This control was formalized in 1923, when the League of Nations issued a mandate for the British to rule in the southern part of what had been Ottoman Syria.[2] The British Mandate for Palestine created two temporary protectorates, both set to expire on May 14, 1948. One protectorate was in Palestine, an attempt to fulfill the promise of the U.K. foreign secretary Arthur James Balfour in 1917 to support the "establishment in Palestine of a national home for the Jewish people."[3] A second protectorate was in Transjordan, and was governed semiautonomously.[4]

A period of growing unrest followed. Jews continued to settle in Palestine even as Palestinian Arabs demanded an independent state.[5] The situation erupted in sporadic violence, with Arabs rioting against Jewish settlers and Zionists resisting—sometimes violently—the efforts of the British government to limit Jewish immigration. Once the horrors of the Holocaust came to light, Britain's policy of resisting immigration of Jewish refugees into Palestine met with wide-scale revolt. Dissident Zionist forces carried out attacks on British forces and officials.

Britain turned the problem over to the newly created United Nations, which developed a plan to partition Palestine into Jewish and Arab states, with Jerusalem under United Nations control.[6] But the Arab League (formed by neighboring nations that claimed to speak on behalf of Palestinian Arabs) denounced the plan, placing the United Nations effort to resolve the conflicting claims in limbo. On the day the mandate was set to expire—May 14, 1948—David Ben-Gurion, the executive head of the World Zionist Organization and president of the Jewish Agency for Palestine, unilaterally declared "the establishment of a Jewish state in Eretz Israel, to be known as the State of Israel."[7] The next day, the neighboring Arab states of Egypt, Syria, Transjordan, and Iraq attacked.[8] It took a year before a cease-fire could be established. Jordan annexed the West Bank, including East Jerusalem. Egypt took control of the Gaza Strip. During the lull, Israel sought and won admission to the United Nations. Significant numbers of states refused to acknowledge its right to exist. Even today, more than thirty United Nations member states refuse to recognize the State of Israel.[9]

The continuing conflict in this region has many causes, and this book does not offer anything approaching a full explanation of it. But at least one reason the conflict has proven so intransigent is that the British mandate expired with no clear plan for the territory it had governed. Palestine became a legal black hole, a territory in which the chain of sovereignty had been broken. The situation was further complicated by the contradictory promises made by the colonial powers to all sides in the conflict throughout the early twentieth century. As British foreign secretary Jack Straw put it in 2002, "A lot of the problems we are having to deal with now, I have to deal with now, are a consequence of our colonial past . . . the contradictory assurances which were being given to Palestinians in private at the same time as they were being given to the Israelis—again, an interesting history for us but not an entirely honourable one."[10]

Israel is far from the only botched handoff. In Korea, Japan's unconditional surrender in 1945 meant the end of Japanese colonial rule. But Japan was in no position to make contingency plans for maintaining legal order. The collapse of colonial rule set off a rush by the Soviets and Americans to establish control. In a hasty deal established to prevent conflicts between wartime allies, the Americans and Soviets drew a line at the 38th parallel to delineate the two occupying forces. The Korean War was the attempt by Koreans on either side of this temporary line to establish their sovereignty over the entire peninsula. Much the same happened in Vietnam, where the sudden end of Japanese rule left uncertainty—and then war—over who was the rightful sovereign after Japan relinquished control. And after India won independence from Britain and split into two independent states, India and Pakistan, in 1947, competing claims to the former Princely State of Kashmir and Jammu on the India-Pakistan border led to repeated wars in the region and fueled a nuclear arms race between the two countries.

In the New World Order, the problems created by clumsy decolonization are devilishly hard to fix. There is no way, short of Security Council intervention, to compel a resolution of the conflict. Conflicts over contested territory can only be resolved by mutual agreement. As a result, blurry lines and botched handoffs are the major reason why the rules against conquest are sometimes broken, even though Might no longer makes Right. Recall that, aside from the immediate postwar transfers, the only other recognized territorial transfers during the 1929–1948 period that were not later reversed were border disputes created by blurry lines: Saudi Arabia's seizure from Yemen in 1934, Paraguay's seizure of border territory from Bolivia in 1935, and Peru's seizure of disputed border territory from Ecuador in 1942. And many of the major conquests in the postwar era—such as Indonesia's seizure of West Papua in 1963 and North Vietnam's conquest of South Vietnam in 1975—took place following botched handoffs. When the rule against conquest is violated, then, it is almost never in cases of naked aggression against foreign sovereign territory, but rather when newly independent states attempt to fill the legal vacuums left by withdrawing empires that failed to ensure a clear chain of sovereignty.

ISLANDS OF UNCERTAINTY

Blurry lines and botched handoffs can lead to long-term conflict when they affect places people deeply care about. A very different route to territorial conflict occurs when land people did not care about—land that nobody bothered to lay firm claim to—suddenly becomes valuable. And nowhere has this been more true than in the archipelago of the South China Sea.

Chances are good that if you look up from this book and gaze around, you will see several items that, in whole or in part, have passed through the South China Sea. Half of the world's merchant fleet tonnage and a third of its crude oil passes through this waterway. That's more than $5 trillion in shipborne trade per year. As goods make their way through the sea, they pass the coasts of Malaysia, Brunei, Philippines, Taiwan, China, Vietnam, Thailand, and Singapore, the same waterway traversed by the *Santa Catarina* when it was captured by Jacob van Heemskerck in 1603.[11]

The hundreds of tiny islands your goods passed were once close to worthless, rocky shoals that offered refuge to little more than resting wildlife and the occasional exhausted fisherman. With the exception of a few large islands that produced something of value—the Spice Islands, for example, that the Dutch and Portuguese fought over so savagely, with Grotius's permission—most islets were more trouble defending than they were worth. Few had fresh water and thus could not support agriculture or permanent settlement. States rarely bothered to establish clear sovereign authority over them.

In a twist of history, it is because these islands were virtually worthless a century ago that they are the source of so much conflict today—bringing the nations of East Asia into dangerous confrontation with one another and even threatening to bring two of the world's greatest powers to the brink of war.

THE COW'S TONGUE LINE

In May 2015, a game of chicken unfolded in the skies over Fiery Cross Reef in the middle of the South China Sea. The United States sent a surveillance aircraft over the reef, where China was dredging sand to create a foundation on which it could build a planned airstrip and seaport. The American pilots ignored repeated demands by Chinese forces that the aircraft leave the area. China's Foreign Ministry later called the confrontation "irresponsible and dangerous." Secretary of Defense Ashton Carter replied, "There should be no mistake about this: The United States will fly, sail and operate wherever international law allows, as we do all around the world."[12]

The Fiery Cross Reef is just one of a vast number of rocks, atolls, and islands in the South China Sea to which the coastal states in the region have made overlapping claims. Airfields have arisen on remote and barren reefs. Immense platforms have emerged on tiny rocks. Satellite images that document this process show five ships dredging sand from the ocean floor, pumping the sand through floating pipes, and dumping it onto an emerald green reef. In successive photos taken over the course of a year, a bloom of brilliant white obscures the reef with a growing sand bar poking up through the surface of the water. The series of images ends with the emergence of a new island over one square mile in area housing numerous buildings, roads, and runways. The images are fascinating but also terrifying. For most of these "reclamations" are taking place on contested territory. No shot has yet been fired, but China has been seeking to establish its claims by gradual occupation.

China's claim in the South China Sea is the most audacious by far—including a vast area within what it has dubbed the "Nine-Dash Line" and others have called the "Cow's Tongue Line"—an accurate description of

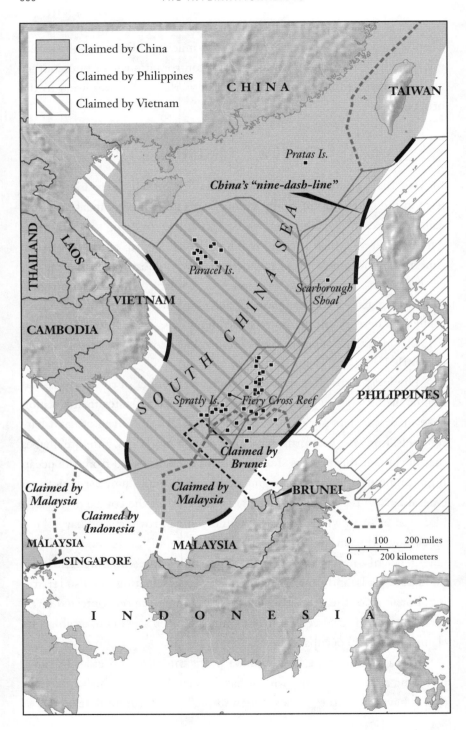

Claimed by China

Claimed by Philippines

Claimed by Vietnam

CHINA

TAIWAN

Pratas Is.

China's "nine-dash-line"

THAILAND

LAOS

VIETNAM

CAMBODIA

Paracel Is.

Scarborough
Shoal

SOUTH CHINA SEA

Spratly Is.   Fiery Cross Reef

PHILIPPINES

Claimed by
Brunei

Claimed by
Malaysia

Claimed by
Malaysia

BRUNEI

Claimed by
Indonesia

MALAYSIA

SINGAPORE

MALAYSIA

0   100   200 miles

0   200 kilometers

I N D O N E S I A

its shape but also of the appetite it represents. Though China claims it has exercised sovereignty over the area within the Cow's Tongue Line for centuries, its neighbors vehemently disagree. Coastal states such as Brunei, Malaysia, the Philippines, Taiwan, and Vietnam point to their own spotty and incomplete historical records to establish their claims to the Paracel Islands, the Pratas Islands, Scarborough Shoal, and the Spratly Islands, among many others. On most of these tiny bits of land, there were—until recently—no structures, no industry, no inhabitants, and little plant or animal life. Thus China's building campaign on contested reefs and rocks is an undisguised bid to create facts on the ground that the other claimants cannot match.

Until recently, this campaign over specks of land would have appeared the height of foolishness. Peace treaties, for example, frequently failed to mention all but the largest islands. At the close of the Sino-Japanese War of 1895, the Treaty of Shimonoseki provided that China ceded to Japan "the island of Formosa [Taiwan] together with all islands appertaining or belonging to said island of Formosa."[13] Which islands, precisely, appertained or belonged to Formosa was not specified. Nobody cared. Even as late as 1945, sovereignty over tiny islands was left vague. After its defeat by the Allies at the close of the Second World War, Japan relinquished its claims to much of the territory it had seized before and during the war, but failed to specify who would take charge of the islands.[14]

All this began to change in the late 1960s. A United Nations–led survey concluded that oil reserves would likely be found in the East and South China Seas.[15] Not coincidentally, that discovery took place as oil companies developed the technology for drilling below the ocean depths.[16]

The rules, too, had begun to shift in ways that would make islands much more valuable. In 1973, the United Nations held a conference on the law of the sea. That conference led to the drafting of a convention—known as the Law of the Sea Convention—that outlined the sovereign rights over the oceans. According to the convention, coastal states could establish an exclusive economic zone out to two hundred nautical miles from the shore. In this area, the coastal state has sole rights over all the natural resources: fish in the sea, minerals on the seabed, oil or natural gas under the sea. And they have sole control over minerals in the subsoil for the continental

shelf—which could extend as far as 350 nautical miles. What's more, islands would get the same rights as any other coastal area.

In a few years, then, insignificant, uninhabited rocks—many barely
peeking above the water in the middle of nowhere—came with over a hundred thousand square nautical miles of ocean that could be exploited (a
circle with a radius of two hundred nautical miles encompasses precisely
125,637 square nautical miles). This development coincided with a drop in
fisheries worldwide, which made exclusive control over any ocean area extremely valuable. Control over the seas also came with oil—in some cases,
lots of it.

One of the sources of conflict in the New World Order, then, is this:
If sovereignty over territory was unclear in 1928, it cannot be resolved
after 1928 except by mutual agreement of all claimants to the territory.
But mutual agreement can be challenging when the stakes are high and
no state with a plausible claim has a better claim than another. Moreover,
military conflict can't resolve the dispute, for waging war and conquering
territory no longer establishes sovereignty. In cases when no one bothered
to draw clear boundaries, there is no way to figure out who's right—and so
the conflict persists.

THE ROLE OF LAW

The South China Sea is the setting for a geopolitical struggle between two
of the world's most powerful states, and thus it would seem that law would
play only a small, even inconsequential role. Indeed, China has shown that it
is willing to flout many of the rules of the system, using its outsized military
to intimidate its neighbors. Meanwhile the United States has responded by
sending its own massive air force and navy to push back against the Chinese
claims. In this clash of military titans, how could legal niceties matter?

But stepping back, it is possible to see that the power struggle is taking
place against a backdrop of law. Why were islands so worthless for hundreds of years? Because barren territory that was difficult to defend against
conquest was more trouble than it was worth. Why did these islands become so valuable? *Because the law changed.* Not only did conquest become

illegal (and thus defending islands unnecessary), but the new law of the sea gave states control over hundreds of miles of ocean and seabed resources surrounding islands. China and the other coastal nations scrambling to establish claims to the islands are doing so because they are pursuing their interests as determined by law. Each state wants these islands because the rules have now made these islands valuable. Law is also the reason the disputes are intractable: In the New World Order, Right cannot be settled with Might. Mere occupation cannot give China what it really wants—the right to lawfully extract the resources that come with recognized sovereignty over the islands. So the standoff continues.

QUIETING SOVEREIGNTY

In a world where Right cannot be established by Might, disagreements over sovereignty can be impossible to resolve. But is there *really* no way to resolve this uncertainty? After all, in the case of property ownership, there are tools to settle exactly these kinds of disputes. A person can buy title insurance at the time he buys the property, just in case a dispute arises in the future. If a dispute does arise, a person seeking to establish title can go to court to "quiet title."

But geopolitics has no such thing as "sovereignty insurance." A state cannot buy an insurance policy from the United Nations to protect it from occupying disputed territory. International law does have a few ways to "quiet sovereignty." The International Court of Justice—often called "the World Court"—was created at the time the United Nations was formed to resolve legal disputes between states, including border disputes and other claims of sovereignty. It has decided fourteen border cases since its inception—most recently a boundary dispute between Malaysia and Singapore over three groups of rocky islands in the Strait of Malacca.[17] The Permanent Court of Arbitration, a more informal version of the International Court, has also resolved territorial disputes as well, though the precise number of such cases is not publicly known.[18] Neither court, however, has compulsory jurisdiction, which means that they can only hear disputes if both sides to the dispute agree to be bound by their decision.

The United Nations Security Council has the compulsory power to resolve sovereignty disputes that the courts lack—and it has used this power to "quiet sovereignty." In the early years of the U.N., eleven former colonies were placed under its trusteeship. The U.N. Trusteeship Council ensured that there was a clear successor to the colonial government, averting many of the problems that often plagued colonial handoffs and the armed conflicts they caused. All eleven trust territories became successfully independent or voluntarily associated with a state.[19] The Security Council has also weighed into a number of territorial disputes.[20] In 1999, for example, the Security Council established a mission to resolve a long-raging dispute over the territory of East Timor.[21] The mission conducted a vote on independence and, when the East Timorese people voted in favor, the U.N. Transitional Authority oversaw the territory's evolution to full and independent statehood. But in others cases, such as the dispute between Russia and Ukraine over Crimea, the threat of a veto by one or another of the permanent members has prevented the Council from acting.

Because the international community lacks a comprehensive and mandatory mechanism for resolving disputes over territory—a Supreme Court of the World, as it were—many clashes can only be worked out in an ad hoc fashion. Individual states simply recognize one or the other claimants and do business with those they recognize. In the particularly fraught cases, there is no consensus over the owner. It is as if half the neighborhood thinks Fred is the rightful owner of the house and the other half thinks Bob is.

This problem applies not only to disputes *between* states over territory. It also applies to disputes *within* states.

THE WORLD'S NEWEST STATE

The world's newest state was born at the stroke of midnight on July 9, 2011. In Juba, the new capital, a jubilant crowd erupted in shouting, singing, drum beating, horn honking, and firework displays. An electronic billboard above the celebrants flashed a picture of the new country's flag with the words "Free at Last" and "Republic of South Sudan." At ceremonies the following day, the fledgling nation's troops marched past bleachers of dignitaries, including former U.S. secretary of state Colin Powell and U.S. ambassador to the United Nations Susan Rice. "We are a nation recognized by the outside world," one reveler explained to a reporter. "We were second citizens, but now we are free at last."[22]

The new country emerged from bloodshed. Africa's longest running civil war in modern history raged in Sudan between the largely Muslim North and the mostly Christian South. In 2003, the war grabbed headlines in the West when it boiled over into a horrific genocide in Darfur. The violence finally abated in 2005, but not before the twenty-two-year war had claimed one and a half million lives and displaced four million people out of a population of just over thirty million. The 2005 Comprehensive Peace Agreement gave the South regional autonomy, representation in a national power-sharing government, and the right to hold a referendum—a referendum in which 99 percent of the voters chose independence.[23]

The high hopes of the South Sudanese, however, were quickly dashed, for South Sudan has become the poster child for the modern failed state. After the Independence Day celebrations were over, ethnic divisions—primarily between the two largest ethnic groups, the Dinka and Nuer—erupted into violence.[24] The economy, disastrously lopsided with few opportunities to earn a living outside the army and oil industry, collapsed in January 2012 when the government of South Sudan shut down oil production over a dispute with Sudan about sharing revenues.[25] Hostilities worsened after President Salva Kiir dismissed his cabinet.[26] His former vice president, Riek Machar, who represented South Sudan at the ceremony adding its flag at the United Nations in 2011, became the leader of a rebel faction. In the fighting that followed, both sides committed horrific war crimes, including indiscriminate killing of civilians, widespread rape, and the torching of entire villages.[27]

South Sudan represents the dark side of the New World Order. Even though it possesses vast oil reserves, South Sudan need not worry about the powers that once ruled the region. Its sovereignty stands as a shield against external violence. Yet its newly won sovereignty has done nothing to prevent internal violence.

The absence of external threats has, if anything, exposed internal tensions. And the absence of external threats means that South Sudan continues to exist as a sovereign state despite the dearth of effective state institutions—police, courts, and military—that are necessary for law and order. The so-called resource curse exacerbates the situation. The state has enough energy reserves to fund itself solely by selling its oil. In 2012, 98 percent of South Sudan's government budget came from the petroleum industry.[29] Most of the population is unnecessary for running the state. And the only people the South Sudanese have to fight for control of South Sudan are one another.

SURVIVAL OF THE WEAKEST

South Sudan is not unique. Figure 6 shows the average number of failed states per year for nearly two centuries. The information comes from the Polity IV project dataset, which follows all major independent states in the world from the early 1800s through 2014. Political scientists use it to assess the characteristics of state governments—whether democratic or authoritarian or somewhere in between. Among the information it captures

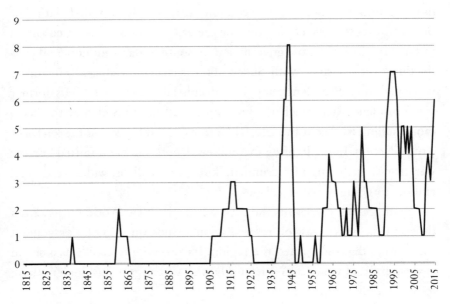

Figure 6: Number of Failed States[28]

is "complete collapse of central political authority" (that is, "state failure or 'interregnum'" so complete that there is no government to assess). The test is stringent—probably *too* stringent.[30] Governments that are very weak or possess control over some, but not all, of its territory do not count as "failed." (According to Polity, Iraq was not a failed state in 2014, but was in 2003.) Thus the startling numbers in the figure likely *understate* the number of failed states in recent decades.

The history of intrastate wars—armed conflicts that take place within states, not between them—follows a similar pattern, as seen in Figure 7.[31] Data drawn from the "Correlates of War" project show that intrastate wars occurred during the 1800s, but there were never more than a dozen in any given year. In the 1950s, however, intrastate wars became *much* more common, rising from a low of 1 in 1955 to a high of 29 in 1992, before falling back down to 4 in 2009. That pause proved ephemeral, with renewed civil wars in Nigeria, South Sudan, Yemen, Syria, Iraq, Afghanistan, Libya, Ukraine, and elsewhere in recent years.

The violence in failed states and intrastate conflicts is often not contained by national boundaries. Terrorist groups that are active in weak

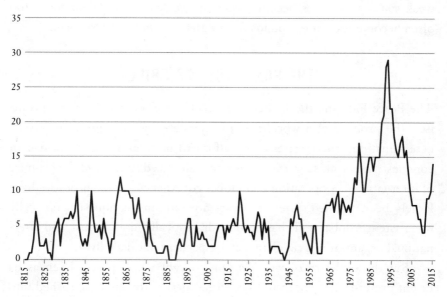

Figure 7: Number of Active Intrastate Wars[32]

and failed states frequently reach across state borders. The Islamic State originated in poorly governed regions of western Iraq and spread into less populated region of eastern Syria before beginning to challenge government control in both countries. It has since expanded into Libya, the Sinai, Algeria, Afghanistan, Yemen, Nigeria—all countries or regions where state control is feeble or nonexistent. Similarly, the chronically fractured state of Afghanistan and the tribal regions of Pakistan served as an incubator for the terrorist group al Qaeda. Similar examples are easy to find: al Shabab in Somalia, Boko Haram in Nigeria, Hezbollah in Lebanon, Tehrik-i-Taliban in Pakistan, the Taliban in Afghanistan, Jabhat al Nusrah in Syria, the Houthi in Yemen.[33]

Though not all failed states breed terrorism and not all terrorism originates in failed states, weak and failed states are a significant source of terrorist threats. States that control their territory suppress violent groups, usually through ordinary law enforcement—police, rather than the military. In states that cannot control their territory, by contrast, violence tends to grow, with no organized force to contain or counter it.

By removing predators from the international ecosystem, then, the outlawry of war has effectively enabled the survival of the weakest. Those weak states sometimes become failed states. And those failed states too often become breeding grounds for internal conflict and terrorism.

THE PRIZE AND ITS PRICE

The Peace Pact and the United Nations Charter embodied grand promises: the promise of a world free of interstate war; the promise of self-determination, where states could afford to be weak without the fear of conquest; the promise of free trade and right-sized states; and the promise of international cooperation and global governance. These promises have largely been fulfilled. Interstate wars are rare and conquests practically nonexistent. Global trade has become dramatically more robust, and international organizations regulate many aspects of our daily lives.

But the outlawry of war has not brought world peace. Even as its bright promises have been fulfilled, other darker threats have rushed into the void. By opting for outlawry, we have traded a world of *inter*state war for one of *intra*state war, a world where only strong states can survive for one in which failed states can survive as well, and a world where imperialism reigned for one where terrorism is on the rise.

It is tempting to think that it is possible to have it both ways—to rid ourselves of both interstate *and* intrastate wars, or prevent the wars we don't want (naked acts of aggression) but allow the ones we do (those that address terrorist threats or solve humanitarian crises). But absent a global police force and a world state to run it (which would have its own risks), the dilemma is real. Either states are allowed to enforce the law unilaterally or they aren't. Either states can use force to do what its leaders believe law and justice requires, or there are strict limits on its use. Either war is a legal method for resolving disputes or it is not.

In the Old World Order, it was, and conquest was common. In the New World Order, states cannot act unilaterally to address violence in other states unless they have been attacked or face imminent attack (or have been asked by a state to assist it in facing such a threat). The prohibition on use of force applies regardless of whether the target state is a model democracy or crushing autocracy, a strong or a weak state, or even a failing one. This is the dilemma: The rules of the New World Order that provide so much benefit protect *all* states from the use of force, including those we do not want to protect because they are too feeble, chaotic, authoritarian, or, for lack of a better word, evil.

To see the difficulty that would arise from giving states the choice to use force when they believed they were acting justly, one need only look at Syria and Ukraine, two places where the rules against force have broken down. The United States regards the regime of Syrian president Bashar al-Assad as illegitimate and believes there is no future for his government in Syria, even as Russia is sending in troops and weapons to protect the regime from collapse. In Ukraine, the story is reversed: The United States is supporting the government against aggressive Russian-backed separatists determined to overthrow the revolutionary government that unseated Yanukovych.

The United Nations Charter has a mechanism for overriding the universal protection provided by Article 2(4)—a vote by the U.N. Security Council. But it has been hamstrung by the very disagreements just described. The permanent five members have been unable to agree to override the protection against the use of force and authorize intervention in either country. Thus the background prohibition remains—no state may use force without violating the most fundamental rule of the system, the prohibition on war. Unless we want more Syrias and Ukraines, we must keep this background prohibition in place.*

But the challenge is even greater than this story suggests. For the prohibition on war not only prevents states from intervening to protect the rights of others, unless the Security Council agrees to authorize an intervention or a state requests assistance defending itself from armed attack, it also prohibits states from using force to vindicate their *own* rights (except in cases of self-defense). States can refuse to join treaties with other states. After all, gunboat diplomacy is no longer allowed. Once states join a treaty, moreover, they might even refuse to comply. As opposed to the Old World Order, where a violation of international law could trigger a military response, the outlawry of war no longer permits states to unilaterally decide to wage war to right wrongs. In what may seem to be a paradox, *international law prohibits states from using force to enforce international law.*

So how does the system work at all? If every sovereign possesses a right to be free from interference—and no state may overcome that right with force—that would seem to create an insuperable barrier to effective law. Yet the system works much more often than this dire description of the situation would seem to suggest—including at times it would seem most likely to fail. For in the New World Order, states have developed a rich set of tools to replace war as a way of enforcing international law—tools we call *outcasting*.

*The founders of the United Nations thought that it would have its own army, assembled from member states. See U.N. Charter, Art. 47. But this vision was never realized, falling victim to the Cold War before it could take shape.

SIXTEEN

OUTCASTING

During his first presidential campaign, in 2000, George W. Bush started out preaching the gospel of free trade, though, in trademark style, the Texas Republican mangled some of its verses. "If the terriers and bariffs are torn down," he proclaimed to a puzzled crowd in Rochester, New York, "this economy will grow!"[1]

Bush was well ahead in the polls when he issued his jumbled ode to international trade. By the end of October, however, his general election opponent, Democrat Al Gore, had caught up. When polls showed a tied race, Bush saw the light. Terriers and bariffs never looked so good.

With the election less than a week away, Bush's running mate, Dick Cheney, made a campaign stop at the Weirton Steel plant in the battleground state of West Virginia. The Weirton factory was once ahead of its time, an integrated manufacturing facility that handled every stage of production from mining ore to shipping finished steel coils to customers. Weirton won the "Battle of Production," according to an army propaganda film, by fabricating thousands of eight-inch howitzer shells to be fired on D-Day.[2] After the war, Weirton was the largest employer in the

traditionally Democratic state. Yet starting in the 1980s, it had been pum-
meled by cheap imported steel from Russia, Brazil, and Japan. Gore himself had visited Weirton as Bill Clinton's running mate in 1992, promising
to help the struggling steelworkers. But he and Clinton had subsequently
concluded that international law ruled out protectionism, and the Clinton
administration had imposed only a few token safeguards. By the turn of the
millennium, Weirton Steel was on the verge of bankruptcy—its furnaces
cold, its plants shuttered. The industrial hero of D-Day had been reduced
to specializing in tinplate, the coated steel used to make soup cans.

Standing in the truck entrance of the blackened mill, Cheney blamed
Weirton's decline squarely on the man against whom Bush was running.
Gore was "a threat to the steel industry," Cheney declared, and if Bush
were elected, he would take a more aggressive stand in defense of beleaguered American workers.[3]

Bush did become president, of course, and in 2002 he kept Cheney's
promise, slapping tariffs as high as 30 percent on steel from abroad. Steel-
worker unions and industry groups cheered. But the countries hit by the
tariffs were not so happy. The European Union filed a case in the World
Trade Organization (WTO) in Geneva challenging the tariffs as a violation of the General Agreement on Tariffs and Trade, the principal treaty
regulating global commerce. The WTO held in the EU's favor: It declared
that the president's policy—a policy on which he had campaigned, a policy
central to his appeal to an important domestic constituency, and a policy
with strong support within Congress—was illegal.

So what did the great defender of the steel industry do? He removed
the tariffs. A treaty caused the world's leading superpower to yield.[4]

President Bush is not known as someone with enormous respect for
international law. In his first year in office, he withdrew from the Anti-
Ballistic Missile Treaty with Russia. During the run-up to the Iraq War, he
promised to wage war regardless of whether the Security Council authorized it.[5] And he made good on that threat, sending 150,000 soldiers into
Iraq without Security Council authorization to depose a sitting head of a
sovereign state. But his scorn for the law of nations may have been most
memorably expressed by his administration's 2005 National Defense Strategy, which darkly predicted: "Our strength as a nation state will continue

to be challenged by those who employ a strategy of the weak using international fora, judicial processes, and terrorism."[6]

Comparing international lawyers to suicide bombers does not suggest a great deal of deference to international law. And yet President Bush beat an embarrassing retreat in the face of an unarmed bureaucracy that told him he couldn't carry out a top campaign promise. Why did he listen to the WTO? The answer, in a word, is outcasting—a practice that took root more than a millennium ago in a tiny outpost of civilization at the top of the world.

THE "FIRST NEW SOCIETY"

Iceland has been described as history's "first new society."[7] When Norse sailors braved the rough and frigid waters of the North Atlantic and landed on the coast of Iceland in 870, they encountered a wild, vast, and uninhabited land ripe for subduing and settling.[8] In colonizing it, they built not only physical structures—the ruins of which still can be found today—but also sophisticated governmental institutions. Within sixty years, Iceland's political structures had taken the form that would last for three centuries.[9]

The society these immigrants created was remarkably egalitarian: Iceland did not have a king, feudal lords, or an aristocracy. There were regional chieftains, but they had little formal power, and Icelanders could switch their allegiances at will.[10] The settlers governed themselves via assemblies, called "Things." These Things had extensive legal procedures and took place at regular intervals in predetermined locations. The most important met each spring (called *vàrping*, or "Spring-Thing") to hear lawsuits and resolve administrative issues.[11]

In addition to these local gatherings, a national assembly, known as the "Althing," began meeting in 930.[12] This congress of notables gathered in the southeast of the island in June, when travel was least treacherous, and functioned as a national court and legislature.[13] The Lawspeaker (*lögsögumadr*), who presided over the Althing, was the only significant national officer, but his role was largely ceremonial. His main task was to recite the laws from memory at the "Law Rock," a grassy hill crowned by a rugged outcropping of volcanic stone around which the Althing convened (early on, the laws were not written down).[14]

While Iceland had legislatures and courts, it lacked public prosecutors.[15] Victims seeking justice had to prosecute the accused in a Thing. If the victim was successful, the Thing would declare the defendant guilty and sentence him to one of several penalties: a fine or compensation for smaller offenses, and "outlawry" for more severe offenses.[16] Someone declared an "outlaw" was cast outside the law, losing the rights normally accorded members of the Icelandic community, including the rights to remain in Iceland, to hospitality, and to own property.[17]

Icelandic outlawry came in two grades. In "lesser" outlawry, the Thing banished the outlaw from the country for three years and confiscated his property, some of which it awarded to the victim. In "full" outlawry, the Thing exiled the outlaw for life. The full outlaw lost his legal personality—from the perspective of the law, he was a dead man. Full outlaws could therefore be killed with impunity. Indeed, the prosecutor of the case was often not only permitted but *obliged* to carry out the punishment himself, assuming the outlaw didn't flee first.[18]

What's striking about this legal system is not so much what it had but what it didn't. Icelandic government was not just missing public prosecutors—it had no executive branch at all. There was no army or fire department, no tax collectors or social workers. Nor were there police, executioners, or jailers to impose sanctions.

By and large, Icelanders paid the penalties. In part, they complied because they believed the legal system was legitimate and disobeying the law shameful. "With laws shall our land be built," an Old Norse proverb went, "but with disorder laid waste."[19] But there was another motivation for Icelanders' obedience: failure to do so—to engage in "judgment breaking"—led to greater sanctions. Icelandic law provided that those who did not pay a fine were subject to lesser outlawry. Lesser outlaws who did not leave the country were subject to full outlawry.[20] Anyone who helped an outlaw could be punished, even outlawed. Full outlawry was a terrible punishment, one Icelanders rightly feared. Iceland is no Eden. Winters are long, dark, and bitterly cold, and summers are brief. To be denied the benefits of membership in the community was not only to be deprived of the normal joys of kinship and camaraderie. It was to lose the tools essential for survival in an extreme climate.

The law was effective even though there were no public institutions of law enforcement, because outlawry turned *all* Icelanders into law enforcers. The community carried out the punishment—the exclusion—itself.

OUTCASTING

Outlaws in medieval Iceland experienced what we call "outcasting." Outcasting occurs when a group denies those who break its rules the benefits available to the rest of the group. Outcasting is nonviolent: Instead of doing something *to* the rule breakers, outcasters refuse to do something *with* the rule breakers.

Though outcasting is not itself violent, it can be combined with violence to create more potent forms of social control. In medieval Iceland, a person declared to be a "full outlaw" not only lost his rights to residency, hospitality, and property, but could also be killed. Being deprived of legal personality—being excluded from the law's protection—was the outcasting part of the outlawry decree. Being hunted down by the prosecutor was the violent part.

The Bible tells us that outcasting was the first punishment. Adam and Eve were cast out of Eden for tasting the forbidden fruit, and Cain was exiled for murdering his brother, Abel. Outcasting is indeed as old as human society itself, but it has largely been ignored by scholars. This neglect is not surprising, for in well-functioning modern states, there are complex professional bureaucracies that enforce the law backed by the threat of violence. If you rob a bank, the police will come to arrest you. If you are convicted of bank robbery, they will throw you in jail. If you don't pay your taxes, the state will garnish your wages, freeze your assets, or impound your property. Try to stop it and you will be arrested for obstructing justice.

International law does not have any of these institutions of law enforcement. There are no world police, no global courts with compulsory jurisdiction. And in a post–Peace Pact world, war is no longer a legitimate means for enforcing the law.

In place of war, international law relies on outcasting. The 1969 Vienna Convention on the Law of Treaties, which is a treaty about treaties, states that a breach of an important provision of a treaty entitles any affected party to terminate it or suspend "its operation in whole or in part."[21] This means that if a state fails to follow a treaty, the states that are affected can refuse to follow it as well. Ironically, international lawyers refer to this peaceful form of retaliation by a military term: "countermeasures." Countermeasures must be proportional to the harm done by the original breach. Countermeasures must also be productive, not punitive. The goal is not vengeance, but rather to bring the bad actor back into line.[22]

A classic example of countermeasures took place in 1978.[23] Pan Am airlines began offering flights from the West Coast of the United States to Paris, with a stopover in London where passengers were moved to a smaller plane. The French objected to this change of aircraft, known in aviation as a "change in gauge," because it gave the United States flexibility not expressly allowed under a treaty, concluded in 1946, that governed air service between the two countries. Pan Am ignored the objection and continued to run the flights. On May 3, French police surrounded a Pan Am airplane after it landed in Paris and refused to allow the passengers off. The United States argued that France's refusal to let passengers disembark violated the 1946 treaty. When the French refused to back down, the United States suspended the West Coast–London–Paris flights. But it did not stop there. It put in place a countermeasure that was calculated to mirror France's illegal behavior: The United States issued an order banning French air carriers traveling from Paris from landing in Los Angeles if they stopped over in Montreal. An arbitral body later upheld the U.S. decision to outcast France—the United States was entitled to refuse France the full benefits of the treaty so long as France refused to give the United States the full benefits of the treaty.

Many treaties are explicit about the right to outcast. Consider airmail. If you want to send a letter from the United States to Germany, you only need American stamps. You don't have to go to the German embassy to purchase a German stamp, much less add a stamp for every country through which your letter will pass. The seamlessness of airmail is made possible by an organization called the Universal Postal Union (UPU) located in Berne, Switzerland. Though few have heard of it, the UPU was created in 1874, and its membership today includes 192 states.[24] The treaty that founded the UPU established a system allowing mail to be delivered from any member to any other member using only the sender's stamp.[25] If one state fails to deliver the mail, the treaty does not direct the UPU to dispatch armed couriers. Rather, it permits the sender to outcast the negligent state. Any member may suspend mail delivery to and from other members who break the rules, thereby depriving them of the benefits of the international postal system.[26]

There are hundreds of similar examples throughout international law, from the International Coffee Organization, which can kick bad actors out of the association, to the Convention on International Trade in Endangered Species of Wild Fauna and Flora, which prohibits members from trading in endangered species unless all parties to the trade follow the rules designed to protect these species.[27] Outcasting, then, is a victim of its own success. It is so ubiquitous and so often effective that it is usually invisible. When is the last time that the evening news reported on a trade war that did *not* erupt, or that mail *was* delivered on time? Outcasting is the Holmesian dog that doesn't bark.

Widespread outcasting was made possible by the change in the law of neutrality triggered by the Peace Pact and that Hersch Lauterpacht identified and explained—first in his memo for Robert Jackson, then in the later editions of *Oppenheim*, and finally in his work for the International Law Commission. As Lauterpacht explained to Jackson, and then Jackson explained to the world, the Peace Pact "did not impose upon the signatories *the duty* of discriminating against an aggressor, but it conferred upon them *the right* to act in that manner."[28] The shift from prohibiting to permitting discrimination meant that states that had once been required to remain impartial could now distinguish between belligerents. Doing so was no longer a violation of neutrality, and therefore no longer a just cause for war.

Outcasting as it exists today, however, did not spring fully formed from the head of Hersch Lauterpacht. It took decades for the tools and techniques of modern outcasting to emerge. Outcasting faced different challenges in trade than it did in human rights, in environmental law than it did in nuclear nonproliferation. In time, new versions of outcasting emerged to meet these challenges.

THE POWER OF OUTCASTING

After the Second World War, the United States and its Allies built a set of international institutions, including the International Monetary Fund and the World Bank, to aid recovery of a global economy devastated by war. But the hallmark of the New World Order was the treaty that led President Bush to back down from his campaign promises in 2003, the General Agreement on Tariffs and Trade (GATT).

Signed by twenty-three nations in 1947, the GATT facilitates and regulates international trade and, in doing so, affects daily life the world over. It influences everything from the price of bananas and iPhones to the text of food and clothing labels, from how tuna and shrimp are caught to the permissibility of excluding genetically modified crops, from the kinds of agricultural subsidies governments can pay their farmers to whether pharmaceutical firms in developing countries can produce generic antiviral drugs to halt the progression of AIDS. The GATT was created to make it easier for states to trade with each other, and it has. Nearly everything you buy today costs less thanks to the increase in free trade enabled by the GATT and its successor organization, the WTO. The ordinary American consumer gains 37 percent in purchasing power thanks to free trade, meaning that she can buy 37 percent more products and services for the same number of dollars. The same is true for the median consumer the world over—with 29 percent gains in France, 24 percent in Japan, 31 percent in Italy, 40 percent in Germany, and 33 percent in Great Britain.[29] By one estimate, the U.S. economy as a whole gains on the order of $1 trillion a year from free trade, and trade drove a threefold increase in the variety of products available to U.S. consumers during the last three decades of the twentieth century.[30]

The main means by which the WTO encourages trade—indeed, the central tenet of the treaty—is the most favored nation principle.[31] According to this principle, any party to the WTO receives the best treatment that any other party receives. If one trading partner has access to lower tariff barriers, every other has to enjoy those lower barriers, too. If one is covered by favorable trade regulations, every other has to be covered by those regulations, too. The most favored nation principle, therefore, is something of a misnomer—since all favorable treatment immediately becomes universal.[32] In effect, the WTO requires all its 164 member states to treat every other as its "most favored" trading partner. States who have signed on give low trade barriers *to* everyone in return for low trade barriers *from* everyone.[33]

All these rules have to be enforced to be effective, and here the founders of the postwar trade system faced a major problem: If war was no longer allowed, how could the WTO force states to comply? To solve this problem, they relied on outcasting.

If a state breaks the rules, another state can file a complaint and prosecute its case before a tribunal. If this tribunal rules in its favor, the WTO does not send in the troops because, of course, it does not have any. Instead, the WTO authorizes the state that filed the complaint to break the rules in return. In a provision that seems lifted straight out of the *Gragas*, medieval Iceland's code of law, the WTO agreements entitle the victorious party to suspend the benefits of membership in the community.[34] Thus, if the tribunal finds that Mexico imposed an illegal tariff on Peru, and Mexico does not lift the tariff, Peru will be authorized to impose an otherwise illegal trade barrier of equal value on Mexico. The WTO is like a global Thing.

While a clever solution, the GATT's initial version of outcasting had a major flaw. It required unanimous agreement among all the member states to resolve any dispute—*including the parties to the dispute*. Predictably, unanimity did not occur often. In fact, it happened once: in 1953, when a GATT panel authorized the Netherlands to retaliate against dairy import quotas imposed by the United States. The United States did not veto the panel's decision and thus allowed itself to be outcasted. It accepted the defeat in part because it realized that its legal position was indefensible. But it also capitulated because it knew that the Netherlands would not impose the penalty. To outcast the United States would have done the Netherlands more harm than good, because the Netherlands needed to trade with the United States more than the United States needed to trade with the Netherlands.[35]

The unanimity requirement was eliminated in 1995, as part of a massive overhaul of the GATT, which created the WTO. States that complain about a violation of the trade rules by another state can now file a complaint with the WTO's Dispute Settlement Body. A panel then hears the case and makes a decision, after which the losing party can appeal. Besides the complaints and responses, the disputing parties must now stay out of decision process altogether.

Thus, in 2002, when Bush boosted steel tariffs from 1 percent all the way up to 30 percent, as Cheney had promised he would, the European Union filed a complaint with the WTO. Japan, South Korea, China, Switzerland, Brazil, Norway, and New Zealand joined the suit. These steel-exporting countries claimed that Bush's actions violated the WTO rules. The United States responded that, under the rules, a state is allowed to raise tariffs temporarily to safeguard domestic industries against an upsurge in imports. Since the American steel industry was being ravaged by a flood of imported steel, such safeguards were appropriate.

The WTO panel rejected this defense. Though it acknowledged that imports had swelled in 2000, by the time that Bush imposed the new tariffs, imports were on the wane. The panel allowed the European Union to retaliate with two billion dollars' worth of tariffs, the highest damage amount ever awarded, if the United States did not remove its "safeguards."

The Europeans then proved to be astute students of American politics. Bush was facing the prospect of a tough reelection the following year. The European Union threatened to train its fire on swing states—to slap high tariffs on Harley-Davidson motorcycles built in Pennsylvania, sport utility vehicles assembled in Michigan, and oranges grown in Florida. Bush succumbed to this clever form of legal blackmail. Removing steel tariffs was politically painful and embarrassing, but the alternative would have been far worse. Bush lifted the steel tariffs, though he refused to credit the WTO ruling when explaining his reversal. Instead, he followed George Aiken's famous advice about Vietnam—he declared victory and went home. "[S]afeguard measures have now achieved their purpose, and as a result of changed economic circumstances it is time to lift them," Bush said as he retreated, going through the motions and fooling no one.[36] The terriers and bariffs were torn down.

THE LIMITS OF OUTCASTING

No method of enforcement is perfect. And outcasting is no exception. It threatens to deny the benefits of cooperation to encourage cooperation. But when states really don't want to cooperate, there isn't much that outcasting can do.

North Korea is the subject of extensive economic sanctions by many countries and has become so isolated from the international community and the global economy that there are few cooperative benefits left to withdraw. The international community thus has relatively little capacity to enforce the law against North Korea using outcasting. It is impossible to outcast a voluntary outcast.

The dependence of outcasting on cooperative benefits also means that, generally speaking, outcasting is more powerful if there are more participants in the outcasting regime. The WTO is so effective in part because more than 160 countries are party to it. As the WTO has grown in size, the cost of exclusion has risen and the power of the system to police the rules has multiplied as a result.

Another drawback of outcasting is that outcasting goes both ways: When a state outcasts another, it also hurts itself. Remember that the single winning case in the pre-WTO GATT was a Pyrrhic victory. Since Dutch farmers could not afford to be cut off from the United States, the Netherlands did not cash the check given them by the GATT. As the political philosopher Thomas Hobbes put the dilemma in the seventeenth century, "[W]hen a pope excommunicates a whole nation, methinks he rather excommunicates himself than them."[37]

Because outcasting hurts both sides, it often favors larger, stronger states over smaller, weaker ones. In 2007, Antigua prevailed against the United States in a WTO arbitration over U.S. restrictions on access to Antiguan Internet gambling sites. The WTO authorized Antigua to put in place retaliatory measures worth $21 million,[38] but Antigua did not impose those penalties. It had far more to lose from cutting itself off from the United States than it had to gain, for the United States accounted for 23.5 percent of Antigua's exports and 58.2 percent of its imports in 2007.[39] By contrast, Antigua was no more than a rounding error for U.S.

exports and imports. From Antigua's perspective, the United States was "too big to outcast."

Of course, Antigua would not have fared better in the Old World Order, where disputes were settled with war. But the "too big to outcast" problem is a reminder that the New World Order is not divorced from global power dynamics; it is, instead, both a producer and a product of them. As Mel Brooks once observed, "It's good to be the king."

But perhaps the biggest problem for outcasting is that countermeasures do not always work. Yes, they are effective for enforcing rules on trade and mail delivery, but there is a whole array of rules that cannot be enforced through simple tit-for-tatting. For example, countermeasures cannot be used to enforce human rights agreements like the United Nations Convention Against Torture.[40] A state cannot torture its own people in response to illegal torture by another state against *its* people. Not only would such retaliation undermine the purpose of the agreement, which is to prevent torture, but it would also be ineffectual. If a government does not care about the torture of its own people, it won't care about the torture of some other people. Many international laws on the environment face the same problem. If a treaty prohibits states from dumping oil in international waters, a state cannot respond to its violation by dumping even more oil into international waters. Like the child who threatens to hold her breath until her parents do something, such threats are simply not credible. They are also self-defeating.

For much of international law, then, simple outcasting, such as WTO countermeasures, won't work. But that doesn't mean outcasting cannot be used. It just needs to be smarter.

SMART OUTCASTING

Cyprus is home to two, largely distinct, ethnic groups: the Greek and Turkish Cypriots. The Greek Cypriots are the more numerous, comprising approximately 80 percent of the population, and have deep roots on the island, tracing their origins back almost four millennia. Turkish Cypriots comprise less than 20 percent of the population. They also arrived later, though still long ago, having settled on Cyprus when the Ottoman Empire conquered Cyprus in 1571. During the Ottoman period, the Turkish ruled the Greek Cypriots.

When Britain granted independence to Cyprus in 1960, it forged a delicate power-sharing arrangement between the Cypriots, granting both the Greek and Turkish communities political authority and constitutional rights. To enforce the compromise, Britain, Greece, and Turkey signed a Treaty of Guarantee permitting military intervention in a case of a constitutional crisis.

The fragile settlement held until 1974, when the military junta in Greece overthrew the binational government in Cyprus and demanded *enosis*—the Greek word for political unification with Greece. Because it had orchestrated the coup, Greece refused to intervene to stop it. Britain refused as well—having lost India, Britain no longer needed Cyprus to protect the sea route to the east. This left Turkey, which asserted its rights under the Treaty of Guarantee and invaded on July 20. By the time a ceasefire was negotiated, Turkey had killed thousands of people, gained control of close to 40 percent of the island, most of which had been owned by Greek Cypriots, and displaced approximately 160,000 people.

Among those who lost their homes was a tour guide named Titina Loizidou.[41] Loizidou decided to create a tour of sorts to publicize the plight of displaced Greek Cypriots. Beginning in 1975, she became an active participant in "Women Walk Home," a group that organized Greek Cypriot women to walk from the southern part of Cyprus through the "Green Line"—the U.N. buffer zone—to reach the occupied Turkish part of the island. Loizidou led contingents of foreign delegates to demonstrate the injustice of the Turkish invasion and occupation. As political theater, the marches were brilliant. Videos of the marches, now posted on YouTube, resemble a surreal reenactment of the playground game "boys catch girls." They show a handful of Turkish soldiers chasing hundreds of women waving white flags, grabbing and tackling a few, losing them as they wriggle away, and then looking around confusedly for new women to catch.[42]

On the last march, held on May 16, 1989, Loizidou made it to the Turkish-occupied North, only to be stopped by Turkish soldiers and driven back to the South by Turkish Cypriot police. At this point, she had had enough of walking home. She was ready to go to court.

Loizidou filed a complaint in the European Court of Human Rights, seeking redress under the European Convention of Human Rights, a treaty that extends human rights protections to the 820 million people of the nations in the Council of Europe. The eighth article of the convention guarantees every individual "the right to respect for his private and family life, his home and his correspondence."[43] Loizidou complained that her arrest by Turkish soldiers the previous year had violated her right to her home in the outskirts of Kyrenia, a picturesque fishing village located between Mount Pentadaktylos and the northern coast of Cyprus—a place, she explained, that "is the place where my family lived for generations, where I grew up, where every stone holds memories and meaning for me."[44] The court ruled in her favor and ordered Turkey to pay Loizidou compensation for property loss and for "the anguish and feelings of helplessness and frustration which the applicant must have experienced over the years in not being able to use her property as she saw fit."[45]

Turkey refused to pay. The Council of Europe, however, would not yield. It demanded that Turkey abide by the court's ruling.[46] On December 2, 2003, Turkey decided to comply, transferring $1.34 million (the full award plus interest) to the Council of Europe for violating Loizidou's human rights.[47]

The Council of Europe has no army, militia, or police force. It did not threaten to invade Northern Cyprus unless Turkey obeyed. What would compel a sovereign state to cave on such a politically sensitive issue? And why would it risk setting such a precedent, one that could not only open it up to billions of additional dollars in compensation for claims of other displaced Greek Cypriots, but also legitimate the claims of Greece and the Republic of Cyprus in their decades-long feud?

The answer, again, is outcasting—but a kind different from that used by the WTO. The court could not allow Cyprus to violate the property rights of a Turkish Cypriot in retaliation for Turkey's denial of Titina Loizidou's property. But it could threaten to take away *another* benefit in return for Turkey's failure to live up to its commitment—specifically, the court could promise to kick Turkey out of the Council of Europe if it failed to meet its obligation to provide compensation for the violation of Loizidou's rights. And it did just that: On November 12, 2003, the Committee of Ministers of the Council of Europe resolved "to take all adequate measures against Turkey if Turkey fails once more to pay the just satisfaction awarded by the Court to the applicant."[48] A week before Turkey relented, the court made clear that these included genuine coercive measures ranging from financial penalties to exclusion from the Council of Europe.

Expulsion would have been humiliating. Turkey had been part of the Council of Europe since the organization's inception in 1949. Membership was a source of national pride and moral legitimacy. Expulsion would also have had far-reaching political and financial ramifications. Not only would Turkey have lost its vote in the Council of Europe, but it would also have lost its chance at being allowed into the European Union with its zero tariffs, labor mobility, and investment capital.

The Council of Europe solved a problem that has plagued other human rights regimes by making compliance a condition of continuing membership. Here outcasting worked by making law-abiding behavior in one arena—human rights—a condition of continued access to the benefits of cooperation in another: membership in the Council of Europe and all the economic benefits that it entails.

MY HAIRSPRAY'S A KILLER

On June 28, 1974, three weeks before Turkey invaded Cyprus, two chemists at the University of California at Irvine, Mario Molina and Frank Rowland, published a paper in the journal *Nature* with the title "Stratospheric Sink for Chlorofluoromethanes: Chlorine Atom-Catalysed Destruction of Ozone."[49] They claimed that chlorofluoromethanes, including chloroflourocarbons (CFCs), popular as propellants in aerosol cans, coolants for refrigeration, and ingredients for making Styrofoam, had the potential to destroy the ozone layer. According to Molina and Rowlands, the property that made CFCs so useful—their inertness—also posed a danger to the environment. Because CFC molecules remain stable in the earth's lower atmosphere, they eventually drift up to the stratosphere, where they are exposed to solar radiation. CFCs degrade there and release copious amounts of free chlorine. These chlorine atoms eviscerate the ozone layer.

Despite the alarming report published in a prestigious scientific journal, almost no one paid attention. Frustrated, Molina and Rowlands held a press conference in September. The press picked up the story, with several articles published in *The New York Times* and *Time* magazine.[50] The report was even featured on the American sitcom *All in the Family*.[51] In a scene from the episode broadcast on October 26, 1974, Michael explains to his wife, Gloria, why he does not want to have a baby with her. He loves children too much, he claims, to bring them into a polluted world. When Gloria says she is sure that people will clean up the environment, Michael responds, "What about spray cans?" Seeing that Gloria is bewildered, Michael goes to their dresser and picks up her hairspray. "Here, right here, this is a killer." "Oh," Gloria responds sarcastically, "so now my hairspray's a killer." "Your hairspray, my deodorant, all spray cans," Michael shouts in panic. "I read that there are gases inside these cans, Gloria, that shoot up into the air and can destroy the ozone." After he finishes explaining how the ozone layer is the planet's protective shield without which there would be no life on earth, Gloria proposes a compromise: "You let me have a baby and I'll let you have my hairspray."

The Molina-Rowlands theory was frightening, but it was just a theory. There was no evidence to suggest that CFCs were actually destroying the ozone layer. That evidence came a decade later when the British Antarctic Survey reported a huge hole in the ozone layer over Antarctica.[52] Just as Molina and Rowlands predicted, CFCs were devouring ozone. Gloria's hairspray really was a killer.

Though galvanized to tackle the problem, governments understood the futility of unilateral action. Even negotiating a global agreement would not work. Though every state in the world had an interest in banning ozone-depleting chemicals, every state had an even greater interest in a ban that included everyone but them. A treaty that required the phase-out of CFCs, even if it could command worldwide assent, would be subject to massive cheating. States might renounce the use of cheap, effective chemicals but would ignore the ban and free-ride off of the sacrifice of others.

An environmental agreement to eliminate CFCs would succeed, in short, only if its provisions were enforceable. But waging war to enforce the law was illegal in the New World Order. And simple outcasting was useless in this context. Emitting CFCs in response to cheating—I'll start destroying the ozone layer unless you stop destroying the ozone layer—would merely make things worse.

But the international community did figure out how to save the ozone layer. CFCs have been phased out all around the world, and the hole in the ozone layer has stopped growing and even begun to shrink. The solution, embodied in the 1987 Montreal Protocol on Substances That Deplete the Ozone Layer, was to create a club of sorts.[53] Like all clubs, this one required members to pay dues. When members signed up, they undertook two obligations. The first one was to phase out their consumption of CFCs according to a schedule listed in the protocol. The phase-out was gradual enough to allow chemical substitutes to be developed and produced, but rapid enough to prevent the eventual destruction of the ozone layer. The second commitment was to sell ingredients for producing CFCs only to other members of the club.[54] These trade privileges gave nonmembers the incentives to join. To be left out of the club meant not being able to buy ingredients from those in the club. The benefits of membership, and costs of nonmembership, increased as the club got bigger. Because of the trade ban, every member that joined the club meant one fewer supplier of CFC ingredients to nonmembers.

EVEN SMARTER OUTCASTING—AND ITS LIMITS

Not all outcasting has worked so smoothly, however. During the 1980s and 1990s, one type of outcasting became ubiquitous: economic sanctions. South African apartheid, communist Cuba's expropriation of private American property, human rights violations by the Chinese government, the takeover of Burma by a military junta, Iraq's invasion of Kuwait—each prompted repeated economic sanctions.

There was only one problem: They often didn't work. In many cases, autocrats already had enough money and clout to insulate themselves from the worst effects, even while their citizens suffered. Kim Jong-un, the leader of North Korea, which has little trade with the West, reportedly favors Johnnie Walker whisky, Yves Saint Laurent cigarettes, and cowboy movies.[55] After the U.S. invasion of Iraq in 2003, U.S. soldiers found a pink Testarossa, a few Porsche 911s, a Ferrari F40, a BMW Z1, and a

Lamborghini LM002 SUV that had belonged to Uday Hussein, the elder son of Saddam Hussein.[56]

Meanwhile, ordinary citizens in the targeted countries—often the intended *beneficiaries* of the efforts to bring their leaders back in line—have found it more difficult to access food, water, and medicine. In Iraq, infant mortality more than tripled after sanctions were put in place to punish Saddam Hussein. According to a 1999 analysis, these sanctions contributed to an increase of forty thousand deaths annually of children under the age of five.[57] Efforts to address these humanitarian complications by exempting food and medicine have alleviated, but rarely solved, the problem. In countries where the economy is ravaged by sanctions, many ordinary citizens have been unable to afford such basic necessities even when available.

For two decades, U.S. sanctions on Iran could have been a case study for the ineffectiveness of sanctions. America began sanctioning Iran after the 1979 seizure of the U.S. embassy in Tehran. President Ronald Reagan lifted the sanctions when the hostages were released, but put them back in place in 1984 after Hezbollah, a Shiite militia funded by Iran, killed 241 American servicemen in a Beirut attack. Over the course of the next two decades, the United States imposed a range of sanctions aimed at blocking Iranian efforts to obtain nuclear weapons.[58] But by 2005, decades of sanctions had produced little, if any, progress. The Iranian economy was relatively healthy, averaging an annual GDP growth rate of 5.5 percent over the first half of the decade.[59] Meanwhile, there was little evidence that the sanctions were dissuading the Iranians from pursuing nuclear research.[60]

The first step toward more effective sanctions was an increase in international cooperation. Outcasting, after all, is not very effective if carried out by a single state—even one as powerful as the United States. The more states participate, the more effective the sanction. The turning point for Iran came in 2006, when the U.N. Security Council joined the American effort. It demanded that Iran stop uranium enrichment and imposed progressively painful sanctions in response to its continued intransigence.[61] As a result, Iran was shut out not only by the United States and a few sympathetic countries but by nearly every nation in the world.

But there was another crucial step, as well: an innovation in the technology of outcasting. An obscure office in the U.S. Treasury Department is tasked with enforcing sanctions rules: the Office of Foreign Assets Control, or OFAC. Over the course of the last two decades, OFAC has developed more targeted—and effective—sanction tools.[62] The biggest innovation came in 2010. At the behest of OFAC, Congress passed the Comprehensive Iran Sanctions, Accountability, and Divestment Act, which strengthened U.S. sanctions on the Iranian energy industry and financial sector.[63] Whereas previous measures had targeted Iranian firms, Congress now authorized the imposition of "secondary sanctions" on any bank, anywhere in the world, that transacted with Iran's central bank. By placing it on the black list, OFAC could cut off any bank from access to the U.S. financial sector. The United States offered banks a choice: You can do business with the United States or you can do business with Iran; you can't do both.[64]

The U.S. coupled the banking freeze with sanctions aimed at individual members of the Iranian regime and their collaborators. In 2011 and 2012, President Barack Obama issued a series of executive orders authorizing the Treasury Department to target those helping Iran circumvent sanctions, acquire U.S. dollars, develop its energy sector, or violate human rights.[65] These orders took advantage of new tools developed by the Treasury Department to hone sanctions very precisely—all the way down to a single person. Unlike the ham-fisted embargoes of the past, sanctions were now being used to shut out individuals from the United States and its economy, freeze any assets they held in the country, and prevent anyone under U.S. jurisdiction from doing business with them.

This ongoing upgrade of the technology of outcasting enables sanctions to be more comprehensive and yet more targeted than earlier versions. It magnifies the power of the sanctions by making access to the U.S. financial sector conditional on cooperation with sanctions. Not only those responsible for the international law violation, *but also those who do business with those responsible* would be outcasted. At the same time, outcasting can now be more narrowly tailored. New sanctions make it possible to target individual banks, individual businesses, even individual persons who are responsible for violations.

What's more, these new outcasting sanctions worked remarkably well: Iran's oil exports fell by more than 50 percent, the value of the nation's currency (the rial) plummeted, and Iran's economy shrank, prompting Iranian president Mahmoud Ahmadinejad to complain: "The enemy has mobilized all its forces to enforce its decision, and so a hidden war is underway, on a very far-reaching global scale."[66]

Ahmadinejad's statement was evidence that the sanctions were imposing costs. But as David Cohen, the Treasury official who oversaw OFAC, pointed out, the sanctions were not part of a hidden war. They were instead "done for all the world to see" and, indeed, "done by all the world." Nor were they a war, Cohen continued, but "the alternative to war."[67] And that alternative worked. Smarter outcasting accomplished what three decades of old-school sanctions had not. In August 2013, Hassan Rouhani succeeded President Ahmadinejad, running on a platform of improving relations with the rest of the world and sanctions relief.[68] The new Iranian leadership began negotiations with the "P5+1"—the permanent five members of the Security Council plus Germany, the economic steward of the EU.[69] In November 2013, they reached an interim agreement limiting Iran's nuclear program and partially lifting sanctions and made plans to complete a more permanent comprehensive agreement. For the first time in decades, there was real hope that a nuclear Iran could be prevented through discussions at the negotiating table rather with military strikes. Whether this will continue to hold depends on many things—chief among them the willingness of both sides to stick to the deal.

UNFINISHED BUSINESS

Even as the new Iranian leadership sat around the table with the P5+1, Russia invaded Crimea. Armed men in unmarked uniforms appeared in Crimea in February 2014, and one month later Russia completed the first successful conquest in Europe since the Second World War. A U.N.-backed military response was impossible, because Russia holds a permanent seat on the Security Council and thus is in a position to veto any authorization. More important, Russia is a nuclear power, and its military strength is second only to the United States'. Even though the U.N. Charter would have allowed the U.S. and others to use force legally to defend Ukraine, a military response was not an option.

Attention thus turned to outcasting. The international community walled off Crimea, in a reaction reminiscent of the League of Nations' response to Japan's seizure of Manchuria nearly eighty years earlier. This time, however, there was much more cooperation to withdraw. The United States and Europe prohibited nearly all investment and trade with the territory.[70] McDonald's, PayPal, Amazon, Visa, and MasterCard all pulled out from Crimea. Fresh water and electricity, more than 80 percent of which had come from Ukraine, was subject to fluctuations in supply. Tourism to Crimea, once flourishing, fell by half in the first year after Russia's annexation.[71] Even the Universal Postal Union suspended mail service.[72] As one U.S. official explained, the sanctions regime carried a message: "It basically says you can claim your war prize, but it's not going to be worth much to you, and we're not going to make it easy for you."[73]

To outcast Russia, the United States and Europe had to work together, a project made difficult not only because the Security Council was hamstrung but also because the Russian economy is so important to the global economy, more important than any previous target of Western sanctions.[74] For Europe, in particular, the costs of sanctions were—and are—immense. Russia supplies 30 percent of Europe's natural gas,[75] and is its third-largest trading partner.[76] With Europe still recovering from the 2008 financial crisis and subsequent recession, political leaders were understandably wary of hurting their own economies.[77] Those members of the EU with significant political and economic ties to Russia—including Greece and Germany— were particularly concerned about the negative impact of economic sanctions.[78]

Yet Europe did act. The European Union declared that "the sovereignty, territorial integrity and independence of Ukraine must be respected. The European Union does neither recognise the illegal and illegitimate referendum in Crimea nor its outcome. The European Union does not and will not recognise the annexation of Crimea and Sevastopol to the Russian Federation."[79] President Obama, too, proclaimed that "Ukraine's sovereignty and territorial integrity must be respected, and international law must be upheld."[80] Both made clear that a bedrock principle of the global legal order had been broken.

Within a week of Russia's annexation of Crimea, the Group of 8 industrialized democracies suspended Russia. Condemning "Russia's illegal attempt to annex Crimea" as a "contravention of international law," the remaining seven members announced they would boycott a planned meeting in Sochi, Russia, and would instead gather without Russia in Brussels, where both NATO and the EU are headquartered. Michael McFaul, who had just stepped down as U.S. ambassador to Russia, explained that although the move was largely symbolic, it sent an important message: "The G-8 was something they wanted to be part of. This for them was a symbol of being part of the big-boy club, the great power club."[81]

The new generation of outcasting tools also allowed for smarter, more narrowly tailored sanctions. The first targets were individuals. President Obama issued an executive order authorizing "sanctions on individuals and entities responsible for violating the sovereignty and territorial integrity of Ukraine, or for stealing the assets of the Ukrainian people." According to the State Department, the travel restrictions demonstrated the U.S. government's "continued efforts to impose a cost on Russia and those responsible for the situation in Crimea."[82] Likewise, the European Union imposed sanctions on those whose actions contributed to "undermining or threatening the territorial integrity, sovereignty and independence of Ukraine," such as Sergei Ivanov, Putin's chief of staff; Vyacheslav Volodin, Putin's first deputy chief of staff, who was responsible for overseeing the political integration of Crimea into Russia; Igor Sechin, the CEO of the Russian state-owned oil giant Rosneft and a close Putin confidant; and Dmitry Rogozin, a Russian deputy prime minister.[83]

The United States and Europe wanted to impose sufficient costs to stop Russian aggression in Ukraine. But they also wanted to minimize collateral damage to the global economy. So instead of targeting the day-to-day health of Russia's economy, they went after its long-term growth. As with the sanctions on Iran, the Russia sanctions cut off access to U.S. and European capital markets. But rather than prohibiting all transactions with large Russian banks as they had in the case of Iran, the United States and Europe tried something new. They blocked only a certain kind of financial transaction—the provision of long-term loans—to certain Russian banks, energy companies, and companies involved in the defense industry. These restrictions made significant capital investment in Russia difficult and expensive. In the long term, they were expected to hinder the Russian economy substantially, but they did not threaten a sudden shock to the global economy.[84]

The United States and Europe also blocked exports of Western technology essential to Russian oil exploration of shale, Arctic, and deepwater oil deposits.[85] The restrictions forced ExxonMobil to abandon a joint venture with the Russian energy company Rosneft in the Kara Sea.[86] These sanctions, like the others deployed against Russia, were fine-tuned to address a state that seemed "too big to outcast." Instead of blockading an entire sector, sanctions pinpointed vulnerabilities—instances where Western resources or technology were valuable and difficult to replace—while minimizing the direct economic impact on the sanctioning countries.

Russia retaliated by adopting what it called "mirror sanctions." A statement posted on the Foreign Ministry's website stressed that sanctions are a "double-edged thing" and put in place "reciprocal sanctions" on several U.S. politicians, including Speaker of the House John Boehner and Senator John McCain, who celebrated their sanctions on Twitter.[87] Perhaps most self-defeating, Russia adopted an import ban on food, prohibiting meat, fish, dairy products, fruit, and vegetables from countries that supported or participated in economic sanctions.[88] When food continued to flood in—the substitute cheese was nearly inedible, as many producers substituted cheap palm oil for expensive milk fat—Putin declared that contraband would be destroyed. The government proceeded to burn and bulldoze tons of confiscated bacon, cheese, and other smuggled foodstuffs. Meanwhile, food prices in Russia rose 20 percent in the first half of 2015.[89]

Together with falling oil prices, the sanctions contributed to a recession in Russia. Trade with the European Union fell by more than a third in the first two months of 2015. Prime Minister Dmitry Medvedev estimated the toll of sanctions to be $106 billion in 2014 and 2015. A report by the IMF a year and a half after the annexation of Crimea stated that it expected Russian GDP to shrink by 3.4 percent in 2015, and it projected that prolonged sanctions could lead to a cumulative output loss over the medium term of up to 9 percent of GDP.[90] In October 2016, Putin publicly admitted the sanctions were taking a toll: "Sanctions are hurting us . . . particularly with technology transfers in oil and gas."[91]

The outcasting of Russia may appear a failure. President Putin has not buckled. If anything, he has doubled down by continuing to foment unrest and conflict in Eastern Ukraine. But the sanctions were precisely designed to burn slow: to avoid crashing the Russian economy—an implosion that would bring Europe down with it—and specifically hurt those who enabled the takeover of Crimea, reduce the size of the war prize, and threaten the overarching trajectory of the Russian economy. The United States and Europe devised a strategy to compel Russia to respect international law over the long term—if the United States and Europe stay the course.

THE ALTERNATIVE TO WAR

If the situation in Crimea offers a sobering reminder of the limits of outcasting, the situation with Iran suggests that even outcasting that fails in the short term can eventually triumph. In August 2015, more than two years of negotiations between Iran and the P5+1 finally produced an unprecedented deal.[92] It provided that the United States, China, Russia, and the European Union would lift many of the most recent sanctions. In return, Iran would drastically scale back its nuclear program. It would remove two thirds of the centrifuges, maintain low levels of enrichment for at least fifteen years, reduce its stockpile of enriched uranium by 98 percent, and allow comprehensive access to the International Atomic Energy Agency (IAEA) to monitor compliance.

A year after the agreement, in May 2016, the IAEA found that Iran had lived up to its commitments. Iran went from over 19,000 uranium enrichment centrifuges to just 5,060. It ended uranium enrichment and removed all nuclear material from its once secret facility at Fordow. It reduced its stockpile of enriched uranium and filled the core of its heavy-water reactor at Arak with concrete, making it permanently inoperable. Together, these terms increased Iran's "breakout time"—the period to produce enough fissile material for a single nuclear weapon—from about two to three months to at least one year.[93] Although critics complained that the deal still allowed Iran to enrich nuclear material, some later acknowledged that it had succeeded in eliminating an imminent threat. In 2016, Moshe Ya'alon, Israel's former defense minister, who had vigorously opposed the deal during negotiations, reversed course and belatedly endorsed it, admitting that

Iran's nuclear program had been "frozen in light of the deal signed by the world powers and does not constitute an immediate, existential threat for Israel."[94]

The evolution of outcasting has not been without setbacks. The path from its emergence in the early 1930s through the present is littered with failures. But over time, through a process of trial and error, the international legal order has developed an extraordinary array of tools to address global challenges that build on the simple system that made Iceland's cooperative civilization without central coercion possible. While not perfect, the tool of outcasting has proven highly flexible, limited chiefly by the creativity of those who wield it. From maintaining global trade, to the international postal service, to human rights protections, to the environment, to nuclear proliferation, outcasting has been used to encourage states to comply and punish those that have not in a world where Might no longer makes Right.

Some may ask whether outcasting—"the alternative to war," as David Cohen put it—is really much better than the war it replaced. After all, states may still be coerced into joining agreements—if not by threat of physical force (which, in the New World Order, would trigger a duress defense) then by threat of economic force (which would not). The outlawry of war and the system of law that has grown up around it are grounded in the principle that the physical destruction of war is uniquely harmful. Political theorist Judith Shklar famously argued that cruelty—"the deliberate infliction of physical, and secondarily emotional, pain upon a weaker person or group by stronger ones in order to achieve some end, tangible or intangible, of the latter"—is the greatest evil.[95] Outcasting replaces this evil with exclusion from the benefits of community membership. Like force and threats of force, outcasting constrains choices. But it does so without the cruelty and destruction that normally accompany war.

That outcasting is not violent has another advantage: It leaves state institutions intact. War is, after all, an exceedingly blunt tool. Using military force to coerce states damages the very institutions necessary to provide basic services and security to residents. In a world where weak states can become failed states and failed states give rise to civil war and terrorism, it is not only good law but good sense to pressure state institutions with outcasting rather than destroy them with war.

SEVENTEEN

SEEING LIKE AN ISLAMIC STATE

In the summer of 2014, just as the Western world was becoming aware of the violent group known as the Islamic State, a video appeared on the web entitled, "The End of Sykes-Picot." As the title implies, the video denounces the 1916 secret agreement between Britain and France that aimed to carve up the Arab world. The star of the show, so to speak, is a young jihadist named Bastián Vásquez, a Norwegian of Chilean descent living in Syria who had become one of the Islamic State's most popular pitchmen.[1]

The video has all the markers of the sophisticated online propaganda that has helped fuel the rise of the Islamic State, a group that not only allows but advocates violent conflict to achieve legal and political aims. Shot in high definition, with male chanting and driving music in the background, it opens with an image of Vásquez raising the black Islamic State flag. He gestures toward an area of desert with a few abandoned buildings. "Right now we are on the site of al Sham," he says in English. "As you can see, this is the so-called border of Sykes-Picot. Al-hamdu lillāh ["Praise Be to God"]. We don't recognize it and we will never recognize it. In shā' Allāh ["God Willing"]. This is not the first border we will break. In shā'

Allāh. We will break all the borders but we will start with this border. In shā' Allāh."

He then moves toward the border. "This is the so-called checkpoint, where the soldiers of Maliki used to stand," referring to Nouri al-Maliki, who was then the Shiite prime minister of Iraq. Vásquez walks over to a toppled sign. "As you can see, here is a sign. It says 'Commander's Battalion Border.' The only commanders and battalions here are the battalions of Islam. In shā' Allāh." He stands on the sign, pressing it underfoot, a sign of deep disrespect in Arab culture, which views the soles of the feet as unclean. "As [self-declared caliph Abu Bakr] al-Baghdadi used to say, he is the breaker of barriers. In shā' Allāh we will break the barrier of Iraq, Jordan, Vietnam, all the countries. In shā' Allāh until we reach consolidation with Allah. It is the first of many barriers we shall break. In shā' Allāh."[2]

This video is less gruesome than others produced by the Islamic State, but it is nonetheless horrific. At one point, Vásquez opens a door of the border station, revealing a room crowded with frightened prisoners. Vásquez explains that the men were Shiite border guards and Yazidis, who "worship Lucifer." He exits the room, and saunters past comrades wiring the building with explosives. The last image in "The End of Sykes-Picot" is shot from inside a truck, the building in the distance. Vásquez has his hand on a detonator. He presses it down and the border police station erupts in a massive explosion. When the dust clears, there is nothing left but rubble. The background music builds to a crescendo.[3]

DIVIDING UP THE SKIN OF THE BEAR

The creation of the border between Iraq and Syria is what the anthropologist James Scott, in his classic book *Seeing Like a State*, described as the process of dividing territory into rational, organized spaces within which a state can exercise power over its population.[4] Vásquez's video makes clear that the Islamic State sees things very differently from the modern state Scott described. It rejects existing state borders and all that they symbolize, and it seeks to organize a global caliphate in their place. To understand this vision—its origins, its scope, and the deep threat it poses to the New World Order—we have to step back just over a century.

When the First World War broke out, the Ottoman Empire was vast. It had lost nearly all of its European holdings in the Balkan wars in 1912 and 1913, and its North African territories in the years before that, but it still retained control over much of what is modern-day Turkey, Syria, Lebanon, Israel, Jordan, Iraq, Iran, Yemen, and Saudi Arabia. The Ottoman caliph—the Islamic political and religious leader—whose authority traced to Murad I's conquest of Edirne in 1362, still existed, though he had been reduced to little more than a figurehead. Caliph Mehmed V declared jihad against the Allied powers on November 11, 1914, but he was merely following a decision made by a triumvirate of ministers who had taken control of the Ottoman government in a coup d'état the year before.[5]

A year after the caliph's call for jihad, Sir Mark Sykes of Great Britain and François Georges-Picot of France began negotiations over the future of their common enemy. The aim of the talks was simple: to determine what the region would look like should their countries prevail in the war. Not surprisingly, they agreed that the region would be sliced into French and British, and, to a lesser extent, Russian, areas of control and influence. As Brigadier General G. M. W. Madonogh, the British director of military intelligence, noted, it was more than a little premature: "[I]t seems to me that we are rather in the position of the hunters who divided up the skin of the bear before they had killed it."[6]

Picot was passionate about the cause of conquest. He hailed from an imperial colonialist dynasty—his father had helped found the Comité de l'Afrique Française, a group of elites devoted to French expansion in Africa, and his brother was its treasurer. In the Quai d'Orsay, he was known as a voice for colonialist interests, and had long been a dedicated advocate of a French Syria.[7] He and the French Foreign Office hoped to establish direct French rule over the Mediterranean coastline, including parts of Syria and Lebanon, and to control most of inland Syria through Arab puppet leaders.

Unbeknownst to Picot, the French plan suited the British just fine. The arrangement would extend French control from the Mediterranean coast to the east, following the Russian-controlled areas along their length. It would create a kind of French sandwich, with France layered between Russian-held territory to the north and British-held territory to the south and southeast. France would be the buffer protecting the British Middle East from Russian aggression.[8]

That the wartime Allies were engaged in secret talks to divvy up the territory of an enemy in war is not so surprising, or even especially noteworthy. Discussions of this kind had taken place for centuries. But what made these talks galling—and why they continue to stir anger in the region today—was that Britain promised Arab leaders the same territory *at the same time* in exchange for their wartime assistance against the Ottomans. The British, moreover, were engaged in secret discussions with the Jewish community about establishing a national home for the Jewish people in Palestine, a commitment that was eventually announced in the Balfour Declaration of 1917.

In a letter to the "Sherif of Mecca," Husayn ibn Ali, Sir Henry McMahon, British high commissioner in Egypt, agreed to recognize Arab independence after the war: "Great Britain is prepared to recognize and support the independence of the Arabs in all the regions within the limits demanded by the Sherif of Mecca."[9] Husayn and his followers saw these promises as a formal treaty. Relying on British assurances, Husayn's son, Faisal, with assistance and encouragement from T. E. Lawrence (immortalized as the romantic figure Lawrence of Arabia), led an Arab uprising against the Ottoman Empire that helped the British defeat the Ottomans in October 1918.

Debate continues as to whether the two commitments—those between France, Britain, and Russia on the one hand and between Britain and Husayn on the other—were, in fact, irreconcilable. Some even maintain that Husayn was not as surprised to learn of the agreement as he later appeared, for he knew of the French and British claims to the region.[10] But this defense seems a thin veil. McMahon well knew that the agreement would have been an affront to Husayn and argued for keeping it secret. "I feel that divulgence of agreement at present time might be detrimental to our good relations with all parties and possibly create a change of attitude in some of them," he warned the Foreign Office.[11] Husayn would not have revolted if he and his men knew they were fighting for European influence rather than the independence they had been promised.

Though the Sykes-Picot Agreement has become a powerful symbol, it never actually took effect. After the Bolsheviks overthrew the provisional government in November 1917, they discovered the secret agreement and exposed it. The revelations led the British and French to drop it altogether. Even the treaty that followed, the 1920 Treaty of Sèvres, which attempted to divide the Ottoman Empire into British, French, Greek, and Italian zones of influence, was never ratified. The Turkish War of Independence erupted before it was concluded. That war ended with the 1923 Treaty of Lausanne, which recognized modern-day Turkey as the successor to the Ottoman Empire.

In the years that followed, the League of Nations granted France a mandate over Syria and Lebanon and the British mandates over Palestine (including Transjordan) and Mesopotamia.[12] The French mandate lasted until October 1945, when Syria and Lebanon joined the United Nations; Iraq gained independence in October 1932; and the Hashemite Kingdom of Transjordan became the independent state of Jordan in 1946. The British Mandate in Palestine ended in May 1948, before the territory could be peacefully divided, leading to a unilateral declaration of independence by Israel and unresolved conflict in the region.

Sykes-Picot, then, is a symbol. The borders of Iraq, Syria, Jordan, Egypt, and the rest of the region are not direct products of the treaty. But while the agreement never went into effect, one need only compare the borders drawn by Sykes and Picot to those that currently define the countries of Syria, Iraq, Turkey, Jordan, Israel, Saudi Arabia, Lebanon, and Iran (as shown in the map on page 401) to notice more than a passing resemblance. Some interpret this resemblance to suggest that Sykes-Picot really did shape the modern map. But it is more likely that long-standing historical claims shaped both the agreement and the modern borders that seem to follow it.

Though the agreement had little real-world effect, linking Sykes-Picot to present-day borders serves a powerful rhetorical purpose. It connects modern borders to the disintegration of the last great Muslim empire and turns these borders into a stark reminder of the history of Western dominance and treachery. Even more important for the Islamic State, it taints the sovereign states that govern within these borders, tying their birth to a

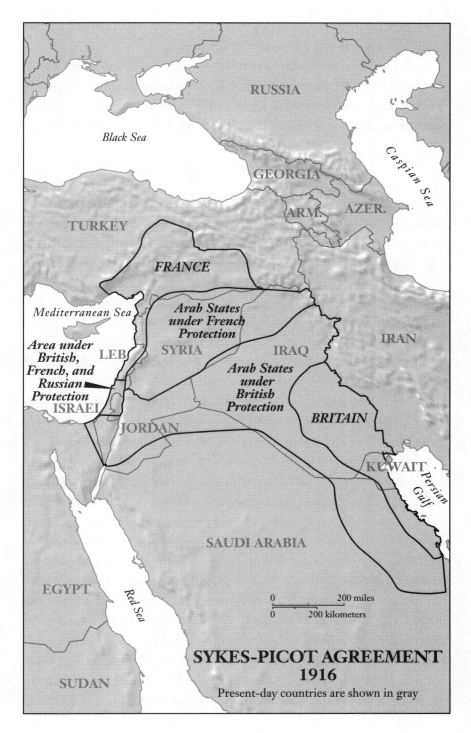

**SYKES-PICOT AGREEMENT
1916**

Present-day countries are shown in gray

secret deal meant to deny Muslims their proper place in the world. Ending Sykes-Picot means ending modern Arab states.

All this does not fully explain, however, why Sykes-Picot is *such* a powerful symbol for the Islamic State and like-minded Islamic fundamentalist groups—a foil for their own vision of world order. For that, we must move forward in time to uncover the origins of modern Islamic extremism.

SAYYID QUTB

The man who would create the intellectual framework of modern Islamic extremism did not look anything like the fearsome young jihadists featured in modern Islamic State propaganda videos. Born in Egypt on October 9, 1906, Sayyid Qutb was short, frail, and in poor health. He had a weak heart and chronic lung problems from a bout of pneumonia in his thirties.[13] Qutb dressed formally and sported a toothbrush mustache, which gave him an antediluvian air.[14] To his many admirers, he exuded the dignity, purity, and serenity of a man of deep, unshakable faith. Others, however, detected in him shiftiness and cunning. Naguib Mahfouz, the first Arab writer to win the Nobel Prize in Literature, was active with Qutb in Cairo's literary scene and in a thinly veiled fictional portrayal expressed reservations about his friend.[15] Appreciating his keen intelligence and impressive learning, especially given his impoverished upbringing, Mahfouz also could not help but be "disturbed by [his] opportunistic side, doubting his integrity. A permanent revulsion . . . settled in my heart."[16] Mahfouz backhandedly observed that Qutb "had the ability, rare in Egyptians, to keep his secrets."[17]

The secrets he kept concerned his ever-growing Islamism. The turning point in his political views can be traced to the two years spent in the United States on an education mission. Though Qutb was skeptical of America before he set off on his trip in 1948, his unease turned to disgust. On the outbound voyage from Egypt, he heard a knock on his stateroom door. A tall, beautiful, "half-naked" woman asked if she could spend the night with him. Resisting temptation, he slammed the door, whereupon he heard a thud. The drunken woman had passed out on the hallway floor.[18]

The moral decadence of American life, and the sexual power of American women, are recurring themes in Qutb's later reflections. "A girl looks

at you, appearing as if she were an enchanting nymph or an escaped mer-
maid," he wrote. "But as she approaches, you sense only the raw instinct
inside her bereft of all radiance, and you can smell her burning body, not
the scent of perfume. Then, she becomes meat." "Truly delicious meat," the
pious man admits, "but meat nonetheless."[19]

While living in the United States, Qutb experienced racism firsthand.
The dark-skinned Egyptian was once mistaken for an African American
and denied entry into a cinema.[20] When the owner apologized after realizing his mistake, Qutb refused to patronize the theater. "I saw the way they
treat the colored people with despicable arrogance and ugly brutality!" he
later reported in his commentary on the Qur'an. "Their swaggering in the
face of the rest of the world is worse than that of the Nazis."[21] But Qutb
was not above racism himself. Jazz, he claimed, was "created by the negroes
to satisfy their primitive inclinations and their desire in noise on the one
hand, and to arouse their vital dispositions on the other hand."[22] The "evil
design" of the Jews, he also wrote, is to ensure that "all of the wealth of
mankind end up in the hands of Jewish financial institutions."[23]

What disturbed Qutb most about the United States was its vacuity.
When he settled in Greeley, Colorado, to attend the Colorado State College of Education, he was struck by the inane materialism of suburbia. Sub-
urbanites filled their weekends with grooming their immaculate lawns. "All
of the homeowners spend their leisure time working hard, watering their
private yards and trimming their gardens. This is all they appear to do."[24]
When they socialized, their conversation consisted of nothing but trifling
small talk. The economic prosperity of the sole remaining superpower did
not lead to spiritual enlightenment. "The soul has no value to Americans,"
he wrote in a letter to a friend. "There has been a Ph.D. dissertation about
the best way to clean dishes, which seems more important to them than
the Bible or religion."[25] The absurdity of America could even be seen in
football. "The foot does not play any role in the game," he observed in
disbelief.[26]

After he returned to Egypt, Qutb joined the Muslim Brotherhood.
The organization had been founded in 1928 by Hassan al-Banna, a primary
school teacher in Ismalia, the Egyptian headquarters of the Suez Canal.
While teaching, Banna became increasingly concerned that the British and

their efforts to modernize Egypt were leading the country away from Islamic principles. The Brotherhood he founded would challenge the forces of colonialism and secularism.[27] In a pamphlet Banna wrote to "inform the people about the mission of the Muslim Brotherhood," he explained that its aim would be "to establish Allah's sovereignty over the world."[28]

Then, as now, the organization was multifaceted—focused not only on resisting secularism, but also on providing a forum for those concerned about colonialism, education, public health, social inequality, and the weakness of the Islamic world on the global stage.[29] Also like now, it contained moderate as well as more extremist elements.[30] Indeed, when Qutb first joined, he shared the Brotherhood's opposition to secular government— the kind whose depravity ran rampant in the United States—but unlike the more extreme elements in the organization, he did not yet advocate violence. Instead, he expected the Egyptian people to rise up against their secular masters and demand an Islamic form of government.

It was the year the Peace Pact was concluded by the Great Powers that a different vision of the world began to emerge in Egypt—a vision that today poses a dangerous challenge to the New World Order made possible by the Pact. For whereas the Pact prohibited war and became the foundation for a world order grounded in sovereign states, the Muslim Brotherhood, founded in 1928, would become the starting point for a vision of the world in which war—*jihad*—was not only allowed but *required* to establish the global sovereignty of Allah.

MILESTONES

On the night of October 26, 1954, Gamal Abdel Nasser, the prime minister of Egypt, addressed a large crowd in the public square of Alexandria, an event broadcast live to the nation on radio.[31] Nasser's goal was to modernize Egypt by establishing a secular government, industrializing the country through large public works programs, and aligning the nation with the atheistic Soviet Union, from which he hoped to receive economic and technical aid.[32]

As he spoke, a radical Islamist from the Muslim Brotherhood pushed his way through the gathering and fired eight shots at the president. Nasser did not flinch as the shots hissed by his head.[33] "Let them kill Nasser!" he cried out. "What is Nasser but one among many? . . . [E]ven if I die, all of you are Gamal Abdel Nasser."[34]

Nasser had scant legitimacy until this point, having overthrown the dissolute and obese King Farouk in a military coup only two years earlier. But his courage in the face of an assassination attempt—miraculously, he was not hit by a single bullet—transformed him into a national hero.[35] Capitalizing on his surging popularity, Nasser moved to wipe out the Muslim Brotherhood. The Security Service caught the main conspirators and hanged six of them. It then threw a dragnet over the rest of the country. Among the thousand Muslim Brothers swept up in the crackdown was Sayyid Qutb, then the editor of the Brotherhood's political magazine.[36]

His arrest, conviction for subversive activities in a show trial, and subsequent incarceration and torture, changed Qutb. In a pattern that would repeat itself many times over, prison turned a moderate Islamist into a radical.[37] During the ten years he spent as a prisoner, Qutb became a zealot and, with the fervor of a fanatic, reworked Islamic political theory so as to justify the use of war as a tool for serving the ultimate aims of Islam. With this conversion, Qutb became the intellectual father of radical Islamism, writing works that would be read throughout the Muslim world. His conceptualization of Islam would give shape, voice, and direction to a generation of jihadists and make him the most cited Islamist writer of the modern age.[38]

It is little wonder that *Milestones*—the manifesto Qutb composed in the dank, fetid Tora Prison where he served his sentence—begins bleakly. "Mankind today is on the brink of a precipice," he warned. The danger is not that "of complete annihilation which is hanging over its head," that is, the threat of nuclear Armageddon. The existential crisis precipitated by the Cold War, Qutb suggested, is merely a symptom of a larger spiritual crisis confronting the modern world.[39]

What's more, Qutb now argued that war was necessary and justified to achieve that progress. Qutb was emphatic that Islam diverges from modern international law with regards to the right to wage war. "The Islamic Jihad has no relationship to modern warfare, either in its causes or in the way in which it is conducted."[40]

Qutb rejected the idea that jihad can only be fought in self-defense. Indeed, he saw treachery behind those who have preached such a doctrine, rebuking the "vicious orientalists" who falsely claim that "Islam has pre-scribed only defensive war!"[41] These apologists for Islam are attempting to subvert it, "depriving it of its method, which is to abolish all injustice from the Earth, to bring people to the worship of God alone, and to bring them out of servitude to others into the servants of the Lord."[42] There is only one sense in which jihad is defensive—it is a defense of man from "the clutches of human lordship and man-made laws."[43]

What causes allow for aggressive war? The causes of jihad, Qutb ar-gued, "should be sought in the very nature of Islam and its role in the world." And Islam, according to Qutb, "is really a universal declaration of the freedom of man from servitude to other men and from servitude to his own desires."[44] Islam seeks to free man from *Jahiliyyah*, the spiritual ignorance that blanketed the world before Islam. The essence of *Jahiliyyah* "is one man's lordship over another"—the elevation of man to divine status and the treatment of him as an ultimate source of sovereignty.[45] The aim of Islam is to annihilate *Jahiliyyah* by persuading mankind that "sovereignty belongs to God alone and that He is the Lord of all the worlds." It cannot permit the existence of any "system in which final decisions are referred to human beings, and in which the sources of all authority are human." Any system that gives man ultimate political authority commits the most grievous of sins: It "deifies human beings by designating others than God as lords over men." Islam cannot abide this blasphemous arrogance. It de-mands that "the usurped authority of God be returned to Him and the usurpers be thrown out."[46]

With these words, the prophet of jihad not only rejected the prohibi-tion on war but he also licensed aggressive war against secular governance as a whole.

BLACK FLAGS

Due to poor health, Qutb spent most of his captivity in the infirmary. It was from his sickbed that he composed *Milestones*, installments of which were smuggled out of prison by his two sisters.[47] He mentored inmates brought to the hospital after having been tortured by interrogators. Young men who were whipped, beaten, hung upside down by their feet for hours, submerged in freezing water and attacked by wild dogs were receptive to Qutb's theories about *Jahiliyyah*, its grip on the Arab world, and the necessity for drastic measures to defeat it.

After having served ten years of his fifteen-year sentence, Qutb was freed. Why he was released is unclear. The president of Iraq interceded on his behalf with the government of Egypt, having read Qutb's commentary on the Qur'an when he himself was in prison, and wished to repay his consoler. Qutb also suffered a heart attack and the Egyptian government may not have wanted to be blamed for his death. His supporters had darker suspicions. To them, the release was a setup: The government expected Qutb to engage in revolutionary activities, giving them an excuse to execute him.[48]

When Qutb walked out of prison in 1966, the British were gone. The economy was booming. Qutb learned that he had achieved a fair degree of notoriety. *Milestones* was published in 1964 and, though it was soon banned, it went through five printings and was read throughout the Islamic world. Yet Qutb could not help but conclude that *Jahiliyyah* was more powerful than ever. Nasser had a lock on Egyptian politics and Western depravity had infiltrated popular culture. Arab nationalism was on the rise outside of Egypt as well. The president of Iraq who helped Qutb was an Arab socialist—indeed, a Nasserite. The Ba'ath Party, an Arab nationalist party, controlled Syria. The Muslim Brotherhood, which had been outlawed in the crackdown of 1956, was disbanded and broken.[49]

Nevertheless, a few diehard Islamists were determined to revive the Brotherhood and chose Qutb as their mentor. In keeping with the plan he had set out in *Milestones*, Qutb was reluctant to sanction violent revolutionary activity. The first phase of the Islamic revival was retreat from society and purification of the soul. Yet Qutb permitted the vanguard to defend itself if attacked and approved weapons purchases and paramilitary training just in case.[50]

The government learned of Qutb's activity and cracked down again. In 1966, Qutb was arrested, convicted of subversive activities, and sentenced to death. The night before his execution, the government sent a message through his sister that the sentence would be commuted if Qutb would admit that the Brotherhood was allied with subversive groups and apologize. Like Socrates before him, Qutb refused to betray his values for clemency and accepted his death sentence.[51]

At 3 a.m. on August 28, 1966, Qutb, along with two other Brothers, were led to the gallows. As hoods were placed over their heads and nooses around their necks, each recited the *shahada*, the fundamental profession of Muslim faith—*lā 'ilāha 'illā-llāh* ("There is no deity except Allah"). Black flags were then hoisted, trapdoors opened, and their bodies sailed through the air until the tug of the ropes snapped their necks.[52]

The prophet had become a martyr.

A WAR OF IDEAS

As Qutb hung from the gallows, fifteen-year old Ayman Mohammed Rabie al-Zawahiri, who had joined the Muslim Brotherhood a year earlier, determined to fight back. Along with four schoolmates, the man who would later take the helm of al Qaeda's terrorist network formed an underground cell devoted to overthrowing Nasser's government and establishing an Islamist state.[53] "The Nasserite regime thought that the Islamic movement received a deadly blow with the execution of Sayyid Qutb and his comrades," he later wrote. But the opposite was true. Instead of putting out a fire, they had fanned it.[54]

Not many years later, another teenager named Osama bin Laden joined the Muslim Brotherhood in Saudi Arabia—where many of the leaders of the Brotherhood had fled after the crackdown of the mid-1960s in Egypt. Several became professors at King Abdul Aziz University in Saudi Arabia. Qutb's younger brother, Mohammed, was among them. A university student from a wealthy family, bin Laden attended Mohammed Qutb's popular public lectures, where Qutb defended his brother's writings against attacks by moderate Islamists. Qutb's call to violence did not initially persuade bin Laden, but his ideas would set him on a path toward becoming the world's most notorious terrorist. Bin Laden's classmate and closest friend during his university years later explained, "We were trying to understand what Islam has to say about how we eat, who we marry, how we talk. We read Sayyid Qutb. He was the one who most affected our generation."[55]

The central intellectual contribution of Qutb—the contribution that made his ideas so influential and placed Islamic radicals on a collision course with the West—is the way in which he turned Grotius's theory upside down. Grotius was the father of natural rights liberalism, a theory that ascribes sovereignty to individuals. The sovereignty of states, in turn, emerges from the pooling together of individual wills through the social contract. Grotius (and much of the canon of Western thought that followed) went so far as to claim that the sovereignty of the individual is ultimate, namely, not derived from God. In his audacious *etiamsi daremus* passage from *The Law of War and Peace*, Grotius claimed that even if there were no God, man would still have natural rights.

In Qutb's worldview, this assertion is blasphemy, for it ascribes to individuals an attribute that only God has—namely, sovereignty. Liberalism, therefore, is the essence of *Jahiliyyah*: it explicitly contradicts the *shahada*, which, according to Qutb, expresses the idea that people "should not decide any affair on their own," but listen solely to God's dictates, for only "He is the Real Sovereign."[56] Liberalism, therefore, is also the paradigm of polytheism, for it ascribes divine status to every individual, not solely to God.

Qutb is the mirror image of Grotius. Grotius sought to ground the right of war on liberalism, on the natural rights of individuals to use force to protect life and property. Qutb grounded the right, indeed the duty, of war in the obligation to annihilate *Jahiliyyah*. Whereas Grotius argued that war could be fought *for* liberal rights, Qutb argued that war had to be fought *against* liberal rights.

The Qutbian enemy, therefore, is breathtakingly encompassing. The realm of *Jahiliyyah* is not merely the West, with its secularism, racism, imperialism, inequality, and sexual promiscuity. Nor is it simply Nasser and his henchmen, the brutes who ran torture chambers like Tora Prison. It encompasses all secular Arab governments—including those in Egypt, Jordan, Iraq, Syria. It also includes the *ulema*, the clergy who claim to speak for Islam, but support the lordship of man. It includes anyone who stands in the way of the establishment of an Islamic State. The enemy is the rest of the world.

The battle between Islam and *Jahiliyyah* is a vicious struggle to the end. It is a fight unto death, because *Jahiliyyah* cannot be defeated only with words.[57] The enemy will never accept Islam, and Islam cannot accept the enemy. There is no room for compromise. The battle is an "eternal state, as truth and falsity cannot co-exist on this earth."[58]

In Qutb's view, those who think that the war is not about ideas but instead about imperialism are fools: "This group of thinkers, who are a product of the sorry state of the present Muslim generation . . . have laid down their spiritual and rational arms in defeat."[59] Even worse, Qutb warned, Christendom is attempting to "deceive us by distorting history and saying that the Crusades were a form of imperialism."[60] The medieval Crusades, the European wars against the Ottoman Empire, Napoleon's invasion of Egypt, the Sykes-Picot Agreement, the establishment of the State of Israel, the support of repressive Arab regimes—these events are presented by the West as though they were the ordinary stuff of power politics, the lamentable, but entirely routine, tendency of the strong to dominate the weak. But this "admission," according to Qutb, is a lie. The Crusades were never about power or territorial control. The war with the West has always been a battle of ideas—between those who recognize that only God possesses sovereignty and those who impute it to man.

Qutb's crusade is not a nationalist one. Seeing the history of the Middle East as a legacy of *foreign* control, he argued, misleads Arabs into thinking that the solution must be *local* control. Arab nationalists think that the antidote to imperialism is nationalism—Churchill must be replaced by Nasser. But that is a trap. Rule by man—any man—is the problem, not the solution. Victory over *Jahiliyyah* cannot be achieved by adopting an Arab form of *Jahiliyyah*. Eastern *Jahiliyyah* is no better than the Western version. In Qutb's messianic view, triumph requires nothing less than a global Islamic state. "Nationalism here is belief, homeland here is *Dar-ul-Islam* [the realm of Islam], the ruler here is God and the constitution here is the Qur'an."[61]

The Sykes-Picot Agreement is such a powerful symbol for the Islamic State, therefore, not because it stands for imperialism and power politics.

It is not the agreement itself, which never entered into effect. And it is not—or at least not only—that it symbolizes the treachery of the West, the collapse of the Ottoman Empire and, with it, the last caliphate. The agreement stands for something much worse: the modern sovereign state.

THE ISLAMIC STATE

In early February 2014, al Qaeda cut ties with its affiliate Al Qaeda in Iraq, largely over the affiliate's policy of terrorism against fellow Muslims. The group assumed a new name—*ad-Dawlah al-Islāmiyah fī 'l-'Irāq wa-sh-Shām*, literally, "the Islamic State in Iraq and the Left." "The Left" (*Al-Sham*) is a term often used to refer to Syria, because Syria is on the left when facing Mecca from the west (for the same reason, the country on the right is Yemen, Arabic for "Right"). Only after this split did many Americans become aware of the group, in part due to the brutal murders of American and British journalists and dramatic territorial gains in Iraq in the summer of 2014.

On the first day of Ramadan in July, Abu Bakr al-Baghdadi (born Ibrahim Awwad Ibrahim al-Badri) made his debut as the self-declared caliph of the Islamic State. Baghdadi had been captured in Fallujah in 2004 and imprisoned at the notorious Abu Ghraib prison, where shocking photographs later revealed horrific abuse of detainees, then transferred to Camp Bucca, where he likely met other future leaders of the Islamic State before being released.[62] Appearing in the Great Mosque in Mosul to give a sermon, Baghdadi's every move was choreographed to mimic practices from the time of the Prophet Muhammad. Indeed, the scene, which was recorded on video and posted on YouTube, almost verges on performance art. Baghdadi, cloaked in black and wearing a black turban, begins by slowly climbing the steps to the pulpit. He sits at the top of the steps while the call to prayer is given and pulls out a "miswak," an ancient wooden toothbrush, and rubs it over his teeth.[63] Only then does he rise to speak. "The religion of Allah, the Exalted, will not be implemented . . . except by the implementation of the Sharia of Allah, and appealing to him, and the application of Islamic law. This can only be achieved by force and power."[64]

The same month, Baghdadi released a message for Ramadan aimed at recruiting new followers. The message is infused throughout by Qutb's worldview. After the fall of the caliphate, Baghdadi explains, the Islamic State ceased to exist: "[T]he disbelievers were able to weaken and humiliate the Muslims, dominate them in every region, plunder their wealth and resources, and rob them of their rights." They accomplished this, he declares, "by attacking and occupying their lands, placing their treacherous agents in power to rule the Muslims with an iron fist, and spreading dazzling and deceptive slogans such as: civilization, peace, co-existence, freedom, democracy, secularism, Baathism, nationalism, and patriotism, among other false slogans." Muslims submit to these "manmade *shirk* (polytheistic) laws of the east and west, living despicably and disgracefully as a follower, by repeating those slogans without will and honor, or he lives persecuted, targeted, and expelled, to end up being killed, imprisoned, or terribly tortured, on the accusation of terrorism."[65]

Baghdadi's message closes with a call to all Muslims to join the Islamic State—a state defined by belief, not ethnicity or nationality: "O Muslims everywhere . . . you have a state and *khilāfah* [caliphate], which will return your dignity, might, rights, and leadership. It is a state where the Arab and non-Arab, the white man and black man, the easterner and westerner are all brothers." He exhorts, "rush O Muslims to your state." "Rush, because Syria is not for the Syrians and Iraq is not for the Iraqis. Indeed, the earth belongs to Allah. . . . The State is a state for all Muslims. The land is for the Muslims, all the Muslims."[66]

Baghdadi's call was effective. The Islamic State has attracted tens of thousands of fighters.[67] It has gained control over large areas of Syria, Iraq, and parts of Libya and Egypt's Sinai Peninsula[68] and received pledges of allegiance from groups in the Philippines, India, Algeria, Afghanistan, Egypt, Lebanon, Indonesia, Pakistan, Tunisia, Nigeria, Mali, Tunisia, and Yemen.[69] It has committed mass atrocities and war crimes on a scale that is hard to fathom, sanctioning violence against Shiite Muslims, indigenous Christian populations, Yazidis, Druze, and others. It has enslaved some members of these ethnic minorities—in many cases under the most brutal possible conditions. But the violence has not stopped with religious and ethnic minorities. It has extended even to Sunni Muslims who do not subscribe to the particular brand of Islam preached by their leader, Baghdadi, or those whose governments cooperate with the United States and Europe.

The Islamic State is not simply seeking revenge against a history of domination and humiliation; it is not solely aiming to end Western intervention in the domestic affairs of Arab countries; nor is it merely trying to establish a theocratic government based on Sharia law. The Islamic State's objective is more distinctive, and radical. It is committed to nothing less than the modification of the fundamental nature of the world order. The Islamic State not only rejects the prohibition on war launched by the Peace Pact, but it embraces the precise opposite: a duty to wage aggressive war. It not only rejects Western influence over Arab states, but it rejects the legitimacy of the sovereign state and the international system as it currently exists. For the international system recognizes the existence of multiple sovereigns, each of whom has the right of self-determination and protection against military attack and conquest. The Islamic State, however, does not accept the possibility that there can be more than one sovereign. Its adherents believe only God, who created the rules as revealed by the Qur'an, Sunna, and Hadith, can truly obligate men to obey.

In the "End of Sykes-Picot" video that opened this chapter, Vásquez puts his right index finger in the air, a gesture so ubiquitous in the Islamic State propaganda that some have taken to calling it "the jihadi equivalent of a gang sign." At a surface level, the gesture alludes to the concept of *tawhid*, or the "oneness" of God. But it has also come to mean something more than simple monotheism. It represents the Islamic State's rejection of any legitimate source of authority but God—including not just the governments of every Western state, but the governments of *every* modern state.[70]

It may seem odd that a group that rejects the idea of the modern state calls itself a state. But again the answer can be found in Qutb's words: "Islam, which is a way of life, takes practical steps to organize a movement for freeing man." "Other societies," Qutb wrote, "do not give it any opportunity to organize its followers according to its own method, and hence it is the duty of Islam to annihilate all such systems, as they are obstacles in the way of universal freedom."[71] It is only in such a state that a Muslim can live according to God.

The Islamic State is the embodiment of Qutb's vision: We see fresh daily evidence that the Islamic State is working to control territory and re-establish the Islamic governance under the caliphate through armed force. When it establishes control, moreover, it acts like a state. The Islamic State has issued its own currency based on gold and silver, which it claims is "far removed from the tyrannical monetary system that was imposed on the Muslims and was a reason for their enslavement and impoverishment, and the wasting [of] the fortunes of the Ummah [nation]."[72] It has established Sharia courts, which issue legal documents such as marriage contracts and birth certificates, resolve private disputes, and determine criminal punishment. It provides policing and protection, manages city services, collects taxes, and engages in military conscription.[73] Even though Baghdadi, as caliph, may oversee day-to-day operations, he and his underlings believe that ultimate political authority derives not from the people, but exclusively from God.

The Islamic State, currently the most successful group to hold this political-theological view, is far from alone. Al Qaeda, from which it split, also aspires to re-create the seventh-century caliphate. In 1994, Osama bin Laden declared that al Qaeda would reclaim "every stolen Islamic land, from Palestine to Al-Andalus and other Islamic lands that were lost because of the betrayals of rulers and the feebleness of Muslims."[74] The chief disagreement between al Qaeda and the Islamic State is not over ends but over timing and means. Bin Laden warned against declaring a caliphate prematurely, without sufficient consultation with other jihadist groups and before firm control could be sustained.[75] As the Islamic State loses its grip over territory, it seems Baghdadi might have done well to heed bin Laden's warnings. But even if the Islamic State is ultimately defeated, its deep commitment to erasing the modern sovereign state system will remain embedded in other groups influenced by Qutb's worldview—including al Qaeda, the Taliban, and Jabhat Fateh al-Sham. Killing tens of thousands of jihadists is not enough to defeat the political idea that animates their movement. Other groups who also see like the Islamic State will simply try to fill the void left by its retreat.

To win a war over the future of the world order, one must fight not simply with powerful weapons but with powerful ideas.

CONCLUSION: THE WORK OF TOMORROW

In November 1940, a few months after German panzers rolled into Paris and the Axis powers signed the Tripartite Pact, Salmon Levinson lay dying. It seemed his dream of outlawry was dying with him. John Dewey wrote a letter to his second wife describing "Sol" as "the man who started the Outlawry of War—poor man—though it will come to something sometime."[1]

Although it seemed impossible at that moment, Dewey was right. Levinson's outlawry movement did "come to something." It led to a global revolution. Less than a decade after Dewey wrote his lament, the Old World Order had given way to the New World Order, with all that the outlawry of war implies. Today conquest has largely ended, as has gunboat diplomacy. The crime of aggressive war, once a logical impossibility, is now one of the four crimes that can be prosecuted before the International Criminal Court in The Hague. And economic sanctions, once prohibited for neutral states, have become a common and crucial tool for enforcing international law.

Yet today the New World Order that Levinson helped launch is at risk. The postwar consensus on the illegality of war is under greater assault today than it has been in seven decades. By looking back, this book seeks to draw attention to these threats and to chart a path ahead.

One source of risk comes from the rise of the Islamic State and other groups inspired by Qutb's jihadist vision. The Islamic State has sought to undermine state control throughout the Middle East, while drawing the West into a confrontation that feeds its worldview and undermines the world order. The Islamic State's videos of beheadings of Westerners are meant to draw converts, but also to provoke a response that will bring about an apocalyptic conflict. In a video of the beheading of Peter (Abdul-Rahman) Kassig, a U.S. aid worker, his masked executioner declares, "Here we are, burying the first American crusader in Dabiq, eagerly waiting for the remainder of your armies to arrive."[2] By attempting to goad the United States, United Kingdom, France, and their allies into responding in ways that undermine the legal order, the Islamic State seeks to accomplish through overreaction what it could never accomplish on its own—a weakening, even the end, of the modern international legal order.

To date, the provocation has not succeded in drawing Western armies to fight on the ground, as the Islamic State clearly hopes.[3] But it triggered another corrosive response: In 2014, the United States launched a massive air campaign against the Islamic State in Iraq and Syria. In order to justify this operation, it claimed that it was acting not only to defend Iraq (which was clearly justifiable), but also in its *own* self-defense (which was not).[4] Unfortunately, the growing reliance on self-defense as a justification for using force—for this and other operations against terrorist groups around the world—threatens to make self-defense the exception that swallows the rule against war. Indeed, it was precisely this concern that led the authors of the Pact to omit an express exception for what they called "defensive wars" and the drafters of the U.N. Charter to adopt a right to self-defense only in cases of "armed attack." If states can always invoke self-defense as a justification to use force, then the prohibition on war becomes meaningless.

Another, equally potent, challenge to the postwar consensus prohibiting use of force outside the Charter framework comes from the clash of the postwar commitment to humanitarian ideals and the prohibition on the use of force for the purpose of righting wrongs except when authorized by the U.N. Security Council.

At the time of this writing, the Syrian conflict has caused nearly a half million deaths. The conflict shows little sign of ending, though there remain glimmers of hope that diplomacy will produce a pause in the killing. President Bashar al-Assad has barrel-bombed and gassed his own people, contributing to an unprecedented refugee crisis. Because Assad has not consented to international intervention to aid his people, and Russia and China have refused to authorize Security Council action to address the humanitarian crisis, the carnage continues.

Many have wondered whether we should continue to abide by the rules of the system if the rules of the system allow such outrages. The potency of war can seem alluring. Indeed, it may seem like the Interventionists—Hugo Grotius, Nishi Amane, Carl Schmitt, and even Sayyid Qutb—were right: War is the only possible solution.

But to hold this view, one must be prepared to embrace all that it entails. If we treat the United Nations Charter like Carl Schmitt treated the Weimar Constitution, the exceptions to the prohibition on war will eventually destroy the New World Order and all it has accomplished. If the United States insists on the right to resort to war in violation of the Charter to address emergencies, it cannot stop others from arrogating to themselves the same powers—and that, in turn, threatens the entire system, which requires states to abide by the prohibition on war.

Russia, once a crucial U.S. partner in the formation of the New World Order, poses another threat to the system. In Eastern Europe, Russia is cementing its control over Crimea and continues to foment unrest in Eastern Ukraine and Georgia. Russia prevented the Security Council from responding to the carnage in Syria while providing support to the Assad government as it slaughtered its citizens. Russia has even joined in the assault, bombing hospitals and schools and killing thousands of civilians. The paralysis of the Security Council in the face of such horrors has dealt a blow to the United Nations' legitimacy. And Russia is not the only state actively undermining the international legal order: China's attempts to assert sovereignty over disputed rocks and islands in the South China Sea,

Iran's support for terrorist groups, and North Korea's repeated threats of military force against South Korea are also deeply corrosive.

In light of these assaults on the system, it is not unreasonable to ask whether the New World Order is simply too far gone to be saved. Why should the United States and its allies continue to support international institutions and the rules of the legal order if others not only refuse to do their share to maintain the system, but are actively working against it?

Rather than viewing these violations of the legal order as reason to abandon it, we should instead see them as reason to redouble our support for it. After all, the health of a legal system is not measured solely by the moments when the law is broken. In 2014, for example, there were 1,165,383 violent crimes reported by law enforcement in the United States.[5] But that does not mean that the laws against violent crimes in the United States are ineffectual. No rule is perfectly effective. What matters is not whether the law is sometimes broken. What matters is whether it is largely effective, even if imperfectly so. And what matters is the response when the law is broken. Violent crime has fallen significantly in the last two decades in the United States. And when there is a violent crime, the police investigate; if they find the offender, he or she is tried; and, if found guilty, sentenced.

The test, then, of the international legal system is not whether we can point to instances where the law is violated. We should instead look to whether the law has largely, if not perfectly, worked. To that, the answer is clearly yes—interstate war has declined precipitously and conquests have almost completely disappeared. Moreover, we should look to what happens when the law is broken. In the international system, the legal order is policed by outcasting, not by war. As we have shown, Russia continues to labor under extensive sanctions cutting it off from valuable trade with Europe and the United States in direct response to its actions in Crimea and Ukraine. And one hundred nations voted in support of a General Assembly resolution calling on states, international organizations, and specialized agencies not to recognize any change in the status of Crimea.[6] States have likewise refused to accept Chinese territorial claims in the South China Sea, the United States chief among them, and the Philippines brought China to mandatory arbitration with U.S. support. The United States and the European Union are working to prevent the flow of money and foreign

fighters into Islamic State–controlled territories. In each case, rule breakers faced consequences. And in each case, the United States has served an
important—indeed, leading—role in policing the system.

The success of the system depends on the willingness of the United States
to continue to play a central role in maintaining the legal order in the face
of these many challenges. Indeed, the greatest threat to the New World
Order comes from those who wish to abandon this role and turn inward.
Throughout the world, anti-internationalist sentiment is growing. In the
United States, the bipartisan consensus in favor of global free trade that
has held strong since the mid-1930s is collapsing. Donald Trump won the
presidency on an anti-internationalist platform that promised to restrict
the movement of goods and people across borders. He has flirted with
defunding the United Nations, pulling back U.S. support for NATO, ignoring the World Trade Organization, seizing Iraqi oil, and abandoning
the policy of resisting Russia's annexation of Crimea with an array of outcasting tools. And he has used force against the Syrian government without
Security Council authorization, in clear violation of the United Nations
Charter.

The United States is not the only state with rising anti-internationalist
sentiment. The unexpected vote by disaffected citizens in the United Kingdom to pull their country out of the European Union and the rise of anti-
EU anti-globalist far-right parties (some clandestinely financed by Russia)
in France, Germany, Greece, Hungary, the Netherlands, Sweden, Austria,
and Slovakia pose a deep challenge to the legal order that the Internationalists built. The postwar consensus in favor of positive-sum peaceful cooperation instead of zero-sum military competition is at greater risk than ever.

For the world order built by the Internationalists to continue, America
and its allies must maintain their commitment to the rules and institutions
that underlie it. The order initiated by the Peace Pact and reaffirmed in the
United Nations Charter was grounded in an understanding that every nation would be more secure and prosperous if nations cooperated with one
another in pursuit of their shared goals. The international institutions that
have grown up since 1928, while imperfect, have brought seven decades of
unprecedented prosperity and peace.

This did not happen on its own. When the world first outlawed war, putting an end to the Old World Order, it failed to create anything to take its place. It took the Internationalists two decades of painstaking efforts before the rules and institutions that could make the decision to outlaw war a reality were in place. Only then was Levinson's dream of a world in which war would no longer be used to resolve disputes between states finally realized. Without continuing U.S. support for those rules and institutions, that accomplishment is unlikely to last long.

It is not enough, moreover, to support the United Nations and related international institutions. Continued commitment to global free trade is also essential. The Internationalists came to understand that when war was outlawed, something else had to take its place. In the postwar world, free trade has filled the vacuum. States can enrich themselves through cooperation, rather than coercion.

Free trade not only channels productive activity away from war making, it provides a legal tool for disciplining states who violate the rules. The tools of outcasting that replaced war as the central international law enforcement mechanism rely on robust global cooperation. If states withdraw from global cooperation or pull back from engaging the global economy, they lose their capacity to exert influence without force.

Reaffirming a commitment to free trade does not require ignoring the dislocation and pain it has caused. The turn in popular sentiment against free trade comes from real harm done to individuals and communities who have seen jobs, even entire industries, disappear. But rather than try to bring those jobs back, we should seek to better support those who have been hardest hit—helping them transition from less to more competitive sectors of the economy. We must also endeavor to spread the gains from trade more evenly. Initiatives to ease the pain of trade competition are the right thing to do, and they will help renew broad-based support for continued global engagement.[7]

Yes, engaging in more cooperation may mean giving up some control, *but it means gaining it, too.* The states that are parties to the World Trade Organization agree to allow goods into their country with minimal trade restrictions, but they gain the same access to markets around the world. This creates jobs and raises wages overall. Indeed, in the years between

1970 and 2000, manufacturing workers in open economies were paid be-ween *three and nine times* as much as those in closed economies, depend-ing on the region.[8] Consumers also benefit from lower prices. And these effects are not limited to trade. The states that agreed to participate in the Paris Agreement on Climate Change in 2016, for example, accepted limits on their climate-harming activities, but in return they gained similar promises from other states to limit their own climate-harming activities. In the process, states made progress toward addressing a collective threat that no state—not even the most powerful—could address alone.

As the world stands on the brink of renouncing the core commitments of the New World Order, this book serves as a reminder of what is at stake. The history we have told demonstrates that in a world of multiple sover-eign states, there are a limited set of legal orders from which to choose. In one—represented by the Old World Order we described in Part I—all states agree that war is legal, a tool to right wrongs. In that world, conquest is permissible, aggression is not a crime, neutrals must stay impartial (thus economic sanctions against aggressors are illegal), and agreements may be coerced. In the second—represented by the New World Order that we described in Part III—all states agree that war is illegal, and refuse to rec-ognize it as a source of legal entitlements, even when used to right wrongs. In that world, conquest is illegal, aggression a crime, economic sanctions are an essential tool of statecraft, and agreements cannot be coerced. In that legal order, moreover, trade plays an essential role not only as a source of beneficial collaboration but also as a collective tool for constraining il-legal behavior.

The third option—represented by the period between the Peace Pact and the close of the Second World War that we described in Part II—falls between these two polar opposites. But this third option is in many ways the worst of all. Inherently unstable, it will generate chaos and disorder until a new, stable equilibrium arises.

Tracing the evolution of the global legal order over the course of four centuries teaches us that international law is a *system* and the rules rise or fall together. It is not possible to pick and choose the rules one at a time. The key rules of the system have a necessary logical connection to one another. (If war is legal, conquest is not far behind.) Nor is it possible to follow one set of rules sometimes, and another set at others. The world cannot juggle two inconsistent legal orders for very long. Sooner or later they will clash and come crashing down.

For all its problems, the New World Order is better than the Old. It is better to live in a world where war is not a permissible mechanism for righting wrongs, even if that means some wrongs remain unaddressed. It is better to live in a world where conquest is not recognized than in one where it is. It is better to live in a world where treaties produced by gunboats can be torn up than in one where they are binding. It is better to live in a world where those who wage aggressive war can be convicted in a court of law than in one where they cannot. It is better to live in a world where states can use economic sanctions to punish aggressors without fear of being drawn into a war as a consequence. In short, it is better to live in the New World Order, with all its real, sometimes terrible, drawbacks, than to go back to a system where war is legal or to a chaotic in-between.

Despite the many challenges, there is reason for optimism. While it is true that things can change for the worse, they can also change for the better. And whether and how they change is largely up to us. We can update the rules to respond to global challenges—as have those who have endeavored to create ever more inventive and creative mechanisms for outcasting rule breakers—or we can disregard them. The choice is ours.

Many have argued that the world is best explained by reference to state power. Law is just words on a piece of paper, incapable of true influence. We reject this account not because states or those within them care more about law than power. Instead, if this book shows anything, it is that the choice between law and power is a false one. *Real* power—power useful for achieving important and lasting political objectives—does not exist in the absence of law. Law *creates* real power. States can reach their goals only if others recognize the results of their actions. As the Japanese found out in 1931, it was not enough to occupy Manchuria if no one treated Manchuria as Manchukuo. Russia is relearning this lesson today in Crimea. It can claim Crimea, but if the rest of the world does not recognize the claim, tourists from everywhere but Russia will vacation elsewhere, ATMs will run dry, and the economy will wither away. China is discovering the same lesson in the South China Sea. It can occupy islands but they are worth little as long as the rest of the world refuses to recognize them.

The account of the world that rests on state power is fatalistic, leaving little room for human agency. But the story of the transformation of the Old World Order to the New demonstrates that even as law shapes power, ideas—and those who develop and spread them—shape the law. Brute force, like rushing water, must be controlled and channeled. Dams need to be built, canals dug, and pipes laid. Those who shape the laws are the hydraulic engineers of the political world. To be effective, they must channel power.

The example of the Internationalists offers a hopeful message: If law shapes real power, and ideas shape the law, then we control our fate. We can choose to recognize certain actions and not others. We can cooperate with those who follow the rules and outcast those who do not. And when the rules no longer work, we can change them.

The Internationalists were transformative figures. They were transformative because of their ideas—and because they were willing and able to use their ideas to change the world.

This is the final lesson we can learn from the Internationalists— from Salmon Levinson, James T. Shotwell, Sumner Welles, Hersch Lauterpacht, and all those who supported their efforts along the way. None of these men is a household name. None held high political office. None found his task easy. None, moreover, was able to accomplish much on his own. But each had a conviction about the way the world should be organized. And each was willing to fight for years, even decades, against long odds to take small steps along the path to constructing a new global order grounded in the rejection of war. The Internationalists worked with one another and with a vast array of grassroots groups, politicians, academics, government bureaucrats, and international colleagues to make progress.

Their example teaches us that we have an opportunity and a burden. Each of us, even those far outside the halls of government, has the capacity to make a difference. We all bear responsibility for the world in which we live. Together we can and must continue to support institutions that have kept the peace, adapt them to changing circumstances, and develop new ones that will further reduce violence.

Aristide Briand understood that renouncing war would not end war. When world leaders gathered at the Quai D'Orsay in August 1928, Briand spoke words that remain true today: "Peace is proclaimed: that is well, that is much. But it still remains necessary to organize it. . . . That is to be the work of tomorrow."

ACKNOWLEDGMENTS

The Internationalists were a group of people who fought together to outlaw war, so it is only fitting that writing their story should be a group effort as well. It is a great pleasure to acknowledge our debts to those who have helped make this book possible.

Our first and greatest debt is to our Dean, Robert Post, who has been unfailingly supportive. His answer to any request has always been "Yes." Without such generous institutional support, we could not have gained access to the archives, data, manuscripts, and other materials that were essential to this project. Equally valuable, and all the more impressive given his unremitting decanal responsibilities, Robert read every workshop paper we presented and gave us characteristically insightful feedback.

The library staff at Yale Law School is unparalleled. This project began under the leadership of Blair Kauffman and concluded under Teresa Miguel-Stearns. They created an environment and facility of which most scholars can only dream. Drew Adan, Alison Burke, Clément Dupuy, Jason Eiseman, Sarah Kraus, Evelyn Ma, John Nann, Michael VanderHeijden, and especially Ryan Harrington hunted down, translated, and analyzed manuscripts, manifestos, archival materials, and rare books from libraries and collections all around the world.

Our administrative assistants, Annie Cooper, Lise Cavallaro, and Deborah Sestito, provided constant support on a daily basis. They helped keep us organized and made it possible for us to focus on the research and writing of this book.

This book ranges widely, and as we researched new people, eras, and parts of the world, we were able to draw on the expertise of a number of extraordinary scholars. Peter Borschberg shared his peerless knowledge of the history of Singapore and Southeast Asia, Randall Lesaffer helped us better understand classical international law, John Witt offered guidance on the finer points of the laws of war and the larger craft of historical explanation, Jim Whitman shared his encyclopedic knowledge of early Modern European understandings of war, Gene Fidel introduced us to Plenty Horses, David Golove suggested Edmond-Charles Genêt as an illustration of the law of neutrality, Meredith Sarkees and Paul Diehl answered our many questions about the Correlates of War Project databases, David Cohen helped us better understand the sanctions work of the Office of Foreign Assets Control at Treasury that he once ran, Claus Kress shared his knowledge of Cologne in the 1930s and his expertise on the crime of aggression, Takeharu Okubo contributed to our understanding of Japan's early engagement with Western international law, Mara Revkin was an invaluable resource on the Islamic State, and Andrew March helped us begin to comprehend Islamic fundamentalist thought. We could not have written this book without access to such a rich reservoir of knowledge and expertise.

Over the five years this book has been in progress, we have benefited from valuable feedback at a number of workshops and conferences, including the U.S. Department of State, Sciences Po, Pantheon-Assas University, New York Institute for the Humanities, University of San Diego, Humboldt University, University of Cologne, Stanford University, University of Michigan, Georgetown University, University of Toronto, University of Antwerp, University of California Los Angeles, Columbia University, New York University, Oxford University, University College London, Yale–National University of Singapore, Sydney University, Fordham University,

Boston University, and the Yale Middle East Legal Studies Seminar conference in Jordan. Special thanks to Mattias Kumm, who hosted us at the Rule of Law Institute in Berlin at which we first presented this project, and to the Grotius reading group (yes, there is such a thing), especially Dennis Klymchuk, Arthur Ripstein, Ernie Weinrib, and Ariel Zylberman. We also were lucky to receive early feedback on drafts from Rob Howse, Mattias Reimann, Rebecca Scott, and Ruti Teitel. We are particularly indebted to our colleagues at Yale Law School, who have read several chapters of this book for the Monday faculty workshop; our drafts improved dramatically as a result of healthy doses of encouragement and criticism. Our colleague Bruce Ackerman not only offered feedback before, during, and after each of those workshops, but also represents an inspiring example of what it is to be an outstanding scholar and institutional citizen.

As the manuscript neared completion, several readers offered feedback on parts of the book, including Naoyuki Agawa, Andrea Ashworth, Peter Borschberg, Mark Greenberg, Randall Lesaffer, Jason Lyall, Gideon Yaffe, and Moran Yahav. Jack Goldsmith and Robert Keohane, both scholars whom we deeply admire, read the entire manuscript and gave us detailed and unsparing—and therefore exceptionally helpful—comments that helped us improve the book considerably. Stuart Proffitt, our editor at Penguin UK, also read the manuscript several times and made numerous suggestions for improvement. Stuart not only lived up to his legendary reputation as an editor, but also an expert in his own right, regularly pointing out historical details few others noticed.

Gordon Silverstein, our Dean of Graduate Studies, once quipped that Yale Law School professors don't want to teach their students—they want to work with them. The pool of talent at Yale Law School is so deep and wide that the opportunity to work with and learn from these brilliant students is irresistible.

Lisa Wang, Jacqueline Van de Velde, and William Holste helped us think through the structure and function of war manifestos—documents in which sovereigns gave their reasons for going to war—and worked with us for more than two years to build the dataset we use in this book (and went from being our research assistants to coauthors on a separate article about manifestos). We are also indebted to students on the team who brought to the project both analytical expertise and extraordinary language skills, including Classical Chinese, Latin, French, German, Portuguese, Dutch, Italian, and Ottoman Turkish: Nico Banac, Jacob Bennett, Perot Bissell, Johannes Buchheim, Varun Char, Idriss Fofana, Sameer Jaywant, Aubrey Jones, Ling-wei Kung, Steve Lance, Gregor Novak, Pedro Ramirez, Britta Redwood, Bonnie Robinson, James Rumsey-Merlan, Ingmar Samyn, David Stanton, and Evan Welber.

For help learning about the rise and fall of territorial conquest from 1816 to the present, we are grateful to a dedicated team of students, whose motto was "Keep Calm and Code On": Megan Browder, John Calhoun, Kevin Chen, Anna Daikun, Leslie Easterbrook, Idriss Fofana, Christopher Galiardo, Sinead Hunt, Alexander Kaplan, Kaitlin Konkel, Robert Nightingale, Daniel Sheehan, Reema Shah, Mike Shih, Julia Shu, Noah Simmons, and Peter Tzeng. Will Smiley and Aimee Genell provided expert advice on the Ottoman Empire and its collapse. Stuart Craig, an exceptionally skilled scholar, brought his expertise to bear on the data we produced, enabling us to shed light most effectively on the questions of importance.

Aaron Voloj Dessauer worked to help us gather information about the Nuremberg Trials, translated a 1946 manuscript by Carl Schmitt, a central figure in the book, and offered very helpful editorial advice. Luciana Sanga—one of a small number of experts in the world on early *kanbun kundokutai*, a process initially used for rendering Chinese texts into Japanese—translated for us the first text on international law written for a Japanese audience, Nishi Amane's *Fisuserinku-shi Bankoku Kōhō* (1868).

For excellent research assistance on a wide range of topics, we thank Dhruv Aggarwal, Ben Alter, Josh Andresen, Una Bergmane, Megan Browder, William Bruno, Celia Choy, Anna Daikun, Leslie Easterbook, Sarah Grusin, Sinead Hunt, Heeyong (Daniel) Jang, Alexander Kaplan, Michael Lemanski, David Louk, Max Mishkin, Tiffany Ng, Robert Nightingale, Raymond Noona, Aadhithi Padmanabhan, Ksenja Pavlovic, Britta Redwood, Lea Schroeder, Kara Sheppared-Jones, Sophia Shin, Will Smiley, Nora Stappert, and Peter Tzeng. Sona Lim worked with us for several years on a variety of tasks related to the book; she was always reliable and always willing to help no matter how big or small the project. Shawn

Moura of the University of Maryland spent countless hours at the National Archives in College Park, Maryland, hunting down references to Carl Schmitt in the war crimes records. Ava Hathaway Hacker helped collect the Sumner Welles Papers at the Roosevelt Library—including what turned out to be a previously unknown early draft of the United Nations Charter. Ava and Liza Mackeen-Shapiro, both emerging writers, also offered editorial suggestions. In addition, a number of research assistants helped us review the penultimate version of the manuscript to ensure our citations and claims were accurate. They include Benjamin Alter, Leslie Arffa, Erin Biel, Emily Chertoff, Eric Chung, Alexandra Francis, William Holste, Michael Lemanski, Aaron Levine, Alina Lindblom, Raymond Lu, Richard Medina, Brian Mund, Arjun Ramamurti, Cameron Rotblat, Max Siegel, Paul Strauch, Jacqueline Van De Velde, and Beatrice Walton. We owe a particular debt to Srinath Reddy Kethireddy, who did the final review of the entire manuscript single-handed, an extraordinarily daunting task.

The team at Simon & Schuster has been a pleasure to work with from beginning to end. Jonathan Karp, President and Publisher of Simon & Schuster, has been an unwavering champion of the book since we first met to discuss it. He shares with us a particular soft spot for one of the Internationalists, Salmon Levinson, who has been largely forgotten, an injustice that this book aims to partly correct. Ben Loehnen, our editor at Simon & Schuster, helped us turn our draft manuscript into the book that we wanted it to be. His judgment on matters big and small was flawless and his manner gentle but firm. Amar Deol shepherded the book through the editorial process with care and attention, and Larry Hughes and his team have worked to put the results of our efforts in the hands of as many readers as possible.

Our agent, Elyse Cheney, has been a passionate and persuasive advocate for this book, and Alex Jacob has been our representative in the international market and an invaluable sounding board throughout the publication process. We feel immensely fortunate to have the support of such a great team.

Our spouses have not only provided unflagging love throughout the writing process, but have deployed their extraordinary talents to help make the project possible. Scott's wife, Alison Mackeen, read and reread our book proposal (and told us, with the honesty that only a spouse can offer, that the first draft needed *a lot* of work). Over the course of many months, she helped us figure out how to make a book about international law sound interesting. She then helped us navigate the unfamiliar world of trade book publishing and offered feedback on several early chapters of the book. Oona's husband, Jacob Hacker, read the entire manuscript. He drew on his own expertise as a leading political scientist to offer nuanced suggestions for strengthening the claims in the book, especially in Part III. A beautiful writer unusually skilled at communicating complicated ideas in a clear way, he also helped us hone the text. In addition, Oona's mother, Anneke Hathaway, made hundreds of after-school pickups so Oona could write; she also helped out with Dutch sources along the way—and even visited Hugo Grotius's prison near her childhood home to help us describe it accurately.

Last, we are grateful to Oona's children, Ava and Owen, and Scott's, Liza and Drin, to whom this book is dedicated. Ranging in age from eight to twelve when this book was first hatched, they had immense fun concocting their own group projects (some of which they unfortunately insisted we taste) as we talked nearby about Grotius, the outlawing of war, and the transformation of international law. The initial idea for the book first emerged during just such a play date. As the manuscript developed, their presence also helped us see that this book was the story not only of the Internationalists and the world they helped create but also of the world that our children, now on the cusp of high school and college, will inherit.

NOTES

ABBREVIATIONS USED IN THE NOTES

BK   Nishi Amane, *Fisuserinku-shi Bankoku Kōhō* (1868) (translated for the authors by Luciana Sanga)

DJB   *De Jure Belli ac Pacis Libri Tres* [The Law of War and Peace in Three Books], translated by Francis Kelsey (Oxford: Clarendon Press, 1925)

DJP   *De Jure Praedae Commentarius* [Commentary on the Law of Prize and Booty], translated by Gwladys L. Williams (Oxford: Clarendon Press, 1950)

FBK   Frank B. Kellogg

FKP MHS   Frank B. Kellogg Papers, Minnesota Historical Society (microfilm edition)

FRUS   United States Department of State, *Foreign Relations of the United States Diplomatic Papers* (Washington, DC: U.S. Government Printing Office)

HLS   Henry L. Stimson

HSP YUL   Henry L. Simson Papers, Yale University Library

IMT   International Military Tribunal, *Trial of the Major War Criminals Before the International Military Tribunal*, "The Blue Series," 42 vols. (Nuremberg: IMT, 1947–1949), www.loc.gov/rr/frd/Military_Law/NT_major-war-criminals.html

JDP CUL   John Dewey Papers, Columbia University Library

JSP CUL   James T. Shotwell Papers, Columbia University Library

JTS   James T. Shotwell

KLP ACL   Karl Loewenstein Papers, Amherst College Library
LNOJ   *League of Nations Official Journal*
PTJ   *The Papers of Thomas Jefferson Digital Edition*, ed. James P. McClure and
             J. Jefferson Looney (Charlottesville: University of Virginia Press, 2008–
             2016)
RJP LOC   Robert Jackson Papers, Library of Congress
RPP HLS   Roscoe Pound Papers, Harvard Law School
SLP UCL   Salmon O. Levinson Papers, University of Chicago Library
SOL   Salmon O. Levinson
SWP FDRL   Sumner Welles Papers, Franklin D. Roosevelt Presidential Library
WBP LC   William E. Borah Papers, Library of Congress
WEB   William E. Borah

INTRODUCTION

1. The events surrounding the signing of the Peace Pact are described in Jacques
   Lefebvre, "Le pacte général de renonciation à la guerre a été signé hier so-
   lennellement, à Paris, par les principales puissances du monde," *L'Ouest-Éclair*
   (Rennes ed.), August 28, 1928, 1–2; J. G. Hamilton, "Movie Atmosphere En-
   velops Treaty Signing Ceremony: Searchlights Play on Chief Actors in Famous
   Clock Room—Shouts of 'Long Live Germany!' Heard in Paris Streets," *The
   Sun*, August 28, 1928, 1; Correspondent, "To-Day's Great Ceremony in Paris:
   Preparations in the Clock Saloon," *Manchester Guardian*, August 27, 1928,
   9; Edwin L. James, "15 Nations Sign Pact to Renounce War in Paris Room
   Where League Was Born; Briand Dedicates It to Nations' Dead," *New York
   Times*, August 28, 1928, 1, 4. The Salle de l'Horloge is depicted and described
   in French Ministry of Foreign Affairs, "The Clock Room," France Diplomatie:
   Ministry of Foreign Affairs and International Development, http://www.diplo
   matie.gouv.fr/en/the-ministry-of-foreign-affairs/a-tour-of-the-quai-d-orsay
   /article/the-clock-room.
2. "Documents Diplomatiques de la Conférence du Mètre," in Diplomatic Documents of the Metre Conference 1875, *Bureau International des Poids et Mesures*,
   accessed June 1, 2016, http://www.bipm.org/en/worldwide-metrology/metre
   -convention/official-texts/.
3. Paul Louis, "La Première Séance de la Société des Nations," *L'Humanité: Journal Socialiste Quotidien* (January 16, 1920), 3.
4. French Ministry of Foreign Affairs, "The Clock Room."
5. Valentine Thomson, *Briand, Man of Peace* (New York: Covici-Friede, 1930), xii;
   Frederick W. Haberman, *Peace 1926–1950, Nobel Lectures, Including Presentation
   Speeches and Laureates' Biographies*, Vol. 2 (River Edge, NJ: World Scientific,
   1999); L. De Saint-Martin, "un Geste: un Acte," *L'Ouest-Éclair* (Rennes ed.),
   August 28, 1928, 1.
6. U.S. Department of State, *Treaty for the Renunciation of War: Text of the Treaty,
   Notes Exchanged, Instruments of Ratification and of Adherence, and Other Papers*

(Washington, DC: U.S. Government Printing Office, 1933), 308–9 (French original text) and 313–14 (English translation).

7. Vegetius rendered it: *"Igitur qui desiderat pacem, praeparet bellum."* Publius Flavius Vegetius Renatus, *Epitoma Rei Militaris,* Book III.

8. Lord Cushendun, the acting foreign secretary, signed for India.

9. Milton Leitenberg, "Deaths in Wars and Conflicts in the 20th Century," 2003, https://pacs.einaudi.cornell.edu/sites/pacs/files/Deaths-Wars-Conflicts3rd -ed.pdf.

10. Human Security Report 2013, *The Decline in Global Violence: Evidence, Explanation and Contestation,* 37. The authors use the standard metric of number of deaths per hundred thousand of population per year.

11. Notable exceptions include the international law historians Stephen Neff in *War and the Law of Nations: A General History* (New York: Cambridge University Press, 2005), 293–96; Randall Lesaffer in "Kellogg-Briand Pact (1928)" in *Max Planck Encyclopedia of Public International Law,* ed. Rudiger Wolfrum (Oxford: Oxford University Press, 2013), 579; and the antiwar activist David Swanson in *When the World Outlawed War* (self published, 2011).

12. Henry Kissinger, *Diplomacy* (New York: Simon & Schuster, 1994), 280.

13. Eric Sevareid, *Radio, Racism and Foreign Policy,* at 19:40, https://archive.org /details/betweenthewarsradioracismandforeignpolicy_20150427.

14. Ian Kershaw, *To Hell and Back: Europe, 1914–1949* (London: Allen Lane, 2015), 181.

15. Kenneth L. Adelman, *The Great Universal Embrace: Arms Summitry—A Skeptic's Account* (New York: Simon & Schuster, 1989), 68; James M. Lindsay, "TWE Remembers: The Kellogg-Briand Pact," *The Water's Edge* (August 27, 2011), http://blogs.cfr.org/lindsay/2011/08/27/twe-remembers-the-kellogg-briand -pact.

16. Independent Cinema Office (U.K.), "Histoire Du Soldat Inconnu," *Essentials: Secret Masterpieces of Cinema,* http://www.icoessentials.org.uk/film/histoire-du -soldat-inconnu.

17. Oona A. Hathaway and Scott J. Shapiro, "On Syria, a U.N. Vote Isn't Optional," *New York Times,* September 3, 2013.

18. Daniel W. Drezner, "International Lawyers Give It the Old College Try," *Foreign Policy,* September 4, 2013.

19. These figures are from the Department of Peace and Conflict Research, UCDP Battle-Related Deaths Dataset v.5-2016, 1989–2015, http://www.pcr .uu.se/research/ucdp/datasets/. They do not include indirect deaths due to disease and starvation, criminality, or attacks deliberately directed against civilians only (one-sided violence).

20. Henry Cabot Lodge, "The Meaning of the Kellogg Treaty," *Harper's Magazine,* December 1928, 41.

21. Carl von Clausewitz, *On War,* trans. and eds. Michael Howard and Peter Paret (Princeton: Princeton University Press, 1976), 87. Howard and Paret translate

the phrase as, "war is simply a continuation of political intercourse, with the addition of other means." Ibid., at 605. We use the better known paraphrase.

22. See Peter H. Wilson, *The Thirty Years War: Europe's Tragedy* (Cambridge: Harvard University Press, 2009), 779–95.

23. See, e.g., Leo Gross, "The Peace of Westphalia, 1648–1948," *American Journal of International Law* 42, no. 1 (1948): 20–41; Stephen D. Krasner, *Sovereignty: Organized Hypocrisy* (Princeton: Princeton University Press, 1999).

24. See Andreas Osiander, "Sovereignty, International Relations and the Westphalian Myth," *International Organization* 55, no. 2 (Spring 2001): 251–87; Ronald Lesaffer, "The International Dimension of the Westphalia Treaties: A Juridical Approach," in *350 años de la Paz de Westfalia, 1648–1998. Del antagonismo a la integración en Europa. Ciclo de conferencias celebrado en la Biblioteca Nacional, Madrid 9 de marzo a 30 de noviembre de 1998*, eds. García García et al. (Madrid: Biblioteca Nacional, 1999), 291–310; Derek Croxton, "The Peace of Westphalia of 1648 and the Origins of Sovereignty," *The International History Review* 21, no. 3 (1999): 569–91.

ONE: HUGO THE GREAT

1. *DJP*, 538.

2. Scott M. Fitzpatrick and Richard Callaghan, "Magellan's Crossing of the Pacific," *The Journal of Pacific History* 43, no. 2 (2008): 148.

3. Martine Julia van Ittersum, *Profit and Principle: Hugo Grotius, Natural Rights Theories and the Rise of Dutch Power in the East Indies (1595–1615)* (Amsterdam: Brill, 2006), 35.

4. *DJP*, 14, 538; Peter Borschberg, "The Seizure of the *Sta. Catarina* Revisited: The Portuguese Empire in Asia, VOC Politics and the Origins of the Dutch-Johor Alliance (1602–c.1616)," *Journal of Southeast Asian Studies* 33, no. 1 (February 2002): 35, 41–44; C. R. Boxer, *The Portuguese Seaborne Empire, 1415–1825* (New York: Alfred A. Knopf 1969), 205–27; Alexander Dean Hazlett, "The *Nau* of the *Livro Nautico:* Reconstructing a Sixteenth-Century Indiaman from Texts" (PhD diss., Texas A&M University, 2007), 4, 30. The Portuguese Chamber of Goa, writing to the king, described the *Santa Catarina* as "the richest and most powerful ship that ever left China." C. R. Boxer, *Portuguese Merchants and Missionaries in Feudal Japan, 1543–1640* (London: Variorum, 1986), 15.

5. *DJP*, 538.

6. Borschberg, "The Seizure of the *Sta. Catarina* Revisited," 47.

7. Robert Fruin, *De Jure Praedae Commentarius: An Unpublished Work of Hugo Grotius's*, trans. H. G. Hamaker (Clark, NJ: Lawbook Exchange, 2003), 18. The Dutch East India Company is commonly called the VOC after its Dutch name: Vereenigde Oost-Indische Compagnie.

8. Formally, the United Amsterdam Company was listed as plaintiff, as was the Advocat-Fiscal, representing Holland. See Verdict of the Amsterdam Admiralty Board, September 9, 1604, in *DJP*, 511.

9. Ibid. Van Heemskerck's sojourn to the East Indies in 1602–1603 is meticulously reconstructed by Martine van Ittersum in "Hugo Grotius in Context: Van Heemskerck's Capture of the 'Santa Catarina' and Its Justification in 'De Jure Praedae' (1604–1606)," *Asia Journal of Social Science* 31, no. 3 (2003).

10. *DJP*, 512.

11. Ibid.

12. Ibid.

13. Ibid., 513.

14. Ibid.

15. Ibid., 514.

16. Borschberg, "The Seizure of the *Sta. Catarina* Revisited," 37–41.

17. Richard Tuck, *The Rights of War and Peace: Political Thought and the International Order from Grotius to Kant* (Oxford: Oxford University Press, 1999), 80.

18. Borschberg, "The Seizure of the *Sta. Catarina* Revisited," 37–38. The surviving crew split 123,380 guilders. Ibid., 57. The States-General eschewed their share in the interest of promoting the Indian trade. Victor Enthoven, *Zeeland en de opkomst van de Republiek* (Leiden: Luctor et Victor, 1996), 208–9.

19. The verdict simply asserted that the capture was "permitted by natural law and *jus gentium* [i.e., the law of nations] and enjoined by the commission of his Princely Excellency" without ever attempting to justify these claims. Verdict of the Amsterdam Admiralty Board, 513; Van Ittersum, *Profit and Principle*, lv, 22–23.

20. See discussions in Fruin, *De Jure Praedae Commentarius: An Unpublished Work of Hugo Grotius's*, 32–36, and Van Ittersum, *Profit and Principle*, 119–22.

21. Van Ittersum, *Profit and Principle*, 24–26.

22. Hamilton Vreeland, Jr., *Hugo Grotius: The Father of the Modern Science of International Law* (New York: Oxford University Press, 1917), 9–10.

23. Caspar Brandt, *Historie van het Leven des Heeren Huig de Groot* (Dordrecht and Amsterdam: Van Braam and Onder, 1727), 7 ("*Fallor? an & talis noster Erasmus erat?*").

24. Ibid., 11 ("*Voy la le miracle d'Hollande! Ziet daer het Wonder van Hollandt!*"). The legend may indeed be a legend. Jean Lévesque de Burigny does not mention the accolade in his account of the meeting with Henry IV, though he does mention the gold pendant bearing Henry's portrait. See Jean Lévesque de Burigny, *Vie de Grotius*, Vol. 1 (Paris: Debure, 1752), 22. Much later de Burigny refers to the use of a similar epithet ("*le miracle, la gloire éternelle de la Hollande & de son siècle*") by Gérard Vossius. Jean Lévesque de Burigny, *Vie de Grotius*, Vol. 2 (Paris: Debure, 1752), 279–80. Grotius himself, in his account of his encounters with Henry IV, never mentions this compliment supposedly paid to him.

25. W. S. M. Knight, *The Life and Works of Hugo Grotius* (London: Sweet and Maxwell, 1925), 36–39. Knight suspects that Grotius bought the degree.

26. Ger Luijten and Ariane van Suchtelen, eds., *Dawn of the Golden Age: Northern Netherlandish Art, 1580–1620* (Amsterdam: Rijksmuseum, 1993), 398–99.

27. The artist commissioned Grotius to pen verses for a series of engravings when Grotius was only thirteen. Ibid., 399.

28. Vreeland, *Hugo Grotius*, 15 ("*[N]amque reliqui viri / Tandem fuere, Grotius vir natus est.*").

29. Ibid., 40.

30. Henk J. M. Nellen, *Hugo Grotius: A Lifelong Struggle for Peace in Church and State, 1583–1645*, trans. J. C. Grayson (Leiden: Brill, 2014), 66.

31. Ibid., 32–34; Christian Gellinek, "The Principal Sources to John Milton's *Paradise Lost*," *Grotiana* 7, no. 1 (1986):112–18. On the general influence of Grotius on Milton, see Philip Dust, "Milton's *Paradise Lost* and Grotius's *De Jure Belli Ac Pacis*," *Cithara: Essays in the Judeo-Christian Tradition* 33, no. 1 (November 1993): 17–26; Elizabeth Oldman, "Milton, Grotius, and the Law of War: A Reading of *Paradise Regained* and *Samson Agonistes*," *Studies in Philology* 104, no. 3 (2007): 340–75.

32. Vreeland, *Hugo Grotius*, 39–40.

33. Ibid., 43 (citing Brandt, *Historie van het Leven des Heeren Huig de Groot*, 23).

34. Knight, *The Life and Works of Hugo Grotius*, 191–92.

35. Ibid., 9.

36. *DJP*, xv.

37. Ibid., xvii.

38. From 1580 to 1640, Spain and Portugal were ruled by the same crown. Philip III of Spain, for example, was Philip II of Portugal. Despite this monarchical union, Portugal was largely independent of Spain; indeed, they were commercial competitors in the Indies. See Malyn Newitt, *A History of Portuguese Overseas Expansion, 1400–1668* (Oxford: Routledge, 2005), 174–75; and Peter Borschberg, *The Memoirs and Memories of Jacques de Coutre: Security, Trade, and Society in 17th Century Southeast Asia* (Singapore: National University of Singapore Press, 2015).

39. Van Ittersum, *Profit and Principle*, 54. Queen Elizabeth did not recognize the sovereignty of the Dutch Republic. Jonathan Israel, *The Dutch Republic: Its Rise, Greatness and Fall, 1477–1806* (Oxford: Clarendon Press, 1995), 301.

40. Private persons could attack enemy vessels if they had a special license called a letter of marque. Heemskerck had such a letter, but there were several technical problems with it. The first was that the letter of marque had come from a dubious source, Prince Maurice. Prince Maurice was the son of William of Orange, who led the Protestant revolt against the Spanish Empire in 1568. When William was assassinated in 1584, Maurice replaced his father as commander of the republic's rebellion against Spain. Maurice had authorized Van Heemskerck's letter of marque in his capacity as Lord High Admiral of Holland and Zeeland. It was unclear as a matter of international law whether Maurice had this power. Maurice was acting on behalf of the individual States of Holland and Zeeland, not the United Provinces, which represented the entire Dutch Republic. Moreover, the Dutch were insurgents and Maurice was their rebel

leader. No European nation recognized the independence of the Dutch Republic and hence accepted Maurice as a legitimate head of state. If Maurice did not have the sovereign power to issue a letter of marque, then Van Heemskerck was indeed a pirate. See Martin van Ittersum's introduction to Grotius, *Law of Prize and Booty*, xviii, xiii; Tuck, *Rights of War and Peace*, 80–81. Another, even more serious, problem was that the letter permitted Van Heemskerck to use force only in self-defense or for the reparation of any injuries he suffered. But the *Santa Catarina* was not the aggressor. Thus, even if Maurice's commission was a valid letter of marque, Van Heemskerck's forceful seizure of the *Santa Catarina* fell outside its terms. Van Ittersum, *Profit and Principle*, 22–23. Despite these technical flaws, Grotius did try to defend Van Heemskerck's action on the basis of the letter. But he did not lead with these arguments—his principal argument is in Chapter 12 of the manuscript, not Chapter 13, which contains his discussion of Van Heemskerck's letter.

41. *DJP*, 102–4.
42. Ibid., 50.
43. For an excellent collection of primary materials on just war theory, see Gregory Reichberg, Henrik Syse, and Endre Begby, eds., *The Ethics of War: Classic and Contemporary Readings* (Oxford: Blackwell, 2006). The label "just war theory" may be used in several different ways. Contemporary writers usually present it as an ethical theory about the conditions under which war may justly be waged (*jus ad bellum*), how it is to be waged (*jus in bello*), and how it should end (*jus post bellum*). See, e.g., Michael Walzer, *Just and Unjust Wars* (New York: Basic Books, 1977). But "just war theory" may also refer to a theological/religious account of when/how it is righteous/sinful to wage/end war, or as a legal theory as to when/how it is legally permissible/forbidden to wage/end war. In the text, we follow the contemporary usage.
44. Cicero, *De re publica*, *De legibus*, trans. C. W. Keyes (Cambridge: Loeb Classical Library, 2000), 3.35: ("Those wars are unjust which are undertaken without provocation. For only a war waged for revenge or defense can actually be just.") (*Illa iniusta bella sunt, quae sunt sine causa suscepta. Nam extra ulciscendi aut propulsandorum hostium causam bellum geri nullum potest.*); Augustine, *Quaestionum in Heptateuchum Libri Septem*, 6.10 ("Quomodo Deus praecipiat insidias fieri") ("But just wars are generally defined as those which avenge wrongs, if some nation or society has to be attacked in war as it either failed to make amends for a wrong done by its subjects, or to return something taken unjustly.") (*Iusta autem bella ea definiri solent, quae ulciscuntur iniurias, si qua gens vel civitas, quae bello petenda est, vel vindicare neglexerit quod a suis improbe factum est, vel reddere quod per iniurias ablatum est.*); Thomas Aquinas, *Summa Theologiae*, IIa – IIae, q. 40 a. 1 co. ("I respond that in order for any war to be called just . . . a just cause, that is that they who are attacked deserve the attack on account of some fault.") (*Respondeo dicendum quod ad hoc quod aliquod bellum sit iustum . . . requiritur causa iusta, ut scilicet illi qui impugnantur*

propter aliquam culpam impugnationem mereantur.); Francisco de Vitoria, *De Indis, Sive De Iure Belli Hispanorum in Barbaros, Relectio Posterior* 13 ("the unique and only just cause of waging war is having received a wrong. . . . Moreover, an offensive war is in order to avenge a wrong and turn against the enemy, as was said. But [things] cannot be avenged where guilt and wrong did not precede.") (*Unica est et sola causa iusta inferendi bellum, iniuria accepta. . . . Item bellum offensivum est ad vindicandum iniuriam et animadvertendum in hostes, ut dictum est. Sed vindicta esse non potest, ubi non praecessit culpa et iniuria.*); Francisco Suárez, *Disputatio XIII de Bello* 4.1 (in *Opera Omnia*, Vol. 12, Tractatus III) ("I therefore say first: no war can be just unless a legitimate and necessary cause underlies it. . . . This just and sufficient cause, in turn, is a grave wrong that was inflicted, which cannot be avenged or repayed in any other way.") (*Dico ergo primo: nullum potest esse iustum bellum, nisi subsit causa legitima et necessaria. . . . Rursus, causa haec iusta et sufficiens, est gravis iniuria illata, quae alia ratione vindicari aut reparari nequit.*); Isadore of Seville, *Etymologiarum* XVIII.1 ("A just war is one that is waged after public proclamation and concerns the recovery of property or [is waged] for the sake of repelling the enemy.") (*Iustum bellum est quod ex praedicto geritur de rebus repetitis aut propulsandorum hostium causa.*). There is some variation between these formulae. As Peter Haggenmacher has pointed out, Aquinas requires fault (*culpa*), in contrast to earlier writers, such as Augustine, who merely require wrongdoing (*iniuria*). Peter Haggenmacher, *Grotius et la doctrine de la Guerre Juste* (Paris: Presses Universitaires de France, 1983), 417–18.

45. *DJP*, 105.
46. Ibid., 103.
47. Ibid., 68, 180.
48. Ibid., 141.
49. Ibid., 302 ("Nature—the mistress and sovereign authority in this matter—withholds from no human being the right to carry on private wars.").
50. Ibid., 35–50.
51. Ibid., 137.
52. Ibid., 17.
53. Ibid., 18.
54. Ibid., 243.
55. Ibid.
56. Ibid., 259–60.
57. Ibid., 256, 258, 275.
58. Ibid., 284, 277.
59. Macao was a *fanfang* (foreigner's quarter) where the Portuguese lived; they did their business in Canton. See the detailed reconstruction of the Dutch expedition to Macao in Leonard Blussé, "Brief Encounter at Macao," *Modern Asia Studies* 22, no. 3 (1988): 647–64.
60. Ibid., 652.

61. *DJP,* 282. Compare with Van Heemskerck's letter to the Directors of the United Amsterdam Company, July 13, 1603, ibid., 531.

62. Ibid., 372–79.

63. Martine Julia van Ittersum, "Dating the Manuscript of *De Jure Praedae* (1604–1608): What Watermarks, Foliation and Quire Divisions Can Tell Us about Hugo Grotius' Development as a Natural Rights and Natural Law Theorist," *History of European Ideas* 35, no. 2 (2009): 125, 145–46. Van Ittersum was responding to the original work of Peter Borschberg. See Peter Borschberg, *Hugo Grotius, "Commentarius in Theses XI": An Early Treatise on Sovereignty, the Just War, and the Legitimacy of the Dutch Revolt* (Berne: Peter Lang, 1994).

64. Letter to G. M. Lingelsheim (November 1, 1606), in P. C. Molhuysen, ed., *Briefwisseling van Hugo Grotius,* Vol. 1 (The Hague: Martinus Nijhoff, 1928), 72, also available at http://grotius.huygens.knaw.nl/letters/0086/; Van Ittersum, "Dating the Manuscript of *De Jure Praedae,*" 130. The work now goes by *De Jure Praedae Commentarius,* usually translated as "Commentary on the Law of Prize and Booty," a name given in the middle of the nineteenth century by a bookseller, not its author. See Robert Fruin, *De Jure Praedae Commentarius: An Unpublished Work of Hugo Grotius's,* 3. (Fruin's essay was written in Dutch in 1868.)

65. In all likelihood, the company had figured out that it could weather the financial expense of war because its shareholders had nowhere else to go. It was a trading monopoly and Dutch merchants were a captive audience. See Van Ittersum, *Profit and Principle,* 188.

66. See also the Courts of Mixed Commission for the Abolition of the Slave Trade, which existed between 1819 and 1866, described in Jenny Martinez, *The Slave Trade and the Origins of International Human Rights Law* (New York: Oxford University Press, 2011).

67. See, e.g., American-Mexican Claims Commission described in Chapter Two.

68. Walter Ullmann, "The Medieval Papal Court as International Tribunal," *Virginia Journal for International Law* 11 (1971): 356–71.

69. The Qing Dynasty ruled from 1644, the Tokugawa Shogunate from 1603.

70. *The Digest* quotes Ulpian: "*Nemo plus iuris ad alium transferre potest, quam ipse habet*" ("No one can transfer greater rights to someone else than he possesses himself.") *The Digest of Justinian,* ed. Alan Watson, Vol. 4 (Philadelphia: University of Pennsylvania Press, 2011), 50.17.54, 474.

71. See, e.g., *DJB,* 2.10.1.2–3. The common law had a less severe rule, which allowed good faith purchasers to acquire ownership when bought in an open market (*market overt*). See Peter M. Smith, "Valediction to Market Overt," *The American Journal of Legal History* 41, no. 2 (April 1997): 225–49.

72. Charter of the Dutch West India Company, June 3, 1621, Art. II in Francis Newton Thorpe, ed., *The Federal and State Constitutions, Colonial Charters, and Other Organic Laws of the States, Territories, and Colonies Now or Heretofore Forming the United States of America* (Washington, DC: Government Printing Office, 1909).

73. Borschberg, "The Seizure of the *Sta. Catarina* Revisited," 37–38.

74. Van Ittersum, *Profit and Principle*, 207, 218–19 n. 28.

75. For the armor, see www.flickr.com/photos/roelipilami/2047595350/in/photo
stream/.

76. *The Poetry of Hugo Grotius*, B. L. Meulenbroek, A. Eyffinger, and E. Rabbie,
eds., 375–91 (Assen, The Netherlands: Van Gorcum, 1970).

77. Ibid, 384.

78. The next three paragraphs rely on Van Ittersum, *Profit and Principle*, 177, 191–
95, 325–30, 345.

79. Spain did not actually recognize Dutch independence, but agreed to treat the
republic as if it were independent. See Israel, *Dutch Republic*, 405; Beatrix C. M.
Jacobs, "The United Provinces: 'Free' or 'Free and Sovereign'?," in Randall
Lesaffer, ed., *The Twelve Years Truce (1609): Peace, Truce, War, and Law in the Low
Countries at the Turn of the 17th Century* (Leiden: Martinus Nijhoff/Brill, 2014),
181-95.

80. Grotius's *The Free Sea* played no role in the negotiations: It was published just
a week or two after the truce was signed. See Martine Julia van Ittersum, "Preparing *Mare Liberum* for the Press: Hugo Grotius' Rewriting of Chapter 12 of
De iure praedae in November–December 1608," *Grotiana* 26, no. 1 (2007): 256.

81. Van Ittersum, *Profit and Principle*, 359–483

82. Ibid., xxi.

83. Archbishop Abbot to Sir Ralph Winwood, June 1, 1613, in *Memorials of affairs
of state in the reigns of Q. Elizabeth and K. James I.*, Vol. 3, ed. Edmund Sawyer
(London: T. Ward, 1725), 459.

84. Ibid.

85. Ibid.

86. See Nellen, *Hugo Grotius*, 95, 167–68, 204.

87. Ibid., 134–35.

88. Ibid., 281–84; C. G. Roelofsen, "Grotius and the Development of International
Relations Theory: 'The Long Seventeenth Century' and the Elaboration of a
European States System," *Quinnipiac Law Review* 17, no. 1 (Spring 1997): 44.

89. For how Grotius spent his imprisonment, see Hamilton Vreeland, *Hugo Grotius*, 124–29; and R. W. Lee, "The Family Life of Grotius," *Transactions of the
Grotius Society* 20 (1934): 13–14.

90. On Grotius's library, see Edwin Rabbie, "The History and Reconstruction of
Hugo Grotius' Library: A Survey of the Results of Former Studies with an
Indication of New Lines of Approach," in *Bibliothecae Selectae da Cusano a Leo-
pardi*, ed. Eugenio Canone (Firenze: Leo S. Olschki, 1993): 119–38.

91. Nellen, *Hugo Grotius*, 304–5.

92. For Grotius's escape, see Knight, *The Life and Work of Hugo Grotius*, 162–63;
Vreeland, *Hugo Grotius*, 121–49.

93. Jesse S. Reeves, "The First Edition of Grotius's De Iure Belli ac Pacis, 1625,"
American Journal of International Law 19, no. 1 (1925): 12–22.

94. Jesse S. Reeves, "Grotius, De Jure Belli ac Pacis: A Bibliographical Account," *American Journal of International Law* 19, no. 1 (1925), 251, 261–62.

95. As Haggenmacher cautioned, "the overall logic of the treatise does not fit into the mould of international law as it crystallized in its classical dimensions a century after the Westphalian peace settlement. Grotius' book essentially contains a theory of just war." Peter Haggenmacher, "On Assessing the Grotian Heritage" in *International Law and the Grotian Heritage*, ed. T.M.C. Assar Instituut (The Hague: T.M.C. Assar Instituut, 1985), 152.

96. Pufendorf referred to the author of *The Law of War and Peace* as "the incomparable Hugo Grotius" who "set out to construct a work wherein he was not ruled by the influence of his predecessors." Samuel Pufendorf, *Eris Scandica: und andere polemische Schriften über das Naturrecht*, Vol. 5, ed. Fiammatta Palladini (Berlin: Akademie Verlag, 2002), 126. His translator Jean Barbeyrac credited Grotius with raising "the Science of Morality . . . again from the Dead." Jean Barbeyrac, "An Historical and Critical Account of the Science of Morality," in Samuel Pufendorf, *Of the Law of Nature and Nations*, 4th ed., trans. Basil Kennett (London, 1729), 78. Barbeyrac credited Francis Bacon as well.

97. *DJB*, 2.2.2.1.

98. Ibid., 2.11.1.4.

99. See, e.g., Ibid., 2.15.8 and 2.2.24. For commercial treaties concluded between agents of the Dutch East India Company in the name of the States General and East Indian nations, see Treaty between Admiral Cornelis Matelieff de Jonge and King of Johor, May 17, 1606, in Peter Borschberg, *Journal, Memorials and Letter of Cornelis Matelieff de Jonge: Security, Diplomacy and Commerce in 17th-Century Southeast Asia*, ed. Peter Borschberg (Singapore: NUS Press, 2015), 158–59, and treaty between same parties signed on September 23, 1606, which incorporated the May agreement by reference, ibid. 160; Treaty between Vice-Admiral Olivier de Vivere and Ali Ri'ayat Shah of Aceh, January 17, 1607, ibid., 397–99; Treaty between Admiral Matelieff and Sultan Modafar of Ternate and his Council, May 26, 1607, ibid., 421–24; Treaty between Samuel Bloemaert with Sebau Tangan Pangeran Adipati of Sambas, October 1, 1609, ibid., 446–48; Van Ittersum, *Profit and Principle*, 267–70. For a discussion of how Grotius used such treaties to advocate for the interests of the Dutch East India Company, see ibid., 359–483.

100. Quoted in G. N. Clark and Jonkheer W. J. M. Van Eysinga, eds., *Bibliotheca Visseriana: Dissertationum Ius Internationium Illustrantium*, Vol. 17 (Leiden: Brill, 1951), 73.

101. *DJB*, 2.1.2.1.

102. Ibid., 3.9.4.2 (emphasis added).

103. Ibid., 3.6.2.1.

104. Ibid., 3.9.4.3.

105. Roman law had *implicitly* accepted the Might is Right Principle by conferring

rights to seizures without distinguishing between just and unjust wars. *Digest* 41.1.5.7: *Item quae ex hostibus capiuntur, jure gentium statim capientium fiunt* ("Likewise, anything which is taken from the enemy immediately becomes by the Law of Nations the property of him who takes it."); *Digest* 49.15.5 and 49.15.19, *Institutes of Justinian*, 1.12.5.

106. Raphael Fulgosius, *In primum Pandectarum partem Commentaria*, ad Dig., 1, 1, 5 (Lyon, 1554), trans. Robert Andrews and Peter Haggenmacher, in Gregory Reichber, *The Ethics of War*, 228–29. See Haggenmacher, *Grotius et la doctrine de la Guerre Juste*, 203–6, 284–86.

107. See Balthazar Ayala, *De Jure et Officiis Bellicis et Disciplina Militari Libri III*, ed. John Westlake, trans. John Pawley Bate, 2 vols. (Washington, DC: Carnegie Institution of U.S.A, 1912), 1.2.34.

108. Victor Hugo, *Les Miserables*, Vol. 2, Bk. 1, Ch. 19.

109. *Oxford English Dictionary*, entry for "Robe" ("Germanic base of Rob, v., the original sense being 'booty,' [hence] clothes regarded as booty.").

110. John Lynn, "How War Fed War: The Tax of Violence and Contributions During the Grand Siecle," *Journal of Modern History* 65, no. 2 (June 1993): 286, 290 ("Abuse did not simply undermine the system; abuse was the system."). For the laws of booty, see Fritz Redlich, *De Praeda Militari: Looting and Booty, 1500–1815* (Wiesbaden: F. Steiner, 1956).

111. *DJP*, 179–80. Grotius agreed with the "exceedingly learned jurist, Fulgosius" because he did not interpret him literally, but disagreed with the "Spaniard Ayala" whom he did interpret literally, though Ayala made it clear in his treatise that he was simply concurring with Fulgosius.

112. Ibid., 180.

113. Grotius's "good faith" exception would not have solved the problem of clean title because merchants would always wonder whether the property seized in war had been seized in good faith.

114. *DJB*, 3.4.4.

115. Ibid, 1.3.4.

116. Nellen, *Hugo Grotius*, 730–34.

117. Samuel Pufendorf, *De jure naturae et gentium libri octo*, 8.6.17 (1688).

118. Emer de Vattel, *The Law of Nations; or, Principles of the Law of Nature, Applied to the Conduct and Affairs of Nations and Sovereigns*, trans. Joseph Chitty (Philadelphia: T & J. W. Johnson & Co., Law Booksellers, 1867 [1758]), 4.4.47.

119. Richard Tuck, "Introduction" in *De Jure Belli ac Pacis* (Indianapolis: Liberty Fund, 2005), xi.

120. James Madison, "Examination of the British Doctrine, Which Subjects to Capture a Neutral Trade Not Open in Time of Peace," in *Letters and Other Writings of James Madison*, Vol. 2, 1794–1815, (Philadelphia: J. B. Lippincott, 1865), 230, 234.

121. John Adams to Thomas Boylston, Washington, DC, January 2, 1801, Adams Papers, reel 4000, cited in and quoted by Richard Samuelson, "The Midnight

Appointments," The White House Historical Association, www.whitehouse history.orge/08/subs/08_b07.html; Charles M. Witlse, "Thomas Jefferson on the Law of Nations," *American Journal of International Law* 29, no. 1 (January 1935): 66–81.

122. Some scholars challenge this attribution. See, e.g., the critiques by Thomas Holland, *Studies in International Law* (Oxford: Clarendon Press, 1898), 1–39; James Brown Scott, *The Spanish Origin of International Law: Francisco de Vitoria and His Law of Nations* (Oxford: Clarendon Press, 1934); and Fruin, *De Jure Praedae Commentarius: An Unpublished Work of Hugo Grotius's*, 60–61.

123. Daniel Patrick Moynihan, *On the Law of Nations* (Cambridge: Harvard University Press, 1990), 7.

124. The classic discussion of Grotius's scholarly influences and antecedents is Haggenmacher, *Grotius et la doctrine de la Guerre Juste*. See also Benedict Kingbury, Hedley Bull, and Adam Roberts, eds., *Hugo Grotius and International Relations* (Oxford: Clarendon Press, 1990); and Hans Blom, ed., *Property, Piracy and Punishment: Hugo Grotius on War and Booty in De iure Praedae* (Leiden: Brill, 2009).

125. *DJP*, 136–37; *DJB*, 1.2.1.4–5 and 1.2.2.1.

126. *DJP*, Prolegomena sec. 15; *DJB*, 1.3.8.2. By defending the right of private war, Grotius was reaffirming an older legal tradition that accorded nobles, not just sovereigns, the right to resort to arms. By contrast to this tradition, however, Grotius affirmed every individual's right to defend himself and his property, not simply the nobility.

127. See, e.g., Arthur O. Lovejoy, *The Great Chain of Being: A Study of the History of an Idea* (Cambridge: Harvard University Press, 1936). Compare the recent discussion of Larry Seidentrop, *Inventing the Individual: The Origins of Western Liberalism* (Cambridge: Harvard University Press, 2014), who locates the origins of individualism much earlier with the rise of Christianity.

128. *DJB*, Prolegomena sec. 16.

TWO: MANIFESTOS OF WAR

1. Edmund Wilson, *Patriotic Gore: Studies in the Literature of the American Civil War* (New York: Oxford University Press, 1962), xi.

2. Ward McAfee, "A Reconsideration of the Origins of the Mexican-American War," *Southern California Quarterly* 62, no. 1 (1980): 49. McAfee offers commentary on standard historical narratives of President Polk.

3. Darryl Dee, *Expansion and Crisis in Louis XIV's France: Franche-Comté and Absolute Monarchy, 1674–1715* (Rochester, NY: University of Rochester Press, 2009), 3–4; François Crouzet, "The Second Hundred Years War: Some Reflections," *French History* 10, no. 4 (1996): 432–33.

4. Reed Browning, *The War of the Austrian Succession* (Stroud and New York: St. Martin's Press, 1993), 32; H. M. Scott, *The Emergence of the Eastern Powers, 1756–1775* (Cambridge: Cambridge University Press, 2001), 23–25.

5. Extract from letter No. 1 of Mr. Clay to Mr. Poinsett, appointed Envoy

Extraordinary and Minister Plenipotentiary of the United States to Mexico, dated Department of State, March 25, 1825, American State Papers Foreign Relations, 1:580. H. Doc. No. 42, 25th Cong., 1st Sess., 8–10 (1837). The principal American strategy was to buy the territory. In 1825 and 1827, John Quincy Adams authorized the purchase of portions of Texas. MSS Archives, Department of State, Instructions to Agents in Mexico, Vol. 15, 53–54. In 1835, Andrew Jackson authorized the purchase of Texas and a large portion of California. H. Doc. No. 351, 25th Cong., 2nd Sess., Vol. 12 (1838).

6. Matias Romero, *Mexico and the United States. A study of subjects affecting their political, commercial and social relations, made with a view to their promotion* (New York: G. P. Putnam, 1898), 374–76; Clayton Charles Kohl, *Claims as a Cause of the Mexican War* (New York: The Faculty of the Graduate School, New York University, 1914), vii–viii. Although Romero provides a list of the regimes, it's uncertain how Kohl counted the repeat administrations, substitutes, *ad interim*, and shared presidencies to calculate the thirty-five total.

7. H. Doc. No. 105, 24th Cong., 2nd Sess., Vol. 3, 24–27 (1838); H. Doc. No. 3, 25th Cong., 2nd Sess., Vol. 1, 40–108 (1837).

8. H. Doc. No. 3, 25th Cong., 2nd Sess., Vol. 1, 109 (1837).

9. Kohl, *Claims as a Cause of the Mexican War*, Appendix.

10. Andrew Jackson, Special Message to Congress, February 6, 1837 ("The length of time since some of the injuries have been committed, the repeated and unavailing applications for redress, the wanton character of some of the outrages upon the property and persons of our citizens, upon the officers and flag of the United States, independent of recent insults to this Government and people by the late extraordinary Mexican minister, would justify in the eyes of all nations immediate war."); Martin van Buren, "First Annual Message," Speech to the Congress of the United States, December 5, 1837.

11. Convention for the Adjustment of Claims of Citizens of the United States Against Mexico, concluded April 11, 1839, ratifications exchanged at Washington April 7, 1840, proclaimed April 8, 1840. For an excellent discussion of the arbitration proceedings between Mexico and the United States, see Kohl, *Claims as a Cause of the Mexican War*, 30–4.

12. Convention for the Adjustment of Claims of Citizens of the United States Against Mexico, art. VII, 1840; Kohl, *Claims as a Cause of the Mexican War*, 33.

13. S. Doc. No. 320, 27th Congress, 2nd Session, Vol. 4, 209–55 (1842). For a commentary on the failure to review all of the claims, see John Bassett Moore, *History and Digest of the International Arbitrations to Which the United States Has Been a Part*, Vol. 2 (Washington, DC: Government Printing Office, 1898), 1244–48. The arbitrators rejected eight on the merits and ten for want of jurisdiction. In total, they accepted the validity of two thirds of the claims considered.

14. Daniel Webster, *The Letters of Daniel Webster: From Documents Owned Principally by the New Hampshire Historical Society*, ed. Claude Halstead Van Tyne (New York: McClure, Phillips & Company, 1902), 269–70.

15. Convention Further Providing for Payment of Awards to Claimants under Convention of April 11, 1839, concluded January 30, 1843, ratifications exchanged at Washington March 29, 1843, proclaimed March 30, 1843.

16. Kohl, *Claims as a Cause of the Mexican War*, 54–56.

17. James Buchanan to John Slidell, November 10, 1854, in S. Doc. No. 52, 30th Congress, 1st Session, 78–79; James K. Polk, *The Diary of James K. Polk During His Presidency, 1845 to 1849*, Vol. 6, ed. Milo Milton Quaife (Chicago: A. C. McClurg & Co., 1910), 33–35 (entry from September 16, 1845).

18. Kohl, *Claims as a Cause of the Mexican War*, 66.

19. James K. Polk, "A special message calling for a declaration of war against Mexico," Speech to the Congress of the United States, Washington, DC, May 11, 1846.

20. Ibid.

21. Ibid.

22. Polk recounted that after war was declared, he explained to James Buchanan, his secretary of state, that "though we had not gone to war for conquest, yet it was clear that in making peace we would if practicable obtain California and such other portion of the Mexican territory as would be sufficient to indemnify our claimants on Mexico, and to defray the expenses of the war which that power by her long continued wrongs and injuries had forced us to wage." Polk, *The Diary of James K. Polk During His Presidency*, 397 (entry from May 13, 1846).

23. U.S. Congress and Thomas Hart Benton, *Abridgement of the Debates of Congress, from 1789 to 1856*, Vol. 15 (New York: D. Appleton & Company, 1861), 506.

24. Kohl, *Claims as a Cause of the Mexican War*, 72.

25. James Polk, "Second Annual Message," Speech to the Congress of the United States, Washington, DC, December 8, 1846.

26. James Polk, "Third Annual Message," Speech to the Congress of the United States, Washington, DC, December 7, 1847. This was not the first time Mexico and the United States had contemplated going to war over such claims. See, e.g., A Treaty of Amity, Commerce, and Navigation, between the United States of America and the United Mexican States, Art. 34, Sec. 3, April 5, 1831.

27. Waging war to collect debts was prohibited in the Hague Convention II of 1907 in *The Hague conventions of 1899 (I) and 1907 (I) for the pacific settlement of international disputes* (Washington, DC: The Carnegie Endowment for International Peace, 1915). Article I states: "The Contracting Powers agree not to have recourse to armed force for the recovery of contract debts claimed from the Government of one country by the Government of another country as being due to its nationals." However, war could still be waged if the "debtor State refuses or neglects to reply to an offer of arbitration, or, after accepting the offer, prevents any compromise from being agreed on, or, after the arbitration, fails to submit to the award."

28. Frederick the Great also justified his invasion of Silesia on the basis of legal

right. See "Rescript, welches Ihro Königl. Maytt. von Preussen an Dero Ministrum zu Regensburg, den Geheimten Justitz-Rath von Pollmann ergehen lassen. Anno 1741" in Reinhold Koser, ed., *Preussische Staatsschriften aus der Regierungszeit König Friedrichs II (1740–1745)* (Berlin: Verlag von Alexander Duncker, 1877), 89: "since we are dealing with the *House of Austria, which refuses to recognize any judge in the Empire, and from whom we can expect no justice*, we have no choice but to present our case and vindicate our rights by those means, which Nature and the Right of Peoples place in the hands of Potentates, who have no judges, and who must deal with each other *Prince à Prince aequaliter* [which is to say, as sovereign equals]" (translated by Jacob Bennett).

29. *DJB*, 3.3.5-14.
30. See generally Alan Watson, *International Law in Archaic Rome* (Baltimore: Johns Hopkins University Press, 1993).
31. Livy, *Ab Urbe Condita*, 1.32. According to Dionysius of Halicarnassus, the fetial priest would return in thirty days. See *Antiquitates Romanae*, 2.72.8.
32. Servius, *In Vergilii Aenid on libri*, 9.52.
33. See Brian Simpson, "The Agincourt Campaign and the Law of War: review of Henry's Wars and Shakespeare's Laws: Perspectives on the Law of War in the Later Middle Ages, by T. Meron," *Michigan Journal of International Law* 16, no. 3 (1995): 653–66.
34. M. H. Keen, *The Laws of War in the Late Middle Ages* (London: Routledge & K. Paul, 1965), 195.
35. Randall Lesaffer, "Defensive Warfare, Prevention and Hegemony: The Justifications for the Franco-Spanish War of 1635 (Part I)," *Journal of the History of International Law* 8 (2006): 91–93.
36. See, e.g., Emer de Vattel, *The Law of Nations; or, Principles of the Law of Nature, Applied to the Conduct and Affairs of Nations and Sovereigns*, trans. Joseph Chitty (Philadelphia: T & J. W. Johnson & Co., Law Booksellers, 1867 [1758]), 3.4.58.
37. Lesaffer, "Defensive Warfare, Prevention and Hegemony," 92.
38. William Shakespeare, *Henry V*, Act 2, Scene 4, 77–105; Theodor Meron, "Shakespeare's Henry the Fifth and the Law of War," *The American Journal of International Law* 86, no. 1 (1992): 1–45.
39. See, e.g., Vattel, *The Law of Nations*, 3.4.52, 55, and 64; Henry Wheaton, *Elements of International Law: With a Sketch of the History of the Science* (Philadelphia: Carey, Lea & Blanchard, 1836), 213.
40. John Milton, "A Manifesto of the Lord Protector of the Commonwealth of England, Scotland, Ireland &c.," in *The Prose Works of John Milton*, Vol. 2, ed. R.W. Griswold (Philadelphia: Herman Hooker, 1845), 464–76.
41. *Contra falsas francor(um) litteras 1491 pro defensione honoris serenissimi Roman(orum) Regis semper Augusti* (Augsburg, 1492).
42. Ibid., 2r. ("*Cum nemo sit qui nesciat francos gallos. . . .*").
43. Mantegna to Francesco II Gonzaga, Margrave of Mantua, October 12, 1494, in *Carteggio inedito d'artisti dei secoli XIV, XV, XVI*, eds. Giovanni Gaye et al.

(Florence: Presso Giuseppe Molini: 1839), 326–27 (translated by William Holste). For a similar description of Charles, see Samuele Romanin, *Storia documentata di Venezia*, Vol. 5 (Venice: Tipografia di Pietro Naratovich, 1856), 13.

44. Ibid. (*"magis semper proditionibus que justi belli potentia aut strenuitate uti solitos: verum etiam varia fictaque mendatia et litteris et nunciis passim vulgare sollere: quibus suas versutas ac perfidas proditiones ob umbrent: et credulum vulgus inanibus suis nugis atque jactantiis pascant. . . ."*).

45. Ibid., 5r. (*"At quis hoc tantum scelus ullo jure dispenset, quod ab omni natura tam alienum est ut nec illius exemplum nec vocabulum proprium habeamus? Qui enim soceri filiam uxoremque detineat, hic et fornicatoris et stupratoris et adulteri et incesti et cujusvis libidinosi nomen vincit ac superat."*) ("But who commits a crime so great with any right, which is so alien from all nature that we have neither an example nor a proper word for it? For one who detains the daughter and wife of his father-in-law, this one conquers and surpasses the name of the fornicator and of the rapist and of the adulterer and of the incestuous and of whosoever libidinous.").

46. The House Committee on Foreign Relations, *"Report, or manifesto of the causes and reasons of war with Great Britain: presented to the House of Representatives by the Committee of Foreign Relations"* (Washington, DC: A. & G. Way, Printers, 1812). Often, these claims would be repeated, modified, or amplified in the State of the Union addresses. For a compilation of these messages and addresses, see *Call to Arms*, ed. Russell Buhite (Wilmington: Scholarly Resources, 2003). Polk's message to Congress in 1846 regarding the outbreak of hostilities on the Texas border, for example, was understood to be a war manifesto. Statement of Senator Cass, *Congressional Globe* (May 11, 1846), 785 ("The message is evidently intended to be a species of manifesto.").

47. Vattel, *The Law of Nations*, 3.4.64. See, e.g., Louis XIV's manifesto for the Nine Years War in 1688 entitled: "The Memorial of the Reasons By which the King is obliged to resume his Arms, and which ought to persuade all Christendom of the sincere Intentions of his Majesty for the Establishment of the Public Tranquillity." Manifestos were often translated into numerous languages. The Milton manifesto was written in Latin and published in English, Dutch, German, French, and Spanish. The manifesto that Gustavus Adolphus used to justify Swedish intervention in the Thirty Years War was distributed in five languages (Swedish, Latin, German, French, and English) and in twenty-three editions (alternate versions were addressed to the concerns of different circles of readers). Peter Wilson, *The Thirty Years War: Europe's Tragedy* (Cambridge: Belknap Press of Harvard University, 2009), 462. For the role of pretext in the law of war, see James Whitman, *The Verdict of Battle* (Cambridge: Harvard University Press, 2012), 125–31.

48. "Message from his Majesty to both Houses of Parliament, May 25, 1790; relative to the capture of certain Vessels, by the Spaniards, in Nootka Sound," reprinted Edmund Burke, *The Annual Register, Or a View of the History, Politics, and Literature, For the Year 1790* (London: J. Dodsley, 1793), 285–86.

49. See the Spanish and British memorials published in *The Annual Register*, 294–300. The Spanish court knew that the letters would be published by the British. As a result, we consider the letters to have been intended for publication, meeting the publication requirement for our definition of manifestos.

50. *The Answer of the States Generall of the United Provinces of the Low Countries to the Declaration of Warr of the King of Great Brittain* (Hague 1674), 12, 18. See also Mexican counter-manifesto to Polk's declaration of war. Dripping with sarcasm, the counter-manifesto stated Mexico's intention to resist "that liberty, peace, and abundance" that the United States had brought to the Indians and "that democracy" that the United States brought to the "people of color." Interim President Mariano Paredes y Arrillaga, *Manifiesto del Exmo. Sr. Presidente Interino de la República Mexicana* (Mexico City, July 26, 1846), 16. ("*Sí, la libertad, la paz y la abundancia que han llevado a las tribus indígenas, precisándolas a vivir errantes: la democracia de que goza la gente de color en los Estados Unidos, privada de todo derecho civil y político y excluida de todos los actos públicos, aún los religiosos.*") (translated by William Holste).

51. "The Letter of King Edward to the Nobles and Commons of France, February 8, 1340, in John Foxe, *The Acts and Monuments of John Foxe*, Vol. 2, ed. Stephen Reed Cattley (London: Seeley and Burnside, 1837), 674–75.

52. Even so, the posting of manifestos in public places continued for centuries. See, e.g., *Ordonnance du Roy, portant Declaration de Guerre contre l'Empereur, l'Angleterre, les États Generaux des Provinces-Unies, & leurs Alliez* (Paris: Frederic Leonard, July 3, 1702). Oona Hathaway, William Holste, Scott Shapiro, Jacqueline Van De Velde, and Lisa Wang, "Just Causes of War: Evidence from War Manifestos" (unpublished manuscript, 2017). Much of the discussion of manifestos in this chapter draws on this work.

53. *Declaration of War on Spain of 1719, With a Manifesto, containing the Reasons, and a Postscript of an intercepted LETTER from Cardinal Alberoni to the Prince de Cellamare* (London: A. Bell, 1719). At the bottom of the title page, the manifesto reads "(Price 6d)"—"d" being the abbreviation for "penny."

54. Hathaway et al., "Just Causes of War."

55. Gottfried Wilhelm Leibniz, *Leibniz: Political Writings*, trans. Patrick Riley (Cambridge: Cambridge University Press 1972), 149.

56. Geoffrey Symcox, *War, Diplomacy and Imperialism, 1618–1763* (New York: Walker, 1974), 102. See also Pärtel Piirimäe, "Just War in Theory and Practice: The Legitimation of Swedish Intervention in the Thirty Years War," *The Historical Journal* 45, no. 3 (Septermber 2002): 499–523.

57. See, e.g, Anuschka Tischer, *Offizielle Kriegsbegründungen in der Frühen Neuzeit: Herrscherkommunikation in Europa zwischen Souveränität und korporativem Selbstverständnis* (Münster: LIT Verlag, 2012). Tischer drew upon the work of Henrich Repgen. Konrad Repgen, "Kriegslegitimationen in Alteuropa: Entwurf einer historischen Typologie," in *Schriften des Historischen Kollegs, Vorträge* 9

(1985): 5–27. See also Bernd Klesmann, *Bellum Solemne: Formen und Funktionen europäischer Kriegserklärungen des 17. Jahrhunderts* (Mainz: Philipp von Zabern Verlag, 2007). Jim Whitman describes Frederick's war manifestos for the invasion of Silesia in Whitman, *Verdict of Battle*, 130–31.

58. Hathaway et al., "Just Causes of War."

59. Ibid.

60. For a discussion of humanitarian intervention in the nineteenth and early twentieth centuries, see Gary Bass, *Freedom's Battle: The Origins of Humanitarian Intervention* (New York: Alfred A. Knopf, 2008).

61. John Milton, *The Works: Historical, Political, and Miscellaneous. To which is Prefixed, An Account of His Life and Writings. In Two Volumes*, vol. 2 (London: Millar, 1753), 263.

62. Theodore Roosevelt, "Fourth Annual Message," Speech to the Congress of the United States, Washington, DC, December 6, 1904, accessed January 31, 2016, http://www.ourdocuments.gov/print_friendly.php?page=transcript&doc=56&title=Transcript+of+Theodore+Roosevelt%27s+Corollary+to+the+Monroe+Doctrine+(1905).

63. Benjamin Franklin remarked that Vattel's book had "been continually in the hands of the members of our Congress now sitting." Francis Wharton, *The Revolutionary Diplomatic Correspondence of the United States*, Vol. 2 (Washington, DC: U.S. Government Printing Office, 1889), 64; see also Ch. 4 (discussing Jefferson's reliance on Vattel).

64. Vattel, *The Law of Nations*, 2.12.164, 3.3.26

65. *The Records of the Federal Convention of 1787*, Max Farrand ed., Vol. 1 (Norwood, MA: The Plimton Press, 1911), 316. Moreover, in advocating for the adoption of the Constitution, John Jay observed that "[t]he just causes of war, for the most part, arise either from violations of treaties or from direct violence." The new national government, he argued, would be better able to avoid giving such just causes than would the thirteen states operating separately. *The Federalist*, No. 3 (John Jay).

66. U.S. Constitution, Art. 4, Sec. 2.

67. See Oona A. Hathaway and Scott J. Shapiro, "Outcasting: Enforcement in Domestic and International Law," *Yale Law Journal* 121 (2011): 253–349.

68. Jerome, Letter CXXVII to Principia 12, quoted in Girolamo Arnaldi, *Italy and Its Invaders*, trans. Antony Shugaar (Cambridge: Harvard University Press, 2005), 4.

69. In order to conquer territory, the conqueror had to control the territory in a meaningful way. Grotius required that the conquered land be defended with permanent fortifications. He illustrated the invalidity of paper conquests with the story of Hannibal's approach to Rome. Hannibal's hold on the territory outside the city walls was so weak, Grotius claimed, that the land he occupied sold for the same price before his arrival as after. *DJB*, 3.6.4.1

70. Whether they could afford to keep the territory is another matter. On the

subject of imperial overextension, see Paul Kennedy, *The Rise and Fall of Great Powers* (New York: Random House, 1989).

71. *DJB*, 3.8.4.1; Vattel, *The Law of Nations*, 3.13.199.

72. Anthony Disney, *Twilight of the Pepper Empire: Portuguese Trade in Southwest India in the Early Seventeenth Century* (Cambridge: Harvard University Press, 1978), 71–72.

73. Doris Graber, *The Development of the Law of Belligerent Occupation: 1863–1914* (New York: Columbia University Press, 1949), 37.

74. Conquest also differs from debellation (in Latin, *debellatio)*. In a debellation, the defeat is so total that one side loses the ability to govern and defend itself—*bellum* means "war" in Latin, so a side is debellated when it is completely vanquished in war. In a conquest, one state seizes territory from another; in a debellation, one state *destroys* another. On debellation, see Ernst Feilchenfeld, *The International Economic Law of Belligerent Occupation* (Washington, DC: Carnegie Endowment for International Peace, 1942); Eyal Benvenisti, *The International Law of Occupation*, 2nd ed. (Oxford: Oxford University Press, 2012), 161–64.

75. *DJB*, 3.20.49.2. Germany and Japan accepted unconditional surrender in 1945.

76. Xenophon, *Cyropaedia: The Education of Cyrus*, trans. Henry Graham Dakyns (London: J. M. Dent & Sons, 1914), 240.

77. The term "international law" was coined by the lawyer and philosopher Jeremy Bentham in 1780. Jeremy Bentham, *An Introduction to the Principles of Morals and Legislation*, eds. J. H. Burns and H. L. A. Hart (London: Athlone Press, 1970), 296 and n. x ("The word *international*, it must be acknowledged, is a new one").

78. *DJB*, 2.22.8.

79. Ibid., 2.22.12.

80. Ibid., 2.22.9.

81. Bartolomé de las Casas, *A Short Account of the Destruction of the Indies*, trans. Nigel Griffin (London: Penguin, 1992).

82. On the Spanish Crown's acceptance of the humanitarian argument, see Tuck, *The Rights of War and Peace*, 72–75; Introduction by Anthony Pagden to Vitoria, *Vitoria: Political Writings*, eds. Anthony Pagden and Jeremy Lawrance (Cambridge: Cambridge University Press, 1991), xxvii. The original justifications for the Spanish conquest derived from papal donation and the natural slavery of Indians. Vitoria delegitimized these arguments in his "On the American Indians," in Vitoria, *Political Writings*, Question 1 and Question 2, Article 2. For extended discussion of these arguments, see Anthony Pagden, *The Fall of Natural Man: The American Indian and the Origins of Comparative Ethnology* (Cambridge: Cambridge University Press, 1986); Hugh Thomas, *The Golden Age of Charles V* (London: Allen Lane, 2010).

83. Vitoria, "On the American Indians" Question 3, Article 5; Francisco de Vitoria, "On Dietary Laws, or Self-Restraint" in Vitoria, *Political Writings*, Question 1, Article 5, Fifth Conclusion. Vitoria specified that humanitarian intervention did

not automatically sanction conquest, but added that "if there is no other method of ensuring safety except by setting up Christian princes over them, this too will be lawful, as far as necessary to secure that end." Francisco de Vitoria, "On Dietary Laws, or Self-Restraint" Question 1, Article 5, Sixth Conclusion.

84. Alberico Gentili, *De Jure Belli Libri Tres*, trans. John C. Rolfe (Oxford: Clarendon Press, 1933), 1.25.198.

85. *DJB*, 2.20.3.

86. *Johnson v. M'Intosh*, 21 U.S. 543, 588 (1823) (emphasis added).

87. Ibid.

88. Ibid., 574.

89. Thomas Jefferson, *A Summary View of the Rights of British America* (Williamsburg, VA: Clementina Rind, 1774), 6.

90. Joel N. Eno, "The Puritans and the Indian Lands," *The Magazine of History: With Notes and Queries*, 3 (1906), 274–75.

91. Yasuhide Kawashima, *Puritan Justice and the Indian: White Man's Law in Massachusetts, 1630–1763* (Middletown, CT: Wesleyan University Press, 1986), 51.

92. Eric Kades, "History and Interpretation of the Great Case of Johnson v. M'Intosh," *Law and History Review* 19, no. 1 (2001): 74.

93. Felix S. Cohen, "Original Indian Title," *Minnesota Law Review* 32 (1947), 36, 45–46.

94. Ibid., 37n. 20.

95. Stuart Banner, *How the Indians Lost Their Land: Law and Power on the Frontier* (Cambridge: Harvard University Press, 2005), 239.

96. Van Ittersum, *Profit and Principle*, 267–70.

97. Jerzy Lukowski, *The Partitions of Poland: 1772, 1793, 1795* (Harlow, Essex: Addison, Wesley, Longman, 1999), 84.

98. Norman Davies, *God's Playground: A History of Poland*, Vol. 1: *The Origins to 1795* (New York: Columbia University Press, 2005), 395.

99. Compare *DJB*, 2.11.7.2 with 2.12.26.1; Vattel, *Law of Nations*, 4.4.37; Georg Friedrich von Martens, *Summary of the Law of Nations, Founded on Treaties and Customs of the Modern Nations of Europe*, trans. William Cobbett (Littleton, CO: Thomas Bradform, 1795), 2.1.3; Lassa Oppenheim, *International Law: A Treatise*, Vol. 1 (Longmans, Green and Company, 1905), paragraph 499. Both Vattel and Martens excluded cases where a state is forced to accept "hard, ignominious and insupportable conditions" (Vattel, in reference to peace treaties) or where "the injustice of the violence employed is so manifest as to leave the least doubt" (Martens, in reference to treaties in general).

100. Treaty of Cahuenga, January 13, 1847.

101. James K. Polk, Fourth Annual Message to Congress, December 5, 1848.

102. Frederick Merk, "Dissent in the Mexican War," *Proceedings of the Massachusetts Historical Society, Third Series* 81 (1969): 120–21; Ralph H. Brock, "'Perhaps the Most Incorrect of Any Land Line in the United States': Establishing the Texas-New Mexico Boundary Along the 103rd Meridian," *The Southwestern Historical*

Quarterly 109, no. 4 (April 2006): 432 n. 5; William R. Nester, *The Age of Jackson and the Art of American Power, 1815–1848* (Washington: Potomac Books, 2013), 240; Richard Griswold del Castillo, *The Treaty of Guadalupe Hidalgo: A Legacy of Conflict* (Norman: University of Oklahoma Press, 1992), 11–12.

103. Abraham Lincoln, "January 12, 1848—Speech in the United States House of Representatives," in *Abraham Lincoln: Complete Works, Comprising His Speeches, State Papers, and Miscellaneous Writings*, Vol. 1, eds. John G. Nicolay and John Hay (New York: The Century Company, 1920), 103.

104. S. Doc. No. 31-18, at 241 (1850).

105. Innocent VIII to Charles of France and Anne of Brittany, dispensation, January 18, 1491, in *Corps universel diplomatique du droit des gens*, eds. Jean du Mont and Baron de Carels-Croon, Vol. 3, pt. 2 (Amsterdam: P. Brunel et al., 1726), 274–76. Charles and Anne were required to do penance and later to appear before the vicar of the Archbishop of Plessis-Le-Parc to assure him that Anne had not been abducted but had married Charles of her own free will.

106. *DJB*, 2.25.4. See also Vattel, *The Law of Nations*, 2.7.168.

THREE: LICENSE TO KILL

1. James Mooney, *The Ghost-Dance Religion and the Sioux Outbreak of 1890* (Lincoln: University of Nebraska Press, 1991), 1060–61. The following account relies on ibid., especially 916–25.

2. Ibid., 917.

3. Ibid.

4. Ibid.

5. Robert M. Utley, "The Ordeal of Plenty Horses," *American Heritage* 26, no. 1 (1974).

6. Nelson A. Miles, "Statement of General Nelson A. Miles on the 'Sioux Outbreak' of 1890," in *Report of the Secretary of War for 1891*, Vol. 1 (Washington, DC: U.S. Government Printing Office, 1892), 133–34, 149.

7. Tasunka Ota literally translates to Many Horses, but the U.S. military and government agents referred to him as Plenty Horses. Roger L. Di Silvestro, *In the Shadow of Wounded Knee: The Untold Final Chapter of the Indian Wars* (New York: Walker, 2005), 3.

8. Utley, "The Ordeal of Plenty Horses."

9. Di Silvestro, *In the Shadow of Wounded Knee*, 102, 134, 138.

10. "He Killed Lieut. Casey: The Trial of Plenty Horses Begun in Sioux City," *New York World*, April 25, 1891.

11. Utley, "The Ordeal of Plenty Horses."

12. Ibid.

13. Robert Lee, *Fort Meade and the Black Hills* (Lincoln: University of Nebraska Press, 1991), 135.

14. *New York World*, May 29, 1891.

15. *DJB*, 3.4.3.

NOTES 453

16. Di Silvestro, *In the Shadow of Wounded Knee*, 151.
17. *DJB*, 3.4.3.
18. Olivier Fatio and Béatrice Nicollier-de Weck, *Comprendre L'Escalade: Essai de Géopolitique Genevoise* (Geneva: Labor & Fides, 2002), 71–79.
19. Ibid., 77.
20. Jean-Pierre Gaberel, *Les Guerres de Genève aux XVIme et XVIIme Siècles et L'Escalade, 12 Décembre 1602* (Geneva: Imprimerie Charles Schuchardt, 1880), 149.
21. Vattel, *The Law of Nations*, 3.4.68.
22. Francisco de Vitoria, *Vitoria: Political Writings*, eds. Anthony Pagden and Jeremy Lawrance (Cambridge: Cambridge University Press, 2003), 313; Andrew Sola, "The Enlightened Grunt? Invincible Ignorance in the Just War Tradition," *Journal of Military Ethics* 8, no. 1 (2009): 48–65.
23. "The Red Man," *The Gentleman's Magazine and Historical Chronicle* 85 (1815): 123.
24. "Manifeste de la justice, de l'importance et de la nécessité que trouve le Roi, notre Seigneur, pour s'opposer à l'agression de l'usurpateur Buonaparte, procurer le repos et la tranquillité à l'Europe, et protéger les droits de l'humanité et de la religion, de concert avec les Souverains qui ont donné à Vienne la déclaration de 13 mars du cette année," in *Louis XVIII of France. Déclaration du Roi de France, adressé au peuple français, suivie du manifeste de Ferdinand VII, Roi d'Espagne, publié à l'occasion de la guerre contre Buonaparte* (Paris, 1815), 29.
25. David A. Bell, *The First Total War: Napoleon's Europe and the Birth of Warfare as We Know It* (New York: Houghton Mifflin, 2007), 251, 255.
26. The unfavorable depiction of Napoleon in the text presents him largely from the Allied perspective. For a recent reassessment of Napoleon's life, one that sees him more charitably as spreading the Enlightenment throughout Europe and ridding it of the oppressive practices of the Old Regime, see Andrew Roberts, *Napoleon: A Life* (New York: Viking, 2014), particularly, xxx–xli.
27. Ibid., 722.
28. Ibid., 723; Philip Dwyer, *Citizen Emperor* (New Haven: Yale University Press, 2013), 501.
29. Philip Mansel, *Monarchy and Exile: The Politics of Legitimacy from Marie de Médicis to Wilhelm II* (New York: Palgrave Macmillan, 2011), 219.
30. Bell, *The First Total War*, 304.
31. Roberts, *Napoleon: A Life*, 732–36.
32. Ibid., 737, 740; Michael John Thornton, *Napoleon After Waterloo: England and the St. Helena Decision* (Stanford, CA: Stanford University Press, 1968), 54.
33. "Declaration at the Congress of Vienna (March 13, 1815)," in Edward Baines, *History of the Wars of the French Revolution, From the Breaking Out of the Wars in 1792, to, the Restoration of General Peace in 1815*, Vol. 2 (London: Longman, Rees, Orme and Brown, 1817), 433.
34. Digby George Smith, *The Greenhill Napoleonic Wars Data Book* (London: Greenhill Books, 1998), 539.
35. Roberts, *Napoleon: A Life*, 776.

36. Ibid., 776–77.

37. Ibid., 781–82.

38. Anthony Mancini, "St. Helena, 'Cursed Rock' of Napoleon's Exile," *New York Times,* May 29, 2012.

39. Ibid.

40. "Liverpool to Castlereagh, July 21, 1815," in *Correspondence, Despatches and Other Papers of Viscount Castlereagh,* Third Series, *Military Diplomatic,* ed. *Charles William Vane,* Vol. 2 (London: William Shoberl, 1851), 434; John Hall Stewart, "The Imprisonment of Napoleon: A Legal Opinion by Lord Eldon," *American Journal of International Law* 45, no. 3 (1951): 571–77.

41. R. A. Melikan, "Caging the Emperor: The Legal Basis for Detaining Napoleon Bonaparte," *Legal History Review* 67, no. 3 (1999): 349–62; Stewart, "The Imprisonment of Napoleon," 571–77.

42. "An Act for the more Effectually Detaining in Custody Napoleon Buonaparte," 56 George III, c. 22 (1816).

43. Sir Neil Campbell, *Napoleon on Elba: Diary of an Eyewitness to Exile,* ed. Jonathan North (Welwyn Garden City: Ravenhall, 2004), 172; Roberts, *Napoleon: A Life,* 729–30.

44. *DJB,* 3.1.2.1.

45. Ibid., 3.1.2.2.

46. Ibid., 3.1.2.1.

47. Grotius went on to argue that the license to kill does not merely protect victims—it protects outside observers as well. For if killing in war were prosecutable as murder, then outsiders to the conflict would be under strong political pressure to prosecute the unjust side, thus putting them in the middle of a tense situation. "To undertake to decide regarding the justice of a war between two peoples had been dangerous for other peoples, who were on this account involved in a foreign war." Ibid., 3.4.4.

48. Ibid.

49. Ibid., 3.4.19. Grotius conceded that the prohibition on rape "is the law not of all nations, but of the better ones."

50. Ibid., 3.7.1.

51. Ibid., 3.7.3.

52. Ibid., 3.4.10.

53. Ibid., 3.5.1.

54. Ibid., 3.4.9.

55. Ibid., 3.4.2-3; Emer de Vattel, *The Law of Nations; or, Principles of the Law of Nature, Applied to the Conduct and Affairs of Nations and Sovereigns,* trans. Joseph Chitty (Philadelphia: T & J. W. Johnson & Co., Law Booksellers, 1867 [1758]), 3.8.137.

56. Samuel Pufendorf, *De jure naturae et gentium libri octo,* trans. Basil Kennett (Oxford: Lichfield, 1703), 8.6.17 (1688). Section 18 follows up on the question of stealthy assassination, where he basically ends up agreeing with Grotius.

57. Cornelius van Bynkershoek, *Quaestiones Juris Publici libri duo* (Oxford: Clarendon Press, 1930), 16.

58. Ibid., 16, 26–28.

59. "Account and translation of Jürgen Ackermann, Kapitän beim Regiment Alt-Pappenheim 1631," ed. R. Volkholz, quoted in Geoff Mortimer, *Eyewitness Accounts of the Thirty Years War, 1618–48* (New York: Palgrave Macmillan, 2002), 67-68.

60. Otto von Guericke, "The Sack of Magdeburg (May 20, 1631)," in *The Thirty Years War: A Documentary History*, ed. and trans. Trytje Helfferich (Indianapolis: Hackett, 2009), 108–9.

61. Mortimer, *Eyewitness Accounts of the Thirty Years' War*, 4–5.

62. Otto von Guericke, "The Sack of Magdeburg (May 20, 1631)," in Helfferich, *The Thirty Years War*, 109.

63. Jeffrey Chipps Smith, "The Destruction of Magdeburg in 1631: The Art of a Disastrous Victory," in *Disaster, Death and the Emotions in the Shadow of the Apocalypse, 1400-1700*, eds. Jenny Spinks and Charles Zika (London: Palgrave, 2015), 247-71.

64. Hans Medick, "Historical Event and Contemporary Experience: The Capture and Destruction of Magdeburg in 1631," trans. Pamela Selwyn, *History Workshop Journal* 52 (2001): 33.

65. Numbers 31:1–2 NIV.

66. Ibid. 31:7.

67. Ibid. 31:15.

68. Ibid. 31:17.

69. 1 Samuel 15:3.

70. Deuteronomy 25:19.

71. 1 Samuel 15:33. On the slaughter of women and children in the Hebrew Bible, Grotius wrote: "For these are the works of God whose right over men is greater than that of men over brutes." *DJB*, 3.4.9.1.

72. Technically speaking, the prohibition against direct attack applied even though civilians were still the enemy. "Women, children, feeble old men, and sick persons," Vattel noted, "come under the description of enemies." Nevertheless these civilians were not threats and killing them would serve no lawful purpose. Vattel, *The Law of Nations*, 3.8.145.

73. Ibid. See also Manifesto written by Count Apraksin on behalf of the tsarina Elizabeth II on the way into Prussia, in *Sammlung der neuesten Staats-Schrifften zum Behuf der Historie des jetzigen Krieges in Teutschland* (Frankfurt and Leipzig, 1757), 144, 149: "Inhabitants who only seek to exercise their profession, especially farmers, have nothing to fear. Rather, they should expect all of the protection that military necessary (*Kriegsraison*) and the circumstances allow. However, we will proceed with all the severity of the laws of war (*Kriegsgesetze*) against those who have taken up arms or have deserted their homes and fatherland" (translation by James Rumsey-Merlan).

74. Ibid.. The last sentence in this passage, however, indicates the tentative nature of enforcement. It didn't go without saying that abuse of civilians was punished by one side, only that prudence and humanity suggested it should. Vattel indicates elsewhere that the laws of war could also be enforced by the retaliatory refusal to give quarter. Ibid., 3.8.141.

75. Eric Robson, "The Armed Forces and the Art of War," in *The New Cambridge Modern History*, eds. G. R. Potter and G. R. Elton, Vol. 7: *The Old Regime, 1713–63*, ed. J. O. Lindsay (Cambridge: Cambridge University Press, 1979), 165. On the humanitarian revolution and Enlightenment humanism, see Steven Pinker, *The Better Angels of Our Nature: Why Violence Has Declined* (New York: Viking, 2011), 129–92.

76. Bell, *The First Total War*; Carl Schmitt, *Theory of the Partisan: Intermediate Commentary on the Concept of the Political*, trans. G. L. Ulem (New York: Telos Press, 2007), 36.

77. James Whitman, *The Verdict of Battle: The Law of Victory and the Making of Modern War* (Cambridge: Harvard University Press, 2012); Randall Lesaffer, "Siege Warfare in Early Modern Europe," in E. J. Broers, B. C. M. Jacobs, and R. C. H. Lesaffer, eds., *Ius Brabanticum, Ius Commune, Ius Gentium: Opstellen Aangeboden aan Prof. Mr. J.P.A. Coopmans ter Gelegenheid van Zijn Tachtigste Verjaardag* (Nijmegen: Wolf Legal Publishers, 2006).

78. Bell, *The First Total War*, 5.

79. Ibid., 46.

80. According to an editorial in *The New York Times*, Wounded Knee was "almost uniformly treated as a bloodthirsty and wanton massacre" by English newspapers. The editorial, however, was critical of this interpretation. January 22, 1891, 4.

81. Ironically, Plenty Horses's acquittal precluded any possibility of war crimes prosecutions—as a political matter, if not a legal one. Though the killing of Casey was legally distinguishable from the massacre of civilians, the public would not have drawn that distinction. There was little chance that a white jury would have convicted white soldiers for killing Indians when an Indian had just gone free for killing a white man.

82. Vattel, *The Law of Nations*, 3.15.226.

83. Convention for the Amelioration of the Condition of the Wounded in Armies in the Field, August 22, 1864, available at https://ihl-databases.icrc.org/ihl/INTRO/120?OpenDocument.

84. Declaration Renouncing the Use, in Time of War, of Explosive Projectiles Under 400 Grammes Weight, November 29 (December 11) 1868, available at https://ihl-databases.icrc.org/applic/ihl/ihl.nsf/Article.xsp?action=openDocument&documentId=568842C2B90F4A29C12563CD0051547C.

85. Hague Declarations of 1899 (IV, 1), (IV, 2), and (IV, 3) in *The Hague Conventions and Declarations of 1899 and 1907*, ed. James Brown Scott (Oxford: Oxford University Press, 1915).

86. Hague Convention (IV) of 1907 Respecting the Laws and Customs of War on Land and Its Annex, Articles 28, 47, 23, and 45, in ibid.

87. *Journal du général Fantin Des Odoards*, 244 (Paris: 1895), translated in Geoffrey Best, *Humanity in Warfare: The Modern History of the International Law of Armed Conflicts* (New York: Columbia University Press, 1980), 168.

88. S. W. Bowman and R. B. Irwin, *Sherman and His Campaigns: A Military Biography* (New York: Richardson & Co., 1865), 235–36.

89. Olaf van Nimwegen, *The Dutch Army and the Military Revolutions, 1588–1688* (Rochester, NY: Boydell Press, 2010), 61–64; Geoffrey Parker, *The Army of Flanders and the Spanish Road, 1567–1659: The Logistics of Spanish Victory and Defeat in the Low Countries' Wars*, 2nd ed. (Cambridge: Cambridge University Press, 2004), 143–44.

90. Nimwegen, *The Dutch Army and the Military Revolutions*, 62.

91. Philippe Contamine, "Ransom and Booty," in *War and Competition Between States*, ed. Philippe Contamine (Oxford: Clarendon Press, 2000), 191.

92. Ibid. For a discussion of prisoner cartels in the American context, see John Fabian Witt, *Lincoln's Code: The Laws of War in American History* (New York: Free Press, 2012).

93. Henry Wheaton, *Elements of International Law: With a Sketch of the History of the Science* (Carey, Lea & Blanchard, 1836), 251 ("Breach of good faith in these transactions can be punished only by withholding from the party guilty of such violation the advantages stipulated by the cartel; or, in cases which may be supposed to warrant such a resort, by reprisals or vindictive retaliation.").

94. Vattel, *The Law of Nations*, 3.8.140, 142.

95. Ibid., 3.8.142.

96. Ibid., 3.8.141.

97. Lassa Oppenheim, *International Law: A Treatise*, Vol. 2 (London: Longmans, Green and Company, 1921), 336.

98. J. M. Spaight, *War Rights on Land* (London: Macmillan, 1911), 462.

99. On these attempts to regulate or eliminate reprisals, see Frits Kalshoven, *Belligerent Reprisals* (Leiden: Martinus Nijhoff, 1971), 1–68. For the use of reprisals in the First World War, see Isabel V. Hull, *A Scrap of Paper: Breaking and Making International Law during the Great War* (Ithaca, NY: Cornell University Press 2014), 64–65, 276–316.

100. Vattel, *The Law of Nations*, 3.8.142.

101. Oppenheim, *International Law*, Vol. 2, 336.

102. While the threat of reprisals often deterred violations, they also raised the risk of "escalating cycles of retaliatory destruction." Witt, *Lincoln's Code*, 64.

FOUR: CITIZEN GENÊT GOES TO WASHINGTON

1. Shortly before Genet was appointed to this post, he had written a report recommending the replacement of the title "Ambassador" with the more

republican-sounding "Minister." Harry Ammon, *The Genet Mission* (New York: W. W. Norton, 1973), 18.

2. Though French counterrevolutionaries assembled in Prussia threatened to attack and drive the revolutionaries from power, the threat was not great. The armed émigrés numbered a mere 20,000. The revolutionaries' views about the emancipatory potential of warfare played a greater role, as evidenced not only by the justifications issued for waging war, but from the fact that France attacked Austria, not Prussia, where the counterrevolutionaries had gathered. David A. Bell, *The First Total War: Napoleon's Europe and the Birth of Warfare as We Know It* (New York: Houghton Mifflin, 2007), 110–11, 114–19, 126.

3. Quoted in "Editorial Note: The Recall of Edmond Charles Genet," in *PTJ*, Vol. 26, 686.

4. Thomas Paine to George Washington, May 1, 1790, Thomas Paine National Historical Association, http://www.thomaspaine.org/letters/george-washington /to-his-excellency-george-washington-may-1790.html.

5. Ammon, *The Genet Mission*, 2–3; Stanley Elkins and Eric McKitrick, *The Age of Federalism* (Oxford: Oxford University Press, 1993), 330.

6. Ammon, *The Genet Mission*, 5–9, 17; Elkins and McKitrick, *The Age of Federalism*, 330–31.

7. Elkins and McKitrick, *The Age of Federalism*, 331–35.

8. Elkins and McKitrick suggest that the French Girondin faction was ignorant of foreign affairs and apparently wanted to "have it both ways" with respect to American neutrality. See ibid., 333–35.

9. Ammon, *The Genet Mission*, 21.

10. Elkins and McKitrick, *The Age of Federalism*, 334, 342.

11. Ibid., 333; Ammon, *The Genet Mission*, 26–27.

12. Gaspard Monge to Citizen Genêt, February 8, 1793, in *Actes et Mémoires Concernant Les Négociations Qui Ont Eu Lieu Entre La France et Les États-Unis de l'Amérique*, Vol. 1 (London: J. G. B. Vogel, 1807), 12; Elkins and McKitrick, *The Age of Federalism*, 333.

13. Elkins and McKitrick, *The Age of Federalism*, 335.

14. Ibid., 345, 348; Gordon S. Wood, *Empire of Liberty: A History of the Early Republic, 1789–1815* (Oxford: Oxford University Press, 2009), 185.

15. Elkins and McKitrick, *The Age of Federalism*, 335.

16. The *Grange* was captured in Delaware Bay—U.S. waters—making the incident less diplomatic still. Ibid., 343; Ammon, *The Genet Mission*, 53–54.

17. Thomas Jefferson to James Monroe, May 5, 1793, in *PTJ*, Vol. 25, 661.

18. "Memorial from George Hammond," May 2, 1793, in ibid., 638.

19. Elkins and McKitrick, *The Age of Federalism*, 314–16.

20. Wood, *Empire of Liberty*, 174, 179–80.

21. Thomas Jefferson to Edmond Charles Genêt, June 5, 1793, in *PTJ*, Vol. 26, 196.

22. Elkins and McKitrick, *The Age of Federalism*, 348.

23. Genêt to Jefferson, June 14, 1793, in *PTJ*, Vol. 26, 281 (*"Mépris des traités qui unissent les Français et les Americains"*).

24. "Treaty of Amity and Commerce Between the United States and France; February 6, 1778," Avalon Law Project, Yale Law School Lillian Goldman Law Library, http://avalon.law.yale.edu/18th_century/fr1788-1.asp ("It shall not be lawful for any foreign Privateers, not belonging to Subjects of the most Christian King, nor Citizens of the said United States, who have Commissions from any other Prince or State in enmity with either Nation to fit their Ships in the Ports of either the one or the other.").

25. Ammon, *The Genet Mission*, 66–67.

26. Thomas Jefferson to Edmond Charles Genêt, June 17, 1793, in *PTJ*, Vol. 26, 298–99; Ammon, *The Genet Mission*, 67.

27. Edmond Charles Genêt to Thomas Jefferson, June 22, 1793, in *PTJ*, Vol. 26, 339 (*"pour justifier ou éxcuser des infractions faites à des traités positifs"*).

28. Alexander Hamilton and Henry Knox, "Reasons for the Opinion of the Secretary of the Treasury, and the Secretary at War, Respecting the Brigantine 'Little Sarah,'" in *The Works of Alexander Hamilton*, Vol. 5, ed. Henry Cabot Lodge (New York: G. P. Putnam's Sons, 1904), 7 (July 8, 1793).

29. Thomas Jefferson to James Madison, August 3, 1793, in *PTJ*, Vol. 26, 606 (emphasis in original).

30. Emer de Vattel, *The Law of Nations; or, Principles of the Law of Nature, Applied to the Conduct and Affairs of Nations and Sovereigns*, trans. Joseph Chitty (Philadelphia: T & J. W. Johnson & Co., Law Booksellers, 1867 [1758]), 3.7.104; Cornelius van Bynkershoek, *Quaestionum Juris Publici libri duo* (Oxford: Clarendon Press, 1930), 1.9.61; Georg Friedrich von Martens, *Summary of the Law of Nations, Founded on Treaties and Customs of the Modern Nations of Europe*, trans. William Cobbett (Littleton, CO: Fred B. Rothman, 1986), 8.6.2; William Edward Hall, *A Treatise on International Law* (Buffalo: William S. Hein & Co., Inc., 1924), 93–94. For a description of state practice in the eighteenth century, see Charles S. Hyneman, *First American Neutrality: A Study of the American Understanding of Neutral Obligations During the Years 1792 to 1815* (Chicago: University of Illinois Press, 1934), 15–16. Hyneman expresses some skepticism about whether jurists were reporting consistent state practice before 1793, but believes that the practice of strict impartiality did firm up after that date. Ibid., 15–19. For a less skeptical take, see Charles Cheney Hyde, *International Law Chiefly as Interpreted by the United States*, Vol. 2 (Boston: Little, Brown, and Company, 1922), 692.

31. Vattel, *The Law of Nations*, 3.7.105; Van Bynkershoek, *Quaestiones Juris Publici*, 63; Martens, *Summary of the Law of Nations, Founded on Treaties and Customs of the Modern Nations of Europe*, 8.5.9. For state practice in the eighteenth century, see Hall, *A Treatise on International Law*, 700–02.

32. As indicated at the end of Chapter Two, allies would be relieved of their treaty responsibilities to assist belligerents if they judged the belligerents to have

waged an unjust war. But if they went further and imposed costs on those belligerents, then they would commit an act of war.

33. Jefferson to Genêt, June 17, 1793, in *PTJ*, Vol. 26, 299 ("But we will not assume the exclusive right of saying what that law and usage is. Let us appeal to
enlightened and disinterested Judges. None is more so than Vattel.").

34. Genêt to Jefferson, June 22, 1793, in ibid., 339.

35. Jefferson to Madison, August 3, 1793, in ibid., 606.

36. Jefferson to Genêt, June 5, 1793, in ibid., 197 (n. 9).

37. Edmund Randolph to Thomas Jefferson, with Jefferson's Note, May 31, 1793,
in ibid., 152.

38. Jefferson to Genêt, June 11, 1793, in ibid., 252. See "Alexander Hamilton's
Report on the American Debt to France," June 8, 1793, in ibid., 183–84.

39. Ammon, *The Genet Mission*, 80.

40. There is some dispute as to whether Genêt actually made this threat. The
origin seems to be Jefferson's *Memorandum on a Conversation with Edmond
Charles Genet*, July 10, 1793, in ibid., 466. Dallas denied the statement in December. See A. J. Dallas, "To the Public," *American Daily Advertiser* (Philadelphia, December 9, 1793), 4575, quoted in *The Historical Magazine* 10 (1866):
339.

41. Elkins and McKitrick, *The Age of Federalism*, 369–71; Ammon, *The Genet Mission*, 107–8.

42. Ammon, *The Genet Mission*, 172.

43. Ibid., 119–20, 155–60, 170–72, 178–79.

44. Thomas P. Jones, "The Baseless Fabric of a Vision," in *American Journal of Science and the Arts* 13 (1828): 90.

45. See, e.g., Henry Wheaton, *Elements of International Law*, 8th ed. (London:
Sampson Low, 1866), 508.

46. Hague Convention (V) of 1907, Art. 9, in *The Hague Conventions and Declarations of 1899 and 1907*.

47. Vattel, *The Law of Nations*, 3.7.104.

48. Ibid. See also Hague Convention (V) of 1907, Art. 7 and 9, in *The Hague Conventions and Declarations of 1899 and 1907*. According to Grotius, the duty of
impartiality applied only in "doubtful matters," but not when it is clear that
"he who supports a wicked cause may be rendered more powerful, or whereby
the movements of him who wages a just war may be hampered." *DJB*, 3.17.3.1
Grotius believed that in clear cases the duty of impartiality did not apply, unlike the rules of conquest, gunboat diplomacy, and the license to kill, which did,
largely because state practice had not yet developed imposing such a duty. See
ibid., 3.1.5.5. ("In this inquiry we have referred back to the law of nature for
the reason that in historical narratives we have been unable to find anything
established by the volitional law of nations to cover such cases.")

49. There was only one limited sense in which states could discriminate. If a state
felt strongly enough about the justice of some cause, it could renounce its

neutrality and join ranks with the victim. A state could remain at peace with both belligerents, but it could also go to war with one side to rescue the other. Vattel, *The Law of Nations*, 3.7.106.

50. Gary Hufbauer et al., *Economic Sanctions Reconsidered*, 3rd ed. (Washington, DC: Peterson Institute for International Economics, 2007), 10.

CODA I

1. For an account of the celebration, see Commission of the United States of America to the International Peace Conference of The Hague, *Hugo Grotius Celebration, Delft: Proceedings at the Laying of a Wreath on the Tomb of Hugo Grotius in the Nieuwe Kerk, in the City of Delft July 4th 1899* (The Hague: Martinus Nijhoff, 1899). For Ambassador White's tribute, see ibid., 14. For a similarly hagiographical description of Grotius as a prince of peace, see C. Van Vollenhoven, "Grotius and the Study of Law," *The American Journal of International Law* 19, no. 1 (January 1925): 1–11, especially p. 3 ("Peaceful though he is in heart and soul").

2. For a definitive discussion of Grotius's lifelong service and commitment to Dutch corporate imperialism and the Dutch East India Company, see Martine Julia van Ittersum, "The Long Goodbye: Hugo Grotius' Justification of Dutch Expansion Overseas, 1615–1645," *History of European Ideas* 36, no. 4 (June 2010): 386–411.

3. Immanuel Kant, "Perpetual Peace: A Philosophical Sketch," in *Kant: Political Writings*, ed. H. S. Reiss (Cambridge: Cambridge University Press, 1991), 103.

4. Jean-Jacques Rousseau, "The Social Contract," in *Rousseau: "The Social Contract" and Other Later Political Writings*, ed. Victor Gourevitch (Cambridge: Cambridge University Press, 1997).

5. Kant, "Perpetual Peace," 103.

6. Martine Julia van Ittersum, "Preparing *Mare Liberum* for the Press: Hugo Grotius' Rewriting of Chapter 12 of *De iure praedae* in November–December 1608," *Grotiana* 26–28 (2005–2007): 256.

7. In 1940 and 1951, Clark and Eysinga published a two-volume collection of archival materials related to the Anglo-Dutch trade conferences. G. N. Clark and Johnkeer W. J. M. van Eysinga, *The Colonial Conferences Between England and The Netherlands in 1613 and 1615*, Parts 1 and 2 (Amsterdam: Brill, 1940, 1951). These materials revealed Grotius's deep involvement with the Dutch East India Company.

8. Robert Fruin, *De Jure Praedae Commentarius: An Unpublished Work of Hugo Grotius's*, trans. H. G. Hamaker (Clark, NJ: Lawbook Exchange, 2003), 7–8.

9. *DJB*, Prolegomena, Sec. 28.

10. Commission of the United States of America to the International Peace Conference of The Hague, *Hugo Grotius Celebration*, 21.

11. *DJB*, Prolegomena, Sec. 29.

12. Ibid, 2.20.47–50.

13. That Grotius developed his liberal theory largely (though not exclusively) to justify Dutch colonial wars and overseas expansion by the Dutch East India Company has become the conventional wisdom among Grotius specialists. See, e.g., Van Ittersum, "The Long Goodbye," 409 ("the imperialist framework of Grotius' thinking on natural law and natural rights . . . is fast becoming the new consensus, endorsed by experts in legal history, IR theory, intellectual history, philosophy and postcolonial theory"). See, e.g., Martine Julia van Ittersum, *Profit and Principle: Hugo Grotius, Natural Rights Theories and the Rise of Dutch Power in the East Indies, 1595–1615* (Amsterdam: Brill, 2006); Peter Borschberg, *Hugo Grotius, the Portuguese and Free Trade in the East Indies* (Singapore: National University of Singapore Press, 2011); Edward Keene, *Beyond the Anarchical Society: Grotius Colonialism and Order in World Politics* (Cambridge: Cambridge University Press, 2002); Richard Tuck, *The Rights of War and Peace: Political Thought and the International Order From Grotius to Kant* (Oxford: Oxford University Press, 1999), 78–108, particularly p. 95 ("*De Iure Belli ac Pacis* reminded [Grotius'] audience that he was still an enthusiast for war around the globe. He was indeed a most improbable figure to be the tutelary deity of the Peace Palace at The Hague.").

FIVE: THE WAR TO END WAR

1. "Austria-Hungary: Ultimatum to Serbia," July 22, 1914, in *International Law Documents 1917: Neutrality, Breaking of Diplomatic Relations, War* (Washington, DC: Government Printing Office, 1918), 38. For more on the events immediately preceding the war, see T. G. Otte, *July Crisis: The World's Descent into War, Summer 1914* (Cambridge: Cambridge University Press, 2014).

2. "Serbian Reply to [the] Austrian Government," July 25, 1914, in *International Law Documents 1917*, 47.

3. "Imperial Rescript and Manifesto," in *New York Times Current History: The European War from the Beginning to March 1915*, Vol. 1, No. 2 (New York: New York Times, 2005), 225. See "The Austro-Hungarian Declaration of War Against Serbia," July 28, 1914, in *International Law Documents 1917*, 49.

4. "Note presented by the German Ambassador at St. Petersburgh," August 1, 1914, in *Diplomatic Documents Relating to the Outbreak of the European War*, ed. James Brown Scott (New York: Oxford University Press, 1916), 763–64.

5. The manifesto usually goes under the name of the *German White Book*. *The German White Book: How Russia and Her Ruler Betrayed Germany's Confidence and Thereby Caused the European War* (Berlin: Liebheit and Thiesen, 1914). The Foreign Office also provided the manifesto to *The New York Times*, which published it in its August 24, 1914 edition. Frederic William Wile, "Full Text of the German White Paper," *New York Times*, August 24, 1914.

6. "Imperial Manifesto," August 2, 1914, in *Documents of Russian History, 1914–1917*, ed. Frank Alfred Golder (New York: Century Company, 1927), 29–30.

7. The Franco-Russian Alliance Military Convention, August 18, 1892, Avalon

Law Project, Yale Law School, Lillian Goldman Law Library, http://avalon .law.yale.edu/19th_century/frrumil.asp; Germany's Declaration of War with France ("Letter Handed by the German Ambassador to M. Rene Viviani"), August 3, 1914, in Scott, ed., *Diplomatic Documents Relating to the Outbreak of the European War*, 693–94.

8. When the British ambassador informed German chancellor Theobald von Bethmann-Hollweg that Britain would go to war over the violation of Belgian neutrality, the chancellor exclaimed that he could not believe that Great Britain would make war on "a kindred nation" over a mere "scrap of paper." Sir E. Goschen's report to Sir Edward Grey on interview with Chancellor von Bethmann-Hollweg (August 4, 1914), World War I Document Archive, http:// www.gwpda.org/1914/paperscrap.html; Isabel V. Hull, *A Scrap of Paper: Breaking and Making International Law During the Great War* (Ithaca, NY: Cornell University Press 2014), 42.

9. "Note Communicated by M. Davignon, the Belgian Minister for Foreign Affairs, to Herr von Below Saleske, German Minister," August 3, 1914, in *Official Diplomatic Documents Relating to the Outbreak of the European War*, ed. Edwin von Mach (New York: Macmillan Company, 1916), 421.

10. Hew Strachan, *The First World War* (New York: Viking, 2004); Barbara Tuchman, *The Guns of August: The Outbreak of World War I* (New York: Presidio Press, 2004), 321.

11. Woodrow Wilson, "An Appeal by the President of the United States to the Citizens of the Republic, Requesting Their Assistance in Maintaining a State of Neutrality During the Present European War," August 19, 2014, *Congress*, 63rd Cong., 2nd Sess., Senate Doc. No. 566 (Washington, DC: U.S. Government Printing Office, 1914), 3–4.

12. Ibid.

13. Howard Jones, *Crucible of Power: A History of U.S. Foreign Relations Since 1897* (Wilmington, DE: Rowman & Littlefield, 2001), 73.

14. "Lusitania Sunk by a Submarine, Probably 1,000 Dead," *New York Times*, May 8, 1915. The Germans claimed that the sinking was entirely justified. The vessel, they argued, contained ammunition bound for the Allies and was therefore a ship of war, a legitimate target under international law. "Sinking Justified Says Dr. Dernberg: Lusitania a 'War Vessel' Known to be Carrying Contraband, Hence Search Was Not Necessary," *New York Times*, May 9, 1915. Recent evidence has bolstered Germany's case: Forensic examination of the wreck suggests there were as many as four million rounds of ammunition on the *Lusitania* when it went down. Sam Greenhill, "Secret of the Lusitania: Arms Find Challenges Allied Claims It Was Solely a Passenger Ship," *Daily Mail*, December 19, 2008.

15. Erik Larson, *Dead Wake: The Last Crossing of the Lusitania* (New York: Crown, 2015), 276.

16. The Secretary of State William Jennings Bryan to the Ambassador in

Germany (Gerard) (May 13, 1915), *FRUS* 1915 (Supplement: The World War), 393; The Secretary of State *ad interim* (Lansing) to the Ambassador in Germany (Gerard) (June 9, 1915) *FRUS* 1915 (Supplement: The World War), 436; The Secretary of State to the Ambassador in Germany (Gerard) (July 21, 1915), *FRUS* 1915 (Supplement: The World War), 480; President Woodrow Wilson to German Foreign Minister (April 18, 1916) (delivered by the Ambassador in Germany (Gerard), pursuant to instructions from Secretary of State Robert Lansing), *FRUS* 1916 (Supplement: The World War), 232-34 ("Unless the Imperial Government should now immediately declare and effect an abandonment of its present methods of submarine warfare against passenger and freight-carrying vessels, the Government of the United States can have no choice but to sever diplomatic relations with the German Empire altogether.").

17. German Foreign Minister Gottleib Von Jagow to U.S. Ambassdor James W. Gerard (May 4, 1916), *FRUS* 1916 (Supplement: The World War), 257.

18. Democratic Party Platform, June 16, 1916, The American Presidency Project, http://www.presidency.ucsb.edu/ws/?pid=29591. See also John Milton Cooper, Jr., *Woodrow Wilson: A Biography* (New York: Alfred A. Knopf, 2009), 342.

19. Zimmermann Telegram as Received by the German Ambassador to Mexico, January 19, 1917, General Records of the Department of State, Record Group 59, National Archives.

20. Ibid.

21. Woodrow Wilson, "Joint Address to Congress Leading to a Declaration of War Against Germany," April 2, 1917, Records of the United States Senate, Record Group 46, National Archives.

22. Derek H. Aldcroft, *From Versailles to Wall Street, 1919–1929* (Berkeley: University of California Press, 1981), 13 ("8 million . . . lost their lives in active service"); Meredith Reid Sarkees, *The COW Typology of War: Defining and Categorizing Wars (Version 4 of the Data)* (showing 8,578,031 battle deaths).

23. Aldcroft, *From Versailles to Wall Street*, 13–14 (noting that the figures for disabled and wounded likely include some civilians). See also Samuel Dumas and K. O. Vedel-Petersen, *Losses of Life Caused by War* (Oxford: The Claredon Press, 1923), 137–45.

24. Wilson borrowed the phrase from H. G. Wells, *The War That Will End War* (New York: Duffield & Co., 1914).

25. Margaret MacMillan, *Paris 1919: Six Months That Changed the World* (New York: Random House, 2003), 53. For more on postwar peace efforts beyond the Covenant and Kellogg-Briand Pact that are the focus here, see Patrick O. Cohrs, *The Unfinished Peace After World War I: America, Britain and the Stablisation of Europe, 1919–1932* (Cambridge: Cambridge University Press 2006).

26. Woodrow Wilson, "President Wilson's Message to Congress," January 8, 1918, Records of the United States Senate, Record Group 46, National Archives.

27. The Covenant of the League of Nations, Arts. 12, 13, 15 (1924).

28. Woodrow Wilson, "Address at Pueblo, Colorado," September 25, 1919, in *Addresses of President Wilson: Addresses Delivered by President Wilson on His Western Tour*, 66th Congress, 1st Sess., S. Doc. No. 120 (Washington, DC: U.S. Government Printing Office, 1919), 359–70.

29. John E. Stoner, *S. O. Levinson and the Pact of Paris* (Chicago: University of Chicago Press, 1943), 8. Levinson and the outlawry movement he began have been largely forgotten. An exception is David Swanson, *When the World Outlawed War* (self-published, 2011).

30. Stoner, *S. O. Levinson and the Pact of Paris*, 1–10.

31. Ibid., 11–13.

32. Ibid., 12 (quoting *The New York Times*). See "Governors Close Stock Exchange," *New York Times*, August 1, 1914.

33. Stoner, *S. O. Levinson and the Pact of Paris*, 12 (quoting letter from SOL to Harry Levinson, September 15, 1914).

34. "Dr. Eliot and Mr. Schiff Discuss Ways to Peace," *New York Times*, December 20, 1914.

35. Stoner, *S. O. Levinson and the Pact of Paris*, 14 (quoting letter from Levinson to his partner, Benjamin V. Becker).

36. Salmon O. Levinson, "The Legal Status of War," *The New Republic*, March 9, 1918, 171.

37. His sons both fought in the war that ensued. SOL, Memo, July 20, 1928, box 28, folder 7, SLP UCL. Both boys enlisted in 1917; in a letter written in 1919, Levinson noted that both of his sons were home for Christmas for the first time since they enlisted "over two years ago." SOL to Knox, December 27, 1919, box 54, folder 7, SLP UCL.

38. Stoner, *S. O. Levinson and the Pact of Paris*, 21.

39. SOL to Jacob Schiff, August 25, 1917, box 44, folder 3, SLP UCL.

40. Ibid.

41. Stoner, *S. O. Levinson and the Pact of Paris*, 25.

42. James H. Tufts to William Rainey Harper, December 1893, quoted in Louis Menand, *The Metaphysical Club* (New York: Farrar, Straus & Giroux, 2001), 288.

43. Ibid., 25–26 (quoting Dewey to Croly, January 28, 1918).

44. Levinson, "The Legal Status of War," 171.

45. Ibid., 172.

46. Stoner, *S. O. Levinson and the Pact of Paris*, 39–41.

47. SOL, Memo, undated, box 28, folder 7, SLP UCL (reporting that Levinson received the call on February 15, the day after the Covenant was made public, and met with Knox on February 17, 18, and 19).

48. Legal experts agreed that the League left the legality of war intact. Oppenheim's third edition stated that: "war is not inconsistent with, but a condition regulated by, International Law. It does not object to States which are in conflict waging war upon each other, provided they have—in compliance with the

Covenant of the League of Nations—previously submitted the dispute to an inquiry by the Council of the League." L. Oppenheim, *International Law: A Treatise*, 3rd ed., ed. Ronald F. Roxburgh (London: Longmans, Green, & Co., 1921), 2: 65–66, §53.

49. SOL, Memo, undated, box 28, folder 8, SLP UCL. Levinson may have been speaking here of the Locarno Treaties, negotiated at Locarno, Switzerland, in October 1925 and formally signed in London on December 3, 1925.

50. Ibid.

51. League of Nations Covenant, Arts. 10, 11, 16.

52. "Henry Cabot Lodge Speaks on the League of Nations," Speech of August 12, 1919, in William Safire, *Lend Me Your Ears: Great Speeches in History* (New York: W. W. Norton, 2004), 314.

53. Levinson decried Lodge's efforts at compromise, stating that it "infuriated us irreconcilables" and noting that "[o]ur valiant senators took hold and are doing the needful." Letter from SOL to Mr. Otto H. Kahn, January 24, 1920, box 54, folder 7, SLP UCL.

54. Thomas A. Bailey, *Woodrow Wilson and the Great Betrayal* (New York: Macmillan, 1945), 49–167.

55. William E. Borah, "The League of Nations," November 19, 1919, in Robert C. Byrd, *The Senate, 1789–1989: Classic Speeches, 1830–1993* (Washington, DC: U.S. Government Printing Office, 1994), 567 (noting he was one of the "irreconcilables"). John Chalmers Vinson, *William E. Borah and the Outlawry of War* (Athens: University of Georgia Press, 1957).

56. Bailey, *Woodrow Wilson and the Great Betrayal*, 59, 63.

57. Ibid., 64.

58. Byrd, *The Senate, 1789–1989: Classic Speeches, 1830–1993*, 573.

59. U.S. Senate, Classic Senate Speeches: William E. Borah, The League of Nations, November 19, 1919, www.senate.gov/artandhistory/history/common /generic/Speeches_Borah_League.htm.

60. "Senate Defeats Treaty, Vote 49 to 35," *New York Times*, March 19, 1919. Two years later, the country entered into a peace treaty with Germany that did not require the U.S. to join the League. "Senate Ratifies German Treaty by 66 to 20 Vote," *New York Times*, October 19, 1921. The treaty was necessary because the congressional peace resolution did not itself effect peace. As Lodge explained: "It ended the war, as far as the United States is concerned, but it was not a treaty of peace." "Opposition Grows to German Treaty; Plea by Harding," *New York Times*, September 25, 1921.

61. Bailey, *Woodrow Wilson and the Great Betrayal*, 132–34, 350.

62. Knox, having defeated the League, co-sponsored the alternative joint resolution later signed by President Warren G. Harding on July 2, 1921, officially ending U.S. involvement in World War I. "Joint Resolution Terminating the State of War Between the Imperial German Government and the United States of America and Between the Imperial and Royal Austro-Hungarian Government

and the United States of America," 42 Stat. 105 (1921); Kurt Wimer and Sarah Wimer, "The Harding Administration, the League of Nations, and the Separate Peace Treaty," *The Review of Politics* 29, no. 1 (1967): 13–24.

63. Plan to Outlaw War (draft), n.d., box 28, folder 9, SLP UCL.

64. SOL, Memo, undated, box 28, folder 7, SLP UCL.

65. "Senate Ratifies German Treaty by 66 to 20 Vote," *New York Times*, October 19, 1921; "Wilson's Hand Seen as Fight on Treaty Stiffens in Senate," *New York Times*, September 26, 1921; "Wilson Senators Plan Reservations in Fight on Treaty," *New York Times*, September 27, 1921.

66. Vinson, *William E. Borah and the Outlawry of War*, 59.

67. SOL to WEB, July 17, 1922, box 3, folder 16, SLP UCL.

68. Ibid. Levinson also encouraged his friend John Dewey to write to Borah to encourage him to lead the outlawry movement, a request Dewey honored after significant prodding from Levinson. See Dewey to WEB, March 6, 1922, No. 04891, The Correspondence of John Dewey, 1871–1952, Electronic Edition. Borah did mount a presidential campaign in 1936, though he won only a handful of delegates.

69. This account is drawn from Levinson's recorded recollection in an undated memo. See SOL, Memo, undated, box 28, folder 7, SLP UCL. According to that memo, the meeting took place in December 1919. It must have been earlier in December, because the pamphlet they reviewed was published on December 25, 1919.

70. Levinson founded the committee, which held its first meeting on December 10, 1921, and served as its chairman. Miscellaneous Papers Associated with the American Committee for the Outlawry of War, box 1, folder 18, SLP UCL.

71. Salmon O. Levinson, *Outlawry of War* (Chicago: American Committee for the Outlawry of War, 1921), 11. The section heading "Plan to Outlaw War" contains an asterisk with the note "Formulated in 1919 by the late Senator Knox and the author." Ibid.

72. John Dewey, "Foreword," in ibid.

73. SOL to Miss Cora Rubin, January 26, 1922, box 117, WBP LC; see Miss Cora Rubin to SOL, January 27, 1922, box 117, WBP LC; Telegraph from SOL to Miss Cora Rubin, January 26, 1922, box 117, WBP LC. The printing and mailing was coordinated through Senator Borah's office, and paid for by the American Committee for the Outlawry of War, of which Levinson was chairman. Letters between SOL and Miss Cora Rubin, box 117, passim, WBP LC.

74. SOL to Miss Cora Rubin, February 7, 1922, box 117, WBP LC.

75. SOL to Miss Cora Rubin, April 28, 1922, box 117, WBP LC; SOL to Miss Cora Rubin, April 5, 1922, box 117, WBP LC; Miss Cora Rubin to SOL, February 13, 1922, box 117, WBP LC.

76. SOL to Miss Cora Rubin, January 27, 1922, box 117, WBP LC; SOL to Miss Cora Rubin, February 10, 1922, box 117, WBP LC.

77. SOL to Miss Cora Rubin, January 27, 1922, box 117, WBP LC.

78. Miss Cora Rubin to SOL, February 7, 1922, box 117, WBP LC; Arthur Capper to SOL, February 1, 1922, box 117, WBP LC.

79. Stoner, *S. O. Levinson and the Pact of Paris*, 61. Levinson corresponded with Jane Addams (president of the Women's International League for Peace and Freedom), box 1, folder 2, SLP UCL; Elinor Byrns (cofounder of the Women's Peace Union), box 11, folder 11, SLP UCL; the Chicago Woman's Club, box 18, folder 3, SLP UCL; and with the Women's Federation of Clubs, Women's International League for Peace, and Women's Overseas Service League, box 50, folders 1 & 3, SLP, UCL. For more on the peace organizations active in the 1920s, see Charles DeBeneditti, *Origins of the Modern American Peace Movement, 1915–1919* (Millwood, NY: KTO Press, 1978); Charles Chatfield, *The American Peace Movement: Ideals and Activism* (New York: Twayne, 1992); Charles DeBeneditti, *The Peace Reform in American History* (Bloomington: Indiana University Press, 1980); Daniel Gorman, *The Emergence of International Society in the 1920s* (Cambridge: Cambridge University Press, 2012); Cecilia Lunch, *Beyond Appeasement: Interpreting Interwar Peace Movements in World Politics* (Ithaca, NY: Cornell University Press, 1999); Harriet Hyman Alonso, *The Women's Peace Union and the Outlawry of War, 1921–1924* (Knoxville: University of Tennessee Press, 1989).

80. SOL, Memo, undated, box 28, folder 7, SLP UCL. It took some effort for Levinson to coax Borah into leading the movement. Letters between the two during this period make clear that Levinson was actively seeking a senatorial ally and public advocate in Borah. See, e.g., SOL to WEB, December 16, 1921, box 117, WBP LC; WEB to SOL, December 10, 1921, box 117, WBP LC; SOL to WEB, December 8, 1921 box 117, WBP LC. By July 13, 1922, Borah had begun working with Levinson on a resolution to outlaw war. WEB to SOL, July 13, 1922, box 117, WBP LC.

81. SOL, Memo, undated, box 28, folder 7, SLP UCL.

82. See, e.g., SOL to WEB, December 2 1922, box 3, folder 16, SLP UCL; SOL to WEB, December 15, 1922, box 3, folder 16, SLP UCL; SOL to WEB, June 12, 1922, box 3, folder 16, SLP UCL; WEB to Morrison, April 9, 1928, box 5, folder 4, SLP UCL (urging Morrison to talk to Levinson to explain that introducing the resolution during the debate over the Peace Pact would undermine the State Department).

83. SOL, "Additional Memoranda Re Outlawry," May 1, 1922, box 117, WBP LC.

84. WEB to SOL, July 13, 1922, box 117, WBP LC.

85. SOL to WEB, June 12, 1922, box 117, WBP LC.

86. SOL, Memo, undated, box 27, folder 18, SLP UCL.

87. Salmon O. Levinson, "Can Peace Be Enforced?" *The Christian Century*, January 8, 1925, 46–47. The evolution of Levinson's and Borah's ideas can be seen in their written exchanges. See, e.g., Salmon Levinson, "Additional Memoranda Re Outlawry," May 1, 1922, box 117, WBP LC; SOL to WEB, June 12, 1922, box 117, WBP LC; WEB to SOL, July 13, 1922, box 117, WBP LC. The two also corresponded on the matter with John Haynes Holmes, a prominent

Unitarian minister and pacifist, who had helped found the National Association for the Advancement of Colored People (NAACP) in 1909 and the American Civil Liberties Union (ACLU) in 1920. WEB to Haynes Holmes, January 31, 1925, box 27, folder 18, SLP UCL; SOL to Haynes Holmes, February 2, 1925, box 27, folder 18, SLP UCL.

88. John Dewey, *Human Nature and Conduct* (New York: Henry Holt & Company, 1922), 109–10.

89. Harold Josephson, *James T. Shotwell and the Rise of Internationalism in America* (Rutherford, NJ: Fairleigh Dickinson University Press, 1975), 39-40.

90. James T. Shotwell, *The Autobiography of James T. Shotwell* (New York: Bobbs-Merrill, 1961), 85.

91. Quoted in Thomas A. Bailey, *Woodrow Wilson and the Lost Peace* (New York: Macmillan, 1944), 108–9. Shotwell claims that he came up with the name "the Inquiry." Shotwell, *Autobiography*, 79.

92. Josephson, *James T. Shotwell and the Rise of Internationalism in America*, 79-98.

93. It was titled *The Economic and Social History of the World War*, and was commissioned by the Carnegie Endowment for International Peace. Josephson, *James T. Shotwell and the Rise of Internationalism in America*, 99–115; Shotwell, *Autobiography*, 134.

94. Shotwell, *Autobiography*, 180.

95. James T. Shotwell, "Locarno and After," *Association Men* 51, no. 6 (February 1926): 269–70.

96. Columbia University and the Carnegie Endowment played an important role in Shotwell's career and in the debate over how to secure the peace. The Carnegie Endowment was founded in 1910 by Andrew Carnegie, at the behest of Nicholas Murray Butler, in order to "hasten the abolition of international war, the foulest blot upon our civilization." Michael Rosenthal, *Nicholas Miraculous: The Amazing Career of the Redoubtable Dr. Nicholas Murray Butler* (New York: Columbia University Press, 2015), 167–68. Butler served as president of both Columbia University and the Carnegie Endowment, and he was a strong supporter of the League of Nations and of Shotwell's work for the cause of peace, though the two were never personally close. Josephson, *James T. Shotwell and the Rise of Internationalism in America*, 136–37; Nicholas Murray Butler, *The Path to Peace: Essays and Addresses on Peace and Its Making* (New York: Charles Scribner's Sons, 1930).

97. Shotwell, *Autobiography*, 182.

98. 1 Stat. 613, January 30, 1799, codified at 18 U.S.C. § 953 (2004).

99. Shotwell, *Autobiography*, 195.

100. "American Arms Plan Taken Up by League: Draft of Treaty to Outlaw Aggressive War Is Presented on Europe's Invitation, N.Y.," *New York Times*, June 18, 1924. See also "An American Contribution," *New York Times*, June 19, 1924 (describing the proposal as providing for the "outlawry of aggressive war").

101. Josephson, *James T. Shotwell and the Rise of Internationalism in America*, 142.

102. James T. Shotwell, "A Practical Plan for Disarmament," *International Conciliation* 10, no. 201 (August 1924): 318.

103. Ibid.

104. "Institute at Vassar Hears Dr. Shotwell: He Discusses the Proposed Disarmament Treaty Drafted for the League," *New York Times*, June 20, 1924.

105. See, e.g., James T. Shotwell, "Working Toward Disarmament," *The Nation* 119, no. 3082 (July 30, 1924): 112.

106. Telegram from SOL to William Hard, October 3, 1924, quoted in Stoner, *S. O. Levinson and the Pact of Paris*, 113. See also SOL, "Memo Re: Geneva," September 20, 1924, box 27, folder 19, SLP UCL. This memorandum enumerates numerous legal vices of the proposed Protocol, particularly emphasizing the various ways in which the Protocol promised to strengthen the League-based sanctions regime, making war more, not less, likely. In an earlier letter to Borah, Levinson wrote: "The whole treaty sounds in the expectation of war. It builds up an expected alliance of so-called defense and relies ultimately upon overwhelming force for the peace of the world. This marks a tremendous difference between our kind of outlawry and theirs." SOL to WEB, June 20, 1924, box 4, folder 5, SLP UCL.

107. Levinson flagged the same problem in his telegraph to Hard: The Protocol created the possibility that the United States would "find ourselves in war with all League nations automatically against us." Telegram from SOL to William Hard, October 3, 1924, quoted in Stoner, *S. O. Levinson and the Pact of Paris*, 113–14.

108. "Protocol for the Pacific Settlement of International Dispute" (Geneva 1924), Art. 10 ("Every State which resorts to war in violation of the undertakings contained in the Covenant or in the present Protocol is an aggressor.").

109. The Protocol specifically required that as soon as the Council of the League of Nations had called on signatory states to apply sanctions, Article 16 of the League Covenant would apply: "As soon as the Council has called upon the signatory States to apply sanctions, as provided in the last paragraph of Article 10 of the present Protocol, the obligations of the said States, in regard to the sanctions of all kinds mentioned in paragraphs 1 and 2 of Article 16 of the Covenant, will immediately become operative in order that such sanctions may forthwith be employed against the aggressor." "Protocol for the Pacific Settlement of International Dispute" (Geneva Protocol 1924), Art. 11.

110. Committee of Imperial Defence: Report of the Sub-Committee on the Geneva Protocol (January 1925), p. 11, The National Archives, http://filestore.nation alarchives.gov.uk/pdfs/small/cab-24-172-CP-105.pdf (page 16 of 99).

111. Protocol for the Pacific Settlement of International Disputes (1924), Arts. 10, 11. As Levinson put it to Hard, "it revives reinforces and make formidable the two dangerous articles of force namely ten and sixteen," which "have been allowed to lie fallow." Telegram from SOL to William Hard, October 3, 1924, quoted in Stoner, *S. O. Levinson and the Pact of Paris*, 113–14.

112. Committee of Imperial Defence: Report of the Sub-Committee on the Geneva Protocol (January 1925), p. 11. Some argued against this view. Professor P. J. Noel Baker, for example, argued against the "fantastic rumour" that "if the Protocol were adopted, the whole British Fleet would be placed unreservedly at the disposition of the League." P. J. Noel Baker, *The Geneva Protocol for the Pacific Settlement of International Disputes* (London: P. S. King & Son, Ltd. 1925), 132.

113. Conclusions of a Meeting of the Cabinet held at the House of Commons (March 2, 1925) (deciding not to ratifiy the Protocol), http://filestore.nation alarchives.gov.uk/pdfs/small/cab-23-49-cc-12-25-21.pdf.

114. John Dewey, "Afterword," in Charles Clayton Morrison, *The Outlawry of War: A Constructive Policy for World Peace* (Chicago: Willett, Clark & Colby, 1927), 301; Charles F. Howlett, *Troubled Philosopher: John Dewey and the Struggle for World Peace* (Port Washington, NY: Kennikat Press Corp., 1977), 96–113. The friendship came to an end roughly a year later, when the two engaged in a hard-edged editorial debate in *The New Republic* entitled "Divergent Paths to Peace." Ibid., 106. (Dewey's contribution was a "Foreword" in the first edition but changed to an "Afterword" in later editions.)

115. The principal treaty was the "Rhineland Pact" in which Germany, France, and Belgium undertook not to attack each other, with the United Kingdom and Italy acting as guarantors. In the event of aggression by any of the first three states against another, all other parties were obligated to assist the country under attack. "Treaty of Mutual Guarantee," October 16, 1925, *League of Nations: Treaty Series*, Vol. 54 (1926), 290–301. In a related set of agreements, Germany committed to submit disputes with France, Belgium, Poland, or Czechoslovakia to arbitration, and France pledged mutual assistance to Poland and Czechoslovakia in the event of a military conflict with Germany.

116. JTS to Arthur Fontaine, March 18, 1927, box AAA, JSP CUL. They had worked together to help to set up the International Labor Organization, whose governing organization Fontaine now chaired. Waldo Chamberlin, "Origins of the Kellogg-Briand Pact," *The Historian* 15, no. 1 (1952): 78.

117. JTS to Arthur Fontaine, March 18, 1927, box AAA, JSP CUL.

118. Here we rely heavily on Chamberlin, "Origins of the Kellogg-Briand Pact," 77–92. Chamberlin's account is widely regarded as authoritative, but it is important to bear in mind that his account is based in part on interviews with Shotwell himself. A comparison of the texts supports Chamberlain's account, as do letters at the time between Shotwell and friends. See, e.g., Earl B. Babcock to JTS, April 20, 1927, box AAA, JSP CUL.

119. JTS, "Notes for a Suggested Statement on Franco-American Policies" (draft message), March 24, 1927, box AAA, JSP CUL.

120. Chamberlin, "Origins of the Kellogg-Briand Pact," 80.

121. JTS, "Notes for a Suggested Statement on Franco-American Policies."

122. Carl von Clausewitz, *On War*, trans. and ed. Michael Howard and Peter Paret

(Princeton: Princeton University Press, 1976), 605. Shotwell made this phrase the title of his own book, James T. Shotwell, *War as an Instrument of National Policy: And Its Renunciation in the Pact of Paris* (New York: Harcourt, Brace & Co. 1929). Nicholas Murray Butler gave himself, not his colleague Shotwell, credit for the adoption of the phrase by Briand in 1926. Nicholas Murray Butler, *Across the Busy Years*, Vol. 2 (New York: Charles Scribner's Sons, 1940), 202–3. Most, however, give little credit to Butler's account. See, e.g., Robert H. Ferrell, *Peace in Their Time: The Origins of the Kellogg-Briand Pact* (New Haven: Yale University Press, 1952), 66–67.

123. "Such a joint engagement for policies of peace would not necessarily call for immediate or compulsory adherence to arbitration or judicial settlement." JTS, "Notes for a Suggested Statement on Franco-American Policies" (Shotwell draft message), March 24, 1927, box AAA, JSP CUL.

124. Josephson, *James T. Shotwell and the Rise of Internationalism in America*, 161. This did not go unnoticed by Levinson, who wrote to Borah that "Coolidge does not use the word. Nor has Kellogg used it so far. . . . I think it is vital to our past and future work to make the Kellogg proposal distinctly Outlawry. You know that the Kirby Pages, the Shotwells and the Butlers are trying to draw a close analogy between the Locarno treaty and the Kellogg proposal and that the latter really adds nothing new, etc. This we can kill with one word." Levinson to Borah, May 31, 1928, box 5, folder 4, SLP UCL.

125. In February 1928, Dewey told Levinson that Shotwell wrote Briand's proposal for the Peace Pact. Dewey to SOL, February 29, 1928, No. 02882, JDP CUL. Levinson replied in March 1928 with skepticism about Shotwell's role, writing, "I have the direct word of one of the biggest men at Quai d'Orsay that Briand did not act on Shotwell's suggestion." SOL to Dewey, March 2, 1928, No. 02883, JDP CUL. Nonetheless, comparing the text of Shotwell's memo and Briand's proposal, it appears that reports of Shotwell's influence were correct, though he did not actually author the text for Briand. See Chamberlin, "Origins of the Kellogg-Briand Pact." Most contemporaries concurred that Shotwell indeed had an important influence on Briand. David Hunter Miller, *The Peace Pact of Paris: A Study of the Briand-Kellogg Treaty* (New York: G. P. Putnam's Sons, 1928), 7.

126. Chamberlin, "Origins of the Kellogg-Briand Pact," 89.

127. Ferrell, *Peace in Their Time*, 74 (describing papers on April 6, 1927).

128. "It happened to be a very busy time for [Dr. Butler], and he asked me to draft a letter substantially in the terms of my oral statement to him. I went back to my office and wrote a draft. . . . Dr. Butler's letter rephrased this statement so as to give it his own peculiar energy of phrase." Shotwell, *Autobiography*, 213.

129. Ferrell, *Peace in Their Time*, 80.

130. Ibid.

131. George Barton French to Dr. Nicholas Murray Butler, January 21, 1930, box

149, Butler Papers, Columbia University (omissions in original) (recounting French's meeting with Kellogg).

132. FBK to Hon Wm. Allen White, April 24, 1933, roll 47, frame no. 533, FKP MHS.

133. Miller, *The Peace Pact of Paris*, 10 (reprinting the text of the proposal).

134. FBK to Hon Wm. Allen White, April 24, 1933, roll 47, frame no. 533, FKP MHS.

135. Ibid., 3. His inference is supported by the title Briand gave the proposal, which he called a "Pact of Perpetual Friendship." Miller, *The Peace Pact of Paris*, 11.

136. Shotwell wrote to Earle Babcock, the Director-Adjoint of the Carnegie Endowment for International Peace, giving detailed instructions for a campaign on behalf of the treaty by the Endowment. JTS to Earle Babcock, May 21, 1927, box AAA, JSP CUL.

137. SOL to FBK, June 24, 1927, roll 47, frame no. 576, FKP MHS.

138. Ibid.

139. Correspondence between SOL and FBK, June 24, 1927–August 9, 1929, roll 47, frame nos. 576–99, FKP MHS.

140. Ibid.

141. SOL to FBK, August 1928, roll 47, frame no. 596, FKP MHS.

142. Dewey to SOL, January 27, 1928, No. 02869, JDP CUL.

143. Ferrell, *Peace in Their Time*, 103. See also SOL to FBK, August 1928, roll 47, frame no. 596, FKP MHS.

144. The Levinson papers contain extensive references to Levinson's agent, Harrison Brown. His role is also recounted in Ferrell, *Peace in Their Time*, 103. The book distributed was Charles Clayton Morrison, *The Outlawry of War: A Constructive Policy for World Peace* (Chicago: Willett, Clark & Colby, 1927) (the second edition was dedicated to "Salmon Oliver Levinson, Author of the proposal for the 'outlawry of war' and its indefatigable apostle," and Dewey's foreword was moved to the back of the book as an afterword).

145. FBK to Hon Wm. Allen White, April 24, 1933, roll 47, frame no. 533, FKP MHS.

146. FBK to Claudel (the "American Note"), December 28, 1927, reprinted in Miller, *The Peace Pact of Paris*, 164–65.

147. For more on Briand's reaction, see Ferrell, *Peace in Their Time*, 145. The text of the two drafts is in Miller, *The Peace Pact of Paris*, 161–63, 170. Prior to the Pact, the alliances were not perfectly symmetrical. For instance, the Locarno Treaties provided that Germany, France, and Belgium would not attack one another. In the event they did so, all the other parties were to assist the country under attack.

148. SOL to President Coolidge, January 24, 1928, roll 47, frame no. 591, FKP MHS. See also SOL to FBK, February 1928, roll 47, frame no. 592, FKP MHS; SOL to President Coolidge, March 1, 1928, roll 47, frame no. 593, FKP MHS; Telegram from SOL to FBK, June 25, 1928, roll 47, frame no. 594, FKP MHS. Kellogg

acknowledged the praise in letters in return. FBK to SOL, February 28, 1928, roll 47, frame no. 593, FKP MHS; FBK to SOL, June 28, 1928, roll 47, frame no. 594, FKP MHS.

149. SOL to Dewey, March 2, 1928, No. 02883, JDP CUL. Indeed, the animosity between Levinson and Shotwell continued to grow. In March 1928, Levinson wrote Dewey, "I just catch in the Times of March 14th Shotwell's real views. He tells Yale that we should enter the League, that Kellogg's offer is 'national hypocrasy' [*sic*]. There is no use of trying to do anything with this animal. He is hopeless and his judgment is a minus quantity." SOL to Dewey, March 14, 1928, No. 02886, JDP CUL. Not long after, he would refer to Shotwell as "an infernal hypocrite" and "a damnable nuisance." SOL to Dewey, February, 15, 1929, No. 03025, JDP CUL.

150. Diary of William R. Castle, January 1, 1928, quoted in Ferrell, *Peace in Their Time*, 147.

151. "If however such a declaration were accompanied by definition of the word 'aggressor' and by exceptions and qualifications . . . its effect would be very greatly weakened and its positive value as a guaranty of peace virtually destroyed." FBK to Claudel, February 27, 1928, quoted in Levinson Memorandum, "Aggression-International," February 1, 1929, box 66, folder 1, SLP UCL.

152. Testimony of Frank Kellogg, Hearings Before the Committee on Foreign Relations United States Senate Seventieth Congress on The General Pact for the Renunciation of War Signed at Paris August 27, 1928 (December 7 and 11, 1928), Avalon Law Project, Yale Law School Lillian Goldman Law Library, http://avalon.law.yale.edu/20th_century/kbhear.asp.

153. Walter Lippmann to Senator Robert F. Wagner (January 9, 1929), in John Morton Blum, ed., *Public Philosopher: Selected Letters of Walter Lippmann* (New York: Ticknor & Fields 1985), 238.

154. Telegram from SOL to Borah, April 12, 1928, box 5, folder 4, SLP UCL.

155. Ibid. Testimony of Frank Kellogg, Hearings on The General Pact for the Renunciation of War.

156. Both Borah and Levinson appear to have found this unobjectionable. Levinson wrote Borah with a suggestion for a "simple exchange of notes" on this point. Levinson to Borah, April 30, 1928, box 254, WBP LC. (Levinson's suggestion was sparked by Lord Grey's comments to the League of Nations' Parliamentary Committee that "The United States might quite consistently agree that any power breaking the treaty should no longer be entitled to the advantage of the protection the treaty gives. In other words, those who are parties to the treaty should be freed of all restraints and obligations of the treaty with regard to any power breaking it.") As Shotwell explained to Babcock, "This device is as near a sanction as the United States can go at present." JTS to Babcock, May 21, 1927, box AAA, JSP CUL. The point was later added to the preamble of the Act.

157. SOL to Borah, April 7, 1928, box 5, folder 4, SLP UCL. Borah had his own

meeting with Kellogg on April 9, and he expressed confidence in a letter to
Levinson the next day that "we are reaching the place where the foreign pow-
ers will have to either accept or reject our proposition substantially as made."
Borah to Levinson, April 10, 1928, box 254, WBP LC. Levinson persuaded
Borah to place outlawry into the Republican Party Platform that summer.
Republican Party Platform of 1928, June 12, 1928, http://www.presidency
.ucsb.edu/ws/?pid=29637. Both Levinsons were delighted when Borah sent his
badge from the convention to Mrs. Levinson as a memento of the occasion.
SOL to Mrs. Borah, June 18, 1928, box 5, folder 4, SLP UCL.

158. The text of the proposal, dated April 13, 1928, is reprinted in Miller, *The Peace
Pact of Paris*, 184–85.

159. U.S. Ambassador to Italy, Henry P. Fletcher, to FBK, June 29, 1928, roll 33,
frame no. 126, FKP MHS.

160. FBK to Borah, Boise, Idaho, July 16, 1928, roll 33, frame nos. 298–300, FKP
MHS.

161. FBK to President Calvin Coolidge, July 13, 1928, roll 33, frame nos. 265–66,
FKP MHS.

162. SOL to Borah, August 27, 1928, box 254, WBP LC.

163. Navy Despatch from American Embassy Paris to U.S.S. Detroit (August 29,
1928), roll 34, frame nos. 316–18, FKP MHS.

164. Initially there were calls to add reservations and understandings to the agreement, but in the end the treaty was ratified without any conditions attached.
Telegraph from Borah to SOL, July 27, 1928, box 5, folder 5, SLP UCL ("The
treaty is to be signed precisely as proposed without any side understandings
protocols or interpretations."). In correspondence between Borah and Levinson regarding proposed reservations, Levinson pressed Borah to insist on a
clean treaty. SOL to Borah, box 5, folder 5, SLP UCL; FBK to Hon. Wm.
Allen White, April 24, 1933, roll 47, frame no. 533, FKP MHS ("I know that
some of the writers on the subject of the Paris pact have claimed there were
many reservations made by the different countries. . . . This is not true. There
was not a single reservation made by any country."). The Senate did not add
any reservations, but it did pass a measure "interpreting" the treaty stating that
the treaty must not infringe upon America's right of self-defense and that the
United States was not obliged to enforce the treaty by taking action against
those who violated it. Multilateral Peace Treaty, 70th Cong., 2nd Sess., *Congressional Record* 70, pt. 2: 1713–31. See also Denna Frank Fleming, *The Treaty
Veto of the American Senate* (New York: G. P. Putnam's Sons, 1930), 251–68.
Blaine was defeated in his reelection bid in 1932.

165. Since early in the negotiations others knew of Kellogg's aspirations for recognition and moved carefully around them. The editor of *The Christian Century*
wrote to Borah: "I do not want to do anything that will tend to divide Mr. Kellogg's interest in the thing that he has done so well thus far or that will suggest
to him that in the last chapter his fame will have to be shared by anyone else.

At the same time the world must eventually know who's who in this business." Editor of *The Christian Century* to Borah, April 12, 1928, box 5, folder 4, SLP UCL (discussing the printing of an editorial calling "attention to the part that you [Borah] are playing behind the scenes in these negotiations").

166. Kellogg was nominated in 1929, but the committee decided not to grant an award at all that year. This decision rankled Kellogg: "If it were not for the fact that this matter [the Nobel nomination] had been advertised all over the world last year, I should not care anything about it now, but to be endorsed last year and not this year would be rather embarrassing." FBK to William H. Beck, December 27, 1929, roll 39, frame nos. 132–33, FKP MHS (asking Beck to help him solicit endorsements to Nobel Committee).

167. Ibid. (asking Beck to help him solicit endorsements to Nobel Committee). Beck is sometimes referred to as "Private Secretary to the Secretary of State" and elsewhere as "Assistant to the Secretary." Letter from the U.S. Legation in Portugal to William H. Beck, May 23, 1927, roll 26, frame no. 120, FKP MHS (referring to him as Private Secretary to the Secretary of State); William H. Beck to Dr. W. H. Wilmer, May 27, 1927, roll 26, frame no. 169, FKP MHS (signed "Assistant to the Secretary").

168. An unsigned memo from January 25, 1930, likely prepared by Beck, shows the breadth and depth of the campaign. "List of conferences, letters, etc." (unsigned), roll 39, frame nos. 409–12, FKP MHS (listing out people who had already or would write letters of recommendation for Kellogg to receive the Nobel Prize). See also, e.g., FBK to Willis Van Devanter, January 16, 1930, roll 39, frame no. 294, FKP MHS (notifying Van Devanter that Justice Butler wrote a nomination letter to the Nobel Committee and suggesting that he do the same); Willis Van Devanter to FBK, January 23, 1930, roll 39, frame no. 393, FKP MHS (enclosing letter from Attorney General William Mitchell endorsing Kellogg for Nobel); FBK to Donald J. Cowling, December 28, 1929, roll 39, frame nos. 154–55, FKP MHS (regarding nomination procedures for Nobel prize). By the end of the campaign, Kellogg (via Beck, Culbertson, Van Devanter, Carr, Marriner, and Cowling) had secured endorsements from Chief Justice of the Supreme Court William Taft, four associate justices of the Supreme Court, Attorney General William Mitchell, almost all members of the Senate Foreign Relations Committee (Borah, Swanson, Moses, Walsh, Capper, Gillett, George, Fess, Goff, Harrison, Vandenberg), many other prominent senators and representatives, several U.S. ambassadors, and over a dozen additional civil society leaders and university presidents. FBK to Laurite Swenson, January 27, 1930, roll 39, frame nos. 414–15, FKP MHS (updating Swenson on who had written letters and asking whether more should be written).

169. Meanwhile, Levinson was working with Elihu Root and others to try to smooth the way for the U.S. to join the Permanent International Court of Justice. Correspondence between HLS and Elihu Root from June 28, 1929 to May 7, 1935, box 43, folder 9, SLP UCL. Stimson provided Levinson with a letter of

introduction to Root on June 28, 1929, which led to their first in-person meeting not long after. Levinson also worked on securing debt relief for Europe. Levinson did not go entirely unrecognized for these efforts, or for his work on outlawry. The majority of contemporary accounts credited him as the father of outlawry and a key figure behind the Paris Peace Pact. He received several honorary degrees from universities. And in 1934, he was made a chevalier of the French Legion of Honor for "his efforts in laying the ground work for the Briand-Kellogg pact of Paris outlawing war, and for his other efforts in behalf of amity among nations." Newspaper Clippings, March 29, 1934, box 29, folder 3, SLP UCL. He also won the $50,000 Bok Peace Prize "for his plan of adjusting War reparations and debts"—a plan to which he devoted himself after the conclusion of the Paris Pact. "Mr. Levinson's Way," *Time*, October 13, 1930, 15.

170. FBK to Laurite S. Swenson, December 28, 1929, roll 39, frame nos. 152–53, FKP MHS. Kellogg also solicited negative letters regarding Levinson's role in the evolution of the Pact almost as eagerly as he solicited positive letters to support his own bid. See, e.g., Spence Phenix to FBK, April 26, 1933, roll 4647, frame no. 541, FKP MHS ("My recollection of the Levinson matter is very much the same as yours. It is absurd for him to claim that he had any part in the negotiations of the Anti-War Treaty.").

SIX: THINGS FALL APART

1. We have written Japanese names in the Japanese order, with the family name first, followed by the given name.
2. *LNOJ* 12, no. 12 (1931): 2248 (meeting held on September 19, 1931); "League Intervenes for Peace in China," *New York Times*, September 20, 1931.
3. *LNOJ* 12, no. 12 (1931): 2248 (meeting held on September 19, 1931).
4. Ibid., 2266 (meeting held on September 22, 1931) (reprinting telegram dated September 21, 1931).
5. Ibid., 2267 (meeting held on September 22, 1931).
6. Ibid., 2310–11 (meeting held on October 13, 1931).
7. Ibid., 2310–13.
8. Ibid., 2321.
9. "By means of steam one can go from California to Japan in eighteen days." *Treaties and Other International Acts of the United States of America*, Vol. 7, ed. Hunter Miller (Washington, DC: U.S. Government Printing Office, 1942), 1090.
10. Hirohiko Otsuka, "Japan's Early Encounter with the Concept of the 'Law of Nations,'" *Japanese Annual of International Law* 13 (1969): 37.
11. The 1842 Treaty of Nanjing, imposed on China at the close of the First Opium War, had opened Chinese ports to trade with Great Britain. The Americans followed two years later with the Treaty of Wangxia.
12. Perry recommended a policy of "masterly inactivity" with regard to the

ongoing conflict in China. John H. Schroeder, *Matthew Calbraith Perry: Antebellum Sailor and Diplomat* (Annapolis, MD: Naval Institute Press, 2001), 210–11.

13. The 1842 Treaty of Nanking, August 29, 1842, in *Treaties, Conventions, etc. Between China and Foreign States*, Vol. 1 (Shanghai, 1917), 351–56.

14. Miller, ed., *Treaties and Other International Acts*, Vol. 7, 1070.

15. Otsuka, "Japan's Early Encounter with the Concept of the 'Law of Nations,'" 36–37.

16. Schroeder, *Matthew Calbraith Perry*, 187.

17. Matthew Perry, *The Japan Expedition, 1852–1854: The Personal Journal of Commodore Matthew C. Perry*, ed. Roger Pineau (Washington, DC: Smithsonian Institution Press, 1968). For more on the Perry expedition from an American perspective, see Francis L. Hawks, *Narrative of the Expedition of an American Squadron to the China Seas and Japan Performed in the Years 1852, 1853, and 1854, under the Command of Commodore M.C. Perry*, United States Navy, Vols. 1–3 (Washington, DC: Beverley Tucker, Senate Printer, 1856).

18. In addition to the limited trade with the Dutch and Chinese at Nagasaki, Japan also traded with China through the Ryukyus, with Korea through the Tsushima Domain, and with the Ainu people through the Matsumae Domain. See Robert I. Hellyer, *Defining Engagement Japan and Local Contexts, 1640–1868* (Cambridge: Harvard University Press, 2009). The reasons offered by scholars for this period of significant closure—*sakoku*, literally "closed country"—are varied. Some point to concerns over external interference by the Spanish (expelled in 1624), Portuguese (expelled in 1639), and Dutch (expelled in 1640)—including efforts to spread Christianity. Others have hypothesized that the policy was more inward looking, primarily aimed at strengthening the government's central power within Japan. See James Murdoch with Ishoh Yamagata, *A History of Japan Volume II: During the Century of Early Foreign Intercourse (1542–1651)* (London: Kegan Paul, Trench, Trubner & Co., 1925), 696–714; Michael S. Laver, *The Sakoku Edicts and the Politics of Tokugawa Hegemony* (Amherst, MA: Cambria Press, 2011).

19. Miller, *Treaties and Other International Acts*, Vol. 7, 1063. Notably, the Japanese had allowed limited Dutch trade with the port of Nagasaki, but there was no other foreign trade at the time of the Perry mission.

20. John S. Sewall, *The Logbook of the Captain's Clerk: Adventures in the China Seas* (Bangor, ME: C. H. Glas & Co. 1905), 124–26.

21. Ibid., 124.

22. Ibid., 143.

23. Perry, *The Japan Expedition*, 3.

24. Schroeder, *Matthew Calbraith Perry*, 79.

25. Sewall, *The Logbook of the Captain's Clerk*, 143–44.

26. Perry, *The Japan Expedition*, 91-92.

27. Ibid., 93–94. All negotiations between Perry's expedition and the Japanese

were carried out through interpreters in Chinese and Dutch—and the treaty was translated into four languages—Japanese, English, Chinese, and Dutch. See De-min Tao, "Negotiating Language in the Opening of Japan: Luo Sen's Journal of Perry's 1854 Expedition," *Japan Review* 17 (2005): 91–119. As we shall see, however, the translations were not perfect replicas of one another.

28. Sewall, *The Logbook of the Captain's Clerk*, 145.

29. Perry, *The Japan Expedition*, 94. Perry's journal refers repeatedly to the "emperor" in Edo. At the time Perry arrived, the Imperial Court (headed by the emperor) was located in Kyoto and did not play a significant role in governance. It was not until the Meiji Restoration in 1868 that the emperor (then a seventeen-year-old boy) would be made the notional head of the government in the newly named Tokyo (Edo). Meirion and Susie Harries, *Soldiers of the Sun: The Rise and Fall of the Imperial Japanese Army, 1868–1945* (London: Heinemann, 1991), 12. It is likely, therefore, that Perry was in fact corresponding with the taikun (shōgun), not the emperor. Indeed, later agreements between the United States and Japan were expressly concluded with the taikun. See Cyril H. Powles, "The Myth of the Two Emperors: A Study in Misunderstanding, Pacific Historical Review," 37, no. 1 (February 1968); Hamish Ion, *American Missionaries, Christian Oyatoi, and Japan, 1859–73* (Vancouver and Toronto: University of British Columbia Press, 2009), 38–39.

30. Perry, *The Japan Expedition*, 95.

31. Ibid.

32. Ibid.

33. Ibid., 96.

34. Hugo Grotius, *The Freedom of the Seas, or The Right Which Belongs to the Dutch to Take Part in the East Indian Trade*, trans. Ralph van Derman Magoffin (New York: Oxford University Press, 1916), 7.

35. Ibid.

36. Miller, ed., *Treaties and Other International Acts*, Vol. 7, 1090.

37. Perry, *The Japan Expedition*, 98.

38. Ibid., 98, 102–3.

39. "Perry's Letter in Connection with the Delivery of a White Flag, [July 14,] 1853," trans. Masatoshi Knishi, in *Meiji Japan Through Contemporary Sources*, 2: 15–16. See Schroeder, *Matthew Calbraith Perry*, 286 n. 44. A reprint of the letter, in Japanese, and a brief account of its presentation, in English, appear in Miwa Kimitada, "Perry's White Flags: From the Deletion in His Own Records to Their Reemergence in Historical Writings," in *Jochi Daigaku Gaikokugo Gakubu kiyo* 29 (1994): 225–49 (this account mentions two, not one, white flags, but is otherwise consistent with the other accounts). As Kimitada rightly notes, Perry's own writings do not mention the letter or any white flags. See Kimitada, "Perry's White Flags," 225.

40. Perry, *The Japan Expedition*, 159.

41. Ibid., 162.

42. Ibid., 163.

43. Ibid., 233 ("List of American Presents brought ashore in Japan, March 13, 1854").

44. The books are listed by Perry as "Kendall, *War in Mexico* and Ripley, *History of the War in Mexico*." Ibid. They are almost certainly Roswell Sabine Ripley, *The War with Mexico*, Vol. 2 (New York: Harper & Brothers, 1849); and George Wilkins Kendall and Carl Nebel, *The War Between the United States and Mexico, Illustrated* (New York: D. Appleton & Co., 1851). The man Perry refers to as "Abe, Prince of Ise, first councilor" is most likely Abe Masahiro, chief senior councilor (*rōjū*).

45. Ripley, *The War with Mexico*, Vol. 2, 87–89, 139–42.

46. Perry, *The Japan Expedition*, 163–64.

47. Sewall, *The Logbook of the Captain's Clerk*, 125.

48. Perry, *The Japan Expedition*, 172; Treaty of Peace and Amity, U.S.-Japan, March 31, 1854 (known as the Treaty of Kanagawa), in Miller, ed., *Treaties and Other International Acts*, Vol. 6, 439–40.

49. Harris had traveled to China and the Dutch East Indies and was living in Shanghai in 1853 when Perry passed through on his way to Japan. Perry rejected Townsend's bid to join the mission, but Harris succeeded in getting himself named to the new post two years later. Townsend Harris, *The Complete Journal of Townsend Harris: First American Consul General and Minister to Japan* (Garden City, NY: Doubleday, 1930), 2–3.

50. Miller, ed., *Treaties and Other International Acts*, Vol. 7, 617.

51. Otsuka, "Japan's Early Encounter with the Concept of the 'Law of Nations,'" 52–53; Harris, *The Complete Journal of Townsend Harris*, 208–10.

52. Unlike Perry's negotiations, Harris's did not take place in the shadow of a line of gunboats. But the threat was no less felt. Indeed, Harris made it explicit at least once. He reported, "I stated, that the terms, demanded by a Negociator [sic], supported by a fleet, would not be as moderate as those asked, by a Person, placed as I was, and to yield to a fleet, what was refused to me, would degrade the Government in the eyes of the People of Japan, and thus actually weaken its power." Miller, ed., *Treaties and Other International Acts*, Vol. 7, 1054.

53. Americans would pay a set tariff to the Japanese government on all goods brought into the country—5 percent on listed items including whaling gear, salted provisions, live animals, timber for building houses, lead, tin, steam machinery, and silk, and 20 percent on nearly everything else. Any exports would be assessed a duty of 5 percent, with the exception of coinage. Treaty of Amity and Commerce, U.S.-Japan, July 29, 1858, in Miller, ed., *Treaties and Other International Acts*, Vol. 7, 971–73.

54. For the text and negotiating histories of the 1857 and 1858 treaties, see Miller, ed., *Treaties and Other International Acts*, Vol. 7, 595–648, 947–1170.

55. See Miller, ed., *Treaties and Other International Acts*, Vol. 7, 1095. The conversation took place on December 21, 1857. One source claims that Nishi

Amane, discussed below, was one of the Japanese interpreters during the Harris expedition—translating from Japanese to the common diplomatic language of Dutch and back again. Alexis Dudden, *Japan's Colonization of Korea: Discourse and Power* (Honolulu: University of Hawaii Press, 2005), 42.

56. Perry's mission was not the last lesson Japan would receive in the Grotian legal order. In 1863, when the Prince of Nagato closed the Shimonoseki Straits to foreign shipping in defiance of the treaty—firing on and damaging the American steamer *Pembroke* in the process—British, Dutch, and French warships, accompanied by another American steamer, bombarded Shimonoseki until the prince capitulated. *Claims of Citizens of the United States Against Foreign Governments*, in *Compilation of Reports of Committee on Foreign Relations, United States Senate, 1789–1901*, 56th Cong. 1st Sess., Senate Report No. 752 (Washington, DC: Government Printing Office, 1901), 437–40 (recounting claims against Japan as of January 13, 1881).

57. Compare Matthew Lamberti, "Tokugawa Nariaki and the Japanese Imperial Institution: 1853–1858," *Harvard Journal of Asiatic Studies* 32 (1972): 97–123, with Harris, *The Complete Journal of Townsend Harris*.

58. Bob Tadashi Wakabayashi, "In Name Only: Imperial Sovereignty in Early Modern Japan," *Journal of Japanese Studies* 17, no. 1 (1991): 27–28. The shōgun used the diplomatic title "Nihon-koku Taikun" (Tycoon of Japan) when negotiating with foreign leaders.

59. James Murdoch, *A History of Japan*, Vol. 3: *The Tokugawa Epoch, 1652–1868* (London: Kegan Paul, Trench, Trubner & Co., 1926), 569–662; Donald Keene, *Emperor of Japan: Meiji and His World, 1852–1912* (New York: Columbia University Press, 2002).

60. Harris, *The Complete Journal of Townsend Harris*, 558. The illness is also mentioned in Murdoch, *A History of Japan*, Vol. 3, 652.

61. Ibid.

62. Lamberti, "Tokugawa Nariaki and the Japanese Imperial Institution: 1853–1858," 119–20. Harris's own journal from this period was lost. Harris, *The Complete Journal of Townsend Harris*, 559.

63. Murdoch, *A History of Japan*, Vol. 3, 652.

64. Letter from Townsend Harris to His Excellency Hotta Prince of Bitsu, July 24, 1858, reprinted in Miller, ed., *Treaties and Other International Acts*, Vol. 7, 1064. See also Murdoch, *A History of Japan*, Vol. 3, 655–56. The next day the commander-in-chief of the U.S. Naval Forces in the India, China, and Japan Seas arrived and confirmed the news that the British were on their way. Miller, ed., *Treaties and Other International Acts*, Vol. 7, 1065. The events are described from the U.S. perspective in Ibid., 947–1170.

65. Murdoch, *A History of Japan*, Vol. 3, 656.

66. Lamberti, "Tokugawa Nariaki and the Japanese Imperial Institution: 1853–1858," 119–20.

67. At the time, under the most favored nation principle, states commonly insisted

on the right to terms equal to the "most favored" nation. See J. H. Richardson, *Economic Disarmament: A Study on International Cooperation* (London: Allen & Unwin Brothers Ltd., 1931), 81–82.

68. Miller, ed., *Treaties and Other International Acts*, Vol. 7, 1044, 1095.

69. The events are detailed in Murdoch, *A History of Japan*, Vol. 3, 697–703. A manifesto was found on one body that spelled out their grievances. Ibid., 702. Though their tactics were brutal, the conspirators reflected the views of many Japanese. Otsuka, "Japan's Early Encounter with the Concept of the 'Law of Nations,'" 54. The episode is also described in Lamberti, "Tokugawa Nariaki and the Japanese Imperial Institution: 1853–1858," 120.

70. Havens, *Nishi Amane and Modern Japanese Thought*, 106, 218; Gino K. Piovesana, S.J., "The Beginnings of Western Philosophy in Japan: Nishi Amane, 1829–1897," *International Philosophy Quarterly* 2, no. 2 (1962): 295-306.

71. Havens, *Nishi Amane and Modern Japanese Thought*, 24–27.

72. Ibid., 26–29. Much of the story of Nishi Amane's early life is also detailed in Roger F. Hackett, "Nishi Amane—A Tokugawa-Meiji Bureaucrat," *The Journal of Asian Studies* 18, no. 2 (February 1959): 213–25. For a discussion not only of Nishi Amane, but also of the encounter between the Japanese and Dutch during this period, see Ōkubo Takeharu, *The Quest for Civilization: Encounters with Dutch Jurisprudence, Political Economy, and Statistics at the Dawn of Modern Japan*, trans. David Noble (Boston: Global Oriental, 2014).

73. Havens, *Nishi Amane and Modern Japanese Thought*, 29.

74. Ibid., 33–39.

75. Hackett, "Nishi Amane—A Tokugawa-Meiji Bureaucrat," 214. See also Havens, *Nishi Amane and Modern Japanese Thought*, 36.

76. Douglas Howland, *Translating the West: Language and Political Reason in Nineteenth Century Japan* (Honolulu: University of Hawaii Press, 2002), 124.

77. Havens, *Nishi Amane and Modern Japanese Thought*, 42–43.

78. Ibid., 42.

79. Ibid., 47–48.

80. Ibid., 49.

81. Ibid., 49–50.

82. "Students Studying in the Netherlands at the End of the Edo Period, 1865, National Diet Library," http://dl.ndl.go.jp/info:ndljp/pid/3851065 (Amane is front row, far right); "Students Studying in the Netherlands at the End of the Edo Period, Japan-Netherlands Exchange in the Edo Period," http://www.ndl.go.jp/nichiran/e/s2/s2_6.html.

83. Havens, *Nishi Amane and Modern Japanese Thought*, 50–56.

84. Ibid., 42–56. In addition to Nishi's *Fisuserinku-shi Bankoku Kōhō*, there is a copy of Tsuda Mamichi's lecture notes in Dutch. Entitled "Volkenregt," the manuscript remains in the collection of the library of Japan's National Diet. Takeharu, *The Quest for Civilization*, 194.

85. Ibid., 183.

86. *BK*, Introduction. He created two versions—one for popular use, and a second for the government. Only the second is still known to exist. Thomas R. H. Havens, *Nishi Amane and Modern Japanese Thought* (Princeton, NJ: Princeton University Press 1970), 51.

87. Dudden, *Japan's Colonization of Korea*, 41–42; Rune Svarverud, *International Law as World Order in Late Imperial China: Translation, Reception, and Discourse, 1847–1911* (Leiden: Brill, 2007), 98–100. See Henry Wheaton, *Wanguo gongfa*, trans. W. A. P. Martin, reprinted as *Bankoku kōhō* (Edo: Kaiseijo, 1865); Tsutsumi Koshiji, *Bankoku kōhō yakugi* (Kyō[Kyoto]: Zeniya Soshirō, 1868); Shigeno Yasutsugu, *Wayaku bankoku kōhō* (Kagoshima: Kagoshima han shuppan, 1870); and Nakamura Masanao and Takatani Ryūshū, *Bankoku kōhō reikan* (Tōkyōfu: Kitabatakemohee, 1876). On Martin's translation, see Rune Svarverud, *International Law as World Order in Late Imperial China*, 87–112.

88. *BK*. Ōkubo Takeharu compares Nishi's text to Wheaton's in Takeharu, *The Quest for Civilization*, 215–23.

89. It is worth noting that Nishi's use of invented terms makes translating his texts challenging. In some cases, Nishi's terminology became widespread, but in others his invented terms fell out of use and therefore do not appear in any extant dictionary. Our translator, Luciana Sanga, has in many cases had to reconstruct the meaning of terms based on context and the meaning of root characters. For more on *kanbun kundokutai*, see Atsuko Ueda, "Sound, Scripts, and Styles: Kanbun Kundokutai and the National Language Reforms of 1880s Japan," *Review of Japanese Culture and Society*, Vol. 20 (2008): 133–56.

90. Howland, *Translating the West*, 64.

91. Ibid., 65; John Peter Stern, *The Japanese Interpretation of the "Law of Nations," 1854–1874* (Princeton: Princeton University Press, 1979), 80–92; Kido Takayoshi, *The Diary of Kido Takayoshi*, Vol. 1, trans. Sidney Devere Brown and Akiko Hirota (Tokyo: University of Tokyo Press, 1983), 148.

92. *BK*, Introduction.

93. *BK*, Vol. 1, ch. 1, secs. 11–12.

94. The word used throughout is commonly translated as "humiliation." Compare to *DJP*, 3.1.

95. *BK*, Vol. 3, ch. 1, sec. 6.

96. *BK*, Vol. 3, ch. 1, sec. 16.

97. *BK*, Vol. 3, ch. 1, sec. 17.

98. "Recently, in western public law, when declaring war, there have been no ceremonies. Here are various examples of how to declare war: Making a concise written or oral statement that you will start a war, and the reasons for that; Attack, after having declared you will start a war unless the final requests concerning an incident are met within a short period of time; Publicly distribute a written declaration and explain through speeches the reasons for starting a war; Promulgate an imperial order to the subjects of one's country and give orders of mobilization to the army; Discharge the ambassadors of the enemy country

and send them back, or call back one's ambassadors to the enemy country." *BK*, Vol. 3, ch. 1, sec. 24.

99. *BK*, Vol. 2, Ch. 1 ("Countries have the following rights in order to protect their freedom: 1) The right to be equal. . . . These laws stem from natural law. . . .")

100. The table of contents for the last book shows how important this subject was to Nishi:

VOLUME IV: RULES ON INTERNATIONAL VISITS AND CORRESPONDENCE

Ch. 1:   Social Intercourse Between Sovereigns and Their Relatives—8 sections

Ch. 2:   Outlines of the Rights of Diplomats—12 sections

Ch. 3:   Etiquette of Dispatching Government Officials—8 sections

Ch. 4:   The Rights and Duties of Diplomats—18 sections

Ch. 5:   Special Envoys and Ambassadors—6 sections

Ch. 6:   Consulates—15 sections

Ch. 7:   Exchange of Gratitude, Congratulations and Etiquette of Correspondence—28 sections

Ch. 8:   Etiquette at Sea—12 sections

BK, Vol. 4.

101. Havens observes: "It is not uncommon to find scholars such as Nishi serving their governments in the modern world, but it is unusual for them to manage to write their most important works while simultaneously holding public office. Rarer still is the intellectual who is able to maintain his scholarly integrity by putting his theoretical ideals into political practice." Havens, *Nishi Amane and Modern Japanese Thought*, 192. Harries and Harries, *Soldiers of the Sun*, 14 ("For the Shogun he had expounded 'barbarian' military science; for Omura and Yamagata, he advised on international diplomatic practice and military capabilities, and he was appointed a lecturer to the Emperor on western thought in general.").

102. Hackett, "Nishi Amane—A Tokugawa-Meiji Bureaucrat," 215.

103. Ibid., 215–16. The connection between Nishi's scholarly and political career is also discussed thoughtfully in Havens, *Nishi Amane and Modern Japanese Thought*, 191–221.

104. Havens, *Nishi Amane and Modern Japanese Thought*, 194.

105. Ibid., 192–93; Hackett, "Nishi Amane—A Tokugawa-Meiji Bureaucrat," 217.

106. Havens, *Nishi Amane and Modern Japanese Thought*, 207.

107. Hackett, "Nishi Amane—A Tokugawa-Meiji Bureaucrat," 221.

108. Havens, *Nishi Amane and Modern Japanese Thought*, 195.

109. Hackett, "Nishi Amane—A Tokugawa-Meiji Bureaucrat," 220–21 (these quotes are from lectures delivered by Nishi between 1878 and 1881, later published serially in the army newspaper).

110. Piovesana, "The Beginnings of Western Philosophy in Japan," 295–306, 299–300.

111. The phrase was reportedly coined by German military adviser Major Klemens Wilhelm Jakob Meckel, who was brought to Japan in 1885 to help modernize the military. He described the Korean Peninsula as "a dagger pointed at the heart of Japan." James L. McClain, *Japan: A Modern History* (New York: W. W. Norton, 2002), 296. The Japanese initially sought out advice on modernizing the military from the French. But after the French defeat in the Franco-Prussian War, they turned to the winner of the conflict—Germany. The Meiji government brought Meckel to Japan in 1885, where he assisted in structural reforms that helped pave the way for the Imperial Army's later victories against China and Russia. See Marius B. Jansen, *The Making of Modern Japan* (Cambridge: Belknap Press of Harvard University, 2002), 396–97; Joachim Burgschwentner, Matthias Egger, and Gunda Barth-Scalmani, eds., *Other Fronts, Other Wars? First World War Studies on the Eve of the Centennial* (Leiden: Brill, 2014), 135; D. Eleanor Westney, *Imitation and Innovation: The Transfer of Western Organizational Patterns to Meiji Japan* (Cambridge: Harvard University Press, 1987), 40–100.

112. Hackett, "Nishi Amane—A Tokugawa-Meiji Bureaucrat," 224; Havens, *Nishi Amane*, 196, 200–201.

113. Dudden, *Japan's Colonization of Korea*, 49, 51.

114. Ibid., 51. For more on Japanese-Korean relations in the early 1870s, and events leading to war, see Marlene J. Mayo, "The Korean Crisis of 1873 and Early Meiji Foreign Policy," *Journal of Asian Studies*, 31 (1972): 793–819; Donald Keane, *Emperor of Japan: Meiji and His World, 1852–1912* (New York: Columbia University Press, 2002), 229–62

115. The treaty is known as the Japan-Korea Treaty of 1876, the Japanese-Korean Treaty of Amity (in Korea), Korean-Japanese Treaty of Amity (in Japan), and the Treaty of Ganghwa Island. See The Japanese-Korean Treaty, Japan-Korea, February 26, 1876, in *Korean Treaties*, ed. Henry Chung (New York: H. S. Nichols Inc., 1919), 205–9.

116. The events are described in some detail in Keane, *Emperor of Japan*, 249–62.

117. The Japanese-Korean Treaty, Japan-Korea, February 26, 1876. See Dudden, *Japan's Colonization of Korea*, 45–55.

118. Ibid., 54.

119. Ibid.

120. Treaty of Ganghwa Island, February 26, 1876, Art. 1, in Chung, ed., *Korean Treaties*, 205.

121. Dudden, *Japan's Colonization of Korea*, 54–55.

122. Frederick Foo Chien, *The Opening of Korea: A Study of Chinese Diplomacy, 1876–1885* (Hamden, CT: Shoe String Press, 1967), 63; Peter Duus, *The Abacus and the Sword: The Japanese Penetration of Korea, 1895–1910* (Berkeley, CA: University of California Press, 1995), 49–51.

123. Convention of Tientsin (Tianjin), April 18, 1885 in *Treaties, Conventions, etc. Between China and Foreign States*, Vol. 2 (Shanghai, 1908), 1316–17.

124. McClain, *Japan*, 297.

125. Duus, *The Abacus and the Sword*, 49.

126. Ibid., 29–102.

127. "The Declaration of War by Japan," in Vladimir (pseud. for Zenone Volpicelli), *The China-Japan War: Compiled from Japanese, Chinese, and Foreign Sources* (New York: Charles Scribner's Sons, 1896), 245; Sakuyei Takahashi, *The Influence of Grotius in the Far East* (Brooklyn, NY: Brooklyn Institute, 1908), 13. The Japanese text of the declaration uses the now common word *kokusaihō* to refer to the law of nations, or international law.

128. Japan exercised economic and military dominance over Korea beginning in 1895, but it would not annex the country until 1910. Treaty Between Japan and Korea (Japan-Korea Annexation Treaty), August 22, 1910, in *Papers Relating to the Foreign Relations of the United States with the Annual Message of the President Transmitted to Congress December 6, 1910* (Washington, DC: U.S. Government Printing Office, 1915), 682–83. The proclamation issued with the treaty explained that the annexation was necessary because the "existing system of government in that country has not proved entirely equal to the duty of preserving public order and tranquility." It continued, "In order to maintain peace and stability in Korea, to promote the prosperity and welfare of Koreans, and at the same time to ensure the safety and repose of foreign residents, it has been made abundantly clear that fundamental changes in the actual regime of government are absolutely essential." Proclamation of Japan Annexing Korea, August 22, 1910, in *Supplement to the American Journal of International Law*, Vol. 4 (New York: Baker, Voorhis & Co., 1910), 280–82.

129. S. C. M. Paine, *The Sino-Japanese War of 1894–1895: Perceptions, Power, and Primacy* (Cambridge: Cambridge University Press, 2003), 270 (quoting Count Itō).

130. Treaty of Shimonoseki, April 17, 1895, in *Treaties, Conventions, etc. Between China and Foreign States*, Vol. 2 (Shanghai, 1908), 1318–24. This story is told from the U.S. perspective in Senate Report No. 752, 46th Cong., 3rd Sess. (January 13, 1881). A transcript of a portion of the negotiations can be found in Pei-Kai Cheng, Michael Lestz, and Jonathan Spence, eds., *The Search for Modern China: A Documentary Collection* (New York: W. W. Norton, 1999), 172–77. An overview of the events can be found at Paine, *The Sino-Japanese War of 1894–1895*, 247–93.

131. See, e.g., William L. Langer, *The Diplomacy of Imperialism, 1890–1902* (New York: Alfred A. Knopf, 1956), 167–94.

132. Ernest Batson Price, *The Russo-Japanese Treaties of 1907–1916 Concerning Manchuria and Mongolia* (Baltimore: Johns Hopkins University Press, 1933), 15.

133. Sino-Russian Railway Agreements, 1896, in Cheng, Lestz, and Spence, eds., *The Search for Modern China*, 177–81.

134. Paine, *The Sino-Japanese War of 1894–1895*, 293.

135. Ibid., 290.

136. Ibid., 290–93.

137. The Japanese Declaration of War, which was delivered to the Russian tsar hours after the Japanese launched an attack on Port Arthur (thus leading to later charges of an illegally waged war), explained, "Russia, in disregard of her solemn treaty pledges to China, her repeated assurances to other powers, is still in occupation of Manchuria and has consolidated and strengthened her hold upon three provinces, and is bent upon their final annexation. And since the absorption of Manchuria by Russia would render it impossible to maintain the integrity of Korea and would in addition compel the abandonment of all hope for peace in the Extreme East, We determined in those circumstances to settle the question by negotiation, and to secure thereby permanent peace." Those negotiations had failed, however: "She has rejected the proposals of Our Government; the safety of Korea is in danger, the vital interests of Our Empire are menaced. The guarantees for the future which we have failed to secure by peaceful negotiations. We can only now seek by an appeal to arms." Declaration of War, February 10, 1904, in *Papers Relating to the Foreign Relations of the United States, with the Annual Message of the President Transmitted to Congress December 6, 1904* (Washington, DC: U.S. Government Printing Office, 1905), 414.

138. The Treaty of Portsmouth, September 5, 1905. In addition, the southern part of Sakhalin Island below the 50th parallel reverted to Japan, while Russia retained the northern section. Japan renounced its claims of sovereignty over southern Sakhalin and the nearby Kuril Islands in the 1951 Treaty of San Francisco, but there remains a dispute about the four offshore islands of Hokkaido. Modern disputes over islands are discussed in greater detail in Chapter Fifteen.

139. He later wrote a book on the topic: Sakuyé Takahashi, *International Law Applied to the Russo-Japanese War* (London: Steven & Sons, Ltd., 1908). The preface, he noted, was written on the "325th Anniversary of Hugo Grotius' birthday." Ibid., vi. For more on Takahashi, see Fujio Ito, "One Hundred Years of International Law Studies in Japan," *Japanese Annual of International Law* 13 (1969): 23–27.

140. Takahashi, *The Influence of Grotius in the Far East*, 12.

141. Ibid., 13.

142. David J. Lu, *Agony of Choice: Matsuoka Yosuke, and the Rise and Fall of the Japanese Empire, 1880–1946* (Lanham, MD: Lexington Books, 2002), 44; Masayoshi Noguchi and Trevor Boyns, "The South Manchuria Railway Company: An Accounting and Financial History, 1907–1943," Kobe University Discussion Paper Series (March 15, 2013). Japan further expanded its control in 1915 after making the "Twenty-one Demands," which led to significantly greater Japanese control in the region. The day China capitulated became known as "National Humiliation Day" in China. Jansen, *The Making of Modern Japan*, 515–16.

143. Sandra Wilson, *The Manchurian Crisis and Japanese Society, 1931–33* (New York: Routledge, 2001), 18–20. For an account of the events from a Chinese perspective, see Whitewall Wang, *Wanpaoshan Incident and the Anti-Chinese Riots in Korea* (Nanking, China: International Relations Committee, 1931).

144. Wilson, *The Manchurian Crisis and Japanese Society*, 18–20; Robert Ferrell, "The Mukden Incident: September 18–19, 1931," *The Journal of Modern History* 27, no. 1 (1955): 66–72.

145. Ferrell, "The Mukden Incident," 67. This came to be known as the Nakamura Incident. See also Daniel B. Ramsdell, "The Nakamura Incident and the Japanese Foreign Office," *Journal of Asian Studies* 25, no. 1 (1965): 53–55.

146. Wilson, *The Manchurian Crisis and Japanese Society*, 18–19; Ramsdell, "The Nakamura Incident and the Japanese Foreign Office," 53–55; Louise Young, *Japan's Total Empire: Manchuria and the Culture of Wartime Imperialism* (Berkeley: University of California Press, 1999), 39.

147. Young, *Japan's Total Empire*, 39.

148. Shigeru Honjō, *Emperor Hirohito and His Chief Aide-De-Camp: The Honjō Diary, 1933–36*, trans. Mikiso Hane (Tokyo: University of Tokyo Press, 1982), 6.

149. Ibid., 5–8, 41–42.

150. To the end of his life, General Honjō insisted the actions were merely defensive. Ibid., 7–8. It is far from clear that he knew of the specific plans in advance of the attack, but he had made clear his intention to solve the "Manchurian problem," and he approved the plan to extend the campaign beyond the railway zone. Ibid., 8–9.

151. League of Nations Special Assembly, *Report of the League Assembly on the Manchurian Dispute* (International Relations Committee, 1933), 4–5.

152. *LNOJ*, Vol. 12 (1931), 2318. In addition to public statements before the League, and private communications, Japan prepared a detailed response to the charges. Much of the material appears in Japanese Delegation to the League of Nations, *The Manchurian Question: Japan's Case in the Sino-Japanese Dispute as Presented Before the League of Nations* (Geneva, 1933).

153. League of Nations, *Appeal by the Chinese Government, Report of the Commission of Enquiry, League of Nations Publications*, No. C.633.M.320 (Geneva, 1932), 5.

154. Memorandum from the U.S. Ambassador in Japan to the U.S. Secretary of State, July 16, 1932, *Papers Relating to the Foreign Relations of the United States, Japan 1931–1941* (Washington, DC: U.S. Government Printing Office, 1943), 93–94.

155. Lu, *Agony of Choice*, 43–65.

156. Ibid., 1–16.

157. Ibid., 86–95.

158. The representatives condemned Japan at a series of special sessions from December 6 through December 8, 1932, *LNOJ Special Supplement*, No. 111 (1933), 32–63.

159. "Discussion and Adoption of the Draft Report Prepared by the Special Committee of the Assembly Under Paragraph 4 of Article 15 of the Covenant," *LNOJ Special Supplement*, No. 112 (1933), 22–23.

160. Ibid.

161. Ibid., 23.

162. For a description of Matsuoka's exit, see "The League: Crushing Verdict," *Time*, March 6, 1933, 21.

SEVEN: THE SANCTIONS OF PEACE

1. See Herbert P. Bix, *Hirohito and the Making of Modern Japan* (New York: Harper-Collins, 2000), 222–23; Hatsue Shinohara, "An Intellectual Foundation for the Road to Pearl Harbor: Quincy Wright and Tachi Sakutaro" (unpublished manuscript) (quoting Tachi Sakutarō, "Fusen Joyaku no Kokusaiho-kan" [View of International Law in the Kellogg-Briand Pact], *Kokusaiho Gaiko Zasshi* 27 (December 1929): 7.

2. See Further Correspondence with the Government of the United States Respecting the United States Proposal for the Renunciation of War, June 23, 1928, Avalon Law Project, Yale Law School Lillian Goldman Law Library, http://avalon.law.yale.edu/20th_century/kbbr.asp; David Hunter Miller, *The Peace Pact of Paris: A Study of the Briand-Kellogg Treaty* (New York: G. P. Putnam's Sons, 1928), 196–200, 232–33.

3. See American Note, June 23, 1928, in Miller, *The Peace Pact of Paris*, 213–19.

4. See, e.g., Hearings Before the Committee on Foreign Relations, General Pact for the Renunciation of War, 70th Cong. (December 7, 11, 1929) (Secretary of State Kellogg). It is worth noting that the exchanges between the parties are not formal reservations, though they are sometimes incorrectly referred to as such. Kellogg expressly denied that notes by the British and French constituted reservations to the treaty. Yet he acknowledged that the exchange of notes would affect the treaty's interpretation. Ibid. ("There is absolutely nothing in the notes of the various governments which would change this treaty, if the treaty had been laid on the table and signed as it is, without any discussion. It is true, of course, that during this discussion, through these notes with the various nations, many questions were raised as to the meaning of the treaty. It was for the reason that I did not care to have any private discussions about the matter that I insisted on carrying out the negotiations by notes.")

5. Shinohara, "An Intellectual Foundation for the Road to Pearl Harbor."

6. For more on the dataset from which these figures are drawn, see Chapter Fourteen.

7. Mark Mazower, *Hitler's Empire: How the Nazis Ruled Europe* (New York: Penguin, 2008), 576.

8. See American Note, June 23, 1928, in Miller, *The Peace Pact of Paris*, 213–19.

9. *Motosada Zumoto, Lytton Report and Japanese Reaction* (Tokyo: Herald Press, 1932), 3.

10. Ibid., 4 (quoting General Muto).

11. Ibid., 10-19.

12. Japan offered a forty-page response, later bound together with similar documents in a book that made a more complete case. The book, which included speeches before the League and other public arguments, was published the following year: Japanese Delegation to the League of Nations, *Japan's Case in the Sino-Japanese Dispute as Presented Before the League of Nations* (Geneva, 1933).

13. Only three members of the League remained outside the Pact. They were Bolivia, El Salvador, and Uruguay. "Participant Status, International Treaty for the Renunciation of War as an Instrument of National Policy," United Kingdom Foreign and Commonwealth Office, accessed January 14, 2016, http://treaties .fco.gov.uk/treaties/treatyrecord.htm?tid=1829; League of Nations Economic Intelligence Service, *Statistical Year-Book of the League of Nations 1942/44* (Geneva: League of Nations, 1945), 291.

14. "Report of the Committee Appointed by the Council on January 15, 1930," *LNOJ*, Vol. 11, No. 5 (May 1930), 353.

15. Kellogg tried to explain away such problems in a widely disseminated speech before the Council on Foreign Relations. Citing a British interpretation of the Covenant, he explained that "[e]ven Article 10 of the Covenant has been construed to mean that League members are not inescapably bound thereby to employ their military forces." Frank B. Kellogg, "The War Prevention Policy of the United States," *American Journal of International Law* 22, no. 2 (April 1928): 260.

16. "Report of the Committee Appointed by the Council," 372. The statements entered by other state parties are available at ibid., 353–83; "Amendment of the Covenant of the League of Nations in Order to Bring It into Harmony with the Pact of Paris," *LNOJ*, Vol. 12, No. 8 (August 1931), 1596–1604.

17. "Report of the Committee Appointed by the Council," 353. The committee began from amendments proposed by the British delegation, which first pointed out the problem. "Amendment of the Covenant of the League of Nations," 1601.

18. "Report of the Committee Appointed by the Council," 367. The representative was Bernhard Wilhelm von Bülow.

19. Ibid., 354.

20. Ibid., 357.

21. Ibid., 353.

22. Ibid., 370.

23. Ibid., 376.

24. The Peruvian delegation offered one possible answer: amending the Covenant to provide that the League could not register "any treaty of peace imposed by force as a consequence of a war undertaken in violation of the Pact of Paris" and that the League would "consider as null and void any stipulations which it may contain, and shall render every assistance in restoring the *status quo*

destroyed by force." "Report of the Committee Appointed by the Council," 364. The proposal met with almost universal silence, possibly because, as one of the few delegates to respond put it, his government was "not prepared to contemplate a situation in which the League should so fail in its duties under the Covenant as to render it possible for the victor of a warlike enterprise carried out in violation of the Covenant to impose a dictated peace upon the vanquished." Ibid., 379.

25. Edwin L. James, "Germany Quits League; Hitler Asks 'Plebiscite,'" *New York Times*, October 15, 1933.

26. Kellogg, then serving as a judge on the Permanent Court of International Justice, insisted that the violation of the Pact required a response. He telegraphed Henry Stimson, his successor: "I believe it is the duty of every country party to Paris Pact as well as Four Power Pacific Treaty to make representations to both countries." Robert H. Ferrell, *The American Secretaries of State and Their Diplomacy*, Vol. 6, *Frank B. Kellogg; Henry L. Stimson* (New York: Cooper Square Publishers, 1963), 133. What he meant by representations was not specified, but the implication was clear: States party to the Pact were obligated to respond in some way to this open and flagrant violation.

27. David Schmitz, *Henry Stimson: The First Wise Man* (Wilmington: Scholarly Resources, 2001), 8; Godfrey Hodgson, *The Colonel: The Life and Wars of Henry Stimson, 1867–1950* (New York: Alfred A. Knopf, 1990), 15.

28. Schmitz, *Henry Stimson*, 11.

29. Hodgson, *The Colonel*, 13.

30. Ibid., 17.

31. Ibid., 16.

32. Ferrell, *The American Secretaries of State*, 161–63.

33. Richard N. Current, *Secretary Stimson: A Study in Statecraft* (New Brunswick, NJ: Rutgers University Press, 1954), 46–47.

34. Ferrell, *The American Secretaries of State*, 162–63.

35. President Herbert Hoover, Remarks Upon Proclaiming the Treaty for the Renunciation of War (Kellogg-Briand Pact) (July 24, 1929).

36. HLS, diary entry, September 23, 1931, reel 3, HSP YUL.

37. Richard N. Current, "The Stimson Doctrine and the Hoover Doctrine," *The American Historical Review* 59, no. 3 (April 1954): 516; Documents on the Tokyo International Military Tribunal: Charter, Indictment and Judgments, ed. Robert Cryer and Neil Boister (Oxford: Oxford University Press, 2008), 1:330.

38. HLS, diary entry, October 8, 1931, reel 3, HSP YUL; Henry L. Stimson, *The Far Eastern Crisis: Recollections and Observations* (New York: Harper & Brothers, 1936), 60.

39. Stimson, *The Far Eastern Crisis*, 60.

40. HLS, diary entry, October 9, 1931, reel 3, HSP YUL.

41. Current, "The Stimson Doctrine," 520.

42. Stimson, *The Far Eastern Crisis*, 60. See also Current, "The Stimson Doctrine," 516–21.

43. HLS, diary entry, November 19, 1931, reel 4, HSP YUL. See Current, "The Stimson Doctrine," 520–21; Ray Lyman Wilbur and Arthur Mastocl Hyde, *The Hoover Policies* (New York: Charles Scribner's Sons, 1937), 599–603.

44. On November 27, Stimson asked Hoover to "reconsider . . . certain elements which lie in favor of an embargo." Stimson worried that "it would be a tremendous loss to the higher motives and the higher policies if Japan really gets away with this, if the army teaches itself, Japan, and the rest of the world that the higher efforts towards peace by the rest of the world can be successfully defied in the way in which Japan is now defying them." But Hoover was intransigent. As Stimson put it in his diary, "The poor old President is in a bad plight. As he says, he has been making speeches against sanctions of force all this time and he cannot reverse himself." HLS, diary entry, November 27, 1931, reel 4, HSP YUL.

45. SOL to HLS, April 5, 1929, box 45, folder 8, SLP UCL.

46. HLS to SOL, telegram, July 17, 1929, box 45, folder 8, SLP UCL.

47. Correspondence between SOL and HLS from April 5, 1929 to September 5, 1930, box 45, folder 8, SLP UCL.

48. HLS to SOL, January 2, 1930, box 45, folder 8, SLP UCL.

49. Salmon O. Levinson, "The Sanctions of Peace," *The Christian Century*, December 25, 1929, 1603.

50. Ibid., 1604. See also David Turns, "The Stimson Doctrine of Non-Recognition: Its Historical Genesis and Influence on Contemporary International Law," *Chinese Journal of International Law* 2, no. 1 (2003): 116. When Stimson first discussed nonrecognition with his advisers, one of them opposed it on the grounds that "Secretary Bryan had tried it in 1915 without results." Current, "The Stimson Doctrine," 522. See also Roy Watson Curry, *Woodrow Wilson and Far Eastern Policy, 1913–1921* (New York: Bookman Associates, 1957), 128; Hersch Lauterpacht, Edwin M. Borchard, and Phoebe Morrison, "The Problem of Non-Recognition," in *Legal Problems in the Far Eastern Conflict* (New York: Institute of Pacific Relations, 1941), 134–36. The British government had also refused to recognize a number of territories' alienation from the sovereignty of the Ottoman Empire in the late nineteenth and early twentieth centuries: the independence of Bulgaria in 1886, the Austro-Hungarian annexation of Bosnia and Herzegovina in 1908, and the Italian annexation of Libya in 1911. Thomas Barclay, *The Turco-Italian War and Its Problems* (London: Constable & Company, 1912), 41–42; Lauterpacht, Borchard, and Morrison, "The Problem of Non-Recognition," 134–35.

51. SOL to James G. McDonald, April 7, 1928, quoted in John E. Stoner, *S. O. Levinson and the Pact of Paris* (Chicago: University of Chicago Press, 1943), 193.

52. Stoner, *S. O. Levinson and the Pact of Paris*, 192 (emphasis added).

53. Stimson, *The Far Eastern Crisis*, 96–97. See also Turns, "The Stimson Doctrine

of Non-Recognition," 117–18; Robert H. Ferrell, *American Diplomacy in the Great Depression: Hoover-Stimson Foreign Policy, 1929–1933* (New Haven: Yale University Press, 1957), 157.

54. Lauterpacht, Borchard, and Morrison, "The Problem of Non-Recognition," 136.

55. The Secretary of State to the Ambassador in Japan (Forbes), telegram, January 7, 1932, in U.S. Department of State, *Peace and War: United States Foreign Policy, 1931–1941* (Washington, DC: U.S. Government Printing Office, 1983), 159–60.

56. Henry L. Stimson, "The Pact of Paris: Three Years of Development," *Foreign Affairs* 11, no. 1 (October 1932). The speech was delivered in August 1932 and reprinted in *Foreign Affairs* that October.

57. Felix Frankfurter to HLS, August 11, 1932, reel 83, HSP YUL.

58. The League grounded its new approach in Article 10 of the League Covenant, by which members undertook "to respect and preserve . . . the territorial integrity and existing political independence of all [other] Members." See generally Joseph Peter Andrew O'Mahoney, "Denying the Spoils of War?: The Politics of the Nonrecognition of Aggressive Gain" (PhD diss., George Washington University, 2012), 117, Proquest (UMI 3524049). The Budapest Articles of Interpretation of the Pact of Paris included a similar statement: "The signatory States [of the Pact of Paris] are not entitled to recognize as acquired *de jure* any territorial or other advantages acquired *de facto* by means of a violation of the Pact." International Law Association, "The Effect of the Briand-Kellogg Pact of Paris on International Law," in *Report of the Thirty-Eighth Conference Held at Budapest in the Hungarian Academy of Science* (London: Eastern Press, 1935), 6. See also Quincy Wright, "The Legal Foundation of the Stimson Doctrine," *Pacific Affairs* 8, no. 4 (December 1935).

59. League of Nations, Report of the League Assembly on the Manchurian Dispute (Nanking: International Relations Committee, 1933), 79.

60. "Measures Proposed by the Advisory Committee in Connection with the Non-Recognition of 'Manchukuo,'" in "Records of the Special Session of the Assembly Convened in Virtue of Article 15 of the Covenant at the Request of the Chinese Government," *LNOJ*, Special Supplement, No. 113 (1933): 10–13. See also O'Mahoney, "Denying the Spoils of War?," 137–38; Westel W. Willoughby, *The Sino-Japanese Controversy and the League of Nations* (Baltimore: Johns Hopkins University Press, 1935), 522–32.

61. For a more skeptical view of the Stimson Doctrine, see Armin Rappaport, *Henry Stimson and Japan, 1931–1933* (Chicago: University of Chicago Press, 1963), 95.

62. Pitt Cobbett, *Cases on International Law*, 5th ed., Vol. 2 (London: Sweet & Maxwell 1937), 1.

63. John Bassett Moore, *Digest of International Law* (Washington, DC: U.S. Government Printing Office, 1906).

64. See, e.g., *Exportation of Arms or Munitions of War: Hearings Before the Committee on Foreign Affairs House of Representatives on H.J. Res. 93*, 73rd Cong., 1st Sess. (March 28, 1933), 12–13 (statement of Edwin M. Borchard, Professor of International Law, Yale University); ibid., 14–17 (letter from John Bassett Moore, read by Borchard); John Bassett Moore, "The New Isolation," *American Journal of International Law* 27, no. 4 (October 1933); John Bassett Moore, "An Appeal to Reason," *Foreign Affairs* 11, no. 4 (July 1933); John Bassett Moore, "Fifty Years of International Law," *Harvard Law Review* 50, no. 3 (January 1937); Edwin M. Borchard, "The Arms Embargo and Neutrality," *American Journal of International Law* 27, no. 2 (April 1933); Edwin M. Borchard, "Sanctions v. Neutrality," *American Journal of International Law* 30, no. 1 (January 1936); Edwin M. Borchard and William Potter Lage, *Neutrality for the United States* (New Haven: Yale University Press 1937).

65. For example, Hersch Lauterpacht, who would become an important figure in the transformation of neutrality law, was much more cautious about concluding that the law had changed. As late as 1935, he still had not yet embraced Stimson's view that the law had changed as a result of the Pact. See, e.g., Lassa Oppenheim, *International Law*, 5th ed., Vol. 2, ed. Hersch Lauterpacht (London: Longmans, Green and Co., 1935), 516–17. He would, however, come around to that view by the end of the decade.

66. International Law Association, "Effect of the Briand-Kellogg Pact," 11.

67. Ibid., 5–6.

68. See, e.g., Quincy Wright and Clyde Eagleton, "Neutrality and Neutral Rights Following the Pact of Paris for the Renunciation of War," *Proceedings of the American Society of International Law at Its Annual Meeting* 24 (April 1930): 79–89; Quincy Wright, "How Should the Neutrality Act of August 31, 1935, Be Revised?," *Georgetown Law Journal* 24 (1935–1936): 420–21. Wright was friendly with Levinson. Wright's wife, Louise, was the chair of the Illinois League of Women Voters' Department of International Cooperation to Prevent War—a group that worked with Levinson on outlawry. Quincy Wright would also go on to be an adviser on international law to the United States at the Nuremberg war crimes trials. See Quincy Wright, "The Law of the Nuremberg Trial," *American Journal of International Law* 41, no. 1 (January 1947): 38–72.

69. Quincy Wright, "The Future of Neutrality," *International Conciliation* 12 (September 1928): 357–58.

70. The volumes of the *American Journal of International Law* during this period were filled with articles on the nuances of neutrality law. In some volumes, more than half of the articles were devoted to the topic. Borchard, however, remained as committed as ever to his traditional view of neutrality. See Edwin Borchard, review of *Draft Convention on Rights and Duties of Neutral States in Naval and Aerial War*, by Research in International Law at the Harvard Law School, *Tulane Law Review* 15 (1940–1941): 640–41.

71. *Exportation of Arms or Munitions of War*, 73rd Cong. 1st Sess., 17 (letter from Moore, read by Borchard).

72. Ibid., 19 (Borchard responding to Rep. Tinkham).

73. Wright, "The Future of Neutrality."

74. Neutrality Act of 1935, 49 Stat. 1081 (1935).

75. The invasion was on October 3. On October 7, the League issued its "Report of the Committee of Thirteen," declaring Italy the aggressor. "Seventh Meeting (Public), Eighty-Ninth Session of the Council," *LNOJ*, Vol. 16, No. 11 (November 1935), 1217–26. For more detail on the war and the reaction of the League, see John H. Spencer, "The Italian-Ethiopian Dispute and the League of Nations," *American Journal of International Law* 31, no. 4 (October 1937): 614–41.

76. Willoughby, *The Sino-Japanese Controversy*, 532.

77. Ibid., 533.

78. M. J. Bonn, "How Sanctions Failed," *Foreign Affairs* 15, no. 2 (1937): 350–61. See also George Baer, *Test Case: Italy, Ethiopia, and the League of Nations* (Stanford, CA: Hoover Institution Press, 1976), Ch. 2.

79. League of Nations, *The League from Year to Year (1935)* (Geneva: League of Nations Information Section, 1936), 80–81.

80. Hugh R. Wilson, *Diplomat Between Wars* (New York: Longmans, Green and Co., 1941), 331. See also Cristiano Andrea Ristuccia, "1935 Sanctions Against Italy: Would Coal and Crude Oil Have Made a Difference?," *European Review of Economic History* 4, no. 1 (2000): 85–100.

81. Cordell Hull, *The Memoirs of Cordell Hull*, Vol. 1 (New York: Macmillan, 1948), 418–19.

82. Statement by the Secretary of State, September 12, 1935, in U.S. Department of State, *Peace and War*, 276.

83. Hull, *Memoirs*, Vol. 1, 428–43.

84. Ibid., Vol. 1, 428–31. For more on the role of American finance, see Gian Giacomo Migone, *The United States and Fascist Italy: The Rise of American Finance in Europe*, trans. Molly Tambor (Cambridge: Cambridge University Press 2015), 287–388.

85. "Second Meeting (Private, Then Public), Ninety-Second Session of the Council," *LNOJ*, Vol. 17, No. 6 (June 1936), 540.

86. "Situation in Ethiopia," *LNOJ*, Vol. 17, No. 12 (December 1936): 1409–10. See also "Situation in Ethiopia," *LNOJ*, Vol. 18, Nos. 8–9 (August 1937): 658–59.

87. "Situation in China," *LNOJ*, Vol. 18, Nos. 8–9 (August 1937): 653–57. See also Rana Mitter, *Forgotten Ally: China's World War II, 1937–1945* (Boston: Houghton Mifflin, 2013), 80.

88. Ibid., 654.

89. "Second Meeting (Private, Then Public)," *LNOJ*, Vol. 19, No. 11 (November 1938): 878–80.

90. Joseph Cummins, *The World's Bloodiest History: Massacre, Genocide, and the Scars they Left on Civilization* (Beverly, MA: Fair Winds Press, 2010), 149–50. At the time, Japan had signed and ratified the Convention for the Amelioration of the Condition of the Wounded and Sick in Armies in the Field (Japan signed on July 27, 1929, and ratified on December 18, 1934) and had signed but not ratified the Convention relative to the Treatment of Prisoners of War (Japan signed July 27, 1929, but never ratified).

91. Iris Chang, *The Rape of Nanking* (New York: Basic Books, 1997); International Military Tribunal for the Far East, *The Tokyo Judgment* (Amsterdam: University Press Amsterdam, 1977), 390.

92. "Second Meeting (Private, Then Public)," *LNOJ*, Vol. 19, No. 2 (February 1938): 82.

93. Ibid., 84.

94. Hull, *Memoirs*, Vol. 1: 544–49; Dorothy Borg, "Notes on Roosevelt's 'Quarantine' Speech," *Political Science Quarterly* 72, no. 3 (September 1957): 413.

95. Sumner Welles, *The Time for Decision* (New York: Harper & Brothers, 1944), 61.

96. Address Delivered by President Roosevelt at Chicago, October 5, 1937, in U.S. Department of State, *Peace and War*, 383–87.

97. Borg, "Notes on Roosevelt's 'Quarantine' Speech," 426–28.

98. Hull, *Memoirs*, Vol. 1: 545.

99. Ibid., 683–84.

100. Ibid., 684. President Roosevelt's case to the American people was more circumspect. He asserted that "by repeal of the embargo the United States will more probably remain at peace than if the law remains as it stands today[.] I say this because with the repeal of the embargo this Government clearly and definitely will insist that American citizens and American ships keep away from the immediate perils of the actual zones of conflict." "Address Delivered by President Roosevelt to the Congress," September 21, 1939, in U.S. Department of State, *Peace and War: United States Foreign Policy, 1931–1941*, 485–87.

101. Robert Dallek, *Franklin D. Roosevelt and American Foreign Policy, 1932–1945* (New York: Oxford University Press, 1995), 200.

102. Ibid., 201–2.

103. Address Delivered by President Roosevelt to the Congress, September 21, 1939; "Neutrality Act of 1939," *American Journal of International Law* 34, no. 1, Supplement: Official Documents (January 1940): 44.

104. Dallek, *Franklin D. Roosevelt and American Foreign Policy*, 209–14; Woodring to Roosevelt, June 20, 1940, box 84, President's Secretary's File (PSF), Franklin D. Roosevelt Papers, Franklin D. Roosevelt Presidential Library, Hyde Park, NY. See also "An American National Policy That Is Unqualifiedly Pro-American (September 14, 1937) (unsigned, but attributed to Woodring), box 84, President's Secretary's File (PSF), Roosevelt Papers (warning that "the influences which led America into the World War are again at work").

105. HLS, radio broadcast, "America's Interest in the British Navy," June 18, 1940, reel 132, HSP YUL.

106. Keith E. Eiler, *Mobilizing America: Robert P. Patterson and the War Effort, 1940–1945* (Ithaca, NY: Cornell University Press, 1997), 37. The idea was not entirely new. Clark and Frankfurter had earlier made the case to the president to appoint Stimson. Ibid., 34–36.

107. Franklin D. Roosevelt to Harry H. Woodring, June 19, 1940, box 84, President's Secretary's File (PSF), Roosevelt Papers.

108. Woodring to Roosevelt, June 20, 1940, box 84, President's Secretary's File (PSF), Roosevelt Papers.

109. Stimson came into office on July 10, 1940, and served until September 21, 1945.

110. "Senate Hearing Ordered on Stimson's Nomination," *New York Times*, June 22, 1940.

111. "Knox and Stimson Approved in Survey," *New York Times*, July 5, 1940.

112. "Roosevelt Move Pleases British," *New York Times*, June 21, 1940 (quoting the *Daily Mirror*, along with several other British papers).

113. Robert H. Jackson, "Opinion on Exchange of Over-Age Destroyers for Naval and Air Bases," August 27, 1940, *American Journal of International Law* 34, no. 4 (October 1940): 728–36.

114. An Act to Promote the Defense of the United States, Pub.L. 77–11, H.R. 1776, 55 Stat. 31 (enacted March 11, 1941).

115. President Franklin Delano Roosevelt, Letter from the President Transmitting Report (June 10, 1941), Report to Congress on Lend-Lease Operations (Washington, DC: U.S. Government Printing Office, 1941).

116. Bix, *Hirohito and the Making of Modern Japan*, 400–401.

117. This is reflected in a memorandum issued by the Japanese Foreign Office after the attack on Pearl Harbor. Japanese Note to the United States, December 7, 1941, Department of State Bulletin, Vol. 5, No. 129 (December 13, 1941) (often referred to as the "Fourteen Part Message"). See also Bix, *Hirohito and the Making of Modern Japan*, 220–24.

118. Bix, *Hirohito and the Making of Modern Japan*, 387-437.

119. Document Handed by the Secretary of State to the Japanese Ambassador (Nomura), November 26, 1941, in U.S. Department of State, *Peace and War*, 810.

120. Bix, *Hirohito and the Making of Modern Japan*, 428–33.

121. *Pearl Harbor Attack: Hearings Before the Joint Committee on the Investigation of the Pearl Harbor Attack*, 79th Cong. (Washington, DC: U.S. Government Printing Office, 1946), 185.

122. "Emperor of Japan Hirohito, Declaration of War Against the United States and Britain," December 8, 1941, *The XXth Century* (Shanghai: XXth Century Publishing Co, 1942), 73.

123. HLS, diary entry, November 25, 1941, reel 7, HSP YUL.

124. Cordell Hull, *The Memoirs of Cordell Hull*, Vol. 2, 1095-96.
125. Japanese Note to the United States United States December 7, 1941.

EIGHT: FIELD MARSHAL IN THE WAR OF BRAINS

1. Sumner Welles, *Seven Decisions That Shaped History* (New York: Harper & Brothers, 1950), 123–26; Benjamin Welles, *Sumner Welles: FDR's Global Strategist* (New York: St. Martin's Press, 1997), 330–31.
2. Welles, *Seven Decisions That Shaped History*, 125–26.
3. "The Brick Balloon," *Time*, August 4, 1948, 14. *
4. Sumner Welles, "An Association of Nations, Address at the Laying of the Cornerstone of the New Wing of the Norwegian Legation in Washington, July 22, 1941," in Sumner Welles, *The World of The Four Freedoms* (New York: Columbia University Press, 1943), 11–15.
5. "American Peace Aims," *New York Times*, July 24, 1941. See also Welles, *Sumner Welles*, 281.
6. "Post-War Aims: World Must Be Guided by Strong League—Views of American," *South China Morning Post*, July 24, 1941, 9.
7. "American Peace Aims," *New York Times*. The *Los Angeles Times* similarly called it "the most specific pronouncement yet given by a high administration official on the postwar aims of the American government." "Welles Urges Peace League: Postwar Association of Nations Favored to Guarantee Disarmament," *Los Angeles Times*, July 23, 1941.
8. "Toward a Better World," *St. Louis Post-Dispatch*, July 24, 1941.
9. "Eden Says Britain Supports Welles' Postwar Program," *Chicago Daily Tribune*, July 31, 1941.
10. "Diplomat's Diplomat," *Time*, August 11, 1941, 11.
11. Welles, *Sumner Welles*, 7–25.
12. "Diplomat's Diplomat," *Time*, 12. See also James Reston, "Acting Secretary," *New York Times*, August 3, 1941.
13. "Diplomat's Diplomat," *Time*, 12 (quoting Blair Bolles). See also Andrei Gromyko, *Memories*, trans. Harold Shukman (London: Hutchinson, 1989), 49 ("By personality and education, Welles had the mark of an Englishman. . . . Everything in Welles's behavior was carefully thought out.").
14. Welles, *Sumner Welles*, 9, 123. Ten years later, Franklin Roosevelt, then assistant secretary of the navy, sponsored Sumner's application to the Foreign Service. Ibid., 123.
15. Harold B. Hinton, "Welles: Our Man of the Hour in Cuba," *New York Times*, August 20, 1933; Welles, *Sumner Welles*, 102–15; "Foreign News: Honduran Strife," *Time*, April 21, 1924.
16. "Diplomat's Diplomat," *Time*, 11. The book was titled *Naboth's Vineyard: The Dominican Republic, 1844–1924*.
17. Welles, *Sumner Welles*, 123.
18. Various correspondence between Eleanor Roosevelt, Franklin Delano Roo-

sevelt, and Sumner Welles, 1928, box 148, folder 8, SWP FDRL. Welles also assisted with a draft of the Democratic Platform. Draft of 1929 Democratic Platform, box 148, folder 8, SWP FDRL. In an early example of their rivalry-to-come, Cordell Hull struck the language Welles had drafted on Latin America (at the future president's request) out of the Democratic platform. Welles, *Sumner Welles*, 139.

19. Eleanor Roosevelt to Welles, October 29, 1928, box 148, folder 8, SWP FDRL.

20. Franklin D. Roosevelt, "First Inaugural Address" (March 4, 1933).

21. Franklin D. Roosevelt, "Address Before the Woodrow Wilson Foundation," December 28, 1933, online by Gerhard Peters and John T. Woolley, *The American Presidency Project*, http://www.presidency.ucsb.edu/ws/?pid=14593. At the Montevideo Conference of December 1933, Hull, on behalf of the United States, backed a declaration favored by most nations of the Western Hemisphere: "No state has the right to intervene in the internal or external affairs of another." Shortly thereafter, Welles engineered the death of the Platt Amendment, a symbol of U.S. military intervention in the hemisphere. "Diplomat's Diplomat," *Time*.

22. A search for "Sumner Welles" yielded four hundred entries in White House logs based on archival sources documenting President Roosevelt's daily activities, including the White House Usher's Log and the White House Stenographer's Diary. See "Franklin D. Roosevelt Day by Day," http://www.fdrlibrary.marist.edu/daybyday/.

23. "Toward a Better World," *St. Louis Post Dispatch*.

24. Welles, *The Time for Decision*, 47–48.

25. Sumner Welles, *Where Are We Heading?* (New York: Harper & Brothers, 1946), 4.

26. Ibid.

27. Se, e.g., Robert E. Sherwood, *Roosevelt and Hopkins: An Intimate History* (New York: Harper & Brothers, 1948).

28. Ibid., 92, 850.

29. Ibid., 6.

30. Welles, *Sumner Welles*, 301 (quoting an interview with Franklin D. Roosevelt, Jr. in 1981).

31. David Dilks, ed., *The Diaries of Sir Alexander Cadogan, O.M., 1938–1943* (New York: G. P. Putnam & Sons, 1971), 397–99.

32. Robert Dallek, *Franklin D. Roosevelt and American Foreign Policy, 1932–1945* (New York: Oxford University Press, 1995), 282.

33. Winston Churchill, *The Second World War: The Grand Alliance* (New York: Houghton Mifflin, 1950), Vol. 3, 394.

34. Dallek, *Franklin D. Roosevelt and American Foreign Policy, 1932–1945*, 282.

35. Churchill, *The Second World War: The Grand Alliance*, 385.

36. Welles, *Sumner Welles*, 304–7.

37. The Atlantic Charter, August 14, 1941. Welles describes the editing process

extensively in Welles, *Where Are We Heading?*, 4–18; Memorandum of Conversation, by the Under Secretary of State (Welles) (August 11, 1941), Avalon Law Project, Yale Law School Lillian Goldman Law Library, http://avalon.law.yale.edu/wwii/at09.asp.

38. Sherwood, *Roosevelt and Hopkins*, 442.
39. Irwin F. Gellman, *Secret Affairs: Franklin Roosevelt, Cordell Hull, and Sumner Welles* (Baltimore: Johns Hopkins University Press, 1995), 272; Churchill, *The Second World War: The Grand Alliance*, 590; 604–5.
40. Churchill, *The Second World War: The Grand Alliance*, 605.
41. "Declaration by the United Nations" (January 1, 1942). Another twenty-one countries would join in the course of the war.
42. "Tripartite Pact," September 27, 1940.
43. Ibid.
44. Memo, Hull to Roosevelt, December 22, 1941, in Harley A. Notter, *Postwar Foreign Policy Preparation, 1939–1945* (Washington, DC: U.S. Department of State, 1950), 63–65. The committee first met on February 12, 1942. Robert Hildebrand, *Dumbarton Oaks: The Origins of the United Nations and the Search for Postwar Security* (Chapel Hill: University of North Carolina Press 1990), 13, 262 n. 16.
45. Welles, *Seven Decisions That Shaped History*, 132–34; Dallek, *Franklin D. Roosevelt and American Foreign Policy*, 149. After the quarantine speech, Welles had privately encouraged Roosevelt to convene a "peace conference" to work out "fundamental norms" and "standards of international conduct." But when Hull had objected, Roosevelt had let it drop. Ibid.
46. Welles, *Seven Decisions That Shaped History*, 132–34. In a rare instance of open criticism of the president, Welles would later write that the decision not to open the international commission the first lady had suggested had been a terrible mistake. The United States' power—its military might and moral authority— were at their height in the year after Pearl Harbor. Had the president sought a firm agreement on postwar political and territorial settlements then—when, among other things, the Soviets relied on Lend-Lease for armaments to allow them to continue to fight—"is it not probable that our influence would have been sufficient to have kept those settlements within bounds that a peace conference would have been disposed to accept as legitimate and fair?" Ibid., 141. Had negotiations been finalized earlier, Roosevelt might not have been forced to make the concessions he would later make to Stalin at Yalta. After the winter of 1943, when the Russian armies had the Germans in retreat, the "moment for negotiation was gone." Ibid.,143.
47. Notter, *Postwar Foreign Policy Preparation*, 79.
48. The committee as a whole, which first met on February 12, 1942, had five subcommittees of which the Special Subcommittee on International Organization was just one. See "Minutes of AC-1, Meeting of February 12, 1942," box 190, folder 5, SWP FDRL. Then-Under Secretary of State Edward Stettinius's

diary makes clear that the committee's work was the foundation for the draft later discussed at the first international conference on what would become the United Nations, even though Cordell Hull and Sumner Welles had by then left the State Department. Thomas M. Campbell and George Herring, eds., *The Diaries of Edward R. Stettinius, Jr., 1943–1946* (New York: New Viewpoints, 1975), 103. For more on the constitution of the committee, see Notter, *Postwar Foreign Policy Preparation*, 73–74.

49. For more on Bowman, see Neil Smith, *American Empire: Roosevelt's Geographer and the Prelude to Globalization* (Berkeley: University of California Press, 2003); Geoffrey J. Martin, *The Life and Thought of Isaiah Bowman* (Hamden, CT: Archon Books, 1980). At the time he was appointed, he was serving at president of Johns Hopkins University. In 1942, he was reportedly spending several days a week at the State Department. In 1944 he would be a member of the London mission led by Stettinius and he would later serve on the American Delegation to Dumbarton Oaks and as an adviser to the American delegation to the United Nations Conference on International Organization in San Francisco. Throughout this period, James Shotwell was one of his key intellectual interlocutors. Martin, *The Life and Thought of Isaiah Bowman*, 141–86.

50. Isaiah Bowman, *The New World: Problems in Political Geography* (Yonkers-on-Hudson, NY: World Book Co., 1921).

51. United States Attorney General, "Opinion on Exchange of Over-Age Destroyers for Naval and Air Bases," *American Journal of International Law* 34, no. 4 (1940): 728–36.

52. Charles Mee, *Meeting at Potsdam* (New York: M. Evans, 1975), 215. See also William Lasser, *Benjamin V. Cohen: Architect of the New Deal* (New Haven: Yale University Press, 2002).

53. Stephen C. Schlesinger, *Act of Creation: The Founding of the United Nations: A Story of Superpowers, Secret Agents, Wartime Allies and Enemies, and Their Quest for a Peaceful World* (Cambridge, MA: Westview Press, 203), 33–35. Pasvolsky's assistant, Harley Notter, served as research secretary. Notter, *Postwar Foreign Policy Preparation*, 82, 108.

54. Notter, *Postwar Foreign Policy Preparation*, 108. In addition to serving on the Special Subcommittee on International Organization, Shotwell served on the main Advisory Committee on Post-war Foreign Policy, ibid., 73, the Subcommittee on Political Problems, ibid., 97; Special Subcommittee on Legal Problems, ibid., 114; and the Subcomittee on Security Problems, ibid., 124.

55. "James T. Shotwell, Historian, 90, Dies," *New York Times*, July 17, 1965.

56. The group met for the first time on July 17, 1942. "Preliminary Memorandum on International Organization," JTS to Sumner Welles, July 30, 1942, box 192, folder 8, SWP FDRL.

57. Ibid., 4.

58. Ibid., 8.

59. Ibid., 8–9.

60. "Preliminary Draft by J.T.S. of Revision of Articles I–VII of the Covenant, for Discussion," August 21, 1942, box 189, folder 6, Document 20, SWP, FDRL.

61. Ibid., 1.

62. Ibid., 1–2.

63. "Provisional Outline of International Organization (prepared by J.T.S., August 31, 1942)" (Document 99), August 31, 1942, box 189, folder 8, SWP FDRL.

64. Ibid., 5.

65. Ibid., 6.

66. Ibid., 7. Another document distributed to the committee around the same time, also likely written by Shotwell and entitled "The Briand-Kellogg Pact," made the same point. After reprinting the two operative articles, the memo noted that the Pact had two key merits: first, it went beyond the League Covenant and provided for "a general prohibition of resort to war," and, second, "it realized a greater degree of universality than the Covenant of the League of Nations." "On the other hand," the memo acknowledged, "unlike the Covenant of the League of Nations, the Paris Pact provides for no permanent organization, no procedure, and no sanctions." "The Briand-Kellogg Pact," August 26, 1942, box 189, folder 6, Document 21, SWP FDRL.

67. "Minutes of October 30, 1942," box 189, folder 4, SWP FDRL.

68. "Preliminary Views on the Nature of Post-War International Organization, Minutes of August 7, 1942," box 189, folder 4, SWP FDRL.

69. Moreover, the final draft of the United Nations Charter would open membership, as well, to "all other peace-loving states which accept the obligations contained in the present Charter and, in the judgment of the Organization, are able and willing to carry out those obligations." United Nations, *Charter of the United Nations*, October 23, 1945.

70. "Minutes of December 11, 1942," box 189, folder 4, SWP FDRL.

71. Although it dropped the repetition of the Pact, it continued to assume that a "threat or act of aggression" was prohibited. The drafts produced in 1943 were largely devoted to describing the architecture of the organization that would ensure the preexisting prohibition would be enforced. "Draft Constitution of International Organization," March 26, 1943, revised April 12, 1943, box 189, folder 1, SWP FDRL.

72. The group set out on September 16, 1940, and the event allegedly took place early on September 17. The political maneuverings took more than three years to unfold. Welles, *Sumner Welles*, 2.

73. Welles, *Sumner Welles*, 271–73.

74. Ibid., 1–3, 27, 272–79, 341–49.

75. Hilderbrand, *Dumbarton Oaks*, 30.

76. Ibid.

77. "Plan for the Establishment of an International Organization for the Maintenance of International Peace and Security," December 23, 1943, *FRUS*, 1944, Vol. 1 (General), 615.

78. Ibid., 614 n. 2.

79. Ibid., 714 n. 94.

80. Memo, Stettinius to the Secretary of State, August 29, 1944, *FRUS*, 1944, Vol. 1 (General), 747. This language would remain in the final agreed draft. U.S. Department of State, *Dumbarton Oaks Documents on International Organization*, publication 2223, 1945. The U.S. influence was unmistakable. "Paragraph 4 had its origin in Section 1, paragraph 3 of the American Proposal and was an idea strongly supported by the British as well as the Soviet Delegations." "Continuing Preparations for a Conference of United Nations," November 20, 1944, *FRUS*, 1944, Vol. 1, 903.

81. Memo, Stettinius to the Secretary of State, August 22, 1944, *FRUS*, 1944, Vol. 1 (General), 716. This reflected earlier internal conversations amongst the Dream Team. "P-I.O. Minutes," January 8, 1943, box 189, folder 4, SWP FDRL.

82. Memo, Stettinius to the Secretary of State, October 2, 1944, *FRUS*, 1944, Vol. 1 (General), 862.

83. Memo, Stettinius to President Roosevelt, August 28, 1944, *FRUS*, 1944, Vol. 1 (General), 738 (describing Gromyko's proposal that "all of the 16 Soviet republics should be included among the initial members"); "Informal Minutes of Meeting No. 6 of the Joint Steering Committee Held at 11 a.m. August 28, 1944 at Dumbarton Oaks," ibid., 743; "Memo by Stettinius, ibid., 751–52 (also describing later conversation regarding the matter).

84. "Informal Meeting Minutes of Meeting No. 6 of the Joint Steering Committee," August 28, 1944, *FRUS*, 1944, Vol. 1 (General), 743 n. 24.

85. Telegram from Stalin to President Roosevelt, September 7, 1944, *FRUS*, 1944, Vol. 1 (General), 782–83.

86. "Informal Meeting Minutes of Meeting No. 6 of the Joint Steering Committee," August 28, 1944, *FRUS*, 1944, Vol. 1 (General), 741.

87. Campbell and Herring, eds., *The Diaries of Edward R. Stettinius, Jr.*, 128–31. See also Dallek, *Franklin D. Roosevelt and American Foreign Policy*, 466–67; "Extracts from the Personal Diary of the Under Secretary of State (Stettinius)," September 7, 1944, *FRUS*, 1944, Vol. 1 (General), 781–82.

88. "Extracts from the Personal Diary of Under Secretary of State (Stettinius)," September 8, 1944, *FRUS*, 1944, Vol. 1 (General), 785–86.

89. Ibid., 786. The cable appears in Telegram, President Roosevelt to the Ambassador in the Soviet Union (Harriman), September 8, 1944, *FRUS*, Vol. 1, 788–89. See also "Informal Minutes of Meeting No. 14 of the Joint Steering Committee," September 13, 1944, *FRUS*, 1944, Vol. 1 (General), 798.

90. Ibid., 799–800.

91. Campbell and Herring, eds., *The Diaries of Edward R. Stettinius, Jr.*, 134.

92. Ibid., 138, 144.

93. Ibid., 139.

94. U.S. Department of State, *Dumbarton Oaks Documents on International Organization*, publication 2223, 1945, 13.

NINE: OPERATION ARGONAUT

1. This section of the journey is described in S. M. Plokhy, *Yalta: The Price of Peace* (New York: Viking, 2010), 4–7.
2. Ibid., 35–36; William M. Rigdon, *White House Sailor* (New York: Doubleday, 1962), 143.
3. The President's Log at Yalta, February 3, 1945, in *FRUS*, 1945 (The Conferences at Malta and Yalta), 549.
4. Rigdon, *White House Sailor*, 143–45; The President's Log at Yalta, February 3, 1945, *FRUS*, 1945 (The Conferences at Malta and Yalta), 550.
5. Steven C. Schlesinger, *Act of Creation: The Founding of the United Nations* (New York: Perseus, 2003), 58.
6. Plokhy, *Yalta*, 10.
7. Letter, Marshal Stalin to President Roosevelt, July 22, 1944, *FRUS*, 1945 (The Conferences at Malta and Yalta), 4. He further cited his doctors' instructions not to undertake any long trips—a shameless appeal given what he likely knew of Roosevelt's own health. Ibid., 12.
8. Telegram, President Roosevelt to Ambassador Harriman (for Marshal Stalin), October 4, 1944, *FRUS*, 1945 (The Conferences at Malta and Yalta), 6.
9. Plokhy, *Yalta*, 28.
10. Rigdon, *White House Sailor*, 137–38.
11. Telegram, Prime Minister Churchill to President Roosevelt, November 5, 1944, *FRUS*, 1945 (The Conferences at Malta and Yalta), 13.
12. See Telegram, Prime Minister Churchill to President Roosevelt, October 22, 1944, *FRUS*, 1945 (The Conferences at Malta and Yalta), 10–11. Under the 1936 Montreux Convention Regarding the Regime of the Straits, Turkey controlled the Bosporus and the Dardanelles, thus controlling access between the Black Sea and the Aegean.
13. See extensive correspondence between Churchill, Roosevelt, and Stalin, *FRUS*, 1945 (The Conferences at Malta and Yalta), 3–40.
14. G. F. Krivosheev, ed., *Soviet Casualties and Combat Losses in the Twentieth Century* (London: Greenhill, 1997), 85–86. There has been some criticism of these numbers from researchers in Russia, who argue that, among other things, Krivosheev's estimate does not sufficiently account for POWs and conscripts. They put the total military war dead at several million higher. Scholars have also debated proper estimates of "excess" wartime deaths. See, e.g., Michael Haynes, "Counting Soviet Deaths in the Great Patriotic War: A Note," *Europe Asia Studies* 55, no. 2 (2003): 303–9.
15. For the United States, the Congressional Research Service estimates 291,557 battle dealths and 113,842 "other deaths" (deaths from other causes, such as accidents, disease, and infection). Nese F. DeBruyne and Anne Leland, *American War and Military Operations Casualties: Lists and Statistics*, Congressional Research Service (January 2, 2015), 2. For the United Kingdom, the Commonwealth Graves Commission reports a total of 383,758 military dead from

all causes for both the U.K. and non-Dominion British colonies (figures include identified burials and those commemorated by name on memorials), and 67,170 civilian deaths due to enemy action. Commonwealth War Graves Commission Annual Report (2014–2015), 39. Others give slightly different numbers. See, e.g., Alan Bullock, *Hitler and Stalin: Parallel Lives* (London: HarperCollins, 1991), 1086 (estimating U.S. losses at 295,000 and Great Britain losses at 388,000).

16. Winston Churchill, *The Second World War: Triumph and Tragedy* (Boston: Houghton Mifflin, 1953), 347. Preparations are also described in The President's Log at Yalta, February 3, 1945, *FRUS*, 1945 (The Conferences at Malta and Yalta), 551–52.

17. Diane Shaver Clemens, *Yalta* (New York: Oxford University Press, 1970), 116.

18. Ibid.

19. Rigdon, *White House Sailor*, 138.

20. The remaining issues left to be decided—all important but none likely to derail plans for the organization—were who should be offered initial membership in the organization, whether there should be provision for territorial trusteeship, where the organization should be located, how to wind up the League of Nations, and arrangements for the final drafting of the legal documents that would establish the new organization and its component parts. Memorandum to President Roosevelt, "Questions Left Unsettled at Dumbarton Oaks," October 27, 1944, *FRUS*, 1945 (The Conferences at Malta and Yalta), 45.

21. Bohlen Minutes, February 4, 1945, *FRUS*, 1945 (The Conferences at Malta and Yalta), 574.

22. Combined Chiefs of Staff Minutes, February 4, 1945, *FRUS*, 1945 (The Conferences at Malta and Yalta), 583.

23. See, e.g., Joint Chiefs of State to the President, January 23, 1945, *FRUS*, 1945 (The Conferences at Malta and Yalta), 396–400. See generally "Entry of the Soviet Union in the War Against Japan," *FRUS*, 1945 (The Conferences at Malta and Yalta), 361–400.

24. An agreement, signed by the U.S., Great Britain, and the Soviet Union at Yalta, stated: "The leaders of the three Great Powers—the Soviet Union, the United States of America and Great Britain—have agreed that in two or three months after Germany has surrendered and the war in Europe is terminated the Soviet Union shall enter into war against Japan on the side of the Allies on condition that: . . . 2. The former rights of Russia violated by the treacherous attack of Japan in 1904 shall be restored, viz.: (a) The southern part of Sakhalin as well as the islands adjacent to it shall be returned to the Soviet Union, . . . 3. The Kuril Islands shall be handed over to the Soviet Union." Agreement Regarding Entry of the Soviet Union Into the War Against Japan, *FRUS*, 1945 (The Conferences at Malta and Yalta), 984. The Soviet Union would seize Sakhalin and the Kuril Islands after World War II, but would not succeed in establishing

claims in Manchuria. The islands remain the subject of dispute between Japan and Russia even today.

25. See, e.g., Bohlen Minutes, February 5, 1945, ibid., 612, 620–21.

26. Bohlen Minutes, February 6, 1945, ibid., 669. Though not a subject of discussion at Yalta, Stalin would also stubbornly insist on retaining control over the Baltic states of Estonia, Latvia, and Lithuania. It had been Hitler's promise of control over these states in the Molotov-Ribbentrop Pact, after all, that had won Stalin's loyalty (until Hitler changed course and invaded Stalin's territory). He would not let the Allies' refusal to recognize the legitimacy of that deal shake his resolve. The Baltics, after all, did not need to prosper. They merely needed to absorb the brunt of any new blows that might come from the west.

27. Memorandum, Soviet Foreign Policy, Acting Secretary of State (Grew) for the President, January 12, 1945, ibid., 449–55.

28. Bohlen Minutes, February 4, 1945, ibid., 589.

29. Andrei Gromyko, *Memories*, trans. Harold Shukman (London: Hutchinson, 1989), 85.

30. Bohlen Minutes, February 4, 1945, *FRUS*, 1945 (The Conferences at Malta and Yalta), 590.

31. Arkady Vaksberg, *Stalin's Prosecutor: The Life of Andrei Vyshinsky* (New York: Grove, 1991) (quoting Sir Frank Roberts), 252–53.

32. Bohlen Minutes, February 4, 1945, *FRUS*, 1945 (The Conferences at Malta and Yalta), 590.

33. Ibid., 590–91; Thomas M. Campbell and George C. Herring, eds., *The Diaries of Edward R. Stettinius, Jr., 1943–1946* (New York: New Viewpoints, 1975), 241.

34. Campbell and Herring eds., *The Diaries of Edward R. Stettinius, Jr., 1943–1946*, at 241. By Stettinius's own account, he later helped the prime minister better understand the issue. Ibid. 241–42.

35. Bohlen Minutes, February 5, 1945, *FRUS*, 1945 (The Conferences at Malta and Yalta), 611–33.

36. Ibid., 661.

37. In the draft under discussion, these were matters within the Security Council's Chapter VIII jurisdiction (today's Chapter VI: "Pacific Settlement of Disputes"). Ibid.

38. Churchill, *Triumph and Tragedy*, 310. The account accords with the minutes of the meeting, Bohlen Minutes, February 6, 1945, *FRUS*, 1945 (The Conferences at Malta and Yalta), 665–66.

39. Bohlen Minutes, February 6, 1945, *FRUS*, 1945 (The Conferences at Malta and Yalta), 666.

40. Ibid., 711–13.

41. Ibid., 712.

42. Stephen Lehnstaedt, "The Minsk Experience: German Occupiers and Everyday Life in the Capital of Belarus," in *Nazi Policy on the Eastern Front, 1941: Total War, Genocide and Radicalization*, ed. Alex J. Kay, Jeff Rutherford, and

David Stahel (Rochester, NY: University of Rochester Press, 2012), 240 (estimating 1.6 million dead in Belarus, out of a total prewar population of 9 million); Paul R. Magocsi, *A History of Ukraine: The Land and Its People* (Toronto: University of Toronto Press: 1996), 638 (estimating 5.5 million fatalities in Ukraine, 15 percent of the population); Timothy Snyder, *Bloodlands: Europe Between Hitler and Stalin* (New York: Basic Books, 2010).

43. Memorandum of Decisions Reached at the Crimean Conference in the Matter of the Two Soviet Republics, March 19, 1945, *FRUS*, 1945 (The Conferences at Malta and Yalta), 991–92. Both were admitted in 1945.

44. Welles, *Seven Decisions That Shaped History*, 193–94.

45. Ibid., 194.

46. John Morton Blum, *From the Morgenthau Diaries: Years of War, 1941–1945* (Boston: Houghton Mifflin, 1967), 416.

47. Samuel I. Rosenman, *Working with Roosevelt* (New York: Harper & Brothers, 1952), 546.

48. Roosevelt wrote these words the night of April 11, the night before he died from a cerebral hemorrhage. They were part of an address he was scheduled to deliver via nationwide radio broadcast from Georgia Hall at Warm Springs the evening of April 14, 1945.

49. Grace Tully, *F.D.R. My Boss* (New York: Charles Scribner's Sons, 1949), 364.

50. Townsend Hoopes and Douglas Brinkley, *FDR and the Creation of the U.N.* (New Haven, CT: Yale University Press, 1997), 129.

51. "Sumner Welles," *Billboard* 57, no. 6 (April 21, 1945).

52. After the close of the conference, President Truman unceremoniously pressed Stettinius, who had led the U.S. delegation at San Francisco, to resign from his position as secretary of state, allowing Truman to replace him with James Byrnes. Truman would offer Stettinius the job of U.S. representative at the new United Nations—a position Stettinius would accept. There, he and Gromyko, who would represent the Soviets, would sit across the table once again.

53. "President Truman's Address to Opening Session of the United Nations Conference on International Organization at San Francisco," April 25, 1945.

54. Campbell and Herring, eds., *The Diaries of Edward R. Stettinius, Jr.*, 374–407.

55. "Summary Report of Twelfth Meeting of Committee," June 5, 1949, in *Documents of the United Nations International Organization San Francisco, 1945*, Vol. 6, *Commission I General Provisions* (New York: United Nations Information Organizations, 1945), 342.

56. Ibid., 346.

57. Ibid., 344.

58. Ibid., 346.

59. Ibid., 344.

60. Welles, *Seven Decisions That Shaped History*, 197.

61. "Summary Report of Twelfth Meeting of Committee," *UNCIO*, 346.

62. There was a provision calling on all members of the United Nations to "make

available to the Security Council, on its call and in accordance with a special agreement or agreements, armed forces, assistance, and facilities, including rights of passage, necessary for the purpose of maintaining international peace and security." U.N. Charter, Art. 43. The standing force envisioned in this article never materialized. Even if it had, its capacity to act would have been constrained by the requirement that the Security Council approve any action taken to enforce peace and security.

63. For more on the United Nations in historical context, see, e.g., Mark Mazower, *Governing the World: The History of an Idea* (New York: Penguin, 2012); Paul Kennedy, *The Parliament of Man: The Past, Present, and Future of the United Nations* (New York: Random House, 2006).

64. *Grundgesetz der Bundesrepublik Deutschland* [Constitution], Art. 26 (1949) (F.R.G.).

65. *Nihonkōku Kenpō* [Constitution], Art. 9 (1946) (Japan).

66. *La Costituzione* [Constitution], Art. 11 (1948) (Italy).

TEN: FRIEND AND ENEMY

1. Index cards to the war crimes case files ("Cases Not Tried"), 1944–1948, and witnesses and defendants in war crimes cases, 1946–1948, Record Group 549, Records of United States Army, Europe 549.2, Records of U.S. Army, Europe (USAEUR) 1933–1964, Records of the War Crimes Branch of the Judge Advocate General Section, U.S. National Archives and Records Administration (College Park, MD).

2. Karl Loewenstein, "Observations on Personality and Work of Professor Carl Schmitt," November 14, 1945, box 46, p. 1, KLP ACL.

3. Ibid.

4. Ibid., 4.

5. Karl Loewenstein, "Library of Professor Carl Schmitt," October 10, 1945, box 46, p. 2, KLP ACL.

6. Carl Schmitt, *Glossarium: Aufzeichnungen der Jahre 1947–1951* (Berlin: Duncker & Humblot, 1991), 264, translation from Gopal Balakrishnan, *The Enemy* (London: Verso, 2000), 254.

7. Ibid.

8. See Dirk Poppmann, "The Trials of Robert Kempner: From Stateless Immigrant to Prosecutor of the Foreign Office," in *Reassessing the Nuremberg Military Tribunals*, eds. Kim Priemel and Alexa Stiller (New York: Berghahn Books, 2012), 38.

9. For the transcript, see Joseph W. Bendersky, "Interrogation of Carl Schmitt by Robert Kempner (I)," *Telos* 72 (1987): 97–129.

10. Ibid., 98. The full sentence is: "I will tell you quite candidly what I am interested in: your participation, direct and indirect, in the planning of wars of aggression, of war crimes and of crimes against humanity." But the interrogations

make clear that Kempner is interested almost exclusively in Schmitt's participation in Nazi aggression.

11. Ibid.
12. Ibid.
13. Schmitt, *Glossarium*, 6.
14. James Shotwell, *Autobiography* (Indianapolis: Bobbs-Merrill, 1961), 200–1.
15. Ibid., 203.
16. Schmitt, *Glossarium*, 7. Schmitt quickly dictated his lecture between March 31 and April 4. Reinhard Mehring, *Carl Schmitt: A Biography*, trans. Daniel Steuer (Cambridge, UK: Polity, 2014), 179.
17. Carl Schmitt, *The Concept of the Political*, trans. George Schwab (Chicago: University of Chicago Press, 2006), 29.
18. Ibid.
19. Ibid., 33.
20. Ibid., 27 ("Emotionally the enemy is easily treated as being evil and ugly, because every distinction, most of all the political, as the strongest and most intense of the distinctions and categorizations, draws upon other distinctions for support").
21. Ibid., 46.
22. Ibid.
23. See, e.g., Joseph Bendersky, "Schmitt's Diaries," in *The Oxford Handbook of Carl Schmitt*, eds. Jens Meierhenrich and Oliver Simons (Oxford: Oxford University Press, 2013), 126.
24. Schmitt, *The Concept of the Political*, 34.
25. Ibid.
26. Ibid., 50–51.
27. Mehring, *Carl Schmitt*, 4.
28. Joseph Bendersky, *Carl Schmitt: Theorist for the Reich* (Princeton: Princeton University Press, 1983), 5; Mehring, *Carl Schmitt*, 6.
29. Piet Tommissen, *Over en inzake Carl Schmitt* (Brussels: Economische Hogeschool Sint-Aloysisus, 1975), 93, quoted and translated in Mehring, *Carl Schmitt*, 7. (Schmitt in conversation with Dieter Groh and Klaus Figge.) At the time, Humboldt was called Friedrich-Wilhelms-Universität.
30. Carl Schmitt, "Berlin 1907," in *Schmittiana I*, ed. Piet Tommissen (Berlin: Duncker & Humblot, 2001), 13–21, translated and quoted in Jan-Werner Müeller, *A Dangerous Mind: Carl Schmitt in Post-War European Thought* (New Haven: Yale Univeristy Press, 2003), 18.
31. Mehring, *Carl Schmitt*, 40. According to Bendersky, Cari claimed to be Serbian. Bendersky, *Carl Schmitt*, 44.
32. Carl Schmitt, *Die Militärzeit 1915 bis 1919*, eds. Ernst Hüsmert and Gerd Giesler (Berlin: Akademie Verlag, 2005), 90.
33. Eric Weitz, *Weimar Germany* (Princeton: Princeton University Press, 2007), 104.

34. Ibid., 136–40. The exchange rate in November was 4.2 trillion marks to 1 US dollar.

35. Ibid.

36. Schmitt, *The Concept of the Political*, 36.

37. Ibid.

38. Ibid., 51.

39. Ibid., 54.

40. Ibid. (modifying an expression of Proudhon).

41. Ibid., 79.

42. Ibid.

43. Friedrich Nietzsche, *Beyond Good and Evil* (1899), Paragraph 146. This is the epigraph to Carl Schmitt, *The Nomos of the Earth in the International Law of the Jus Publicum Europaeum*, trans. G. L. Ulmen (New York: Telos Press, 2003).

44. Jonathan Wright, *Gustav Stresemann: Weimar's Greatest Statesman* (Oxford: Oxford University Press, 2002), 415.

45. Ibid., 66–110.

46. Shotwell, *Autobiography*, 204–6.

47. Ibid., 205.

48. Ibid., 206.

49. For an excellent discussion of Stresemann's plan, see Adam Tooze, *The Wages of Destruction: The Making and Breaking of the Nazi Economy* (New York: Penguin, 2006), 4–20.

50. Walter Gallenson and Arnold Zellner, "International Comparison of Unemployment Rates," in *The Measurement and Behavior of Unemployment*, ed. Universities-National Bureau (Princeton: Princeton University Press, 1957), 455.

51. Tooze, *Wages of Destruction*, 13.

52. Mehring, *Carl Schmitt*, 134.

53. Carl Schmitt, *Dictatorship* (Cambridge, UK: Polity, 2013); Carl Schimtt, *The Crisis of Parliamentary Democracy*, trans. Ellen Kennedy (Cambridge: MIT Press, 1988).

54. Carl Schmitt, *Constitutional Theory*, trans. Jeffrey Seitzer (Durham, NC: Duke University Press, 2007).

55. Diary entry, September 17, 1927, in Mehring, *Carl Schmitt*, 181.

56. Schmitt's carbon copy of a letter dated January 30, 1933, to the journal *Beamtenbund*, in ibid.

57. Weimar Constitution, Art. 48, Clause 2.

58. See Carl Schmitt, "The Guardian of the Constitution," in *The Guardian of the Constitution*, trans. and ed. Lars Vinx (Cambridge: Cambridge University Press, 2015), 125–73.

59. Weimar Constitution, Art. 48. Schmitt claimed that the president had the power to dissolve the Reichstag under Article 25.

60. For Schmitt's role, see Lutz Berthold, *Carl Schmitt und der Staatsnotstandsplan am Ende der Weimarer Republik* (Berlin: Duncker & Humblot, 1999).

61. Mehring, *Carl Schmitt*, 252–53.
62. Peter Hayes, "'A Question Mark with Epaulettes'? Kurt von Schleicher and Weimar Politics," *Journal of Modern History* 52, no. 1 (1980): 35–65.
63. Weitz, *Weimar Germany*, 351.
64. Ibid., 161.
65. Mehring, *Carl Schmitt*, 264. Though Schmitt was one of four lawyers for the Reich, he was the chairman of the group and presented the main theoretical justification for the government's actions.
66. For a thorough discussion of the arguments and decision, see David Dyzenhaus, *Legality and Legitimacy: Carl Schmitt, Hans Kelsen, and Hermann Heller in Weimar* (Oxford: Oxford University Press, 1999).
67. Mehring, *Carl Schmitt*, 265.
68. On the reactions to the decision, see Peter Caldwell, *Popular Sovereignty and the Crisis of German Constitutional Law* (Durham, NC: Duke University Press, 1997).
69. Hans Mommsen, *Aufstieg und Untergang der Republik von Weimar, 1918–1933* (Berlin: Ullstein, 1998), 543.
70. Mehring, *Carl Schmitt*, 204, 242.
71. Franz Neumann, *Behemoth: The Structure and Practice of National Socialism, 1933–1944* (London: Oxford University Press, 1944), 43–44.
72. Ibid., 32.
73. Mehring, *Carl Schmitt*, 255, 264.
74. Ibid., 258, 265.
75. Roscoe Pound, "Law and the Science of Law in Recent Theories," *Yale Law Journal* 43, no. 4 (1934): 532.
76. Tamara Ehs and Miriam Gassner, "Hans Kelsen (1881–1973)," November 8, 2012, www.transatlanticperspectives.org/entry.php?rec=132.
77. Bernhard Schlink, "Best Lawyer, Pure Law," *New York Times Magazine*, April 18, 1999. His colleague, the German law professor Horst Dreier, made a similar assessment, calling Kelsen "the jurist of the century." Horst Dreier, "Jurist des Jahrhunderts?," in *Deutsche Juristen jüdischer Herkunft*, eds., Helmut Heinrichs et al. (Berlin: Verlag C. H. Beck, 1993), 705–32.
78. Only one biography has been published on Kelsen: Rudolf Métall, *Hans Kelsen: Leben und Werk* (Vienna: Verlag Franz Deuticke, 1969). Recently, its accuracy has been called into question. Thomas Olechowski, "Biographical Researches on Hans Kelsen in the Years 1881–1920," *Právněhistorické Studie* 43 (2013): 280–81. We have relied on Olechowski's article in what follows.
79. See, e.g., *Minutes of the Vienna Psychoanalytic Society*, eds. Herman Nunberg and Ernst Federn, trans. M. Nunberg, Vol. 3, *1910–11* (New York: International Universities Press, 1974), 347, as noted in Clemens Jabloner, "Kelsen and His Circle: The Viennese Years," *European Journal of International Law* 9, no. 2 (1998): 382.
80. Bernd Rüthers, "On the Brink of Dictatorship—Hans Kelsen and Carl Schmitt

in Cologne 1933," in *Hans Kelsen and Carl Schmitt: A Juxtaposition*, eds. Dan Diner and Michael Stolleis (Gerlingen: Bleicher, 1999), 119.

81. Hans Kelsen, "Who Ought to be the Guardian of the Constitution?", in Vinx, *The Guardian of the Constitution*, 174–221.

82. Vinx, *The Guardian of the Constitution*, 209–10.

83. Rüthers, "On the Brink of Dictatorship," 119.

84. Hans Mayer, *Ein Deutscher auf Widerruf* (Frankfurt am Main: Suhrkamp Verlag, 1982), 144.

85. Frank Golczewski, *Kölner Universitätslehrer und der Nationalsozialismus* (Cologne: Böhlau Verlag, 1988), 299.

86. Ruthers, "On the Brink of Dictatorship," 120.

87. Mehring, *Carl Schmitt*, 270.

88. Hermann Göring, Dortmund Speech, Spring 1933, quoted in Paul Maracin, *Night of the Long Knives* (Guildford, CT: The Lyons Press, 2004), 91.

89. Mehring, *Carl Schmitt*, 280.

90. Carl Schmitt, *Carl Schmitt Tagebücher 1930 bis 1934*, eds. Wolfgang Schuller and Gerd Giesler (Berlin: Akademie Verlag, 2010), 257, as cited in Bendersky, "Schmitt's Diaries," 126.

91. Ibid., 133.

92. Robert Kempner, *Ankläger einer Epoche* (Frankfurt: Ullstein, 1983), 88–90.

93. See Detlev Vagts, "International Law in the Third Reich," *American Journal of International Law* 84, no. 3 (1990): 661–704.

94. Golczewski, *Kölner Universitätsleher*, 116–17.

95. The petition was drafted by Hans Carl Nipperdey. See Ruthers, "On the Brink of Dictatorship," 120–21.

96. Mayer, *Ein Deutscher auf Widerruf*, 144. See also Golczewski, *Kölner Universitätsleher*, 302 n. 17.

97. Carl Schmitt, "Der deutschen Intellektuellen," *Westdeutschen Beobachter*, March 31, 1933, quoted and translated in Ruthers, "On the Brink of Dictatorship."

98. Schmitt, *The Concept of the Political*, 27.

99. Memo from Planitz, after conversation with Adenauer, June 30,1932, in Golczewski, *Kölner Universitätslehrer*, 299.

100. Golczewski, *Kölner Universitätslehrer*, 299.

101. "Rede Hitlers vor der deutschen Presse 10. November 1938" (Hitler's Speech before the German Press [November 10, 1938]), *Vierteljahrshefte für Zeitgeschichte*, vi, Heft 2 (1958), 188, quoted in Gordon A. Craig, *Germany: 1866–1945* (New York: Oxford University Press, 1978), 638.

102. Carl Schmitt, "Der Missbrauch der Legalität" (The Abuse of Legality), *Tägliche Rundschau*, July 19, 1932, quoted in Balakrishnan, *The Enemy*, 156.

103. Mehring, *Carl Schmitt*, 281.

104. As Bendersky points out, the most frequent phrase in Schmitt's diary is, perhaps, *Angst vor*, "fear of." Bendersky, "Schmitt's Diaries," 4.

105. To be fair to Schmitt, almost no one gave up their job of their own free will. As

Arnold Brecht observed, "[t]here were only relatively few, *really voluntary*, exceptions." Arnold Brecht, *The Political Education of Arnold Brecht: An Autobiography, 1884–1970* (Princeton: Princeton University Press, 1970), 435 (emphasis in original).

106. Schmitt admitted as much later on. Joseph W. Bendersky, "Interrogation of Carl Schmitt by Robert Kempner (I)," *Telos* 72 (1987): 126 ("Fundamentally, Goering's only interests in the institution were nepotism and money.").

107. Mehring, *Carl Schmitt*, 303.

108. Carl Schmitt, "Nationalsozialismus und Rechtsstaat," *Juristische Wochenschrift* 63 (1934): 713–18.

109. Hannah Arendt, *The Origins of Totalitarianism* (New York: Harcourt, Brace, 1951), 339 n65.

110. Carl Schmitt, "The Führer Protects the Law: On Adolf Hitler's Reichstag Address of 13 July 1934," in *Third Reich Sourcebook*, eds. Anson Rabinbach and Sander Gilman (Berkeley: University of California Press, 2013), 64.

111. The description of Schmitt's screed as "little more than a call for a well-organized intellectual pogrom" is from Balakrishnan, *The Enemy*, 207.

112. Carl Schmitt, "Schlusswort des Reichsgruppenwalters" in *Das Judentum in der Rechtswissenschaft* (Berlin: Deutscher Rechts-Verlag, 1936) (translation by Aaron Voloj Dessauer), available at https://ia600500.us.archive.org/11/items /DasJudentumInDerRechtswissenschaftBandDieDeutscheRechtswissen schaft/DasJudentumInDerRechtswissenschaft-1.-DieDeutscheRechtswissen schaftImKampfGegenDenJuedischenGeist193640S.ScanFraktur.pdf.

113. Carl Schmitt to Heinrich Himmler, February 12, 1936, in his Sicherheitsdienst (SD) file: 125, http://carl-schmitt-studien.blogspot.com/2008/05/sicherheits dienst-des-rfss-sd-hauptamt.html.

114. Arendt, *The Origins of Totalitarianism*, 339.

115. Hermann Göring to Carl Schmitt, undated, in SD file, 142–43, http:// carl-schmitt-studien.blogspot.com/2008/05/sicherheitsdienst-des-rfss-sd -hauptamt.html.

116. Bendersky, "Schmitt's Diaries," 139.

117. Hans Frank, *Das Haus des Deutschen Rechts in München* (Munich: Akademie für deutsches Recht, 1939), 14.

118. Carl Schmitt, *Writings on War*, trans. and ed. Timothy Nunan (Cambridge, UK: Polity, 2011), 31.

119. Hans Kelsen to Hersch Lauterpacht, December 3, 1937, in Elihu Lauterpacht, *The Life of Hersch Lauterpacht* (Cambridge: Cambridge University Press, 2011), 87.

120. Martti Koskenniemi, *The Gentle Civilizer of Nations* (Cambridge: Cambridge University Press, 2002), 356.

121. *Oppenheim's International Law*, 5th ed., Vol. 2 (London: Longmans, Green, and Co., 1935), vii.

122. Ibid., 517.

123. Ibid., 518.

124. Schmitt, *Writings on War*, 73.

125. Ibid., 72.

126. Ibid.

127. The minutes of the meeting were drafted by Hitler's military adjutant, Colonel Friedrich Hossbach, in a document usually referred to as the "Hossbach Memorandum." See *Documents on Germany Foreign Policy, 1918–1945*, Series D *(1937–1945)*, Vol. 1, *Neurath to Ribbentrop (September 1937–September 1938)* (Washington, DC: U.S. Government Printing Office, 1949).

128. Adolf Hitler, *Mein Kampf*, trans. Ralph Manheim (Boston: Houghton Mifflin, 1971 [1927]), 652 (emphasis added).

129. Ibid., 654 (emphasis added).

130. Joseph H. Kaiser, "Europäisches Grossraumdenken: Die Steigerung geschichtlicher Grössen als Rechtsproblem," in *Epirrhosis: Festgabe für Carl Schmitt*, eds. Hans Barion et al. (Berlin: Duncker & Humblot, 1968), 538, quoted in Bendersky, *Carl Schmitt*, 258.

131. Bendersky, *Carl Schmitt*, 258.

132. The ultimate objective of Welles's mission has been much debated. See, e.g., Stanley E. Hilton, "The Welles Mission to Europe, February–March 1940: Illusion or Realism?," *The Journal of American History* 58 (1971): 93–120. Welles later described the aim of the mission as follows: to "find out what the views of the four governments [Germany, England, France, and Italy] might be as to the present possibilities of concluding any just and permanent peace." Welles, *The Time for Decision*, 74.

133. Adolf Hitler, Memo of February 29, 1940, in *Speeches and Proclamations, 1932–1945*, ed. Max Domarus, trans. Mary Fran Gilbert (Wauconda: Bolchazy-Carducci, 1990), 1942.

134. Ibid., 1943.

135. Sumner Welles to Roosevelt, Report of March 1, 1940, 1, available at http://www.fdrlibrary.marist.edu/_resources/images/psf/psfa0071.pdf.

136. Ibid., 2.

137. Ibid., 8, 9.

138. James B. Reston, "Acting Secretary: Sumner Welles, Career Diplomat Who Looks the Part, Is Often Called to the White House These Days," *New York Times*, August 3, 1941, 9, 22.

139. Edgar B. Nixon, ed., *Franklin D. Roosevelt and Foreign Affairs*, Vol. 1 (Cambridge: Belknap Press of Harvard University, 1979), 559–60.

140. Sumner Welles, March 1, 1940 Report, 11.

141. Ibid., 12.

142. Sumner Welles to Roosevelt, Report of March 2, 1940, 5.

ELEVEN: "GOD SAVE US FROM PROFESSORS!"

1. Bardo Fassbender, "Hans Kelsen," in *The Oxford Handbook of the History of International Law*, eds. Bardo Fassbender and Anne Peters (Oxford: Oxford University Press, 2012), 1168–72; Rudolf Métall, *Hans Kelsen: Leben und Werk* (Vienna: Verlag Franz Deuticke, 1969), 69.

2. The story is relayed in Hans Georg Schenk, "Hans Kelsen in Prague: A Personal Reminiscence," *California Law Review* 59, no. 3 (1971): 615.

3. Hans Kelsen to Roscoe Pound, October 11, 1938, box 140, reel 7, RPP HLS, 1.

4. Ibid., 2.

5. Roscoe Pound to Hans Kelsen, November 1, 1938, box 140, reel 7, RPP HLS. Brüning was a professor at Harvard from 1939 to 1952.

6. See, e.g., Roscoe Pound to John Fairlie, January 27, 1939, and Hans Kelsen to Roscoe Pound, April 15, 1943, box 140, reel 7, RPP HLS.

7. Hersch Lauterpacht diary entry, October 4, 1940, in Elihu Lauterpacht, *The Life of Hersch Lauterpacht* (Cambridge: Cambridge University Press, 2011), 113.

8. Hersch Lauterpacht to Rachel Lauterpacht, December 3, 1940, in ibid., 130.

9. Hersch Lauterpacht to Sir Stephen Gaselee, February 5, 1941, in ibid., 142.

10. See Hersch Lauterpacht, "Memorandum on the principles of international law concerning the question of aid to the Allies by the United States," reprinted in *International Law, The Collected Papers of Hersch Lauterpacht*, Vol. 5, ed. Elihu Lauterpacht (Cambridge: Cambridge University Press, 2004), 651.

11. Robert H. Jackson, "Address of Robert H. Jackson, Attorney General of the United States, Inter-American Bar Association, Havana, Cuba, March 27, 1941," *American Journal of International Law* 35 (1941): 15.

12. Robert Jackson, *That Man: An Insider's Portrait of Franklin D. Roosevelt*, ed. John Q. Barrett (Oxford: Oxford University Press, 2003), 103. The quotation omits the beginning of the sentence: "the treaty and many others that Germany had entered into," where the "treaty" refers to the Pact.

13. Ibid.

14. Lassa Oppenheim, *International Law: A Treatise*, Vol. 2, 5th ed., ed. Hersch Lauterpacht (London: Longmans, Green and Co., 1935), 517. The citation for the sentence reads "But see Stimson in *Foreign Affairs* (N.Y.), ii, Special Suppl., No. 1, p. iv," referring to the article in which the Stimson Doctrine is set out.

15. Hersch Lauterpacht, "Committee on Crimes Against International Public Order: Punishment of War Crimes," n.d. 1942, OCLC No. 669764519: 5–6.

16. For further discussion on the development of the idea of criminalizing aggression, see Kristen Sellars, *"Crimes Against Peace" and International Law* (Cambridge: Cambridge University Press, 2013).

17. Antoine Prost and Jay Winter, *René Cassin and Human Rights: From the Great War to the Universal Declaration of Human Rights* (Cambridge: Cambridge University Press, 2013), 20–23.

18. "Penal Reconstruction and Development Proceedings of the Conference held

in Cambridge on the 14th November, 1941, Between Representatives of Nine Allied Countries and of the Department of Criminal Science in the University of Cambridge," eds. L. Radzinowicz and J. W. C. Turner. Reprinted by permission from *The Canadian Bar Review* (March 1942): 24.

19. Ibid.

20. Elbert D. Thomas, "What We Must Do with the War Criminals," *American Magazine*, February 1943, 91.

21. Ibid., 90.

22. Bertram D. Hullen, "Roosevelt Says U.S. Will Join in Investigation of Atrocities," *New York Times*, October 8, 1942.

23. Statement on Atrocities, The Moscow Conference, October 1943, Avalon Law Project, Yale Law School Lillian Goldman Law Library, http://avalon.law.yale.edu/wwii/moscow.asp.

24. They discussed the matter, but only in passing, at the Tehran Conference in November and December 1943. Stalin had proposed that 50,000 to 100,000 of the German commanding staff be "physically liquidated." Roosevelt had jokingly responded that perhaps "49,000" would do. Churchill, not getting the joke, objected to "executions for political purposes." Bohlen Minutes, November 29, 1943, *FRUS*, 1943 (The Conferences at Cairo and Tehran), 552–55.

25. Sheldon Glueck, *War Criminals: Their Prosecution and Punishment* (New York: Alfred A. Knopf, 1944), 38.

26. Robert H. Jackson, *Report of Robert H. Jackson, United States Representative, to the International Conference on Military Trials* (Washington, DC: U.S. Department of State, 1949), 295–97, 335; IMT, Vol. 1, 168–69.

27. See, e.g., Lord Wright, "Introduction," in United Nations War Crimes Commission, *History of the United Nations War Crimes Commission and the Development of the Laws of War* (London: His Majesty's Stationery Office, 1948), 10–18.

28. See discussion in Chapter 3, pp. 64–69.

29. Treaty of Versailles, Art. 227. For a detailed history of the debate over the arraignment of the Kaiser at Versailles, see James F. Willis, *Prologue to Nuremberg: The Politics and Diplomacy of Punishing War Criminals of the First World War* (Westport, CT: Greenwood, 1982).

30. Treaty of Versailles, Art. 227.

31. Willis, *Prologue to Nuremberg*, 101–12.

32. Schmitt had made these arguments in defending the *Lex Lubbe*, despite proposing contrary claims in his memo "The international crime of the war of aggression and the principle '*nullum crimen, nulla poena sine lege.*'" See Carl Schmitt, *Writings on War*, trans. and ed. Timothy Nunan (Cambridge, UK: Polity, 2011), 146 ("For a jurist of the Continental European way of thinking, it was self-explanatory that the mere usage of the word 'crime' did not amount to a penalization in the sense of the principle '*nullum crimen, nulla poena sine lege*' in international law so long as the facts of the case, the perpetrators, the

punishment, and the court were not determined and circumscribed by clear wording.").

33. Telford Taylor, "An approach to the preparation of the prosecution of Axis criminality," June 2, 1945, 3: box 7, Record Group 238, U.S. Counsel for the Prosecution, Washington, Correspondence 1945–46, National Archives and Records Administration.

34. See generally "Bohuslav Ečer," *Encyklopedie dějin města Brna* (2004), http://en cyklopedie.brna.cz/home-mmb/?acc=profil_osobnosti&load=5794; "Bohuslav Ečer," *Věda a Výzkum—Právnická Fakulta Masarykovy Univerzity*, available at http://science.law.muni.cz/content/cs/vedecko-vyzkumna-cinnost/vav-minu lost/prvorepublikova-era/bohuslav-ecer/.

35. United Nations War Crimes Commission, *History of the United Nations War Crimes Commission and the Development of the Laws of War*, 94, 99–104.

36. Bohuslav Ečer's memo "The Punishment of War Criminals," in *London International Assembly's Reports on Punishment of War Crimes (Reports of Commission I [Formerly Commission II] on the Trial and Punishment of War Criminals)*, 56–58 (memo dated October 10, 1942).

37. Ibid.

38. Ibid., 57–58.

39. Ibid., 172(f) (memo dated November 1943).

40. "Suggested Post-Surrender Program for Germany," in Henry Morgenthau Jr. Diary, September 5–6, 1944, Book 769, 29-27 available at http://www.fdrli brary.marist.edu/_resources/images/morg/md1062.pdf. We have benefited greatly from the excellent discussion in Gary Bass, *Stay the Hand of Vengeance: The Politics of War Crimes Tribunals* (Princeton: Princeton University Press, 2002).

41. Morgenthau's memo to Roosevelt from September 5, 1944, in Bradley F. Smith, *The American Road to Nuremberg: The Documentary Record, 1944–1945* (Stanford: Hoover Institution Press, 1981), 27–29.

42. HLS, diary entry, September 16–17, 1944, reel 9, HSP YUL.

43. Group Meeting, September 7, 1944, in Morgenthau Diary, Book 770, 19 available at http://www.fdrlibrary.marist.edu/_resources/images/morg/md1063.pdf.

44. Ibid.

45. Ibid., 494.

46. Ibid., 526.

47. Bass, *Stay the Hand of Vengeance*, 150; Smith, *The American Road to Nuremberg*, 9; HLS, diary entries, September 13–14, 1944, HSP YUL.

48. U.S. Department of State, *Foreign Relations of the United States: Conference at Quebec* (1944), 467; Smith, *The American Road to Nuremberg*, 27–29.

49. Cabinet Papers from British Public Records Office, 66/42, Churchill war criminals memorandum, W.P. (43) 496, November 9, 1943, 265–66, available at http://filestore.nationalarchives.gov.uk/pdfs/large/cab-66-42.pdf.

50. Ibid, 266.

51. HLS, Memo to the President, September 5, 1944, reel 128, HSP YUL.

52. HLS, Memo to the President, September 9, 1944, reel 128, HSP YUL; Smith, *The American Road to Nuremberg*, 30.

53. HLS, Memo to the President, September 5, 1944, reel 128, HSP YUL; HLS, Memo to the President, September 9, 1944, reel 128, HSP YUL; HLS, Memo to the President, September 15, 1944, reel 128, HSP YUL.

54. HLS, Memo to the President, September 5. 1944, reel 128, HSP YUL.

55. Bass, *Stay the Hand of Vengeance*, 166–68.

56. *Time*, October, 2, 1944, 21.

57. Michael Beschloss, *The Conquerors: Roosevelt, Truman, and the Destruction of Hitler's Germany, 1941–1945* (New York: Simon & Schuster, 2002), 144.

58. HLS, diary entry, October 3, 1944, reel 9, HSP YUL.

59. "The Gallup Poll #347: field date 05/15/1945–05/15/1945," *Gallup News Service* (1945).

60. G. M. Gilbert, *Nuremberg Diary* (New York: Farrar, Straus & Giroux, 1947), 8.

61. A. N. Trainin, *Hitlerite Responsibility Under the Criminal Law*, ed. A. Y. Vishinski, trans. by Andrew Rothstein (London: Hutchinson & Co., 1945), 96.

62. See, e.g., ibid., 37.

63. For a detailed discussion of Chanler's role in developing the crime of aggression, see Jonathan Bush, "'The Supreme . . . Crime' and Its Origins: The Lost Legislative History of the Crime of Aggressive War," *Columbia Law Review* 102, no. 8 (2002): 2324–2424.

64. Lately Thomas, *The Astor Orphans: Pride of Lions* (New York: William Morrow, 1971). William Chamberlain Chanler was originally named "William Astor Chanler II," but his name was later changed to avoid confusion with his cousin, William Astor Chanler Jr. See ibid., 222–23.

65. Bush, "'The Supreme . . . Crime' and Its Origins," 2351.

66. Harry L. Coles and Albert K Weinberg, *Civil Affairs: Soldiers Become Governors* (Washington, DC: U.S. Government Printing Office, 1964), 187, 206–7, 392.

67. Tornata di Sabato, Anno VII, December 8, 1928, 9768.

68. R. J. B. Bosworth, *Mussolini* (London: Bloomsbury, 2011), 401–2.

69. Telford Taylor, "The Nuremberg Trials," *Columbia Law Review* 55 (1955), 488, 493 n. 29; Telford Taylor, *The Anatomy of the Nuremberg Trials* (Boston: Back Bay Books, 1992), 37.

70. Otto Skorzeny, *Secret Missions: War Memoirs of the Most Dangerous Man in Europe*, trans. Jacques Le Clercq (New York: E. P. Dutton, 1951), 57.

71. Ibid., 102; Glenn B. Infield, *Skorzeny: Hitler's Commando*, 1st ed. (New York: St. Martin's Press, 1981), 12; Skorzeny, *Secret Missions*, 8.

72. Ibid., 96–99.

73. United Nations War Crimes Commission, *History of the United Nations War Crimes Commission and the Development of the Laws of War*, 181–84 (quoting a note to the committee by Arnold McNair, the British legal expert); Bohuslav Ečer, "Minority Report," September 27, 1944, The National Archives, United Kingdom, Foreign Office, 371/39003.

74. Smith, *The American Road to Nuremberg*, 67.

75. Ibid., 69–71.

76. Ibid., 72.

77. Bohuslav Ečer, Report on Professor Trainin's *The Criminal Responsibility of the Hitlerites*, at the Commission's Meeting of October 31, 1944 (November 11, 1944), 107/180/1, War Crimes—Working File, The U.S. National Archives and Records Administration (College Park, MD).

78. Chanler to Telford Taylor, December 28, 1954, in Bush, "'The Supreme . . . Crime' and Its Origins," 2418–19.

79. Smith, *The American Road to Nuremberg*, 69.

80. For December 14 and 18 memos to McCloy and the Judge Advocate General, respectively, criticizing Chanler's theory, see Smith, *The American Road to Nuremberg*, 75–84.

81. Smith, *The American Road to Nuremberg*, 71.

82. Chanler to Taylor, February 25, 1955, in Bush, "'The Supreme . . . Crime' and Its Origins," 2420.

83. Presidential Memorandum for the Secretary of State, January 3, 1945 in Smith, *The American Road to Nuremberg*, 92.

84. Robert H. Jackson, *That Man: An Insider's Portrait of Franklin D. Roosevelt*, ed. John Q. Barrett (Oxford: Oxford University Press, 2003), 167.

85. Ibid.

86. Ibid., 169.

87. Robert H. Jackson, "The Rule of Law Among Nations," American Bar Association Journal 31 (1945): 290–94.

88. See Telford Taylor, "The Nuremberg Trial," *Columbia Law Review* 55, no. 4 (1955): 495 n37.

89. Chanler to Telford Taylor, December 28, 1954, in Bush, "'The Supreme . . . Crime' and Its Origins," 2418–19.

90. "Address of Robert H. Jackson, Attorney General of the United States, Inter-American Bar Association, Havana, Cuba, March 27, 1941," *American Journal of International Law* 35 (1941): 354.

91. See Noah Feldman, *Scorpions: The Battles and Triumphs of FDR's Great Supreme Court Justices* (New York: Hachette, 2010), 44–47.

92. Jackson, *That Man*, 106–7.

93. See, e.g., Colonel Cutter's document, "Punishment of War Criminals," in Smith, *The American Road to Nuremberg*, 173–74.

94. Bosworth, *Mussolini*, 33, 410–11.

95. Ian Kershaw, *Hitler: 1936–1945: Nemesis* (New York: W. W. Norton, 2000), 821, 825. Joseph and Magda Goebbels asked the adjutant to the head doctor of the SS medical administration to give each child a morphine shot. Hitler's personal physician then crushed cyanide capsules in their mouths. Ibid., 832–33.

96. "British Capture Ribbentrop in Apartment," *Pittsburgh Post-Gazette*, June 16, 1945.

97. "Nazi Death Factory Shocks Germans on a Forced Tour," *New York Times*, April 18, 1945.

98. See Edward T. Folliard, "Tour of Horror After Americans Liberate Buchenwald," *Washington Post*, April 18, 1945.

99. "Nazi Death Factory Shocks Germans on a Forced Tour," *New York Times*.

100. HLS, diary entry, January 18, 1945, reel 9, HSP YUL; Stimson, "The Nuremberg Trial: Landmark in Law," *Foreign Affairs* 25, no. 2 (January 1947): 179–89.

101. HLS, Memo to the President, September 9, 1944, reel 128, HSP YUL; Morgenthau Diary, Vol. 1, 614.

102. See Jackson, *Report of Robert H. Jackson*, 331.

103. Smith, *The American Road to Nuremberg*, 182.

104. Jackson, *Report of Robert H. Jackson*, 51.

105. Ibid.

106. Ibid.

107. Ibid., 53.

108. Ibid., 335. See also arguments by Gros on pp. 295, 297.

109. Jackson diary, May 10 1945, box 95, RJP LOC.

110. For an excellent biography of Lauterpacht and discussion of his role in developing the legal foundations of the crime against humanity, see Philippe Sands, *East West Street: On the Origins of "Genocide" and "Crimes Against Humanity"* (New York: Alfred A. Knopf, 2016).

111. Jackson, *Report of Robert H. Jackson*, 383–84.

112. Ibid., 299.

113. Ibid., 384.

114. Hans Kelsen to Roscoe Pound, September 8, 1943, box 140, reel 7, RPP HLS.

115. Hans Kelsen to Roscoe Pound, April 15, 1943, box 140, reel 7, RPP HLS.

116. See, e.g., Archibald MacLeish to Roscoe Pound, September 20, 1943, RPP HLS.

117. Thomas Olechowski, "Kelsen, the Second World War and the US Government," in D. A. Jeremy Telman, ed., *Hans Kelsen in America—Selective Affinities and the Mysteries of Academic Influence* (Switzerland: Springer Verlag, 2016).

118. According to Olechowski, those memos were titled: 1) on the Draft Executive Agreement relating to the prosecution of European Axis War Criminals; 2) on the Agreement for the Prosecution of European Axis War Criminals; 3) on the Rule against Ex post facto laws; 4) on the Definition of Aggression; 5) on the Question: "Is launching a war of aggression a crime?"; 6) on the Instrument of Surrender signed by the Japanese Government; 7) on the Punishment of War Criminals and the Charter of the United Nations; 8) on War Crimes as related to the preparation, launching, and opening of hostilities without previous warning. Ibid., 106.

119. Jackson, *Report of Robert H. Jackson*, 121; "Amendments proposed by the United Kingdom Delegation to the United States Draft Protocol," June 28, 1945, in ibid., 86; "Minutes of Conference Session of June 29, 1945," in ibid., 99.

120. See Memorandum of Hans Kelsen, n.d., box 104, reel 10, pp. 2–3, RJP LOC. For an earlier expression of this idea, see Hans Kelsen, "Collective and Individual Responsibility in International Law with Particular Regard to the Punishment of War Criminals," *California Law Review* 31 (1943): 533.

121. Ibid., 533–34, 538–40.

122. Ibid., 533–34 ("violation" was substituted for "delict" in quotation above).

123. Ibid.

124. Memorandum of Hans Kelsen, at 4–5.

125. Kelsen addressed the problem first in Kelsen, "Collective and Individual Responsibility," an article published in 1943 that Jackson probably read, as he jotted the citation in his papers. Kelsen addressed the issue more fully in Kelsen, "The rule against ex post facto laws and the prosecution of the axis war Criminals," *Judge Advocate Journal* 2, no. 3 (Fall/Winter 1945): 10, which almost certainly derives from the memos he wrote for Weir and which Jackson probably read as well.

126. Ibid. ("The subsequent treaty does not make a legal action illegal *ex post facto*. It only adds to the collective responsibility for an illegal action established by pre-existing International Law, individual responsibility of the perpetrators.").

127. Kelsen also noted the political upside. Reforming international law in this way would make war crimes prosecutions more palatable. "The punishment of war crimes by an international tribunal . . . would certainly meet with much less resistance, since it would hurt national feelings much less if it were to be carried out within the framework of a general reform of international law, the aim of which is to complete the collective responsibility of States for violations of international law by the individual responsibility of the persons who, as agents of the State, have committed the acts by which international law has been violated." Kelsen, "Collective and Individual Responsibility," 565.

128. Memorandum of Robert Jackson, July 5, 1945, box 104, reel 10, RJP LOC.

129. Jackson, *Report of Robert H. Jackson*, 137–38, 395.

130. Ibid., 423.

131. On the back of the folder containing his legal opinion, Schmitt wrote that it was commissioned by the lawyer Walter Schmidt. Helmut Quaritsch, "Zur Entstehung des Gutachtens 1945," in Carl Schmitt, *Das internationalrechtliche Verbrechen des Angriffskrieges und der Grundsatz "Nullum crimen, nulla poena sine lege,"* ed. Helmut Quartisch (Berlin: Duncker & Humblot, 1994), 125. Schmidt was almost certainly acting on behalf of Flick, through his associate, Konrad Kaletsch. Hubert Seliger, *Politische Anwälte? Die Verteidiger der Nürnberger Prozesse* (Baden-Baden: Nomos, 2016), 228.

132. For more background on this memo, see Helmut Quaritsch's Introduction in Schmitt, *Verbrechen*, and Timothy Nunan, Notes on the Text, in Schmitt, *Writings on War*, 125.

133. For Schmitt's discussion of the Kellogg-Briand Pact, see "The International Crime of the War of Aggression," in Schmitt, *Writings on War*, 155–64.

134. Ibid., 161.
135. Ibid., 159 (quoting William Borah, Testimony Before the United States Senate) ("The treaty is not founded upon the theory of force or punitive measures at any place or at any time. . . . There are no sanctions; the treaty rests in a wholly different philosophy. . . . In other words, when the treaty is broken the United States is absolutely free. It is just as free to choose its course as if the treaty had never been written.").
136. Ibid., 190.
137. Ibid., 150.
138. Flick was eventually prosecuted by the Allies in 1947.
139. Ibid., 125–26.
140. Konrad Kaletsch, Flick's deputy, who hired Schmitt for Flick's defense, also retained Dix. See Nobert Frei, Ralf Ahrens, Jörg Osterloh, and Tim Schanetsky, *Flick: Der Konzern, die Familie, die Macht* (Munich: Karl Blessing Verlag, 2009), 405.
141. Schmitt, *Glossarium*, 138 ("Dix nannte mein Exposé vom Sommer 1945 damals eine 'volkerrechtliche Seminarübung.'").
142. Schmitt, *Writings on War*, 196.
143. Ibid.
144. See, e.g., ibid., 197.

TWELVE: NAZI CIRCUS TOWN

1. Hersch Lauterpacht to Rachel Lauterpacht, November 30, 1945, in Elihu Lauterpacht, *The Life of Hersch Lauterpacht* (Cambridge: Cambridge University Press, 2010), 277.
2. Joseph E. Persico, *Nuremberg: Infamy on Trial* (New York: Viking, 1994), 39.
3. See Thomas Dodd to Grace Dodd, August 14, 1945, in Christopher S. Dodd, *Letters from Nuremberg: My Father's Narrative of a Quest for Justice* (New York: Crown, 2007), 90.
4. Airey Neave, *On Trial at Nuremberg* (Boston: Little, Brown, 1978), 42.
5. Persico, *Nuremberg*, 40.
6. Rick Atkinson, *The Guns at Last Light: The War in Western Europe, 1944–1945* (New York: Henry Holt, 2013), 606.
7. Rebecca West, "Extraordinary Exile," *The New Yorker*, September 7, 1946, 38.
8. Dan Kiley, "Architect of Palace of Justice Renovations," in *Witnesses to Nuremberg: An Oral History of American Participants at the War Crimes Trials*, eds. Bruce M. Stave, Michele Palmer, and Leslie Frank (New York: Twayne, 1998), 24.
9. Roger Manvell and Heinrich Fraenkel, *Goering: The Rise and Fall of the Notorious Nazi Leader* (New York: Simon & Schuster, 1962), 114. When weighed after his arrest, Göring weighed 120 kilograms, approximately 265 pounds. Burton C. Andrus, *I Was the Nuremberg Jailer* (New York: Coward-McCann, Inc. 1969), 31.

10. IMT, Vol. 13, 7 (May 3, 1946) (testimony of Schacht); Andrus, *I Was the Nuremberg Jailer*, 29–30. In his meeting on March 3, 1940, Welles reported that Göring's "face gave the impression of being heavily rouged but, since at the end of our three-hour conversation the color had worn off," suggesting that his facial color was due to "some form of facial massage." Sumner Welles to FDR, Report of March 3, 1940, 1, available at http://www.fdrlibrary.marist.edu/_resources/images/psf/psfa0071.pdf.

11. West, "Extraordinary Exile," 35.

12. G. M. Gilbert, *Nuremberg Diary* (New York: Farrar, Straus, 1947), 11.

13. Andrus, *I Was the Nuremberg Jailer*, 30; Manvell and Fraenkel, *Goering*, 425.

14. Ibid., 12.

15. *War Office Intelligence Review* 110 (December 19, 1945): 11. Schacht on Ribbentrop: "For Ribbentrop there was only one excuse, even according to the most charitable estimation—his extraordinary stupidity." Hjalmar Schacht, *Confessions of "the Old Wizard": The Autobiography of Hjalmar Horace Greeley Schacht*, trans. Diane Pyke (Boston: Houghton Mifflin, 1956), 406.

16. Albert Speer, *Inside the Third Reich* (New York: Macmillan, 1970), 243–44, 321; Schacht, *Confessions of "the Old Wizard,"* 406.

17. Gilbert, *Nuremberg Diary*, 9.

18. West, "Extraordinary Exile," 34.

19. For Schacht's low opinion of Göring, see Schacht, *Confessions of "the Old Wizard,"* 406.

20. Speer, *Inside the Third Reich*, 186.

21. Ibid., 511.

22. Gilbert, *Nuremberg Diary*, 35.

23. IMT, Vol. 2, 95 (November 21, 1945); "I: Defense Motion Challenging Jurisdiction of Tribunal."

24. IMT, Vol.1, "Chapter V: Opening Address for the United States" (November 21, 1945).

25. IMT, Vol. 2, 115 (November 21, 1945).

26. Gilbert, *Nuremberg Diary*, 37.

27. IMT, Vol. 2, 129–30 (November 21, 1945).

28. Ibid., 146–47.

29. Ibid., 150.

30. Ibid., 155.

31. "Lord Shawcross," *The Telegraph*, July 11, 2003, http://www.telegraph.co.uk/news/obituaries/1435769/Lord-Shawcross.html.

32. Hersch Lauterpacht to Rachel Lauterpacht, November 29, 1945, in Lauterpacht, *The Life of Hersch Lauterpacht*, 276.

33. Lauterpacht's drafts for the opening and closing arguments have since been published by Philippe Sands. See Hersch Lauterpacht, "Draft Nuremberg Speeches," *Cambridge Journal of International and Comparative Law* 1, no. 1 (2012): 45–111.

34. IMT, Vol. 3, 100 (December 4, 1945) (opening statement of Shawcross).

35. Hans Kelsen, "Collective and Individual Responsibility in International Law with Particular Regard to the Punishment of War Criminals," *California Law Review* 31 (1943): 530–39.

36. IMT, Vol. 3, 105 (December 4, 1945) (opening statement of Shawcross); Lauterpacht, "Draft Nuremberg Speeches," 62.

37. IMT, Vol. 3, 106 (December 4, 1945) (opening statement of Shawcross).

38. West, "Extraordinary Exile," 34.

39. Ibid.

40. Taylor, *The Anatomy of the Nuremberg Trials*, 225.

41. Gilbert, *Nuremberg Diary*, 45–46.

42. Persico, *Nuremberg*, 145.

43. Gilbert, *Nuremberg Diary*, 49.

44. Airey Neave, *They Have Their Exits* (London: Hodder & Stoughton, 1953), 184.

45. Taylor, *The Anatomy of the Nuremberg Trials*, 133.

46. Neave, *They Have Their Exits*, 181.

47. See Luise Jodl, *Jenseits des Endes: Leben und Sterben des Generaloberst Alfred Jodl* (Munich: Molden, 1978), 184–85, and interview with Wechsler recorded in Persico, *Nuremberg*, 95–96. The Jodls first considered the historian of law Prof. Heinrich Mitteis, but weren't sure how he had fared under the Russians. Dr. Schlögl, the director of the Red Cross in Nuremberg, suggested Exner to Luise; she wrote her husband about this suggestion, who replied that he had met Exner in Vienna at some point and could not imagine a more suitable candidate.

48. Annette Weinke, "Hermann Jahrreiss (1894–1992): Vom Exponenten des völkerrechtlichen 'Kriegseinsatzes' zum Verteidiger der deutschen Eliten in Nürnberg," in *Kölner Juristen im 20. Jahrhundert*, eds. Steffen Augsberg and Andreas Funke (Tübingen: Mohr-Siebeck, 2013), 170.

49. Golczewski, *Kölner Universitätslehrer*, 412.

50. Weinke, "Hermann Jahrreiss," 179.

51. Hermann Jahrreiss, "Völkerrechtliche Grossraumordnung. Bemerkungen zu einer Schrift von Carl Schmitt," *Zeitschrift der Akademie für Deutsches Recht* 6 (1939): 608–9; Hermann Jahrreiss, "Wandlung der Weltordnung. Zugleich eine Auseinandersetzung mit der Völkerrechtslehre von Carl Schmitt," *Zeitschrift für öffentliches Recht* 21 (1941): 513–36.

52. See Abby Mann, *Judgment at Nuremberg* (London: Cassell, 1961), xi–xii. Mann describes his conversation with a general's wife whose husband had been executed at the International Military Tribunal and who was writing a memoir. Luise Jodl, née von Benda, published a memoir about her husband, *Jenseits des Endes: Leben und Sterben des Generaloberst Alfred Jodl*, in 1976.

53. Jahrreiss was only one of three defense counsel familiar with the laws of war. The other two were Herbert Kraus and Otto Kranzbühler.

54. IMT, Vol. 17, 463–75 (July 4, 1946)(statement of Jahrreiss); Carl Schmitt, *Writings on War*, trans. and ed. Timothy Nunan (Cambridge, UK: Polity, 2011), 173.

55. Ibid., 472

56. Ibid., 480.

57. Taylor, *The Anatomy of the Nuremberg Trials*, 475.

58. For similar speculation, see Kristin Sellars, "'Crimes Against Peace' and International Law" (Cambridge: Cambridge University Press, 2013): 125–26.

59. IMT, Vol. 19, 460 (July 26, 1946) (statement by Shawcross).

60. Ibid. ("Did the aggressions of Japan and Italy . . . followed by the German aggressions against Austria and Czechoslovakia, deprive those obligations of their binding effect simply because those crimes achieved a temporary success?").

61. Ibid.

62. Ibid.

63. Ibid.

64. Ibid., 461.

65. Ibid., 462 (emphasis added).

66. IMT, Vol. 22, 462 (September 30, 1946).

67. Ibid., 464.

68. "'The Supreme . . . Crime' and Its Origins: The Last Legislative History of the Crime of Aggression," *Columbia Law Review* 102, No. 8 (2002): 2373.

69. Ibid., 498.

70. See discussion in Chapter 10, pp. 217–19.

71. See Markus Lang, *Karl Loewenstein: Transatlantischer Denker der Politik* (Stuttgart: Franz Steiner Verlag, 2007).

72. Karl Loewenstein, "Office Diary, August 1945–August 1946," box 46, folder 1, 3, https://acdc.amherst.edu/explore/asc:18140/asc:18148, KLP ACA. See Joseph W. Bendersky, "Carl Schmitt's Path to Nuremberg: A Sixty-Year Reassessment," Telos 139 (2007): 6–34.

73. Loewenstein, "Office Diary," entry for August 14, 1945, box 46, KLP ACL.

74. Ibid., entry for August 15, 1945.

75. Ibid., entry for August 16, 1945.

76. Ibid., entry for September 13, 1945.

77. Memo from Loewenstein to McLendon, October 10, 1945, box 46, folder 1, KLP ACL.

78. Ibid.; Loewenstein, "Office Diary," entry for October 4, 1945, box 46, KLP ACL. In "Carl Schmitt's Path to Nuremberg," Bendersky claims a meeting about arresting Schmitt took place on September 21, citing Loewenstein's office diary, but no mention of Schmitt appears on the entries for September 21, 26, or 29.

79. Werner Sollors, *The Temptation of Despair* (Cambridge: Belknap Press of Harvard University, 2014), 176.

80. Karl Loewenstein, "Observations on Personality and Work of Professor Carl Schmitt," November 14, 1945, box 28, folder 1, KLP ACL.

81. Ibid., 3–4.

82. Carl Schmitt, *"Ius Publicum Europaeum,"* Archiv Der Max-Plank-Gesellschaft, Rep. 13 Schmitt, Nr. 2/1, trans. Aaron Voloj Dessauer (unpublished manuscript on file with authors), 1.

83. Ibid.

84. Ibid.

85. Ibid.

86. Ibid.

87. Ibid., 4.

88. Ibid.

89. Ibid., 2.

90. Ibid., 8.

91. He was cleared by a German court and American authorities certified that they had no grounds to hold him. Bendersky, "Carl Schmitt's Path to Nuremberg," 20. The discussion in this section is much indebted to Bendersky's masterful discussion.

92. Duška Schmitt to Hermann Jahrreiss, April 1, 1947, cited in Reinhard Mehring, *Carl Schmitt: A Biography*, trans. Daniel Steuer (Cambridge, UK: Polity, 2014), 416.

93. Index cards to the war crimes case files ("Cases Not Tried"), 1944–1948 and witnesses and defendants in war crimes cases, 1946–1948, Record Group 549, Records of United States Army, Europe 549.2, Records of U.S. Army, Europe (USAEUR) 1933–1964, Records of the War Crimes Branch of the Judge Advocate General Section.

94. On the many inconsistent accounts Kempner offered about Schmitt's rearrest, see Bendersky, "Carl Schmitt's Path to Nuremberg," 7–8, and Helmut Quaritsch, ed., *Carl Schmitt: Antworten in Nürnberg* (Berlin: Duncker & Humblot, 2000), 11–47.

95. Bendersky, "Carl Schmitt's Path to Nuremberg," 20–21.

96. Ibid., 23–24. It is possible that Kempner was trying to bully Schmitt, threatening to prosecute him for war crimes unless he cooperated with the "Ministry Cases" currently taking place and for which Kempner was the lead prosecutor. Quaritsch, *Carl Schmitt: Antworten in Nürnberg*, 11–47. The Ministry Cases tried the leading Nazi lawyers and Schmitt would have been of invaluable help to the prosecution.

97. Another possibility is William Dickman, a Jewish émigré working for the Legal Advice Branch of the Legal Division of OMGUS. In a memo dated February 6, 1947, he wrote: "To my mind, Carl Schmitt is a war criminal similar to other leading figures of Nazism. While, e.g., Fritzsche used the instrumentality of the radio for propagandizing the ideas of Nazism, Schmitt used the media of legal journals and periodicals, articles and books." Memo to Mr. Alvin J.

Rockwell, February 6, 1947, "Carl Schmitt Library" File, in Record Group 260: Records of U.S. Occupation Headquarters, World War II, 1923–1972, Series: Legal Files, compiled 1944–1950, box 61.

98. Bendersky, "Carl Schmitt's Path to Nuremberg," 23.

99. The transcripts have been translated and published by Joseph Bendersky. For the first (April 3), third (April 23), and fourth (April 28) sessions, see Bendersky, "Carl Schmitt at Nuremberg," 91–129; for the second session (April 11), only found much later, see Carl Schmitt, "The 'Fourth' (Second) Interrogation of Carl Schmitt at Nuremberg," introduction by Joseph W. Bendersky, *Telos* 139 (2007): 35–43.

100. Bendersky, "Carl Schmitt at Nuremberg," 98.

101. Ibid., 100.

102. Ibid., 101.

103. Ibid., 114.

104. Ibid., 124.

105. Ibid., 125.

106. Ibid., 107.

CODA II

1. Elihu Lauterpacht, *The Life of Hersch Lauterpacht* (Cambridge: Cambridge University Press, 2010), 11, 280.

2. Ibid., 277.

3. Ibid., 278.

4. Ibid.

5. On the last day of 1945, just a month after he returned from Nuremberg, he wrote that he was working on an article to mark the tercentenary of the death of Grotius. The article would later appear in the *British Yearbook of International Law*, of which he was the editor. Ibid., 279. McNair remembered Lauterpacht telling him that the article "contained more of his essential thinking and faith than anything else he had written." Arnold McNair, "Hersch Lauterpacht: 1897–1960," *Annals of the British Academy* (London: Oxford University Press, 1961), 79.

6. Elihu Lauterpacht, ed., *International Law: The Collected Papers of Hersch Lauterpacht*, Vol. 2 (Cambridge: Cambridge University Press, 1970), 308. Lauterpacht was the Whewell Professor of International Law at the University of Cambridge. William Whewell, the man after whom the chair is named, had translated Grotius's *The Law of War and Peace* in three volumes of about 1,400 pages.

7. Lauterpacht, ed., *International Law*, 310.

8. Ibid. Itaw Commission, which was originally cited, has slightly different language.

9. Ibid., 311.

10. Ibid.

11. Ibid.

12. Ibid., 320.

13. Ibid.

14. Ibid.

15. Ibid., 327 (emphasis added).

16. Ibid., 364–65.

17. Ibid., 327.

18. U.N. General Assembly resolution 174 (II), Statute of the International Law Commission, November 21, 1947, http://legal.un.org/ilc/texts/instruments /english/statute/statute.pdf. One of the General Assembly's first acts was the creation of the International Law Commission for the "promotion of the progressive development of international law and its codification." Ibid., Art. 1, ¶1. The U.N. Charter gave the General Assembly the power to "initiate studies and make recommendations for the purpose of . . . encouraging the progressive development of international law and its codification." Charter of the United Nations, Art. 13, ¶1. During its first session, on December 11, 1946, the General Assembly adopted Resolution 94 to consider procedures to be recommended for the discharge of these responsibilities. The committee recommended establishing an international law commission. On November 21, 1947, the General Assembly adopted Resolution 174 establishing the International Law Commission and approving its statute.

19. Lauterpacht, *The Life of Hersch Lauterpacht*, 356.

20. Ibid., 357.

21. Hersch Lauterpacht, *Report on the Law of Treaties*, in *Yearbook of the International Law Commission*, Vol. 2 (New York: United Nations, 1953), 147 ("Treaties imposed by or as the result of the use of force or threats of force against a State in violation of the principles of the Charter of the United Nations are invalid if so declared by the International Court of Justice at the request of any State.").

22. Hersch Lauterpacht, *Private Law Sources and Analogies of International Law: With Special Reference to International Arbitration* (London: Longmans, 1927), 167.

23. Lauterpacht, *Report on the Law of Treaties*, 147.

24. Ibid.

25. Ibid.

26. Ibid., 147–48. Lauterpacht was far from alone in this view. By the time he worked as special rapporteur, the view had become conventional wisdom: "Writers on international law appear to be unanimous in the opinion that, with the possible exception of treaties of peace which are often imposed by a victorious belligerent upon a State which has been defeated in war, freedom of consent by the parties is an essential condition of the validity of a treaty." Harvard Research in International Law, "Draft Convention on the Law of Treaties," *American Journal of International Law* 29, Supplement: Research in International Law (1935): 1149.

27. Lauterpacht, *Report on the Law of Treaties*, 148 ("[I]n so far as war or force or threats of force constitute an internationally illegal act, the results of that illegality—namely a treaty imposed in connection with or in consequence thereof—are governed by the principle that an illegal act cannot produce legal rights for the benefit of the law-breaker.").

28. "Comments by Government of the United States of America on Parts I, II and III of the Draft Articles on the Law of Treaties Drawn up by the International Law Commission at its Fourteenth, Fifteenth and Sixteenth Sessions," *American Journal of International Law* 61, no. 4 (October 1967): 1145–46.

29. The about-face in the law would later be enshrined in an international treaty, the 1969 Vienna Convention on the Law of Treaties. Article 52 provided: "A treaty is void if its conclusion has been procured by the threat or use of force in violation of the principles of international law embodied in the Charter of the United Nations." Vienna Convention on the Law of Treaties, May 23, 1969, 1155 U.N.T.S. 331, at 344.

30. Mark R. Peattie, *Ishiwara Kanji and Japan's Confrontation with the West* (Princeton, NJ: Princeton Univeristy Press, 1975), 352–53.

31. Hersch Lauterpacht, *Recognition in International Law* (Cambridge: AMS Press, 1947).

32. The International Court of Justice, established in 1945, is the principal judicial organ of the United Nations and is the successor to the inaptly named Permanent International Court of Justice established under the Covenant of the League of Nations in 1922.

33. Lauterpacht, *The Life of Hersch Lauterpacht*, 414.

34. Elihu Lauterpacht, "Sir Hersch Lauterpacht: 1897–1960," *European Journal of International Law* 8, no. 2 (January 1997): 313–15.

THIRTEEN: THE END OF CONQUEST

1. "The First Day of Ukraine's EuroMaidan Protests. November 21, 2013. Kyiv, Ukraine," YouTube video, 2:20, posted by ромадське Телебачення (Hromadske), November 1, 2014, https://www.youtube.com/watch?v=K6hsBASbX5Y.

2. "In pictures: Inside the Palace Yanukovych Didn't Want Ukraine to See," *The Telegraph*, February 27, 2014.

3. Andrew Higgins and Steven Erlanger, "Gunmen Seize Government Buildings in Crimea," *New York Times*, February 27, 2014; Marie-Louise Gumuchian, Laura Smith-Spark, and Ingrid Formanek, "Gunmen Seize Government Buildings in Ukraine's Crimea, Raise Russian Flag," CNN, February 27, 2014, http://www.cnn.com/2014/02/27/world/europe/ukraine-politics.

4. Judgement of the Constitutional Court of Ukraine on the All-Crimean Referendum in the Autonomous Republic of Crimea, Case No. 1-13/2014 (March 14, 2014).

5. Luke Harding and Shaun Walker, "Crimea Applies to Be Part of Russian Federation After Vote to Leave Ukraine," *The Guardian*, March 17, 2014.

6. "Executive Order on Recognising Republic of Crimea," March 17, 2014, http://en.kremlin.ru/events/president/news/20596; "Ukraine Crisis: Putin Signs Russia-Crimea Treaty," BBC, March 18, 2014, http://www.bbc.com /news/world-europe-26630062.

7. "Direct Line with Vladimir Putin," April 17, 2014, http://en.kremlin.ru/events /president/news/20796.

8. The dataset and documentation can be obtained at The Correlates of War Project, Territorial Change (v5), as described and documented in Tir, Jaroslav, Philip Schafer, Paul Diehl, and Gary Goertz, "Territorial Changes, 1816–1996: Procedures and Data," *Conflict Management and Peace Science* 16 (1998): 89–97.

9. Other work, often drawing from different sources, has arrived at conclusions consistent with ours. Mark W. Zacher's excellent article "The Territorial Integrity Norm: International Boundaries and the Use of Force," *International Organization* 55, no. 2 (Spring 2001): 245, concludes that "[t]he decline of successful wars of territorial aggrandizement during the last half century is palpable." Unfortunately, the work—like nearly all empirical work of its kind—treats 1945 as the relevant break point in the twentieth century, and thus does not inspect the changes that occurred between 1928 and 1945. Moreover, it speaks of a "norm" against territorial aggrandizement, rather than the legal prohibitions embodied in the Paris Peace Pact and U.N. Charter. See Tanisha M. Fazal, *State Death: The Politics and Geography of Conquest, Occupation, and Annexation* (Princeton: Princeton University Press, 2007) (documenting the radical decline of state death after 1945); Gary Goertz, Paul Diehl, and Alexandru Balas, *The Puzzle of Peace: The Evolution of Peace in the International System* (New York: Oxford University Press, 2016), 156 (finding that "[a]fter World War II, territorial acquisition through military seizure is rare" and that "[e]ven in the few instances in which states have recently violated the norm against conquest, the international community has responded in ways that seek to maintain the norm").

10. The dataset also occasionally contains outright mistakes—classifying a transfer as taking place in a different year than it occurred. For instance, the "Correlates of War" dataset in Observation 225, indicates that the Ottoman Empire gained 107,120 square kilometers of contiguous land from Al Hasa in 1875. That transfer took place in 1871. More rarely, the "Correlates of War" dataset misidentifies the countries involved in a transfer. In each of these cases of clear error, we have corrected the borrowed data. Our posted data files indicate each of these changes.

11. We drew the number of states from Correlates of War Project, "State System Membership List, v2011" (2011), at http://correlatesofwar.org. This figure necessarily excludes a number of the conquests that took place in this period. Many of the entities involved in conquests during this period were nonstate entities. The data include 137 conquests in the period, in 133 of which the gainer was a state. In 79 instances, territory was conquered from defined

nonsovereign entities and in 58 instances, territory was conquered from other sovereign states. A state during this period therefore had a 3.0 percent (133/ state year) chance of gaining from a conquest. It also had a 1.33 percent (93 /state year) chance of being a *victim* of a conquest. Overall, a state had a 4.3 percent (191/state year) chance being involved in some way (as either gainer or loser) in a conquest.

12. This calculation is for illustrative purposes only. It is an average across all states, as recognized by the "Correlates of War," and years. In reality, of course, some states are more likely to be victims of conquest, probabilities change across years, and probabilities are not independent. In addition, this figure excludes the 79 conquests in which a nonstate entity was the victim of a conquest.

13. Crimea is 27,000 square kilometers.

14. Dan Altman finds that where there has been only one "coerced cession" after 1945, there have been a significant number of what he calls "land grabs" by "fait accompli"—which involve seizure of a *disputed* piece of territory with the intention to assume lasting control. Dan Altman, "By Fait Accompli, Not Coercion: How States Wrest Territory from Their Adversaries," November 5, 2016 (working paper). These findings are consistent with our claim that conquest (coerced cession) is rare in the modern world order. They are also consistent with our claim, developed *infra* Chapter 14, that territories with uncertain sovereign authority are a continuing source of conflict.

15. S. O. Levinson to James G. McDonald, April 7, 1928, quoted in John E. Stoner, *S. O. Levinson and the Pact of Paris* (Chicago: University of Chicago Press, 1943), 193.

16. Ibid., 192 (emphasis added).

17. The territory is the same or nearly the same if the territory was identified as the same geographic area and if the size of the territory was within ±10 percent or 10 square kilometers of the territory that initially transferred.

18. The "Correlates of War" database records the transfer in 1920.

19. Egypt's seizure of territory in 1879 from an Ethiopia weakened by war with the British was one of the few reversed shortly thereafter—in 1884. But by then Egypt had itself been rendered a "protectorate" of the United Kingdom, an arrangement that was not reversed until the 1922 unilateral declaration of Egyptian independence, formalized in a 1936 treaty. France's seizures of Tunisia in 1881, and of Laos, Benin, and the Malagasy Republic in the 1890s, were not reversed until the period of rapid European decolonization that began in the 1950s.

20. "Oral History Interview with Loy W. Henderson," Harry S. Truman Library and Museum, (1973), http://www.trumanlibrary.org/oralhist/hendrson.htm (indicating that Welles spoke with Roosevelt about the drafting of the declaration and that they heavily revised a draft by Henderson).

21. Statement by the Acting Secretary of State, the Honorable Sumner Welles (July 23, 1940), https://history.state.gov/historicaldocuments/frus1940v01/d412.

22. The declaration not only stood as a statement of principle, but it also enabled the Baltic states to maintain independent diplomatic missions, and Executive Order 8484 protected their financial assets. John Hiden, Vahur Made, and David J. Smith, eds., *The Baltic Question During the Cold War* (New York: Routledge, 2008).

23. U.S. Department of State, *Peace and War: United States Foreign Policy, 1931–1941* (Washington, DC: U.S. Government Printing Office, 1943), 28–32. The other objectors were Mexico, China, New Zealand, the Soviet Union, and the Republic of Spain.

24. While not annexed by the United States, the Okinawa and Ryuku Islands were occupied and administered by the United States for decades after the War. Under Article 3 of the Treaty of San Francisco of 1952, Japan agreed to give the United States not only base rights on the islands but also powers of administration, legislation, and jurisdiction. Under this regime, Okinawans did not possess either American or Japanese citizenship. In 1972, the U.S. returned the islands to Japanese administration, but numerous U.S. bases remain on the islands.

25. One case not included in this list is Tibet. In 1950, the People's Liberation Army defeated the Tibetan army, and in 1951 the Tibetan representaives signed a seventeen-point agreement with the Chinese Central People's Government affirming China's sovereignty over Tibet and the incorporation of Tibet. This is not included as a "conquest" in our dataset, because the autonomous sovereign status of Tibet prior to 1950 was unclear. In order for a transfer of territory to be classified as a conquest in our dataset, the losing entity must have clear sovereignty over the lost territory.

26. Quincy Wright, "The Stimson Note of January 7, 1932," *American Journal of International Law* 26, no. 2 (April 1932): 342–48.

27. League of Nations, Report of the League Assembly on the Manchurian Dispute (Nanking: International Relations Committee, 1933), 79.

28. Atlantic Charter, Art. 8, Avalon Law Project, Yale Law School Lillian Goldman Law Library, http://avalon.law.yale.edu/wwii/atlantic.asp.

29. Another possible argument is that nuclear states use nuclear weapons to prevent rather than pursue conquest not because of the Peace Pact, but because using nuclear weapons would destroy the value of the conquest—at least for some time. (This is a variation on the argument that nuclear weapons are too powerful to use.) If that were the case, however, the emergence of nuclear weapons still would not be able to explain the decline of conquest. Another explanation would be necessary.

30. Bruce Russett, *Grasping the Democratic Peace: Principles for a Post–Cold War World* (Princeton: Princeton University Press, 1993); Spencer R. Weart, *Never at War: Why Democracies Will Never Fight One Another* (New Haven: Yale University Press, 1998); Paul K. Hutt and Todd L. Allee, *The Democratic Peace and Territorial Conflict in the Twentieth Century* (Cambridge: Cambridge University

Press, 2002); Michael W. Doyle, *Liberal Peace: Selected Essays* (New York: Routledge, 2011).

31. See, e.g, Steven Pinker, *The Better Angels of Our Nature: Why Violence Has Declined* (London: Penguin, 2011); Joshua Goldstein, *Winning the War on War: The Decline of Armed Conflict Worldwide* (New York: Dutton, 2011); Azar Gat, *War in Human Civilization* (Oxford: Oxford University Press, 2008); Azar Gat, "Is War Declining and Why?," *Journal of Peace Research* 50, no. 2 (2013): 149–57; *The Waning of Major War: Theories and Debates*, ed. Raimo Vayrynen (London: Routledge, 2006); Nils Petter Gelditsch, "The Decline of War—The Main Issues," *International Studies Review* 15, no. 3 (2013): 397–99; Lawrence Freedman, "Steven Pinker and the Long Peace: Alliance, Deterrence, and Decline," *Cold War History* 14, no. 4 (2014): 657–72; John Mueller, *Retreat from Doomsday: The Obsolescence of Major War* (New York: Basic Books, 1989).

32. Mueller, *Retreat from Doomsday*, 3.

33. Freedman, "Steven Pinker and the Long Peace," 658.

34. Ibid.

35. One of the frequently used datasets, Peter Brecke's "Conflict Catalog," http://www.cgeh.nl/data, includes 3,708 conflicts, with data on parties, fatalities, date, and duration. But for the first 100 conflicts, for example, there are data on fatalities for only 13. Many of those reported numbers, moreover, appear to be low. Tanisha Fazal is critical of all the available datasets. She argues in particular that advances in military medicine have made battle deaths less likely and nonfatal battle casualties more likely over the last several centuries, especially since 1946. Tanisha M. Fazal, "Dead Wrong? Battle Deaths, Military Medicine, and Exaggerated Reports of War's Demise," *International Security* 39, no. 1 (Summer 2014): 96–98.

36. Pinker, *The Better Angels of Our Nature*, 231.

37. There have been a number of recent critics of the declinist hypothesis, including, for example, Bear F. Braumoeller, "Is War Disappearing?" (unpublished paper) (August 27, 2013); Fazal, "Dead Wrong? Battle Deaths, Military Medicine, and Exaggerated Reports of War's Demise," 95–125; Meredith Reid Sarkees and Jeffrey S. Dixon, "The Waning of Intra-State War? The 'Decline of War' Thesis Revisited" (unpublished paper) (March 1, 2017). As Nils Petter Gleditsch put it, "Despite the various critiques, there is wide agreement on the decline of war and other forms of violence. . . . However, the reasons for the decline are less clear." Nils Petter Gleditsch, ed., "The Decline of War," *International Studies Review* (2013) 15: 396–419.

FOURTEEN: WAR NO LONGER MAKES STATES

1. The flags also include nonmember observer states maintaining permanent observer missions—Palestine and the Holy See. "Dag Hammarskjöld Library," United Nations, accessed January 14, 2016, http://ask.un.org/faq/98140.

2. "Fact Sheet, History of the United Nations," United Nations, last modified

February 2013, accessed January 14, 2016, http://www.un.org/wcm/webdav/site/visitors/shared/documents/pdfs/FS_UN%20Headquarters_History_English_Feb%202013.pdf.

3. Robert John Araujo, "Objective Meaning of Constituent Instruments and Responsibility of International Organizations," in *International Responsibility Today, Essays in Memory of Oscar Schachter*, ed. Maurizio Ragazzi (Leiden: Martinus Nijhoff Publishers, 2005), 343–44. Some of the predicted increase undoubtedly came not from his expectation that there would be more states in the world but because there were, at the time, a number of states that had not yet been admitted to the United Nations. Both the United States and Soviet Union used their power on the Security Council to exclude states from membership up until the mid-1950s, when they effectively declared a truce and admitted the states that each had prevented from joining.

4. "Newly Renovated UN General Assembly Hall Will Greet World Leaders Next Week," *UN News Centre*, September 15, 2014, 2.

5. Data for this figure come from "State System Membership List, v2011," "Correlates of War" project (2011), accessed January 14, 2016, http://cow.dss.ucdavis.edu/data-sets/state-system-membership. We have extended the series from 2011 through 2015 by adding one state—South Sudan—in 2014.

6. Or reinvention. A good argument can be made that the Sumerians, Athenians, Romans, Persians, and Chinese had states as well.

7. Max Weber, "Politics as a Vocation," in H. H. Gerth and C. Wright Mills, eds., *Max Weber: Essays in Sociology* (New York: Oxford University Press 1946), 78.

8. Charles Tilly, *Coercion, Capital, and European States, AD 990–1992* (Cambridge, MA: Blackwell, 1992), 67.

9. Ibid., 69.

10. Ibid., 75. Geoffrey Parker's *The Military Revolution* offers a detailed account of military innovation and its impact on the global legal order. Geoffrey Parker, *The Military Revolution: Military Innovation and the Rise of the West, 1500–1800* (2nd ed. New York: Cambridge University Press, 1996). John Brewer's *The Sinews of Power* explores the connection between England's system of taxation and its rise as a dominant global military power. John Brewer, *The Sinews of Power: War, Money, and the English State, 1688–1783* (Cambridge, MA: Harvard University Press 1990).

11. Ibid., 26.

12. Waging war takes more than men and money, of course, and doing so successfully is a complicated business. Historians and political scientists have spilled a great deal of ink debating the precise secret behind the rise and fall of empires and nations. See, e.g., Paul Kennedy, *The Rise and Fall of the Great Powers: Economic Change and Military Conflict from 1500 to 2000* (New York: Vintage, 1989); Robert Gilpin, "Theory of Hegemonic War," *The Journal of Interdisciplinary History* 18 (1988); James D. Fearon, "Rationalist Explanations for War," *International Organization* 49 (1995).

13. Tilly, *Coercion, Capital, and European States*, 75.
14. The point has been made that there are many variations on mercantilism—perhaps even, as one historian put it, as many "mercantilisms as there are mercantilists." Ferand Braudel, *The Wheels of Commerce*, trans. Siân Reynolds (New York: Harper & Row, 1981), 542 (quoting Henri Chambre, "Pososkov et le mercantilisme," *Cahiers du monde russe* 4, no. 4 (1963): 358). Nonetheless, the term is a helpful blanket for a school of thinking about economic relations that dominated until it came under attack by Adam Smith in 1776.
15. Braudel, *The Wheels of Commerce*, 544, quoting Voltaire in 1764.
16. Tilly, *Coercion, Capital, and European States*, 42.
17. Though precise estimates vary, most political scientists agree that state size continued to grow over the course of the eighteenth century. David Lake and Angela O'Mahony show that the average state grew from 870,000 square kilometers in 1815–1820 to 1.75 million square kilometers at the close of the century—or about double the size. David Lake and Angela O'Mahony, "The Incredible Shrinking State: Explaining Change in the Territorial Size of the Countries," *Journal of Conflict Resolution* 48, no. 5 (2004): 699–722. The number of "states" in the international system slightly rose over the course of the nineteenth century, even as the average size of states grew. See, e.g., ibid. Those may appear to be inconsistent trends, but they make sense when one recognizes that "states" in the state system did not control all or even nearly all the territory of the world until the beginning of the twentieth century. Instead, much territory was in the hands of tribes and other nonstate entities until the late 1800s. Notably, however, a recent paper questions what it calls the "bellicist" consensus regarding state formation, arguing that between 1100 and 1790, "variation in patterns of economic development and urban growth caused fragmented political authority in some places and the construction of geographically large territorial states in others." See Scott F. Abramson, "The Economic Origins of the Territorial State," *International Organization* (forthcoming, 2016).
18. Lake and O'Mahony document the decrease in the side of states over the twentieth century and come to the "tentative conclusion . . . that the rise in state size during the nineteenth century is the product of a growing number of federal democracies, which tend to be large, and the decline in average size during the 20th century is produce by the growing number of unitary democracies." Lake and O'Mahony, "The Incredible Shrinking State," 700. They speculate that this "uncaused cause" is brought about by growing economic liberalism. Our argument is consistent but goes a step further—we argue that the outlawry of war reversed several dynamics that pushed states to be larger, of which protectionism is one element. Lake and O'Mahony show the decline in state size begins in the late 1800s. Our own calculations show state size leveling off around 1920 and remaining largely stable until 1950, at which point it declines by a third. This appears to be consistent with calculations in Lars-Erik Cederman,

"Generating State-Size Distributions: A Geopolitical Model" (unpublished manuscript, Center for Comparative and International Studies, Zurich, Switzerland, 2003).

19. Our claim that weak states were no longer threatened with conquest is consistent not only with the data in the previous chapter but also with the argument and findings of Tanisha Fazal, who documents the decline of state death in the second half of the twentieth century. Tanisha Fazal, *State Death: The Politics and Geography of Conquest, Occupation, and Annexation* (Princeton, NJ: Princeton University Press, 2007).

20. Adam Smith, *An Inquiry into the Nature and Causes of the Wealth of Nations* (London: W. Strahan and T. Cadell, 1776).

21. David Ricardo, *On the Principles of Political Economy and Taxation* (London: John Murray, Albermarle-Street, 1817).

22. Mohamed Nagdy and Max Roser, "International Trade (2016)," OurWorld InData.org, accessed January 17, 2016, http://ourworldindata.org/data/global -interconnections/international-trade/.

23. Robert Powell, "Absolute and Relative Gains in International Relations Theory," *The American Political Science Review* 85, no. 4 (1991): 1303–20.

24. John A. Vazquez, "Why Do Neighbors Fight? Proximity, Interaction, or Territoriality," *Journal of Peace Research* 32, no. 3 (1995): 277–93. See Halvard Buhaug and Kristian Skrede Gleditsch, "Contagion or Confusion? Why Conflicts Cluster in Space," *International Studies Quarterly* 52, no. 2 (2008): 215–33.

25. Robert O. Keohane's book *After Hegemony* (Princeton: Princeton University Press, 1984) is considered the leading text.

26. Nagdy and Roser, "International Trade (2016)."

27. John Kenneth Galbraith, *A Journey Through Economic Times: A Firsthand View* (Boston: Houghton Mifflin, 1994), 158–59. See also Erik Gartzke and Dominic Rohner, "The Political Economy of Imperialism, Decolonization and Development," *British Journal of Political Science* 41 (2011): 525–57 (arguing that economic development led nations to prefer commerce to conquest because "capital abundance makes empire expensive, shifting incentives away from appropriating inputs to production and towards efforts to influence the terms under which nations interact"). This in turn contributed to the decline of mercantilism and the rise of free market policies.

28. International Convention for the Regulation of Whaling, December 2, 1946, 62 Stat. 1716, 161 U.N.T.S. 72

29. Atlantic Charter, U.S.-U.K., August 14, 1941, 55 Stat. 1603.

30. U.N. Charter, Art. 1, ¶ 2.

31. Lieutenant Colonel A. J. F. Doulton, *The Fighting Cock: Being the History of the 23rd Indian Division, 1942–1947* (Aldershot: Gale & Polden, 1951), 237.

32. Ibid., 230–48.

33. See Neta Crawford, *Argument and Change in World Politics: Ethics, Decolonization,*

and Humanitarian Intervention (Cambridge: Cambridge University Press, 2002); Robert H. Jackson, "The Weight of Ideas in Decolonization: Normative Change in International Relations," in Judith Goldstein and Robert Keohane, eds., *Ideas and Foreign Policy: Beliefs, Institutions, and Political Change* (Ithaca, NY: Cornell University Press, 1993), 112; Michael W. Doyle, *Empires* (Ithaca, NY: Cornell University Press, 1986); David Strang, "From Dependency to Sovereignty: An Event History Analysis of Decolonization 1870–1987," *American Sociological Review* 55, no. 6 (1990): 846–60.

34. Jaroslav Tir, Philip Schafer, Paul Diehl, and Gary Goertz, "Territorial Changes, 1816–1996: Procedures and Data," *Conflict Management and Peace Science* 16 (1998): 89–97; "Territorial Change (v.5)," "Correlates of War" project (2014), accessed January 17, 2016, http://cow.dss.ucdavis.edu/data-sets/territorial -change. Data calculated for (tc_indep=1). Note that the first and last decades are only partial.

35. As we explain in the codebook, available at www.theinternationalistsbook .com, "Independence occurs when a part of a territory governed by one sovereign entity splits off and becomes its own distinct state governed by a new, independent, self-governing sovereign entity. Independence is distinct from forced dissolution in that it is motivated in significant part by a desire for self-governance. If a territory gains independence but is placed under trusteeship, this is still independence as long as the trustee does not make claims to sovereignty and is intended to be temporary and transitional."

FIFTEEN: WHY IS THERE STILL SO MUCH CONFLICT?

1. Department of Peace and Conflict Research, UCDP Battle-Related Deaths Dataset v.5-2016, 1989-2015.

2. League of Nations Covenant, Art. 22 ("Certain communities formerly belonging to the Turkish [Ottoman] Empire have reached a stage of development where their existence as independent nations can be provisionally recognized subject to the rendering of administrative advice and assistance by a Mandatory until such time as they are able to stand alone.").

3. James A. Balfour, "Balfour Declaration 1917," Avalon Law Project, Yale Law School Lillian Goldman Law Library, http://avalon.law.yale.edu/20th_century /balfour.asp.

4. David Fromkin, *A Peace to End All Peace: The Fall of the Ottoman Empire and the Creation of the Modern Middle East* (New York: Holt, 1989), 339, 500–08.

5. Tom Segev, *One Palestine, Complete: Jews and Arabs Under the British Mandate* (New York: Henry Holt, 2000), 158–62.

6. U.N. General Assembly Resolution 181, U.N. GAOR, 1st Sess., at 131, 139, U.N. Doc. A/64 (1946); Carol Migdalovitz, *Israel: Background and Relations with the United States* (Washington, DC: Congressional Research Service, 2009), 7.

7. "The Declaration of the Establishment of the State of Israel (May 14, 1948),"

Israel Ministry of Foreign Affairs, accessed January 13, 2016, http://www.mfa
.gov.il/mfa/foreignpolicy/peace/guide/pages/declaration%20of%20establish
ment%20of%20state%20of%20israel.aspx.

8. Saudi Arabia sent a contingent to operate under Egyptian command and
Yemen declared war but did not take direct action. David Ben Gurion, "Israel:
A Personal History," in *Israel in the Middle East: Documents and Readings on Society, Politics, and Foreign Relations, Pre-1948 to the Present*, ed. Itamar Rabinovich
and Jehuda Reinharz (New York: Oxford University Press, 1984), 15.

9. "Israel's Diplomatic Missions Abroad: Status of Relations," Israel Ministry of
Foreign Affairs, accessed January 13, 2016, http://www.mfa.gov.il/MFA/About
TheMinistry/Pages/Israel-s%20Diplomatic%20Missions%20Abroad.aspx.

10. John Kampfner, "NS Interview: Jack Straw," *New Statesman*, November 18,
2002, http://www.newstatesman.com/node/156641.

11. Jeff Himmelman, "A Game of Shark and Minnow," *New York Times*, October
27, 2013.

12. Matthew Rosenberg, "U.S. Rebukes China on Efforts to Build Artificial Islands," *New York Times*, May 27, 2015.

13. Treaty of Shimonoseki, China-Japan, April 17, 1895, Art. 2(b).

14. Treaty of Peace, Art. 4, September 8, 1951, 3 U.S.T. 3169, 136 U.N.T.S. 48 ("It
is recognized that all treaties, conventions and agreements concluded before
December 9, 1941, between China and Japan have become null and void as a
consequence of the war."); Ibid., Art. 4 ("Japan has renounced all right, title and
claim to Taiwan [Formosa] and Penghu [the Pescadores] as well as the Spratly
Islands and the Paracel Islands").

15. Victor H. Li. "China and Off-Shore Oil: The Tiao-yii Tai Dispute," *Stanford
Journal of International Studies* 10 (1975): 143 ("In November 1967, the Republic of China [Taiwan], the Republic of Korea, and the Republic of the Philippines under the sponsorship of the United Nations Economic Commission
for Asia and the Far East [E.C.A.F.E.] formed a Committee for Coordination of Joint Prospecting for Mineral Resources in Asian Offshore Areas. This
body . . . concluded that the organic matter deposited by the Yellow River and
the Yangtse River may make the continental shelf in this region one of the most
prolific oil and gas reservoirs in the world.").

16. In 1947, the first U.S. well was placed just over ten miles off the Louisiana
coast, at a water depth of about eighteen feet. Technology continued to improve and by the 1980s deepwater drilling technology began to emerge. "A
Brief History of Offshore Oil Drilling, Staff Working Paper No. 1," *National
Commission on the BP Deepwater Horizon Oil Spill and Offshore Drilling* (2010),
accessed January 13, 2016, http://www.cs.ucdavis.edu/~rogaway/classes/188
/materials/bp.pdf.

17. Case Concerning Sovereignty over Pedra Branca/Pulau Batu Puteh, Middle
Rocks and South Ledge (Malaysia/Singapore), International Court of Justice, May 23, 2008. See Brian Taylor Summer, "Territorial Disputes at the

International Court of Justice," *Duke Law Journal* (2004) (describing nine boundary disputes at the ICJ prior to 2004); Frontier Dispute (Burkina Faso/ Niger) (July 20, 2010); Carter Center, Approaches to Solving Territorial Conflicts: Sources, Situations, Scenarios, and Suggestions (May 2010) (describing fourteen territorial conflicts addressed by the ICJ). In addition, there have been numerous maritime disputes resolved by the ICJ, in part because the Law of the Sea Convention requires states to choose a means of dispute resolution, with the International Court of Justice as one option.

18. Some known cases are summarized in Carter Center, Approaches to Solving Territorial Conflicts. In addition to the Permanent Court of Arbitration cases, there have been an unknown number of private *ad hoc* arbitrations and other mediated resolutions. Ibid.

19. The United Nations and Decolonization: Trusteeship Council, http://www.un .org/en/decolonization/trusteeship.shtml.

20. United Nations Office of Legal Affairs, *Handbook on the Peaceful Settlement of Disputes Between States* (New York, 1992), 111–23.

21. U.N. Security Council Resolution 1246 (1999).

22. "South Sudan—Birth of a Nation—July 9, 2011," YouTube video, 2:07, posted by ForPolExmnr, July 11, 2014, https://www.youtube.com/watch?v=M8xP BE5ccpc.

23. "South Sudan Profile—Overview," *BBC News*, accessed January 17, 2016, http://www.bbc.com/news/world-africa-14019208.

24. Carol Berger, "Old Enmities in Newest Nation: Behind the Fighting in South Sudan," *The New Yorker*, January 23, 2014.

25. Jairo Munive, "Invisible Labour: The Political Economy of Reintegration in South Sudan," *Journal of Intervention and Statebuilding* 8, no. 4 (2014): 334, 339.

26. Simon Tisdall, "South Sudan President Sacks Cabinet in Power Struggle," *The Guardian*, July 24, 2013.

27. Alastain Leithead, "South Sudan's Men of Dishonour," *BBC News*, September 28, 2015.

28. Calculated from "Polity IV Annual Time-Series, 1800–2014," accessed January 18, 2016, http://www.systemicpeace.org/inscrdata.html. The graph is compiled by summing all instances where polity2=0, indicating a period "of 'interregnum,' during which there is a complete collapse of central political authority.").

29. Munive, "Invisible Labour," 339.

30. Monty G. Marshall, Ted R. Gurr, and Keith Jaggers, "Polity IV Project: Political Regime Characteristics and Transitions, 1800–2015," *Center for Systemic Peace*, May 19, 2016, 19.

31. "Intrastate wars" includes civil wars, in which military action is internal to the state, the national government is involved, both sides actively resist, and the death toll exceeds 1,000. It also includes "intercommunal wars," wars involving two parties, none of which is the government; and regional wars, which involve

a local or regional government as one of the parties to the war. See Meredith Reid Sarkees, "The COW Typology of War: Defining and Categorizing Wars (Version 4 of the Data)," "Correlates of War" project.

32. Meredith Reid Sarkees and Jeffrey S. Dixon, "The Waning of Intra-State War? The 'Decline of War' Thesis Revisited" (unpublished paper) (March 1, 2017). This graph, provided by the authors in advance of publication, includes all four types of war classified in "Correlates of War" as "intrastate wars" (civil wars for central control [type 4], civil wars over local issues [type 5], regional internal [type 6], and intercommunal [type 7]). For more information on the typology, see Sarkees, "The COW Typology of War."

33. The State Department lists several "terrorist safe havens" in its country report on terrorism: Office of the Coordinator for Counterterrorism, "Chapter 5: Terrorist Safe Havens (Update to 7120 Report) 5.1.a - 5.1.b. Strategies, Tactics, and Tools for Disrupting or Eliminating Safe Havens," U.S. Department of State, July 31, 2002, accessed January 18, 2016, http://www.state.gov/j/ct/rls/crt/2011/195549.htm.

SIXTEEN: OUTCASTING

1. John W. Dietrich, ed., *The George W. Bush Foreign Policy Reader: Presidential Speeches with Commentary* (New York: Routledge, 2005), 5.

2. "Weirton Steel," YouTube video, 32:51, from a film by the Ordnance Department and Signal Corps, United States Army, posted by todengine, March 1, 2012, https://www.youtube.com/watch?v=A4euorued9E (14:43).

3. Toby Harnden, "Cheney at the Coal Face to Woo 'Pick-up Truck Man,'" *The Telegraph*, October 28, 2000, http://www.telegraph.co.uk/news/worldnews/northamerica/usa/1372247/Cheney-at-the-coal-face-to-woo-pick-up-truck-man.html; "Enforcement of Trade Laws Cheney Focus," *Lubbock Avalanche-Journal*, October 28, 2000, http://lubbockonline.com/stories/102800/nat_102800045.shtml.

4. Richard W. Stevenson and Elizabeth Becker, "After 21 Months, Bush Lifts Tariff on Steel Imports," *New York Times*, December 5, 2003.

5. "President Bush to Send Iraq Resolution to Congress Today." September 19, 2002, U.S. Department of State, http://2001-2009.state.gov/p/nea/rls/rm/13565.htm.

6. U.S. Department of Defense, "The National Defense Strategy of the United States of America," March 2005, http://www.au.af.mil/au/awc/awcgate/nds/nds2005.pdf.

7. Richard F. Tomasson, *Iceland: The First New Society* (Minneapolis: University of Minnesota Press, 1980).

8. Gunnar Karlsson, *The History of Iceland* (Minneapolis: University of Minnesota Press, 2000), 11–15.

9. William Ian Miller, *Bloodtaking and Peacemaking: Feud, Law, and Society in Saga Iceland* (Chicago: University of Chicago Press, 1990), 16–17.

10. Karlsson, *The History of Iceland*, 24–26; Jesse L. Byock, *Medieval Iceland: Society, Sagas, and Power* (Berkeley: University of California Press, 1988), 120.

11. Byock, *Medieval Iceland*, 59–60; Jesse L. Byock, *Viking Age Iceland* (London: Penguin, 2001), 171.

12. According to the traditional account, a man named Ulfljotur was sent to eastern Norway around 927 to study the law of the "gulathing." On the basis of this study, he compiled and brought back a new law code. This code was adopted in 930 as the law of the land by the community of settlers. Tomasson, *Iceland*, 15. The national parliament of Iceland is still called the Althing.

13. Byock, *Medieval Iceland*, 61.

14. Byock, *Viking Age Iceland*, 175–76. See also Miller, *Bloodtaking and Peacemaking*, 227–28. At the Althing, there were Quarter Courts, which "provided the forum for those cases in which no judgment could be reached at the local Thing, and they served as courts of first instance for cases between litigants who were attached to different local Things." Ibid., 17.

15. Karlsson, *History of Iceland*, 21, 24.

16. Miller, *Bloodtaking and Peacemaking*, 223–28.

17. Haraldur Bessason and Robert J. Glendinning, eds., *Laws of Early Iceland: Gragas I*, trans. Andrew Dennis, Peter Foote, and Richard Perkins (Winnipeg: University of Manitoba Press, 1980), 7–8.

18. Byock, *Viking Age Iceland*, 231–32; Miller, *Bloodtaking and Peacemaking*, 234–35. The outlaws could enlist others to help, and often did so. They sometimes turned to their chieftains for help, but the chieftains in turn relied on those who voluntarily pledged their allegiance. They were, in effect "unifiers in the self-protection of the local community." Karlsson, *History of Iceland*, 25.

19. Miller, *Bloodtaking and Peacemaking*, 229.

20. Byock, *Medieval Iceland*, 29; Bessason and Glendinning, *Laws of Early Iceland*, 92.

21. Vienna Convention on the Law of Treaties Art. 60, May 23, 1969, 1155 U.N.T.S. 331.

22. United Nations International Law Commission, Draft Articles on Responsibility of States for Internationally Wrongful Acts, with Commentaries, *Report of the International Law Commission on the Worl of its Fifty-Third Session* [2001], U.N. Doc. A/56/20.

23. Case Concerning the Air Service Agreement of March 27, 1946 between the United States of America and France, Reports of International Arbitral Awards, Vol. 18 (December 9, 1978).

24. Treaty Concerning the Formation of a General Postal Union, October 9, 1874, 19 Stat. 577. The UPU was originally called the "General Postal Union."

25. Ibid.

26. Ibid. ("When a country does not observe the provisions of Article 28 concerning freedom of transit, Administrations have the right to discontinue postal service with that country. They must give advance notice of that measure by telegraph to the Administration concerned"). See also George A. Codding, Jr.,

The Universal Postal Union: Coordinator of the International Mails (New York: New York University Press, 1964), 112 (noting that "a similar article has been included in postal conventions since 1920").

27. International Coffee Agreement, September 28, 2007, http://www.ico.org /documents/ica2007e.pdf; Convention on International Trade in Endangered Species of Wild Fauna and Flora, March 3, 1973, 993 U.N.T.S. 243.

28. Robert H. Jackson, "Address of Robert H. Jackson, Attorney General of the United States, Inter-American Bar Association, Havana, Cuba, March 27, 1941," *American Journal of International Law* 35, no. 2 (April 1941).

29. Pablo D. Fajgelbaum and Amit K. Khandelwal, "Measuring the Unequal Gains from Trade," NBER Working Paper No. 20331 (July 2014): 39, Table 4 (gains from trade for median consumer, by country).

30. Scott C. Bradford, Paul L. E. Greico, and Gary Clyde Hufbauer, "The Pay-off to America from Global Integration," in C. Fred Bergsten, ed., *The United States and the World Economy: Foreign Economic Policy for the Next Decade* (Washington, DC: Institute for International Economics, 2005), 69; Christian Broda and David E. Weinstein, "Globalization and the Gains from Variety," *The Quarterly Journal of Economics* 121, no. 2 (2006): 541–85.

31. Russian president Vladimir Putin recognized its importance enough to write his undergraduate thesis on the topic: "The Most Favored Nation Trading Principle in International Law." Allen C. Lynch, *Vladimir Putin and Russian Statecraft* (Washington, DC: Potomac Books, 2011), 15.

32. There are a few exceptions. In particular, countries involved in regional trade union—like the EU or NAFTA—may provide more favorable terms to those within the trade union without being required to offer those same terms to all members of the WTO.

33. General Agreement on Tariffs and Trade, January 1, 1948, 55 U.N.T.S. 194.

34. Ibid., Art. 23.

35. R. Rajesh Babu, *Remedies Under the WTO Legal System* (Leiden: Martinus Nijhoff Publishers, 2012), 240.

36. "United States—Definitive Safeguard Measures on Imports of Certain Steel Products," World Trade Organization, accessed January 26, 2015, https://www .wto.org/english/tratop_e/dispu_e/cases_e/ds248_e.htm; Warren Vieth, "Steel Tariffs Are Judged Illegal," *Los Angeles Times*, November 11, 2003; Jonathan Weisman, "Bush Rescinds Tariffs on Steel," *Washington Post*, December 5, 2003.

37. Thomas Hobbes, *Behemoth*, ed. Ferdinand Tonnies (London: Frank Cass, 1969), 7.

38. "United States—Measures Affecting the Cross-Border Supply of Gambling and Betting Services," World Trade Organization, accessed January 25, 2016, http://www.wto.org/english/tratop_e/dispu_e/cases_e/ds285_e.htm.

39. Karen Jacobs Sparks, ed., *Encyclopedia Britannica Book of the Year 2011* (Chicago: Encyclopedia Britannica, 2011), 512.

40. Convention Against Torture and Other Cruel, Inhuman or Degrading Treatment or Punishment, October 12, 1984, 1465 U.N.T.S. 85.

41. The story of Titina Loizidou in this section draws on the following sources: Michel Faure, "L'espoir de Titina" ("Titina's Hope"), *L'Express* (Paris), March 22, 2004, http://www.lexpress.fr/actualite/monde/europe/l-espoir-de-titina_490287 .html; Janet McMahon, "European Court of Human Rights Rules in Favor of Woman Seeking to Regain Family Home in Kyrenia," *Washington Report on Middle East Affairs* (September 1999), http://www.wrmea.org/1999-septem ber/european-court-of-human-rights-rules-in-favor-of-woman-seeking-to-re gain-family-home-in-kyrenia.html. For Loizidou's statement to the European Court of Human Rights, see "Statement of Applicant Titina Loizidou," December 14, 1990, Hellenic Resources Network, accessed January 28, 2016, http:// www.hri.org/news/special/loizidou/tstatemnt.html.

42. "Cyprus—'Women Walk Home,'" YouTube video, 33:51, posted by "grokked," March 11, 2014, www.youtube.com/watch?v=AbMLVo6cw0M (9:50).

43. European Convention for the Protection of Human Rights and Fundamental Freedoms, November 4, 1950, 213 U.N.T.S. 222. Article 46 of the Convention requires state parties to the convention to comply with decisions of the court ("The High Contracting Parties undertake to abide by the final judgment of the Court in any case to which they are parties."). After rendering a final judgment, the court automatically transmits the file to the Committee of Ministers of the Council of Europe, which is then charged with executing the judgment.

44. Statement of Applicant Titina Loizidou, Loisidou v. Turkey, December 14, 1990.

45. *Loizidou v. Turkey*, Article 50 (Just Satisfaction) Judgment, 1998-IV Eur. Ct. H.R. 1807 (July 1998), ¶39.

46. Interim Resolutions ResDH(2000)105, July 24, 2000, and ResDH(99)680, October 6, 1999, in Council of Europe Committee of Ministers, "Collection of Interim Resolutions, 1988–2008," 237–38, https://www.coe.int/t/dghl/moni toring/execution/Source/Documents/IntRes2008_en.pdf. See also "Implementation of Decisions of the European Court of Human Rights by Turkey," Recommendation 1576, September 23, 2002, Council of Europe Parliamentary Assembly, http://assembly.coe.int/nw/xml/XRef/Xref-XML2HTML-en .asp?fileid=17036&lang=en. The assembly encouraged further measures be taken to ensure Turkey's compliance with human rights rulings, especially *Loizidou*. The statement emphasized the importance of member-state compliance with the legal processes of the Council of Europe.

47. "Turkey Compensates Greek Cypriot for Property," *Asbarez*, December 2, 2003, http://asbarez.com/49301/turkey-compensates-greek-cypriot-for-property/.

48. Interim Resolution ResDH(2003)174, November 12 2003, in Council of Europe Committee of Ministers, "Collection of Interim Resolutions," 235.

49. Mario J. Molina and F. S. Rowland, "Stratospheric Sink for Chlorofluorometh-

anes: Chlorine Atom-Catalysed Destruction of Ozone," *Nature* 249 (June 28, 1974): 810–12.

50. Walter Sullivan, "Tests Show Aerosol Gases May Pose Threat to Earth," *New York Times*, September 16, 1974; "Death to Ozone," *Time*, October 7, 1974, 95.

51. *"All in the Family*, S[eason] 5 E[pisode] 7—*Gloria's Shock*," YouTube video, 23:55, from an episode that aired on October 26, 1974, posted by "TobiasParaone," September 3, 2013, www.youtube.com/watch?v=Jncz_um7OOs (12:20).

52. Walter Sullivan, "Low Ozone Level Found Above Antarctica," *New York Times*, November 7, 1985.

53. The Montreal Protocol is a protocol to the Vienna Convention for the Protection of the Ozone Layer, March 22, 1985, 1513 U.N.T.S. 293.

54. Montreal Protocol on Substances that Deplete the Ozone Layer, September 16, 1987, 1522 U.N.T.S. 3, Arts. 2–4.

55. "Kim Jong-un 'Loves Nukes, Computer Games and Johnny [*sic*] Walker,'" *Chosun Ilbo*, December 20, 2010, http://english.chosun.com/site/data/html_dir /2010/12/20/2010122001136.html.

56. Mihnea Radu, "Luxury Cars Belonging to Saddam Hussein's Son," autoevolution, June 27, 2012, http://www.autoevolution.com/news/luxury-cars-belonging -to-saddam-husseins-son-46640.html.

57. John Mueller and Karl Mueller, "Sanctions of Mass Destruction," *Foreign Affairs* 78, no. 3 (May/June 1999).

58. Gary Samore, ed., "Sanctions Against Iran: A Guide to Targets, Terms, and Timetables," addendum to *Decoding the Iran Nuclear Deal* (Cambridge, MA: Harvard Kennedy School, 2015), http://belfercenter.ksg.harvard.edu/files /Iran%20Sanctions.pdf.

59. "Data: GDP growth (annual %)," The World Bank, http://data.worldbank.org /indicator/NY.GDP.MKTP.KD.ZG.

60. Shreeya Sinha and Susan Campbell Beachy, "Timeline on Iran's Nuclear Program," *New York Times*, April 2, 2015.

61. United Nations, S.C. Res. 1696 (July 31, 2006); S.C. Res. 1737 (December 23, 2006); S.C. Res. 1747 (March 24, 2007); S.C. Res. 1803 (March 3, 2008); S.C. Res. 1929 (June 9, 2010).

62. Juan C. Zarate, *Treasury's War: Unleashing a New Era of Financial Warfare* (New York: PublicAffairs, 2013), 287–316.

63. Comprehensive Iran Sanctions, Accountability, and Divestment Act of 2010, 22 U.S.C. § 8501 (2010). In addition, Section 1245 of the 2012 National Defense Authorization Act provided that foreign financial institutions that knowingly facilitate significant financial transactions with the Central Bank of Iran or with Iranian financial institutions designated by Treasury would risk being cut off from direct access to the U.S. financial system.

64. David S. Cohen, "Remarks of Under Secretary for Terrorism and Financial Intelligence David Cohen at the Foundation for Defense of Democracies Washington Forum," December 6, 2012, U.S. Treasury Department, https://

www.treasury.gov/press-center/press-releases/Pages/tg1790.aspx. The United States was not alone in targeting Iran's financial sector. In March 2012, the European Union ordered the Society for Worldwide Interbank Financial Telecommunication, or SWIFT, to block Iranian banks from using their service. Rick Gladstone and Steven Castle, "Global Network Expels as Many as 30 of Iran's Banks in Move to Isolate Its Economy," *New York Times*, March 16, 2012. At the same time, Europe adopted a complete embargo on imports of Iranian oil. Samore, ed., "Sanctions Against Iran," 12.

65. Exec. Order No. 13,590, 76 C.F.R. 72,609 (2011); Exec. Order No. 13,599, 77 C.F.R. 6659 (2012); Exec. Order. No. 13,606, 77 C.F.R. 24,571 (2012); Exec. Order No. 13,608, 77 C.F.R. 26,409 (2012); Exec. Order No. 13,622, 77 C.F.R. 45,897 (2012).

66. Zarate, *Treasury's War*, ix.

67. Cohen, "Remarks at the Foundation for the Defense of Democracies" (emphasis added).

68. Suzanne Maloney, "Why Rouhani Won—And Why Khamenei Let Him," *Foreign Affairs*, June 16, 2013, https://www.foreignaffairs.com/articles/iran/2013 -06-16/why-rouhani-won-and-why-khamenei-let-him.

69. For more on the deal, see The White House, "The Iran Deal: Joint Comprehensive Plan of Action," July 14, 2015, https://medium.com/the-iran-deal /joint-comprehensive-plan-of-action-5cdd9b320fd#.v8ykblagu.

70. Peter Baker, "U.S. Tightens Crimea Embargo to Pressure Russia," *New York Times*, December 19, 2014.

71. Alexey Eremenko and Carlo Angerer, "Crimea One Year After Russia Referendum Is Isolated from World," NBC News, March 16, 2015, http://www .nbcnews.com/storyline/ukraine-crisis/one-year-after-annexation-sanctions -isolate-crimea-world-n324131; Dimiter Kenarov, "Putin's Peninsula Is a Lonely Island," *Foreign Policy*, February 6, 2015, http://foreignpolicy.com/2015 /02/06/putin-peninsula-lonely-island-crimea-annexation-russia-ukraine/.

72. "International Mail Services to Crimea via Ukrainian Post Suspended," *Post and Parcel*, April 7, 2014, http://postandparcel.info/60771/news/companies /international-mail-services-to-crimea-via-ukrainian-post-suspended/.

73. Baker, "U.S. Tightens Crimea Embargo to Pressure Russia."

74. David S. Cohen, "Remarks of Under Secretary for Terrorism and Financial Intelligence David S. Cohen at the Practicing Law Institute," December 11, 2014, U.S. Treasury Department,https://www.treasury.gov/press-center/press -releases/Pages/jl9716.aspx.

75. James Kanter, "E.U. to Extend Sanctions Against Russia, but Divisions Show," *New York Times*, December 19, 2015.

76. "Russia—Trade Picture," European Commission, last updated February 22, 2017, http://ec.europa.eu/trade/policy/countries-and-regions/countries /russia/.

77. There were also legal impediments. The EU needs to renew its sanctions every

six months, which requires unanimity among the twenty-eight member states. James Kanter, "Italy Delays E.U.'s Renewal of Sanctions Against Russia," *New York Times*, December 15, 2015.

78. Carol J. Williams, "Russia and Greece Consider Collaborating to Circumvent Western Sanctions," *Los Angeles Times*, June 21, 2015.

79. Herman Van Rompuy and José Manuel Barroso, "Joint Statement on Crimea," March 18, 2014, European Union Delegation to the United Nations, http://eu-un.europa.eu/articles/en/article_14755_en.htm.

80. Barack Obama, "Statement by the President on Ukraine," March 17, 2014, The White House, https://www.whitehouse.gov/the-press-office/2014/03/17/statement-president-ukraine.

81. European Commission, "The Hague Declaration Following the G7 Meeting," March 24, 2014, http://europa.eu/rapid/press-release_STATEMENT-14-82_en.htm; Alison Smale and Michael D. Shear, "Russia Is Ousted from Group of 8 by U.S. and Allies," *New York Times*, March 24, 2014.

82. Exec. Order No. 13,660, 79 C.F.R. 13,493 (March 6, 2014); "Ukraine and Russia Sanctions," U.S. Department of State, accessed January 29, 2016, http://www.state.gov/e/eb/tfs/spi/ukrainerussia/.

83. "Council Implementing Regulation (EU) No 477/2014," *Official Journal of the European Union* 137, no. 3 (December 5, 2014), http://eur-lex.europa.eu/legal-content/EN/TXT/?uri=uriserv:OJ.L_.2014.137.01.0003.01.ENG#ntr1-L_2014137EN.01000301-E0001; "Ukraine Crisis: Russia and Sanctions," *BBC News*, December 19, 2014, http://www.bbc.com/news/world-europe-26672800; "Announcement of Additional Treasury Sanctions on Russian Government Officials and Entities," April 28, 2014, U.S. Treasury Department, https://www.treasury.gov/press-center/press-releases/Pages/jl2369.aspx; "Treasury Sanctions Russian Officials, Members of the Russian Leadership's Inner Circle, and an Entity for Involvement in the Situation in Ukraine," March 20, 2014, U.S. Treasury Department, https://www.treasury.gov/press-center/press-releases/Pages/jl23331.aspx; "Issuance of a New Ukraine-Related Executive Order; Ukraine-Related Designations," March 17, 2014, U.S. Treasury Department, https://www.treasury.gov/resource-center/sanctions/OFAC-Enforcement/pages/20140317.aspx.

84. Cohen, "Remarks of Under Secretary for Terrorism and Financial Intelligence David S. Cohen at the Practicing Law Institute"; "Information Note on Capital Markets," European Union Newsroom, accessed January 29, 2016, http://europa.eu/newsroom/files/pdf/info-note-capital-markets.pdf. The program was not without its bumps. One question that quickly emerged was whether U.S. companies that had not been paid by their Russian business partners—sometimes in violation of their contractual obligations—were effectively offering prohibited loans when they charged interest on the unpaid balance.

85. Cohen, "Remarks of Under Secretary for Terrorism and Financial Intelligence David S. Cohen at the Practicing Law Institute."

86. Stanley Reed and Clifford Krauss, "New Sanctions to Stall Exxon's Arctic Oil Plans," *New York Times*, September 12, 2014.

87. "Sanctions Tit-for-Tat: Moscow Strikes Back Against US Officials," *Russia Today*, March 20, 2014, https://www.rt.com/news/foreign-ministry-russia-sanctions-133/.

88. Ivana Kottasava, "Russia Bans More Foreign Foods," *CNN Money*, August 13, 2015, http://money.cnn.com/2015/08/12/news/economy/russia-western-food-embargo/.

89. Ibid.; Anastasia Bazenkova, "Fake Cheese Floods Russian Stores," *Moscow Times*, October 2, 2015.

90. International Monetary Fund, "Cheaper Oil and Sanctions Weigh on Russia's Growth Outlook," *IMF Survey*, August 3, 2015, http://www.imf.org/external/pubs/ft/survey/so/2015/CAR080315B.htm; Ivana Kottasava, "Russia's Slump Pushes 3 Million into Poverty," *CNN Money*, July 22, 2015, http://money.cnn.com/2015/07/22/news/economy/russia-crisis-poverty-three-million/index.html?iid=EL; "Historic Inflation Russia—CPI Inflation," Worldwide Inflation Data, accessed January 29, 2016, http://www.inflation.eu/inflation-rates/russia/historic-inflation/cpi-inflation-russia.aspx.

91. Kenneth Rapoza, "Putin Admits Sanctions Sapping Russia," *Fortune*, October 21, 2016.

92. See The White House, "The Iran Deal: Joint Comprehensive Plan of Action," July 14, 2015, https://medium.com/the-iran-deal/joint-comprehensive-plan-of-action-5cdd9b320fd#.v8ykblagu.

93. Ambassador Stephen D. Mull, Lead Coordinator for Iran Nuclear Implementation Senate Committee on Banking, Housing, and Urban Affairs (May 25, 2016).

94. William Booth, "Former Israeli Defense Minister Calls Nethanyahu a Fearmonger Who Hypes Threats," *Washington Post*, June 16, 2016.

95. Judith N. Shklar, "The Liberalism of Fear," in Nancy L. Rosenblum, ed., *Liberalism and the Moral Life* (Cambridge: Harvard University Press 1989).

SEVENTEEN: SEEING LIKE AN ISLAMIC STATE

1. Angus McNeice, "Police Launch Investigation into Chilean-Norwegian Jihadist in Syria," *Santiago Times*, July 3, 2014. Vásquez is believed to have died in early 2015.

2. Hayāt Media Center, "The End of Sykes-Picot," June 29, 2014, https://archive.org/details/sykespicotend.

3. "The End of Sykes-Picot" is not the only piece of Islamic State propaganda to focus on the 1916 agreement. Indeed, it is fair to say the organization is obsessed with the agreement. "The End of Sykes-Picot" was released alongside its Arabic-language counterpart, "Kaser al-Hudud" (The Breaking of the Borders) as well as a photo campaign called "Smashing the Sykes-Picot Border" and a Twitter hashtag, #SykesPicotOver.

4. James C. Scott, *Seeing Like a State: How Certain Schemes to Improve the Human Condition Have Failed* (New Haven: Yale University Press, 1998).

5. Lawrence Sondhaus, *World War One: The Global Revolution* (Cambridge: Cambridge University Press, 2011), 91; David Fromkin, *A Peace to End All Peace: The Fall of the Ottoman Empire and the Creation of the Modern Middle East* (New York: Holt, 1989), 43–44, 71–76.

6. Marian Kent, *Oil and Empire: British Policy and Mesopotamian Oil, 1900–1920* (London: Macmillan Press for the London School of Economics, 1976), 122.

7. Fromkin, *A Peace to End All Peace*, 190; Jonathan Schneer, *The Balfour Declaration: The Origins of the Arab-Israeli Conflict* (New York: Random House, 2012), 78.

8. Fromkin, *A Peace to End All Peace*, 191. See also Jukka Nevakivi, "Lord Kitchener and the Partition of the Ottoman Empire, 1915–16," in Bourne and D. C. Watt, eds., *Studies in International History* (Hamden, UK: Archon, 1967), 327 (noting Kitchener's desire to put space between the British and Russian territories); Kent, *Oil and Empire*, 122.

9. Henry McMahon, *Letter to Sharif Hussein*, October 24, 1915.

10. Schneer, *The Balfour Declaration*, 85.

11. Ibid., 80.

12. British Mandate for Palestine, *LNOJ*, Vol. 3, No. 8 (August 1922), 1007–12; French Mandate for Syria and the Lebanon, *LNOJ*, Vol. 3, No. 8 (August 1922), 1013–17. The mandate over Mesopotamia never went into effect. It was replaced by a treaty with the Kingdom of Iraq.

13. John Calvert, *Sayyid Qutb and the Origins of Radical Islamism* (Oxford: Oxford University Press, 2010), 106; Adnan Musallam, *From Secularism to Jihad: Sayyid Qutb and the Foundations of Radical Islamism* (Westport, CT: Greenwood, 2005), 69; James Toth, *Sayyid Qutb: The Life and Legacy of a Radical Islamic Intellectual* (Oxford: Oxford University Press, 2013), 4.

14. Calvert, *Sayyid Qutb and the Origins of Radical Islamism*, 62.

15. Ibid., 106.

16. Naguib Mahfouz, *Mirrors*, trans. Roger Allen (Cairo: Zeitouna Press, 1999), 120.

17. Ibid., 122.

18. Calvert, *Sayyid Qutb and the Origins of Radical Islamism*, 142, citing Salah al-Khalidi, *Sayyid Qutb: Min al-Milad ila al-Istishhad* (Damascus: Dar al-Qalam, 1994), 27–28.

19. Sayyid Qutb, "Hama'im fi New York," al-Kitab, Sana 4, no. 10 (December 1949): 666 (translated by Mara Revkin).

20. Calvert, *Sayyid Qutb and the Origins of Radical Islamism*, 148, citing Daniel Brogan, "Al Qaeda's Greeley Roots," *5280 Magazine: Denver's Mile-High Magazine* (June 2003), 162–63, http://www.5280.com/magazine/2003/06/al-qaeda%E2%80%99s-greeley-roots?page=full.

21. Sayyid Qutb, *Fi Zilal al-Quran*, "Surah 6: Al-Anām" (Cattle), 1091 (Cairo: Dar al-Shuruq, 1978) (translated by Mara Revkin).

22. Adnan Musallam, *From Secularism to Jihad*, 117.

23. Sayyid Qutb, *Milestones* (New Dehli: Islamic Book Service, 2002), 111.

24. Sayyid Qutb, "Hama'im fi New York," al-Kitab, Sana 4, no. 10 (December 1949): 668.

25. Dan Caldwell, *Vortex of Conflict: U.S. Policy Toward Afghanistan, Pakistan, and Iraq* (Stanford, CA: Stanford University Press, 2011), 17; Calvert, *Sayyid Qutb and the Origins of Radical Islamism*, 152.

26. Lawrence Wright, *The Looming Tower* (Toronto: Alfred A. Knopf, 2006), 19. See also Calvert, *Sayyid Qutb and the Origins of Radical Islamism*, 152.

27. Andrea Mura, "A Genealogical Inquiry into Early Islamism: The Discourse of Hasan al-Banna," *Journal of Political Ideologies* 17, no. 1 (February 2012): 61–85.

28. "The Complete Works of Imam Hasan al-Banna, 1906–1949," *The Quran Blog*, accessed February 19, 2016, http://thequranblog.ÒˋÅles.wordpress.com/2008 /06/_2_-to-what-do-we-invite-humanity.pdf.

29. Mura, "A Genealogical Inquiry into Early Islamism," 71.

30. Calvert, *Sayyid Qutb and the Origins of Radical Islamism*, 191; Toth, *Sayyid Qutb*, 75–76.

31. Calvert, *Sayyid Qutb and the Origins of Radical Islamism*, 191–92.

32. "The Revolutionary," *Time*, September 26, 1955, 27–34.

33. Calvert, *Sayyid Qutb and the Origins of Radical Islamism*, 192.

34. Muhammad Haykal, *The Cairo Documents: The Inside Story of Nasser and His Relationship with World Leaders, Rebels and Statesmen* (Garden City, NY: Double-day, 1973), 25; Peter Mansfield, *Nasser's Egypt* (London: Penguin, 1969), 88.

35. Toth, *Sayyid Qutb*, 80.

36. Calvert, *Sayyid Qutb and the Origins of Radical Islamism*, 181–95.

37. Toth, *Sayyid Qutb*, 63–64.

38. William McCants, ed., *Militant Ideology Atlas* (West Point: Combatting Terrorism Center, 2006), 13, https://www.ctc.usma.edu/wp-content/uploads/2012 /04/Atlas-ExecutiveReport.pdf. Abu Muhammad al-Maqdisi, a Salafi Islamist writer who was the spiritual mentor of al-Zarqawi (the two met in prison in Jordan in the late 1990s) as well as one of al Qaeda's important spiritual guides, is a particularly prominent modern exponent of Qutb's vision. Ibid., 8–13. Maqdisi's book, *Democracy: A Religion*, argues that democracies rely on man-made laws, which he considers to be polytheistic idols and therefore a violation of the Islamic requirement of a monotheistic belief in God (*tawhid*). Maqdisi explains that the "plurality of sources of legislation" found in modern constitutional democracies implies "the plurality of lords and gods served besides God" and therefore constitutes polytheism. But these ideas are not original to Maqdisi. They are taken almost whole cloth from Qutb. Ibid., 8, 13.

39. Qutb, *Milestones*, 7.

40. Ibid., 57.

41. Ibid.

42. Ibid.

43. Ibid., 45.

44. Ibid., 57.

45. Ibid., 45–46. Qutb departs from standard usage, which takes *Jahiliyyah* to refer to this precise historical, pre-Islamic period, Qutb claims that *Jahiliyyah* persists even today. Indeed, he argued that *Jahiliyyah* rules the Muslim world—or more accurately, that there is no Muslim world, for even those who call themselves Muslims are not true Muslims. They still wander in the spiritual desert of *Jahiliyyah* as though the truth of the Qur'an had never been revealed to the Prophet.

46. Ibid., 58.

47. Calvert, *Sayyid Qutb and the Origins of Radical Islamism*, 231.

48. Ibid., 236–37.

49. Ibid., 229–71.

50. Ibid.; Toth, *Sayyid Qutb*, 89–90.

51. Calvert, *Sayyid Qutb and the Origins of Radical Islamism*, 261–63.

52. Ibid.

53. Wright, *The Looming Tower*, 37.

54. Ibid. (quoting Ayman al-Zawahiri, "Knights Under the Prophet's Banner," in Laura Mansfield, *His Own Words: Translation and Analysis of the Writings of Dr. Ayman Al Zawahiri* [Lulu.com, 2006]).

55. Ibid., 78–79.

56. Qutb, *Milestones*, 47.

57. Ibid., 59.

58. Ibid., 65.

59. Ibid., 56.

60. Ibid., 160.

61. Ibid., 126.

62. Joshua Eaton, "U.S. Military Now Says ISIS Leader Was Held in Notorious Abu Ghraib Prison," *The Intercept*, August 25, 2016, https://theintercept.com /2016/08/25/u-s-military-now-says-isis-leader-was-held-in-notorious-abu -ghraib-prison/.

63. Ed Husain, "How 'Caliph' Baghdadi Aimed His Sermon at the Muslim Devout," *The Telegraph*, July 18, 2014, http://www.telegraph.co.uk/news /worldnews/middleeast/iraq/10975807/How-Caliph-Baghdadi-aimed-his -sermon-at-the-Muslim-devout.html#disqus_thread.

64. "ISIS Abu Bakr al-Baghdadi First Friday Semon as So-Called 'Caliph,'" *Al Arabiya News Reports*, July 5, 2014, http://english.alarabiya.net/en/webtv/reports /2014/07/07/ISIS-Abu-Bakr-al-Baghdidi-first-Friday-sermon-as-so-called -Caliph-.html.

65. Abū Bakr al-Baghdādī, "A Message to the Mujahidin and the Muslim Ummah

in the Month of Ramadan," http://www.gatestoneinstitute.org/documents/baghdadi-caliph.pdf.

66. Ibid.

67. Ashley Kirk, "Iraq and Syria: How Many Foreign Fighters Are Fighting for ISIL?," *The Telegraph*, August 12, 2015; Eric Schmitt and Somini Sengupta, "Thousands Enter Syria to Join ISIS Despite Global Efforts," *New York Times*, September 26, 2015; "Islamic State Group: Crisis in Seven Charts," *BBC News*, accessed June 13, 2016, http://www.bbc.com/news/world-middle-east-27838034; "ISIS Sanctuary Map: May 25, 2016," *Institute for the Study of War*, accessed June 13, 2016, http://www.understandingwar.org/backgrounder/isis-sanctuary-map-may-25-2016.

68. Karen Yourish, Derek Watkins, and Tom Giratikanon, "Recent Attacks Demonstrate Islamic State's Ability to Both Inspire and Coordinate Terror," *New York Times*, December 7, 2015.

69. "Islamic States 43 Global Affiliates: Interactive World Map," IntelCenter, December 15, 2015, http://intelcenter.com/maps/is-affiliates-map.html#gs.1B wx8RE.

70. Nathaniel Zelinsky, "ISIS Sends a Message: What Gestures Say About Today's Middle East," *Foreign Affairs*, September 3, 2014.

71. Qutb, *Milestones*, 75.

72. "The Islamic State Announces Its Own Currency," *Insite Blog on Terrorism & Extremism*, November 13, 2014, http://news.siteintelgroup.com/blog/index.php/entry/311-the-islamic-state-announces-its-own-currency.

73. Mara Revkin, "The Judicial Construction of Citizenship in the Islamic State: Evidence from Iraq and Syria," Yale Law School Middle East Legal Studies Seminar paper.

74. Bruce Lawrence, ed., *Messages to the World. The Statements of Osama bin Laden* (New York: Verso, 2005), 14.

75. Greg Miller and Julie Tate, "Osama bin Laden Warned Against Almost Every Aspect of Islamic State Playbook," *Washington Post*, March 1, 2016. An affiliated group, Al Qaeda in the Islamic Maghreb, similarly argued that declaration of the caliphate was premature. Thomas Joscelyn, "AQIM Rejects Islamic State's Caliphate, Reaffirms Allegiance to Zawahiri," *Long War Journal* (July 14, 2014), http://www.longwarjournal.org/archives/2014/07/aqim_rejects_islamic.php.

CONCLUSION: THE WORK OF TOMORROW

1. John Dewey to Robbie Tunkintell (Roberta Lowitz Grant Dewey), November 30, 1940, JDP CUL. The letter is addressed to "Robbie Tunkintell," which was apparently an affectionate nickname for Dewey's second wife, Roberta L. G. Dewey. See, e.g., John Dewey to Roberta Lowitz Grant Dewey, undetermined month, 1945, No. 09978, JDP CUL. Levinson died on February 2, 1941.

2. Graeme Wood, "What ISIS Really Wants," *The Atlantic*, March 2015. As of this

writing, the video remains posted at al-Furqān Media Foundation, "Although the Disbelievers Dislike It," November 16, 2014, https://archive.org/details /disbelievers (at 15 min, 12 sec) (readers should be warned that the video is extremely graphic and disturbing).

3. While the U.S. has not sent large numbers of combat troops as of this writing, it has sent more than three hundred Special Operations Forces to recruit, assist, and train local fighters. One of these service members was killed in November 2016. Alissa J. Rubin, Karam Shoumali, and Eric Schmitt, "American Is Killed in First Casualty for U.S. Forces in Syria Combat," *New York Times*, November 24, 2016.

4. Ambassador Samantha J. Power, Permanent Representative of the United States of America to the United Nations, to Mr. Ban Ki-moon, Secretary-General of the United Nations, September 23, 2014. Actions of this kind can become self-fulfilling prophesies. When the United States launches attacks on groups, they are more likely to engage in armed attacks against the United States. This can give rise to armed attacks that *do* satisfy Article 51 of the U.N. Charter.

5. Federal Bureau of Investigation, 2014 Crime in the United States: Violent Crime, https://ucr.fbi.gov/crime-in-the-u.s/2014/crime-in-the-u.s.-2014/offenses -known-to-law-enforcement/violent-crime.

6. U.N. General Assembly Resolution 68/262, *Territorial Integrity of Ukraine* (March 27, 2014).

7. See Oona A. Hathaway, "Positive Feedback: The Impact of Trade Liberalization on Industry Demands for Protection," *International Organization* 52, no. 3 (1998): 575–612.

8. Organization for Economic Cooperation and Development, Trade and Jobs, http://www.oecd.org/tad/tradeandjobs.htm.

ILLUSTRATION CREDITS

INSERT 1

1. Hendrik Cornelisz Vroom, *The Return to Amsterdam of the Second Expedition to the East Indies.* 1599, oil on canvas. Rijksmuseum, The Netherlands.
2. Ignatius Lux, *Jacob van Heemskerck.* c. 1659–1713, engraving. Rijksmuseum, The Netherlands, F. G. Waller Bequest, Amsterdam.
3. *Corte ende sekere beschrijvinghe vant veroverern der rijcke ende gheweldighe krake comende uyte gheweste van China,* 1604. National Library of the Netherlands.
4. Jan Anthonisz van Ravesteyn, *Hugo de Groot at the Age of Sixteen.* 1599, oil on panel. Fondation Custodia.
5. Workshop of Michiel van Mierevelt, *Portrait of Hugo de Groot (1583–1645).* 1631, oil on panel. Rijksmuseum, The Netherlands.
6. *Grotius's Escape from Loevenstein Castle in 1621.* c. 1790, engraving.
7. *Contra falsas francorum litteras 1491 pro defensione honoris serenissimi Romanorum Regis semper Augusti.* Augsburg, 1492. Beinecke Rare Books Library, Yale University.
8. Jacques Callot, *Le Pillage d'une Ferme.* 1633. From *Les Misères et les Malheurs de la Guerre.* Alamy, Image ID EDPC4K.
9. Johann Philipp Abelin, *Sack of Magdeburg 1631.* 1659, engraving.
10. Adolf Ulrich Wertmüller, *Edmond Charles Genêt (1763–1834).* 1784, oil on canvas. Albany Institute of History and Art.
11. Thomas Rowlandson, *The Devils Darling,* 1814, hand-colored etching. Getty Images, Editorial # 590683301.

12. *Napoleon I Submitting to the British Law and Surrendering, 14 July 1815.* c. 1815, lithography. Getty Images, Corbis Historical Collection, Editorial # 587492778.
13. Paul J. Pugliese.
14. John C. H. Grabill, *Tasunka Ota (alias Plenty Horse[s]), the Slayer of Lieut. Casey, near Pine Ridge, S.D.*, 1891, photographic print. U.S. Library of Congress.
15. Mathew B. Brady, *Commodore Matthew Calbraith Perry*, c. 1856–58, salted paper print from glass negative. Metropolitan Museum.
16. American Warship. c. 1854, woodblock print. Nagasaki Prefecture.
17. *Students Studying in the Netherlands.* c. 1861–64, photograph. National Diet Library.
18. BK, 3. Waseda University Library.
19. *Nishi Amane.* c. 1870–1897, photograph. National Diet Library.
20. *The landing of the forces of the* Un'yo *at Ganghwa Island.* c. 1875, woodblock print.
21. *A Chicago Lawyer Salmon Levinson Drafted the Plan for Relief.* January 21, 1933. Acme News Pictures, Inc.
22. *John Dewey.* c. 1910–1920, photograph. New York Public Library Digital Collections, The Miriam and Ira D. Wallach Division of Art, Prints and Photographs.
23. *Washington State Branch (Seattle) Members with No More War Signs.* September 1922, high sepia photograph. Swarthmore College Peace Collection, Photograph Exhibit, 1920–1929 Events, Group Photos of the Women's International League for Peace and Freedom, #B3.
24. Staff of the Inquiry at the Paris Peace Conference, 1919. Box 296, JSP CUL.
25. *James T. Shotwell.* March 1, 1927, photograph. Box 296, JSP CUL.
26. *Aristide Briand and Gustav Stresemann.* 1926, photograph. Dutch National Archives, The Hague, Fotocollectie Algemeen Nederlands Persbureau, 1945–1989.
27. Ullstein Bild, *Briand-Kellogg Treaty.* August 27, 1928, photograph. Getty Images, Editorial # 545728479.
28. Bettmann, *Frank Kellogg and M. Briand at Office.* August 30, 1928, photograph. Getty Images, Editorial # 515302928.
29. National Council for Prevention of War, *Help "Tell the Last Man" About the Pact.* 1928, postcard.
30. *Japanese Ambassador Signing Kellogg-Briand Pact.* July 24, 1929, photograph. Library of Congress. Getty Images, Corbis Historical Collection, Editorial # 640475759.
31. *Secretary of State Henry L. Stimson and former Secretary Frank B. Kellogg leaving the State Department.* July 25, 1929, photograph. U.S. Department of State.
32. *Lytton Commission.* 1931. Alamy, Image ID FGD7M.
33. League of Nations, *Chart of the Mukden Incident, Report of the Commission of*

Enquiry, League of Nations Publications: Political, Official No. C.663.M.320, Map No. 6, 1932.

34. Bettmann, *Sumner Welles Smoking with George Kennan*. March 22, 1940, photograph. Getty Images, Editorial # 515167444. (Though dated March 22, the photo was almost certainly taken earlier, since, by his own account, Welles left Europe from Rome on March 20. Welles, *The Time for Decision*, 144.)

35. Bettmann, *Hull and Welles Call at White House*. May 10, 1940, photograph. Getty Images, Editorial # 515347010.

36. L. C. Priest, *President Roosevelt and Winston Churchill seated on the quarterdeck of HMS* Prince of Wales *for a Sunday service during the Atlantic Conference*. August 10, 1941, photograph. Imperial War Museum. Photograph A 4815.

37. "Provisional Outline of International Organization (prepared by J.T.S., August 31, 1942)" (Document 99), August 31, 1942. Box 189, folder 8, SWP FDRL.

38. *James T. Shotwell*. Undated, photograph. Box 296, JSP CUL.

39. *Picknickers from Dumbarton Oaks*. Sept. 9, 1944, photograph. Alamy, Keystone Pictures USA, Image ID EOKPF3.

40. PhotoQuest, *At Yalta for "The Big Four."* February 1, 1945, photograph. Getty Images, Editorial # 149012879.

41. PhotoQuest, *Stalin & Churchill at Crimea Conference*. February 14, 1945, photograph. Getty Images, Editorial # 525184973.

INSERT 2

1. Ullstein Bild, *Carl Schmitt, Jurist*. April 8, 1930, photograph. Getty Images, Editorial # 537152649.

2. Ullstein Bild, *Hans Kelsen, Portrait*. Jan. 1, 1930, photograph. Getty Images, Editorial # 541040891.

3. Ullsein Bild, *Carl Schmitt, Jurist*. January 1, 1932, photograph. Getty Images, Editorial # 541055955.

4. Index cards to the war crimes case files ("Cases Not Tried"), 1944–48 and witnesses and defendants in war crimes cases, 1946–48, Record Group 549 Records of United States Army, Europe 549.2, Records of U.S. Army, Europe (USAEUR) 1933–64, Records of the War Crimes Branch of the Judge Advocate General Section, U.S. National Archives and Records Administration (College Park, MD) (photograph taken for authors by Sidney Cheser).

5. Bettmann, *Defendants at Nuremberg Trials*. 1946, photograph. Getty Images, Editorial # 515586328.

6. Bettmann, *Robert H. Jackson at Nurnberg Trials*. 1946, photograph. Getty Images, Editorial # 549379825.

7. *Hersch Lauterpacht*. Undated photograph. Courtesy of Sir Elihu Lauterpacht.

8. *The Illustrated London News*, December 8, 1945.

9. *First General Assembly, The First Session of the United Nations General Assembly Opened on the 10th January 1946 at Central Hall in London*. January 10, 1946, photograph. United Nations Photo # 71048.

10. Evy Mages, *The United Nations Security Council Vote*. November 29, 1990, photograph. Getty Images, Editorial # 51533322.

11. *A Month and a Half After the State*. June 30, 1948, photograph. Getty Images, AFP Collection, Editorial # 102248160.

12. David Rubinger, *Greeks Search for Relatives*. October 29, 1974, photograph. Getty Images, Editorial # 530701316.

13. Chappatte, *WTO rejects U.S. Steel Tariffs*. November 12, 2003, cartoon. *International Herald Tribune*.

14. Elizabeth Arrott, *Unidentified Gunmen on Patrol at Simferopol Airport in Ukraine's Crimea Peninsula*. 28 February 2014, photograph. Voice of America.

15. National Aeronautics and Space Administration, *NASA Ozone Watch*. 2016, https://ozonewatch.gsfc.nasa.gov/monthly/climatology_10_SH.html.

16. CSIS/Asia Maritime Transparency Initiative, Fiery Cross Reef Tracker, Photo Gallery, https://amti.csis.org/fiery-cross-reef/.

17. *Ibid.*

18. *Sayyid Qutb (Sayed Kotb) meeting with Dr. William Ross*. 1949, photograph. Colorado State College of Education Bulletin, October 17, 1949, No. 12.

19. *Sayyid Qutb*. Undated, photograph. LexLex Encyclopedia, http://i?cias.com /e.o/qutb_s.htm.

20. *Abu Bakr al-Baghdadi*. 2014, image grab from propaganda video. Getty Images, Editorial # 632521832.

21. *The End of Sykes-Picot*. 2014, image grab from propaganda video. YouTube (since removed under YouTube's Terms of Service).

INDEX

Page numbers in *italics* refer to illustrations.